MW00605039

Figure 1. George Washington in Masonic Regalia, 1794. *Engraving from Sidney Hayden,* Washington and His Masonic Compeers, *6th ed. (New York, 1867), after oil painting at George Washington National Masonic Monument, Alexandria, Virginia. Courtesy American Antiquarian Society*

STEVEN C. BULLOCK

Revolutionary Brotherhood

Freemasonry and the Transformation

of the American Social Order,

1730–1840

Published for the Omohundro Institute

of Early American History and Culture,

Williamsburg, Virginia, by the

University of North Carolina Press

Chapel Hill & London

The Omohundro Institute of Early American History and Culture
is sponsored jointly by the College of William and Mary and the Colonial
Williamsburg Foundation.

Library of Congress Cataloging-in-Publication Data
Bullock, Steven C. Revolutionary brotherhood : Freemasonry and the
transformation of the American social order, 1730–1840 / Steven C. Bullock.
p. cm. Includes bibliographical references and index.
ISBN 0-8078-2282-5 (cloth : alk. paper)
ISBN 0-8078-4750-X (pbk. : alk. paper)
1. Freemasonry—United States—History—18th century. 2. Freemasonry—United
States—History—19th century. I. Title.
HS523.B85 1996 95-39554
366'.1'0973—dc20 CIP

The paper in this book meets the guidelines for permanence and durability of
the Committee on Production Guidelines for Book Longevity of the Council
on Library Resources.

This volume received indirect support from an unrestricted book publication
grant awarded to the Institute by the L. J. Skaggs and Mary C. Skaggs
Foundation of Oakland, California.

04 03 02 01 00 8 7 6 5 4

This study examines the history of American Freemasonry, tracing its beginnings from the learned circles around Sir Isaac Newton in London during the early eighteenth century to the considerably less lofty world of Andrew Jackson more than a hundred years later. I argue that Masonry played an important role in shaping the momentous changes that first introduced and then transformed the eighteenth-century Enlightenment in America, helping to create the nineteenth-century culture of democracy, individualism, and sentimentalism. Freemasonry was so significant in this process partly because it came to be closely identified with the Revolution that encouraged and accelerated these developments. More important, the shifting meanings of fraternity helped people experience and interpret the confusions, contentions, and cross-purposes that helped mold the American ideals of liberty and equality. Early American Masonry, this study suggests, created a "revolutionary brotherhood."

After years of studying a group that emphasizes fraternal feeling and mutual aid, I am particularly aware of how heavily this project depends upon others—and how unable I am to repay my debts to those who have assisted me. The fraternity of Free and Accepted Masons deserves to be mentioned first. Their stewardship, both in preserving and disseminating their history, has made this work possible. I am also indebted to the Masonic antiquarians whose studies served as the foundation for my own. In particular, S. Brent Morris has provided valuable aid. The libraries of the Museum of Our National Heritage (especially John D. Hamilton and Carolyn Riccardelli), the Massachusetts Grand Lodge, and the Grand Lodges of Pennsylvania and New York (especially William D. Moore) allowed me to use their materials.

Four scholarly institutions have played an important part in my work and deserve to be singled out. The National Endowment for the Humanities supported this work directly and through the American Council of Learned Societies. Worcester Polytechnic Institute provided not just employment but also leave, release time, and financial assistance that helped me finish this work. Thanks are due to my chair, Lee Fontanella, for his helpful support. The Humanities and Arts Department provided a congenial professional setting for my work. Bill Baller, Joel J. Brattin, David Samson, and (especially) Peter Hansen, four valued department colleagues, must be particularly singled out, not only for their helpful readings of my work but for their willingness to help me think about Freemasonry, history, and just about everything else. Jo Ann Manfra provided encouragement and support as well as exemplary leadership and example. Finally, the Institute of Early American History and Culture has played a particularly important role in shaping this study. Even before he became a friend, Mike McGiffert shaped and prodded an early version of some of this work into publishable shape. His patient advice and insightful editing introduced me to the Institute's awe-inspiring professional standards. Fredrika Teute has been an exemplary editor of this study. Gil Kelly copyedited the manuscript with a sharp eye and a sharp wit. I am grateful to them as well as to all the other workers who helped correct and polish this work at the Institute and at the University of North Carolina Press.

My greatest institutional debt is to the American Antiquarian Society, my scholarly home for more than a decade. Under the presidencies of Marcus A. McCorison and Ellen S. Dunlap, John B. Hench provided me with settings where I could try out my ideas. Fellows and readers offered more informal opportunities. Although I cannot name them all, I am grateful for their encouragement and advice. Georgia B. Barnhill, curator of graphic arts at the Society, has been a wise tutor in the mysteries of learning from and using images. Other members of the staff were similarly helpful, particularly Nancy H. Burkett, Keith Arbour, Joanne D. Chaison, and Thomas G. Knoles. Along with Marie E. Lamoureux and others, they went beyond simply providing books in a shorter time than any researcher could reasonably expect, to providing extensive bibliographic advice—and an atmosphere that somehow combined complete professionalism with extraordinary personal warmth.

Others scholars, both in and outside the American Antiquarian Society, have also provided extensive aid. The people who provided me with references, encouragement, stimulating ideas, helpful readings, criticism, and academic friendship are legion—beyond my ability to cite here. Readers for the *William and Mary Quarterly,* the *Journal of the Early Republic,* and the Institute provided valuable (if not always immediately welcome) criticism. Jan Lewis, one of the readers for the book manuscript, offered particularly helpful advice. Among the many other scholars who read my work, I especially want to thank Edward L. Ayers, Philip Benedict, Cathy Brekus, John L. Brooke, Scott Casper, Ronald P. Formisano, Wayne Franklin, Robert A. Gross, Lee Heller, Christine Leigh Heyrman, Reeve Huston, Drew McCoy, Stephen Marini, Lou Masur, Pauline Maier, James H. Merrell, Charles Royster, John Shy, David Underdown, Mark Valeri, David Waldstreicher, and Conrad E. Wright. William Gilmore-Lehne provided helpful comments on a number of sections as well as valued encouragement and advice at a crucial point in this project. Douglas M. Strong sacrificed uncounted hours to discuss the project with me. Fred Anderson, Christopher Clark, Christopher Grasso, and Rosemarie Zagarri offered wise comments on the entire manuscript.

Four scholars made notable contributions to the development of this work from its beginnings as a dissertation. Peter S. Onuf became an unofficial adviser during its earliest days and has continued to be a supporter. At Brown University, John L. Thomas taught me the importance of writing and teaching well. Donald M. Scott helped me think about reading texts and has continued to provide valued encouragement and stimulating advice. Gordon S. Wood acted as my dissertation adviser. His wisdom, learning, and scholarly standards continue to serve as a model and an inspiration.

Finally, my family deserves particular thanks. Besides my father, my brothers Todd and Neil, and their families, I want especially to thank my mother for her support and her example and my son Christopher for immeasurably enriching my life. My wife, Sylvia, has helped me in so many ways that I cannot adequately express my gratitude—so it is only fitting that this book should be dedicated to her.

CONTENTS

Part Three. Republican Masonry

Chapter Nine

Into the Secret Place: Organization and Sacrilization, 1790–1826 239

Part Four. Masonry and Democracy

Chapter Ten

The Lion and the Crows: Antimasonry, 1826–1840 277

Epilogue.
Losing the Right to Reverence: Masonry's Decline and Revival 309

REVOLUTIONARY BROTHERHOOD

Understanding
Salem Town's Fraternity

In 1800, a young man with the unlikely name of Salem Town waited outside the Masonic lodge in Granville, New York, wondering who would enter. Town had grown up in western Massachusetts hearing "flying reports . . . of a marvelous character" about the Freemasons. His mother believed the fraternity practiced the "black art, or some of its kindred magical alliances," and she warned him to stay away from "that wicked society." But, after moving to Granville, Town found the attraction too great. He began to watch the "mysterious order of men" in order "to fathom their purposes." "I made it convenient to be in the neighborhood of the lodge room at the time when the members were assembling," he recalled, "and though apparently careless, yet I marked every man." To his "astonishment," Town recognized "a number of the most prominent men in the village." He scrutinized their behavior for more than a year. As his fascination grew, "something of a secret desire sprang up in my mind to see the inside of the lodge rooms." Determined "to risk [his] life for once," he applied for entrance.[1]

What he found there overwhelmed him. Masonry, he decided, was nothing less than an organization "divinely taught to men divinely inspired." Already it had saved the Books of the Law, God's holy word, from destruction in Old Testament times. Now it would spread Christianity and civilization to the entire world. So important was Masonry in this divine purpose that Town expected the fraternity to play a prominent role in the coming reign of Christ on earth, the promised millennium. Just as Masonry brought together a family of brothers, he predicted in 1818, so it would allow the world to "rejoice together as brethren of one common family."[2]

Town's fascination with and faith in Freemasonry were widely shared. During the generation after the Revolution, Masonic rituals solemnized dedications of churches, universities, and the United States Capitol. Its symbols adorned quilts, drinking glasses, and tavern signs—as well as the nation's Great Seal. Its lodges attracted Benjamin Franklin, George Washington, and Andrew Jackson as well as tens of thousands of less eminent members. Indeed,

Masonry seemed so significant to some brothers that in 1826 they abducted and perhaps killed a renegade member who threatened to publish its secrets. The resulting reaction against the fraternity inspired the first third-party political movement in American history. From its origins in early-eighteenth-century London, through its expansion into nearly every American community by 1820, to its near destruction a decade later by a massive Antimasonic agitation, Freemasonry fascinated Americans.

Despite this prominent place, scholars have found little reason to wait outside the lodge room like Town or take his statements seriously after he entered. The fraternity has seemed too obscure, too unusual to hold much interest. Indeed, the angry attack on Freemasonry that erupted during the 1820s and 1830s, the culmination of a century of Masonic expansion, seemed so inexplicable to scholars in the 1950s and 1960s that many considered this opposition mere expressions of paranoia.[3] This study suggests a different starting point. The very obscurity of early Americans' interest and emotional investment in Masonry, I argue, creates, not a barrier to understanding, but a point of entry that offers a new perspective on more familiar features of early America. As Robert Darnton writes: "When we cannot get a proverb, or a joke, or a ritual, or a poem, we know we are on to something. By picking at the document where it is most opaque, we may be able to unravel an alien system of meaning. The thread might even lead into a strange and wonderful world view."[4] This study of American Masonry's first century attempts to unravel the complexities of one of early America's most opaque organizations. Taking the claims of Masonic brothers and their opponents seriously and attempting to explain—rather than explain away—their excitement, this work seeks to understand the appeal of Masonry for eighteenth- and early-nineteenth-century Americans and, from that perspective, to illuminate the society and culture that first nurtured and then rejected it.

Such an examination makes clear that Masonry, rather than being entirely separate from the world, changed dramatically in conjunction with it. Four major shifts in the fraternity and its context are examined, in chronological sections. The story begins with the fraternity's creation in England and its transit to colonial America, where it helped provincial elites separate themselves from the common people and build solidarity in a time of often bitter factional divisions (Part I). These leaders, however, would be overtaken in the Revolutionary period as lesser men appropriated the fraternity for their own purposes, spreading it to inland leaders as well as Continental army officers (Part II). These changes prepared the way for the period of Masonry's greatest power and prestige, the years from 1790 to 1826, when Americans used Masonry to respond to a wide range of needs, including their hopes for an enlightened Republic, their attempts to adapt to a mobile and increasingly commercial society, and their desire to create a separate refuge from this confusing outside world (Part III). This multiplication of uses involved Masonry

Figure 2. Masonic Temple, Aurora, New York. Cornerstone laid by De Witt Clinton, 1819. *Photograph by Sylvia D. Bullock*

in conflicting and even contradictory activities and ideas, a situation that exploded in the midst of a widespread attempt to reform and purify American society based on the principles of democracy and evangelicalism. The resulting Antimasonic movement virtually destroyed Masonry in the North and crippled it in the South. The fraternity revived in the 1840s and 1850s but without the high pretensions to public honor and influence that had made it seem so overwhelming to men such as Salem Town (Part IV).

Masonry's mysterious world, seemingly so alien, was intimately intertwined with the central themes of American history. As a secret organization that sought public honor and attention, Freemasonry is an especially sensitive indicator of the changing boundaries between private and public. Colonial Masons considered their order a means of entering public life, of teaching the manners necessary for genteel behavior, and of encouraging the love that held society together. The growing post-Revolutionary disjunction between a competitive, impersonal public world and an affective private world, however, changed Masonry. The rapidly expanding fraternity gained a new role in civic ritual and came to be seen by many as a key element in republican attempts to spread liberty and create public virtue. At the same time, however, the fraternity intensified affectionate ties between its members that both separated Masonry from the outside world and helped provide the business and political contacts necessary in a rapidly expanding commercial society. Brothers increasingly described the lodge as a haven from a cold public world, a vision of separate spheres that only later became fully attached to women and the home. At the same time, brothers also used their fraternity to pioneer a new romantic vision of the self, an internal identity based in the heart and expressed through emotional outpourings rather than through controlled and polished public self-presentation. The growing tensions between these disinterested public and self-interested private roles spurred Antimasonic anger. In turn, the attempt to destroy Masonry developed new means of arousing and focusing public opinions, pioneering methods of channeling and disciplining popular expression that presaged the rise of single-issue pressure groups.

Just as it illuminates the zones of participation and freedom that constitute liberty, Masonry also reveals crucial changes in the ideal of equality. Masonry's first century spans the period when equality became a central and explicit national value. The fraternity served as a focal point for this transformation from a hierarchical society of superiors and inferiors to a republican society of independent citizens. Colonial Freemasonry offered the urban elite an important symbol of gentility and honor. In the years surrounding the Revolution, aspiring urban artisans like Paul Revere elbowed their way into lodges, claiming a fraternal standing that paralleled their new political position. This Revolutionary transformation allowed Masonry to become closely identified with the new nation's ideals, a position symbolized by the cornerstone ceremony that allowed Revere (and his brothers) to stand atop Beacon Hill in 1795 to dedicate the new Massachusetts statehouse.

Masonry's significance for this central American narrative, however, goes beyond merely providing a particularly powerful example of these well-known changes. The fraternity also reveals their larger ambiguities, the ways that these shared values could be used by individuals and groups for particular purposes. As both an honorable society, aiming to provide its brothers with high standing and public reputation, and a brotherhood, suggesting equality in a nonpaternalistic family, Masonry simultaneously emphasized exclusiveness and inclusion. The situation of Revere and his artisanal brothers suggests this ability to unite theoretically contradictory but situationally complementary ideals and practices. For these men, the values of fraternal equality reinforced their identification with their community and the attempt to reshape the boundaries of status. But Masonic honor also helped provide them with the high standing that justified the leadership of men new to the centers of power. Revere's Masonry thus attempted to put into practice the peculiar post-Revolutionary ideal of a "natural aristoi" suggested by the non-Mason Thomas Jefferson, an aristocracy based on equality.

Despite its close connection with liberty and equality, fraternity never entered the canon of great American ideals in the same way that French revolutionaries linked "Liberté! Egalité! Fraternité!"—partly because American Revolutionaries needed to stir up war with the very people even the Declaration of Independence called "our British brethren." But there is a larger difficulty. Liberty and equality easily translate into noble ideals expressed in marble inscriptions; fraternity more often expresses the living, confusing uncertainties of everyday life where practice and theory come together, sometimes to reinforce each other, sometimes to clash. What is a weakness for theorists and moralists seeking clarity and certainty, however, provides an extraordinary opportunity for the historian interested in the forms and ideals by which people order their experience—what might be called the social order.[5]

Seen from this perspective, the forms and ideals of fraternity (and Masonry itself, the preeminent fraternity in this period) are central to American development. "The American has dwindled into an Odd Fellow" with an overdeveloped "organ of gregariousness, and a manifest lack of intellect and cheerful self-reliance," Henry David Thoreau complained in 1849.[6] In tracing this seeming process of dwindling, this study challenges Thoreau's negative assessment. Rather than mindless abdication of responsibility, voluntary associations based upon the ideal of fraternity represented a creative response to extraordinary changes, whether attempting to meet the challenge of colonial ethnic and religious divisions or the dangers of a post-Revolutionary society where movement and commerce threatened to overwhelm people's sense of responsibility to each other and to society as a whole. Just as important, fraternity was not as politically and intellectually inert as Thoreau suggested. Masonry's first century provided ideals and social forms that could be used to challenge the established order, both for artisans left out of a haughty colonial elite and for the black Bostonians who used Masonic values to challenge post-Revolutionary white society as a whole. Masonry's legacy suggests that this tradition continued. In the half-century after 1840, both the agricultural Grange and the industrial Knights of Labor drew upon Masonic forms and language to attack injustice and oppression. Even in the 1960s and 1970s, feminists and African Americans each used the terms of sorority and fraternity—sister and brother—to express their solidarity. Rather than a prescription for mindless conformity (a concern sometimes reinforced by the college fraternities that provide the most common use of the term today), the fraternalism expressed in Masonry offered a set of resources that could be used for a wide range of purposes. Although the order cannot be seen as a master key to all early American history, it opens up that mysterious ground where pragmatic action (behaving in ways that "work") intersects with attempts to create moral and intellectual coherence out of experience.

This study attempts to explore both sides of this complex equation. Placing Masonic developments into this larger context has required two primary techniques: identification of membership and close readings of Masonic documents and rituals. Information from a wide variety of lodges on brothers' identities makes it possible to locate Masonry within specific social settings. At each stage of the argument, I draw heavily upon intensive investigations of particular people, lodges, and localities. But, as Salem Town realized, simply attempting to mark every man (or even a large sample) does not penetrate deeply enough into the mystery of Masonry's popularity. I also examine the fraternity's symbols, rituals, and public display through close anthropological readings that place language and action in a context of shared attitudes and understandings. Such thick descriptions provide a means of exploring the complex and sometimes baffling set of codes that created and expressed Masonry's social and cultural position. These two modes of investigation have often been separated into two distinct genres, quantitative social history and ethnographic cultural history. But such an artificial distinction clearly cannot do justice to American Masonry and its development. In this book, I examine the interaction between these two spheres, showing how Masonic ideas gave meaning to specific circumstances and how, in turn, changing social situations affected these ideas.

Fittingly, my attempts to understand Masonry and interpret it to a broader audience are similar to Salem Town's. I began this project as an outsider with little prior knowledge of the fraternity and quickly found myself lost in a confusing new world with its own terminology and enthusiasms. My attempt to comprehend these strange structures and experiences and then to integrate them into more familiar historical settings required arduous struggle (if seldom a fear of risking my life). But the results of this scholarly rite of passage may provide fraternal aid for others who wish to explore further the Ancient and Honorable Society and the context in which it grew. What its brothers sometimes called "traveling east for more light" should prove as exciting and enlightening for future voyagers as it was for Salem Town—and for me.

PART ONE

Colonial Masonry

CHAPTER ONE

Newton and Necromancy

The Creation of the Masonic Fraternity

As a fellow of the Royal Society, a member of its Council, censor of the College of Physicians, secretary of the Society of Antiquaries, and master of a Masonic lodge, brother William Stukeley was a respected figure in the learned circles of early-eighteenth-century London. Financial distress forced the young physician's move to Lincolnshire in 1726, but, he wrote to a friend, the provinces offered many metropolitan advantages: "We have settled a monthly assembly for dancing among the fair sex and a weekly meeting for conversation among the gentlemen." "We have likewise erected," he also noted, "a small well-disciplined Lodge of Masons." Lincolnshire offered another benefit. Stukeley, whose interest in the stone circles of Stonehenge was already well known, erected a "Temple of the Druids" in his backyard. Two years after his move, he solemnly buried his miscarried child there "under the high altar." [1]

The peculiar combination of modern science and ancient religion that preoccupied Stukeley lay at the heart of the new Masonic fraternity as well. The order took shape in the social and cultural settings that encouraged the Enlightenment emphasis on order, rationality, and sociability, within the culture of assemblies, clubs, and scientific societies. But Masonry also expressed Stukeley's continuing fascination with the seemingly purer wisdom of the ancient world that impelled his Druidic worship. By uniting elements that would soon be divided in British and American culture, the first English brothers created a society that attracted not only early-eighteenth-century gentlemen like Stukeley but thousands of later Europeans and Americans—and provided raw materials that allowed them to fashion Masonry to their own particular circumstances. [2]

Although it claimed antiquity at least as great as the Druids, the fraternal order Stukeley joined in 1720/1 was still quite new. Noncraftsmen had taken decisive control of the builders' legacy only with the creation of a supervisory grand lodge in 1717. Even thirteen years later, an author felt compelled to explain: "In these latter Days, Masonry is not composed of Artificers, as it was in its primaeval State."[3] Freemasonry had become, to use its own terms, *speculative* rather than *operative:* a male fraternal order, not an association of stonelayers.

Early brothers like Stukeley built speculative Masonry on a foundation of three traditions. Belief in the great antiquity of the builder's practices provided the transformation's original impetus. Learned gentlemen like Stukeley saw the Freemasons' histories, forms, and rituals as a direct link to the primeval world that loomed so large in the imagination of educated Britons, promising a deeper insight into the nature of God and the world. But the creators of the speculative fraternity also sought to do more than preserve and refurbish this precious inheritance. By identifying their brotherhood with sociability and science, they also made it a potent symbol of gentility and the emerging enlightened theories of nature and human society. Masonry drew upon and codified the practices of early clubs, exemplified the ideals of Newtonian social and moral regularity, and helped establish the often-shaky authority of English elites.

The popularity of this complex combination of esoteric and enlightened worlds facilitated the development of Masonry's third tradition, its link to high social status. Although tradesmen continued to predominate numerically within English Masonry, the aristocrats and learned gentlemen who also belonged dominated not only the fraternity's leadership but its public image. By 1730, the speculative order that claimed to be "the Royal Art" had spread throughout the British Isles and beyond into both the Continent and the empire.

The cultural moment of early Masonry can be more closely defined by looking at the great scientist Sir Isaac Newton, a man that Stukeley claimed as his "particular friend." Newton also drank deeply from the mysteries of alchemy and biblical prophecy even as he forged many of the concepts that underlay the later mechanistic science that ultimately denied these occult connections. But Masonry's founders largely came, not from Newton's generation, but from his immediate heirs—and that cultural difference shaped the fraternity in two crucial respects. First, Masonry participated in fashionable London society in a way that the socially puritanical scientist never did, giving the fraternity the cachet that allowed rapid expansion within London and then beyond. Just as important, Masonry had already begun the broader cultural movement away from occult beliefs. Although its creators drew upon the forms and the allure of these seemingly ancient mysteries, the fraternity would not become a latter-day meeting of magis studying alchemical texts.

Even the attenuated ancient mysteries represented in Masonry lost their standing in learned and polite circles within a generation. In the 1720s, Stukeley could still discuss the mystic significance of Solomon's Temple with his "particular friend" Newton. Twenty years later, Stukeley's contributions at Royal Society meetings provoked barely suppressed disdain. The ancient mysteries lost their intellectual respectability, as science and social thought grew increasingly mechanistic and rational. As heir to that earlier-eighteenth-century world, Masonry continued to join together what subsequent generations put asunder—the polite, learned world of cosmopolitan society and the mysterious wonders in which Stukeley participated both in his backyard temple and in his lodge.

1. The Remains of the Mysterys of the Ancients

According to the Master's degree given by speculative Masons in the 1730s, the murder of Hiram Abiff, the master workman at the building of Solomon's Temple, took place at "high 12 at Noon." A group of disgruntled craftsmen accosted him in the temple demanding the secret "Master's word"—a term used primarily to differentiate the pay and assignments of workers but also, the ritual implied, bearing deeper, mystical significance. Refusing the conspirators' demands, Hiram was killed and his body thrown into a grave, where it lay until found by a party sent out by Solomon. On the way, the workmen agreed that, if there was no clue on Hiram's body to the powerful but now-lost word, their first statement would become its substitute. Finding the grave beneath a covering of "green Moss and Turf," they exclaimed, according to an early exposé, "Muscus Domus Dei Gratia, which, according to Masonry, is, *Thanks be to God, our Master has got a Mossy House.*" Thereafter, explained the ritual, the Master's Word became "*Macbenah,* which signifies *The Builder is smitten.*"[4]

The mysterious story of Hiram's death, with its implications of necromantic discovery of secrets from bodies, would encourage subsequent Masons to devise elaborate explanations and narrative continuations. But, for the first generation of speculative brothers, the obscurity later members sought to dispel might have been precisely the point. The earliest brothers experienced the Hiram story, not as moral allegory, but as a link to primeval times. Through the rituals and teachings of Masonry, they sought to recover the wisdom of the ancient world, the still-bright divine illumination that shone before corruption and neglect tarnished human perception. Speculative Masonry eventually incorporated very different ways of thinking, but the fraternity's origin lay in this primitivist ideal of direct contact with the foundations of knowledge and religion.

These hopes arose out of the interaction between the craftsmen's practices and organizations and the learned world's expectations about the nature of antiquity. The craft's legendary histories and initiation rituals located the origins of their architectural and building knowledge far in the past. To the educated Britons who increasingly entered these trade organizations in the seventeenth century, they seemed to promise something further, the deep wisdom of primeval times. In the years around 1717, these expectations became so powerful that some noncraftsmen who had been admitted into these groups transformed them into something quite different, a fraternity dedicated to morality and wisdom that would be open to all men. In the process of creating this speculative Masonry, organizers formulated rituals and new lines of authority that dramatically changed earlier practices.

In making these modifications, Masons drew upon common expectations about the ancient world. Inherent in the hope of recovering a pristine primeval experience was a belief in intervening corruption and degradation. But in attempting both to recover and to refurbish these supposedly ancient relics, brothers also invested them with contemporary relevance, making them more than an antiquarian expedition into the past. If brothers did not (as subsequent brothers and scholars have sometimes maintained) claim the tradition of occult magic as their own, they linked their fraternity to even more important issues about the origins and development of civilization and religion. At a time when learned Europeans were being confronted with the unexpected diversity of their contemporary world and the past, Masonry's seeming connection with antiquity provided both powerful confirmation of a Judeo-Christian genealogy of learning, and insight into the world's primeval religion. The link to the past promised by the murder in the temple offered not just an experience of ancient times but a particular vision of contemporary cultural issues.

Interest in Masonry developed long before the creation of the speculative fraternity. Popular culture, especially in Scotland, identified craft secrets—the so-called Mason word—with occult involvement. In 1696, neighbors hinted that a Scottish Mason's house was haunted because he had "devoted his first child to the Devil" when "he took the meason-word." [5] Elite culture shared this curiosity. "Those that have the Mason's word," the seventeenth-century poet Andrew Marvell suggested, can "secretly discern one another." The new genre of local natural history that became popular later in the century often made Masonry one of the topics of investigation. Robert Plot's 1686 book on Staffordshire, for example, reported that the craftsmen admitted people primarily through "the communication of certain *secret signes* whereby they are known to one another all over the *Nation*." By 1710, Richard Steele could assume that the *Tatler*'s genteel readers would understand a reference to the craftsmen. Steele wrote that London's "idle Fellows" recognized each other so easily that they must have "some secret Intimation of each other, like the Free Masons." [6]

The proverbial nature of the artisans by 1710 grew out of two circumstances that allowed noncraftsmen to take control of craft organizations over the next decade. The builders' activities encouraged speculation about antiquity. The legendary histories they handed down within the trade claimed great age for groups further distinguished by rituals and organizational forms. Just as important, these legends and ceremonies were available to outsiders. Since the early seventeenth century, noncraftsmen had been admitted into Masonic groups. What these initiates discovered seemed exciting, for their experiences matched learned beliefs about antiquity. In an age that venerated the distant past, Masonry's intimations of antiquity allowed a new stage of Masonic history, the appropriation of the builders' forms and activities by noncraftsmen.

The Masonic lore common within learned and popular British culture originated within the craft itself. Although nearly all early modern trades asserted high standing and great antiquity, the Masons' claims were unusually elaborate. According to their manuscript constitutions, Masonry was the most important of "the seven Liberall Sciences," since the others were "all found by one science . . . Geometrye." Masons argued that their craft had been practiced and patronized by the ancient world's most learned and powerful men. As one typical early history noted, Hermarynes, "afterward called Hermes the father of wise men," discovered the principles of geometry and Masonry after the Flood upon a pillar where they had been written down by Jaball, the original discoverer of "the Craft of Geometrye." The patriarch Abraham eventually received this information and taught it to "the worthy Clarke Euclid." In turn Euclid passed it on to "Aymon," "master of Geometrie and the chiefest master of all his masons" at Solomon's Temple. From there this learning spread to France and then England.[7]

Although probably originally written by a learned patron of a guild in the late Middle Ages, this genealogy seemed powerful confirmation of the hopes raised by the distinctive nature of other elements within the craftsmen's organizations. Ceremonies initiating craftsmen into the hierarchy of the trade had long included reading these manuscript histories. By the mid-seventeenth century in Scotland and England, Masons supplemented these recitations with rituals involving secret words and signs, perhaps helping to shore up guild restrictions at a time when the expanding use of stone in buildings allowed the entrance of competitors. The earliest version of this esoteric information dates from 1696. Although the prescribed ceremonies vary greatly, the surviving Scottish and English manuscripts suggest a rough consensus on the nature of the apprentices' initiation and a growing standardization.[8]

The Freemasons' craft was unusual, finally, because of its structure. Like other artisans, stoneworkers organized legally established guilds to regulate their trade. These local bodies passed along craft traditions, provided charitable aid, encouraged conviviality, and created the tradition of a fictive family among its "fellows." Members also gained the economic and political privileges of full citizenship. As craftsmen who were "free of the city," Masons became known as "Freemasons," a designation similar to the informal usage of other guilds that sometimes referred to themselves as "free vintners" or "free carpenters."[9] Unlike these other trades, however, Masons also included a more informal organization alongside the guild. The lodge had first met in medieval times, bringing together a small group at a work site for business and conviviality. By the seventeenth century, these groups had lost many of their craft functions. In Scotland, lodges met in formal groups apart from the incorporations that regulated Masonry and related buildings trades. Although the situation is less clear in England, lodges there seem to have been more informal, perhaps operating beyond the control of any larger group. Indeed, English lodges might have been primarily ad hoc groups pursuing social and charitable purposes. Like their better-established Scottish counterparts, they also initiated fellows from both within the trade and without.[10]

As some of these outsiders realized by 1717, the specific circumstances of the Masons' craft pointed to powerful cultural themes. Ancient origins commanded great respect in post-Restoration England. The superiority of modern achievements could be argued by the beginning of the eighteenth century, but Biblical and classical antiquity still formed the standard for comparison. Law, religion, and politics all believed precedent the primary means of asserting present legitimacy. Even the Society of Antiquaries, the learned group of historians that Stukeley helped form, felt compelled to describe the new group as a revival of an earlier (though actually unrelated) circle.[11]

Connection with the past seemed so significant partly because of the continuing belief that the ancients had possessed secret wisdom of great, even occult, power. Although neglect and moral decay had obscured this knowledge, many educated Britons confidently expected that at least a portion might still be recovered. This ancient wisdom (even when discovered through means that would later seem irrational or superstitious) promised a deeper and more holistic understanding of God's truth. Sir Isaac Newton made such a recovery a major part of his work, attempting for years to decipher the wisdom hidden in biblical prophecy and alchemy. Indeed, Newton's *Principia,* ironically one of the later symbols of modern superiority, held that all its discoveries had been known in ancient times. This archaeology of wisdom seemed especially relevant to Masonry. Its histories specifically linked the craft to the accepted genealogy of learning, both to Solomon, the exemplar of Biblical wisdom, and to Hermes, the legendary Egyptian magus often seen as the font of occult magical knowledge. Masonic forms seemed to corroborate these assertions. According to widely accepted learned tradition, the ancient world had conveyed knowledge, not through books, but by instruction of a select few through symbolic language and secret ceremonies. The analogous craft structures and their admissions rituals seemed to suggest that initiation into craft mysteries might provide a latter-day entrance into ancient wisdom.[12]

This hope seemed particularly significant, because seventeenth-century craft practice made these experiences available to outsiders. Since at least the beginning of the seventeenth century, noncraftsmen had been admitted into guilds and lodges. In London, a separate group called the "acception" brought together Masons with non-Masons like the learned antiquarian and scientist Elias Ashmole. These admissions might have been a recognition of the craft's relatively weak place in the hierarchy of guilds in London and elsewhere as well as of builders' need for patrons and wealthy customers—or simply an expression of the informal conviviality of the lodge. Whatever the reason, the intersection between the builders' practices, with their intriguing hints of ancient origins, and the learned men who increasingly participated in them allowed the creation of something quite new.[13]

In June 1717, a group of four London lodges made up of both craftsmen and noncraftsmen met to create a grand lodge. At its head they placed, not an operative Mason, but a gentleman. This shift of leadership symbolizes the shift to the new speculative Masonry that Londoners were then beginning to create, a new organization unconnected to the actual practice of building. No craft Mason would ever serve as grand master.

In the ten years after this meeting, nonoperatives transformed the craft lodges. The new grand lodge took on powers quite different from previous trade practice. New genealogies stressed the speculative group's continuity with the past. The rituals themselves, the ultimate evidence for connection with antiquity, changed dramatically by severing the vital link with the actual trade of masonry. Despite these developments, however, the speculative brothers' purposes remained the same, a link to the ancient world promised by the builders' experiences.

Although the creation of a fraternal order followed the 1717 meeting, the original purposes of the new grand lodge remain unclear. The 1738 *Book of Constitutions,* seeking to bolster the fraternity's claims to continuity with older craftsmen, represented the new body as seeking to "revive the Quarterly Communication," but, on its own evidence, none was held until 1721. Most likely, the grand lodge was created merely to sponsor an annual feast for craftsmen and Accepted Masons. Whatever its original intent, however, the grand lodge rapidly expanded its powers. What had been a meeting of all London Masons soon became a separate institution with its own officers. In 1721, the grand lodge claimed the right to control the creation of new lodges and to serve as the final authority in Masonic matters. Grand lodge members now spoke of prohibiting "Alterations or Innovation" and of dangerous "*Rebels*" who needed to "humble themselves." These claims, however, still only extended to "the Lodges in and about *London* and *Westminster*." In the following decade, even this limitation would be removed. The grand lodge soon claimed authority over all of Britain and even America.[14]

This expansive sovereignty required explanation. Previous English lodges might have had no superintending authority at all. Even guilds, the only legally sanctioned bodies in English operative Masonry, exercised power only within the limits of a locality. Innovating speculative brothers, however, soon mobilized historical precedents for their actions, drawing, for example, upon traditions of medieval national assemblies of the craft. Brothers also revised the legends contained in earlier histories, complaining of their "gross Errors in History and Chronology . . . to the great Offence of all the learned and judicious Brethren." In this revision, a number of English kings, Solomon, and even Augustus Caesar posthumously received the title of grand master. By the time of the 1738 *Book of Constitutions,* speculative Masons referred to the 1717 meeting as merely the "resumption" of grand lodge assemblies.[15]

Ancient lineage (or at least the illusion of it) seemed even more important in ritual activity. Ceremonies provided the central means of connecting the new club, often made up entirely of gentlemen, with the myths and practices of the tradesmen whose name it now bore. Just as important, the craft rituals themselves seemed to reinforce the claims to antiquity found in the guild's histories. The speculative brothers needed to preserve and to restore these connections even as they adapted craft practices for new purposes. To do so, they reshaped the two operative ceremonies and created a third from other sources to form rituals that fitted their expectations about antiquity. These three degrees, performed by the lodge and regulated by the grand lodge, formed the foundation for all subsequent Masonry. A look at these degrees, focusing on the first and third, suggests the significance of these developments.

Speculative brothers inherited two degrees, corresponding to the craft statuses of young trainees and guild members recognized in nearly all organized English trades. By 1723, these ceremonies had become relatively established and entitled, following Scottish terminology, the "Entered Apprentice" and "Fellow Craft" degrees. Both drew heavily upon earlier lodge practices, warning initiates of the importance of secrecy (important in a trade organization that fixed prices and disciplined members), providing information about lodge structure and craft practices, and passing on the secret means of identifying Masons of the same degree through gestures, words, and handshakes (originally designed to identify levels of skill and status within a relatively mobile trade). The Entered Apprentice ritual particularly stressed the need for secrecy and, at least in the earliest years, continued the tradition of reciting the craft's regulations and legendary history. The Fellow Craft degree revealed the more esoteric significance of geometry and God, both symbolized by the letter G placed "in the midst of *Solomon's* Temple."[16]

Ritual action reinforced the importance of this information. According to a 1730 exposé, the Entered Apprentice degree began with the partially undressed initiate entering the lodge after three knocks on the door. Taken to the lodge master (the presiding officer) and made to kneel within a square, the candidate suddenly felt the point of a drafter's compass against his exposed left breast. He then took an elaborate oath promising not to reveal the laws of Masonry. With his hand on the Bible, the initiate swore not to "Write them, Print them, Mark them, Carve them or Engrave them, or cause them to be Written, Printed, Marked, Carved or Engraved on Wood or Stone." To reinforce this agreement, he obligated himself "under no less Penalty than to have my Throat cut, my Tongue taken from the Roof of my Mouth, my Heart pluck'd from under my Left Breast, then to be buried in the Sands of the Sea . . . my Body to be burnt to Ashes . . . So help me God." [17] Only then was the new Mason taught the arrangement and contents of the lodge. The ritual ended with the degree's secret sign, token (handgrip), and word.

The ceremony explicitly conveyed Masonic lore; implicitly it taught much more. The strange attire and ritual solemnity placed the candidate in a vulnerable position, taking him out of his former social context. The shock of the metal point further disoriented the initiate, preparing him for the solemn oath of secrecy and the mysteries of Freemasonry. His ritual humiliation before the lodge marked the end to his old position as a "cowan" and prepared him for a new relationship—that of a brother. Later-eighteenth-century rituals reinforced this change by blindfolding the candidate, underlining his inability to see Masonic truth, what the ritual called "more light." The fraternal bonds forged at this initiation bound brothers together by common concern and a common secret. An early Masonic song emphasized this division between the fraternity and outsiders:

> As Men from Brutes distinguish'd are,
> A Mason other Men excels.[18]

Although these early rituals continued and elaborated operative practices, the very nature of the new speculative fraternity transformed their meaning. Operative ceremonies primarily marked new economic status, either as an apprentice or a qualified tradesman. Speculative Masonry, shorn of its connection with craft functions, made these rituals a means of attaining particular degrees that measured progress in the lodge's moral and esoteric teachings. When the question, "What do you come here to do?" was asked at the lodge, the reply was to be

> The Rules of Masonry in hand to take,
> And daily Progress therein make.[19]

Stressing moral improvement rather than economic or social standing, speculative rituals became increasingly solemn and complex. A 1696 Edinburgh ritual, the earliest extant operative ceremony, required the new initiate to make "a ridiculous bow" while "putting off his hat after a very foolish manner." Speculative Masons attempted to suppress such merriment. In 1724, the grand lodge recommended that a Norwich lodge include a bylaw requiring "that no ridiculous trick be played with any person when he is admitted." Increased seriousness required more intensive moral teaching. Over time, masons' tools became increasingly important as symbols of ethical values. The early speculative rituals contained symbolism that was rudimentary by later standards. The Entered Apprentice, according to a 1730 exposé, served the master "with Chalk, Charcoal and Earthen Pan" representing "Freedom, Fervency and Zeal." By the 1760s (the next clear indication of English practice), Masonic ceremonies included extensive glosses on a wide range of symbols, material that before had been conveyed only informally, if at all. The square, for example, represented honesty; the level, the equality of brotherhood.[20]

Besides these Entered Apprentice and Fellow Craft rituals, early speculative brothers also created a third ceremony, which raised members to the degree of Master Mason. Probably emerging after 1723, the new degree's history and meanings are unclear. Given only by the grand lodge in its earliest years, the ritual was perhaps intended originally for lodge masters. By 1730, lodges gave it to any approved and willing Fellow Craft brother. Both the degree and the ritual lacked clear craft precedent. Guild masters held an office, not a peculiar economic or esoteric status. Lodges and guilds considered Master Craftsmen fellows of the craft. Indeed, the new speculative ceremony included little that had been in earlier craft rituals. Presumably the story of Hiram came from an older legend (perhaps fittingly, now lost). The range of explanations of the Master's Word itself in different sources suggests that even early recipients found it unclear. Most commonly, exposés claimed that the word came from a craftsman's exclamation upon discovering that Hiram's flesh slipped off his finger when he was lifted out of the grave. Even spellings of the Master's Word differed; it became variously "mal-ha-bone," "Mahalbyn," and "Machbenah."[21]

The lack of clarity within Masonic rituals, however, might have increased its appeal. Early brother and Royal Society fellow Martin Clare believed that the story of Hiram "seems to allude in some Circumstances to a beautiful Passage in . . . Virgil." He also cited precedents for the story in Herodotus, Ovid, and other parts of Virgil. For learned men such as Clare, the operative ceremonies were, not recent expansions of old informal practices, but relics of ancient solemnities that needed to be restored and preserved. "The [Masonic] System," Clare wrote in 1730, "may have some Redundancies or Defects, occasioned by the Indolence or Ignorance of the old Members." Still, "there is (if I judge right) much of the old Fabrick still remaining; the Foundation is still intire" despite "the many Centuries it has survived" and "the many Countries, and Languages, and Sects, and Parties it has run thro'." Masonry thus bore the marks of the long tradition of hidden wisdom that linked the Egyptian mysteries, the mystical Pythagoreans, Jewish Essenes and Cabalists, and even the English Druids. Thus Masonry "ought to be received with some Candour and Esteem from a Veneration to its Antiquity." Other Masons agreed.

> Antiquity's Pride
> We have on our side,

boasted an early song. Stukeley, whose social circle included Clare and other early Masons, joined the fraternity from a similar apprehension. He suspected, he wrote later, that it represented "the remains of the mysterys of the ancients." [22]

Although the ultimate meanings of the Hiram story were unclear, and perhaps were meant to be, some of its elements carried rich connotations for early-eighteenth-century Britons, meanings that help reveal the broader significance of Masonry's links to antiquity. The mysterious words of the Hiram story recalled the tradition of magic that had recently come under heavy attack. The setting within the temple connected the fraternity to an even more important dispute about the origins of religion and civilization—and how each related to the biblical record and Christian revelation. The speculative brothers' attempt to revive and reexperience ancient mysteries was not mere idle curiosity. They expected to learn about a past that was eminently usable.

Despite the necromantic elements of the Hiram story, Masonry's relationship to magic was ambiguous. The fraternity clearly scorned popular magic, using occult forces solely for physical purposes. Although these beliefs remained strong within parts of popular culture for more than a century, early-eighteenth-century elite culture increasingly rejected them. Not surprisingly, Masons explicitly disavowed identification with these beliefs. The first speculative *Constitutions* scorned the Middle Ages as "ignorant Times, when true Learning was a Crime, and *Geometry* condem'd for *Conjurnation*." Although some "People in former Ages, as well as now," a brother noted as late as 1738, "alleged that the *Free Masons* in their *Lodges* raise the *Devil* in a *Circle*," the brothers "innocent and secure within" laugh at such "gross Ignorance." [23]

Another realm of magic growing out of Renaissance learning rather than medieval ignorance, however, possessed a closer relationship with speculative Masonry. The recovery of ancient texts had spurred interest not only in Plato and the Platonic tradition (particularly suited to magical ideas of correspondences) but also in works of explicit magic and wisdom. These learned traditions of alchemy and spiritual magic were often lumped together under the name of Hermes, reputedly an ancient Egyptian magus with a precocious understanding of Christianity. This type of magic seemed to involve, not a selfish desire for wealth or power, but a sacred quest for the divine secrets of the universe made possible only by holiness. Alchemy thus was a spiritual as much as a chemical pursuit seeking to recover the ancients' religious understanding—and their deep insights into the nature of the material and spiritual world.[24]

Masonry only partially participated in this tradition. Even in the Master's ritual, with its mystical attempt to recover a spiritually charged phrase, the new word was found, not through divination, but through natural means. Furthermore, even though Hermes, a key symbol of learned magic, already appeared in the traditional histories of Masonry, the first speculative brothers did not magnify his role. Instead, they removed him from their histories, re-routing the transmission of antediluvian wisdom through Noah rather than the pillars discovered by Hermes. Not surprisingly, Masons never explicitly claimed any kind of occult power for their secrets.

In this distancing, Masonry participated in a larger trend. Learned magic had already begun to lose some of its authority by the late seventeenth century. Increasingly, educated Britons considered it senseless superstition indistinguishable from popular magic. Even Newton, the last major scientist to take the tradition seriously, identified alchemical ideas more with natural than with supernatural explanations.[25]

Like Newton, however, Masonry still found the symbols and structures of learned magic valuable. The discovery of the Master's Word bore more than passing similarities to magical attempts to gain wisdom. Both Masons and magi held hidden meetings of the initiated, shared secret words, and were open only to men who had passed certain tests of morality and religion. In both traditions as well, certain words and numbers held deeper meaning (three and seven were especially significant in each). Although Masonry explicitly disavowed these connections, its appeal clearly rested at least in part on the expectation that its secret words and rituals offered a wisdom deeper than what was available through other means.

Like the denouement of the Hiram story, its setting at Solomon's Temple carried rich symbolic lessons of great importance for the new speculative Masonry. Not only did contemporaries see the temple as a central element in the biblical tradition, but it also played a more than incidental role in the great debate about the relative claims of reason and revelation that emerged in the years before the speculative fraternity's creation.

Interest in Judaism and its central architectural monument was particularly intense in the seventeenth century. The first English translation of the complete works of Josephus, a key source of temple lore for Masons and others, appeared after the Restoration. Newton's Cambridge successor and close associate, William Whiston, published his own version. The temple itself provided a key focus of this curiosity about Judaism. John Bunyan taught morality using *Solomon's Temple Spiritualiz'd*. The less orthodox Whiston, after his views cost him his clerical career, earned money in the 1720s by preparing models of the rebuilt temple envisioned by Ezekiel and the earlier Mosaic tabernacle and giving lectures on their meanings. Newton himself participated in this curiosity. Calling the temple "the noblest monument of antiquity," he placed it at the center of ancient history. Masonic brother William Stukeley discovered in an 1725 discussion with the great scientist that they shared similar views on the importance of the temple. "Sir Isaac," he noted, "rightly judged [the temple] older than any other of the great temples mention'd in history; and was indeed the original model which they followed." They also agreed that Jewish workmen taken to Egypt built many of the temples there and "from thence the Greeks borrow'd their architecture, as they had the good deal of th[e]ir religious rites, th[e]ir sculpture and other arts."[26]

This widespread interest in the ancient Hebrews and their temple involved more than piety or simple curiosity. It also responded to two key intellectual developments of the previous two centuries. The Reformation set off explosive controversies about religion. Not only did Christians disagree among themselves, but, by the early eighteenth century, rationalist and deist voices challenged them all. At the same time, the expansion of encounters with people and cultures beyond Europe revealed a shocking variety of religious and moral beliefs. This unexpected diversity challenged the belief of complacent Europeans in the superiority of their religion. Christianity and its predecessor, Judaism, had seemed the foundation of world history. Now the influx of new information raised the possibility that they were merely another parochial set of events and beliefs. The resulting skepticism about specific religious beliefs and, even more troubling, about Christianity itself sparked renewed researches into the ancient world. These inquiries centered on two intertwined issues: the historical centrality of the biblical tradition and the nature of revelation and early religion. These controversies helped shape Masonry's teachings and religious position—and ultimately prepared the ground for Masonry's second primary intellectual tradition, the Enlightenment.

Masonry took an unambiguous stand on the lineage of learning and civilization. Its *Constitutions* and rituals firmly placed the Jewish biblical tradition at the heart of all Masonry and the subsequent history of knowledge. According to the fraternity's *Constitutions,* the temple formed "the constant Pattern" for the ancient world. Visitors, returning home after seeing "the Wonder of all Travellers," used the temple "as . . . the most perfect Pattern" to improve "the *Architecture* of their own Country." After completing the temple, furthermore, "the many Artists" who worked on its construction "dispers'd themselves" into Africa, Europe, and even India, where they served as "the GRAND MASTERS" of each nation. The Masonic *Constitutions* carefully claimed that Nebuchadnezzar's Hanging Gardens and Ephesus's Temple of Diana, two of the wonders of the ancient world, were both influenced by Hebrew examples or workers. Even Pythagoras, the official history noted, "borrow'd great Knowledge" from "the learned . . . JEWS" held captive in Babylon.[27]

The care with which speculative Masons asserted the centrality of Hebrew contributions reveals their contested nature. Increased knowledge about the past, particularly its chronology, sharpened the problem of relating the history of the sacred and the profane. New information about classical pagan civilization even raised the possibility that it predated Hebrew culture. A new genealogy of learning could now be imagined that undercut the centrality of the Biblical record.[28]

Such a possibility created a flurry of post-Restoration interest in Judaism and other ancient religions that often centered on the temple. Masonic brother

Figure 3. Front View of the Temple of Solomon. *Engraving by John Senex, London, 1725. Courtesy of Scottish Rite Museum of Our National Heritage, 75.46.16. Photography by David Bohl*

William Stukeley published a pamphlet that showed "how heathen mythology is derived from sacred history." His friend Newton pursued the question obsessively during his later years. Recognizing that claims to great antiquity among other traditions undermined Judaism's centrality, Newton attempted to harmonize their chronologies with the Bible, seeking to show that other ancient cultures exaggerated their age and that Solomon's kingdom represented human history's first great civilization.[29]

For Newton, the importance of Solomon's Temple went even beyond its apologetic and historic value. It also prefigured the heavenly Jerusalem, the ultimate expression of God's wisdom. Thus, rigorous study of even the temple's smallest details revealed the nature of God himself. Newton's view might have been idiosyncratic, but his attitudes about the significance of the temple underline the continuing emotional power of the biblical past with which speculative Masons, claiming descent from the temple's builders, identified themselves.[30]

This ancient world could also be seen as the foundation of true religion, as the original model from which later beliefs had declined. Particularly in the

early eighteenth century, religious debate often focused on gaining control of this primeval terrain. Brother William Stukeley's Druidic ideas arose out of this desire for ancient antecedents. Like Newton, Stukeley believed that the earliest English people arrived from the Middle East around the time of the patriarchs, carrying the religion of Abraham—what Stukeley called "Patriarchal Christianity"—and the world's primeval language, Hebrew. This Druidic worship later degenerated, but Stukeley believed that its earlier purity resulted in a knowledge of the Trinity through reason alone, a discovery that he believed offered a strong argument for Christian orthodoxy. Stukeley's ancient researches thus involved, in the words of a friend, "reconciling Plato and Moses[,] and the Druid and Christian religion." [31]

Masons seem not to have made similar claims to antiquity about their religious beliefs, but their unwillingness to prescribe particular beliefs clearly harked back to those early "Patriarchal" times preceding both the complex legalism and ritualism of classic Judaism and the exclusive dogmas of contemporary Christianity. The 1723 *Constitutions* argued that Masonry bound its members "Only to . . . that Religion in which all Men agree." Pointing out that Masonry was "found in all Nations, even of divers Religions," the 1738 *Constitutions* went even further. The brothers, it argued, were "true *Noachida*," the medieval Jewish scholar Maimonides' term for the righteous gentile who could be saved by keeping the moral law. Like Stukeley as well, however, Masonry also went beyond this simple primitive religion. The histories in the Masonic *Constitutions* also declared Masonry part of the later Jewish and Christian tradition. The discussion of the origins of Masonry in the 1723 version referred to the temple as that of the "TRUE GOD" and called Jesus "*God's* MESSIAH, the great Architect of the Church." [32]

Masonry took a moderate position in the debate about ancient religions. Although the fraternity clearly rejected both atheism and claims to a monopoly on religious truth, Masonic teachings refused to define this position any further. Rationalists and even moderate deists could agree that primitive religion had become tarnished in later years, even if Judaism and Christianity perhaps held more truth than other religions. At the same time, more orthodox Christians could hold that ancient beliefs confirmed the truths of Christianity and provided an entry into the higher truths issuing from revelation.[33]

But the same issue could also lead to more intractable problems for this broad middle way—difficulties that helped legitimate Masonry's other intellectual tradition. As research into this past increasingly revealed, the search for certainty in ancient origins could generate claims that challenged Christianity itself. At the heart of these difficulties lay the shocking recognition of widespread religious diversity both in the eighteenth-century world outside Europe and in the past. Examination of the past and other religious traditions uncovered, not unity, but diversity. Fuller knowledge of early practices and beliefs, furthermore, revealed how seldom they met eighteenth-century expectations. These troubling discoveries thus lacked the satisfying apologetic results earlier thinkers had expected. Devout Christians seeking reform could turn this argument upon established churches, using ancient religion to challenge beliefs they could claim were later additions to primitive purity. Newton believed the idea of the Trinity a corruption of original monotheism. More troubling, opponents of all established beliefs could wield these same weapons against orthodoxy itself. Deists pointed out that even the Bible showed that religion emerged before God revealed himself, not afterward, thus undercutting the necessity of revelation. Indeed, Judaism and Christianity themselves might be seen as further examples of degeneration from first principles.

The faith in the ancient world that made first operative and then speculative Masonry so compelling to learned Britons thus raised major difficulties. Increasing historical knowledge led, not to a resolution of contemporary problems, but to a recognition that the past might have been as confusing as the present. Increasingly, eighteenth-century Europeans realized the need for some suprahistorical standard to adjudicate the questions raised by the ancient world, a standard they increasingly found in enlightened ideas of universal reason, ideals that would also be incorporated into the speculative fraternity then taking shape.[34]

The power of Masonry over the next hundred years rested in large part upon the flexible way the fraternity aligned itself with the ancient world and its worship. Although the fraternity clearly linked itself to religion, it also allowed a range of interpretations that prevented Masonry from becoming narrowly sectarian. But this openness to a variety of opinions could also prove a liability. People seeking to tighten the boundaries of religious belief and expression found the fraternity a tempting target. This sort of attack, however, would not become a serious problem for another century, when evangelicals attacked and nearly destroyed the American fraternity. Before then, however, Masonry provided a religious experience that was, as the early-eighteenth-century brothers expected, both emotionally powerful and rational. These rituals, with the temple and the dead body of Hiram at their mythical center, drew initiates into a world of ancient experiences that attended to both mystical wisdom and rational inquiry.

Masonry's complex connections with the wisdom and mysteries of the distant past were profoundly ironic. A group of learned Englishmen discovered in the relatively recent histories and rituals of a contemporary group of artisans the signs of an antiquity that powerfully expressed their deepest beliefs about God and the nature of truth. To protect this link with the past, they created a new organization with unprecedented powers. But, even at their culmination, the rituals they formed revealed the growing problem at the heart of the early-eighteenth-century faith in the ancients: primeval experience had been complex rather than simple and authoritative.

The increasing challenges to simple trust in ancient wisdom, however, did not destroy the power of Masonry. Although the learned often came to see the speculations of the ancients as early errors rather than obscure emblems of deeper insight, primeval mysteries retained their fascination in other cultural settings. Inside the Royal Society, Stukeley's Druidical theories were increasingly scorned. Outside, his ideas sparked a powerful enthusiasm for the Druids that lasted a century. Long after serious scientists stopped searching for a key to the ancients' obscure figures, the rich hints of past mysteries and links to the ancient world, discovered and then expanded by early speculative brothers, continued to promise a unified knowledge that went beyond empirical observation.[35]

II. The Augustan Style

According to the Master Mason's ritual, the workmen who found Hiram's body could not lift it because his flesh came off in their hands. They succeeded only through use of "the lion's grip," lifting him "Hand to Hand, Foot to Foot, Cheek to Cheek, Knee to Knee, and Hand in Back." Hiram was raised, the ceremony commented, "as all other Masons are. . . . By the Five Points of Fellowship."[36]

If Hiram's death placed speculative Masonry within one set of meanings, his raising connected it with another. Fellowship had been a key concept in operative Masonry. Craftsmen were fellows, and thus associates, equal partners. Although not yet connected to Hiram or the giving of the word, the five points of fellowship had been part of some operative lodge ritual. In adapting these practices, speculative Masons gave the ceremonial embrace new significance. They placed it in the climactic story of their rituals, using it to communicate the Master's Word that Hiram had died to protect. This increased importance deepened the meanings attached to the idea of fellowship by the speculative Masons. They first expanded the term's meaning to make members more than fellows; they were now members of a fictive family. Just as important, this brotherhood was no longer limited to craftsmen. All men, regardless of their occupation, residence, and nation, could now become Masonic brothers.

In the hands of the new speculative Masons, the idea of a universal family tied together by affection became the central public and private explanation of their organization, now known explicitly as a "fraternity." Just as the idea of ancient mysteries created the basis of one part of Masonry, the ideal of brotherhood provided a foundation for another. The term "brothers" significantly appears but is never explained in the rituals; the concept pointed to another, virtually distinct set of meanings that went beyond the esoteric cult of primitivism suggested by the degree ceremonies. By embracing the ideal of brotherhood, Masonry became a vital part of early-eighteenth-century cosmopolitan society.

The ideal of brotherhood did more than simply identify Masonry with its social context. Masonry linked itself closely to two major shifts developing at the time. It first followed the practices of genteel society that built upon the ideal of polite sociability emerging after the Restoration. Second, the fraternity also powerfully expressed the ideas of the early Enlightenment, especially its order, simplicity, and social harmony. By blunting the force of local peculiarities and individual idiosyncrasies, Masonic brotherhood provided an organizing principle that allowed truly universal fellowship.

The elaboration of these practices and ideas through the principle of brotherhood helped ensure the new fraternity's success. In ways that ancient mysteries could not, the idea of brotherhood spoke to one of the central social problems of the early eighteenth century, the difficulties of ordering authority and social life in a rapidly changing world that was undermining older patterns and boundaries. Masonry's family provided personal relationships and social standing without rejecting the new opportunities offered by the expan-

Figure 4. The Five Points of Fellowship. The climactic moment in the Master Mason's ritual, the raising of Hiram Abiff by the lion's grip. *From Avery Allyn,* A Ritual of Freemasonry *(Philadelphia, 1831). Courtesy American Antiquarian Society*

sion of commerce, science, and communications. In this, Masonry was not so much unique as archetypal. Much of its power came from arranging and purifying common elite practices and ideas in ways that allowed Masonry to express its central concerns in a particularly powerful way. Drawing upon cultural models that would shape eighteenth- and nineteenth-century Europe and America, the first speculative Masons created a fraternal organization that could encompass the world. An exploration of the origins of Masonry's genteel practices and its enlightened ideas—as well as their relationship to their early-eighteenth-century context—may explain this success.

The antiquarian Dr. William Stukeley seems to have joined the London lodge that met at Christopher Cat's Fountain Tavern in the Strand soon after his 1720/1 initiation, for he was present when the duke of Wharton, grand master of the new speculative fraternity, visited the group on November 3, 1722. Although Stukeley failed to record the details of the visit, the lodge undoubtedly drank to the grand master's health, perhaps after singing the still-new Warden's Song, which mentioned Wharton's name, or the more elaborate Master's Song, with toasts punctuating each section. Perhaps, as well, a brother read a learned lecture to the assembly. Less than a year later, Dr. Stukeley, now master of the lodge, discussed his research on a Roman ruin in Dorchester with the group, passing out the printed version of the lecture to each of the members.[37]

Lectures, toasts, and singing were not uniquely Masonic. They formed part of the cosmopolitan society in which the speculative fraternity was being created. Even the location of Stukeley's lodge suggests this connection, for until about 1720 Christopher Cat's tavern had been the meeting place of the celebrated Kit-Cat Club. Limited by rule to forty members and by practice to stalwart members of the Whig party, the group was noted for both its elaborate toasts and a brilliant membership that included the duke of Wharton's father (an important Whig political leader) as well as Joseph Addison and Richard Steele, the authors of the *Spectator,* the most popular periodical of cosmopolitan London.[38]

The world of the Kit-Cat Club and the *Spectator,* with their genteel social practices, provided a key model for Masonic lodges. Clubs developed rapidly in urban society after the Restoration. The new fraternity built upon this foundation, explicitly stating and practicing the principles and ideas pioneered, often only implicitly, by these groups. In seeking to blunt political, religious, and national divisions, the fraternity paralleled as well a related impulse in society that attempted to reconstitute social relationships through the ideals of politeness and toleration. Masonry's fictive kinship provided a rich language that helped, as the 1723 *Constitutions* suggested, to "conciliate true Friendship among Persons that must else have remain'd at a perpetual Distance."[39]

Masonic activities often drew upon the practices of other clubs. Both groups usually met in the private rooms of taverns, denying entrance except to members. Newcomers were admitted only by general consent. Within these rooms, eating and drinking formed a central activity. In early lodges, food and drink were served throughout the meeting, with a supper usually following. Both groups closed with members "clubbing" together to pay the bill. Not surprisingly, contemporaries sometimes suggested that both clubs and lodges encouraged overindulgence. Brother William Hogarth, ironically later a grand steward responsible for the annual feast's wine supply, depicted an aproned and (seemingly) besotted Freemason being helped home in his engraving *Night.*[40]

The brothers' appropriation of club practices rested partly on their active involvement in other such institutions. Stukeley, for example, was an avid creator and joiner of clubs, joining the Society of Antiquaries in the 1710s and the Egyptian Society in the 1740s. In between, he helped found the Society of Roman Knights, the Brazen Nose Society, and the Clergyman's Book Club. Along with the local lodge master and the early speculative leaders Jean Theophile Desaguliers and the Reverend James Anderson, Stukeley also belonged to the Gentleman's Society of Spaulding, a group founded to discuss the *Spectator.*[41]

By the 1710s, participation in clubs was becoming a regular part of social life among the upper levels of English society. The club had first become popular in the later seventeenth century, simultaneous with the evolution of the term itself from a clump to a select group of men knotted together. By the early eighteenth century, London hosted an estimated two thousand such organizations, a circumstance often noted in the *Spectator.*[42] "Man is said to be a Sociable Animal," wrote Addison in a 1711 number, "and, as an Instance of it, we may observe, that we take all Occasions and Pretences of forming our selves into those little Nocturnal Assemblies, which are commonly known by the name of *Clubs.*" Whenever "a Sett of Men find themselves agree in any Particular, tho' never so trivial, they establish themselves into a kind of Fraternity, and meet once or twice a Week, upon the account of such a Fantastick Resemblance." The *Spectator,* fictively set in one such association, altogether mentions nearly thirty groups, including imaginary bands of the quiet and the dull, the Mum and the Hum-Drum Clubs. As Addison suggested, the club could be used for a wide variety of uses from dissipation and blasphemy, like the Hell-Fire Club headed by the duke of Wharton, to simple eating and drinking, like the Beefsteak Club. Addison thought the latter the most popular, as they were "the points wherein most men agree."[43]

The enormous popularity of the club formed part of a larger transformation. Beginning in London, English society experienced major changes that reshaped modes of sociability. The communal and kinship bonds that had held together village life no longer proved adequate to the world of increased social diversity and widened cultural horizons experienced by Britons who moved beyond the narrow world of the parish but not yet within the circles of court society. The club, and its stepchild Masonry, provided a means of recreating the close ties of local friendship in a larger, more cosmopolitan world.

London experienced these developments first. Having tripled in size in the seventeenth century to become the largest urban area in Europe, the eighteenth-century city no longer possessed a unified center. Addison in 1712 noted that "the inhabitants of St. James' are a distinct people from those of Cheapside." Rather than a single community, "I look upon it [London] as an aggregate of several nations." These nations, furthermore, were in constant motion. Stukeley entered the city as a young man, left it soon afterwards, and then returned in middle age. Foreign immigration, an even greater cultural dislocation, also expanded markedly in these years. Perhaps not coincidentally, two of the key figures in the creation of the new brotherhood, the Scot James Anderson and the Huguenot Jean Theophile Desaguliers, were both born outside England.[44]

Expanding networks of commerce and communications centered in London further diminished complacent parochialism. The Commercial Revolution that began in the seventeenth century brought the goods and merchants of both foreign and domestic trading partners to the city. Addison described the Royal Exchange, London's mercantile and financial center, as a "kind of *Emporium* for the whole Earth." "Sometimes I am justled among the Body of *Armenians:* Sometimes I am lost in a Crowd of *Jews:* and sometimes make one in a Groupe of *Dutch-men*." Increased access to printed materials, particularly after the lapse of effective censorship in 1694, further broadened the horizons of literate Britons. What one journalist deplored as an "immoderate Appetite of Intelligence" made casual acceptance of local beliefs and practices more difficult.[45]

The changes that transformed London also affected the provinces, although later and on a lesser scale. The Commercial Revolution reached there as well, bringing them into closer contact with the metropolis. "This whole kingdom, as well as the people, as the land, and even the sea, in every part of it," wrote Daniel Defoe in the 1720s, exaggerating only slightly, "are employ'd to furnish something . . . to supply the city of London with provisions." In the opposite direction, a flood of printed materials issued from the metropolis. Newspapers arriving from London spurred provincial competitors near the beginning of the eighteenth century. Expanded transportation networks, the natural result of commercial expansion, further changed provincial life. Rural and urban elites increasingly met together in resorts like Bath or Tunbridge Wells.[46]

Clubs provided an important means of adjusting to these changes. Amid weakened parochial ties, they created small, select groups that helped order economic, political, and social life. Masonry went even further, articulating ideals that most clubs paid homage to only implicitly. To the closed door that expressed the club's exclusivity, Masons added a guard with a drawn sword and an extensive initiation that decisively marked the distinction between the lodge and the outside world. Instead of the often informal rules ordering most clubs, Masonry created a *Book of Constitutions*. Even in 1723, Masonic regulations filled eighteen printed pages.

Masonry's clearest enunciation of club ideals, however, lay in its formalization of the idea of brotherhood. In this metaphor, Masonry was not entirely original. Addison had referred to clubs as "a kind of Fraternity," and Jonathan Swift, Henry St. John Bolingbroke, and later Mason Dr. John Arbuthnot had formed a "Brothers' Club" in 1711 among the leaders of the Tory party. Typically, however, Masonry gave greater definition and consistency to the metaphor, extending and exploring the meanings of ties between members. Even singing, an important part of many meetings, was allowed only when the lodge included no brother "*to whom Singing is disagreeable*." According to the 1723 *Constitutions*, the fraternity offered a "*Center* of *Union*" in a world of "perpetual distance."[47]

More than distance, however, separated English people. The problem of factionalism bedeviled early-eighteenth-century cosmopolitan society. Addison considered clubs "very useful," but only if "Men are thus knit together, by a Love of Society, not a spirit of Faction." Although Addison sought forms of association that transcended the divisions created by differing beliefs, clubs more often reinforced existing disagreements. Even Swift and Bolingbroke's Brothers Club, despite claiming that its "great ends" included "Improvements of friendship," was actually a partisan institution designed to unite Tories in imitation of the Whig Kit-Cat Club. The attempt to mute such divisions became a central issue for the early-eighteenth-century English elite. "We should not any longer regard our Fellow-Subjects as Whigs or Tories," pleaded Addison in 1711, "but should make the Man of Merit our Friend, and the Villain our Enemy."[48]

Early speculative Masons made this unity a central Masonic ideal. By allowing all "Men of Honour and Honesty" to join, the first article of the charges read to new brothers noted, Masonry rose above parochial differences. The early "Fellow-Crafts Song" similarly boasted:

> Ensigns of State, that feed our Pride,
> Distinctions troublesome, and vain,
> By *Masons* true are laid aside:
> *Art's* free-born *Sons* such Toys disdain.

"Sweet Fellowship," the song continued, formed the "*Lodge's* lasting Cement." Masonic rules of behavior also recommended this ideal. Members meeting on the street were "to salute one another in a courteous Manner, . . . calling each other *Brother*." Within the lodge, rules banned discussion of controversial topics. "No private Piques or Quarrels must be brought within the

Door of the *Lodge*," brothers were warned, "far less any Quarrels about *Religion*, or *Nations*, or *State-Policy*."[49]

Such disagreement deeply troubled early-eighteenth-century England. "The Minds of many good Men among us," mourned Addison in 1711, "appear sowered with Party-Principles, and alienated from one another in such a manner, as seems to me altogether inconsistent with the Dictates either of Reason or Religion." Masonry could not entirely ignore these quarrels, but its fraternal prescriptions sought to carve out a broad middle ground that could unite *"good men and true."*[50]

By the early years of the eighteenth century, many Britons craved relief from nearly a century of political instability. The revolutions of the 1640s and the 1680s deeply divided the body politic. Defense of the Protestant monarchy in the wars against France after the Glorious Revolution and the question of succession raised by the failure of Queen Anne to produce an heir sustained a rivalry between Whigs and Tories that continued with unprecedented intensity after 1688. "If an *English* Man considers the great Ferment into which our Political World is thrown at present, and how intensely it is heated in all its parts," Addison suggested in 1711, "he cannot suppose that it will cool again in less than three hundred Years." Although stability actually came much sooner, British political culture remained contentious long after the Hanoverian succession in 1714.[51]

Religious issues also remained troublesome. Neither the eclipse of the Anglican establishment during the Civil War nor its restoration in 1660 brought harmony. Religious debates continued to divide the country in the early eighteenth century, particularly because the church's concern with legitimacy and obedience inevitably involved it in political issues. While High Church Tories called for exclusion of dissenters and complete obedience to church and monarch, increasing numbers of deists rejected the power of the church and even the possibility of revelation. In the period just before and during the 1717 creation of the speculative grand lodge, the fate of two celebrated churchmen suggests the extent of this polarization. Dr. Henry Sacheverell faced parliamentary impeachment in 1709 for urging the church to coerce dissenters; Bishop Benjamin Hoadley met with church discipline eight years later for claiming the church had no right to do so.[52]

Speculative Masonry sought to avoid the shoals of this intolerance. The new group's irenic course in both religion and politics excluded extremes but otherwise prescribed little. Like the latitudinarian position of many moderate churchmen and dissenters, the fraternity rejected both narrow High Church beliefs and the deists' entirely natural religion. Such a liberal attitude can be seen in the membership of the new fraternity. The Presbyterian minister the Reverend James Anderson and the Anglican priest the Reverend Jean Theophile Desaguliers cooperated in preparing the 1723 *Book of Constitutions*. Stukeley, although he later took Anglican orders, attended no church at all during the same period. By 1731, Jews belonged to at least two London lodges.[53]

Such doctrinal and sectarian differences were to be laid aside within the Masonic family. The very first charge read to new brothers after they had completed the deliberately obscure rituals told them that the fraternity no longer required conformity to prevailing local beliefs. "'Tis now thought," the charge pointed out, "more expedient only to oblige them to that Religion in which all Men agree, leaving their particular Opinions to themselves . . . , by whatever Denominations or Persuasions they may [be] distinguish'd." Although this came close to endorsing natural religion (the fundamental principles of religious truth known through reason alone), Masonry also warned against irreligion and deism: "If he [the Mason] rightly understands the Art," the first article of the charges noted in terms commonly used for early deists, "he will never be a stupid *Atheist,* nor an irreligious *Libertine.*"[54]

The new fraternity took up a sort of nonpartisan latitudinarianism in politics as well. Many of the early brothers were Whig leaders—including the powerful prime minister Sir Robert Walpole—and Anderson's history of Masonry explicitly linked the rise of the speculative group to the Hanoverian succession. According to its regulations, however, speculative Masonry did not require adherence to any particular political opinion beyond a refusal, as "a peaceable Subject to the Civil Powers," to countenance rebellion. Even a rebel could not be automatically expelled from the lodge. In the absence of other crimes, the fraternity judged, "his Relation to it remains indefeasible." The staunch Tory Dr. John Arbuthnot, a visitor to France in the late 1710s when such visits seemed suspect as evidence of support for the Pretender, participated actively in Masonry during its early years.[55]

The fraternity's desire to remove obstacles to friendship and harmony can be seen finally in its attempt to unite men of different social standing. "All *Masons,*" argued the charges, "are as *Brethren* upon the same *Level.*" But they also noted that this equality did not involve omitting the deference due to men of high degree. "*Masonry* takes no Honour from a Man that he had before"; rather, Masonry "adds to his Honour." By exquisitely balancing social standing and brotherly equality, Masonry sought to unify the divided English elite.[56]

In this goal, Masonry expressed key changes in early-eighteenth-century cosmopolitan society. Especially in London, social life increasingly involved easier interaction among different levels of society. Nobles such as the duke of Montague attended clubs with urban gentry and professionals. Swift proudly reported to Stella that the Brothers Club in 1711/2 numbered "9 L[or]ds, and ten Common[e]rs." Former punctilios of social standing also began to loosen. In the city, Addison noted, "our Manners, sit more loose upon us." "An unconstrained carriage, and a certain openness of behaviour, are the height of good breeding." By contrast, the country lagged behind "the politer Part of Mankind": "A Polite Country Squire shall make you as many Bows in half an

Hour, as would serve a Courtier for a Week." The provincial resort towns that modeled themselves on London similarly sought to reduce attention to what Addison called "obliging Deferencies, Condescensions and Submissions, with many outward Forms and Ceremonies." Scarborough authorities in the 1730s asked that visiting gentlemen not wear swords, since "all distinctions ought to be lost in a general complaisance."[57] This new attempt to blur rather than reinforce distinctions among the elite can be seen most fully in the relatively unornamented male clothing becoming popular in the period, the breeches with coat and waistcoat worn by professionals and urban gentry as well as great aristocrats.

These new practices were summed up and given meaning by the ideal of *politeness,* a term that, like *club,* took on its present meaning in the years after the Restoration. Originally "smooth" and "polished," *polite* now referred to refined manners and self-presentation. In polishing their manners, gentlemen stressed decorous speech and carefully controlled bodily movement, what a 1702 book subtitled *The Manners of the Age* called "a dextrous management of our Words and Actions." Such politeness sought to forge a common elite culture that differentiated its adherents from the lower orders that Addison called the "Rustick part of the Species (who on all Occasions acted bluntly and naturally)." "Romping, struggling, throwing things at one another's head are the becoming pleasantries of the mob," noted Lord Chesterfield, an early speculative Mason, "but degrade the gentleman." Such control also encouraged peaceful interaction within a divided society growing beyond personal acquaintance, serving, as *The Manners of the Age* continued, to "make other people have better Opinions of us and themselves." Through careful attention to manners and speech, gentlemen could move easily within a polite social world that reached across local and even national boundaries.[58]

Masonry explicitly identified itself with these new models of social practice. According to early speculative brothers, classical architecture, revived in the Renaissance by "the polite Nations," signaled increasing civilization:

> View but those Savage Nations, where
> No Masonry did e'er appear,
> What strange unpolish'd Brutes they are.

The speculative *Constitutions* likewise warned that brothers "must avoid *ill Manners.*" The fraternity's ability to encourage proper values was even celebrated in song:

> It makes us courteous, easy, free,
> Generous, honourable, and gay;
> What other Art the like can say?
> We make it plainly to appear,
> By our Behaviour everywhere,

> That where you meet a Mason, there
> You meet a Gentleman.[59]

Masonic ideals thus richly embodied early-eighteenth-century models of sociability. The fraternity's forms made the ideals of clubs and polite society explicit. But Masonry's cultural meanings went beyond symbolizing new social practices. Its ideas of unity and brotherhood expressed new ways of organizing and thinking about the nature of society, providing a powerful language for the changing ideas of the Enlightenment, ideas encoded not only within Masonry's idea of fraternity but also in its celebration of the Augustan style of architecture.

The first history of speculative Masonry, written by Royal Society fellow the Reverend James Anderson, portrayed the recovery of a hidden knowledge far different from the Master's Word discovered at Hiram's grave. Just as much as Solomon's Temple, Anderson celebrated Rome's "*Zenith* of Glory, under AUGUSTUS CAESAR," identified as "the *Grand-Master* of the Lodge at *Rome*." According to Anderson, the buildings of that period provided "the Pattern and Standard of *true Masonry* in all future Times . . . which we often express by the Name of the AUGUSTAN STILE, and which we are now only endeavouring to imitate, and have not yet arriv'd to its Perfection." This period, however, marked also by the birth of "*God's* MESSIAH, the great-Architect of the Church," did not last, since "The GOTHS and VANDALS . . . with warlike Rage and gross Ignorance . . . utterly destroy'd many of the finest Edifices, and defac'd others." In place of the ideal Roman structures, they erected buildings of "Confusion and Impropriety." Only later did the Renaissance emerge from these "Ruins of *Gothic* Ignorance." After "the AUGUSTAN STILE was rais'd from its Rubbish in *Italy*," England too participated in this development, setting the early model of royal patronage of the style in the employment by Charles I of Inigo Jones. After the Glorious Revolution, Anderson suggested, the example of William III led "the *Nobility,* the *Gentry,* the *Wealthy* and the *Learned* to affect much the *Augustan Style*."[60]

The Augustan style formed the centerpiece of Masonry's second set of meanings—the world of Enlightenment and genteel sociability. Unlike the obscurity and complexity of ancient mysteries, neoclassical architecture based on Roman models symbolized simplicity and balance, the central themes of the early Enlightenment. Through its celebration of classical buildings and its praise of fraternity, the new speculative group placed itself firmly within these developing ideas. The Enlightenment aesthetics, cosmology, and sociology wrapped up in the idea of the Augustan style provided an intellectual framework as important for later American Freemasonry as the social framework of clubs and genteel society—and just as crucial for making sense of developments within the fraternity.

Speculative Freemasonry began in the circles formulating and enunciating these new enlightened ideas. Fellows of the Royal Society, like Anderson and Stukeley, made up more than one-quarter of the fraternity's membership in its first decade. Brother Jean Theophile Desaguliers, the society's demonstrator, suggests these close ties. The Anglican priest played a key role in shaping the speculative fraternity. Not only did he serve as grand master in 1719 and deputy grand master in 1722 but was similarly at the center of the intellectual world of the early Enlightenment. His work spreading and popularizing Newton's ideas brought him into close contact with the great scientist, who stood as godfather to one of his sons. Besides his work with Newton, Desaguliers served as a key citizen in the emerging republic of letters. He translated a number of French scientific works into English, by authors such as the important Dutch mathematician Willem Jakob Gravesende. Christian Huygens and Hermann Boerhaave, two of the best scientific minds of the next generation, attended Desaguliers's lectures on the Continent. His writings later inspired his Masonic brother Benjamin Franklin's scientific work. Desaguliers's demonstrations helped spread enlightened science in England as well. In 1719, while serving as grand master, he gave a series of lectures in the great rooms owned by Sir Richard Steele, the coauthor of the *Spectator* and, according to some evidence, Desaguliers's Masonic brother. This connection between enlightened ideas and the fraternity continued throughout the century. Franklin, whose newspaper reprinted a story about Montesquieu's 1730 initiation, led the aged Voltaire into a Parisian lodge for his initiation forty-eight years afterward.[61]

For both early and later brothers, the new group's celebration of architecture and fraternity expressed central elements of these new enlightened ideas. The Augustan style that Anderson made central to his official 1723 history of Masonry first celebrated the growing importance of neoclassical aesthetic principles. Even before the creation of the speculative group, Joseph Addison had used architectural metaphors to convey his artistic ideas. Praising "majestick simplicity," Addison in 1711 labeled bad poets "Goths in Poetry, who, like those in Architecture, not being able to come up to the beautiful Simplicity of the old Greeks and Romans, have endeavoured to supply its Place with all the Extravagances of an irregular Fancy." By contrast, Augustan poets, like neoclassical buildings, did not need to "hunt after foreign Ornaments."[62]

Such neoclassical aesthetic principles became increasingly popular in early-eighteenth-century England. The first English translation of Andrea Palladio's complete *Four Books of Architecture,* a central text in the Renaissance revival of classical buildings, appeared in the 1710s, the decade of Addison's important aesthetic statements and the speculative fraternity's creation. By then, the term *Gothic* had become a common term of abuse. In 1710, Stukeley scorned Oxford's new All Souls' quadrangle as "an anachronism of the *Gothic* degenerat[e] taste." Fearing the destructiveness of "Goths and barbarians," he formed the Society of Roman Knights in 1722 to study and preserve the remains of Roman Britain. One of the society's members, writing in the 1730s, remarked sarcastically: "I my self have admired the laborious Dullness and Stupidity which appear in all Gothick contrivances of any kind."[63]

Proper artistic principles energized only part of this scorn. The power of Augustan aesthetics largely lay in their apparent congruence with the Newtonian idea of a regular universe governed by simple mathematical principles. "The grand secret of the whole machine," wrote later Masonic brother John Arbuthnot around the turn of the century, "proves to be (like the other contrivances of infinite wisdom) simple and natural." Thus mathematical learning encouraged Augustan standards. "The mathematics," Arbuthnot claimed, "charm the passions, restrain the impetuousity of imagination, and purge the mind from error and prejudice." A 1728 poem by Desaguliers similarly promised a "plain and intelligible account of the system of the world" in the course of proving *The Newtonian System of the World the Best Model of Government.*[64]

Masonry's promotion of geometry, mathematics, and architecture thus celebrated and represented this enlightened world of simplicity, clarity, and regular proportions, allowing early speculative brothers to imagine Masonry as more than a trade followed by lowly mechanics, more than a mere club of gentlemen. Because of its basis in order and harmony, Anderson suggested, Masonry provided a measure of civilization and learning. Only "the polite *Nations*," he pointed out, perceived "the Confusion and Impropriety of the *Gothick* Buildings." "Let those that do despise the Art," boasted an early (and less polished) Masonic song,

> Live in a Cave in some Desart,
> And herd with Beasts from Men apart
> For their Stupidity.[65]

Just as Masonry's geometric metaphors spoke eloquently of enlightened principles of art and the world, they also embodied new ways of thinking about society and human nature that would be deeply influential in eighteenth-century England and America. Early-eighteenth-century intellectuals, most notably Anthony Ashley Cooper, the third earl of Shaftesbury, portrayed society as bound together by sympathy and natural desire for interaction, simple and natural processes analogous to the neoclassical, Newtonian world. Masonry's fraternal figures of speech also reveal another element of this transformation, the way that these ideas met some of the pressing needs of the British elite. Seventeenth-century instability had challenged the power and standing of this group, calling its very legitimacy into question. By reshaping notions of the social order, enlightened ideas of society helped reinforce the standing of the elite. Masonic fraternity provided a way of thinking through and experiencing new kinds of social relationships better suited to both the realities of eighteenth-century society and the social metaphors that explained and justified it. The close connection between Masonry and the social order that gave it birth can be seen in the development of enlightened ideas of natural sociability during the seventeenth-century crisis of the English elite.[66]

The dominant seventeenth-century image of society was "the Great Chain of Being," a hierarchy of ranks linking the monarch to the lowliest peasant, with each level fulfilling its duties by commanding its inferiors and obeying its superiors. This vision of a society held together by authority and submission lost its power over the next century. Increased commercialization, inflation, and population growth put pressure upon village hierarchies that had previously been relatively self-contained, and growing numbers of merchants, middlemen, and professionals fitted awkwardly in the metaphor of the Great Chain.[67]

Thomas Hobbes's bleak vision of Leviathan, written during the great debate of the midcentury Civil War, revealed the breakdown of older metaphors. For Hobbes, human existence originally lacked elaborate hierarchy and structures of authority, leading individuals to fear for their own existence. Social order was thus a human creation, designed to end the "war of every man against every man." "Men," he wrote, "have no pleasure, (but on the contrary a great deale of grief) in keeping company, where there is no power able to over-awe them all." Only complete submission to authority could resolve conflict.[68]

Elite Britons would be able to reimpose a measure of subordination after 1660, particularly through the restoration of the monarchy and a changing demographic setting that eased economic pressures. But, especially for cosmopolitan urban gentlemen experiencing the uncertainties created by commercialization, political and religious turmoil, and a flood of printed information, the challenges posed by Hobbes and others remained troubling. British elites had to turn back the demands of monarchical or religious absolutism even as they upheld the social hierarchy that provided their own authority. Attempting to redefine society in response to these pressures, late-seventeenth- and early-eighteenth-century English theorists molded the Enlightenment social theory powerfully expressed in Masonry.

The basis of this transformation lay in a two-pronged critique of Hobbes. First, Britons suggested that humans naturally approved good actions because of their innate sentiments—perhaps even a sixth sense—of benevolence, what Henry More called a "boniform faculty" and Shaftesbury a "moral sense." A new psychology, envisioned most fully by John Locke, similarly reshaped views of the self, removing the hidden conflicts and passions that had justified the strong hand of social and political power.[69]

Just as important, theorists now suggested, humans naturally enjoyed each other's company. "If any Appetite or Sense be natural," Shaftesbury argued, "the Sense of Fellowship is the same." By the early eighteenth century, these ideas of benevolence and sociability had become a central tenet of nearly all enlightened thinking about society.[70] By denying Hobbes's view of humanity, post-Restoration thinkers argued, society could avoid his world and his solution. Innate propensities could do naturally what absolutisms based on monarchy or religion claimed to do artificially.

Speculative Masonry became a powerful tool for thinking about and experiencing these values. The new group defined itself as a fictive family, as a fraternity held together by brotherly love—a conception reinforcing and reinforced by the ideals of benevolence and sociability. Masonic fraternity gave emotional weight to enlightened social relations by asserting their similarity to the widespread, seemingly natural experience of the family. Members were knit together by the same permanent bonds of affection and responsibility as actual kin, even during a period of intense political and religious disagreements.[71]

Masonry's fraternal metaphor also suggested that the group was held together, not by authority or coercion, but by social affections among relative equals. Rather than a hierarchical family headed by a commanding paterfamilias, Masonry prescribed a world of siblings where, as their official regulations stated, "all *Masons* are as *Brethren* upon the same *Level*." "All Preferment among *Masons*," boasted early brothers, "is grounded upon real Worth and personal Merit only," not social or political position. Although the grand master had to possess high social standing, that alone was not sufficient for a post that required "singular great Merit."[72]

As their balance between social hierarchy and merit suggests, Masons did not imagine a world of complete equality. Indeed, they implicitly supported social distinctions. The fraternity's special clothing, its emphasis on charity, and its processions all proclaimed high standing. The closed nature of the group, along with its high fees, excluded men without adequate financial resources. According to a prologue delivered at the Drury Lane Theater in 1728 by an actor in Masonic dress:

> But now the Honourable Badge I wear,
> Gives an indelible high Character.[73]

The ideals of benevolence and sociability thus reinforced, rather than undermined, elite status. At the close of the eighteenth century in America, these ideals would be used to challenge not just absolutism but all forms of social superiority (why was authority necessary if society naturally cohered?). Early-eighteenth-century proponents of Enlightenment social ideas, however, saw no such tension. These new ideals, they believed, actually strengthened the old order. Only the elite, they argued—often only implicitly—possessed the education and the cosmopolitan outlook necessary to cultivate these qualities fully. Common people, limited by superstition, ignorance, and parochial vision, lacked the moral and aesthetic sensitivity required to understand and lead society. According to Shaftesbury, "a man of thorough good breeding," that is, one with the proper "liberal education" in virtue, "is incapable of doing a rude or brutal action" and thus does not require the threat of punishment. "The mere vulgar of mankind," on the other hand, "often stand in need of such a rectifying object as the gallows before their eyes." Enlightened ideas provided alternative ways of supporting the social order, not leveling it. As Chesterfield told his son, "A drayman is probably born with as good organs as Milton, Locke, or Newton; but by culture they are much more above him, than he is above his horse."[74]

These attitudes first expressed a concurrent reshaping of status boundaries that helped break down the division between court and country that had bedeviled the seventeenth century. Urban merchants, professionals, and even intellectuals, previously lacking elite status, now could claim high standing. By including people who were often as wealthy as and better educated than the older gentry, the new categorization of society provided a more defensible definition of social standing. Older status divisions remained, but now the broader category of gentlemen allowed lower levels of the elite to escape categorization among Shaftesbury's "mere vulgar."[75]

Just as important, this rethinking of hierarchy in enlightened terms found confirmation in—and provided justification for—the world of clubs and politeness developing in early-eighteenth-century England. The relatively easy mixing of aristocrats and urban professionals in genteel society suggested natural harmony between the elements of this redefined society. At the same time, the voluntary organization of clubs underlined what Shaftebury called the "combining principle" among just those groups that seemed to possess it most abundantly.

Speculative Masonry was deeply embedded in the complexities of these new social definitions. As a part of the new genteel world, it provided a means of entry for urban men of wealth and learning, allowing Desaguliers and Stukeley to claim brotherhood with leading aristocrats and even members of the royal family. Furthermore, Masonic rituals, moral symbols, and instruction taught values that both justified elite status and provided a means of identifying with it.[76] As in the larger issue of ancient mysteries and modern enlightenment, Masonry's treatment of social distinctions explicitly symbolized a new vision of society even as it implicitly buttressed much of the old. Thus the "Enter'd 'Prentices Song," the most popular piece of early Masonic music, both celebrates Masons' high standing and asserts their equality with others.

> Great *Kings, Dukes, and Lords,*
> Have laid by their Swords,
> Our *Myst'ry* to put a good Grace on,
> And ne'er been ashame'd
> To hear themselves nam'd
> With a *Free* and an *Accepted Mason.*[77]

This tradition, however, was balanced by another. Even as Masonry proclaimed its centrality to the enlightened world of science and politeness, brothers also employed a different set of ideas to locate it within the world of ancient builders linked by a fellowship of adepts. Brotherhood and architecture could refer to the ancient mysteries as well as to a club of the genteel bound together by the simple principles of a Newtonian universe. Masonry's power lay in both meanings, allowing members to live simultaneously within worlds that were rapidly diverging. This powerful combination propelled the expansion of speculative Masonry into England, Europe, and America during the generation after its formation.

III. An Honour Much Courted of Late

When brother James Anderson revised the Masonic *Book of Constitutions* in 1738, he added a revealing history of speculative Masonry's earliest days. Tracing the 1717 "revival" and subsequent development of the grand lodge, Anderson ignored the growth of the new organization's jurisdiction, the development of its degree rituals, and the elaboration of enlightened ideas. Instead, his account focused on the installation of noble grand masters beginning in 1721. When grand lodge members elected John, duke of Montagu, Anderson noted, "they all express'd great Joy at the happy Prospect of being again patronized by *noble Grand Masters,* as in the prosperous Times of *Freemasonry.*" This aristocratic patronage spurred new success: "*Masonry* flourish'd in Harmony, Reputation and Numbers." Although three men, including Desaguliers, had held the position of grand master before Montagu, Anderson ended his history with a separate roster of noble grand masters that enabled the duke to head the list.[78]

Such aristocratic endorsement—and the "Reputation" Masonry gained thereby—seemed so important to Anderson because it reinforced a final element in the creation of the speculative fraternity. Masonic ideas and identifications asserted high social standing, but only the actual patronage by elite groups could validate these claims. The high status their membership conferred on Masonry (members of the royal family such as the future George IV served as grand master in later years) provided an important part of its appeal over the next century.

This identification allowed Masonry to spread rapidly in London and beyond. The fraternity's connection with the noble and the powerful attracted not only aristocrats but a substantial number of middling professionals, merchants, and tradesmen drawn by the new group's images of mystery, enlightenment, and social standing. Imitations, both jesting and serious, bore further witness to this appeal. Within a few years after its creation, Masonry spread beyond the learned circles of London that had created it into all of Britain and across the channel. After a shaky start made worse by the difficulties of transatlantic communications, the fraternity also took firm root in the American colonies among groups that looked to the English metropolis as a model.

The early 1720s marked the beginning of a great Masonic expansion. If the 4 original lodges of the 1717 meeting had become only 12 by 1721, probably largely the result of the affiliation of older operative lodges, the development of new lodges proceeded quickly thereafter. In 1724, the grand lodge, extending its reach beyond the metropolis, approved lodges in Carmarthenshire, Cheshire, Bristol, Hampshire, Norfolk, Somersetshire, and Sussex. By 1725, the grand lodge supervised some 70 lodges and had begun creating subordinate provincial grand lodges for more direct oversight. Despite this expansion, London dominated early speculative Masonry. More then 100 of the 140 lodges on the rolls in 1735 met within the city. Provincial lodges caught up with their metropolitan counterparts only around the middle of the century.[79] A song from 1721 had already foretold this expansion:

> And Thence in ev'ry Reign
> Did Masonry obtain
> With Kings, the Noble and the Wise,
> Whose Fame resounding to the Skies,
> Excites the present Age in Lodge to join.[80]

As the song suggested, the excitement around Masonry arose first among the prominent. The new group caught the attention of so many men of rank that by 1722 a clergyman noted that it had become "an honour much courted of late by quality." William Stukeley noted in his diary that the 1721 ceremony installing the duke of Montagu also was attended by Lord Herbert and Sir Andrew Fountain. Philip Dormer Stanhope (later the Lord Chesterfield who wrote the celebrated *Letters to His Son)* joined the fraternity about that time as well.[81]

Growing elite interest in the fraternity can be seen in the membership of Westminster's Horn Tavern Lodge, the highest-toned of the four represented at the 1717 formation of the grand lodge. The duke of Richmond, a lodge master, described the group in the 1720s as "being for the most part persons of quality and Members of Parliament." Besides the duke, the group also claimed nine other noblemen as well as grand master Jean Theophile Desaguliers. Four baronets and knights, three other men labeled "Honorable," and twenty-four noted as "esquire" also were part of the seventy-one members listed in 1725. Later the lodge initiated Montesquieu.[82]

These luminaries, however, did not monopolize the fraternity. Masonry's evolution from operative lodges and its universal pretensions left the door open for humbler men. The majority of the new members after 1717 came from the middling ranks just below the nobility and gentry, the expanding group of men who, like Stukeley, were unable to live off their estates but still possessed education, financial resources, or professional credentials that distinguished them from the rest of English society.[83] Fraternal charity, mutual aid, and economic contacts were more useful to them than to aristocrats. Their affiliation linked them to the cosmopolitan world of learning and gentility—and to the highest levels of society. Besides the aristocratic Horn Tavern Lodge, none of the other lodges in 1723 contained any members denominated "esquire." Only four lodges among the twenty in the 1723 *Constitutions* boasted officers with honorific designations. A high proportion of these members appear to have been professionals or prosperous tradesmen; some might have had connections with the operative craft. Thomas Morris, a 1718 grand warden, made his living as a stonecutter. Operative affiliations, however, usually faded. Among the early masters of Lodge No. 18, formed in 1722/3, were a physician, a surgeon, a tobacconist, a boatbuilder, a brewer, and two biscuit bakers. A mid-century list of the lodge's members shows a similar range of occupations.[84]

The desire for public honor that attracted both of Masonry's key constituencies helped encourage the speculative group to act more visibly than the ideals of ancient mysteries or polite fraternity required. With the installation of the first noble grand master in 1721, the grand lodge began holding an annual public procession, a practice that continued until 1747. Local lodges held theater nights attended by members in their regalia. To encourage such patronage, theater managers often added Masonic songs, prologues, or epilogues to the program. These public activities as well as accounts of prominent men joining or taking office all made regular appearances in the growing number of newspapers printed in London and the provinces. "In the Dearth of News," noted a 1730 letter writer to London's *Daily Journal,* "the subject of Free-Masonry has . . . filled up many a Paper."

> The world is in pain
> Our secrets to gain,

boasted the fraternity as early as 1723.[85]

Not all of this attention was welcome. Along with the positive reports of processions, theatergoing, and various meetings came less admiring attempts to penetrate fraternal secrets. At least half a dozen articles and pamphlets purporting to expose Masonic rituals appeared in the 1720s. Samuel Pritchard's *Masonry Dissected,* published in 1730, proved so popular—and presumably so accurate—that the grand lodge was forced to make changes to prevent an influx of illegitimate masons.[86] The attention given these secrets also inspired a variety of imitators, ranging from jesters to organized groups claiming to represent a more authentic Masonic tradition. Ridicule of the speculative fraternity began in the 1720s. The rival Khaibarites poked fun at Masonic myth-making in a 1726 poem:

> To see the Roll of Masons good
> So boasted of, must move your Laughter
>
> .   .   .   .
>
> The less of History they saw,
> Their kind Invention flow'd the faster;

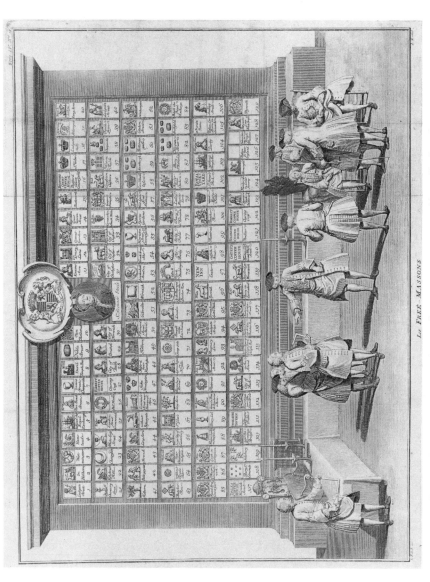

Les Free-Massons

Figure 5. Les Free-Massons. Amsterdam, 1735. An engraved list of lodges from 1735, with portrait of Sir Richard Steele at top. *Courtesy of Scottish Rite Museum of Our National Heritage, 91.008.4. Photography by Bill Wasserman*

So *Jews* made Bricks without their Straw,
When *Pharao* was the true *Grand Master.*

Their organization, however,

wise disdains
To idle Dreams or Shifts to flee,
Unmov'd, immortal it remains,
Firm founded on SOCIETY.

Newspapers in the 1740s recounted processions of "Scald Miserable Masons" marching through London streets dressed in outlandish costumes to mock the speculative brothers' pretensions to honor.[87]

"The truly ANTIENT NOBLE ORDER of the Gormogans" made a more direct bid through much of the 1720s to supersede the fraternity. According to the newspaper accounts, this bizarre (and perhaps even fictitious) society claimed descent from the first emperor of China and introduction into England by a Mandarin. Dismissive references to the "Ancient and Honorable Society" filled the notices of the group. "There will be no drawn sword at the Door," it announced in contrast to the Masonic practice of "tyling" the entrance. Indeed, Masons could not become members unless they had renounced their "Novel order and been properly degraded." A 1724 report claimed that "a Peer of the first Rank, a noted Member of the Society of Free-Masons," probably the eccentric duke of Wharton (the 1722 grand master), had gone through this ceremony of burning his Masonic gloves and leather apron. Other accounts asserted a Roman Catholic role in the society. All of the College of Cardinals, a newspaper suggested, were already members, and the Mandarin creator of the English chapter would soon hand it over to the pope. Newspaper reports of the group continued until 1730.[88] The precise meaning of these accounts remains uncertain, but they point to a recurrent problem for Masons—the inclusive universalism supported by the brothers left them open to suspicions of subversion and alien influence (encouraging Roman Catholic and Chinese activities in Protestant Britain).

Operative Masons also attempted to assume the high reputation of the speculative group. Imitating the London body's penchant for fabricating tradition, both Scottish and Irish Masons soon set up grand lodges that claimed the same powers as the earlier speculative order. The lodge in York, made up of nonoperatives as well as craftsmen, also sought special status. Although still attached to the mason's craft, York members in 1725 began to assert that they had formed a speculative grand lodge before the London body. Drawing upon an old tradition found in some manuscript constitutions of an alleged medieval national Masonic convention in York, the new grand lodge proclaimed authority over all English Masonry. These pretensions proved insupportable. The York grand lodge survived only to about 1750, warranting few, if any, subordinate bodies. The legend of earlier York precedence that it helped popularize, however, would assume mythic significance for later American Freemasons who often styled themselves Ancient York Masons.

Interest in the fraternity quickly spread beyond the British Isles. By 1735, lodges met in Madrid, Paris, Hamburg, and The Hague. Continental Masonry seems to have been primarily restricted to the upper levels of society most affected by the Enlightenment ideas and fascination with England. Partly because of this aristocratic character, European Masons denied connection with building trades, linking themselves instead with learned architects or medieval military orders. Revealingly, German Masons named their lodges and kept their records in French, the language of diplomacy and the court.[89]

The growth of Continental Freemasonry also drew the attention of the Catholic Church. In 1738, the pope issued an encyclical banning all participation in Masonry under pain of excommunication. But the restriction barely slowed the growth of Freemasonry. One of the fraternity's most public French exponents, the Scottish-born Chevalier de Ramsey, belonged to a Catholic religious order. Indeed, in Protestant Britain and its colonies with their strong anti-Catholic traditions, the papal prohibition might even have encouraged Masonry by identifying opposition to the group with Catholic tyranny and superstition.

The speculative fraternity inevitably reached across the Atlantic as well. By the time of the 1738 papal ban, lodges had already been organized in Philadelphia, Savannah, Boston, New York, Charleston, and Cape Fear, North Carolina. Despite this early start, American Freemasonry (like the American colonies themselves) developed haphazardly and sporadically, victim of confusion on both sides of the Atlantic. For American colonials, the authority of Masonic rules and secrets along with the rich ideals of brotherly connections provided them with the resources necessary for creating lodges virtually on their own, even if they often also felt the need for the stronger signs of legitimacy available only from Britain. At the same time, however, the metropolis's desire for control and elaboration of orderly authority would also be subverted by the lack of consensus about the proper means of creating it. The result was a tangled move toward Masonic order on the American Atlantic seaboard that bears witness to the strong desire of colonials to appropriate, like their Continental brothers, Masonry's rich connections with English gentility and enlightenment.

The London grand lodge originally expected that these colonies would follow the model of subordinate provincial grand masters and grand lodges already established in the British Isles. But these plans hardly fitted the realities of a rapidly developing group of provinces more than a month's journey from London. The experience of Philadelphia's St. John Lodge, almost certainly America's first organized Masonic group, illustrates some of this complexity. The lodge began to meet sometime around 1730 without the authorization of the central body. Although still only a single lodge, the brothers also, by the following year, formed a grand lodge. Such a self-creation had not been the plan of the London grand lodge. It had already appointed Daniel Coxe as provincial grand master for Pennsylvania, New Jersey, and New York in June 1730. Although Coxe came to America, he never seems to have used his authority, and the Philadelphia brothers perhaps never even knew of this appointment.[90]

Undaunted by, or perhaps also unaware of, the failure of the first American grand master, the London body appointed Henry Price, a Boston merchant tailor, as "Provincial Grand Master of New England and Dominions and Territories thereunto belonging" in April 1733. Price, unlike Coxe, wasted no time in using his authority; in July, he created a provincial grand lodge and a subordinate "First Lodge" in Boston. Hearing through the Boston newspapers (falsely, it turned out) that Price's commission had been extended to the remaining American colonies, the Philadelphia brothers wrote to him asking for a deputation as a grand lodge. Their body, they explained, "seems to want the sanction of some authority derived from home, to give the proceedings and determinations of our Lodge their due weight." Grand master Benjamin Franklin revealed in a separate letter that a number of "foreigners" were illegally initiating outsiders in return "for a bowl of punch." Freemasonry, Franklin noted, "is like to come into disesteem among us unless the true Brethren are countenanced and distinguished by some such special authority." Price sent a deputation. Soon afterward Philadelphia's Masons fell upon hard times, reviving again under another Boston authorization provided to Franklin in 1749. The Philadelphia brethren, however, seem to have distrusted this arrangement. The following year, they asked for and received a deputation directly from the London grand lodge.[91]

Even the intricacies of Philadelphia brothers' experience, however, did not exhaust the possibilities for the creation of a new lodge. The English grand lodge also warranted individual lodges in America, whether or not they fell under a provincial grand lodge. The lodge in Savannah, Georgia, for example, began to meet on its own authority in 1733/4, perhaps under the leadership of James Oglethorpe. It received a charter in 1735, along with a warrant for a provincial grand lodge, but, when the grand master died three years later, no successor was chosen until 1760. The lodge at the Royal Exchange in Norfolk, Virginia, chartered in 1753, operated without a provincial grand lodge, even though the London body chartered at least two more lodges in the colony in the 1770s.[92]

By the middle of the century, the London grand lodge had formed provincial grand lodges in most of the major cities on the mainland. The bodies meeting in Charleston, Philadelphia, New York, and Boston, however, exercised their power to create other lodges sparingly. Only the Boston and New York bodies organized more than three or four, and the latter concentrated primarily on its own city. Even the Bostonians expanded slowly. Outside of the

ambiguous grant to Pennsylvania, the Massachusetts provincial grand lodge
warranted only three or four other lodges before 1745: in Portsmouth, New
Hampshire, Antigua, Nova Scotia, and perhaps Charleston, South Carolina.
The pace picked up after 1745, but even these lodges remained limited to similar mercantile centers like Annapolis, Newport, and Providence. Only in 1760
did the Boston brothers create another lodge within their province—in the
port city of Marblehead.[93]

The limited geographical penetration of Masonry within the American
colonies did not suggest provincial indifference. By 1755, provincial grand
master Henry Price could boast to the London grand lodge, "Masonry has had
as great Success in America since my settling here as in any part of the World,
(except England)."[94] Indeed, the plausibility of Price's point undercut his request to allow the Massachusetts provincial body authority over "all North
America." The London grand lodge presented the Boston brothers only with
power over areas with no existing provincial grand master. Even from across
the Atlantic, English Masons realized that colonial Masonry had become too
big for a single local authority.

Speculative Masonry in the previous generation had moved far beyond its
origins in London's learned and polite circles. Buoyed by public attention
and the patronage of the powerful, the fraternity developed simultaneously
within Britain, on the Continent, and in America. Although the identification of Masonry with ancient mysteries, with enlightened attitudes, and with
high social standing would continue, subsequent brothers, in America as elsewhere, would increasingly reinterpret the rich legacy of the speculative fraternity's first generation for their own purposes.

Speculative Masonry developed within the London intellectual and social
circles that surrounded Newton, partaking of the same confusions, the same
mixing of traditions that marked him and his Masonic friends such as Stukeley and Desaguliers. The origins of the fraternity lay in the encounter between these cosmopolitan groups and operative Masons' mysterious heritage
and practices. To protect the antiquity they perceived there and the hope for
a deeper knowledge of universal truth, early speculative brothers created a
powerful organization and a regular series of degrees that reaffirmed the link
between the new group and ancient wisdom.

They also embedded another set of elements within Masonry. Following
genteel social practices and enlightened ideas, speculative brothers created
both a club and a fictive family. These ideas were already at odds with certain
interpretations of antiquity, and the two traditions would diverge even further as the century progressed. Masonry, however, remained rooted in both
traditions, making available to its members a powerful range of symbols and
identifications largely unavailable elsewhere. The resulting popularity of these

connections within London's polite and learned social circles formed the final Masonic tradition, providing the fraternity the social cachet its ideas continued to claim even as it spread beyond the aristocratic circles the brothers boasted of so loudly.

Closely linked to Newton in its origin, the speculative fraternity, perhaps not coincidentally, soon identified itself with the other great hero of the eighteenth-century Enlightenment, John Locke. In 1753, the *Gentleman's Magazine,* heir to the *Spectator* in its influence upon the polite world, published a 1696 letter from Locke to the earl of Pembroke passing on a translation of an early-fifteenth-century Masonic document said to have been originally copied by Henry VI. The material, the magazine claimed, had been published in Frankfurt several years previously. The catechism noted Masonry's claims to universality, learning, and antiquity, suggesting that "Peter Gower," the Greek who introduced the craft to England, was also learned in Egyptian and Syrian mysteries. Locke's note on the passage identified Gower as Pythagoras, the great mathematician, who "knew the true System of the World lately revived by *Copernicus.*" Although his annotations expressed doubts about some Masonic claims, Locke concluded by noting his awakened interest: "I cannot deny that it has so much raised my Curiosity, as to induce me to enter myself into the Fraternity; which I am determined to do (if I may be admitted) the next Time I go to London." [95]

The document seems to have been an elaborate forgery. Neither the original manuscript, the Locke transcription and commentary, nor the Frankfurt imprint has yet been found. But the ready acceptance of the material within both Masonic and non-Masonic circles underlines its larger symbolic significance. German interest in the great Enlightenment philosopher and the fraternity revealed the growing truth of Masonic claims to universality. The manuscript's royal origin suggested the speculative order's high social aspirations. Most important, the document's association of Masonry with Locke, Copernicus, and Pythagoras as well as with the hidden knowledge of the East captured the close connection early speculative brothers forged between Enlightenment and ancient mysteries—between the mathematical universe of Newton and the mystical secrets of necromancy.

CHAPTER TWO

The Appearance of So Many Gentlemen

Masonry and Colonial Elites, 1730–1776

One night in June 1737, the Philadelphia apothecary Dr. Evan Jones and some of his friends, all non-Masons, led Jones's apprentice, Daniel Rees, into a garden. Jones had learned of Rees's desire to join the fraternity and decided to initiate him. Teaching Rees meaningless signs, the pranksters made the young apprentice swear an oath of allegiance to the devil. Then imitating the Christian sacrament, they gave Rees a cup, making him drink, not wine, but a laxative. Finally, telling Rees he would need to seal the obligation and "kiss the book," one of Jones's friends pulled down his pants and had the blindfolded apprentice kiss his "posteriors." [1]

Sitting in a tavern several days later, Jones and his lawyer, John Remington, one of the conspirators, related the story to Benjamin Franklin, a member of a group of arbitrators appointed to hear a lawsuit involving Jones. When the other party failed to arrive, the two jesters regaled the audience with their exploits. Soon afterward the still-unsuspecting brother appeared, looking for his master. Pointing to Franklin, Jones urged, "Daniel, that Gentleman is a Freemason; make a Sign to him." Franklin ignored the boy but took a copy of the blasphemous oath home with him, often reading it aloud to neighbors and visitors.

Two nights later, the conspirators led Rees into a dark cellar to initiate him into what they called "a higher degree." Removing his blindfold, they showed him strange figures. One of the pranksters donned a "Cow's Hide with Horns" to impersonate the devil. Others played "Snap Dragon," lighting their faces grotesquely by holding pans of burning brandy under their faces. When Rees refused to acknowledge any fear, Jones accidentally spilled—or threw—a pan of burning spirits onto the boy. Rees's burns were so severe that he died three days later.

Jones and Remington were quickly brought to justice. Although Jones's lawyer challenged all the Freemasons returned on the jury, the two defendants were still convicted of manslaughter. Remington was ultimately pardoned by the governor's Council. Jones was branded on the hand.

Blaming Rees for his own death would be neither fair nor just. But clearly his naïveté about the fraternity at least encouraged his tormentors. As Jones and Remington knew, a young apprentice stood little chance of entering a group consisting largely of the province's leading gentlemen. Rees also misunderstood Masonic secrecy. Imagining lodge practices as a world apart from everyday standards, he accepted as genuine the tricksters' sophomoric inversions of church and court rituals.

These confusions about Masonry were not minor misunderstandings; they were profound misapprehensions about the very nature of the colonial fraternity, misunderstandings that still obscure early American Masonry and the social and cultural world that reshaped it. Colonial Masonry was not a middle-class order that embraced a wide range of members. Instead, membership was restricted almost exclusively to men of rank. The fraternity's intimate relationship with these genteel urban elites profoundly shaped its forms and ideas, most importantly in the fundamental continuity between its public representations and its private activities. Unlike nineteenth-century brothers, the Anglo-American gentlemen who swelled early lodges did not seek to sequester themselves from the world, but to establish their place within it.

In this project, colonial Masons recreated the fraternity in their own image. American gentlemen found connection with kings and nobles and with enlightened ideas and images nearly irresistible. But the ancient mysteries that impelled the speculative fraternity's creation proved much less appealing and played little role in colonial Masonry. The spread of Masonry across the Atlantic formed part of the eighteenth-century anglicization of American elites, their increasing adoption of English ways. But their selective reshaping of Masonry suggests that this emulation involved more than simply attempting to replicate English society. Colonial Masons took up metropolitan practices and attitudes only to the extent that they fitted their particular needs. Even then these selected elements were adapted to a new setting. Rather than wholesale imitation, colonials engaged in a selective anglicization.[2]

The two central terms of colonial Masonry, love and honor, suggest the significance of this American context. Colonial leaders saw the fraternity as a means both to build elite solidarity and to emphasize their elevation above common people. Masonry's public processions and orations portrayed colonial elites as they wished to be seen, secure in their dignity and open in their sympathies. Although analysis of lodge meetings reveals a more complex underside to these images, Masonry's private activities ultimately pursued the same goals of love and honor as its public display. The very success of colonial gentlemen in adapting Masonry to their needs, however, weakened the fraternity's impact. Other practices and organizations within genteel society also fulfilled Masonic functions without raising the suspicions encouraged by Masonry's novelty and mysteriousness. Ironically, Masonry never became central to the lives of its members, in large part because of the colonial fraternity's success in representing the values of elite colonial society.

Like his acquaintance Daniel Rees (who also yearned to join this gentlemanly world), the young Benjamin Franklin also stumbled in his quest for higher status, most notably when the aftermath of the Rees incident revealed Franklin's ambiguous involvement. But he ultimately succeeded in negotiating his ascent. Although this rise obviously involved large measures of luck and talent, it also rested largely on a worldly wisdom that might have saved the life of an unfortunate apprentice. Even Franklin's involvement in Masonry suggests his shrewd understanding of the social and cultural boundaries being constructed by colonial elites—standards that the fraternity came to embody in its passage to the American provinces.

1. The United Party for Virtue

When the Masons marched through the streets of Boston in June 1739 to mark the feast day of their patron, John the Baptist, the brothers wore aprons and jewels and were accompanied by "a band of music." They went first to the house of the governor, a Masonic brother, who joined them for a concert and a "sumptuous" dinner. In the harbor, a sloop flying flags (and a Masonic apron) fired its guns at five, six, and seven o'clock. "A vast concourse of People," a newspaper reported, "attended to see this Procession. Almost all Occupation ceas'd, the Streets were covered; Windows, Balconys; Battlements of Churches and Houses were full of Spectators, who were highly pleased with the Appearance of so many Gentlemen." [3]

The brilliant public processions of the Masons that began in the late 1730s (first held in Boston and Charleston in the months before Daniel Rees's death) dramatized the brothers' interpretation of themselves and their fraternity. Masonry's public display drew upon a widely recognized visual vocabulary that proclaimed the order's high status. In the public addresses that often accompanied these activities, brothers similarly claimed standing by presenting the fraternity's ideal of universal love as a counterweight to the centrifugal forces that threatened to divide the colonial city. These representations of social status and public concern were reinforced by the high standing of the "many Gentlemen" who marched through the streets in Masonic aprons and jewels.

As the Rees case suggests, the development of Masonry's public display in the late 1730s took place in an atmosphere of intense interest in a group widely known for possessing a closely guarded "secret." "The newspapers," a New Yorker noted in 1738, "furnish us with daily examples of many of the Nobility's being of that Society." [4] Readers of the *Virginia Gazette* had learned the year before of the London initiation of both James Thompson (the author of the very popular poem "The Seasons") and the prince of Wales. The precise meaning of the fraternity, however, remained elusive and troubling.

The *Virginia Gazette* reprinted an English magazine article in 1739 arguing that any "mysterious society" meeting "in such dark and clandestine Assemblies" must be plotting against king and state and should be crushed. Five years later, a Philadelphia taverngoer repeated a similar view to Annapolis's Dr. Alexander Hamilton. Hamilton replied with the more skeptical view that "their secret, which has made such a noise, I imagine is just no secret at all." Franklin had argued similarly in 1730, "Their Grand Secret is, That they have no Secret at all." [5]

Such confident denials betrayed more than a tinge of curiosity—both Franklin and Hamilton became brothers soon after their statements—but assertions of Masonic foolishness injured the fraternity just as much as fears of conspiracy. Revealingly, Masons reacted, not by becoming more secretive, but by staging public appearances that invited, even demanded attention. The processions that began in the late 1730s partly sought to allay fears about the fraternity and to create a new image for the order. Through these processions, Masonic brothers dramatized their commitment to both gentility and social distinctions, with a set of symbols drawn from eighteenth-century elite culture. An examination of another procession, the 1755 Philadelphia ceremony marking the opening of the first Masonic hall in America, suggests the ways Masons communicated these messages.

According to an admiring observer, the parade of brothers that made its way to Christ Church was "the Greatest Procession of Free Masons . . . that ever was seen in America." At its head marched a sword-bearer, his drawn sword warning against interference and, as the weapon of officers and gentlemen, affirming the status of the brethren. Next came musicians playing marches, followed by six stewards, two from each of the city's three lodges, carrying white rods symbolizing authority. Then came the officers of the grand lodge and other dignitaries, some of the most prominent and influential men in Pennsylvania. The grand secretary, William Franklin (now holding his father Benjamin's former position of clerk of the Assembly), and the grand treasurer, Mayor William Plumstead, each carried a cushion of crimson damask with, respectively, an open Bible and the Masonic Book of Constitutions. Behind them marched the grand chaplain, William Smith, provost of the Academy and College of Pennsylvania. Grand master William Allen, the provincial chief justice, and deputy grand master Benjamin Franklin then marched side by side, each "supported" by two gentlemen. Allen's attendants were Pennsylvania governor Robert Hunter Morris and his immediate predecessor, James Hamilton. Three more lodge officers, in front of the brothers "two by two," carried columns representing the orders of architecture. At the end of the procession came the brothers' coaches and chariots, including probably Justice Allen's magnificent crested carriage with its English driver guiding four black horses. The 127 Freemasons, the newspaper account concluded, "all new cloathed with Aprons, white Gloves and Stockings, and the Officers in

The Second grand anniversary Procession.

Figure 6. The Second Grand Anniversary Procession. By Dr. Alexander Hamilton. A rare picture of a colonial procession. *From* The History of the Ancient and Honorable Tuesday Club. *Permission of John Work Garrett Library, Johns Hopkins University*

the proper Cloathing and Jewels of their respective Lodges, with their other Badges of Dignity, made a handsome and genteel Appearance."[6]

The fraternity's display, similar to that used by Masons in nearly all seaboard cities, drew upon a familiar vocabulary of hierarchy taken from early modern civic processions and celebrations. Swords and rods called attention to Masonry's high social position. White stockings and gloves, jewels, elevation of books on crimson cushions, and learned reference to the orders of architecture further displayed Masonry's gentility. Even the brothers' aprons, the clearest reminder of Masonry's artisan roots, set them apart from common tradesmen (the so-called leather-apron men), for the brothers donned, not cowhide, but soft white lambskin.[7]

The ceremonial form itself also underlined the fraternity's standing. Primarily expressions of civic unity and religious devotion in medieval times, processions, in the wake of the Reformation and the growth of urban oligarchy, became reminders, not of unity, but of hierarchy. Increasingly, common people participated only as onlookers. Councilmen and mayors, judges and courts, kings and queens, wealthy leaders of guilds, and elites of every description now dominated civic ritual. Moving through the streets in rich regalia, participants commanded attention, asserting power by incarnating the structure of authority. Such a theater of dominance, asserting the elite's growing social and cultural distance from the people, played a major role in maintaining power and order in eighteenth-century England.[8]

Processions held particular significance in the American context. The relatively narrow gap in living standards between different levels of society during the seventeenth century expanded in the eighteenth, allowing displays of wealth and taste unattainable by common people. Partly because of this economic differentiation, native-born elites were also able to consolidate their hold on colonial politics. The widespread instability of the seventeenth century—culminating in a series of rebellions—encouraged emerging elites to close ranks and, despite continued disagreement, to recognize a common stake in preserving both the political system itself and their place in it.[9]

Masonic processions drew on this growing eighteenth-century differentiation of prosperity and power. Ships, symbols of wealth and commerce, often played a role in Masonic activities; in Charleston harbor, they were sometimes decorated and illuminated during Masonic activities. The December 1738 celebration there reportedly included an unmathematical 250 salutes by 39 guns. Charleston brothers usually began their St. John's Day by marching to the house of the grand master, just as the Bostonians in 1739 waited upon the governor. After dinner, sometimes held on board a navy ship, they often held a ball. The *Hallowell*, lying in Boston harbor during the December 1739 ceremony, even flew a lambskin apron.[10]

Other processions accompanied funerals or theatergoing. After about midcentury, the fraternity, especially in the South, began to participate in brothers' funerals, a practice already common among military and other voluntary societies. More distinctively, Masons followed the English practice of attending the theater as a group. Indeed, the first Masonic public appearance on the continent came in May 1737 when Charleston brothers saw George Farquhar's *Recruiting Officer*. The aproned brothers in the pit, clearly visible to the audience, joined in the Masonic songs also presented by the actors. A special prologue and epilogue further distinguished the occasion. When the New York grand lodge attended the theater in 1761 and 1763, an actor spoke a prologue "in the character of a Master Mason," presumably in apron and gloves. Philadelphia playgoers in 1759 enjoyed the same as well as an epilogue by a "Master Mason's wife." More than gratitude for increased ticket sales perhaps impelled the Philadelphia additions. At a time when theatrical performances encountered widespread hostility, Philadelphia brothers had played a key role in bringing plays to the city. After the governor and the chief justice (both brothers) refused to follow precedent and forbid the American Company's request to perform, the performances took place in a warehouse owned by another Mason.[11]

Fraternal symbols could even be displayed in less formal settings. Colonial merchants stocked glasses and jewelry marked with Masonic emblems for use in houses as well as lodge rooms. William Burrows, a Charleston lawyer, advertised in 1752 for the return of his watch, a possession (like a carriage) generally limited to the well-to-do, carrying a "silver badge of Masonry" attached to the string. In March 1774, Philip Vickers Fithian observed the Virginia brother Colonel Joseph F. Lane wearing "black superfine Broadcloth; Gold-Laced hat; laced Ruffles; black Silk Stockings; and to his Broach on his Bosom he wore a Masons Badge inscrib'd 'Virtute and Silentio' cut in a Golden Medal!" The impressed Fithian exclaimed, "Certainly he was fine!"[12]

Undoubtedly dressed in similarly elegant clothing, the brothers in the 1755 Philadelphia procession entered Christ Church only after all others had been seated. The service that followed further highlighted the fraternity's connection with cosmopolitan society by asserting ties to love and public concern. After prayers and psalms, grand chaplain William Smith proclaimed Masonic allegiance to the ideals of benevolence and sociability, the central concepts of enlightened social theory. To the non-Masons in the church he described the fraternity as "a Society of Friends"—significant words in the Quaker City— "linked in a strong bond of Brotherly Love." "Let no rude Gust of Passion," he warned the brothers, "extinguish that Candle of Brotherly Love, which illuminates your Souls, and is the Glory of your Nature." Smith's invocation of benevolence was as much a Masonic ritual as the procession; the Masonic orations published around midcentury characteristically stressed its importance to the fraternity. In the architectural metaphors of other speakers, love was the "Pillar of *Masonry*," "the *Foundation* and *Cape-Stone* [*sic*], the Cement and Glory of the Ancient and Honorable *Fraternity*." [13]

Although love, as another Masonic orator noted, was "an Affection too well understood to need defining," Masonic use of the term applied enlightened social theory to the American situation. Taking eighteenth-century emphases on sociability and benevolence as their foundation, Masons pointed out these qualities varied according to "proximity." Family formed the primary circle of benevolence, the most natural level of sympathy and affection. "It is not to be doubted," a brother noted in 1749, "that nearer Relations do challenge from us, higher measures of Affections and Assistance." But concern for people farther away proved more difficult. As affections moved outward, they naturally diminished and therefore could not easily include everyone. Colonial brothers suggested that Masonry provided a mechanism for enlarging this sympathy. By building bonds of affection that moved outward from the innermost circles of benevolence, Masonic brotherhood attempted to expand the "particular love" of families and neighbors into a "universal love" that would eventually include the entire world.[14]

This model of social harmony had deep intellectual roots in England and America. The very popular English latitudinarian Samuel Clarke cited a similar process as the "the foundation, preservation, and perfection of . . . universal friendship or society." Starting with children or posterity, "natural affection" was expanded through a process of "multiplying affinities . . . till by degrees the affection of single persons, becomes a friendship of family; and this enlarges itself to society of towns and cities and nations; and terminates in the agreeing community of all mankind." Only "perverse iniquity and unreasonable want of natural charity" kept the world from "so happy a state." [15]

By midcentury, when American Masons began to publish their addresses, the importance of love had also become a key theme in American religious thought, not only in Jonathan Edwards's extraordinary rethinking of enlightened ideas but also in less exalted discourse. The Reverend brother Charles Brockwell's December 1749 sermon to Boston brothers, *Brotherly Love Recommended*, would have appeared in booksellers alongside a number of addresses with a similar theme by non-Masons. Another sermon on brotherly love had already appeared in Boston that same year. A second, *Love to Our Neighbors Recommended*, had been given in 1727 but was reprinted in 1749 "at the Desire and Expence of One that lately perused and very much approved of it"; a third edition appeared later that year. Indeed, Brockwell's December address carried the same title as a Gilbert Tennent sermon printed the previous year by Franklin. Although not a brother, the Presbyterian revivalist used terms strikingly reminiscent of earlier Masonic discourse to suggest that "Mutual *Love* is the *Band* and *Cement*" of society.[16]

Masonic use of the idea rested just as much on particular American circumstances as on the English or colonial antecedents, for fraternal orators found the theme of love a means of deploring the particular divisiveness of American society. Newport brother Thomas Pollen made this point explicitly. Universal love was a "blessing" in any society, he argued, "but most especially when a monstrous diversity of religious tenets, a mad contention about little honours, a furious clashing in worldly interests, and an unchristian enmity between rival families are rending the very bowels of a society in pieces."[17] Pollen's view clearly expressed his horror at Rhode Island's specific problems—the colony's extraordinary religious diversity and the beginnings of the political infighting that agitated Rhode Island politics for more than a decade. Few Masonic orators took as bleak a view of their situation, but others similarly warned against divisions based upon what Smith in 1755 called the "little and . . . trifling . . . ordinary Causes of Contention." From the vantage point of eternity, he argued, these divisions "are seen but as Feathers dancing on the mighty ocean"—an extraordinary comment at a time when the Assembly and governor were locked in a convulsive struggle over provincial finances. Such political factionalism, spurred by demographic and economic expansion, became increasingly intense in all American colonies north of South Carolina by midcentury. At the same time, the great increase in non-English immigration expanded ethnic diversity. The Great Awakening intensified these divisions even further by expanding religious differences. Together, the Reverend Arthur Browne suggested to Bostonians in 1755, the divisions of the American city had created a situation like the ancient world, where people "made all their concern terminate in themselves." In such a situation, Pollen asked, "What greater blessing can descend from heaven . . . than universal love *with healing in its wings*[?]"[18]

Masonic assertions that they were "a society, the badge of whose profession is to promote" universal love, suggested the brothers' commitment to a society that seemed to inspire little loyalty in others. By encouraging friendship and brotherhood among members chosen "without regard to party disputes, or religious differences," the fraternity inspired the natural sympathy that ought to obtain among all people. In words that echoed the *Book of Constitutions*, Browne argued that Masonry "has been a means of conciliating persons, who otherwise must have lived, (without extraordinary interposition) in perpetual discord and contention."[19]

Through its concern for the common good and its use of the verbal and visual symbols of enlightened gentility, Masonry thus identified itself as a brotherhood of cosmopolitan and respected men joining together to better society. Such an image of a cultivated, orderly society where a benevolent elite would be clearly recognized and honored for its selfless devotion to the public good was deeply embedded in the Enlightenment. Franklin had envisioned just such an organization in his "united Party for Virtue," a plan he devised only months after joining the Masons. Complaining that "few act from a Principle of Benevolence" and most follow their own "particular private Interest," he suggested a group that would bring together "the Virtuous and good Men of all Nations."[20]

The fraternity sought to do precisely that. Like Franklin's proposed organization, Masonry erected no formal barriers, either of religion or of nationality, to membership. Philadelphia's St. John's Lodge included not only Quakers and Anglicans but also local Baptists and Presbyterians. Jews from Portugal, the Caribbean, and elsewhere formed a large proportion of the lodge set up by the Bostonians in Newport, Rhode Island. Boston's First Lodge initiated a French (and presumably Catholic) prisoner of war in 1744, even waiving the normal fee. Similarly, the fraternity could soften the asperity of party conflict, bringing together Franklin and Governor Morris in a 1755 display of fraternity despite their bitter dispute over provincial finances. Of course, Masonry did not succeed fully. Philadelphia's Quaker elite generally remained unmoved by the prospect of Masonic fraternity. Only a few Friends joined the brotherhood there.[21]

Nonetheless, colonial Masonry helped blunt and buffer the divisive forces of ethnicity, religion, and nationality—but it did so, ironically, by reinforcing the crucial eighteenth-century social division, that between gentlemen and others. Although brothers might sometimes boast that "neither rich nor poor are excluded, provided they are duly qualified," in practice the poor seldom possessed the proper qualifications.

The dimensions of Masonic elitism can be seen in a sample of nearly two hundred Masonic brothers—members of the original Philadelphia lodge in the 1750s and the Masons who attended Boston celebrations between 1768 and 1770.[22] Almost all these brothers stood high on the occupational ladder (Table 1). More than 60 percent of those whose occupations are known were merchants, and another large segment (14 percent in Boston, 21 percent in Philadelphia) can be classified as professionals. Fewer than 10 percent were artisans, a category that probably included about one-half of each city's workers. The rest were retailers or sea captains.[23] Even the artisans in the sample—craftsmen possessing little prestige—often turn out to be atypical in wealth or attributes of gentility. Many of the artisanal brothers, particularly in Philadelphia, pursued trades requiring close contact with gentlemen or large amounts of capital. Clock- and watchmakers such as Emanuel Rouse of Philadelphia and printers such as Thomas Fleet of Boston regularly worked for the wealthy and influential. Other Masonic artisans engaged in crafts that, although not connected to genteel activities, still required heavy investment. Robert Smith, Philadelphia's most eminent colonial builder and architect, designed and supervised the construction of Carpenter's Hall, the Walnut Street prison, and the Christ Church steeple. Besides serving as Boston tax collector from 1767 to 1774, Abraham Savage possessed a sawmill, a gristmill, and

Table 1. Occupations of Modern Masons, Boston, and St. John's Members,
Philadelphia, 1750–1770

Occupation	Boston Moderns, 1768–1770[a]	St. John's Lodge, Philadelphia, 1750–1760[b]
Merchant	64 (66.0%)	32 (61.5%)
Merchant	63	
Merchant tailor	1	
Professional	14 (14.4%)	11 (21.2%)
Attorney	4	2
Doctor	6	4
Minister	1	1
Military	2	1[c]
Postmaster	1	1
Governor		1
Nephew of proprietor		1
Artisan	8 (8.2%)	4 (7.7%)
Bricklayer		2
Bookbinder, bookseller		1
Silversmith, clock- and watchmaker		1
Cooper	2	
Butcher	1[d]	
Carver	1	
Forge, sawmill, gristmill	1	
Glazier	1	
Printer	1	
Ropewalk	1	
Retailer	2 (2.1%)	3 (5.8%)
Shopkeeper	2	3
Sea captain	9 (9.3%)	2 (3.8%)[e]

[a] 97 of 138 (70.3%) identified.   [b] 52 of 72 (72.2%) identified.   [c] Colonel in army.
[d] Listed with title of captain.   [e] May be army or militia rank.

Sources: Boston: Masons who attended Boston St. John's Day celebrations are listed
in Massachusetts Grand Lodge, Proceedings in Masonry, 137–182. The key sources for
identification of occupations are Henry J. Parker, "The Masonic Register of Boston
Masons, 1733–1800," MS, Massachusetts Grand Lodge Library; the list of Boston
merchants in John W. Tyler, Smugglers and Patriots: Boston Merchants and the Advent
of the American Revolution (Boston, 1986); James H. Stark, The Loyalists of Massachusetts and the Other Side of the Revolution (Boston, 1910); Oliver Ayer Roberts, History
of the Military Company of the Massachusetts, Now Called the Ancient and Honorable
Artillery Company of Massachusetts, 1637–1888, 4 vols. (Boston, 1895–1901).

Table 1. Continued

Philadelphia: Labaree et al., eds., *Papers of Franklin,* V, 235–237, supplemented by Julius F. Sachse, *Old Masonic Lodges of Pennsylvania: Moderns and Ancients, 1730–1800 . . . ,* 2 vols. (Philadelphia, 1912), I, 1, 47–49. For identification of occupations, Hannah Benner Roach, "Taxables in the City of Philadelphia, 1756," *Pennsylvania Genealogical Magazine,* XXII (1961), 9–41; Kenneth Scott, *Abstracts from Benjamin Franklin's Pennsylvania Gazette, 1728–1748* (Baltimore, 1975); Kenneth Scott and Janet R. Clarke, *Abstracts from the Pennsylvania Gazette, 1748–1755* (Baltimore, 1977); Stephen Brobeck, "Revolutionary Change in Colonial Philadelphia: The Brief Life of the Proprietary Gentry," *WMQ,* 3d Ser., XXXIII (1976), 410–434; and G. B. Warden, "The Proprietary Group in Pennsylvania, 1754–1764," *WMQ,* 3d Ser., XXI (1964), 367–389.

---

a forge. These activities sometimes meshed closely with mercantile concerns. Philadelphia's Charles Stedman was an ironmaster as well as a merchant; merchants William Allen and Robert Ellis also invested in ironworks.[24] Sea captains (almost 10 percent of the Boston group but fewer than 4 percent of the Philadelphians) enjoyed a status somewhat similar to that of these artisans. Their work brought them into close contact with shipowners and merchants, into whose ranks they might rise through careful investment. Boston merchant brother Christopher Prince had made just such a transition.

Merchants who belonged to the lodges were not always as close to the upper reaches of their occupational group as were their brother artisans. Even so, the lodges still included many men of high status. Nearly half of the Philadelphia merchants in the sample belonged to the city's elite Dancing Assembly, which met, after 1755, in the new Masonic hall. This group included Mayor William Plumstead, who, besides his Masonic position as grand treasurer, served as a trustee of both Philadelphia's hospital and academy and a member of the governor's Council. His 1756 tax assessment placed him in the top 2 percent of the city's inhabitants. Other Philadelphia merchants included grand master Allen (the city's richest man), Tench Francis, Jr. (son of the attorney general), and Michael Hillegas (the musically minded merchant and land speculator who became the first treasurer of the United States). Boston's merchant Masons included a number of the city's most important men. Benjamin Hallowell, perennial master of First Lodge, served as collector of the port and a customs commissioner, and Ezekiel Price acted as confidential secretary to a number of the colony's governors. All but one of the colonial Massachusetts grand masters came from this commercial group.[25]

Merchants made up the majority of lodge members, but their prestige was nearly matched by the smaller and more diverse group of men here classified as professionals. Although few ministers seem to have joined the lodges (the samples include only one from each city), lawyers and physicians were prominent. Boston lawyers and Philadelphia physicians, especially, were leaders in their professions. Boston's attorneys included the most important members of the legal community. Grand master Jeremiah Gridley was a key figure in the professionalization of the Boston bar. When he argued the government's position in the writs of assistance case, his opponent was another brother, James Otis, Jr. The judge of the vice-admiralty court and the solicitor to the Board of Customs Commissioners belonged to the Boston fraternity, as did Andrew Oliver, provincial secretary and lieutenant governor.[26]

Such important physicians as Dedham almanac maker Nathaniel Ames, Revolutionary leader-turned-traitor Benjamin Church, Jr., and William Lee Perkins, whose establishment included two servants and a reported annual income of six hundred pounds per year, attended the Boston lodges. The Philadelphia fraternity included John Kearsley, the leading Pennsylvania physician of the period; Edinburgh-trained Adam Johnson; Thomas Bond, projector of the Pennsylvania Hospital and the first to give a course of clinical lectures in America; and Thomas Cadwallader, a physician at the hospital and a member of the governor's Council for nearly twenty years. Like Johnson, Bond and Cadwallader had received their training in Europe.

Men engaged primarily in government service may also be included among this professional group. This category was small in colonial America, yet the lodges included, besides those noted in the 1755 Philadelphia ceremonies, Thomas Penn, nephew of the proprietor and a member of the Council, and Boston postmaster Bartholomew Stavers. Several professional soldiers also belonged to the lodges. These included the commissary of Boston troops, Colonel Joseph Goldthwait, an alumnus, like a number of the Boston brothers, of Boston Latin School, as well as artillery officer and engineer Richard Gridley and Philadelphia's Colonel Joseph Burd, who married into the wealthy Shippen family.[27]

Masonic lodges thus brought together a large cross section of their city's most important men. Philadelphia's St. John's Lodge alone carried on its rolls about one-quarter of the city's corporation. High fees and the unanimous votes required for initiation, membership, and additional degrees (usually requiring separate ballots) kept out those of limited means. In Philadelphia, both St. John's Lodge in the late 1730s and the slightly less genteel Third Lodge charged five pounds for initiation—more than a month's wages for a common sailor. Boston's First Lodge soon after its foundation raised its initiation fee to ten pounds. The increase, the lodge committee reasoned, would not exclude "any man of merit" but would "discourage those of mean Spirits, and narrow, or Incumber'd Fortunes." To admit such men into the lodge would be "Disparagement to, and prostitution of Our Honour."[28]

Masonic honor as expressed in the eminence of its members, the display of its processions, and its claims to public leadership attempted to gain the respect of the genteel and the admiration of the common people, still referred to as the "vulgar." Colonial Masonry looked outward, claiming to be promoting the public good and, in turn, demanding public respect. Even the parts of the 1755 Philadelphia ceremony restricted to Freemasons alone could be used to gain attention and honor. Local gossip noted that the dinner at the new Masonic Hall included such delicacies as turtle. The toasts that followed were marked by cannon blasts in the public square adjoining the lodge room.

II. The Greatest Order and Regularity

"The lodge," a now-anonymous Mason told Boston brothers in 1734, is like "a Paradice or Heaven." Men of "all Religions, Sects, perswasions and denominations, of all nations and countrys" made up both. Furthermore, "universal understanding" and "human Kind and fraternal treatment of each other" distinguished the lodge and heaven from less exalted societies. This similarity could be seen in less obvious ways as well. Like paradise, the lodge refused "admission to improper persons." Only "the human Benevolent mind . . . deserves and is capable" of attaining and enjoying the special "felicity" of each.[29]

The values of brotherly love and honor that marked the fraternity's public appearances permeated the lodge room as well. But the brothers' private activities did more than provide additional expressions of these ideals. Unlike the polished presentations of the pulpit or the procession, lodge meetings revealed even more clearly the tangled reality of an elite that sought to sustain the fiction that social divisions were clear and obvious to all. Brothers had to face the everyday difficulties of attempting to keep out the improper and to build a "society of Friends" when actual worthiness was often difficult to assess and ties usually involved more than high-minded universal love. These themes of worthiness and fraternity appealed strongly to a colonial elite assimilating the ideals of politeness, establishing clubs at a rapid rate, and attempting to prevent the necessary bonds of patronage from becoming mere bondage. If the lodge attempted to put into practice the brothers' highest values, the actions and attitudes they expected to experience in heaven, Masonic meetings also had to deal with the human confusions and ambiguities from which paradise was to be free.

The deliberately high expense of Freemasonry formed only one of a series of barriers meant to keep out the improper. Wealth in itself was a significant sign but was not enough. According to the 1734 orator, the fraternity was to be restricted to "good and worthy men who are so in practise, and the general conduct of their lives." To ensure that only men of "Benevolent mind" entered the doors of the lodge, brothers established a complex admission process that allowed careful scrutiny of prospective family members, as illustrated by the admission of Charles Pelham to Boston's First Lodge in 1744.[30]

Pelham's father, longtime lodge secretary, had suggested that his son, then

in his early twenties, replace him as lodge secretary. The office seldom attracted more genteel members, as seen by the gratuities sometimes voted
by lodges. Accepting the outgoing secretary's suggestion, past grand master
Henry Price proposed Charles Pelham for initiation on August 8.[31]

The requirement that a lodge member sponsor a prospective member was
only the first hurdle. Voting on Pelham's petition had to wait until the next
regular meeting two weeks later. Only exceptional circumstances (such as a
ship's captain about to embark) allowed the lodge master to grant a dispensation permitting quicker disposition. Active members voted on prospective
brothers by dropping a ball into the ballot box passed around the room, white
for acceptance, black for rejection. A single black ball excluded a candidate.
"Certainly," argued the 1733 Philadelphia bylaws, "more Regard ought to be
had in this way to a Brother who is already a Mason, than to any Person who
is not one, and we should never in such cases disoblige a Brother, to oblige a
Stranger." Suggesting earlier lapses, they recommended that "the use of Balls
be established in its full Force and Vigour; and that no new Member be admitted against the will of any present Member." [32] Charles Pelham, of course,
had no such trouble; he was accepted "Nemini Contra."

The lodge room, however, was still closed to him; his initiation came only at
the next meeting. Pelham "was made a Mason in due form" on September 12,
more than a month after being proposed. Pelham took up his post at the following lodge meeting. The process was deliberate, but other lodges, particularly later in the colonial period, lengthened it. Besides a separate lodge vote
on the question, they required the Master's degree before a brother could sign
the lodge bylaws and take up full membership. These other lodges gave the
degree in regular lodge meetings (after dismissing brothers of lower degrees)
or held a separate "Master's Night." Boston's First did not even perform the
ritual, since brothers had formed a separate Master's lodge in 1738 to confer
the degree, an unusual organization that confused even the Newport, Rhode
Island, lodge formed by the Boston grand body. They immediately granted
the Master's degree "not thinking but that they had Authority," to the later
disapproval of the Bostonians.[33]

These variations extended into the degree ceremonies themselves. Since English ritual had not yet been standardized, uniformity among different lodges
or even over time would have been difficult. America's distance from the London grand lodge probably increased the problem. In some cases, simply learning basic forms might have been a problem. The records of Boston's First
Lodge make no mention of the Fellow Craft degree until 1736/7. Even arrival
of a brother with full knowledge of an English lodge's practices would not
have created uniformity. American Masons did not create formal procedures
for either teaching rituals or superintendence by a central body until the next
century.[34]

The range of practice possible within colonial Masonry suggests that

brothers did not regard regulations or forms as central. Although these ceremonies provided the means of entering the order, they lacked the independent significance they gained in the nineteenth century. For colonial brothers,
consistent procedure was less important than keeping out the wrong people.
The key division was, not between Masonry and the outside world (as post-
Revolutionary brothers would come to argue), but between different social
ranks.[35]

This hierarchical vision could be seen even within the structure of the
lodge. On the lowest rung stood the "tyler," the officer paid to guard the door
against intruders. Usually appointed by the master rather than elected by the
members, he was often a poorer man initiated for the purpose, like Samuel
Fisher, who asked Philadelphia's Third Lodge for the post, stating that "he
was in a Distress'[d] Condition having a Wife and Five small children." As
the lodge's presiding officer, the master marked the other end of the scale. The
1734 Boston orator compared the lodge to an enlightened despotism, calling
it "an absolute Monarchy, in which the Will of the Sovereign is a law." In the
early years of Boston's First, the master even appointed the next two officers
of the lodge, the senior and junior wardens, officers that in later Boston and
American practice were chosen by the membership. Like other masters, Boston's presiding officer also granted dispensations for initiating Masons without the normal waiting period, sanctioned "private meetings" (those held outside the regularly scheduled times, usually for initiations), regulated drinking
and the expense of refreshments, examined the books of outgoing treasurers,
and was consulted before the proposal of an applicant. The master thus had
a great deal of power; but he was to be a patriot king, not a tyrant. Masonic
rules, the orator stated, were "so wisely contrived and established, that the
Sovereign can never will nor command any thing which is not exactly agreeable to the nature and reason of things . . . the pecul[i]ar light of Masonry
Enabling to discern what is best with regard to the Lodge."[36]

The master's role suggests the power of social distinctions even within the
brotherhood of the lodge. As in England, American brothers were warned
that respect for high status was not to be diminished because of fraternal ties.
Members seem to have followed such a calculus in elections; outside of the
always exceptional Franklin, who became Pennsylvania grand master in the
early 1730s while still a struggling printer, artisans or sea captains rarely held
Masonic office. Even more revealing is the list of Boston brethren compiled
in 1736. The list included Luke Vardy, keeper of the tavern where the grand
lodge and First Lodge met, but the lodge secretary placed Vardy's name at the
bottom and, as with no other member, specified his occupation.[37]

The private world of the lodge was thus not the counterworld created by
Rees's tormentors—swearing to the devil instead of the deity and kissing the
behind rather than the book. Despite their careful attention to initiates' character, Masons drew no sharp distinction between their fraternity and the

standards of elite society. The essential dividing line in Masonry and pre-Revolutionary society was, not the distinction between public and private, but, as Jones and his friends correctly realized, the social barrier between those who could claim honor and gentility and those who could not.[38]

In attempting, as the 1734 orator suggested, to keep out the "illnatur'd" and to admit only those of "Benevolent mind," Masonry expressed the emerging standards of eighteenth-century gentility. The consolidation of political authority and economic position by increasingly distinctive American elites also included the erection of new cultural boundaries. In this cultural differentiation, they drew upon their expanding knowledge of British developments. Increased trade, swifter communication, and growing numbers of imperial officials after the Restoration brought American elites into closer contact with Britain and thus with both enlightened social theory and the cosmopolitan ideal of politeness. In the period after 1700, and especially after 1720, emerging American elites drew upon this increased awareness to reconfigure their social and cultural lives. The most obvious evidence of these changes lay in the growing size and majesty of houses and public buildings like Philadelphia's Palladian Christ Church. Genteel institutions like dancing assemblies and clubs also developed rapidly in this period.[39]

The heart of gentility, however, was, not buildings or institutions, but the ideal of politeness. "Politeness," the Reverend William Smith wrote several years before his 1755 Masonic oration, "is the Bond of [s]ocial life,—the ornament of human nature." These attitudes, closely related to the Masonic idea of love and drawing upon similar roots in enlightened social theory, required a clear distinction between gentlemen (another word that took on increased importance as a social marker) and others often labeled "barbarous." Unlike common people, gentlemen's manners were refined, showing consideration for equals and a gracious condescension to inferiors through a polished self-presentation. Smith judged "a certain Easiness of Behavior" produced by "a softening" of "our natural Roughness" the central "Characteristic of the Gentleman."[40]

This context clarifies the challenge posed to Benjamin Franklin when a rival newspaper accused him of complicity in the Rees affair. The author first questioned the call for further punishment for Rees's murderers recently published by Franklin. Significantly terming the demand "Barbarous," he went on to argue that Franklin had not been simply a bystander in the death. The printer had laughed when Jones and Remington showed him the oath, encouraged Rees in his attempted signs, and even asked to be present at the next ceremony. When he was not invited, he denounced his friends before the magistrates and then gave evidence against them. Such a record clearly indicated that Franklin (and his fraternity) could hardly claim moral authority in this incident: "How far this Part, acted by an accepted Free-Mason tend to the Honour of that Society, I shall not contend about . . . but leave an indifferent Reader to judge."[41]

Accused of profanity, cruelty, and disloyalty as well as dishonoring Masonry, Franklin defended himself in the very next edition of the *Gazette*. He admitted that he had laughed at Jones and Remington's account, but only at the beginning of the story. When Rees came in, he had turned his head to avoid involvement. Later he tried, too late, to inform the apprentice of the deception before he left—"I was acquainted with, and had a Respect for the Young Lad's Father." His interest in the oath arose from its "very extraordinary nature." To his consternation, it had quickly become a problem; "so many People flooded to my House for a Sight of it, that it grew troublesome." His readings of the oath, he asserted, had "always" been "accompanied . . . with Expressions of Detestation." "I think I may reasonably hope," he pleaded, "that I am so well known in this City, where I have liv'd near 14 Years, as that the false and malicious Insinuations contain'd in the Mercury, will not do the Injury to my Reputation that seems intended." Franklin appended a deposition, signed by the two other participants in the tavern conversation, attesting to the truth of Franklin's account. His Masonic brother William Allen, acting as justice of the peace, took the statement.[42]

Franklin's desperate tone and his resort to a powerful patron suggest the significance he attached to the accusation. Caught in ambiguous involvement in a crude and vulgar joke (surely his popular and repeated readings of the oath involved more than making a moral point), Franklin realized that the attack threatened his carefully cultivated identification with genteel culture, the cultural positioning that had allowed growing contact with the city's elites. Franklin's preferred public image involved not just appearing industrious but creating a seeming distance from the rowdy, undisciplined popular culture revealed in Daniel Rees's initiation.

What Franklin called the "principal People" had first noticed him because of his polite knowledge and manners. After receiving the ultimately worthless attentions of Governor William Keith upon first moving to Philadelphia, a more important moment occurred in 1728, when Franklin's master, Samuel Keimer, won the contract to print New Jersey's paper money. A number of provincial leaders were deputized to supervise the process. With little to do, they struck up conversations with the journeyman whose reading had included close study of Shaftesbury and the *Spectator,* key texts of eighteenth-century gentility. Keimer felt envious of the attention but lacked the cultural and social polish necessary to impress the New Jersey gentlemen. He was, Franklin wrote later, "an odd fish, ignorant of common life, fond of rudely opposing received opinions, slovenly to extreme dirtiness, enthusiastic in some points of religion, and a little knavish withal"—in short, the worst attributes of the culture that genteel elites (and the ambitious Franklin) were trying to distance themselves from. Franklin's ability to follow genteel conventions paid off. The "Friends" made during his stay, Franklin noted, "were afterwards of great Use to me."[43]

Franklin received his first public position the following year through a simi-

lar recognition of polite standards. William Bradford, the Assembly's printer
and proprietor of a rival Philadelphia newspaper, had printed the Assembly's
address to the governor "in a coarse blundering manner." Determined to show
his awareness of genteel conventions, Franklin stepped in and reprinted the
address "elegantly and correctly." This incident "strengthened the hands of
our friends in the House, and they voted us their printers for the year ensu-
ing," a long-lasting relationship that later resulted in Franklin's appointment
as Assembly clerk.[44]

The shortcomings of even literate artisans such as Bradford and Keimer
(and perhaps momentary lapses like Franklin's handling of the Rees affair)
led gentlemen to strengthen the boundaries of gentility by creating settings
that excluded coarse and blundering common people. William Smith, the 1755
Philadelphia orator, believed such a segregation of the genteel so significant
that he reacted vehemently against plans to place a proposed New York college outside the city. Proper learning, he protested, required "uniting the
Gentleman with the Scholar," a union possible only within the city. "The rural
Situation," he warned, lacked the "polished and learned" models of cities. In
the countryside students would "only see a few illiterate Artificers, whom they
soon learn to look upon as tasteless unpolish'd Clowns." The arguments for an
urban (and thus urbane) location were so strong that they could be countered,
Smith claimed, only by the clearly unacceptable position that "politeness . . .
is to be acquir'd by conversing with inanimate Nature, or is altogether unnecessary." "This would discover," Smith argued, such "a Barbarity of Taste
and Sentiment, that I am far from expecting to hear that any One, who assumes the Name of a Gentleman, will henceforth shew himself a Stickler for
the rural Situation."[45]

The separation of elites from commoners that Smith suggested for the college
was already taking place within the city itself. Expressing the new values of
gentility, gentlemen increasingly met apart from common people in assemblies for dancing and music as well as in clubs. Masonic brothers seem to have
seen themselves as part of the rapid development of these selective groups
after 1720. The grand master of South Carolina at Charleston's June 1738 celebration made "a very eloquent Speech of the Usefulness of Societies, and the
benefits arising therefrom to Mankind." Organized in 1736, the Charleston
lodge began only seven years after the city's first recorded society. At least fifteen such groups met in the city from 1729 (the date of the first recorded club)
to 1750, and residents formed at least twenty-six more from 1751 to 1775. An
examination of these organizations helps sort out some of their purposes and
activities—and the many roles played by Freemasonry.[46]

The earliest societies recorded in Charleston were charitable groups, organized at first around national origins. The St. Andrew's Society that assembled

first in 1729 (perhaps in imitation of an earlier Boston group) originally brought together Scots who wished to aid new immigrants from their homeland. Like its membership rolls, its charity soon became open to all. By 1732, the group numbered some fifty members, each subscribing 7s. 6d. each quarter to "assist all People in Distress, of whatever Nation or Profession they be," and their yearly St. Andrew's Day dinner had become a major social occasion. Both the governor and the chief justice attended the 1732 celebration, which included a "handsome Entertainment, of about 40 Dishes." The South Carolina Society, which grew out of the Huguenot Two-Bitt Club, performed similar functions. It likewise soon claimed an impressive membership of all nationalities. The popularity of such charitable organizations, built upon previous national loyalties, was not limited to Charleston. St. Andrew's Societies also met in New York and Philadelphia.[47]

Besides forming Scottish and Huguenot organizations, Charleston residents also created a Welsh Club, an Irish Society and a Sons of St. Patrick, a German Friendly Society, and a St. George's Society. Besides aiding immigrants, these groups often provided benefits to sick or poor members as well as to their widows. By 1778, the German Friendly Society, formed in 1766, held £4,678 for these purposes. Other such mutual aid societies in Charleston included the Friendly Society, for fire insurance, and the Fellowship Society, which also set up a hospital.[48]

The conviviality that was a secondary purpose of nearly all charitable groups became the primary purpose of many others. These tended to be the most elusive of all organizations, partly because their rules and spending could be informal. Josiah Quincy, Jr., a Bostonian who visited Charleston in 1773, attended otherwise unrecorded Friday night and Monday night clubs. On Friday, he spoke of politics, rice, and slaves, with "the more elder substantial gentlemen," and on Monday, he ate, drank and played cards with a younger assemblage. The Candlestick Club, the Smoking Club, the Segoon-Pop Club, and the Beef-Steak Club all seem to fit in this classification, as does "the valiant Company of Volunteers, who . . . engaged in a desperate Attempt upon Fort Jolly" in 1732 and again in 1733. These purely social clubs were often ephemeral; after 1733, the jovial volunteers seem to have given up their assaults.[49]

Clubs could also be used for practical purposes beyond conviviality or charitable aid. Following Franklin's example, Charleston residents formed a library company in 1748. A number of education societies, all organized after 1750, helped fill the gap created by the lack of public schooling. Other groups spread knowledge of indigo planting and agricultural improvement or worked to encourage manufactures. Recreation and culture provided the focus for still other societies. A St. Andrew's Hunting Society set out hounds for the chase, perhaps even before the first mention of the organization in 1757, and the Orpheus Society and the St. Cecilia's Society provided concerts for members and their guests. Quincy attended a performance sponsored by the latter, an elite group limited to 120, at which he noted that many of the men were clothed "with richness and elegance uncommon with us—many with swords on." The awe-struck Quincy even noted two foppish "Macaronis . . . from London.[50]

Besides Masonry, at least two other fraternal orders built around central metaphors met in colonial Charleston. Such was the "antient, venerable, and honorable Society of BROOMS" that celebrated its anniversary on November 5, 1753. The failure of this group within two years probably stemmed partly from the limited appeal of a "special SWEEP . . . on affairs of great importance," or even a "grand SWEEP." [51]

"The Right worthy and amicible order of Ubiquarians," formed at Charleston in 1741, seemed more promising. Rather than cleaning or building, the Ubiquarians selected "the Roman Constitution, in its most perfect State" and its "Virtue and Morality" as their basis. A praetor headed the Charleston "Convention," with censors, senators, and even aedils as other officers. Drawing on the powerful image of Roman virtue, the Ubiquarians attracted a number of "Gentlemen of the first Distinction." Charles Pinckney, Esq., formerly the province's attorney general, headed the group in 1742; Gabriel Manigault, the richest merchant in colonial Charleston, and Lieutenant Governor William Bull, Jr., served as officers. Like the Masons, the Ubiquarians made brilliant public appearances, meeting in a tavern to elect their officers, then marching "in a very decent and regular manner" to "an elegant Entertainment" that included dinner in the chambers of the governor's Council. Despite this dignified display, however, the Ubiquarians lasted only about three years.

The collapse of an order attracting as many leading gentlemen as the Masons (both Pinckney and Bull were brothers at some time in their lives) is difficult to explain.[52] Like Masonic processions, the Ubiquarians' public display identified its members with genteel values. Furthermore, the group organized itself around a compelling metaphor rooted deeply in the neoclassical eighteenth-century imagination. Yet the Romans probably proved less appealing than the builders in certain ways. The Ubiquarians, whose failure to attend divine service on their anniversary might have been telling, seem to have lacked the religious roots of the fraternity connected with Solomon, Paul, and both Saint Johns. More important, the Ubiquarians failed to arouse the intense public interest generated by Freemasonry. The appeal of the Romans lay in their heroic, stark simplicity, not their mysteriousness.

Perhaps most crucially, however, the Ubiquarians lacked a supporting organization of the strength and stature of the London grand lodge, headed by royalty and nobility. Although American Freemasons seldom communicated with the central body, newspaper reports of its activities and infrequent contacts gave colonial brothers a focus and a model in the metropolitan center of culture. The Ubiquarians's corresponding "GRAND CONVENTION" in England never gained similar notice or reputation. In both practice and theory, Masonry was a universal organization crossing local boundaries.[53]

If Masonry's inclusiveness and range of cultural meanings distinguished it from the Ubiquarians, the fraternity's long-run (if not always short-term) success also reflected its ability to combine nearly all the functions of colonial voluntary societies. John Gordon suggested to Annapolis brothers in 1750 that Freemasonry grew up for the same reasons as other "Combinations of men"; "as social Affection first drew Men into Society, so the same Affections not finding sufficient Scope in more general and public Associations, led them into Private Fellowships."[54] Like clubs, Masonry gave both public and mutual charity; it offered a satisfying ritual to bind the group together; it sponsored activities such as music, theater, and dining; and it furnished opportunities for conviviality. Masonry's private fellowship was not only the most universal in its reach but the broadest in its practices.

The Savannah, Georgia, lodge was too active, a resident complained to the colony's trustees soon after the city's founding in the mid-1730s. The lodge held "a fine Supper every Satterday Night and often 2 or 3 in the Week besides." "Where such an expence can be born," the correspondent grumbled, "I am at a Loss to know." A later witness reported that the lodge often "revell'd" at a Tavern "'till 2 a clock next morning, when they would reel home." During one especially notable night, the brothers set upon the captain of the watch and stole his sword as a practical joke; they later initiated the victim to buy his silence.[55]

The high spirits of the Savannah brothers clearly expressed a conviviality similar to that of the Charleston residents who stormed Fort Jolly. But Masonry officially deplored such undisciplined revelry. According to its public pronouncements and private regulations, the fraternity sought not just to encourage social interaction; it was also to be a family that increased the social respect due its brothers. The ideals of love and honor expressed in Masonry's public processions and private regulations were to dominate its activities as well. The tension between the search for internal fellowship and for external respect that the Savannah brothers neglected was a central concern for most lodges. In their charity, discipline, and fellowship, Masonic brothers attempted to bridge the difficult gap between affectionate love and stern public honor. Such a tension was deeply felt within urban elites in a society where patron-client ties still were necessary but where independence increasingly was cherished: a conflict seen within the lodge and the lives of its brothers, and only partially bridged by the ideal of Masonic family ties.

The practice of Masonic charity reveals the strains created by the desire for both fraternal love and public reputation. Like English lodges, colonial groups received numerous requests for aid and responded in a variety of ways. Boston's First Lodge in 1740 chose a committee to investigate "poor Masons and their widows," providing up to three pounds each. The body seems to have been limited only to this duty, however, and it lapsed afterward. The lodge also took up collections for designated purposes. Dinners after public processions sometimes included such informal giving; at the 1768 installation of a new grand master in Boston, the grand secretary "carried about a Hat to the Brethren" for Jonathan Clark Lewis. Most often, however, the lodge itself voted money from its funds; specifically designated charity funds came later. The grand lodge in Boston created one in 1755. Philadelphia's Tun Tavern (Third) Lodge formed a standing committee two years later to hear appeals for aid but took the money from the common account. Its grand lodge created a regular charity committee only in the early nineteenth century.[56]

The relatively small size of the colonial fraternity allowed unsystematic responses, but these improvisations also represented something larger, a desire to avoid becoming simply another mutual benefit society. Masonic brothers wanted to be able to provide aid beyond the bounds of the Masonic family. Solomon's Lodge at Charleston subscribed the substantial sum of $250 in 1740 for the relief of those affected by the fire that had swept the city. After the installation of George Harison as New York's provincial grand master, brothers there first donated £15 from the treasury to clothe students at the local charity school and then took up "a handsome private donation for the relief of indigent prisoners."[57] Although these gifts perhaps reduced the amount of aid available to brothers, they also reinforced the fraternity's reputation by underlining its honorable concern for the public.

The difficulty of balancing these issues can be seen in Masonic discipline as well. Colonial lodges considered conflicts between brothers a Masonic matter. Pelham recorded a 1751 disagreement between Benjamin Hallowell and David Littlejohn in which the Boston lodge appointed a committee to reconcile the two, a procedure followed by Philadelphia's Tun Tavern Lodge two years later. According to the latter's bylaws, the entire lodge would consider the matter if the smaller group failed to resolve it. The 1732 bylaws of Philadelphia's St. John's Lodge even required, under pain of expulsion, that disputes between brothers could not be made public until the lodge had discussed the matter. Such extreme penalties were seldom followed, except in the case of illegal Masonic meetings and initiations. Philadelphia's Third Lodge imposed this penalty on John Riley in 1749, twelve years after Philadelphia brothers connected the Rees affair to such clandestine meetings. The general refusal of lodges to expel brothers for other reasons suggests again colonial Masonry's characteristic tensions between love and honor. Spurning a brother for unfraternal conduct might strengthen the lodge's internal harmony, but it posed a more immediate threat to the fraternity's all-important self-presentation.[58]

Lodge business like discipline, charity, rituals, and elections formed only one portion of the lodge meeting. After these matters, the lodge would then be "called from labor to refreshment." These times of conviviality were not merely frivolous; they also fulfilled a serious purpose: drinking, dining, and conversing expressed and reinforced fraternal ideals. "Since Love and Good

Will are the best Cement of any Society," the Philadelphia St. John's by-laws explained, "we endeavor to encrease it among ourselves by a kind and friendly conversation." As in other areas, Masonic rules attempted to prevent lodge practice from damaging fraternal friendship or public reputation. Boston's First Lodge's 1733 bylaws stipulated that no brother could eat or call for liquor or tobacco without the permission of the master or his wardens until after the business of the meeting. No more than three shillings per brother could be spent at each meeting.[59]

Celebrations provided further scope for Masonic friendship. The early charters granted to and by Boston Masons required that the groups dine together on the feast of St. John the Evangelist (December 27). Often described as "elegant" or "Sumptuous," these fraternal suppers held on this or the other St. John's Day (June 24) were followed by toasts to the king and craft. Sometimes, again expressing the tensions between public presentation and private fellowship, even non-Masons attended. The organist of King's Chapel, the minister of Trinity Church, and the twelve other musicians at the 1768 dinner after the installation of a new Massachusetts grand master were all nonmembers.[60]

Published accounts reveal the ideals of conduct expected, if not always followed, at these dinners. The *Gazette* reported that "the greatest Order and Regularity was observed" at the 1755 Philadelphia celebration: "Chearfulness, harmony, and good Fellowship abounded, during the whole time of the meeting." According to a Charleston report from the same year, "None being present but those of the Fraternity, the whole was conducted with decency and decorum, so peculiar to the Society." In 1767, the same group "passed the afternoon with that decent festivity and social delight which those who meet with a sincere desire of pleasing and being pleased seldom fail of, and which have long been among the distinguishing characteristics of every regular assembly of the true and faithful brotherhood."[61]

Of course, as the early Savannah brothers reveal, not all Masons exhibited these characteristics of "decent festivity," but such violations seemed to most brothers to attack the essence of Masonic love and honor. Colonial Masonry did not view fraternal fellowship as a withdrawal into a private world of freedom. Rather, the honorable met within the lodge to learn the virtue and polite ways necessary for public honor. In William Smith's metaphor, the fraternity sought to regulate the winds of passion so that they would not extinguish "the candle of Brotherly love." Just as important, such behavior jeopardized Masonic honor. "You should Consider," the 1734 orator warned the Boston brethren, "that not only your own Reputation, but the Reputation of all the fraternity, is affected by your behavior. Invested as you are with that distinguishing Badge which has been worn with pride by the most noble and most worthy of mankind: you should Scorn to do a mean thing: Walk worthy of your vocation, and do honour to your profession."[62]

Masonry's ideal of honorable brotherhood spoke to key themes in colonial

society. Fraternal metaphors first extended the theme of particular and universal love. As the primary expression of benevolence, family relations provided
a seemingly natural way of describing the universal love that Masonry sought
to develop. Sympathy and affection, however, did not exhaust the meaning
of kinship ties. By creating bonds that went beyond narrow calculations of
self-interest, kinship networks facilitated long-distance commerce and often
provided the core of political groups.[63]

Masonry's expansion of familial ties beyond literal kinship also spoke to
the inherent tensions between the bonds created by love and the independence
required by honor. Despite their increasing size and heterogeneity, colonial
cities still lacked impersonal mechanisms like bureaucracies or professional
organizations to order opportunity. Personal ties of patronage, often created
by family connection or political influence rather than merit, provided the
primary means of advancement. Even the powerful William Allen (whom
Franklin turned to when threatened by the Rees case) gained his position
through close ties with what Franklin called the "principal people." His connection with the Penn family, aided by his familial ties with the influential
Shippens, brought him both a business partner whose father was a close
friend of the proprietors and an appointment as chief justice of the colony.
One of his daughters would marry into the Penn family, just as Allen married
the daughter of Assembly speaker Andrew Hamilton.[64]

The ties that smoothed Allen's rise would be more problematic for men such
as William Smith and Benjamin Franklin who could not depend upon the web
of family connections enjoyed by the wealthy merchant. Their situations demanded the aid of outsiders. Yet this dependence also seemed both a symptom
of the corruption deplored by eighteenth-century thinking and an admission
of personal inadequacy. Encouraging William Smith to visit Philadelphia in
1753, shortly before his appointment as head of the new academy and college,
Franklin recommended bringing a letter of introduction to William Allen.
This reference, Franklin argued, would allow Smith to be "more notic'd here."
Yet, realizing that Smith might resent the necessity of using the powerful to
gain attention, Franklin went on to argue that, since the letter itself "will be
founded on your Merit," the attention gained thereby would also be the result
of Smith's own qualities.[65]

Ironically, after Smith moved to Philadelphia and Franklin moved away
from Allen's political tutelage, Smith would use the same tension between
dependence and independence against Franklin himself. The former printer's
progress, Smith suggested in 1764, had been entirely the result of Allen and
his circle. Franklin, he wrote, would "probably . . . never [have] been of consideration enough to give the least disturbance to this province, but for the
numerous favours so ill bestowed on him, by this gentleman and his friends.
They were the persons who first raised him from his original obscurity, and
got him appointed *Printer* to the province, and *Clerk* to the house of assem-

bly." Franklin in his *Autobiography* (and subsequent Franklin folklore) would later suggest, "I have raised myself," but such a claim represented posthumous editing. Franklin actually less aggressively wrote of his "having emerg'd"—and his own description of his rise clearly shows conscious concern with building ties with the gentlemen who could provide "favours."[66]

Franklin's election as Assembly printer was engineered, he wrote in his *Autobiography,* by "our Friends in the House," particularly Andrew Hamilton. The speaker of the Assembly, Franklin later noted, "interested himself strongly in that instance" and continued "his Patronage till his Death." Franklin became a Freemason about this time, joining many of Philadelphia's "principal people" of the city in St. John's Lodge, including Hamilton's son and his son-in-law Allen. In 1736, the Assembly elected Franklin its clerk. The post was valuable, Franklin explained to his son, not only because of the pay (which the printer still needed) but also because of the connections it offered: "The Place gave me a better opportunity of keeping up an Interest among the Members, which secur'd to me the Business of Printing the Votes, Laws, Paper Money, and other occasional Jobs for the Public, that, on the whole, were very profitable." These ties paid off further when, in 1737, he was appointed deputy postmaster.[67]

With this aid, Franklin prospered; he was able to leave "private Business" in 1748. His new status as a gentleman, however, entailed other concerns. "The Public," he recalled, "now considering me as a Man of Leisure laid hold of me for their Purposes—every Part of our Civil Government, and almost at the same time, imposing some Duty upon me." Franklin's surprise was almost certainly feigned, for social and economic prominence in the colonial city naturally implied political leadership. Yet, even then, Franklin continued to need the help of the "leading men"; when he sought the post of deputy postmaster general in 1751, he drew upon William Allen's London connections. Allen, when Franklin's quest was successful, also offered to post the substantial security required, but Franklin, assuming the role of an independent gentleman, looked elsewhere.[68]

Like Masonry's other central themes and practices, its ideal of brotherhood spoke to key experiences of colonial gentlemen. Masonry's fraternal metaphor provided a way of thinking about ambiguous relationships of patronage and loyalty that both downplayed the power inherent in the competing metaphor of patriarchy and gave such ties a moral significance beyond selfish, calculating plays for advantage or ruthless attempts at control. Masonry thus helped to create and sanctify bonds that could be exploited to personal advantage. But Masonry served the interests of colonial gentlemen in another way besides simply aiding their individual situations. By extending fraternity beyond the family—by creating fictive kin—Masons argued, their order merited public honor because it helped both to hold together society and to serve the common good. Rather than building a separate private world, as Rees had thought, the fraternity helped provincial leaders identify their own interests with the interests of the whole. "Our Ancient Society," William Smith assured the brothers and their onlookers in Christ Church during their 1755 procession, "assumes no other foundation, than that which every happy Society has, and must have, . . . fundamental Principles" that ought "to render GOD more *feared* and more adored, and Mankind more happy and more in *Love* with each other." [69]

III. A Very Harmless Sort of People

Franklin and the Freemasons found it difficult to maintain their footing in the aftermath of the Daniel Rees case. Four months after the newspaper exchange about Franklin's involvement, his *Gazette* published its normal announcement of the 1738 St. John's Day elections. It printed no news of the grand lodge for the two following years, however. The next notice of Masonic activity appeared only in June 1741. Silence reigned again for the next eight years. From 1741 to 1749, no mention of Philadelphia Masonry appears in either newspapers or other contemporary reference.[70]

Franklin faced more personal difficulties when news of the murder and trial reached his parents in Boston. Fearing for his child, Josiah Franklin wrote to Benjamin about his opinions. His wife, Josiah noted, was deeply concerned about Benjamin's Masonic connections. The printer prepared at least two partial responses in his commonplace book before finally completing a letter to his "Honour'd Father and Mother" on April 13, 1738.[71]

"As to the Freemasons," he explained, "I know no Way of giving my Mother a better Opinion of them than she seems to have present, (since it is not allowed that Women should be admitted into that secret Society)." Although, he conceded, she may dislike it for that reason, "for any thing else, I must entreat her to suspend her Judgment until she is better inform'd, . . . unless she will believe me when I assure her that they are in general a very harmless sort of People, and have no principles or Practices that are inconsistent with religion and good manners." [72]

The reactions of Franklin and the Pennsylvania fraternity to the Rees case suggest a final characteristic of the colonial fraternity—its relative weakness. Never very large even at their greatest extent (probably Boston and Philadelphia had at most two hundred Masons each at any one time), colonial Masonic bodies tended to be fragile. Charleston brothers, like the Philadelphia lodges, also seem to have suspended their activities for about a decade. After 1742, when the city's newspaper reported a celebration, the grand lodge appeared again only in 1752. Later, both Philadelphia and Boston brothers faced rival Masonic groups that far outstripped them in size and expansiveness.[73]

The institutional fragility of colonial Masonry partly reflected brothers' restrained attitudes about the institution. Franklin's endorsement of the fraternity contrasts markedly with the attitudes of later Masons. While many post-Revolutionary brothers boasted of Freemasonry as a divine institution with worldwide importance, Franklin merely called them "harmless." Indeed, the letter to his parents is one of the very few references to the fraternity in Franklin's vast correspondence. His slight emotional investment in Freemasonry seems not to have been unusual. Personal letters even between brothers seldom mention the fraternity.[74]

Like so many other aspects of the fraternity, colonial Masonry's frailty was closely related to the social and cultural experiences of the urban elite—indeed, perhaps too closely related. Masonry fitted so well into the emerging institutions of genteel culture that it never gained independent significance. The fraternity's public display and explanations as well as its more private sociability, secrecy, and exclusivity all followed the standards that increasingly shaped the lives of urban elites. While much of Masonry simply followed these practices, the fraternity's most distinctive trait turned out to be a liability. Masonry's links to impenetrable mysteries (an aspect of the fraternity virtually ignored by colonial brothers) sometimes raised the suspicions of outsiders. Both the forms of elite social life and the specifics of public suspicion shed light on colonial Freemasonry's fragility.

By midcentury, Masonic activities formed only part of an array of similar practices within the emerging American culture of gentility. John Rowe, a Boston brother who recorded many of his 1760s social engagements, provides an entry into this world. Although his social circle was not the highest (the governor appears only intermittently), Rowe was one of Boston's principal people, serving as a selectman, town meeting moderator, and Anglican vestryman. A prosperous merchant, Rowe traded with England, Madeira, and other American colonies as well as owning a wharf, a warehouse, and shares in a number of ships (the cargo of one would spark the Boston Tea Party). He also was active in genteel elite society. When a provincial grand lodge committee visited him with a deputation appointing him grand master on October 5, 1768, he had already eaten his early-afternoon dinner, but his activities had barely begun. After receiving the brothers, Rowe went to a meeting with the Boston selectmen, attended "the Charitable Society," and finally spent "an hour at the Coffee House."[75]

Rowe's schedule during June of the previous year, while unusually heavy, illustrates the texture of this experience—and the place of Masonry within it. On May 30, he dined at "the Club" with ten others before going fishing, one of his favorite activities. The "Artillery election" the day after the fishing trip concluded with a dinner at "Fanewill Hall," open only "by invitation." The governor and the Council joined the company, which heard the Reverend Daniel Shute of Hingham give "a sensible Discourse." Following the meal, Rowe rode to Needham, continuing on the next day to Natick for more fishing. For dinner, he ate with fourteen others at a tavern. "We were," he recorded in his diary, "very merry." On June 3, he spent two hours as part of the board of arbitrators. The following day, "High Training Day," saw another dinner at Faneuil Hall, with the governor's Council again in attendance. A selectmen's meeting filled the afternoon and evening of the next day, discussing aid to sufferers of a February fire. On June 6 and 8, Rowe again went fishing, followed on the latter evening with a meeting of "the Posse," another club. Rowe dined at a tavern "on Turtle" with twenty-eight others on the eleventh, seemingly for no specific reason, and hosted a dinner five days later for two military officers. On the twenty-fourth, St. John's Day, he "dined at Mr. Greatons" with forty-three brothers. Rowe, in the absence of grand master Jeremiah Gridley, presided. A charity school inspection filled July 1, ending with yet another Faneuil Hall meal. This time, the diners included the selectmen, the overseers of the poor, "Mr Secretary Oliver, Mr Treasurer Gray etc. others."[76]

Neither the private nor the public elements of Freemasonry presented unique or strange experiences to Rowe. Other selective clubs played a major role in his activity. Besides the three groups he attended in June 1767, the Posse, the otherwise unidentified "the Club," and the Freemasons, he also belonged to the Wednesday-Night Club, the No. 5 Club, and the Merchant Club, served as treasurer of the Charitable Society, and participated in the annual celebration of the Sons of St. Patrick. The Fire Club he joined in September 1768 even had a secret mode of recognition: "The Word 'Ask More.' " The secrecy of such clubs extended into other parts of elite life. The "principal people" often met apart from the lower orders, whether in the selectmen's meetings or at clubs. Political leadership was virtually restricted to these elites, as Benjamin Franklin, who held no elective office before, discovered when he retired from trade. After marriage to a wealthy widow brought George Washington similar elevation, he seems to have considered the resulting public offices as much a perquisite of rank as a position of responsibility. In his eleven years on the Truro Parish vestry from 1763 to 1774, Washington attended fewer than half the meetings. He waited four years after his election to attend a meeting as a trustee of Alexandria.[77]

Late-colonial society replicated not only Masonry's sociability and secrecy but also its public processions and descriptions. Charleston's 1753 King's Birthday celebration followed the pattern of many Masonic celebrations. In the morning, with the ships in harbor decorated, the troops paraded through the streets. At noon, they, with the lieutenant governor (a Masonic brother), the Council, the Assembly, and other government officers, marched to a fort where they toasted the king's health amid the firing of cannons. An "entertainment" and a ball closed the day—"the most numerous, brilliant, and polite Assembly," judged the *Gazette*, "ever seen here on any public Occasion." Processions also marked the opening of court sessions. The Savannah Court of Oyer and Terminer marched to church before their June 1767 charge to the grand jury.[78]

Funerals provided further opportunities for public display. Two months after the Savannah court ritual, Jeremiah Gridley's funeral in Boston—which included the fraternity, Gridley's regiment, robed lawyers, and the "Gentlemen of the Town"—provoked Rowe's displeasure: "I do not much approve of such parade and show but as it was his Relatives desire, I could not well avoid giving my Consent." Rowe seemingly objected to the ceremony's excess, for he spoke approvingly of John Box's "handsome Funerall," where the Masons also "walked in Proper Form." Even Rowe's descriptions of other social events mirror the language used of Masonic celebrations. When Ralph Inman's son, George, received his Harvard degree in 1772, the proud father gave "the Genteelest Entertainment I ever saw," with 347 "Gentlemen and Ladies," including the governor and the lieutenant governor, the admiral of the port, and their families, "and all the Remainder, Gentlemen and Ladies of Character and Reputation." The dinner, Rowe recorded, "was conducted with much Ease and Pleasure and all Joyned in making each other Happy."[79]

By then, the distinction between gentle and common that Masonry helped to reinforce had become a central principle of urban society. Ties between gentlemen crossed the boundaries of age and formal status. When George Washington's stepson, John Parke Custis, attended King's College in New York during the early 1770s, he alone of the students, as the most socially prominent, ate with the faculty. He noted happily to Washington, "There is as much distinction made between me and the other students as can be expected." William Allen joined the Philadelphia corporation when he was only twenty-two—and within the next ten years became an alderman, a justice of the peace, the mayor of Philadelphia, and an assemblyman. The social and political distance possible within the small and geographically compact colonial cities can be seen in the relationship between John Rowe and the fairly prosperous artisan Paul Revere. Although Rowe assiduously recorded the participants at the dinners and meetings he attended, Revere appears only once before the Revolution—when Rowe served on a committee in 1773 considering streetlamps. Significantly, Revere oversaw his own ward; Rowe, as a gentleman, dealt with the entire city.[80]

The growing distinctiveness of elite social experiences also encouraged interactions that made Masonic sociability less important. The small-scale world of the colonial city offered a variety of means to bring together gentlemen. Rowe met Masonic brothers in many contexts besides the lodge. Brother John Box, Sr., for example, served with him as an officer of the Charitable Society, and a December 1766 dinner put on by Boston merchants and presided over by Rowe included brothers James Otis, Benjamin Hallowell, and Edmund Quincy. Philadelphia grand lodge officers often had similar points of contact with each other. In 1737, the year of the Rees murder, the Library Company directors included brothers Allen, Franklin, William Plumstead, Philip Syng, Jr., and James Hamilton. All had previously held the office of Masonic grand master except Hamilton, and he would be elected to the position later.

Business also brought brothers together. The wealthy Charleston merchant James Crokatt, who later trained brother Henry Laurens, exemplifies these commercial ties. When Crokatt became master of Solomon's Lodge in 1738 (the year he joined the governor's Council), the grand master was his lawyer James Graeme. His predecessor as master, George Seaman, had been a business partner. Also among the lodge members was a future partner, Benjamin Smith, who in 1743 would serve on the St. Philip's vestry with two other Freemasons, one of whom was former master George Seaman.[81]

In such a world where both Masonry's practices and ideals of love and honor could be experienced outside the lodge as well, the fraternity's primary distinction was its supposed possession of secrets; and, although these mysteries excited interest in the fraternity, they also encouraged apprehensions. The 1734 Boston orator, speaking only a year after the formation of the city's fraternity, warned brothers "that people of dark Suspitious minds, have Imagined that Something Extremely Wicked must be the Cement of our fabrick, and the tribe of Scorners affect to Represent it as Some What mighty Ridiculous." Fulfilling these complaints, the *Boston Post-Boy* in 1750/1 published a scurrilous poem (with an accompanying illustration) suggesting that the trowels carried in the processions were used for anal tortures. Angry at the slur, the fraternity voted to boycott the paper and apply to the governor for a suit against the publisher; it also celebrated the next St. John's Day in Roxbury. Four years later, the Boston wit Joseph Green satirized the fraternity in a poem that claimed that the brothers chose a temporary master by testing his ability to endure having his nose pulled and his "posteriors" beaten. As the Reverend Michael Smith told the brethren in New Bern, North Carolina, later that same year, "There are many in the World who entertain strange and unreasonable Notions of the Craft."[82]

Masonry's possession of what Green termed a *Grand Arcanum* sparked public interest, but it also hindered full acceptance of the fraternity. Green's satiric vision of beaten posteriors and pulled noses misrepresented Masonry in a manner similar to Rees's laxatives and satanic oaths. These imagined counterworlds reveal the dangers inherent in Masonry's tradition of primeval mystery within colonial America. The larger problem of early Masonry, however, lay, not in such criticism, but in the failure of the fraternity's distinctive elements to do more than raise curiosity and doubts. By successfully reshaping the fraternity to their own setting, colonial elites unwittingly limited Masonry to only a minor role in their identity as genteel social leaders, to being called by a former grand master merely "a very harmless sort of people."

Boston wit Joseph Green perhaps intentionally distorted Masonry's private activities in 1755 in *The Grand Arcanum Detected,* but his earlier poem of 1750, *Entertainment for a Winter's Evening,* suggests a sharp understanding of the fraternity's public images. Green, a Harvard graduate and a justice of the peace, would later be a frequent member of John Rowe's social circles. But his account of the December 1749 procession, the most widely read and longest account of the colonial fraternity by an outsider, attempted, not to praise, but to satirize Masonry by mocking its hypocrisy and pretensions.[83]

Set in clever couplets, the account begins as the group marches to church as "the bells in steeple play." The sermon on love is given full treatment:

> While other sects fall out and fight
> About a trifling mode or rite,
> We firm by *Love* cemented stand,
> 'Tis *Love* unites us heart and hand,
> *Love* to a party not confin'd,
> A *Love* embracing all mankind,
> Both catholick and protestant,
> The *Scots* and eke *New-England* saint
>
> . . . .
>
> And light that's *new,* and light that's *old*
> We in our friendly arms enfold.

The poet protests the lodge's evident lack of love:

> Did there not (for the Secret's out)
> In the last LODGE arise a rout?
> Mackenzey with a fist of brass
> Laid Trail's nose level with his face,
> And scarcely had he let his hand go,
> When he receiv'd from Trail a d—— blow,
> Now, parson, when a nose is broken,
> Pray, is it friendly *sign* or *token?*

The minister replies that this event was extraordinary:

> 'Tis true—but trifling is th' objection,
> All general rules have an exception
>
> . . . .
>
> But what I've said, I'll say again,
> And what I say I will maintain:
> 'Tis *Love,* pure *Love,* cements the whole,
> *Love*—of the BOTTLE and the BOWL.

The long discussion ends:

> This having said the reverend vicar
> Dismiss'd them to their food and liqour.[84]

After the sermon, the brothers again march through the street, with Green commenting on individual members' traits. He mentions, sometimes crudely, several of the tradesmen's occupations, including the apothecary's use of the enema. He describes personal weaknesses

> Sage Hallowell of public soul,
> And laughing Frank, friend to the bowl,
> Meek Rea, half smother'd in the crowd,
> And Rowe who sings at church so loud.[85]

Though it mocks the fraternity for the benefit of Green's elite friends (many of whom were brothers), the poem shows the power of Masonry's public messages as it underlines the confusions the fraternity sought to clarify. Green recognizes the ideal of love as a counterweight to religious, political, and national divisions—and an attempt to tame a more vulgar popular culture of smashed noses. His account of the public procession then sets the brothers' less polished occupational and personal foibles in opposition to the polite and honorable ideals of the fraternity's symbolic display. Like all satire, Green's poem upholds the ideals even as it emphasizes that people fall short.

Green ends the poem as the Freemasons head to their tavern meeting room. The audience in the street grows larger and louder, compared by the poet to spectators following a shamed London bawd drawn through the streets:

> Just such the noise, just such the roar,
> Heard from behind and from before,
> 'Till *lodg'd* at STONE's, nor more pursu'd,
> The mob with three huzzas conclude.[86]

The attempt of brothers to give Freemasonry a genteel and honorable reputation, despite occasional jests and suspicions, largely worked. Although the fraternity never became central to their identities or their social lives—perhaps leaving room for gibes like Green's about the fraternity's pretensions to deep mysteries and elevated goals—it attracted the participation of many of the colonial city's principal people. What Green called "the *apron'd train*" also aroused the interest of the common people. In Green's poem, "they should'ring close, press, stink and shove" to glimpse the fraternity. As yet, however, men below the rank of gentleman could not go behind the closed doors, except perhaps at the behest of the elite. Their appetite for Masonic honor (as well as mystery), however, was whetted, as Daniel Rees's had already been a decade earlier. Given the opportunity, they would attempt to enter the ranks of the "ancient and honorable society." Such a thing would have scarcely seemed possible to the genteel brothers marching through the Boston streets, but it would soon happen.[87]

PART TWO

The Revolutionary Transformation

CHAPTER THREE

Where Is Honour?

The Rise of Ancient Masonry, 1752–1792

Philadelphia's Masonic lodges did not participate in the 1790 funeral of brother Benjamin Franklin. Twenty thousand people watched the funeral procession — "a concourse of Spectators," judged the *Pennsylvania Gazette,* "greater than ever was known on like occasion." The Society of the Cincinnati, the American Philosophical Society, and the Council and Assembly of the state all took part as did "all the Clergy of the City, including the Ministers of the Hebrew Congregation."[1]

The city's Masonic lodges, however, completely ignored the event, failing even to note the death of one of the first Freemasons in America and the former head of the order in Pennsylvania. By 1790, Franklin was simply the wrong sort of Freemason for the Philadelphia brothers. Their refusal to acknowledge his death underlined the social and institutional transformation that had occurred within the fraternity the sixty years Franklin had been a member.

While Franklin lived abroad (virtually the entire period between 1757 and 1785), a new set of men took over Pennsylvania Masonry. The new group's first lodge had already been organized in 1757 when he left Philadelphia for England. Its founders, drawing upon English example, called it "Ancient" to distinguish it from previous lodges that, Ancient brothers claimed, had profaned the fraternity's sacred traditions. By the title and their labeling the older group as "Moderns," the new Masons laid claim to priority and precedence despite their later organization.

The immediate occasion of the Ancients' indictment of the Moderns probably lay in an English disagreement about rituals, but this argument was only the external cause of the division. Social differences gave meaning and passion to the division in England and America. Whereas Franklin's Moderns had brought together many of the province's most prominent men in a society that proclaimed their gentility, cultivation, and high social standing, the Ancients included many who lacked political power and social distinction. The new Ancient lodges proved the more popular and adaptable body. By the time Franklin returned from England for good in 1785, he could not enter a Pennsylvania lodge. The grand lodge he had headed no longer existed, and its past grand master could not even set foot in a lodge room without a ceremony of "healing" to convert him from an unacceptable Modern Mason into an Ancient brother.

Other areas experienced a similar transformation. Indeed, by 1792—the year the Massachusetts Ancients dictated terms of a merger with the Moderns—the Ancients had triumphed almost everywhere in America, from seaboard cities like New York (where they organized during the Revolutionary war) to the swiftly developing interior (where their lodges had expanded far more rapidly than the Moderns'). By opening Masonry to social groups outside the elites of the principal seaports and by preserving the Modern identification of the fraternity with genteel cosmopolitan culture, Ancient Masons created an organization of extraordinary appeal.[2]

This reordering was more than an internal affair. It also reflected larger changes in American society. Masonry's transformation began in the 1750s, shortly before the Revolutionary developments in society and culture that accompanied the fight for Independence. The groups that embraced Ancient Masonry most strongly, furthermore, were the chief beneficiaries of Revolutionary changes. Urban artisans took on new political importance during the Revolutionary crisis, demanding and gaining representation on the committees that wrested power from the British governments. Similarly, elites outside the capitals also sought and received increased political power, symbolized most clearly in the transfer of state capitals into the interior. These two developments seem in many ways unrelated. Although artisans appear to exemplify urban crowd action and perhaps even class resentment, interior elites seem part of the westward movement that encouraged economic development and democratic ideals.[3]

An examination of Masonic changes suggests another perspective: one that highlights the cultural and social changes that lay behind the new political assertiveness of both groups. For each, economic and cultural expansion broadened horizons and heightened aspirations to the social distinctions and cosmopolitanism offered by Masonry. Like the committees organized during the imperial crisis, Ancient lodges offered a way to assert a new importance— and a concrete example of Revolutionary equality and participation. Masonic affiliation also provided a means of redefining social position and claiming the honor previously reserved for gentlemen of wealth, education, and family. The same upheaval that shaped the new political geography of post-Revolutionary America also created Ancient Masonry.

1. The Good Old Way

Almost from the start, the older Philadelphia Masons distrusted the new lodge they created in 1757. Perhaps they worried because the members of No. 4 had already been meeting for some time before they petitioned for a warrant, or perhaps they disliked the artisanal membership of the new group. Whatever the reasons for their concern, however, the older lodges soon decided to investigate. On September 13, less than three months after the charter was issued, four brothers visited the new lodge. They were not subtle: lodge minutes noted that "all behaved as spies from an enemy's camp." Despite their clumsiness, the visitors found out what they wanted to know. They summoned the officers of the new lodge to a meeting eight days later and "Charged [them] with being Antient Masons," part of a new faction of British Masons that rejected the legitimacy of the old London grand lodge. The officers of No. 4 "plead[ed] Guilty." The committee, after extensive debate, referred the matter to the grand lodge. When an accused officer again admitted to being "Antients," the lodge later recalled, the grand lodge asked "Whether we would become what they were in manner and form to which we answer'd neither Could nor would." The grand lodge confiscated their warrant, removing its sanction from the meetings.[4]

The new lodge continued unrepentant. Though their rough prose suggests the gap between themselves and the genteel "principal people" of the grand lodge, they continued to meet in defiance of the older body and applied to the London Ancient Masons for another charter. "We are determined," they told its grand lodge, "never to forsake the good old way at this Distressing and Critical time."[5]

The ultimate success of the Pennsylvania Ancients depended first upon their ties to this English movement. The London Ancients had emerged around midcentury to suit the needs of lesser men, often of Irish descent, but had gone beyond simply creating a new lodge. Soon, they also organized their own grand lodge and claimed superiority to the original Masons. Their language and military organizations (as well as their unofficial ally, the Scottish grand lodge) would help spread Ancient Masonry to the colonies.

When the Philadelphia Ancients made the rather audacious claim that the officers of the original grand lodge, formed from the first lodge on the Continent and chartered by the inventors of speculative Freemasonry, were "Moderns" departing from the "good old way," they drew upon British ideas and support. "The Grand Lodge of Antient Masons," alleged Laurence Dermott, the ideologist and driving force of the London body formed in 1751, "received the old system without adulteration." "A person made in the modern manner, and not after the antient customs of the craft," however, "has no right to be called free and accepted—his being unqualified to appear in a master's lodge." The new British body seized upon small changes in the degree rituals made by the original grand lodge in 1739, alterations made to keep out pretenders not made in regular lodges, as evidence of departure from true Masonry. Turning the older brothers' penchant for precedent against them, the new group denounced the original lodges as "moderns"—"defective in

Figure 7. Lodge Summons, Philadelphia Ancient Lodge No. 2. Philadelphia, 1757, altered 1761. *Courtesy of Scottish Rite Museum of Our National Heritage, 1993-076. Photography by David Bohl*

form and capacity." The clever appropriation of the title "ancient" to describe newly formed bodies succeeded fully. Even the older lodges finally accepted the inferior designation of "moderns," sometimes in their own minutes.[6]

The dispute between the two groups involved more than a concern for the exact wording of the ritual. The ideology of Ancient Masonry served a particular British social need. By 1740, the original impetus of speculative Freemasonry within London had worn off, symbolized by the leadership of William, fifth Lord Byron. Elected grand master in 1747 at the age of twenty-five, he attended only three meetings during his five years at the head of the grand lodge—once to be installed, once to suggest a successor, and once to install him. In the provinces, only about a dozen new provincial lodges were formed in the 1740s; the number of London lodges actually declined from 128 to 73. Already in 1742, the grand master warned of "the Great Decay of many Lodges," and Horace Walpole, himself a Mason, told a correspondent, "Nothing but a persecution could bring them into vogue here again."[7]

The weakness of Masonry in the 1740s allowed a number of Irish brothers to establish their own London lodges without the original grand lodge's approval. In 1751, the new Masons, probably including some men first inducted into the older bodies, formed their own supervisory body. With the choice of Laurence Dermott as their grand secretary the following year, they gained a forceful leader who encouraged expansion. The 10 lodges formed by 1753 mushroomed to more than 140 by 1771.[8]

Serving as grand secretary for thirty-five years, Dermott proved the ideal leader for the new group. He had participated in the formative experiences of many of its members. Born in Ireland and emigrating to London as an adult, Dermott had followed a common path. Most of the first Ancient members shared his Irish background; many probably became Masons even before moving to London. Twenty years after the formation of the new lodges, despite the great influx of English members, the rival grand secretary still referred to the Ancients as "the Irish Faction."[9]

Dermott also shared the economic experiences of many Ancient brothers. Although he later became a wine merchant, he was, at the time of his election, only a journeyman painter "obliged," he noted in the 1753 records, "to work twelve hours in the day for the Master Painter who employed him." Most of the early Ancients similarly worked as artisans; only one attorney appeared on the 1751 rolls. The following year the grand lodge voted to provide seven shillings a week from the Grand Charity Fund for each member in debtor's prison.[10]

Dermott's shaky economic footing, however, did not imply lack of intellectual curiosity. Indeed, he was something of a linguist, reading and speaking both Latin and Hebrew. According to Dermott's later description, the new Ancient brothers also followed this pattern: "Men of some Education and an honest Character but in low Circumstances."[11]

Dermott played cleverly upon the social differences between his group and its rivals. His *Ahiman Rezon,* the Ancients' Constitutions, claimed that the fastidious moderns had originally objected to the wearing of aprons, "which made the gentlemen look like so many mechanicks." Unable to dispense with this ancient custom, they turned the aprons upside down "in order to avoid appearing mechanical." Ironically, with the strings now hanging to the floor, the masons, in Dermott's fanciful description, were forced to walk like drunken peasants to avoid tripping.[12]

The Ancients' more humble social rank encouraged their interest in creating military lodges. Although other British grand lodges similarly organized groups attached to individual regiments, the Ancients were the most active supporters of the practice, warranting 62 lodges by 1813. These bodies provided Masonic fellowship for lower ranks of soldiers who could not, like their superiors, mingle in polite local society. With the increasing number of soldiers in America after midcentury, military lodges helped spread Ancient Masonry to the colonies. Philadelphia's No. 4 included at least one British soldier in its earliest years, and its second master, John Blackwood, probably also served in the military. According to the minutes, he missed a meeting "in the Interest of the Public, and returned Victoriously crowned with laurels."[13] Blackwood's advice persuaded the lodge to apply to the London Ancient grand lodge, instead of the Irish body, for a warrant. Ancient soldiers similarly participated in the development of the Boston Ancients. When the Scottish Lodge of St. Andrew's sought to form a grand lodge in 1769, it called upon the aid of three regimental lodges to support its petition.

Without the example and aid of the English Ancients and their Scottish and Irish allies, the split in American Masonry might never have developed. What eventually made the division irreconcilable, however, was, not the English quarrel, but the social situation of the two groups. The rise of Ancient Masonry formed part of the American redefinition of honor and social status.

ii. The Mason's Arms

When the Boston Ancients wanted to visit the grand lodge in 1758, the Moderns appointed a committee to examine the upstarts' dubious credentials. Noting the illegal initiation of some of the members, the Moderns refused to admit a fraternal bond. Instead, they insultingly offered to initiate, upon payment of a fee, any members of the new group who possessed a "good character." The Ancients rejected such elite condescension. Eleven years later, they formed their own grand lodge.[14]

Although Philadelphia brothers had also organized an Ancient grand lodge in 1760, the divisions within the two cities were short-lived. The disorders of the Revolution crippled the Moderns. Loyalty to the crown, though hardly absent from the Ancient fraternity, was widespread among the leaders of Modern Masonry. Boston's Moderns, reduced to one lodge from their former three, finally accepted a merger on Ancient terms in 1792. Philadelphia's Moderns simply ceased to meet sometime around the end of the war. By 1800, nearly all American lodges identified themselves as Ancient.[15]

The ultimate victory of the Ancients, like their earlier refusals to accept the dictates of their social betters, reveals the changing nature of both Masonry and American society. The membership rolls of the Philadelphia Ancient lodge during its earliest years (1757–1760) and the original Boston Ancient group (later St. Andrew's Lodge) before the war indicate that the Ancient Masons, like their British counterparts, occupied a social stratum significantly below the Moderns. In turn, the changes within the lives of these artisans and lesser merchants suggest the social and cultural developments behind the new artisanal assertiveness of the Revolutionary period.

The two Ancient lodges attracted few gentlemen. Although the first master of the Philadelphia body ranked in the top third of the 1756 tax assessment, he was only a master plumber and painter recently arrived from Ireland. His even more obscure Boston counterpart appears in town records as a constable, a post traditionally given to poorer Bostonians. Of the eight original Boston members, only two others held a public position. One had spent some time as a fireman; the other later served as scavenger and hogreeve—responsible for cleaning the streets and rounding up stray swine.[16]

The Masonic experiences of the two most distinguished pre-Revolutionary St. Andrew's members suggest the limits of the Ancients' appeal. Joseph Warren, the first Ancient grand master, had a Harvard education and eventually became an important political leader. But he originally joined the lodge after spending a year teaching school and dropped out soon after beginning his medical apprenticeship. Upon his return five years later, he quickly became master and then grand master. The recorded participation of future governor John Hancock suggests a similar lack of enthusiasm. After becoming a Mason in Canada, Hancock attended St. Andrew's meetings for about a year and a half. The death of his uncle in 1764, making him enormously wealthy, marked the end of his affiliation with the lodge.[17]

Warren and Hancock were exceptional not only in their wealth and Harvard education but also in their occupations. The mercantile and professional sectors that provided the bulk of the Modern membership made up a much smaller part of the Ancient lodges. St. Andrew's merchants were neither as numerous nor as affluent as those in the Modern lodges. There they made up more than two-thirds of the identifiable members; among the Boston Ancients, they composed about one-quarter. The 1771 assessment of the merchandise and factorage held by Ancient merchants averaged less than one-third that of the Modern merchants. The earliest Philadelphia Ancients included no merchants at all. Neither lodge contained any lawyers, and only a handful of physicians, none with a European education, belonged to St. Andrew's. Sea captains formed a more significant part of the St. Andrew's membership (36 percent) than in the Modern Boston lodges (7 percent) (Tables 2, 3).[18]

Two-thirds of the Philadelphia and more than one-quarter of the Boston Ancients worked as "mechanics"—artisans and small retailers. Few in either Ancient lodge engaged in trades that required heavy capitalization or close

Table 2. Occupations of Ancient Masons, St. Andrew's Lodge, Boston, and Lodge No. 2, Philadelphia, 1752–1775

Occupation	St. Andrew's, Boston, 1752–1775[a]	No. 2, Philadelphia, 1756–1760[b]
Merchant	32 (26.7%)	0
Clerk	1	
Merchant	31	
Professional	5 (4.2%)	0
Physician	4	
Schoolteacher (public)	1	
Luxury goods artisan	4 (3.3%)	4 (16.7%)
Jeweler	1	
Clock- and watchmaker		1
Engraver		1
Goldsmith		1
Goldsmith and engraver	1	
Printer	1	1
Bookbinder	1	
Mercantile-related craft	10 (8.3%)	3 (12.5%)
Cooper	2	
Blockmaker		1
Shipbuilding	8	2
Sailmaker	2	1
Shipwright	2[c]	
Ropemaker	1	
Ship joiner	1	
Ship chandler	1	
Boat builder	1	1
Building crafts	7 (5.8%)	4 (16.7%)
Housewright	2	
Carpenter		1
Carver	2	
Bricklayer	2	1
Glazier	1[d]	
Glazier, plumber, and painter		1
Plaisterer		1
Other artisanal	13 (10.8%)	5 (20.8%)
Sugar refiner	2	
Baker	2	
Blacksmith	2	
Gunsmith	2	
Cabinetmaker	1	
Chairmaker	1	
Hatmaker	1	

Table 2. Continued

Occupation	St. Andrew's, Boston, 1752-1775[a]	No. 2, Philadelphia, 1756-1760[b]
Leather dresser	1	
Tin plate worker	1	
Barber		1
Shoemaker		1
Stonecutter		1
Tailor		1
Upholsterer and undertaker		1
Retailer	4 (3.3%)	3 (12.5%)
Innkeeper	2	1
Auctioneer	1	
Victualler	1	
Shopkeeper		1
Tavernkeeper		1
Seagoing	44 (36.7%)	4 (16.7%)
Sea captain	43	2
Pilot	1	
Flatman		1
Unidentified		1
Agriculture	1 (.8%)	1 (4.2%)
Husbandman	1	
Farmer		1

[a] 120 of 153 (78.4%) identified.   [b] 24 of 65 (36.9%) identified.   [c] 1 also a painter.
[d] Also a cooper?

Sources: The Lodge of St. Andrew, and the Massachusetts Grand Lodge . . . 5756-5769, 231-234; Barratt and Sachse, *Freemasonry in Pennsylvania,* I, 11, 52-54, 73-74; and sources in Table 1.

contact with the elite. While Modern artisans published newspapers, crafted silver, or owned ropewalks, St. Andrew's members more often built boats or baked bread.[19]

The gap between the two groups appears most strikingly in the tax assessments made in Philadelphia in 1756 and in Boston in 1771. Boston Ancients' real estate assessment averaged about half that of the Moderns', and twice as many Moderns were rated for ownership of other buildings besides their houses. The contrast in the Philadelphia 1756 tax ratings is even more pronounced. Only about one-quarter of the Ancients ranked as high as the top nine-tenths of the Moderns, and about one-quarter of the Moderns were assessed higher than any Ancients (Tables 4, 5).[20]

Table 3. Summary of Occupations of Ancients and Moderns

	Boston Moderns	Boston Ancients	Philadelphia Moderns	Philadelphia Ancients
Merchant	66.0%	26.7%	61.5%	0%
Professional	14.4	4.2	21.2	0
Artisan	8.2	28.3	7.7	66.7
Retailer	2.1	3.3	5.8	12.5
Seagoing	9.3	36.7	3.8	16.7

Note: Figures for Ancients do not total 100% because of omission here of one agricultural occupation in each lodge.
Sources: See Tables 1 and 2.

Table 4. Boston Masons in 1771 Provincial Tax

	Moderns ($N = 78$)	Ancients ($N = 65$)
Average value of real estate	£30.25	£15.45
Average value of merchandise and factorage	£495.75	£154.51
Proportion owning ships	12.8%	1.5%
Proportion assessed for houses	74.4%	70.8%
Proportion assessed for other buildings	37.2%	21.5%
Proportion listed as boarders	6.4%	20.0%

Source: Bettye Hobbs Pruitt, ed., *Massachusetts Tax Valuation List of 1771* (Boston, 1978).

Ancient Masonry's success rested on more than changing the American fraternity's socioeconomic profile. The new lodges reflected a rearrangement of urban social categories—a transformation that upset older definitions of society based on a dichotomy between the elite and everyone else. The growing cosmopolitanism of a number of artisans placed them outside the older sphere of tradesmen but not yet within the circle of the elite. The rocky initiation of the *Boston Magazine* in 1783 reveals this ambiguity.

The magazine briefly edited by William Billings—the composer, singing master, and tanner who had joined St. Andrew's in 1778—sought to imitate the polite English culture popularized by such London publications as the *Spectator* and the *Gentleman's Magazine*. Such periodicals represented the

Table 5. Philadelphia Masons in 1756 City Tax

Tax Range (£)	Proportion Assessed		
	All (N = 2,397)	Moderns (N = 47)	Ancients (N = 23)
0–3	1%	0%	0%
4–10	18	0	0
11–15	26	2	26
16–20	24	11	17
21–25	5	0	30
26–30	7	15	4
31–40	7	11	9
41–50	4	26	4
51–60	3	13	9
61–80	2	6	0
81–100	2	4	0
101–600	2	13	0
Total	101	101	99

Note: Deviations in totals from 100% in tables are due to rounding.
Source: Hannah Benner Roach, "Taxables in the City of Philadelphia, 1756," *Pennsylvania Genealogical Magazine,* XXII (1961), 9–41.

pinnacle of cultural aspirations for genteel Americans. Philadelphia Modern brothers Benjamin Franklin and William Smith had each published one for a short time. At first glance, the *Boston Magazine* fitted the pattern established by its London and American predecessors. Its first issue included "Poetical Essays" and an "Essay on Moral Reflections." Some of the contents, however, failed to meet the standards of polite society. A particularly shocking piece entitled "Life of Sawney Beane" detailed in a decidedly ill-mannered fashion the story of a Scottish family who robbed, murdered, and ate its victims. When a woman was taken by the Beanes, "the female Cannibals cut her throat, and fell to sucking her blood with as great a gust[o] as if it had been wine; this done, they ript up her belly, and pulled out all her entrails." Such indelicacy appalled the proper gentlemen of Boston. They quickly removed Billings and set about making the magazine "more respectable," asking in the next issue that it "be considered as their first number."[21]

That the artisan Billings lacked the nice taste necessary for such a magazine came as no surprise to some of the Boston elite. The Reverend John Eliot, a member of the "society of gentlemen" that took over the *Boston Magazine,* despaired of the periodical after hearing that "Mr. Billings, the psalm singer," would direct it. With rare exceptions like Franklin, who carefully studied the style and attitudes of the *Spectator,* artisans seldom played any part in polite society. Gentlemen might sometimes refer to them as "the middling people," but in the end they fell into the vast category of the vulgar. Even the pupils of a Philadelphia Latin school in the 1760s, weary of Greek and Latin, knew where the social lines were drawn. "We cheerfully renounced the learned professions," Alexander Graydon later recalled, "for the sake of the supposed liberty that would be the consequence. We were all, therefore, to be merchants, as to be mechanics was too humiliating."[22]

Billings and his Ancient brothers, even such well-known figures as St. Andrew's master Paul Revere and printer Isaiah Thomas, lacked many of the essential qualifications for gentility. Most important, their learning was usually rudimentary. For Billings, a near-contemporary noted, "opportunities for even common education were very limited." Revere received only a little formal education before his apprenticeship, at North Writing School rather than an elite Latin school. Thomas, who probably joined an Ancient Boston lodge around the time of the Revolution, was apprenticed to a printer at the age of six and had no formal education at all. He recalled that his master could not understand the catechism and found punctuation a mystery.[23]

Though Ancient brothers lacked the central qualifications of gentlemen, they were not really part of the vulgar either. Ancients tended to come from the upper ranges of men outside the elite. Close to half of the Philadelphia Ancients ranked in the top third of the city's wealthholders, and nearly three-quarters of the Boston Ancients on the 1771 tax rolls owned their own houses, approximately the same proportion as the Moderns (Tables 4, 5). More important, the experiences of Billings and others placed them outside the narrow world of artisans like Thomas's marginally literate master or Franklin's former employer, Samuel Keimer. The cultural and economic horizons of the Ancient Masons were expanding beyond the parochial limits of the vulgar. Billings's desire and ability to edit a magazine was just as significant as his failure to follow elite norms.

These expanding aspirations can be seen first in the area of culture. By the advent of the *Boston Magazine,* Billings had composed and partially written three books of music, including the 1770 *New-England Psalm Singer,* the first book to include only American music and the first authored by a single American composer. Billings did not aim at the audience that read polite magazines. Psalms, despite the bewigged men in his first book's frontispiece, appealed more to the vulgar than to the genteel — as Eliot's harsh dismissal of the composer as "the psalm-singer" suggested. Billings's genre, however, was not merely vernacular. It drew upon a long British and Continental tradition, particularly as exemplified by William Tans'ur, the eighteenth-century British composer whose work Billings knew intimately.[24]

Perhaps not coincidentally, the artisans of St. Andrew's played an important role in the growth of this genre in New England. Another member of St. Andrew's lodge published the first American edition of Tans'ur's work; two others participated in Billings's historic 1770 publication. Paul Revere, soon to be master of the lodge, engraved the frontispiece. The jeweler Josiah Flagg engraved the music. The two had already published and sold their own "collection of Psalm Tunes . . . from the most Celebrated Authors" four years previously.[25]

Such efforts show an expansion of economic activities as well. Revere's engraving, for example, sometimes placed him beyond the world of the personal bespoke work of the goldsmith. His print depicting the Boston Massacre sold by the hundreds in various stores, including those run by Thomas Crafts (the father of another St. Andrew's brother) and Isaiah Thomas. In 1771, Thomas himself sought and received the contract for printing the Harvard master's theses, provoking a rival to slur him as a "dunghill-bred Journeyman Typographer." The printer with no formal education now signed the Latin theses "Typis Isaiae Thomas" and began publishing his own magazine. His most important endeavor was his newspaper. Appearing first in 1770, the *Massachusetts Spy* was established "on a new plan." Newspapers had previously sought elite readers, but Thomas saw the opportunity for a new audience: "The Massachusetts Spy was calculated to obtain subscriptions from mechanics, and other classes of people who had not much time to spare from business."[26]

The expanding cultural and economic horizons of the Boston Ancients and their involvement in a new, middling level of culture suggest a coalescing and maturing of a group of artisans and lesser merchants outside the ranks of gentlemen. Men such as Thomas, Revere, and Billings—literate, entrepreneurially active, and culturally aware—could not fit easily into the elite's bifurcated social vision. Their learning and experiences separated them from the provincialism and parochialism of vulgar artisans such as Thomas's master and Samuel Keimer. Franklin and his debating club, the Junto, had pioneered these new territories in the 1730s. But, though he continued to attempt to spread "Instruction among the common People" through Poor Richard, Franklin wholly assimilated into elite culture.

The newly cosmopolitan Ancients, like Franklin's printing office successor, Ancient brother David Hall, would be unable to follow Franklin's example, but their new lodges allowed them to appropriate the symbols of distinction and honor. Ancient Masonry did not challenge the old order of society through a counterculture like that of the contemporaneous Virginia Baptists. Even as they implicitly redefined old categories, Ancient Masons sought to keep social distinctions meaningful. An application by an even poorer group of Boston men for a Scottish warrant in 1763 brought a hostile reaction from St. Andrew's. The petitioners, they warned, were "very improper Persons" who "will inevitably bring the Craft into the greatest Disgrace imaginable."[27]

The display of the Ancients further suggests this attempt to shore up an uncertain status. In Boston, the 1769 organization of a grand lodge, an attempt to "render Ancient Masonry more respectable," brought the same "elegant oration" and "grand entertainment" enjoyed by Modern predecessors. The Ancients even tried to rename their meeting place "the Mason's Arms," feeling perhaps the impropriety of the name by which all knew it—the "Green Dragon." The 1772 Ancient celebration in Philadelphia used Masonic verses by the Modern lieutenant governor of South Carolina in a song echoing the language of genteel magazines. "'Tis from the watchful culture of the mind," declaimed one verse loftily,

> A well-directed soul, a sense refin'd,
> That heav'nly virtues spring to grace the man.

When the Pennsylvanians marched in public during their 1778 St. John's Day celebration, the order of procession followed its 1755 predecessor almost exactly. The once-white wands of authority, however, were now "tipt with Gold."[28]

III. The Country People

In the summer of 1766, Wilton Atkinson, a "Gent[leman] from Lancaster," Pennsylvania, arrived in Philadelphia seeking grand master William Allen. Atkinson hoped to secure an Ancient Masonic lodge for his town, then perhaps the largest in the colonial interior, but had not realized that Allen was head of the Moderns, not the Ancients. Discovering his mistake, he applied to Philadelphia's Lodge No. 2. Even there things did not go smoothly. Atkinson had to be reinitiated because his earlier Masonic initiation had been irregular. Only then could the Ancient grand lodge grant a warrant.[29]

The stumbling beginnings of the Lancaster fraternity reveal the second primary focus of American Masonry's Revolutionary transformation. Beginning slowly before the Revolution but then picking up rapidly, Ancient Masons spread their fraternity into the interior. By the beginning of the next century, more American lodges met in inland villages than on the urban seaboard.

The changing center of American Masonry was part of a larger series of social changes that transformed the geography of American settlement. The vast expansion of population and commercial activity beyond the older capital cities in the mid-eighteenth century challenged the elite's dismissive view of these areas as lacking political standing, genteel manners, and cosmopolitan knowledge. As the case of Atkinson, the Lancaster "gent[leman]," suggests, the leaders of these commercial villages often lacked the cosmopolitan experience of urban elites. But inland development made simple scorn increasingly less plausible. The new village elites that developed outside the capital cities after midcentury shared the relative wealth, power, and cosmopolitanism that, on a different scale, characterized the urban Moderns. Yet, despite this new group's growing distinction from the common people around them, they still, like the urban Ancients, lacked the standing of urban gentlemen.

The continued indifference of these seaboard elites only partly reflected the standards of gentility. Just as important, it also grew out of their continued refusal to relinquish their position even as they faced a new social landscape. This situation began to change only during the Revolutionary period, when the interior gained new political representation and power.[30]

Closely intertwined with these developments, the spread of Ancient Masonry reveals the cultural and social dimensions of this change. First formed about midcentury among the elite groups developing beyond the principal ports, Ancient Masonic lodges helped solidify their local prestige. More important, the fraternity provided a way of asserting standing that carried weight even in the capitals. Masonry's powerful symbols of high status and style helped bolster the social and cultural position of interior elites at a time when they were becoming less geographically and economically marginal.

Brother Robert Gilchrist was one of the leading merchants of Port Royal, Virginia. Indeed, he became so successful by importing such genteel goods as silk stockings and shoe buckles that he retired from business and bought a chaise—a polite conveyance he failed to report to the tax collector in 1762. Despite this transgression, Gilchrist was an active local leader, serving as a justice on the county court as often as he headed Port Royal's lodge. The rise of the Scottish immigrant mirrored that of his adopted home. Gilchrist had arrived in 1744, the year the Assembly created the new town on the Rappahannock River. Despite occasional downturns, Port Royal (like Gilchrist) prospered from the 1740s to the Revolution. Its success was built upon the links Scottish merchants created between inland Virginia's tobacco farmers and the larger Atlantic trading network. By 1765 a visitor could describe Port Royal as "a considerable town of trade furnishing the country around."[31]

By the 1760s, similar changes were transforming much of the American interior. The mainland colonies had once been a series of discrete European-American population centers connected primarily with England rather than with each other. Now demographic and economic expansion swelled the population, pushing European settlement inland. The new elites of these expanding areas, the local men who profited most from growing wealth, population, and commercial ties, made up the bulk of the new Ancient lodges that were being formed outside the major seaports from New England to the South. Like the urban Moderns, these brothers typically occupied the highest levels of their societies, following high-ranking occupations, holding substantial political offices, and possessing wealth and education that identified them as their villages' leading men. This social position can be seen in the two earliest interior Ancient lodges, the Port Royal group often headed by Gilchrist and the nearby Fredericksburg lodge that met farther up the Rappahannock.[32]

The two lodges united many of their towns' principal men. Despite the overwhelmingly agricultural nature of the area's economy, merchants formed a

Table 6. Occupations of Port Royal Lodge Members

Occupation	No.	Occupation	No.
Trade	20 (38.5%)	Professional	14 (26.9%)
Merchant	14	Lawyer	10[c]
Warehouse owner	2	Physician	3
Factor	3	Minister	1
Clerk	1		
		Artisanal and	
Land	15 (28.8%)	proprietorial	3 (5.8%)
Planter	11[a]	Tavern owner	1[d]
Landowner	4[b]	Millwright	1
		Seagoing	1

[a] 1 is also a lawyer.   [b] 1 is also a millwright.   [c] 1 is also a planter.   [d] 4 more are listed with other occupations.

Note: Of 103 members, 52 (50.5%) are identified. Occupations are as listed in the sources and reflect their biases, the county order book.

Sources: T. E. Campbell, *Colonial Caroline: A History of Caroline County, Virginia* (Richmond, Va., 1954); Marshall Wingfield, *A History of Caroline County, Virginia from Its Formation in 1727 to 1924* (Richmond, Va., 1924).

large proportion of both these groups. Of the thirteen original members of the Port Royal lodge that formed in 1754 and received a Scottish charter in 1755, at least seven were merchants. The charter senior warden and the first steward both owned ships. Three other pre-1781 members served as factors for Scottish mercantile houses. Port Royal brothers also owned, at various times, two of the town's chartered warehouses that held tobacco before shipping. The Fredericksburg lodge, formed at least by September 1752 and chartered by the Scottish grand lodge six years later, also included a number of men involved in trade. The Fredericksburg merchant James Hunter (the Younger) received his education in Scotland and England, worked for a time in France, and shipped tobacco to Liverpool. A number of neighboring planters also joined, although they probably, as was common practice, also engaged in trade, as did the Taliaferros, the influential local family that contributed five members to the lodge (Table 6).[33]

The professions made up another important part of the early Virginia Ancients. The nine lawyers on Port Royal's pre-Revolutionary roster formed a large proportion of the county's bar. Of the ten Caroline County residents qualified to practice in the county court between 1743 and 1762, seven became Fredericksburg brothers. Three medical doctors also attended their lodge meetings, including Dr. Charles Mortimer, the Fredericksburg magistrate who served as Mary Washington's physician.[34]

Besides their relatively high-status occupations, the Virginia brothers were

Table 7. Public Offices of Port Royal Lodge Members

Office	No.	Office	No.
Magistrate	17	Tobacco inspector	2
Vestry	8	Flour inspector	1
Captain[a]	7	Governor's Council	1
Sheriff	4	County lieutenant	1
Ensign[b]	2	Deputy county	
Warden	2	attorney	1
County clerk[c]	2	Jailer	1

[a] Probably militia title.   [b] Militia title.   [c] 1 as first clerk, 1 as second clerk.

Note: It is unclear how many of the remaining 103 members held no office or were simply unidentified as officeholding. Furthermore, many members held more than one office. John Catlett, for example, served as vestryman of St. Mary's parish, as magistrate, as inspector of flour, and as inspector of tobacco.

Sources: See Table 6.

also distinguished by their local prominence. Seventeen of the fifty-four identifiable pre-1781 Port Royal lodge members served as magistrates. Four, including Gilchrist, became sheriffs. Seven held the title of captain — most likely from the militia — while at least eight others served on local vestries (Tables 6, 7). Other Ancient lodges outside the seaboard cities suggest the same pattern. The charter master of Lodge No. 8, the first Pennsylvania lodge outside Philadelphia, served as a captain in the Seven Years' War and, during the Revolution, became a member of the county and then the state Committees of Safety. The lodge's junior warden was already a county commissioner.[35]

Not surprisingly, given these characteristics, early Ancient Masons tended to be wealthy. Not all could retire from trade as Gilchrist did, but nine other members of his lodge were also indicted in 1762 for failing to report their chaises. The charter junior warden of the lodge owned a gristmill as well as, by the 1770s, a chartered warehouse. The high standing of the new Ancient lodges outside the principal ports seems to hold even for the rising seaport of Gloucester, Massachusetts. The petitioners to the new Boston grand lodge in 1770 included Epes Sargent, Jr., the owner, according to the tax assessment the following year, of four warehouses, 535 tons of shipping, 1,600 feet of wharf, and 1,500 pounds worth of merchandise.[36]

Although the occupations, offices, and wealth of these brothers paralleled Modern brothers', the new group received their Masonry, not through the more genteel Moderns, but through the urban Ancients. Modern Masons had shown little interest in making the fraternity available beyond the urban seaboard. The Pennsylvania Modern grand lodge authorized only three lodges during its more than forty years of operation, all in Philadelphia. The more prolific Massachusetts Moderns chartered approximately forty subordinate groups, but their warrants went primarily to seaports in other colonies. During its sixty-year existence, the grand lodge formed only five Massachusetts lodges outside Boston—all along the coastline. By contrast, Pennsylvania's Ancients set up eight lodges in their state by the end of the Revolution as well as groups in other smaller towns such as Cantwell's Bridge, Delaware, and Winchester, Virginia. By 1792, the Boston Ancients had created eleven Massachusetts lodges outside Boston as well as four in New Hampshire and two in Vermont. In the following three years, the united grand lodge (essentially under Ancient control) created eleven more lodges in the state.[37]

As the earlier Modern indifference suggests, the increasing gap between the Ancient brothers and their surroundings did not translate easily into prominence on a wider stage. The increasing wealth and high status of these secondary centers failed to impress more cosmopolitan urban gentlemen. They continued to refer to the country as rustic and uncivilized, a characterization that, while it reflected the smaller scale of the wealth and power of lesser villages, increasingly failed to fit the reality of a rapidly growing interior.

Like urban mechanics, inland leaders had often been scorned by cosmopolitan gentry. Their category of "rustic" included not just people who failed to follow genteel ways but also those whom John Rowe indiscriminately called "the Country People." The tory Peter Oliver, whose sibling Andrew helped reject the Boston Ancient's petition in 1758, challenged the legitimacy of Revolutionary leaders by citing their insignificant rural or artisanal origins. Oliver attributed the success of the wealthy James Otis, Sr., the father of the Boston leader and Modern Freemason, to his influence over country juries "who were too commonly Drovers, Horse Jockies, and of other lower Classes in Life." Even in the Massachusetts General Court—a body dominated numerically by the country—Otis consorted with similar people, Oliver suggested, for in it were "too great an Ingredient of . . . Innkeepers, Retailers, and yet more inferior Orders of Men." The Philadelphia Modern officer, Dr. Thomas Cadwallader, similarly warned Dr. Alexander Hamilton (himself soon to be a brother) that the New Jersey House of Assembly "was chiefly composed of mechanicks and ignorant wretches, obstinate to the last degree."[38]

In this urban (and supposedly urbane) vision, cities served as the center of power as well as of gentility. To be away from the capital meant absence not only from the most lucrative appointments but from the "principal people" who controlled them. Although Dr. Joseph Warren was the son of a Roxbury selectman, Oliver considered him only "a bare legged milk boy to furnish the Boston Market" before his success in the metropolis. John Adams, coming from a similar small-town background, feared such elite snobbery when he

Figure 8. Saint Peter's Lodge Night. Lodge Summons, Newburyport, Massachusetts. *By Paul Revere, Boston, 1772. Courtesy American Antiquarian Society*

contemplated meeting the prominent Massachusetts Moderns Jeremiah Gridley and James Otis, Jr. "I felt Shy," he confessed in his diary, "under Awe and concern."[39]

For colonial gentlemen, residence in the country, when it was not an occasional retreat, served primarily to repair wounded fortunes or reputations. Evan Jones and John Remington both seem to have left Philadelphia after the Rees incident. The Reverend William Smith, the speaker at the Modern's

1755 procession and, after transferring his membership, at the Ancients' similar celebration in 1778, moved to a small town on Maryland's Eastern Shore after losing his position as provost of the College of Philadelphia—ironically, an example of the "sorry places" he had warned New Yorkers against in their plans for a new college.[40]

Compared to the primary seaboard ports, secondary villages were small indeed. Boston numbered about fifteen thousand people between 1750 and 1770. Philadelphia in the same years grew from about twelve thousand to twenty thousand. But Fredericksburg, the larger of the two Virginia Ancient villages, reached three thousand only in 1769. By then, Boston and Philadelphia each cleared more than forty thousand tons of shipping; Fredericksburg handled about sixty-six hundred. Distance created another barrier to provincial pretensions; Atkinson's trip from Lancaster to Philadelphia probably took two days.[41]

These limitations kept most local elites from entering the inner circles of power, a difficulty made greater by apportionment schemes that commonly gave disproportionate representation to the capitals and more established areas. Gilchrist was an active and responsible magistrate, but he proved unable to get himself placed back on the bench when a new governor failed to reappoint him in the late 1760s. The case of the young George Washington further suggests the limits of Ancient Masons' standing. When Washington became a brother in Fredericksburg on November 4, 1752, he had just completed a failed campaign to succeed his brother as the colony's adjutant general. The young man not only could not prevent the division of the job into three separate positions, but his extensive lobbying got him only one of the lesser appointments. After Washington left for a military position farther west the following year, he attended only one more meeting of the Fredericksburg lodge.[42] Marriage to one of the colony's wealthiest widows brought him colonywide prominence—he became a burgess after his marriage—and distanced him further from the Fredericksburg Masons; he seems to have visited lodges again only during the Revolution.

Such inland leaders found it difficult to measure up to the high standards of men such as Smith or Otis. The group that created the first Pennsylvania interior lodge, formed in Chester County the year Atkinson made his way to the capital, began with less Masonic experience than that irregular brother. Even the petitioners had to request initiation so that "they might be qualified to hold a Lodge in their own Neighborhood." The Fredericksburg Masons similarly might have begun with only a rough conception of Masonic practice. They inducted sixteen Entered Apprentices, but twice as many were "made a member" or "admitted" as actually took degrees.[43]

Despite these limitations, economic developments were transforming these localities. International commerce increasingly relied upon the products of the interior. At the same time, inland inhabitants provided a growing market for international goods. These developments meant that many urban fortunes depended heavily upon trade with and investment in the interior. Charleston brother Henry Laurens created a flourishing wagon trade with the South Carolina backcountry. Pennsylvania grand master William Allen financed interior storekeepers to gain better access to agricultural produce. Land speculation also helped swell Allen's wealth, just as huge tracts in Maine enlarged the fortunes of William Hallowell, master of Boston's first lodge.[44]

Such expanding economic activity helped create a disjunction between accepted ideas and actual situations—a disjunction like that faced by the urban artisans who also pioneered Ancient Masonry. Although men such as Gilchrist and Atkinson might not have measured up to the highest urban standards, they possessed relatively substantial wealth and broadened horizons that distinguished them from the common people around them. Yet urban gentlemen refused to admit their claims. The inland elites' growing participation in Masonry's cosmopolitan honor helped challenge this subordinate position. The fraternity offered a means of bringing together these developing groups and of claiming high standing in terms accepted by men above them. A further look at the activities of Ancient Virginia lodges suggests the particular attraction of Masonic love and honor.

The ideal of love, of fraternal connection among diverse men, provided the first appeal of Masonry. In the scattered settlements of Virginia, the fraternity increased opportunities for contact and sociability. The pre-Revolutionary members of the Fredericksburg lodge represented eighteen different counties, uniting cosmopolitan men such as Dr. Thomas Walker, the former Fredericksburg resident who joined the lodge after moving to Albemarle County. Fraternal ties developed between lodges as well. Fredericksburg brothers sometimes met with their Port Royal counterparts. The two groups joined together in a Fredericksburg lodge dinner in 1769, just as they helped mark the postwar revival of the town's lodge in 1783. Business experiences underlined the interdependence proclaimed by fraternal metaphors. Shortly after emigrating from Scotland, the later Fredericksburg brother James Hunter (the Younger) formed a mercantile partnership with two of his relations and John Taliaferro, probably already a Port Royal lodge member. While James's sibling Adam set up trade agreements with their British relatives, James bought goods from Virginians such as Port Royal lodge member James Robb.[45]

The Scottish background of many Virginia Ancient brothers further added to the significance of Masonic love. Brother Robert Bogle (or Boogle) represented his father's Glasgow firm in Port Royal. Fredericksburg members included Scots such as Andrew Beaty, Walter Stewart, and John Paul Jones (of later Revolutionary naval fame). Another lodge member, Daniel Cambell, stayed in town only a short time before returning to Scotland. These immigrants faced not only the difficulty of adapting to a new location but pervasive popular prejudice.[46]

Besides helping build solidarity among men often distinguished by national origins as much as social and economic standing, Masonry also offered symbols of gentility and honor seldom available in small towns. Port Royal brothers held a "Masons Ball" in December 1783. Three months previously, they had participated in a brilliant Fredericksburg procession. The plans of the master for that occasion suggest the appeal of these activities. "I wish with all my soul You could be with us on the 19th Inst," George Weedon wrote to James Hunter in Richmond, "when the Lodge moves in full Prossession to our Old[?] Sanctum Sanctorum." There "we [will] form us as working Masons, and repare a Principal Arch under our Old Lodge room in the Key stone of which will be inserted a Silver Plate, to hand to Posterity the Liberal Donation granted by the Brotherhood for the purpose of reclaiming that Noble Structure."[47] Like the language describing it, the procession both emulated the practices and values of colonial gentlemen and claimed fraternal equality with them.

The Ancient lodge in Winchester, Virginia, a town even further inland, attempted to draw the social boundaries of their fraternity as tightly as the urban Moderns. "[You] may think strange at our being so Few in Number," the lodge explained to the Philadelphia's Ancient grand lodge in 1770: "The Reason is we have not a Man in the Lodge that is not an Ornament to the Society nor will we suffer any other to Enter in among us." Their description of the lodge's 1785 St. John's Day celebration, like the Fredericksburg procession two years earlier, reveals the strong appeal of Masonic status to an inland elite that craved cosmopolitan status. On that day, the lodge officers "put on the Ornaments of their Office with new Aprons and Gloves and formed as near to the Order of Procession" in the new book of Constitutions "as possible Considering the difitiency in Number." Although lacking the band commonly used in urban processions, they carried velvet cushions, pillars, and even wands tipped with gold as they marched to church. There they heard psalms "Sung by a numb'r of Boys and Girls genteely dressed . . . each in a broad light blew Sash in Hon'r. to Masonry." The secretary was careful to note that even the children were no ordinary urchins: they were, he put down parenthetically, "the first mens['] Children of the Borough."[48]

When the cornerstone of Charles Bulfinch's elegant Massachusetts State House was laid on July 4, 1795, the governor was Samuel Adams, the dominant figure in the pre-Revolutionary mobilization of the Boston artisans and the inland towns—and an avid psalm singer. The new united grand lodge of Massachusetts (created in 1792 when the Ancients merged with the nearly moribund Moderns) performed the ceremony. Its senior grand warden was Isaiah Thomas, the urban artisan who moved inland during the Revolution. At the head of the fraternity, representing the Ancients as well as the Moderns who had originally demanded "SUBMISSION" from them, was the Boston mechanic Paul Revere.[49]

The ceremony marked the culmination of the American fraternity's Revolutionary transformation. Ancient Masonry had developed more than forty years before, during the 1750s when similar Ancient lodges had been formed in Philadelphia and Virginia. Peopled by men of lesser rank, the groups developed slowly before the Revolution but then quickly picked up momentum during and after the war. By 1795 Ancient Masonry dominated the American fraternity.

The changes that began after midcentury placed the Ancient fraternity not only atop Beacon Hill (the height of Boston prestige) but at the center of Revolutionary changes in definitions of power and hierarchy. The early Ancient lodges drew upon groups that claimed increased political participation—and that saw their situations and aspirations reflected in republican ideology.

Ancient Masons helped reshape the social distribution of power in America. The higher levels of urban artisans were the first to bid for new standing during the imperial crisis, and in Boston, at least, Ancient Masons helped lead the call for these changes. "It is necessary," Thomas told his readers before the war, that "it should be known what common people, even COBBLERS, *think* and *feel* under the present administration." [50] Revere, Warren, and other members of St. Andrew's lodge—including William Palfrey, secretary of the Sons of Liberty, and Thomas Crafts of the Loyal Nine—helped plan much of the growing resistance to the British, including perhaps the Tea Party, in the Ancient's Green Dragon Tavern.

The Ancients also spread Masonry to the other group that broke the elite monopoly on status and position—the leaders of the interior. These men also gained new political importance in the emerging republican structure. State constitutions almost universally required equitable apportionment, opening up new avenues of influence and advancement for inland leaders. The resulting redistribution of power can be seen symbolically in the relocation of state capitals after the Revolution. New York moved its seat of government to Albany, South Carolina created a new town one hundred miles from the coast, and the Pennsylvania capital became Harrisburg, even farther inland than Lancaster, from which Wilkins Atkinson had traveled in 1766 to get the first Ancient lodge for his town.[51]

Just as important, Masonry played a role in the redefinition of power and status itself. Although Isaiah Thomas felt obliged to apologize for his lack of "learning and eloquence" when he addressed a group of inland Massachusetts Masons in 1779, he boldly questioned older ideas of social standing. "Where is *Honour*?" he asked. "Shall we look for her in the courts of the most mighty potentates on earth, or in the stately palaces of the great—alas! we know too well that *self-interest* is the chief end of their politicks." For Masons who, like Thomas, were seeking parity with the elite, republican ideas had particular significance. The concepts of disinterested virtue and equality helped both to buttress the claims of artisans and inland elites to social distinction and to destroy the pretensions of the potentates who scorned their claims.[52]

The ideals of the Revolution thus appeared to be closely related to the transformed American fraternity and its social constituency—indeed, so intimately related that many post-Revolutionary American came to see Masonry as an archetype of the republican society based on virtue and talent they were attempting to build. This new position highlights the ambivalence in the Ancients' relationships with their Modern predecessors. On one hand, the expanded social boundaries of the new lodges ensured they would not suffer in the Revolutionary discrediting of elite practices and pretensions. On the other, many Ancient ideas and purposes were hardly new. Republican values, in some ways, extended the enlightened vision of an inclusive society. The older group's genteel image likewise laid the foundation for Ancient Masonry's ability to reinforce and proclaim status. The new place of Masonry defined during the Revolutionary years rested on the brothers' ability to reshape the social and intellectual boundaries of the fraternity even as they retained colonial Masonry's connection with the symbols of gentility and high social standing. For a post-Revolutionary society in which nearly all forms of distinction remained suspect but many sought high social status, the transformed fraternity would be extraordinarily powerful.

To realize this potential, however, the fraternity first would have to survive the challenges of the war itself.

CHAPTER FOUR

According to Their Rank

Masonry and the Revolution, 1775–1792

The king of Sweden, the Reverend William Smith informed the Boston Ancients in October 1780, attended the recent installation of the new Swedish grand master. According to the newspaper account Smith quoted in the letter, the monarch first gave the grand master "an ermin'd cloke." Then he "was placed upon a Throne, clothed with the marks of his new Dignity, and there received the Complements of all the members." The Masons came up "according to their rank . . . to kiss the Hand, Sceptre, or Cloke of the new Grand Master." In turn, he gave each a silver medal prepared for the ceremony. "This solemnity," stated the newspaper, "hath raised the Order of Freemasons from a kind of Oblivion into which they were sunk."[1]

Smith, speaker at both Philadelphia's 1755 Modern and the 1779 Ancient processions, did not recount this story as a mere curiosity. As grand secretary of the Pennsylvania Ancients, he hoped to persuade the Massachusetts grand lodge to support Pennsylvania's proposal of a grand master general—an officer to preside over all American lodges. The "magnificent" Swedish ceremony, he suggested, "may serve . . . as a model for us."[2]

Despite Smith's dreams of magnificence, fears of the oblivion that nearly engulfed the Swedish brothers could not have been far from his mind. The Revolution created a multifaceted crisis within the American fraternity. It disrupted meetings and split lodges as brothers took differing positions. The break from Britain also raised questions about the ultimate legitimacy of the American fraternity—for the mother country had been the source of Masonic authority as well. Even in the Continental army, the one bright spot in the wartime fraternity, the brothers were at times preoccupied with these difficulties. Making the original proposal for a national grand lodge at the beginning of 1780, they warned not only of "the relaxation of virtue amongst individuals" but also about "the present dissipated and almost abandoned condition of our lodges in general."[3]

The military lodges that met within the army's camps faced no such difficulties. Officers flocked into Masonry during the Revolution. But the success of Masonry within the Continental army only highlights the crisis the officers themselves faced. They felt acutely their lack of the social standing deemed necessary for their positions and were apprehensive about the diversity of local origins, religion, and rank created among them by their new circumstances. Masonry's ideals of honor and love offered them a powerful means of addressing these difficulties, so powerful that Masonic bonds played an important role in building the camaraderie necessary for the survival of the army—and thus the American republic.

The fraternity that emerged from the war was stronger than ever before. This rather unexpected result came, not because it took up the scepters and thrones prescribed by Smith, but because the fraternity, despite the uncertainties created by the war, was able to align itself with both the Revolutionary cause and the republican society it attempted to create. To understand this unanticipated result, the problems of the civilian lodges deserve attention first, difficulties visible in another attempt to create magnificence in the midst of near oblivion.

1. Great Trubles amonge Masons

When General Joseph Warren, grand master of the Ancient grand lodge of Massachusetts, died at the Battle of Bunker Hill in June 1775, the British threw his body into an unmarked grave. British evacuation the following March allowed recovery of the body and a funeral organized by Warren's Masonic brothers. Accompanied by their Modern counterparts (invited for the occasion) and two companies of soldiers, Boston's Ancients marched from the Council chambers to the Anglican King's Chapel. The Reverend Dr. Samuel Cooper, a Revolutionary leader, led the prayer; Perez Morton, a Harvard-educated lawyer and a new member of St. Andrew's, gave the oration. Portraying Warren as the embodiment of virtue, Morton recalled that the former grand master believed "that nothing so much conduced to enlighten Mankind, and advance the great End of Society at large, as the frequent Interchange of Sentiments, in friendly Meetings." Morton noted that Warren often followed his own advice: "We find him constantly engaged in this eligible Labour; but on none did he place so high a Value as on the most honorable of all the detached Societies, THE FREE ACCEPTED MASONS."[4]

The rich images of the celebration contrasted strongly with the actual condition of Boston Masonry. Even before the Declaration of Independence, the Ancient St. Andrew's Lodge had faced problems that plagued American brothers during the war and afterward. Simply continuing to meet proved difficult. Hindered by British occupation, the lodge stopped meeting in April 1775 just before Lexington and Concord. It revived only in the following year. The issue of Revolutionary loyalty further weakened the lodge. While General Warren led American troops at Bunker Hill, his lodge brother Dr. John

Jeffries aided the British. Jeffries and a number of other members left with the British in 1776—after he revealed the location of his grand master's body.[5]

Disruption and divided loyalties were not unique to Boston Ancients. Fighting, mobilization, and occupation impeded Masonic activities throughout America, particularly in the interior. Indeed, Boston's Ancients were unusual in their quick recovery, a reorganization made possible because fighting shifted to other areas. Their strong patriot contingent furthermore kept the loyalists in their ranks from having much influence, preventing division and further disruptions that many other lodges, even in Boston, could not escape. While these problems of continuing meetings and determining loyalties would sometimes be easily resolved, they also created unforeseen consequences, hastening the demise of the Moderns in many areas and contributing to Masonry's later reputation as a strongly patriotic organization.

Boston lodges, at the center of the earliest fighting of the Revolution, were only the first to face the problems of wartime activity. The eight years of hostilities disrupted lodges in all parts of America. New York's Modern Lodge No. 3 held no meetings at all during the war. Charleston Masons seemingly did not assemble from 1778 to 1780. In Philadelphia, Lodge No. 8 stopped meeting during the British occupation while No. 2, the city's oldest Ancient lodge, had its jewels and paraphernalia stolen by British soldiers. Even as late as 1785, the Pennsylvanians excused the inaction of their subordinate in Winchester, Virginia, noting, "The late War has caused great trubles amonge Masons of which you have had more than Common Share."[6]

These "great trubles" affected the interior most heavily. With smaller populations to draw from and sometimes heavier burdens of mobilization, country lodges often found even continued existence difficult. What they called "the general calamities of the war" kept the Guilford, Connecticut, Masons from meeting after 1776. St. Patrick's Lodge in Johnstown, New York, received no new members from 1774 to 1784. Pennsylvania's No. 17, in Queen Anne County, Maryland, similarly explained to their grand lodge in 1779 that "the late and present Exigencies of the times [had] prevented them from meeting for a considerable time."[7]

Calamitous as the experiences of war were, however, the random and relatively short-lived nature of these disruptions meant that they had little lasting impact on American Masonry. Only in Boston and Philadelphia would this disorder have any discernible long-term effects. Hostilities there helped destroy the already-declining Moderns.[8] Philadelphia Modern Masons seem to have met sporadically, if at all, after 1776; their lodges probably did not even last to the end of the conflict. The more active Boston Moderns met only irregularly; the grand lodge granted its final warrant in 1780 and assembled thereafter primarily to celebrate St. John's Days. The master's lodge met only

seven times between 1780 and 1782. The following year, the First and Second Lodges received grand lodge permission to form a single body called St.
John's, a new body joined by Boston's other Modern lodge in 1791.[9]

More than the difficulties of wartime survival crippled the Moderns. They also
had to face, in a particularly sharp way, the second major problem of wartime
Masonry, the question of loyalty to the Revolution. Although, following Masonic tradition, lodges and grand lodges took no official stance, the loyalism
of key Modern members in both Philadelphia and Boston undermined their
organizations. In this as in the more general disruption, the comparatively
greater damage done to the Moderns was partly a matter of chance. Affiliation with particular lodges seems not to have determined individual political
loyalties. Moderns and Ancients, Masons and non-Masons, ended up on both
sides of the Revolution. Like the more general wartime disruption, this confusion of loyalties and the largely unintended success of the new Masonic
groups can be seen in the Warren celebration.

Modern grand master John Rowe also marched in the funeral procession
with the Ancients, but with quite different results. After arriving at the Council chambers and joining the other Moderns in the procession, he found, "To
my great mortification [I] was very much Insulted by some furious and hot
Persons with'o the Least Provocation[.] [O]ne of [the] Brethren thought it
most Prudent for me to Retire. I accordingly did so—this has caused some
Uneasy Reflections in my mind as I am not Conscious to myself of doing anything Prejudicial to the Cause of America either by will or deed." [10]

Rowe's humiliation arose, not from outright loyalism, but from attempted
neutrality. In 1775, Rowe had feared that "this Unhappy affair" of Lexington and Concord was "a Shocking Introduction to all the Miseries of a Civil
War." The imposition of British military rule in Boston led him to explore
moving inland, but, after being denied a pass to leave with his substantial
goods, he chose to stay, explaining to his diary that he wanted to protect them
from British looting. Even then he did not shun British officers; he visited
Admiral Molyneux Shuldham, "a Genteel man," and invited others to dinner.
When the American army arrived, Rowe similarly dined with Generals Israel
Putnam and Nathanael Greene, and "paid [his] Respects to Generall Washington." The British evacuation also allowed Rowe to meet with his deputy
grand master, Colonel Richard Gridley, an early supporter of Independence.
The wound Gridley suffered at Bunker Hill placed him alongside the Ancient
grand master Warren as an early hero of the Revolution.[11]

Not all Boston Moderns, however, shared Gridley's enthusiasm for the
American cause—or even Rowe's cautious neutrality. The customs commissioner and Modern brother Benjamin Hallowell had been "abused" publicly
before the Revolution by an angry crowd led by the Ancient Paul Revere.

When the British pulled out of Boston, Hallowell left with them and his brother Robert, a fellow First Lodge member, for Canada and then England. At least twenty members of the Second Lodge accompanied them, as did the St. John's Lodge and grand lodge secretary carrying the lodge records and the grand lodge jewels.[12]

The disarray of the Boston Moderns contrasted strikingly with the growing prestige of their Ancient brothers, a new self-confidence seen in their invitation of the Moderns to the Warren funeral. St. Andrew's was not free from loyalism — at least half a dozen members left Boston with the British troops — but its intimate involvement with the Revolutionary cause closely identified it with the patriots. Grand master Warren had helped lead such Whig groups as the North-End Caucus and the Sons of Liberty in meetings held at the Ancients' Green Dragon Tavern. Later, St. Andrew's members would even claim that the Boston Tea Party was planned at their hall. Whether or not this was the case, lodge minutes reveal a close connection with the event. St. Andrew's convened for its annual election the night before the first public meeting discussing the tea's arrival, but adjourned because of low attendance. "Consignees of TEA," the secretary noted, "took the Brethren's time." On the night of the event itself, the lodge also held a scheduled meeting. The group conducted some business, but the minutes perhaps suggest a desire for an alibi to prevent connecting lodge members with the activities in the harbor. Only five members attended that night: the master, the two wardens, and the two deacons.[13]

Closely tied to the Revolutionary movement, Boston's Ancients increasingly appropriated the high standing of the weakening Moderns. The Ancients expanded rapidly. Their grand lodge formed nineteen new lodges during the war; St. Andrew's alone accepted thirty new members in 1777, twenty-five in 1778, and forty-one over the next two years. Their extraordinary December 15, 1777, meeting included thirty-five visitors and considered thirty petitions. The grand lodge also began to give to the town poor and, at their June 1782 celebration, even dined with the selectmen and the French consul at Faneuil Hall, the site of dinners formerly held for the colonial elite.[14]

The pattern of Ancient patriots and Modern loyalists in the two grand bodies, however, was not universal among Masons, even in Boston. Tories formed the majority of the most militantly Ancient lodge in Boston. Lodge No. 169 received a charter from London in 1771 after the local Ancients rejected its petition. Angered by St. Andrew's attempts to win Modern approval, the new group protested both to St. Andrew's and to London about visits between Ancients and Moderns. Yet they shared more with the latter in their political sympathies. When the British left Boston with many of the city's loyalists, lodge members carried the charter to Canada and then to New York City, where they formed the nucleus of the Ancient grand lodge created there in 1781. The Reverend William Walter, a British Army chaplain who had been Rowe's rector at Trinity Church, became its first grand master.[15]

Other cities show similarly complex patterns of loyalties. In New York, the success of the imported Ancients was made possible partly by the patriotism of the older Modern groups and their consequent relative weakness during the British occupation.[16] Charleston Modern lodges elected their own grand master after the loyalist Egerton Leigh left for Britain, but the occupation of the city led to another election in 1781, this time controlled by the tories. Philadelphia's Ancient Lodges No. 3 and 4 welcomed many British soldiers into their meetings. Their influence facilitated the recovery of the heavily patriotic No. 2's stolen property. Prevented from meeting during the British occupation, Lodge No. 2 revived soon afterward. By the end of the war, its members included sixteen colonels, ten majors, and twenty-eight captains.[17]

Masonic divisions thus did not determine larger loyalties. Only in the interior is a relatively consistent pattern visible. Even there, however, the strong patriotism of most lodges may simply suggest the successful suppression of overt toryism. More than one-half of the members of St. George's Lodge in Schenectady, New York, between 1774 and 1800 (77 of 134) served in the Revolution. In Poughkeepsie, New York, Solomon's Lodge quickly voted to erase the name of member Benedict Arnold from lodge records after his defection.[18]

The diverse loyalties within lodges, like the other disruptions created by wartime, in the end perhaps did little to harm Masonry's reputation and expansion. Ironically, it might even have aided this growth. The flight of loyalists along with the heavy participation of American soldiers in local and military lodges helped obscure earlier divisions, allowing Masons to claim that their order had been a patriotic organization all along. Similarly, the largely fortuitous weakening of Modern Masonry in many areas encouraged a quicker end to internal dissension.

The problems of the war also allowed an easier end to British Masonic control. The troublesome problem of fraternal subordination to a country whose political control was being repudiated would, strangely enough, be more easily faced when Masonic scruples were loosened by the disorders of war. This last major component in the wartime crisis of Masonry can be seen in the fate of the proposal for a national grand lodge, an idea originally proposed as a means to remedy the wartime disruptions and divisions.

11. Free and Independent

In 1786, almost ten years after the American Declaration of Independence, the Pennsylvania grand lodge still found Masonic independence a troubling issue. Some members supported removing the statement of "subordination" to England included in their warrants. Others objected so strenuously that the body decided to solicit advice from its lodges. In September, the grand lodge voted that it was not under "any ties to any other grand lodge except those of Brotherly Love and Affection." It did so, however, despite a strong dissent from the Alexandria, Virginia, lodge that would soon elect George Washington as its master. Accepting their opponents' major premise, they agreed that "Americans are certainly separate and independent of Great Britain." But this fact, while "politically true," did not resolve the issue of fraternal independence: the question remained, "How this political truth may, with propriety, be applied to the Masonic Order?" Since Masons "do not intermeddle in State matters," the Alexandia brothers argued, they "ought not to draw arguments from thence to dismember themselves from the jurisdiction of those they hold under." [19]

The Alexandria response cut to the heart of the problem faced by American Masons in the wake of the Revolution—the relationship of political loyalties to fraternal relations. Many brothers wished to end Masonic subordination to Britain just as they had rejected its rule in other parts of their lives. But the fraternity claimed independence from political affairs, and American Masonic legitimacy clearly rested on British foundations. As the Alexandria brothers noted, losing contact with Britain threatened destruction of the Masonic family and perhaps their right to claim its ancient inheritance.

Facing two opposing imperatives, the debate about Masonic independence bedeviled American brothers for more than a decade, from 1778, when Virginia lodges elected their own grand master, to 1790, when Massachusetts Moderns closed the matter by doing the same. The ultimate success of this decision for independence did not represent a clear-cut victory for that side's argument. American lodges sometimes issued bold declarations of independence, including a 1780 attempt by Continental army officers to create a national grand lodge. But such strong stands seldom led to bold action. The national proposal failed, sunk by the difficulties of organizing on such a broad scale and by fears of precipitous action. Brothers instead muddled through on the state level, compromising the issue at nearly every turn until practical issues and experiential independence forced them to recognize the need for separation.

However confused, the unclear decision for Masonic independence allowed the fraternity to move successfully into the new, post-Revolutionary world. Anxieties about independence focused attention on Masonic legality, fostering a new concern with procedure that helped grand lodges manage the explosive growth of the fraternity over the next generation. More important, by preventing a breach with either American patriotism or fraternal relations, cautious brothers paved the way for later claims that the Republic and Masonry were actually closely linked. Although the final element of the Masonic revolutionary crisis might not have led to the triumphant magnificence that Smith imagined, ultimately American brothers avoided the dangerous alternative of either British subordination or Masonic dismemberment—choices that threatened the honor and the fictive family created by the fraternity.

Ironically, Continental army officers, fighting to end the political connection with England, were among the first American brothers to mourn the separation of lodges from "the grand lodge in Europe." Meeting in Morristown, New Jersey, on the December 27, 1779, a number of officers turned from a brilliant celebration to consider the dangers facing Masonry. "Political dispute and national quarrels," they warned, should not hinder Masonic meetings or charity. To prevent such disruption, they recommended a national grand lodge to "preside over and govern all other lodges of whatsoever degree or denomination." This new superintending body, headed by a general grand master of "merit and capacity," would not be independent. The officers asked that "the Present Provincial grand masters in Each of the Respective United States of America" nominate a national grand master and petition "our mother Lodge in Britain" for such an appointment.[20]

Promising to fulfill British requirements and American aspirations, the officers' proposal attracted many brothers, including Pennsylvania grand secretary William Smith, whose letter transmitting the proposal to the Massachusetts Ancients included his call to imitate the Swedish ceremony. Despite its attractiveness to some brothers, however, the general grand master scheme eventually failed, falling victim, like concurrent attempts to strengthen national political institutions, to the problems of uniting a vast and diverse range of polities. Local prerogatives, Masonic divisions, misunderstandings, and the problems created by communications over long distances doomed the bold initiative even before it could be discussed fully.

Meeting in nearby Philadelphia soon after the officers' action, the Pennsylvania Ancient grand lodge heartily endorsed the officers' suggestions—voting unanimously to accept the proposal even before the officers completed the final version of the petition. For the general grand master, they proposed a brother who had attended the Morristown meeting, General George Washington. Even though clearly working in collaboration with the officers, the Philadelphia body also attempted to change the proposal. Rather than approaching the British grand lodge—or, as would be necessary, the several British grand lodges—the Pennsylvanians suggested that the national organization would require only "the concurrence of all the grand lodges in America to make this election effectual."[21]

Even such American unity proved elusive. Despite the enthusiastic support of the Pennsylvania Ancients (who called it "a Measure highly approved by all the brethren"), the Massachusetts Ancients immediately raised the question of local prerogatives. Their grand master asked that the Pennsylvanians determine whether the new body would infringe on the "right" of the present grand lodges to elect their own officers. The Pennsylvanians wrote back that they had not fully considered the question, although admitting that some brothers had believed the state grand masters would serve only as deputies to the national leader. The grand lodge would be willing, however, to let the question of local powers be "fixed by a convention of committees." The Massachusetts Ancients found such assurances unconvincing. St. Andrew's Lodge unanimously opposed the idea, and, in January 1781, its grand lodge recommended that the proposal be deferred "until a general peace" when other grand lodges could be consulted. But the brothers did not even wait for the end of the war to reject the idea. Less than a month later they judged the new national body not "expedient." [22]

The actions of the Massachusetts Ancients alone doomed the proposal, but other difficulties had already arisen that suggest the impracticality of the scheme. Distance hindered even discussion of the plan. The Philadelphia Ancients had learned of the Massachusetts Ancient grand lodge only through the chance presence of a visiting soldier. The Virginia grand lodge formed in 1777 remained only an unconfirmed report to Philadelphians in 1780. Realizing their limited knowledge, the Ancient brothers there reassured their Massachusetts counterparts that newspaper advertisements would alert any other grand lodges "which we may not have heard of." The difficulties of communication, obscuring even the number of parties to the agreement, also hindered a clear sense of what the proposal entailed. While the soldiers sought a single grand lodge to break down the division between Ancients and Moderns—even as they blithely spoke of getting approval from a single "Mother Lodge" in Britain—the Pennsylvanians considered their proposed body solely an Ancient body. They voted to invite the rumored Virginia grand lodge only if it proved to be Ancient. [23]

The grand master general proposal had been so appealing to the Pennsylvanians partly because it seemed to minimize the difficulties raised by political separation from England. A national American body, approved by all American grand lodges and headed by the universally acknowledged leader of the American cause, would simply take over the role of the older provincial grand lodges, perhaps even with British blessing. But the general grand master plan faced the same difficulties of local jealousies and parochial visions faced by the nationalist attempts to strengthen political ties. Masonry never created a federal Constitution, or even a national confederation. Too many difficulties stood in the way of such large-scale solutions. But the fluidity of the Revolutionary situation also allowed American brothers to become independent in fact without necessarily making (or heeding) bold Declarations of Independence—an ability seen in the experiences of the New York grand lodge.

Having papered over the split between Ancients and Moderns simply by declaring itself and its subordinate lodges Ancient, the postwar New York grand lodge attempted to deal with the issue of independence in a similar way—by ignoring it. New York brothers continued to act as a grand lodge without definitively deciding whether they were separate from Great Britain or still a provincial body. When a subordinate lodge received a demand for payment of dues from the London Ancients in 1786, however, New York brothers could no longer disregard the question. The dunned lodge demanded that the New York group prove its legitimacy before it declined the London request. "Doubts are entertained," explained another lodge, "concerning the propriety of Holding a grand lodge under the Present Warrant, and [the] Authority from which it is derived." In June 1787, the grand lodge voted to assert its independence—by firmly reasserting the status quo. "Nothing is necessary or essential" for continued sovereignty, they declared, since their grand lodge had been correctly established by lodges "legally warranted." This declaration seemingly quelled doubts; it also allowed previous practices to continue. In September, a more scrupulous grand lodge member pointed out that their seal still referred to the group as a provincial body.[24]

The New Yorkers' ambiguous passage to independence reveals some of the key elements of Masonry's Revolutionary settlement. As the continuation of older activities suggests, the practical issues of independence were not especially complex. The connections between British bodies and their American subordinates had been relatively loose, with American provincial grand lodges operating on their own in nearly all situations. The theoretical issues were more troublesome. Like other American Masonic bodies, the New Yorkers realized that such questions admitted of few means of balancing the claims of British ties and American freedom. Ultimately, even the legitimacy of brothers' claims to connection with Masonic honor and antiquity could be threatened. The resulting solutions, mostly blurring the theoretical issues until the practical experience of independence seemed overwhelming, allowed Masonry to emerge in a strong position, perhaps even stronger than might have been possible with a more tidy resolution.

Pre-Revolutionary Masonic authority in general had been only loosely articulated. Subordinate lodges seldom paid regular dues, either to Great Britain or to the provincial grand lodges. Their American supervisory bodies often did not report even the formation of new lodges to Britain. Boston Moderns seem to have contacted London only to request the appointment of a new provincial grand master after the old one died. The more diligent St. Andrew's brothers sent dues to their Scottish superiors just twice in the decade before their request for their own grand body. Ties with Great Britain further loosened during the Revolution.[25]

Although practice seldom acknowledged British authority, such ties remained essential in theory. As early as the 1730s, Benjamin Franklin had noted that the Philadelphia lodges needed to be "distinguished by some such special authority" in order to fight off illegitimate Masonic pretenders.[26] The development of Ancient lodges in the decades before the Revolution further focused attention on Masonic rules, since disputes about the regularity of the new lodges could be explicitly argued only in legal terms. When the St. Andrew's members faced the Modern grand lodge in 1772, the Moderns based their demand for "SUBMISSION" upon the Ancients' failure to follow proper forms. The Boston Ancients, on the other hand, could only hold that the approval of the Scottish grand lodge erased previous irregularities. Even the wartime disruption of lodge activities encouraged concern with Masonic legality, since warrants required regular gatherings.

The question of legality thus raised serious concerns. In a Revolution where colonial charters and American constitutions played a central role in the debates, Masonic warrants could not be taken lightly. Nor could brothers easily consent to an unprecedented self-creation when Masonic myth gloried in its unbroken connection with remotest antiquity. Reconstitution and redefinition in the present seemed threatening, virtually un-Masonic. The search for continued legitimacy helped motivate the Pennsylvania Ancients' quick endorsement of the national grand lodge scheme. Their letter to the Boston Ancients confessed that their lodge had "granted warrants beyond its bounds to the Delaware and Maryland States . . . but we know that necessity alone can be a plea for this." Necessity, however, could not suffice in the long run. A number of Massachusetts Ancients even argued that the death of grand master Joseph Warren had closed their grand lodge, since the Scottish grand body had named Warren without creating an autonomous grand lodge. When the Massachusetts body finally moved to explicit independence in 1782, St. Andrew's brothers refused to make the move. Despite the grand lodge's claim to "Precedents of the Most approved Authority," the lodge considered the assumption of power "inconsistent with the principles of Masonry, necessary to be observ'd for the good of Craft." Besides, Scotland had not been the source of the oppression that had created the Revolution. "When Massachusetts breaks from Scotland," some members argued, "St. Andrew will break from her." The members rejected affiliation with the state body until 1807; Paul Revere led a minority into a new lodge under the independent grand lodge.[27]

That the only long-term division over Masonic independence took place over a Scottish, not an English, warrant reveals the strength of the competing argument cited by the Boston dissenters. Continued ties with England raised the specter of American disloyalty. Feeling the tensions created by these conflicting imperatives, the Pennsylvania Ancients in 1784 again called for a national meeting to resolve the matter. Some Maryland lodges had petitioned the Pennsylvania body for authority to create a state grand lodge, an action clearly outside the boundaries of a provincial grand lodge charter. But, the Pennsylvanians also noted, allowing the Maryland groups to apply to Britain might result in "greater evils." "Prevailing opinion" argued "that the alteration of the political relation . . . renders it improper to continue any acknowledgment of dependency and ought to exclude every kind of foreign jurisdiction." But this bold argument against "dependency" actually led to no concrete action by the Pennsylvanians. As they realized, direct assaults on the issue created difficulties. Their final declaration of independence two years later followed an elaborate procedure to forestall hints of rebellion or irregu-

Figure 9. Membership Certificate, Rising States Lodge, Boston. The lodge
created by the St. Andrew's minority. *By Paul Revere, 1780.*
Courtesy American Antiquarian Society

larity. Forced to resolve the issue by the vast expansion of their domain, they
"closed for ever" the old grand lodge in September and, on the following day,
formed a new body through a "Grand Convention."[28]

By 1790, the year the Massachusetts Moderns elected their own grand master, the problem of American Masonic legitimacy had been resolved. The Bostonians had simply waited until the death of their grand master, John Rowe,
who had been appointed by the English Moderns before the Revolution, and
then elected a grand master on their own. Such an action no longer seemed
very controversial. State bodies, not a general grand lodge or British authorities, now held ultimate control of the future of American Masonry.

In appearance, these new state structures of authority might have resembled the old system of provincial grand lodges; but, underneath, a number of changes prepared Masonry for its greatest period of expansion. First, the slow end to subordination prevented the dangers of either a potentially damaging connection to a former enemy or an unraveling of the fraternal fabric that constituted Masonry's main claim to public honor. The consolidation of power on the state level, aided by the growing attention to Masonic legality, helped provide a solid foundation for a fraternity growing beyond all previous expectations. Increasingly, grand lodges encouraged fuller attendance at their meetings and attempted to cull inactive or noncontributing lodges. But these powers remained in relatively familiar hands. Rather than a national body, Masonry continued to be rooted in the states and localities even as it preserved its international connections and perpetuated its universal pretensions.

In the end, the soldiers' hope of a united and active fraternity would be realized in America, although not precisely in the way they envisioned it. The strength of the order after the war rested not only on resolving the issues of disruption, loyalty, and legitimacy but also on the active involvement of the soldiers themselves. The Continental army officers, blocked in their attempts to advance honor and fraternity both in a national grand lodge and in their own Society of the Cincinnati, discovered in their military lodges a means of dealing with the questions of reputation and friendship that they—like the whole of post-Revolutionary society—would face. The officers' attraction to Freemasonry can be glimpsed in their celebration half a year before the meeting to propose a national grand lodge.

III. The Cares and Fatigues of the Soldier's Life

On June 24, 1779, more than one hundred Masonic brothers, all Continental army officers, marched from West Point. General Samuel Holden Parsons, General John Paterson, and General John Nixon joined in the procession, along with the then-obscure Captain Daniel Shays. Behind a band, "the Sword of Justice," the Bible, and the Square and Compass, the brothers proceeded to the Robinson House. There they were met by "a number of gentlemen" and brother George Washington. After a sermon, a Masonic address, and dinner, the brothers toasted "the Arts and Sciences" as well as the trio of martyred Masons "Warren, Montgomery, and Wooster." Members of the American Union Lodge, the group sponsoring the celebration, sang "The Virtuous Science." After the entertainment, Washington, "amidst a crowd of brethren," the lodge officers, and the band playing "God Save America," returned to his barge on the Hudson. "His departure was announced," the secretary recorded, "by three cheers from the shore, answered by three from the barge, the music beating the 'Grenadier's March.'"[29]

The celebration, with its rich images of honor and brotherhood among the very highest levels of the army, attracted a great deal of attention. Colonel Rufus Putnam, stationed nearby, became a Mason in American Union Lodge at its very next meeting; Captain Henry Sewall, an Entered Apprentice for about two years, took the final two degrees the following month. General Paterson applied for his own military lodge only three months after the ceremony. Nine of the thirteen present at the new group's first meeting had attended the June celebration. Not surprisingly, they called it Washington Lodge.[30]

The fraternity's appeal to army officers went far beyond West Point. Washington Lodge listed 250 members by the end of the war, and hundreds more met in other military lodges. Besides the two Massachusetts lodges, eight military groups met in Continental army camps; still other officers joined lodges near their posts. This extensive involvement can be seen most clearly at the highest levels of the army: at least 42 percent of the generals commissioned by the Continental Congress were or would become Freemasons.[31]

For these officers, Masonry's values of love and honor held particular attraction. By balancing inclusiveness and exclusivity, the fraternity spoke directly to the peculiar needs of men who sought both to uphold their seemingly precarious social position and to build ties with a diverse group of fellow officers separated by local origin, religious affiliation, and military rank. The impact of military Masonry, however, went beyond the officers' individual situations. Fraternal ties among the officers helped create and sustain the sense of common purpose necessary for the survival of the Continental army—and thus the winning of the war. The success of this esprit de corps would be represented in the postwar Society of the Cincinnati, an attempt to continue the officers' corporate identity using language and symbols that recalled Masonry's earlier significance.[32]

"Honor," argued American Union brother Rufus Putnam, formed "the first Prinsible of a Soldier," a dictum to which his fellow lodge member Samuel Holden Parsons clearly subscribed. His August 1777 marching orders used the word three times. Even to his wife, Parsons excused his failure to visit by arguing that, despite his superior's permission, he could not have left his troops "without staining my honor." "Although I am willing to devote my life to the service of my country," he wrote to a congressman upon hearing that a junior brigadier general had been promoted ahead of him, "I shall never be persuaded 'tis my duty to continue that service under such circumstances as will reflect personal dishonour upon me." "If I submitted to take any command in the army under these circumstances," he argued, "[I] must join my fellow citizens in despising myself." Parsons had heard incorrectly, but his indignation hardly matched his seniority. His seeming rival's original appointment had followed his by only five weeks.[33]

Such disputes about precedence pervaded the Continental army. American officers like Parsons often seemed obsessed with their honor. The cases of Parsons, Putnam, and their brother officers reveal the roots of their anxieties—as well as Masonry's ability to legitimate authority and honor in a context where such public recognition seemed the soldier's first principle.[34]

According to eighteenth-century theory, military rank should reflect social standing. The patriot David Ramsay, in his 1785 *History of the Revolution of South-Carolina,* even complained of the quality of the British officers occupying Charleston. "In former wars," he argued, "dignity, honour, and generosity, were invariably annexed to the military character." But, though the older officers "were for the most part gentlemen," new positions were often filled "by a new set greatly inferior in fortune, education, and good breeding." John Adams singled out Parsons among others in proposing higher qualifications for American officers. "A General Officer," he wrote to Nathanael Greene in 1776, "ought to be a Gentlemen of Letters and General Knowledge, a Man of Address and Knowledge of the World. He should carry with him Authority, and Command."[35] Higher-ranking officers often came from established families. Parsons was a Harvard graduate, a prominent lawyer, and a Connecticut assemblyman.

As Adams also suggested, however, men such as Parsons were exceptional. The wealthiest and most influential Americans seldom joined the Continental army. Many remained loyal to the crown. Others headed local militias, served in the government, or simply tended their estates. Even in the highest ranks, many Revolutionary officers came from outside the genteel elite that had previously held the highest political offices.[36] Colonel Benjamin Tupper, the original senior warden of Washington Lodge, possessed only a short public school education and a knowledge of tanning when he completed his indenture at age sixteen. He served as a farmhand until he entered the army during the Seven Years' War, rising only to the rank of sergeant. Rufus Putnam similarly came from a home where, he recalled, "I was made a ridecule of, and otherwise abused for my attention to books" by a "very illiterate" stepfather. Enlisting in the Seven Years' War for three years, he served as an ensign, the lowest commissioned rank. Although he held no further public office during the intervening period, he entered the Continental army as a lieutenant colonel and became a brigadier general.[37]

High military rank brought anxiety not only because it raised expectations about social position but because military effectiveness seemed to depend upon personal honor. In theory at least, military command seemed inextricably linked to social authority based on reputation and high status. As Adams had written, an officer "should carry with him Authority, and Command." Although later a general, judge, and Masonic grand master of Ohio, Putnam never lost the sense of dependence upon those above him. He recorded his experiences for his "decendents," he suggested, so that they would know "in what estimation I was held by my superiour officers."[38]

For men uncertain of their honor and fearful of their reputation among their superiors, peers, and subordinates, Freemasonry helped provide the endorsement they craved. The order had, until recently, been highly selective and open only to the highest levels of society. It sponsored public processions rich with symbols of high status identifying its members with military heroes such as Joseph Warren, David Wooster, and Richard Montgomery as well as the universally admired Washington.

Masonry also offered training in the polite manners that marked gentlemen. American Union Lodge's bylaws provided for Masonic instruction and a system of fines to punish unfraternal—and ungenteel—conduct. Such rules helped keep Masonry's reputation honorable so that it and its members would not "be Liable to the aspersions or Censure of the World." According to a Masonic petition from New Jersey officers, the fraternity developed "that order and decency which are the ornaments of sober and rational men." [39]

Masonry also helped mitigate the dangers of a world defined by authority and command. Hierarchy seems partially at odds with the other side of Masonry's appeal, its promotion of love and social harmony. Yet the officers also needed fraternity, perhaps even more because of their prickly concern with their standing. Just as much as its promotion of honor, Masonic ideals of harmony and brotherhood fitted closely the officers' peculiar circumstances.

Masonry built fraternity among men uprooted from their households and neighborhoods, forbidden from "fraternization" with enlisted men, and often separated by jealousy and fears of dishonor from their peers and superiors. "I have no way to tell you where I am," Samuel Holden Parsons wrote to his wife in 1777, "but by describing the place which has no name." "You ask me where I can be found?" he noted the following year from West Point. "This is a puzzling question." "News," he complained, "arrives here by accident only." Freemasonry helped build new ties among similarly misplaced men, creating structures and attitudes "whereby," the members of a Pennsylvania lodge later stated, "we were Enabled to Converse with More Ease." [40]

This enabling function can be seen in another Pennsylvania lodge, No. 19 of the Pennsylvania Artillery, which first met in central Pennsylvania and upstate New York during the 1779 Sullivan expedition. On the edge of the frontier far from the their homes (and the trappings of polite culture), the Masons initiated "brothers," sang songs, and read Masonic pamphlets, including the sermon delivered by William Smith the previous December to a group of Philadelphia Masons that included General Washington. In the address given at the city's elegant Christ Church, Smith had spoken of the fraternity's ability to provide "that Strength which . . . is . . . a Band of Union among Brethren, and a Source of Comfort in our own Hearts." Providing a physical expression of this unity and comfort, the traveling lodge reinterred two brother officers who had been part of an advance party killed by Indians. Accompanied by

General John Sullivan and brother General William Maxwell, the lodge presided over the necessary ceremonies for comrades who had previously had only boards marking their resting place.[41]

Parson's lodge, American Union, began in more settled surroundings, but it met similar needs. Its first bylaws, prepared during the siege of Boston in February 1776, provided for meeting three times each month, but the lodge soon convened more often. In the three months after February 1779, it met eighteen times, providing relief from the extended periods of inactivity that marked wartime duty. On May 7, 1779, just before much of the Connecticut Line moved to New York, the brothers gave the Fellow Craft degree at 3:00 P.M., the Master's degree at 5:00, the Fellow Craft again at 7:00, and formed as a Master's lodge at 8:00.[42]

These meetings brought together men from a variety of localities. Although officially attached to the Connecticut Line, at least four among the sixteen men who organized American Union lived outside Connecticut. Maryland resident Colonel Otho Holland Williams belonged to a Virginia brigade. Two others lived in Massachusetts; another served in the Delaware line. Even the twelve Connecticut brothers hailed from at least eight different towns.[43]

Military rank further complicated geographical diversity. Continental officers never developed the close ties with their troops that sustained militia units or the provincial armies of the Seven Years' War, partly by conscious design. From the start of his tenure as commander of the Continental army, George Washington stressed "Discipline and Subordination" as the key to a successful fighting force. The informal interaction between officers and common soldiers that had sustained earlier American forces (and would later revealingly be called "fraternization") seemed to Washington an affront to basic military principles. He sought all possible means to reinforce the distinction between officers and men. Even at a time of financial stress in September 1775, when he feared "Winter, fast approaching upon a naked Army," the general established "Proportions of Rations" that gave colonels six times the provisions allotted to common soldiers. Washington also endorsed higher pay for the lowest-level commissioned officers (whose rations were twice those of their underlings), warning that the present level of compensation was "one great Source of that Familiarity between the Officers and Men, whch is so incompatible with Subordination and Discipline."[44] Local ties, another foundation of colonial military life, seemed similarly suspect. Even a year before the Declaration of Independence, Washington's July 4, 1775, general orders "hoped that all Distinctions of Colonies will be laid aside." Indeed, Washington hoped to dissolve "all particular Attachments."[45]

The structure of the Continental army also helped weaken these attachments. Revolutionary soldiers tended to be drawn from a number of localities, restricting the easy transfer of local authority into the military hierarchy — and the continuing bonds that nurtured a common purpose. The permanence of

Table 8. Military Ranks of Members of Three Lodges

Rank	American Union Lodge	Lodge No. 29, Pennsylvania Line (Ancients)	Lodge No. 36, New Jersey Brigade (Pennsylvania Ancients)
Company-grade	61 (67.8%)	23 (56.1%)	16 (80.0%)
Lieutenant	32 (35.6%)	14 (34.1%)	12 (60.0%)
Captain	29 (32.2%)	9 (22%)	4 (20.0%)
Field-grade	29 (32.2%)	18 (43.9%)	4 (20.0%)
Colonel	10 (11.1%)	9 (22%)	1 (5.0%)
Lieutenant colonel			2 (10.0%)
Major	8 (8.9%)	6 (14.1%)	
Surgeon		1 (2.4%)	1 (5.0%)
Doctor	8 (8.9%)		
Chaplain	1 (1.1%)		
Adjutant	2 (2.2%)		
Regimental quartermaster		1 (2.4%)	
Regimental paymaster		1 (2.4%)	

Sources: Plumb, *American Union Lodge,* 8, 78–82; Johnston, *The Record of Connecticut Men, in the Military, and Naval Service; Massachusetts Soldiers and Sailors of the Revolutionary War,* I, 541; Sachse, *OMLPa,* II, 68–73, 130–134.

the Continental army further heightened the distinction between officers and common soldiers. Unlike the annually recreated provincial troops, the Revolutionary army drew men away from their localities for years. Not surprisingly, common soldiers increasingly came from the lower orders of society, expanding the distance between men now defined as "common" in two senses and superiors with a burning desire to be considered gentlemen. Reflecting their growing distance from these men, officers like Parsons demanded promotion, not on the basis of local standing or geographical balance, but on their date of commission.[46]

Besides the fundamental barrier between officers and enlisted men, a less formal division existed between higher and lower grades of officers. Baron von Steuben, a Masonic brother, was considered unusual because he entertained company-grade officers at dinner. Masonic lodges also helped bridge this divide. At least one Pennsylvania lodge included noncommissioned officers, but American Union, like most military lodges, consisted exclusively of commissioned officers, with the higher ranks proportionately overrepresented (Tables 8, 9). Although more lieutenants joined American Union Lodge than all field officers combined, nearly one-third of American Union members ranked as field officers (above the company-grade ranks of captains and lieu-

Table 9. Military Ranks of Members of Lodge No. 19 (Ancient),
Pennsylvania Artillery

Rank	No.	Rank	No.
Noncommissioned officers	7 (26.0%)	Field-grade officers	9 (33.3%)
Sergeant	4	Brigadier general	1
Corporal	2	Colonel	2
Quartermaster	1	Major	3
		Adjutant	1
Company-grade officers	11 (40.7%)	Surgeon	1
Captain	4	Chaplain	1
Lieutenant	6		
Ensign	1		

Source: Sachse, *OMLPa,* II, 34–36.

tenants), in great disproportion to the number of lower-ranking officers in the forces (regiments typically had twenty-four captains and lieutenants but only two colonels and a major). For these junior officers, such connections with their superiors must have been valuable.[47]

Fraternal ties, however, did not entirely obliterate distinctions of rank, as the special treatment of General Washington at the 1779 celebration makes clear. Higher-ranking officers usually held higher Masonic offices as well. General Paterson served as the charter master of Washington Lodge. Colonels Benjamin Tupper and John Greaton were the next two officers.[48] But the Masonic hierarchy did not blindly follow military rank. Colonel Parsons served only as treasurer at the creation of American Union, and, when the lodge replaced him as master in June 1779, they chose a captain.

Rank also affected patterns of affiliation. Some officers on the higher social rungs had already joined the fraternity. Parsons had received his degrees in the 1760s. Brigadier Generals George Weedon and Hugh Mercer, like Washington, had been members of the Fredericksburg, Virginia, lodge. Even during the Revolution, higher-ranking officers often became Masons in local nonmilitary lodges, largely because they tended to stay in closer contact with nearby communities. Captain Daniel Shays, Colonel John Greaton, and Captain William Sewall all joined the fraternity in Albany during the early years of the war.[49] Philadelphia's earliest Ancient lodge, No. 2, became a center for Continental and state officers. At the meeting of December 8, 1778, for example, the members voted to initiate Captains Thomas Huston and William Bradford, Jr., and Majors Evan Edwards and Jonathan Gostelowe. The lodge also chose Colonel Thomas Proctor as master, Colonel Isaac Melchior as senior warden, Captain Gibbs Jones as junior warden, and initiated (besides those balloted for) Major Archibald Dick. Finally, they received petitions from Majors William

West, David Lenox, and Isaac Budd Dunn—the last recommended by Colonel George Noarth.[50]

Stationary lodges, however, could not fulfill officers' needs for continuing sociability. Military life simply required too much movement. American Union Lodge met in Connecticut and New Jersey as well as New York and Massachusetts. Colonel Otho Holland Williams, the Maryland resident who joined American Union Lodge in Massachusetts, later served as the original senior warden of another military lodge whose warrant would be captured by the British in Camden, South Carolina. To meet the difficulties created by this travel, American grand lodges created ten different military lodges, the first soldiers' lodges created by American bodies (except for a group organized briefly by the Massachusetts Moderns during the Seven Years' War). Seven of these Revolutionary groups held warrants from Pennsylvania: three among their state's troops and one each in the North Carolina, Maryland, Delaware, and New Jersey lines. New York and the two Massachusetts grand lodges organized the remaining three.[51]

These military groups helped build ties among the officer corps when organized religion often proved unhelpful. Christian worship had nurtured both local identity and previous American military activities, but circumstances prevented it from taking a similar role in the Revolution, at least for officers. The army chaplaincy remained chronically understaffed and focused its attentions on the needs of the common soldiers rather than the officers. Furthermore, the diversity of religious denominations among both the officers and the chaplains exacerbated rather than healed divisions. Both the orthodox Congregationalist stalwart Timothy Dwight and the Universalist pioneer John Murray held chaplain's appointments under officers who were Masonic brothers.[52]

Masonic fraternity even cut across the most basic wartime division—that between friend and foe. According to its Massachusetts charter, American Union Lodge's meetings in New York required the sanction of the area's grand lodge. Yet loyalists, hardly inclined to support the cause of the American Union Lodge, dominated the New York grand lodge's top offices. The grand master by then lived upstate, stirring up Indians to raid patriot settlements and attack soldiers. His deputy grand master in New York City, however, confirmed American Union's warrant despite refusing to refer to the lodge as "American Union," calling it instead "Military Union Lodge." Although they were on different sides, the New York official could not prohibit Masonic activity, for fraternal ties bound together even enemies—a point also noted by Parsons. When he discovered shortly after the June procession that his men had captured a trunk containing a British regimental lodge's charter, he insisted upon returning the material. Even during war, he wrote the lodge, "as Masons we are disarmed of that resentment which stimulates to undistinguished desolation; and however our political sentiments may impel us in the public dispute, we are still Brethren, and (our professional duty apart) ought to promote the happiness . . . of each other." [53]

In theory at least, gentlemanly ties continued even without Masonic affiliation. A captured officer could move about freely after giving his word—his "parole"—not to harm his captors.[54] But, as Parsons suggested, these ideals were often ignored during the heat of battle. American officers, furthermore, often could not claim the social rank necessary for such consideration. Masonry provided an additional bond, a credential of status, that might encourage better treatment. Washington Lodge member William Sewall joined the fraternity because, he thought, "I should fare better in case I should be made a prisoner." Indeed, both Boston and Philadelphia brothers used their "influence" to aid jailed British brothers. Lieutenant Colonel William Stacy, captured in 1778, was tied to a stake by tories and Indians before his Masonic distress signal released him from torture and death.[55]

Officers felt psychologically threatened even in less physically precarious situations. Status insecurities, localism, and jealousies all worked to pull apart rather than unite Continental officers, especially within a larger society that was suspicious of military aspirations and, at least from the military perspective, seemed determined to demand sacrifices they would not take on themselves. Officers joined the fraternity primarily to satisfy these deeply felt personal needs, but Masonry's impact went beyond the level of the individual. By building organizations that stressed familial affection within a profoundly disorienting situation, Masonry provided a counterweight to the fragmentation that threatened the officer corps, helping create the sense of common purpose necessary for the survival of the army—and thus the success of the Revolution itself. Among the rank and file, such a disintegration actually took place during the later years of the war. Precisely the opposite, however, occurred among the officers. Rather than rebelling for release, their so-called Newburgh conspiracy (the 1783 attempt to coerce Congress into a financial settlement) threatened, not the dissolution of the army, but its peacetime continuation.[56]

Masonry alone did not create this new corporate identity, but its lodges helped build and sustain the connections necessary for its formation. By forging associations of unity and honor, the fraternity helped overcome the centrifugal tendencies of a Continental system that destroyed local bonds without providing anything concrete in their place. Masonry created these connections, furthermore, not by reinforcing previous associations based on locality, religion, or ethnicity, but by transcending them. Lodges offered moral instruction without sectarian divisions, a symbolic language of social distinction that did not depend upon local associations, and (not least of all) a means of creating and justifying a space for the relaxed sociability of eating, drinking, and singing. Through membership in a fraternity that ignored (or rejected) traditional boundaries and divisions, officers built a larger republican identity that rejected the colonists' pervasive localism and contractualism without accepting the class-structured professionalism of the British military. With its ideals of love among men divided by irrelevant distinctions and of honor attained solely by merit, Masonry could even be seen as an embodiment of the enlightened republican principles for which the officers were fighting.[57]

Besides the ultimate success of the Revolution itself, the Society of the Cincinnati created by the officers at the end of the war constituted the most visible result of the solidarity Masonry had helped to create. Not surprisingly, then, the Cincinnati shared a rhetoric of fraternal affection and honor as well as a significant number of members with Masonry. The failure of the officers' group to match the earlier fraternity's extraordinary post-Revolutionary success suggests the ways that American ideas about social standing changed during the Revolution—and the ways that Masonry fulfilled these new ideals.

Like the brotherhood, the Cincinnati promoted charitable giving. County groups were to meet regularly to collect charitable contributions for needy officers. "Friendship and Brotherly kindness," recalled Mercy Otis Warren, "were held up as the basis of the institution." In a term that had been previously used of Masonry (and, ironically, the pacifist Quakers), Henry Knox and George Washington each referred to the new officers' group as a "Society of Friends."[58]

Even more than love, honor lay at the heart of the officers' expectations for the Cincinnati. Only officers who served to the end of the war or who had "resigned with honour" after at least three years service could join. Members displayed a golden eagle hung from a buttonhole by a blue and white ribbon, a badge similar to European orders of honor—and to Masonic regalia. The Cincinnati's eagle obviously held similar power for its members. Its organizers spent so lavishly in preparing them that they exhausted their original funds. Their presentation at the New York society in 1786 came at a splendid ceremony created by Baron von Steuben, a member of the German Order of Fidelity (whose badge he wore throughout the Revolution) and a Freemason. Rising from his "Chair of State," President Steuben welcomed new members amid flourishes of trumpets and drums. "Receive this mark," he told each as he attached the order, "as a recompense for your merit."[59]

As Steuben's involvement suggests, Masonry and the Cincinnati shared many of the same members. Rufus Putnam attended the committee meeting that set up the organization; Samuel Holden Parsons served as the first president of the Connecticut society. Forty percent of the first generation of that state's group were or would become Freemasons.[60]

Although Masonry and the Cincinnati shared ideas and membership, their fortunes diverged sharply after the Revolution. Masonry prospered and grew enormously in size and in prestige. The Society of the Cincinnati provoked angry criticism that soon made it a marginal institution. The roots of this divergence lay not just in the pervasive fear of military power but also in the redefinition of honor during the Revolutionary years. Masonry was able to fit into, even epitomize, these new standards; the Cincinnati became one of their first victims. A brief look at the attack on the officers' group suggests the outlines of these new ideas and how Masonry, unlike the Cincinnati, met their cultural requirements.[61]

According to Mercy Otis Warren's famous attack on the Cincinnati, American army officers at the end of the war sought "to follow the fantastic fopperies of foreign nations and to sigh for the distinctions acquired by titles, instead of that real honor which is ever the result of virtue." The officers realized, she suggested, that "new exigencies might arise, that would open new sources of wealth to favored titles and distinguished orders." In a less well known passage, Warren also argued that opposition to the Cincinnati arose just as much from those who envied the order's claim to high status as from "the sincere votaries of . . . the natural equality of men." These opponents, she suggested, included "Ambassadors abroad, who had adopted a fondness for nominal distinctions, members of congress and of state legislatures, and many others who had acquired a taste for the external superiority that wealth and titles bestow." Such men, Warren noted, "could not be pleased to see themselves and their children thus excluded from hereditary claim to the honor, privileges, and emoluments of the first order of American nobility."[62]

Warren saw clearly the two sides of the Cincinnati's opposition, the desire for social equality and the desire for high personal position, but failed to realize their close relationship. The Revolutionary attack on colonial elites helped redefine the social location of, and the requirements for, distinction. Republican ideals of virtue and talent provided new standards to measure social standing. But attacks on the old aristocracy did not attempt to abolish distinction. They sought to allow the formerly obscure to make an influential and honorable place for themselves, to enjoy the stature commanded by "Real honor." Like the urban artisans or the village elites that pioneered Ancient Masonry, Continental officers often could not command it through their "fortune, education, and good breeding." But they could claim new standing on the basis of virtue and patriotic devotion.[63]

Yet, ironically, the two sides of Revolutionary honor worked against each other. The same groups that coveted newly available standing undercut some of the very means they needed to assert it. The Cincinnati stumbled over these conflicting cultural desires. Made up of men who believed they had earned true honor through virtue, the officers' group seemed to outsiders only a demand for external superiority.

In this perspective, the post-Revolutionary success of Masonry seems even more extraordinary. The fraternity's growing prestige, seen both in the rapid expansion of lodges and the cornerstone ceremonies at the United States Capitol and other public buildings, reflected its ability to fit new standards of honor, to balance Revolutionary demands for inclusiveness and exclusivity — for inclusive love and exclusive honor. Freemasonry was open to all, not handed down like the standing of the old elite or the Cincinnati. The fraternity's ability to unite previously unconnected men in the bonds of brotherhood, so important for the Revolutionary officers, provided a legacy of continuing significance in a post-Revolutionary society as fluid and confusing as the officers' wartime experiences. Perhaps not coincidentally, American Union Lodge re-formed after the war on the northwestern frontier, in the first town of the Ohio territory.[64]

Just as important, Masonry also provided social standing in a society where the jealousy seen in the Cincinnati's opponents continued to flourish. The fraternity's acknowledged antiquity and strict rules against religious and political discussion kept it from being termed "self-created" or eager for power. Furthermore, Masonry's structure, unlike the Cincinnati, rooted it in the locality while offering more than local prestige. Masonry was, the noncommissioned members of Pennsylvania's Lodge No. 19 wrote, "a most Ancient Society where no exception is made of any Man providing he is found worthy of Obtaining it."[65]

Ultimately, William Smith's vision of a grand ceremony installing a grand master general was not as completely removed from reality as it seemed in the midst of the Revolution. As Smith hoped, American Masonry would be raised from the danger of oblivion, from the difficulties of disruption, loyalty, and legitimacy. The post-Revolutionary fraternity gained new position and standing; but the social context would not tolerate the magnificent ceremonies based on the models of courts and palaces, a position underlined by the failure of the officers' order of the Cincinnati. Instead, Masonry, formerly known as the "royal art," came to be seen as a decidedly republican institution. That it should gain this position after a period of crisis, marked by a continuing desire among many to remain subordinate to Britain and a mixed record of loyalty to the Revolution, was doubly ironic.

In 1830, during the great reaction against this post-Revolutionary success, former Continental captain and Washington Lodge officer Henry Sewall, a soldier stationed near the June 1779 procession, would excuse his fraternal involvement by claiming that he had joined during the Revolution, when Masonry possessed little importance. "The frequent meetings of the lodge which I attended during this period," he wrote, "were merely convivial, serving no other purposes than to mitigate in some degree the privations, and beguile the cares and fatigues of the soldier's life." Sewall's attempt to minimize Masonry's significance distorted the particular meanings of the order to the Continental army's troubled officer corps. Uprooted from familiar settings and troubled by social shortcomings, Continental officers could not take conviviality for granted, especially during a period when the boundaries and perquisites of social rank seemed uncertain. With its ability to combine exclusive honor and inclusive love, Masonry helped unite the officers, enabling them (as the Pennsylvania brothers stated) "to Converse with More Ease" in ways that fed their needs both for high social standing and new friendships. The esprit de corps built during the Revolution by these fraternal meetings provided some of the sense of common purpose that helped the Continental army survive to win the war. Even Sewall, despite his later protestations, had not been immune to Masonry's attractions. He went on to take further degrees only two months after some of his future lodge brothers marched from West Point to meet their brother and his, George Washington.[66]

PART THREE

Republican Masonry

CHAPTER FIVE

A New Order for the Ages

Public Values, 1790–1826

On September 18, 1793, President George Washington dedicated the United States Capitol. Dressed in Masonic apron, the president placed a silver plate upon the cornerstone and covered it with the Masonic symbols of corn, oil, and wine. After a prayer, the brethren performed "chanting honors." Volleys of artillery punctuated the address that followed. Like the entire ceremony, the silver plate identified Freemasonry with the Republic; it was laid, it stated, "in the thirteenth year of American independence . . . and in the year of Masonry, 5793." [1]

If, as Thomas Jefferson argued, the Capitol represented "the first temple dedicated to the sovereignty of the people," then the brothers of the 1793 ceremony served as its first high priests. [2] Clothed in ritual vestments, Washington and his brothers consecrated the building by the literal baptism of corn, oil, and wine — symbols of nourishment, refreshment, and joy, or, as some versions interpreted them, Masonry, science and virtue, and universal benevolence. In exemplifying the goals of a free and prosperous society, Masons mediated between the sacred values of the community and the everyday world of stones and mortar.

The fraternity's position on Capitol Hill, one of the many such consecration ceremonies over the next generation, provided a powerful symbol of Masonry's new place in post-Revolutionary America. No longer an expression of the honor and solidarity of a particular social class, the fraternity increasingly identified itself with the ideals of the nation as a whole. The order, brothers argued, represented, taught, and spread virtue, learning, and religion. Masons thus did more than lay the Republic's physical cornerstones; they also helped form the symbolic foundations of what the Great Seal called "the new order for the ages."

The success of these new Masonic ideas, seen in the growth of cornerstone ceremonies as well as their endless repetition over the next thirty years, rested on two sets of interrelated changes. First, the new vision of the fraternity fitted into the widely shared desire to reconceive the character of American society as it emerged from the Revolution. By celebrating morality and individual merit, Masonry seemed to exemplify the ideals necessary to build a society based on virtue and liberty. But Masonry did more than represent proper values; it also taught them in peculiarly successful ways, making the brothers not just the priests but the teachers and missionaries of the new order. Such standing attracted large numbers of Americans eager to associate themselves with these cosmopolitan ideals. Fraternal membership and ideology helped bring high standing to a broad range of Americans, breaking down the artificial boundaries of birth and wealth. To men engaged in learned and artistic occupations, rural men with cosmopolitan aspirations, and even Boston's women and blacks, Masonry offered participation in both the great classical tradition of civilization and the task of building a new nation. Just as important, the fraternity also seemed to provide the leaders for these enterprises.

Besides expressing powerful ideological and cultural impulses, Masonry's new explanations and ideals seemed so compelling because they also were intertwined with a great fraternal expansion. The rise of Ancient Masonry and the resolution of wartime troubles launched the fraternity into a period of unparalleled growth. Within a generation after the Revolution, American Masonry grew from a few scattered groups of brothers to a well-organized and pervasive organization gathering in nearly every locality in America. Indeed, more lodges met in the United States in 1825 than in the entire world fifty years before. This extraordinarily rapid growth both fed upon and reinforced the fraternity's claim to exemplify and lead the new nation. But expansion also complicated the fraternity's relationship to its larger setting. For many, Masonic membership became a means of gaining practical (even perhaps selfish) benefits, not only charity but political and economic advantage. At the same time, Masons created a new, private sphere of ritual that bonded them together through intense experiences and feelings far different from the enlightened values proclaimed in Masonry's public rituals and explanations.

These increasingly separate spheres of fraternal experience grew up in the shadow of the powerful and persistent ideas that expanded virtually in proportion to Masonry itself. From 1793, when brothers dedicated the Capitol, to 1825, when they did the same for the Concord Minutemen monument, Americans identified their order with the values of virtue, learning, and religion. Despite the nagging doubts expressed by some skeptics, the fraternity seemed well prepared to help preserve the new order created by the Revolution—and to provide virtuous and learned leaders. Such a position seems to have been on the mind not only of those who invited the fraternity to lay the Capitol cornerstone but also of the editor of Charleston's 1825 city directory. Rather than listing the officers of South Carolina's grand lodge among the more ordinary benevolent, charitable, and friendly societies, he placed them among the public officials—between the state's military officers and its legislators.[3]

1. Temples of Virtue

Virtue provided the central exhibit in the identification of the fraternity with the new Republic's foundations. For Salem Town, who had joined the fraternity despite his mother's warnings about Masonry's dangerous magic, virtue was the essence of the fraternity itself. "Speculative Masonry," he argued, "has an ultimate reference to that speculative building erected by virtue in the heart."[4] New York brother (and political leader) De Witt Clinton made a similar point in his overview of Masonic history. In the years after the Renaissance, he suggested, the fraternity's primary purpose became the spread of virtue. Building upon the "pure and sublime system of morality" of earlier scientific brothers, the order's "principal attention" was now directed "to the cultivation of morality." "Masonry," he explained, "may now be defined" as "a moral institution, intended to promote individual and social happiness."[5]

Such arguments became ubiquitous in post-Revolutionary discussions of Masonry. The fraternity, brothers asserted, provided a peculiarly effective means of teaching morality at a time when such education seemed increasingly necessary—and increasingly perplexing. Masonry not only avoided the pitfalls of other institutions, but its symbols and rituals followed Enlightenment theories about pedagogy. As one orator noted in 1812, Masonry provided a powerful "school of moral virtue."[6]

Moral training had been a goal of Masonry since its creation, but post-Revolutionary Americans gave this activity powerful new ideological meaning. Virtue, the rejection of self-interest in favor of moral rules and the good of the whole, seemed to provide the essential foundation of a republican society. Leaders had always required self-control to withstand the temptations of power and corruption. But republics, unlike monarchical or aristocratic governments, did not depend solely upon their leaders. The people's character ultimately determined the health and prosperity of a society without the strong government and traditional restraints that had previously undergirded the social order. And many post-Revolutionary Americans feared that virtue could not be sustained, allowing the Republic to degenerate into either despotism or anarchy. George Washington's 1796 Farewell Address thus called morality one of the "great Pillars of human happiness" and "political prosperity." Masonry helped to provide the foundation for this building, training and teaching Americans to reinforce "the duties of men and Citizens." As Washington noted to his brothers only a few months later, America needed to become what Masonry already was: "a lodge for the virtues."[7]

Masonry's "decided and unquestionable excellences as a moral institution," the Reverend brother John Clark told upstate New York brothers in 1827, helped rescue people from the dangers of "moral degradation." "The object for which Masonry is instituted," he explained, "is none other than to make better and happier the human race." The foundation of this moral purpose lay in two extraordinarily effective "mode[s] of inculcating duty," methods of moral training that reinforced the fraternity's claim to lay the foundation stones of the new nation.[8]

Clark first noted the "peculiar advantage of [the lodge's] discipline." Masonic fraternity created a moral watchfulness that protected members' character not only through informal concern but through reproof, suspension, and expulsion. Through these means, Clark argued, lodges held "an almost perfect control over the moral deportment of their members." As a Virginia brother noted, Masonry created a "rigid school of social virtue."[9]

The fraternity also practiced a more complex but similarly powerful means of moral instruction. According to Clark, Masonic rituals provided a "long and continued training" through "signs, addressed to the *eye,* the *ear,* and the *touch*." Such emblematic education, De Witt Clinton suggested, formed the fraternity's "peculiar utility," distinguishing it from other ethical traditions with similarly pure morals. Through these means, Clinton argued, Masonry could "impress" its lessons "with a greater force upon the mind." As the physical imagery suggests, brothers interpreted their rituals in the terms of contemporary pedagogy. Lockean epistemology suggested that information obtained by the senses formed the raw material for later thought. "We are creatures of sense rather than intellection," noted Clark; therefore, the fraternity used "sensible signs." Such information created an impression, almost a literal mark, upon the mind. In the rituals, another brother noted, "the signet of heavenly TRUTH stamps [morality] . . . in characters indelible."[10]

The power of post-Revolutionary Masonic education, however, rested on more than simply displaying truth. The fraternity also drew upon mid-eighteenth-century elaborations of Lockean ideas. According to the associationalist ideas most closely identified with David Hartley, sense data arriving in the mind together remained linked. Taking advantage of this seeming law, Masons carefully prepared their classroom so that it presented a unified lesson. Proposed members were screened so that only men ready for these truths received them. A Connecticut brother recommended a proposed member to a lodge, calling him "a feeling and an understanding man." If "his mind" was "properly imprest with the importance of the institution" and the ceremony "given . . . with Solemnity," the testimonial noted, the prospective brother would be certain to gain its benefits. To ensure this proper solemnity, older members carefully learned the rituals. After 1800, officers and traveling teachers (known as lecturers) increasingly emphasized the memorization of the ceremonies' exact wording, celebrating (in the words of a contemporary song) "the Mason's glory"

> whose prying mind doth burn,
> Unto complete perfection;
> Our mysteries to learn.[11]

The arrangement of lodge rooms received similar attention. According to a Masonic handbook, "Every character, figure, and emblem, depicted in a Lodge has a moral tendency, and inculcates the practice of virtue." Visual signs thus reinforced verbal instruction. Theorists had already pointed out that combining different types of impressions aided learning. "It is a law in our natures," suggested the non-Mason Dr. Benjamin Rush, "that we remember *longest* the knowledge we acquire by the greatest number of our senses." Recognizing that "every thing that strikes the eye, more immediately engages the attention," brothers created an artificial environment that made Masonic symbols a central means of education. Such training seemed to link visual images directly to their moral associations. "Whenever any of these acts or objects are presented to the eye, the ear, or the touch," Clark argued, "the moral duty associated with that act or object is immediately brought before the mind." [12]

In their attempt to make virtue second nature, Masons drew upon powerful ideas that had inspired other enlightened plans to transform education in the Western world. Jean Jacques Rousseau's *Émile* (1762) recommended controlling children's impressions; Jeremy Bentham's Panopticon proposed (in 1791) a prison where guards constantly watched prisoners. In America, the same vision of a mechanical mind gave power to new ways of thinking about women's roles. "Mothers, or all ladies should have cultivated minds," argued one young woman, "as the first rudiments of education are always received from them, and at that early period of life when the mind is open to every new impression." Proclaiming motherhood "of more importance than the government of provinces, and the marshalling of armies," another author in 1791 suggested that "heaven hath reposed its supreme confidence" in woman by giving her "the care of making the first impressions on the infant minds of the whole human race." Fraternal, rather than maternal, teaching allowed similarly effective training of students who were more mature. At a time when virtue appeared necessary for social prosperity and political health, Masonry formed the most popular and widespread attempt to achieve what the non-Mason Dr. Benjamin Rush recommended as "possible" — to "convert men into republican machines." [13]

Masonry's moral training seemed particularly significant because the new importance attached to virtue only heightened its difficulties. Late-seventeenth- and early-eighteenth-century English social theorists such as the earl of Shaftesbury had explored the idea of natural sociability and benevolence. Attempting to refute Thomas Hobbes's bleak picture of a humanity so selfish that it required despotism, they argued that people naturally were concerned for the well-being of their neighbors and that people naturally got along with one another. But such benevolence, although universal, could be relied upon only among gentlemen; common people needed more direct forms of authority. Post-Revolutionary Americans dramatically changed the social refer-

ents of this idea. What had been an attempt to justify the rule of the aristocracy and gentry now became a means of holding together an entire society.
Not only would virtue have to be extended to all; it would have to be the fundamental source of public order.[14]

Not surprisingly then, the new emphasis on morality highlighted the difficulties of achieving it. Many Americans began to stress, not the ubiquity of
virtue, but the need to nurture and encourage it. The non-Mason Samuel Harrison Smith's 1796 American Philosophical Society prize essay on education
defined virtue, not as a universal and natural reaction, but as "active exer-
tion." The old identification of benevolence as spontaneous moral sympathy
became "pity . . . a mere natural impulse." Thus, Smith argued, "there is no
merit in obeying its voice." True "benevolence" required "reflection."[15] De
Witt Clinton went even further. "We must not expect," Clinton warned his
Masonic lodge in 1793, "that virtue will rise up spontaneously in the heart."
"If some men have a natural propensity to benevolence," he noted, "others
perhaps are under an opposite bias." Even among those with a "natural propensity" toward goodness, "thinking and cultivation must cherish and mature
the benign tendencies of our nature."[16]

Just as the universality of virtue came to be questioned, so too the means
of cultivating it seemed increasingly problematic. Religion continued to be
regarded as a primary teacher of morality. But individual churches, in the
wake of disestablishment and increasing pluralism, could not train everyone. Furthermore, their sectarian sympathies often narrowed their interests
and their loyalty to the whole of society.[17] Schools seemed more promising
in theory but similarly inadequate in practice. "We find an universal accor-
dance in opinion on the benefits of education," Clinton complained in 1809,
"but the practical exposition of this opinion exhibits a deplorable contrast."
Although Noah Webster similarly considered universal schooling a "*sine qua
non*" of the Republic, he also pointed out that even existing schools often did
not meet the high standards necessary for proper education. Since students
imitated the character of their instructors, "the instructors of youth ought, of
all men, to be the most prudent, accomplished, agreeable, and respectable."
Instead, he complained, they were often immoral and immature.[18]

As "the sacred asylum of temperance, order, and decorum," Masonry
seemed to transcend these limitations. It possessed the virtuous teachers necessary for inculcating the practice of morality, since merit formed the only
criterion of membership and office. Furthermore, its rejection of particular
religious and political opinions allowed it to reach out to all men. Finally, the
fraternity's principles, uncorrupted by the false standards of hierarchy or sectarian prejudice, were "simple, pure, and universal."[19]

Such purity of teachings, teachers, and methods all reinforced the fraternity's claim to act as what one brother called "the nursery of VIRTUE." In a
society that considered moral nurture a problematic necessity, the fraternity's

enlightened means of education seemed to be more than private or individual; it benefited the entire nation—and even the world. If, as the Reverend Wilkes Allen asserted simply in 1809, "the cause of Masonry is the cause of virtue," then it followed logically that "the promotion of [Masonry's] interests" led to "the increase of human happiness."[20]

11. The Great Instrument of Civilization

Before the Renaissance, brother De Witt Clinton told his New York lodge in 1793, the fraternity had kept knowledge safe in an inhospitable world. "Scientific and ingenious men . . . assembled" in the lodge, he explained, "to improve the arts and sciences, and to cultivate a pure and sublime system of morality." The majority of the people, by contrast, "were kept in a state of profound ignorance and considered as the profanum vulgus." Government policy restricted intellectual merit to a favored few, "to the Aristotles, the Virgils, and the Plinys of the age."[21]

The invention of printing changed this ancient order. Seeing the possibility of bringing "the means of instruction to all ranks of people," brothers unselfishly and "with cheerfulness" shared "with the world, those secrets of the arts and sciences, which had been transmitted and improved from the foundation of the institution." As a result, "the sunshine of mental and moral illumination" shone across the world, revealing the importance of freedom and "natural equality"—a concept Clinton believed "one of the most significant discoveries in the history of the world."[22]

Clinton's history articulated one of the central claims of post-Revolutionary Masonry, its intimate relationship with what contemporaries called "science," organized learning beyond everyday knowledge. American brothers now began to argue that their order had helped nurture and spread civilization, serving as a beacon of proper principles even in times of darkness. As Clinton's scenario suggested, such a view encompassed several important elements. The new language of Masonic science first placed the fraternity into the accepted genealogy of learning and civilization, giving it a central role in the lineage of progress. The scientific principles that underlay these changes, furthermore, had continuing significance at a time when Americans had embarked on an unprecedented experiment in liberty and equality. As a result, the fraternity became a powerful tool for raising people from their old status as the "profanum vulgus" to fulfill the enlightened hope of a society of Aristotles, Plinys, and Virgils. Finally, Masonry did more than simply spread learning. It also helped teach and identify men who possessed the "mental and moral illumination" necessary to continue this republican course—leaders who were well prepared to lay the foundations of the new nation. As the outgoing grand master of Massachusetts argued in 1810, American Masons are "justly ranked . . . with the benefactors of mankind" because "with magna-

Figure 10. Prostyle Temple. Depiction of Masonic and biblical figures, memorializing De Witt Clinton at base. *From Jeremy Cross*, The True Masonic Chart *(New Haven, Conn., 1819). Courtesy American Antiquarian Society*

nimity and zeal, they have resisted the . . . influence of ignorance" and its attendant vices, "superstition and prejudice."[23]

Clinton's attempt to identify the fraternity with the learned men of the past represented a new theme in the American fraternity. Early English brothers had emphasized the links between their order and the ancient mysteries, but colonial Masons paid little attention to this idea, preferring to stress, not mystical knowledge, but the broader themes of love and honor. Post-Revolutionary brothers gave learning a central place in their new descriptions of the fraternity, in many cases by reshaping the fraternity's history. Rather than the hidden knowledge or the "royal art" celebrated by James Anderson's early history, Masonry increasingly seemed to be descended primarily from the "scientific and ingenious men" commemorated by Clinton. This involved, first, a reassertion of links with ancient mysteries. One Massachusetts brother claimed Moses as a progenitor, since he had been "initiated in the knowledge of the wisemen" and versed in "all the wisdom of the Egyptians." Other speakers celebrated the roots of Masonry in the Essenes, the Delphic mysteries, and even "our celebrated brother Pythagoras." Echoing this genealogy, Tom Paine (like John Cleland, who wrote *Fanny Hill*) linked the fraternity to the Druids, the mysterious order English brother William Stukeley had helped popularize.[24]

Despite the similarities of this genealogy to earlier Masonic histories, however, post-Revolutionary claims seldom emphasized the hidden, esoteric wisdom early-eighteenth-century brothers had celebrated. Rather, American Masons stressed the significance of their supposed predecessors' scientific learning. A New Hampshire orator in 1798 celebrated the fraternity's popularity in ancient Greece, viewed, not as the fountainhead of deep mystical learning, but as "that nation of taste and refinement." Since the fraternity, he explained, "was connected as nearly with all the liberal arts and sciences, which were then mostly cultivated by the craft," membership "became the first ambition of the lovers of learning, taste and philosophy."[25]

The search for new ancestors involved more than mere antiquarianism. By recreating the Masonic past, brothers hoped to reinforce their order's connection with learning in the present. Claims about the fraternity's support of learning filled secret lodge meetings as well as public orations. Brothers officially sponsored educational endeavors that reached beyond the fraternity. This encouragement of broader education seemed to link the fraternity to the post-Revolutionary vision of an enlightened society built around equality and openness, values that brothers came to see expressed even in their order's structure. By supporting learning and by teaching and embodying republican relationships, Masonry seemed to be upholding and advancing the Revolutionary experiment itself.

Figure 11. Tracing Board. Illustrating the Masonic symbols taught within the lodge, this would have been hidden from public view. *Circa 1800, Western Star Lodge No. 15, Bridgewater, New York. Courtesy of the Livingston Masonic Library, New York, New York; gift of Western Star Lodge No. 15*

The new view of Masonic history made the search for learning an important theme within American lodges. Besides delineating Masonic genealogy, Clinton's 1793 address also suggested that "mental improvement" was "an essential requisite, an indispensable duty" for current Masons. "The study of the liberal arts," second-degree initiates were similarly instructed, "is earnestly recommended to your consideration." Masons even began to argue that fraternal membership itself provided education. Candidates for the second degree heard (and then memorized) a lecture on the significance of the liberal arts, calling it "that valuable branch of education, which tends so effectually to polish and adorn the mind." As a song of the period claimed, Masonry provided "the compendious way to be wise."[26]

The new stress on learning encouraged some lodges to support educational activities for a broader audience. The lodge in Danville, Virginia, like many other southern and frontier bodies, opened its lodge hall to a fledgling school; the Marietta, Ohio, group helped finance the local public school building; and the Troy, New York, lodge aided the town's lending library when it experienced financial difficulties. The lodge in Alexandria, Virginia, formerly headed by George Washington, even created a museum based on the collections of its members. Although primarily designed to bolster their charity funds through admission fees, members also expected a larger and more important result. Like the lodge itself, the new institution was to be "a Seminary" where people "may all come and learn Wisdom, from the stupendous Works of the Great Architect of the World."[27]

Despite these high-minded actions and words, however, lodge meetings did not actually provide a seminary in the accepted meaning of the term. Second-degree members were required to memorize an introduction to the seven liberal arts, but this was a short set piece, not a regular course of reading or study. Similarly, lodge masters might sometimes provide lectures on related subjects, but these remained occasional and dependent upon individual initiative, hardly the high-minded school celebrated by countless orators. At least one contemporary noticed this gap between rhetoric and actions. Excited by his friends' claims that "*the sciences were taught in the lodges,*" Nathaniel Very joined the fraternity in the mid-1810s. The central Massachusetts resident quit the fraternity after a year, however, complaining later that it had held "out the false banner of religion, science and philosophy."[28]

Yet the widespread and continuing desire, in Very's language, to "prate . . . of the Liberal Arts" must have been something more than rhetorical flourishes or, as the suspicious Very suggested, a "treacherous lure" for unsuspecting victims.[29] The brothers' praise of learning served as a cultural marker that identified them with particular beliefs. Emphasis on liberal education first involved rejection of parochialism. Just as important, Masonic talk of learning linked brothers to the growth of the enlightened world and the survival of the new nation. Through their emphasis on science, members argued, their order provided the foundations of both an informed public opinion and a republican social order.

Masonry's celebration of science first distinguished it and its members from the narrow localism of less cosmopolitan Americans. The orator at the 1820 consecration of Maine's grand lodge noted that the slow development of schools partly resulted from widespread popular suspicion of "the apparent indolence of men of learning, and the small benefit the community seems to derive from their manner of life." Yet such narrow views failed to recognize the significance of science, he suggested, for learned men and institutions "are infinitely important in the support of a republic government." In this project, Masons were crucial: "To no order in society is the encouragement of schools and the advancement of knowledge more valuable than to the Fraternity." "The liberal arts and sciences were formerly taught in Lodges," he noted, "and brethren imparted instruction to their children and others with more attention than was found in any except masonic families."

For men attempting to free themselves from the narrow horizons of loyalty to family and locality, fraternal celebrations of cosmopolitanism and universal science offered a powerful counterimage. Schoharie, New York, brothers petitioned the grand lodge for a local body in 1795, writing that they hoped that the new lodge would help wipe "away those narrow and contracted Prejudices which are born in Darkness, and fostered in the Lap of Ignorance." Even at the height of the Quasi War with France three years later, the Reverend brother Preserved Smith counseled western Massachusetts brothers to avoid small-minded emphasis on local and family loyalties by considering "the world as one great republic." [30]

By linking brothers with the larger world, Masonry more particularly connected them to the American republic. Since Masonry was both "hostile to arbitrary power" and "republican in its elements," De Witt Clinton proclaimed in 1825 that the fraternity's "doctrines" were "the doctrines of patriotism." The fraternity and the broader education it encouraged rejected what Clinton had earlier identified as "the fundamental error of Europe"—restricting "the light of knowledge to the wealthy and the great." Clinton attacked even John Locke, the central figure in Enlightenment views of education, because his program was "professedly intended for the children of gentlemen." Clinton considered such a restriction "a radical error," "a monstrous heresy." "The general diffusion of education," he noted in 1823, was "the palladium [safeguard] of liberty." [31]

Learning seemed to protect liberty in two primary ways. First, it helped ensure enlightened policies that could protect and extend the Republic. Proper education combined the "mental and moral illumination" Clinton hailed as the product of printing and the fraternity. Nearly all Americans believed learning without moral discipline dangerous. But Masons, embodying the enlightened elements within republican theory, went further, stressing that morality needed education to survive. "Without the cultivation of our rational powers," Clinton warned, "we can entertain no just ideas of the obligations of morality or the excellencies of religion." Republican citizenship also required knowledge. "Institutions for the general diffusion of knowledge," brother George Washington argued in his Farewell Address, should be "an object of primary importance," since "in proportion as the structure of a government gives force to public opinion, it is essential that public opinion should be enlightened." The president had specifically requested that the topic be included in the document, calling education "one of the surest means of enlightening and giv[in]g just ways of think[in]g to our Citizens." "Ignorance is the cause as well as the effect of bad governments," Clinton argued more aphoristically in 1809, a formulation he liked so well that he merely changed the terms fourteen years later to suggest that "knowledge is the cause as well as the effect of good government."[32]

Knowledge created good government not only by encouraging enlightened participation but by helping reshape society according to republican principles. Widely available education would end the monopoly of power that had artificially reinforced the older aristocracies' monopoly on learning. Since, Clinton argued in 1828 as governor of New York, education provided "the obscure, the poor, the humble, the friendless, and the distressed, the power of rising to usefulness and acquiring distinction," the state should provide free college tuition to these groups. This action would "place the merits of transcendent intellect on a level, at least, with the factitious claims of fortune and ancestry." Perhaps not coincidentally, the non-Mason Thomas Jefferson used a Masonic metaphor to describe a similar plan. The schools and scholarships his program would create, Jefferson wrote in 1813, would prepare "worth and genius" from "every condition of life" to rise above the "Pseudo-aristocracy" who had only "wealth and birth" as qualifications." Thus, it would be "the key-stone of the arch of government."[33]

Post-Revolutionary brothers argued that their order did more than encourage and teach the values that allowed the success of the true aristoi. Masonry's membership criteria and internal rules exemplified republican social arrangements. Brotherhood, members argued, was open to "the candid and the wise of every nation . . . through every grade of life, from the monarch on the throne to the honest and industrious peasant that turns the globe." Even within the fraternity, Masons suggested, leadership depended, not upon social rank, but, as the initiation ritual of one degree argued, "upon superior attainments." "No Free-Mason should be elected to an office in consideration of his fortune or rank in society," South Carolina's Masonic Constitutions similarly declared, "but from a consciousness of his real merit and ability." Clinton's 1793 description of the fraternity even anticipated Jefferson's later discussion of a natural aristocracy. Masonry, Clinton argued, "admits of no rank except the priority of merit, and its only aristocracy is the nobility of virtue."[34]

Masonry might not have provided rigorous reading courses or academic training, but its support for and celebration of learning placed it at the center of widespread attitudes about the survival and prosperity of the new nation. Such a vision made Masonry a constituent part of the rise of liberty that seemed to have culminated in the formation of the American republic. "Is it not indisputable," asked Newburyport lawyer and later United States attorney general Caleb Cushing in 1826, "that Free Masonry has spread and flourished and become invigorated in the same proportion, and step by step, with the advancement of civilization?" "An intimate correspondence exists between them," he argued, since "they harmoniously co-operate in refining and purifying the human race."[35]

Other Americans, however, considered even this expansive vision too narrow. Masonry was not simply a sign of growing enlightenment; the order was actually its cause. The fraternity, insisted Preserved Smith, was "the great instrument of civilization." Washington newspaper editor Anne Royall, the widow of a brother, made the point with her characteristic bluntness: "If it were not for Freemasonry, the world would become a herd of savages; and more, if it had not been for Masonry, it never would have been anything else but savages."[36]

Masonry's connections with civilization and the Republic (created in large part by the new fraternal language of virtue, learning, and religion) received ultimate confirmation in the spread of cornerstone ceremonies. In the years after the Revolution, and especially after 1790, American officials increasingly called upon brothers to solemnize public enterprises. The fraternity anointed bridges, boundary stones, Erie Canal locks, and the Universities of Virginia and North Carolina. Government buildings, such as the Massachusetts and Virginia State Houses, and memorials to the creation of the Republic, such as the Bunker Hill and Concord Minutemen monuments, also were baptized by the symbolic corn, oil, and wine. Even churches received Masonic blessing.[37]

The new ceremonies reveal the double-edged character of the new Masonic rhetoric, its continuing ability to serve both inclusivity and exclusiveness. As brothers often pointed out, ideals of virtue, learning, and religion opened opportunities for people by challenging older criteria of exclusion; but these values also created new ways to limit high status. The fraternity's extraordinary standing in post-Revolutionary America rested in large part on its ability to negotiate the tricky requirements of elitism in a society that claimed equality as an essential goal.

The practice of Masonic cornerstone laying began in England, but it took on particular significance in a country attempting to redefine its metaphorical foundations.[38] The American ceremonies were part of a self-conscious attempt to create new images that could celebrate and inculcate Revolutionary ideals.

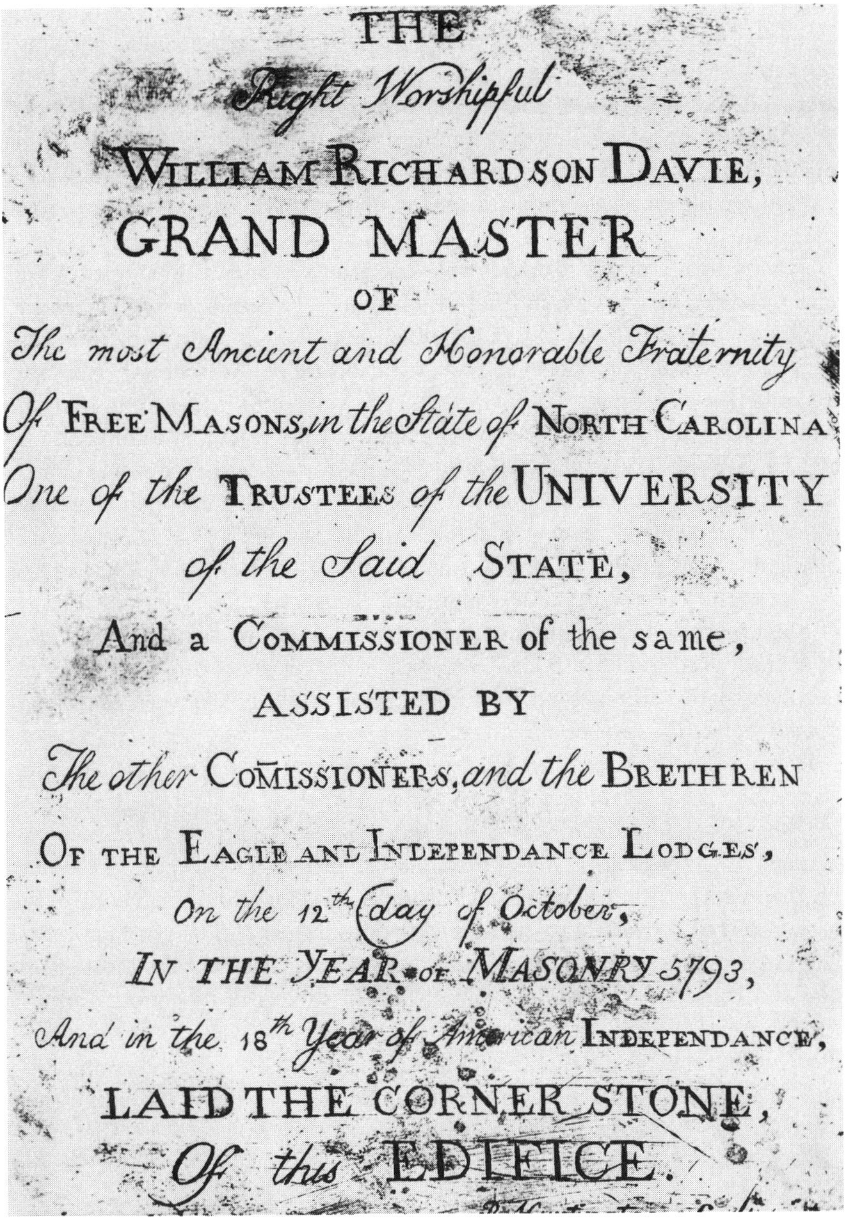

Figure 12. "Old East" Cornerstone Plate, University of North Carolina, Chapel Hill. *1793. North Carolina Collection, University of North Carolina Library at Chapel Hill*

During the colonial period, civic ritual had centered on the monarchy and its underpinnings—the elite and the church. The Revolution called each into question. The overthrow of the king's rule undermined the power of the hierarchy he had symbolized, and the separation of church and state weakened the ability of a single church or clergyman to represent religion itself. Rebuilding the foundations of society, post-Revolutionary America found Masonry's republican ideals and symbols a means of incarnating the "new order for the ages."

The fraternity could take this role because Masonry's organization and ideals seemed to prevent it from seeking any interest beyond that of the society as a whole. "The object for which MASONRY is instituted," the Reverend John Clark told Geneva, New York, brothers, "is none other than to make better and happier the human race." Masonry's national and worldwide membership, its lack of explicit exclusions, its voluntary nature, and its ancient origins all seemed to refute any suspicion of a desire for power or selfish advantage. At the same time, lodges kept out the unsuitable and carefully trained its members, making it difficult for designing men to use the fraternity against the public good. The fraternity fulfilled such high expectations, the Reverend Preserved Smith explained, because it sought "to unite all men of good morals, and enlightened understandings . . . by the great principles of virtue." "From such a union," Smith argued, "the interest of the Fraternity becomes that of all mankind." Another orator similarly identified Masons as "the associated friends of humanity." [39]

Even as they pledged their loyalty to republican values of equality, however, such claims paradoxically also allowed brothers to assert high standing for themselves. Orators often warned brothers that their role as symbolic exemplars required high admission standards. Instead of accepting everyone, brother George Hume Stewart told Baltimore Masons at the 1814 laying of the Masonic Hall cornerstone, the fraternity encouraged and taught high moral and intellectual standards by creating "select associations of the most exemplary individuals." "Every man cannot be a fit subject of its honors," argued the Reverend William Bentley in 1797. A person who was a "slave to prejudice" or "unable to separate the social character from the religious opinion" and "destitute of an ingenious mind in private life" could not "be enlightened by truth" or "exercise a rational and universal benevolence." Brothers also claimed that Masonic training increased this original superiority. According to a Vermont orator, Masonry "justly stamps an indelible mark of preeminence on its genuine professors, which neither chance, power, nor fortune can give." [40]

The address given by grand master Paul Revere at the July 4, 1795, laying of the cornerstone of the Massachusetts State House sums up the carefully shaped means by which Masons asserted this preeminence. Revere began his short talk (perhaps the only public address he ever made) by identifying the nation with the values brothers were already claiming for their fraternity. America was a country where "the Arts and Sciences are establishing themselves" and "where liberty has found a safe and secure abode." Revere then admonished brothers to "live within the compass of Good Citizens" in order to show "the World of Mankind . . . that we wish to stand upon a level with them, that when we part we may be admitted into the Temple where Reigns Silence and Peace." If Revere's talk explicitly spoke of equality and citizenship, his words and their setting also gave his fraternity a special position. The fraternity provided the language, the metaphors with which Revere addressed the public and dedicated the new symbol of the commonwealth. Just as important, it was the self-selected fraternity that stood on Beacon Hill dressed in ritual vestments who, along with the officially elected state governor, accepted "the cheers of the multitude and the booming of cannon."[41]

A newspaper account of the ceremony praised the day's orator, a non-Mason, as "truly republican." Masonic ceremonies and addresses made the same sort of claim. Like Jefferson's proposed school system, the fraternity's role as exemplar, priest, and teacher of the new order allowed it to create men "worthy to receive . . . the sacred deposit of the rights and liberties of their fellow citizens." As a minister told Revere and his officers just days before the Beacon Hill ceremony, Masons were "the Sons of REASON, the DISCIPLES of WISDOM, and the BRETHREN of Humanity."[42]

III. Around the Enlightened World

Clinton's 1806 description of Freemasonry as "co-extensive with the enlightened part of the human race" fitted not only his cosmopolitan vision of a free nation but his personal experience. Clinton became a Mason in Holland Lodge, a group originally founded in 1787 to work in the Dutch language that quickly became a center for New York City's lively cultural life. Lodge master William Irving, Jr., helped his non-Masonic brother Washington write *Salmagundi*. Another Irving brother also belonged to the lodge, as did the poet Fitz-Greene Halleck. Two organists (one of whom owned a music store) as well as a painter and the owner of a picture gallery featuring Shakespearean scenes also attended meetings. Besides Clinton himself, an important educational reformer and later the president of the Literary and Philosophical Society, the American Academy of Arts, and the New-York Historical Society, Holland Lodge also included another central figure in New York's intellectual life, John Pintard. Pintard, like Clinton, played an important role in establishing many of the city's intellectual institutions, from the American Bible Society and the Episcopalian General Theological Seminary to the Tammany Museum (for which another Holland Lodge member served as treasurer) and its successor the New-York Historical Society.[43]

Holland Lodge was unusual within the post-Revolutionary fraternity, attracting an exceptionally high proportion of learned, wealthy, and powerful men, but its members' cultural cosmopolitanism suggests key ways in which Masonic affiliation fitted into particular social settings. For men involved in artistic occupations, the fraternity allowed association with fellow artists and possible patrons as well as teachings that asserted the dignity of their professions. Masonic membership also reinforced the intellectual interests of men unable to participate in the richer cultural life of the nation's largest cities, helping men in provincial locations to identify themselves with the broader cosmopolitan world. Finally, the fraternity's ideas found a ready hearing among marginal men and women far from the elite circles of Holland Lodge. Boston's blacks and women found the fraternity a means of claiming full participation in the liberty and equality that many Americans celebrated as the foundations of enlightened society.

Masonry's cosmopolitan membership proved particularly attractive for men involved in the visual and performing arts. The colonial fraternity had included important silversmiths like Philip Syng, Jr., and Revere as well as engravers like Peter Pelham, stepfather of John Singleton Copley and presenter of one of the first musical concerts in the colonies. Post-Revolutionary lodges attracted an even greater proportion of cultural leaders. Holland Lodge's membership after 1800 included both Stephen Price, the most important theatrical manager of the period, and William Dunlap, the painter and writer whose pioneering dramatic work led to his being called "the father of the American stage." For such artistic men, the fraternity offered important benefits for their careers, providing fellowship with culturally aware men, increased status, and opportunities to gain business.

Theater people like Price and Dunlap often found the lodge a congenial place. Thomas Wade West, who received a Masonic funeral by Washington's Alexandria lodge less than half a year before Washington's own, set up an ambitious series of theaters in the South in the 1790s, even commissioning his fellow Mason Benjamin Henry Latrobe to design a new building in Richmond. By inviting his brother-in-law Matthew Sully to America, West also brought Sully's son Thomas, to be one of the most accomplished painters of next generation. In Philadelphia (where Thomas Sully eventually settled), the actor William Francis offered his dancing academy for meetings of the temporarily homeless grand lodge in 1802, two years after being reprimanded by that body for unauthorized use of lodge regalia on stage.[44]

Other types of artists also showed interest in the fraternity. After renting quarters for some years after 1802, the Pennsylvania grand lodge built one of the first Gothic Revival buildings in America. Designed by brother William Strickland, a young pupil of Latrobe and eventually a significant figure in his own right, the building completed in 1811 would later include emblematic figures by William Rush, the first American-born sculptor to gain national

renown. Musicians were similarly active in the fraternity. Boston lodges supplied many of the earliest members of the Handel and Haydn Society, including its first president and conductor. Brother William Rowson, who often
played trumpet at their concerts, also participated in the city's fledgling theater with his better-known wife, Susanna Rowson, author of the popular novel
Charlotte Temple.[45]

Masonry's attractions went beyond providing a place where creative artists
and cultural organizers could meet. For artists struggling to be regarded as
more than either skilled workmen or dangerous corrupters of public morality,
the fraternity's claims to public leadership and support of cosmopolitan values
helped reinforce their status. Furthermore, Masonic teaching celebrated the
arts, linking the order's beginnings to ancient architects equally conversant in
science and aesthetics. At the same time, Masonry served economic ends. It
first brought cultural entrepreneurs into contact with wealthy men with wide-
ranging interests. Samuel Maverick, son of Dunlap's engraving teacher and
lodge brother, included Masonic symbols in an 1816 advertisement, hoping to
gain fraternal patronage for his engraved calling cards. Other brothers placed
emblems on clocks, tavern signs, and liquor flasks for the use of Masons and
others.[46]

The lodge itself could even become a source of business. The great expansion of the post-Revolutionary fraternity along with increased attention
to internal decoration encouraged lodges to seek out men who could prepare jewels, lodge furniture, and membership certificates. Maverick engraved
certificates for Virginia as well as New York lodges. He also worked in partnership with the period's most active Masonic entrepreneur, Connecticut engraver Amos Doolittle. Forming alliances with artists in Albany, Philadelphia,
and New York, Doolittle and his associates created and sold printed aprons,
books, and certificates sometimes printed in Latin, French, or Spanish.[47]

These connections suggest that the fraternity should be considered part of
the post-Revolutionary art world—the structures and institutions that facilitated artistic production. At a time when popular suspicion of and indifference toward high culture also continued to be strong and academies providing
training and meeting places for established artists existed only sporadically
even in the largest cities, lodges provided a center for culturally active men
that both encouraged their ambitions and helped provide them with business.
Lodges did not offer academic instruction in the arts any more than in mathematics or literature, but brothers were pointing to something significant when
they claimed, as a Massachusetts orator did in 1798, that their order sought
to bring together men "by love of the polite arts." [48]

Nearly thirty years later, in 1826, brother Caleb Cushing reminded brothers
that they were "not only Masons, but Free Masons." The title was significant,
he argued, because it originally meant more than the possession of particu-

lar privileges. The early brothers "were also denominated *free*, because they soared above the prejudices of their co[n]temporaries, and were free in soul, free in the use of their intellectual powers, and free from the slavery of opinion, which palsied the minds of uninitiated men." Such a characterization seems to have been particularly meaningful to the young lawyer who had recently returned to his relatively provincial hometown of Newburyport. As a Harvard tutor, Cushing had sometimes been invited to "the great balls, and to parties in the fashionable circles," "a very great favor," he told his mother, because, despite his inability to dance, he could learn "how people look, dress, and behave in the best families." The eminent lawyer Daniel Webster, one of Cushing's mentors, commended his attempt to establish a law career first in Newburyport. Cushing noted in his diary the year before his Masonic oration that Webster considered "practice in a small town . . . very useful as a means of getting experience." But success in Newburyport should not be an end in itself. In the same conversation, Webster also warned that Cushing "ought always to keep in view the object of a permanent residence elsewhere." [49]

Masonry's connection with cosmopolitan culture proved particularly attractive for men outside the centers of intellectual life. Towns and villages (and even small cities) provided fewer opportunities for men who thought of themselves as part of the nation's cultural elite. Fraternal affiliation became a key means of asserting that standing. Just as it did for artists, lodges provided a means of meeting with like-minded men in a setting that valued their aspirations, brought them public prestige, and helped form international connections. These qualities were particularly significant in post-Revolutionary America, as an expanding communications network allowed growing numbers of Americans to seek participation in the international republic of letters that Masonry seemed to symbolize.

Such a broader vision seems to have been one of the key concerns of the Reverend William Bentley, the Congregational minister who resided in Salem, Massachusetts, all his adult life. In 1797, Bentley called upon the brotherhood to prepare an international Masonic history, contemplating the pleasures of viewing "the hospitable lodges distributed around the enlightened world . . . in one evening of meditation." Masonry provided a similarly cosmopolitan experience when he visited Boston in 1800 for the funeral commemoration of brother George Washington's death. Among his Masonic dining partners afterward were Paul Revere, Isaiah Thomas, and Jacob Perkins, an inventor who had already developed the leading method of preventing the counterfeiting of banknotes and would later print the world's first postage stamp. Bentley called it "a Feast . . . which the most exalted genius might enjoy with enthusiasm." [50]

Bentley's enthusiasm for Masonry is particularly significant, for the minister was one of the early Republic's most knowledgeable men, not just about the deeper (and slower-moving) intellectual currents of the learned world but about the faster eddies of politics and diplomacy. The learned New York brother John Pintard called Bentley's weekly summaries of world news—published first in a Salem paper—"the best brief chronicle of the times in this or perhaps the European world." His interest in German culture encouraged the later thinking of the Transcendentalists. Jefferson even sought him for the presidency of his new Virginia university.[51]

The fraternity's connection with cosmopolitan men can also be seen in the example of another brother even farther from the centers of intellectual life. Wilkins Tannehill, grand master of Tennessee and sometime mayor of Nashville, helped organize that town's first dramatic society in the 1810s. Brother John Eaton, later secretary of War, served as an officer; Andrew Jackson was also a member. At least one other significant Mason, Sam Houston, later president of Texas, appeared in an early production. Tannehill's interests went beyond the theater. In 1827, he published *Sketches of the History of Literature*. Although protesting that the substantial book was only a "work of humble pretensions" by a "*backwoodsman*," he included extensive discussions of ancient, medieval, and even Arabic texts.[52]

While still exceptional, the activities of Bentley and Tannehill were no longer as extraordinary as they would have been before the Revolution. Travel and trade eased the isolation of areas outside the major cities. Books, pamphlets, and newspapers were published in much greater quantities and in many different places; they were also distributed and republished much farther afield. The example of brother Isaiah Thomas, a participant at the 1800 dinner that so impressed Bentley, suggests this new range. One of the two most important publishers in the first generation after the Revolution, Thomas could by 1789 print more than thirty thousand copies of a single book—and still publish, besides a newspaper and magazine, some twenty-seven other titles the same year, including the first novel written by a native-born American (William Hill Brown's *Power of Sympathy*). Indeed, more books and pamphlets were printed in America during the first two decades after 1800 than in the previous two centuries. Such a torrent of materials required distribution beyond the commercial networks of colonial America. Thomas eventually created partnerships in at least four different states to sell his products.[53]

As a symbol of this new cosmopolitan reach, Masonry attracted men at nearly every level of this expanding communications network. Lexington, Kentucky, brother Alexander M'Calla served as the first librarian there as well as one of the town's postmasters. Printers and publishers, the linchpin of these changes, were often brothers as well. Isaiah Thomas also founded the American Antiquarian Society, the first national historical society, and pursued extensive research into the history of printing, leading Bentley to dub him "the father of the press in New England."[54] Although never rising to the grand master position held by Thomas and Tannehill, Hezekiah Niles served as master of a Baltimore lodge as well as editing one of the country's most cosmopolitan newspapers, the influential *Weekly Register*.

Of course, brothers' participation in this broadening cultural world varied greatly. John Woodworth, founder of the local library, author of a poetic satire on the 1797 Lyon-Griswold fight in Congress, and coauthor of the 1813 revision of state laws, presided over a Troy, New York, lodge that included the eccentric enthusiast Benjamin Gorton. Gorton's scriptural study led him to believe he had discovered the date of the Second Coming. According to nearly contemporary tradition, he rode through town that day announcing the impending event. Nathaniel Very, after resigning from his central Massachusetts lodge, commented that "not three" members of his lodge "knew Geometry from Demonology."[55]

For most brothers (as for most Americans), however, the expansion of civilization and knowledge seemed much more important than its continued limitations. Both Clinton and Cushing boasted that Masonry no longer remained restricted to, as Cushing suggested, "the gifted few, whose mental energy placed them in the fore ground of their age." Especially in towns and villages where the learned circles possible in major cities were seldom sustainable, Masonry's expansion and strength seemed to symbolize the period celebrated by Cushing as a time "when reason is no longer compelled to creep in cautious navigation along the shores of knowledge, but . . . boldly pushes her prow abroad upon the boundless ocean of space and time."[56]

Sometime in the 1790s, a number of Boston women came to Hannah Mather Crocker. Her friends, Crocker later recalled, were "very anxious" because their husbands were becoming Masons. More than the late evenings bothered the women; they feared that the fraternity might "injure their [husbands'] moral and religious sentiments." Crocker investigated. "To my great joy," she wrote, "I soon restored peace of mind to my anxious friends; and satisfied them respecting the value of the institution." Indeed, Crocker's faith in Masonry became so strong that she later wrote a fictional dialogue in which she persuades a doubting man to join the fraternity.[57]

Ultimately, the power of Masonry's new explanations can be seen most tellingly, not among artistic and cultural leaders or provincial intelligentsia, but in its significance to educated women and ex-slaves in post-Revolutionary Boston. For Hannah Mather Crocker and Prince Hall, just as much as for Clinton and Cushing, the fraternity's close connection to learning, virtue, and religion offered a set of vital ideas that spoke deeply to their situations and identities. Masonic values could even be used to challenge the injustices of the dominant culture, an ability seen in the experiences of Prince Hall and the "African Lodge" he headed.

According to the learned Salem minister William Bentley, Prince Hall was "the leading African of Boston." Born into slavery in 1735, Hall received his freedom in 1770 and then lived and worked as a leather dresser in his native Boston. His leadership in the black community (emancipated over the course of the 1780s) led him to prepare a number of petitions against slavery and the slave trade. Hall's fraternal affiliation began with the Revolution. Along with a number of other Boston blacks, he was made a Mason by a British soldier in a Masonically irregular action. Hall went on to form African Lodge, gaining a charter from England in 1785. Later he assumed the title of grand master to provide Masonic authority for black lodges in Providence and Philadelphia during the 1790s and 1800s, groups that included the Philadelphia minister Absalom Jones, the country's first black Episcopalian priest. Hall's Masonic group suggests a similar social position. Boston's black brothers were not a random sample of the African-American community. Although clearly none ranked in the upper levels of the city's society, the members, like their white brothers, possessed high rank within their own group. African Lodge Masons, Bentley noted, were "many grades above the common blacks of Boston." [58]

Masonry provided Hall with a public identity and a platform for speaking to the community. Although Boston's white brothers refused to accept fully the legitimacy of Hall's lodge, contemporary references to him almost always included his Masonic standing. Jeremy Belknap, the learned Boston minister, identified Hall to a correspondent solely as "the grand master of the black Lodge." Even the Boston tax records of 1788 and 1789 note him as a "Free Mason" and "Worshipful Grand Master." Masonry also allowed Hall a public voice. A sermon by the chaplain of the lodge appeared in print in 1789 after revisions by Hall; he published his own Masonic addresses in 1792 and 1797. Such standing as a community spokesperson was generally available to blacks only through religious office; significantly, historians for many years wrongly believed Hall a Methodist lay minister as well as a Mason.[59]

If the fraternity created a platform, its teachings provided the moral authority to challenge the marginal status of his race. The "two grand pillars of Masonry," Hall wrote in 1782, were "love to God and universal love to all mankind." For Hall, Masonic connections with religion and fraternity were more than inert commonplaces of post-Revolutionary ideology. These values served as a means of denouncing Boston's treatment of black Americans. The close ties between Masonry and Christianity, Hall argued, gave black brothers a genealogy that placed them at the center of the history of Christianity and learned culture. As Masons, they were descended from the African Queen of Sheba — received with friendship and equality by King Solomon, the legendary Masonic grand master — and from the Knights of Malta, a group considered a forerunner of the Masons. The Knights, Hall argued, very probably had African members, since "at that day . . . there was an African church, and perhaps [it was] the largest Christian church on earth." [60]

Even more distinctively, Hall emphasized the leaders of the early church, mentioned in two of the three African Lodge addresses and a long series of biographies entered by Hall into the lodge records. The church fathers were not Masons, Hall admitted, but they offered proof of African learning and religion, of full participation in Western and Christian history. The early Christians of North Africa (including Augustine, Tertullian, Cyprian, and others) became for Hall "some of our fore-fathers . . . who were not only examples to us, but to many of their nobles and learned." Thus, the chaplain of Hall's group noted, "the truly great will never disdain to take an African Brother by the Hand for they [know] there hath been . . . great and learned men of that Nation." In this long perspective, even African slavery was just an episode. The present position of blacks "is not a just cause of our being despised" by other peoples, "for there is not one of them that hath no[t] be[e]n in bondages under sum Nation or other from the Jews down to the English Nation."[61]

If Masonry's religious elements encouraged blacks to revalue themselves and their history, Hall's use of the fraternity's other "grand pillar," brotherly love, was directed outward at white society. By invoking fraternity as a member of an international brotherhood, Hall gained the moral authority necessary to challenge the inconsistencies of a white orthodoxy that praised equality, religion, and fraternity yet treated blacks as inferiors. A long list of biblical examples of kindness to strangers ends with "our blessed Lord" who was willing to "call us . . . his brothers." Anticipating the objection that these religious exemplars were not all Masons, Hall retorts that not all were even Christians "and their benevolence to strangers ought to shame us both, that there is so little, so very little of it to be seen in these enlightened days."[62]

A similar pattern can be seen in the ideas of Hannah Mather Crocker. Crocker's social position differed greatly from that of Hall. While Hall had been born a slave, Crocker was a descendant of the preeminent ministerial family of Massachusetts. Samuel Mather was her father; Cotton, her grandfather. While Hall's lodge included many who could not even read, Crocker's group developed out of a number of women studying ancient languages. Yet the two used Masonry in much the same way—as a means of rethinking the status of their group and challenging the powerful to do likewise.[63]

As might be expected of a Mather, Crocker's 1790s investigation of Masonry led to more than an intellectual answer. Determining to her and her friends' satisfaction the value of the fraternity, Crocker went on to form them into "a regular lodge." Women, of course, were not allowed into orthodox lodges, but Crocker's group claimed to be "founded on the original principles of true ancient masonry, so far as was consistent for the female character." According to Crocker's later account, the organization even received some male encouragement. Although her Masonic newspaper pieces "gave umbrage to a few would-be-thought Masons; . . . by the most respectable part of them we were treated like Sisters." Crocker served as mistress of the organization, calling it St. Ann's, after the mother of Mary.[64]

The group, despite its invocation of a saint, was no deviation from the moralistic tradition of the Mathers. St. Ann's was not a frivolous group; rather, it was an improving society, what her grandfather called an "essay to do good." The personal morality taught by the fraternity through its metaphorical language received particular attention. "Within *due Square*," Crocker noted later of the experience, "we marked our lives by the parallel line of integrity." Crocker, like Hall, also used Masonry to challenge the position of women within Boston society. Masonry first encouraged women to seek education. "The prime inducement for forming the lodge," she wrote, "was a desire for cultivating the mind in the most useful branches of science, and cherishing a love of literature." In this, Crocker saw the group as pioneering a new path: "At that period," she recalled in 1815, "female education was at a very low ebb. If women could even read and badly write their name it was thought enough for *them,* who by some were esteemed as only 'mere domestick animals.'" The lodge seems to have been organized within a group of women who "even then, dared to study the languages," a particularly significant activity for Crocker, whose father had stressed the importance of ancient languages as the only means to determine the proper meaning of Scripture. Masonry's moral teachings and connection with the great and learned women of the past—like Hall, Crocker saw the Queen of Sheba as a symbolic precursor—helped spur Boston women's desire to gain the learning denied to them. "I have reason to think," Crocker claimed later, "this institution gave the first rise to female education in this town, and our sex a relish for improving the mind."[65]

Masonic ideas, while helping to reshape women's ideas of themselves, could also be used to challenge male prejudices. Like Hall, Crocker used Masonry's ideals—what she called "that universal benevolence, which would promote 'peace on earth and good will to men'"—to question received views of women's capacity.[66] One of her published Masonic poems notes the difference between heaven, where Masonic brothers and sisters will meet in equality, and Boston, where Masonry's "sacred plan" was

> Held *here* by man,
> as far beyond *our* reach.[67]

St. Ann's Lodge was not as public or as strong a challenge to accepted thinking as the African Lodge. Symbolically, Crocker's first poetic address appeared in the newspaper prefaced by a letter of introduction from a male patron. Furthermore, by the time Crocker published her pamphlets on Freemasonry and women's intellectual capacity in the 1810s, her ideas about women were on their way to becoming orthodoxy. But St. Ann's Lodge cannot be dismissed as unimportant. According to Crocker, Masonry, along with the Christian religion to which she saw it closely allied, played a central role in the Revolutionary-era transformation of women's position. The fraternity, Crocker argued, helped women throw off the "cramp to genius" imposed by false expectations and helped them see that "they were given by the wise author of nature, as not only helps-meet, but associates and friends, not slaves to men."[68]

Just as much as the 1793 Capitol cornerstone ceremony, the Masonic writings of Hall and Crocker reveal the power of post-Revolutionary Masonic explanations. Of course, an extraordinary social distance existed between President Washington, universally admired as leader of the Revolution, and Hall, who, like other Boston blacks, suffered "daily insults . . . in the streets of Boston." But for each the same set of ideas, the virtue, learning, and religion that brothers increasingly identified with their fraternity, proved deeply meaningful—and a powerful means of reshaping their society. For Washington and other white brothers, Masonry helped challenge the exclusivity of the colonial aristocracy by creating new standards of judgment that helped establish brothers as exemplary leaders. For Hall's and Crocker's challenge to post-Revolutionary America's continuing exclusions, Masonry offered moral ideals and standards that helped them rethink their status and encourage others to do likewise. The same ideals that could be used by the president of the United States in 1793 to dedicate the nation's Capitol could be used the previous year to challenge the marginal status of America's most oppressed citizens by a self-educated ex-slave who also could call Washington his brother.[69]

CHAPTER SIX

An Appearance of Sanctity

Religion, 1790–1826

By 1818, when his lectures appeared in book form as *A System of Speculative Masonry*, brother Salem Town had decisively rejected his boyhood fears of the fraternity. Growing up in 1780s and 1790s Belchertown, Massachusetts, the young Town often heard warnings from his mother about the "wicked society" she believed involved in the "black art, or some of its kindred magical alliances." The mistrust expressed by his mother, he suggested in his book, was now possible only "in the abodes of ignorance, where the genial rays of science have but dimly shone." "It is no secret," he proclaimed, "that Masonry is of divine origin." Before Christianity made the truth known to all, Freemasonry "was divinely taught to men divinely inspired" in order to preserve true religion. God's revelation of himself through the Bible and Jesus Christ transformed Masonry into a "speculative" group unconnected with stonework, but its ultimate principles remained the same. Masonic ideas, he argued, still "have the same co-eternal and unshaken foundation, contain and inculcate, in substance, the same truth, and propose the same ultimate end, as the doctrines of Christianity taught by Divine Revelation." [1]

Town's enthusiastic embrace of Masonry as what a Pennsylvania grand master called "a religious institution" marked the culmination of an unexpected transformation.[2] Colonial descriptions of the fraternity primarily stressed its universality and its broad acceptability rather than its religious merits. This situation would change dramatically after the Revolution. Like Town, a substantial number of Masonic brothers (and even non-Masons) came to see their order not simply as representing universal moral principles but as a unique order that fulfilled the purposes and proclaimed the truths of Christianity. As a representative of the Virginia grand lodge told a new Masonic body in 1826, their meeting within a church was entirely appropriate, for religion and Masonry were "upheld by the same Omnipotence—nurtured by the same divine influence—inspired by the same God!" [3]

The fraternity's new position grew out of several related developments. A broad spectrum of post-Revolutionary American believers embraced religious attitudes that made Masonry's nonsectarianism and promotion of active benevolence outside the church an integral part of their religious outlook. At the same time, brothers began to invest Masonry with explicitly Christian values and beliefs. These claims would be validated and strengthened by the growing numbers of ministers and church members who joined the order.

The widespread attempt to connect Masonry with Christianity was part of what might be called the politics of the sacred, the struggle to enshrine certain beliefs and attitudes as above criticism and able to convey holiness. Masonry moved within the boundaries of the sacred for many Americans largely because it fitted into and provided support for a particular part of the religious spectrum. For cosmopolitan Americans eager to avoid both a narrow and parochial sectarianism on one hand and an equally dangerous nonbiblical rationalism, Masonry seemed to reinforce an enlightened middle way.

These new links to religion formed some of the most powerful, and the most troubling, elements of the fraternity's new, post-Revolutionary identity. The connections forged in this period reinforced Masonic claims to teach the morality that undergirded the Republic. But, as Town suggested, Masonry could also be seen as something more than a human institution promoting the public good; it might itself be sacred. If pretensions to Masonic piety were powerful, however, they also provoked more serious objections than any other part of the fraternity's post-Revolutionary rhetoric. Some sectarian religious groups explicitly forbade fraternal involvement, seeing Masonry's inclusiveness as a threat to their own exclusivity. Less suspicious Christians held back from believing the fraternity and religion synonymous but accepted Masonry as a powerful aid to the church. Yet even among the most evangelical denominations, large numbers of believers came to view Masonry as what one brother termed "the herald of universal peace and tranquillity," the harbinger of the coming millennium.[4]

The vigorous religious attack on Masonry after 1826 not only successfully challenged this close identification between church and lodge but also obscured its earlier power and widespread acceptance. Contemporaries, however, knew better. As the anti-Masonic Baptist Barre Association realized in 1830, they were fighting "the alliance of Free Masonry with the churches."[5]

1. Neutral Ground

This alliance was not forged by Masonic actions alone. At the same time brothers moved vigorously to identify their order with Christianity, changes within religion made the association plausible. During the years after the Revolution, a wide spectrum of religious thought moved toward the enlightened ideals represented in Freemasonry, a development summed up in an address given by New York grand master De Witt Clinton in 1823.

Clinton's address praised the "preeminent merits" of the organization. It served, he noted, as "neutral ground, on which all the contending sects of Christendom may assemble in peace" around a "common center." Despite differences in "doctrine or discipline," these various persuasions "must all, notwithstanding, recognize the divine origin, and the sacred character of the Bible." Such agreement united "in the bonds of friendship and charity all their cultivators without regard to kindred, sect, tongue, or nation."[6]

Clinton's address drew upon a well-rehearsed Masonic language that since its early-eighteenth-century English beginnings had praised Masonry as "the center of union." But Clinton was not describing the fraternity. Rather, he was speaking as vice-president of the American Bible Society. His description of that group reveals an increasing interpenetration of discourses, a development of common ground between ideals of Masonry and a wide range of post-Revolutionary religious positions. To many Christians in these years, the nonsectarian friendship and active benevolence symbolized by Masonry increasingly lay at the heart of their religious commitments.

These values, however, were not universally shared. Many religious groups continued to fear that cooperation with outsiders might dilute the all-important identification of believers with their local church. The issue of Masonry revealed the fault lines that divided visions of the church's social relationships and responsibilities. Proponents of Masonry celebrated cooperative activity as a means of enlightening the world; opponents believed they needed to preserve a select few from its clutches. As a group that claimed to promote Christian piety, benevolence, and fraternity outside the church and boasted of its opposition to strict theological boundaries, Masonry challenged the claims to exclusive ultimate truth and the complete loyalty asserted by sectarian religious groups. The close connections between this sectarianism and opposition to Masonry can be seen in discussions within the Shaftesbury Association of Baptists located in western Vermont and eastern New York.[7]

"For a number of years," a contemporary Baptist historian noted, the Shaftesbury Association "was considerably occupied in discussing" Freemasonry. The question of Baptist membership in the fraternity first arose in 1798, when representatives voted to require association members "to desist" from Masonic activities "for the peace of the churches." Baptists who "continue obstinately in such practice ought to be rejected from fellowship." Participation, they argued in biblical terms, was "sinning against the weak brethren," because it tempted more scrupulous church members to act against their conviction that Masonry was evil. Yet even this forceful decision did not satisfy everyone. Disgruntled members complained that other associations continued to send delegates who were Masons to Shaftesbury meetings. In 1804, the association decided not to press the issue further. Reiterating their opposition to Baptist membership in the fraternity, they also reaffirmed the autonomy of other associations.[8]

The Shaftesbury Association decisions reveal some of the central characteristics of religious hostility to Masonry. Like most official opposition,
the Shaftesbury Association met far from cosmopolitan centers. Attacks on
Masonry seem to have been particularly strong in western New England
(where Salem Town had grown up), North Carolina, and western Pennsylvania. Religious affiliations also influenced the pattern of hostility. Although
a few Congregational and Presbyterian churches opposed Masonry, official
action was concentrated among Baptists. A North Carolina Baptist and Masonic brother noted as late as 1825, "I have long known that the generality of
[Baptists] entertain no very favorable view of the Masonic institution."[9]

The Shaftesbury Baptists were typical as well in their explanations. Church
harmony provided the rationale for nearly all official actions against the fraternity. Noting "the tender feelings of their brethren," the Primitive Baptist
Neuse Association of North Carolina declared in 1819 that Masons and prospective Masons in their group "would Do well to . . . appreciate the importance of maintaining Christian union."[10] The Baptist Church of Addison,
Vermont, "excluded" a member who maintained his Masonic affiliation after
an 1814 church vote, complaining that his persistence proved "that he is more
attached to Masonry . . . than . . . to the peace and harmony of the Church
of Christ." With the church battling a hostile world, internal dissent based
on loyalty to outsiders was something akin to treason, collaboration with the
ungodly enemy. The 1820 Pittsburgh Presbyterian Synod warned against accepting an order that "embraced with equal affection the Pagan, the Deist,
the Turk and the Christian" during this "present crisis of the kingdom of God
with the kingdom of darkness."[11]

The sectarian emphasis on close-knit fraternity reveals as well the limitations of religious proscription. "Weaker brethren" who believed Masonry
intrinsically evil could only be successful beyond their local group by citing
the dangers to internal unity. The North Carolina Primitive Baptist decision
carefully asserted, "We as an association Do not profes to know any thing
about masonry and therefore would not presume to Justify nor Condem the
principles thereof." The Shaftesbury Association similarly remarked that it
knew of "no moral evil in joining with the Masons" and would say only that
"a *number* of our brethren, and *some* of our churches . . . cannot walk in fellowship with" active Masons. These careful preambles suggest that outright
condemnation, although clearly the goal of some members, was controversial.
As Baptist historian David Benedict noted of the Shaftesbury deliberations in
1813, Masonry "was a question of . . . a very embarrassing nature" since "it
could not be proved" that fraternal membership "violated any moral rule."[12]

The issue of Masonry was difficult as well because membership seldom
raised such suspicions outside rural areas. The prominent Baptist minister
Samuel Stillman had addressed Boston Masons as early as 1785, allowing his
sermon to be published. The Rhode Island historian Benedict clearly found the

Shaftesbury actions somewhat awkward. Expecting other associations not to send Masons to the Shaftesbury meetings, he commented, "was not the most grateful to some members of corresponding Associations, who had been let further into the secrets of Masonry, than their proscribing brethren." Benedict judged that the Shaftesbury Baptists had invested "much labour and time spent to little purpose": they "manifested some part of wisdom" in their deliberations, but "they showed by far the most when they gave [them] up." [13]

The 1821 General Assembly of the Presbyterian Church exhibited a similar lack of wider sympathy when it took up the Pittsburgh presbytery's complaint against Masonry. Although a committee of the national body discussed the petition at "considerable length," the subject was "indefinitely postponed." The assembly made the decision, a newspaper piece claimed, "deeming it inexpedient to decide upon a subject on which they did not possess sufficient information, and considering that some of their own pious and excellent members belonged to the Masonic fraternity." "We deem their 'indefinite postponement,' " commented another editor more pointedly, "only as a gentle mode of reprobating an act of their misguided brethren." [14]

Attempting to preserve the all-important identification of believers with the local church, sectarians rejected the cooperative action among Christians that others saw as a major religious advance. The General Assembly had already argued that united action among people of different beliefs advanced the coming of God's kingdom—not, as the Pittsburgh group suggested, hindered it. To more cosmopolitan Presbyterians, Masonry's ideals of nonsectarianism and organized benevolence expressed essential methods of Christian witness. The growing power of these ideas played a key role in reshaping post-Revolutionary Masonry's religious standing.

Masonry first represented an attack on religious exclusivity. The fraternity's opposition to religious discussion within the lodge had originally sought primarily to avoid arguments. Now it seemed a positive virtue, an attempt to grasp essential truth rather than a desire for a lowest common denominator. The fraternity, Clinton argued in 1794, rejected "the contracted views of faction" as well as "sect." Its beliefs were not "the religion of an hour, a priest, a sect." "A lodge," the grand master of North Carolina noted in 1816, "is, perhaps, the only asylum upon earth where the benevolent feelings serve as a principle of union among men of different religions and politics." [15]

Masonry's opposition to sectarian exclusivity, forged in seventeenth-century English dissension, gained new cultural force in post-Revolutionary America. With Christianity facing disestablishment and growing diversity as well as a seeming threat of heresy and even complete infidelity, many believers judged the beliefs and moral standards shared by all Christian groups more important than their disagreements over specific dogmas. Parochial views of truth now seemed particularly dangerous because they hindered the spread of religion and the morality it encouraged. As a result, churches began to speak of themselves as "denominations," distinguished from each other by name but sharing the essence of Christianity. At its most evangelical extreme, this view led to groups calling themselves simply "Christians" who shunned human titles and claimed to find guidance solely in the Bible. This sense of a larger Christian unity, however, spread far beyond these small groups, permeating the mainline orthodox denominations and spreading as well into more populist groups. Bible societies, spreading nonsectarian Christianity by distributing the text of the Bible rather than human commentaries, provided a popular means of expressing this new sense of common purpose. "Within the hallowed circle of their operation," noted the Presbyterian General Assembly in 1817, "all denominations of Christians have met." [16]

Like its celebration of a common foundation, Masonry's promotion of benevolence through united action expressed increasingly popular ideas. As an international fraternity in what the 1817 Presbyterian General Assembly called "the age of christian charity," Masonry seemed to embody this spirit.[17] Thus a song written by novelist and Masonic wife Susanna Rowson for performance at an 1812 Boston Masonic benefit asked:

> Who feels this blest impulse, to mortals so dear?
> Who cheers the lone widow, and wipes off the tear?
> Who raises the mourner, the orphan protects?
> 'Tis the true loyal Mason, who never neglects
> With fervour to join, in a work so divine.[18]

Boston's Baptist leader Samuel Stillman, although not a brother, had already recognized these claims to divine activity. He included the fraternity in his 1801 list of the city's "Charitable Institutions." [19]

Ultimately these cosmopolitan attitudes about what was divine work involved not just the ideal of toleration and cooperation but a view of the world at odds with sectarian expectations, a division seen in the conflicting assessments of the church made by the two bodies involved in the Presbyterian controversy. "The general aspect of its churches is dark and calls for deep humiliation and sorrows," the Pittsburgh synod warned after the national decision about the fraternity, largely because of "organized infidelity." Their opinion directly contradicted the 1817 assessment of the denomination's national body, which had judged that "the general aspect of the church of God has never been more favorable within our knowledge, than at the present time." Indeed, the General Assembly pronounced in 1819—the year before the Pittsburgh synod condemnation—that "infidelity, as formerly practiced in our country, can scarcely be said to exist." "We have, perhaps, never, Dear Brethren, been called to address you, when we had fewer causes of mourning grief than at present." "The day of Millennial Blessedness," they predicted, would "soon . . . burst with all its *splendour* upon our *world*." [20]

For the growing numbers of post-Revolutionary Christians who expected millennial dawn rather than darkness, Masonry could play an important role in hastening the spreading light. Its values and activities encouraged the unity, morality, and benevolence necessary for the advance of Christianity and civilization. Although some parochial groups found Masonic brotherhood a challenge to their fellowship, other, less sectarian believers believed the order helped lay the foundation of a Christian society. Since "charity . . . and . . . Brotherly-Love . . . are fundamental principles of both," an Episcopal clergyman declared in 1823, "Genuine Free Masonry is a powerful auxiliary to the religion I profess."[21]

II. Dedicated to the Worship of God

Changing religious values made possible the alliance between Masonry and the churches, but developments within the fraternity helped seal the union. At the same time post-Revolutionary American Christians increasingly accepted the values represented within Masonry, the fraternity itself embraced Christianity. Public addresses and secret rituals proclaimed Masonic piety. Lodges increasingly encouraged religious activities. The result was a dramatic reorientation. Rather than universal love, brothers now began to argue that religion formed the fraternity's "grand cornerstone."[22]

This new sense of religious purpose was apparent right from the start of many lodge meetings. New York brothers often began their assemblies by praying "that all our doings may tend to thy glory and the salvation of our souls." They further prayed God "that our new brother may dedicate his life to thy service," hoping "that he may, with the secrets of Free Masonry, be able to unfold the mysteries of Godliness and Christianity." The prayer ended by noting that these requests were made "in the name and for the sake of JESUS CHRIST, our Lord and Saviour."[23]

In the years after the Revolution, the fraternity developed new expressions of explicit piety. Early speculative Masonry had presented itself as a recovery of ancient wisdom, imparting deep truths that only incidentally included religious belief. According to early exposés, Masonic ceremonies of the 1720s seldom included prayers or Bible readings. Public explanations also gave precedence to religious universality rather than close identification with particular beliefs. This situation began to change in the years surrounding the Revolution. New rituals developed or adapted in America prescribed extensive prayers and Bible readings. In the additional degrees that expanded upon the first three, Biblical settings and narratives became increasingly common. The Royal Arch ceremony alone required reading of more than a dozen Scripture passages. Knights Templars initiates viewed a representation of the Crucifixion and solemnly swore, under pain of death, to fight for the Christian religion.[24]

As the Templar ritual suggests, the fraternity's new self-description stressed

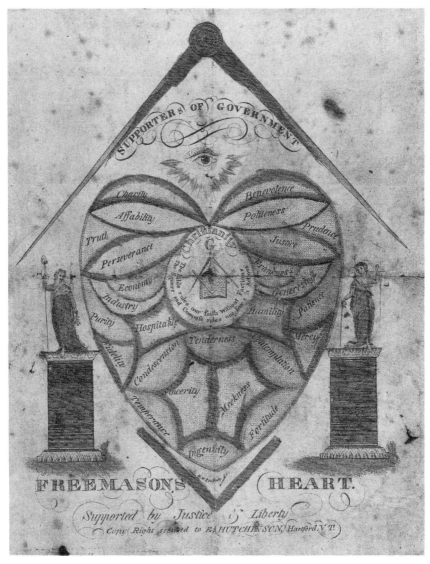

Figure 13. Freemason's Heart Supported by Justice and Liberty. *M. M. Peabody,
Hartford, Vermont, circa 1818–1820. Courtesy American Antiquarian Society*

Masonry's identification not simply with religion in general but with explicit
Christianity. Members continued to celebrate Masonic universality and to accept non-Christians into their lodges. But even celebrations of openness often
labeled American brothers "Christian Freemasons."[25] Brothers increasingly
argued that a refusal to accept revelation was impossible for a lodge member.
"A deistical mason," argued a Connecticut Episcopalian priest and brother in

1807, "is a solecism, and can no more join in the service of the lodge than he can in the service of the church." Rather than abandoning religion, brothers suggested, their fraternity actually brought people closer to its essentials. Elaborating the most common description of Masonry's religious position, Baltimore brothers in 1825 toasted the fraternity as "the Handmaid of Religion—like Martha and Mary, both devoted to the service of the Master." The popular metaphor of the personal servant made Masonry clearly subordinate, but it also claimed the sanctity that came from close interaction. According to the Reverend Ezra Ripley, the Unitarian minister of Concord, Massachusetts, the fraternity was "a bright, but lesser LIGHT" than the Bible, "dispersing its rays where revelation is not known, and operating in concert with it, where it is enjoyed." [26]

Some brothers found even these claims too restricting. They argued that Masonry did more than fulfill divine purposes: it was itself a sacred institution. Vermont's Episcopal bishop claimed in 1807 that attacks on the order had failed because Masons "gave their hearts to God." A decade later, Maryland's grand master described the new Baltimore Masonic Hall as "dedicated to the worship of God" and "intended to celebrate His praise." [27]

Brothers increasingly moved to bring their activities into line with these claims. Grand lodges admitted ministers into the fraternity free of charge.[28] Masonic halls were opened for religious activities. The Pennsylvania grand lodge organized a Sunday school in its building to teach Bible reading to illiterate adults. According to one Maryland lodge in 1829, its planned hall was to serve "not only a means of accommodation to the Lodge . . . but of advancing the interests of Masonry and religion generally." "The basement story of the building," they noted, "is intended for a place of public worship, free for all denominations of Christians." The earlier Lynchburg, Virginia, hall served the same purpose. After Methodist bishop Francis Asbury preached there, the building hosted groups of Baptists, Episcopalians, Reformed Methodists, and New School Presbyterians.[29]

The strongest indication of Masonry's new sense of religious purpose, however, lay, not in explicit claims or meeting places, but in the attempts of some grand lodges to institute religious tests despite the explicit prohibition of all previous Masonic teaching. After 1823, Tennessee initiates declared their belief in "God and a future state of rewards and punishments." The Maryland grand lodge in the early 1800s considered requiring all initiates to affirm the Bible "as the will of God revealed to men." The proposal failed, but only after two years of "considerable discussion." [30]

These extraordinary changes suggest the role Masonry was coming to play in the post-Revolutionary attempt to reshape religious boundaries. If the nonsectarian side of Masonic discourse placed it in opposition to narrow localism, the fraternity's newly explicit Christianity helped erect another set of limits. Increasingly, brothers stressed that their broad-minded toleration and inter-

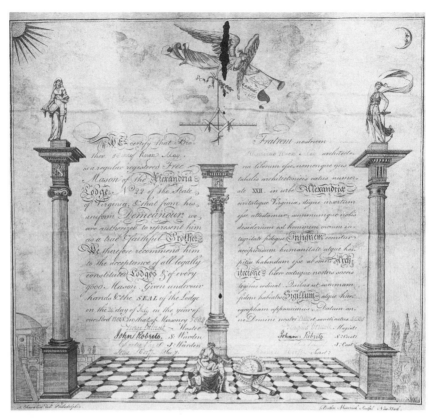

Figure 14. Membership Certificate, Alexandria, Virginia, Lodge. Lodge once headed
by George Washington. *Engraved by Peter Rushton Maverick, New York, circa
1789–1792. Courtesy American Antiquarian Society*

national brotherhood did not allow the rationalist extreme of rejecting revelation and all religious authority. In this new emphasis, brothers drew not only
upon long-standing fraternal ideas that linked the order to the Bible and biblical times but also upon a powerful new cultural impetus. For many influential
Christian leaders in the years after the Revolution, the greatest danger now
seemed to be, not popular superstition or corrupt Christianity, but complete
irreligion. Disestablishment and the popularization of deistic ideas, especially
in the midst of the period's social, political, and religious ferment, seemed to
make the denial of Christianity a real possibility. For some orthodox religious
leaders, these fears centered on the image of the anarchistic French Jacobins.
Masonry represented a much broader spectrum of views, but its new religious orientation played a similar role in marking the limits of the sacred. The
fraternity first rejected deism and skepticism because they jettisoned crucial
elements of Christianity. At the same time, Masonry also opposed the narrow
views of truth promoted by sectarians.[31]

The new alignment made possible by these changes allowed brothers to place their fraternity within the realm of the sacred, even, Salem Town believed, as a crucial part of the coming "day of Millennial Blessedness" expected by the Presbyterians. "A happy Masonic millennial period will soon commence," Town predicted, "to the inexpressible joy of all the inhabitants of the earth." "Speculative Free-Masonry," he wrote enthusiastically, "is about to enter a very glorious and happy era when this institution will appear in beautiful garments, shine forth in the glory and excellence of her principles, the world be enlightened by her radiance, united in friendship, and rejoice together as brethren of one common family." [32]

III. Spiritual Masonry

"The unexampled spread of Masonry through our country of late years," the 1831 Massachusetts Antimasonic Convention complained, resulted from the fraternity's successful attempt to ensnare ministers and church members. According to these opponents, religious suspicions had once kept church members from the fraternity. "But few if any of the members of the lodge," the report asserted, "were found in the churches of Christ." "Not many years since," however, the grand lodge voted to allow ministers to enter without fee: "The pastors of churches being thus gained, an appearance of sanctity was thrown around the Institution, which gave it a credit and currency with serious people, which it had never before obtained." As a result, "multitudes around them, emboldened by such examples, viewed the Institution with a favorable eye." [33]

As opponents realized, the alliance between Masonry and the churches involved a third element beyond religious ideology and fraternal activity. The plausibility of Masonry's claim to sanctity ultimately rested upon the increasing involvement of active church members. Although the clergy were perhaps not as influential in this process as Antimasons suggested, still, church members looking for guidance on membership would have discovered prominent ministers from a wide variety of denominations active in the fraternity, often in very public circumstances.

As the report also suggested, this relationship sometimes got off to a rocky start. Particularly in rural areas where Masonry arrived only after the Revolution, religious suspicions were common. The Illuminati controversy of the late 1790s brought many of these fears to the surface. Yet these concerns abated markedly over the next years. The Reverend Thomas Robbins, although never a Masonic brother, illustrates these suspicions—and their decline.

In June 1799, a Vermont lodge invited Robbins to its annual celebration. The Connecticut Congregationalist, then on a preaching tour, attended but was not impressed. Although the members "were pretty orderly," he noted grudgingly in his diary, "still I hate Masonry." The main influence on his thinking seems to have been his previous summer's reading of John Robison's *Proofs of a Conspiracy against All Religions and Governments of Europe*, which located the origins of the French Revolution "in the Secret Meetings of the Free Masons." Robbins found utterly convincing Robison's charges that Continental Freemasonry had been corrupted by the atheistic Illuminati (an actual, though short-lived, secret order opposed to the Roman Catholic church founded in Bavaria in 1776 that died out within a decade). These Illuminati-infected brothers then allegedly went on to plot the further spread of infidelity. "*Laus Deo*" ("Praise to God"), he wrote in his diary, "that that conspiracy has been detected." [34]

When Jedidiah Morse had first raised American fears of the Illuminati in May 1798, he meant more to awaken people to the dangers of the Francophile Jeffersonian party than to attack the American fraternity.[35] Morse, speaking as a staunch Federalist in the midst of a cold war with France and a heated Jeffersonian attack on the government, argued that Robison had revealed the reason for this crisis—a French conspiracy to use the Jeffersonian party against government and religion. Morse, however, did not indict the Masons as conspirators. He had already given a prayer at a Masonic function the previous year and, less than two months after his call to alarm, would present an address at another Masonic gathering, allowing both to be published. The printed version of Morse's Illuminati sermon included extensive notes assuring readers that he had "ever entertained a respect for [Masonry], as promotive of private friendship and benevolence, and public order." [36]

As subsequent rebuttals suggest, the hint of American Masonic complicity proved one of the weakest links in Morse's case. After all, Federalist hero George Washington belonged to the fraternity, and many of its brothers shared Morse's political position. Only after relentless demands for specific examples, led by the Reverend brother William Bentley, would Morse and his allies finally be forced to suggest that American members were involved. Even then, Morse only pointed to French émigrés following an obscure higher-degree ritual. These men, he hastened to add, were actually "imposters," not "true and good Masons." [37]

If Morse was circumspect in accusing American brothers, however, the volume of Masonic response suggests that even such oblique criticism touched a nerve. Published attacks on the fraternity were rare before 1826, and American Masons responded sharply. A month after Morse's attack, Massachusetts brothers presented a loyal address to President John Adams. The speech given by William Bentley on the occasion devoted eleven printed pages to the question. Over the next two years, New England Masonic sermons and orations often mentioned the issue.[38]

Although, as Episcopalian minister and brother Roger Viets argued in July 1800, charges of Illuminism needed to be answered because they were made publicly and by educated men of stature rather than privately or by lesser men, the attacks must have been particularly troubling because they expressed popular concerns about the fraternity that had been acute in the 1790s. Masonry had spread rapidly since the Revolution, entering new social and geographical territory. These fraternal outposts evoked the same suspicions that had marked the introduction of Masonry in colonial cities. Not surprisingly, the first wave of official Baptist opposition in New England began in the west, where the fraternity was still relatively unfamiliar.[39]

The Illuminati controversy, however, marked the zenith of public questioning and private anxieties. Over the next years, Masonic refutations, increasing familiarity with the fraternity, and a changing political climate all weakened opposition. "His whole soul caught the flame," confessed a repentant Connecticut minister of himself in 1800 to a new Masonic lodge, "every passion was aroused and prejudice sat brooding on his heart" at the fraternity he believed corrupted by the Illuminati. But, he noted, "truth has at length burst the clouds of prejudices and calumny, and convinced, at least the considerate part of the community." Even for the less thoughtful, an increasing familiarity with Masonic activities and brothers could also ease tensions. "Do we appear as a junto of atheists, traitors, and criminals?" the Reverend brother Viets had asked in Connecticut that same year. "Do you . . . suspect that we are conspired to destroy religion, liberty and social felicity?"[40]

Thomas Robbins, like Morse a staunch Federalist and Trinitarian Congregationalist, would also change his opinion of Masonry. Although he never became a member, he lent his presence to a number of its celebrations. His first post-1799 involvement came on an 1802 New York missionary journey when the fraternity invited him to speak. Robbins failed to note his reactions, but the following year he attended a Masonic celebration even without an official invitation. In 1804 and 1807, he addressed the fraternity at its public meetings. The minister who had praised God for revealing the fraternity's evil deeds in 1798 prepared for the latter occasion by reading, seemingly without hostility, a Masonic handbook. Even the brothers themselves seemed less troubling. While before they had seemed only "pretty orderly," members now appeared "quite respectable."[41]

In 1826, a rural Vermont brother celebrated this decline of hostility as "the extension of the true principles of Masonry." "But a few years since," recalled James Johnson, "prejudices, unyielding prejudices, were existing in our religious community against this ancient Order, and seldom did a professing Christian, and still more seldom did a minister of the Gospel, seek admittance into our lodges." This situation, however, had changed: "This prejudice has been chased away by the light of Masonry." The fraternity now included "many eminent Christians . . . and many learned, pious, and laborious ministers of the Gospel."[42]

As Johnson realized, the fraternity's standing gained enormously from the growing numbers of eminent laypeople and clergy in its ranks. Prominent clergymen from rationalist, conservative orthodox, and evangelical denominations all contributed to the roster of the fraternity—and its claims to religious sanction and purpose.[43]

Although conservative orthodox ministers like Robbins often harbored early doubts about the fraternity, many of their number were already involved in Masonry. Robbins's own unofficial mentor, Nathan Strong, belonged to the fraternity. A former Yale tutor, author of an extensive refutation of Universalism, and founding editor of the *Connecticut Evangelical Magazine,* the Hartford minister moved in the highest ranks of Connecticut Congregationalism. His February 1799 discussion of the fraternity with Robbins came soon after Strong led in creating the Connecticut Missionary Society, a group he helped direct for nearly a decade. The first missionaries to Palestine appointed by the American Board of Commissioners for Foreign Missions were members of the fraternity, raising support partly through this affiliation. The board's missionary to Ceylon also received aid from his lodge.[44]

Presbyterianism, closely linked to Congregationalism but stronger outside New England, also contributed important clergy, including John Taylor, the first acting president of Union College (named for the missionary alliance between the Presbyterians and the Congregationalists). His Masonic brother Alexander MacWhorter moved within the inner circles of Presbyterianism, serving as one of the original trustees when the denomination's national body was incorporated in 1799, the year he preached a sermon on the death of George Washington at the request of his brothers.[45]

Episcopalian clergymen like John Wesley had been among the first ministers to address and attend American Masonic meetings, and the fraternity continued to attract denominational leaders. The future bishop of New York, the Reverend Jonathan M. Wainwright, served as a grand chaplain of that state's grand lodge in 1826. That same year, the Reverend Alexander Viets Griswold, the bishop of the Eastern Diocese (encompassing all of New England except Connecticut), joined the Providence Knights Templars organization, a group that required the possession of ten Masonic degrees. Indeed, so close did the order and the church seem that at least three Episcopal clergymen entered their vocation by way of Masonry. In 1811, while still a lawyer and congressman, Pennsylvania grand master James Milnor told brothers that speculative Masonry was "incorrectly" named; it should be "Spiritual" Masonry. Two years later Milnor began religious study. He continued to hold state Masonic offices during this training and afterward upon moving to New York.[46]

If Masonry penetrated deeply into the groups that thought of themselves as the center of the American Christian spectrum, the fraternity also drew upon the two outer wings that conservative Trinitarians often regarded with hostility. Unitarians and Universalists seem to have been proportionally overrepresented within the fraternity that shared their enlightened goals of order, simplicity, and benevolent works. Massachusetts Unitarians William Bentley and Thaddeus Mason Harris were among the most popular (and most published) of all turn-of-the-century Masonic orators. Similar Masonic involvement can be seen among the Universalists. Denominational pioneer Hosea Ballou was a Massachusetts member, as were two other important Universalist members of his family: Adin, founder of the utopian Hopedale community, and Hosea, II, founding president of Tufts University.[47]

Rationalist religion incurred the wrath of Robbins and Morse, but such conservative Trinitarians often found the evangelical populist groups that occupied the other end of the spectrum almost as troubling. A month after his 1799 encounter with Vermont Masons, Robbins noted that "infidelity" did not seem to be the major religious problem there; rather, Vermonters were "infected" with the "erroneous views" spread by Methodists and Baptists. Perhaps linking the fraternity with such dangerous groups, Robbins finished his diary entry by pointing out (incorrectly) that "Masonic lodges are forbidden to meet by law in Great Britain."[48]

Although some Baptist bodies opposed the fraternity, a number of their most prominent ministers participated actively. The Reverend William Rogers, grand chaplain at an 1820 Philadelphia Masonic ceremony, was, a contemporary periodical noted, "undoubtedly one of the most influential Baptist clergymen of his day in the country." Stephen Gano, pastor of the flagship First Baptist Church of Providence for more than thirty years, joined the Masonic Knights Templars organization in 1826 in the same ceremony that admitted the region's Episcopal bishop.[49]

Twenty-five years earlier, Gano had preached at the ordination of another Baptist minister who would soon also become a brother. Joshua Bradley had been offered positions as colleague to Samuel Stillman and to Isaac Backus, central figures in the history of New England Baptists, but settled first in Newport. The former shoemaker's apprentice fitted the experience of many Baptist ministers more than the settled Gano, for Bradley soon began a series of moves that led him to New York and Missouri, among other states. While serving in Connecticut, he regularly visited New Haven on Saturday evenings to preach to the small Baptist group meeting in the Masonic Hall.[50]

The peripatetic life chosen by the Baptist Bradley was a virtual requirement for Methodist ministers, and many used fraternal ties to ease the difficulties of a system that assigned clergy to a different location every few years. In 1826, a Masonic newspaper editor in Boston claimed that "the greatest portion of the Methodist preachers of the New-England Conference are zealous and good Masons."[51] These Methodist brothers included the ministers most often cited as the model for Father Mapple of Melville's *Moby Dick*: Enoch Mudge, the first native New Englander to become a Methodist itinerant and later the minister at New Bedford Seaman's Chapel, and Father Edward Taylor, later hired by Boston Unitarians to minister to the poor. A more influential denominational leader was Solomon Sias, member of the same Knights Templars group as the Baptist Gano. Sias, presiding elder of the New Hampshire district for several years in the 1810s, published the denomination's newspaper, *Zion's Herald*, in the 1820s, raising its circulation during his three-year tenure to six thousand.[52]

The strongest evidence of Masonry's appeal among Methodist clergy, however, comes from the membership of perhaps the most evangelical and populist minister of that (or perhaps any other) denomination, "Crazy" Lorenzo
Dow. With his shoulder-length hair and his radical message of opposition to
traditional physicians and clergymen, the self-proclaimed "cosmopolite" traveled tirelessly to spread evangelical Christianity, speaking perhaps to more
people than any other minister in the period. In 1830 Dow addressed a Maryland lodge meeting, exhorting the brothers "to show," as a number of other
leading clergymen had done over the previous forty years, "that Masons can
be good men as well as good Christians." 53

This connection between Masonry, morality, and Christianity was dramatized in ceremonies in nearby Alexandria the same year. On March 29, more
than five hundred brothers assembled to lay the cornerstone of the Associated Methodist Church. They then proceeded to Mount Vernon to visit the
grave of brother George Washington. After an address, the brothers stood in
a "Cordon around the Grave" to deposit "the emblematical evergreen *sprig*"
symbolizing the Resurrection.54

Uncommon before 1820, Masonic church dedications spread throughout
the country during the following decade. Massachusetts brethren laid cornerstones for both Baptist and Methodist groups.55 An Episcopalian church
received the same dedication in Carlisle, Pennsylvania. In 1821, Savannah
brothers led the ceremony for a "Church of All Denominations," a building
sponsored by the fraternity to be used by all Christian groups. The Louisiana grand lodge in 1828 laid the "Foundation Stone" of the New Orleans
Mariner's Church.56

For some, these rituals represented primarily a recognition of Masonry's
moral and charitable purposes. But the symbolic message of the ceremony
went much deeper. Brothers previously had called upon ministers such as
Morse and Robbins to bless their gatherings. The new practice of church
cornerstone ceremonies suggested precisely the opposite. Now clergymen and
church members invited Masonry to sanctify their churches and their mission.
The grand master at the Alexandria ceremony asked that "the all bounteous
Author of all good, bless the inhabitants of this town," praying as well that
God would "enable the religious society to carry on and finish the work." 57

Masonry never commanded the allegiance or even the acceptance of all post-
Revolutionary Christians. But the spread of church cornerstone ceremonies,
the growing popularity of Masonry's nonsectarian benevolence, and the fraternity's explicit identification with Christianity, when added to a membership
list that included eccentrics like Lorenzo Dow as well as the establishment
editors of the Methodist *Zion's Herald* and the Congregationalist *Connecticut Evangelical Magazine,* provide strong evidence for "the alliance of Free
Masonry with the churches" noted by later Antimasons. The success of this

Antimasonic movement makes it difficult to recover these earlier religious associations. Yet even brother Andrew Jackson held a view of Masonry's religious standing similar to that of the New England school teacher and spelling-book author Salem Town. Expressing his regrets at being unable to attend the 1830 Alexandria cornerstone ceremony, President Jackson suggested that "the memory of" Washington "cannot receive a more appropriate honour than that which Religion and Masonry pay it, when they send their votaries to his tomb, fresh from the performance of acts which they consecrate." Even at the height of Antimasonic opposition, Jackson suggested that Masonry first acted to "consecrate," to make holy, a church building. Then religion sent its votaries, its devout worshipers, to the tomb, not as members of the church, but as brothers of the fraternity. According to Jackson and many post-Revolutionary Christians, Masonry represented the deity as effectively as local congregations or individual denominations—even in sanctifying the two key loci of nineteenth-century piety, the church and the grave.[58]

IV. Cavils, Objections, and Calumnies

The high claims of post-Revolutionary Masonry did not go unchallenged. A widespread and persistent criticism of the gap between Masonic pretensions and reality dogged the fraternity. Although John Payson argued in 1800 in New Hampshire that "the cavils, objections, and calumnies raised and vented against our institution . . . have been too often refuted to need a repetition," the extensive apologetics that became a standard part of Masonic sermons and orations failed to quiet the criticism completely. Besides questions about religion and continuing doubts about Masonry's secrecy, a number of critics wondered aloud why immoral men were still Masonic brothers and why no women could join. Masonry's heightened prestige did not quell these doubts; if anything, it sharpened them. "No inconsiderable pains have been taken," mourned Richard Eliot in an uncharacteristically gloomy 1803 assessment, "but all that has been said, and done . . . has proved to be ineffectual" to remove such "mistaken apprehensions." [59]

Despite Eliot's frustration, what is the most striking about these criticisms of Masonry is, not their existence, but their weakness. The new position of the fraternity in public ceremonies and rhetoric inspired no organized protest. Even questioning remained localized and, except for isolated comments by religious groups, seldom reached print. Indeed, the primary evidence of mistrust of the fraternity before the mid-1820s lies in the refutations made by Masons themselves. These questions, however, were not insignificant. Besides helping to shape Masonry's self-descriptions, the issues of immoral men and excluded women also reveal the hegemony of the new Masonic language, for even criticisms tended to assume the high view of the fraternity insisted on by brothers.

Besides explaining Masonry's secrecy and its religious role, Masonic apologists most often discussed fraternal membership policies. Non-Masons pointed out that Masons did not always live up to the high moral claims of the order. "Some of those who belong," Thaddeus Mason Harris represented critics as saying, "are intemperate, profligate, and vicious." On one level, this question was easily answered. "Nothing can be more unfair or unjust," Harris responded, "than to deprecate or condemn any institution, good in itself, on account of the faults of those who pretend to adhere to it. The fact is, the best things may be abused." [60] As Harris and others pointed out, the unworthiness of some members could also be used as an argument against Christianity. Yet both the church and the fraternity—brothers often mentioned the membership of George Washington and, particularly after his 1824–1825 tour of the United States, General Lafayette—clearly contained a preponderance of good and virtuous members.

If this objection could be easily answered on one level, it also raised deeper questions about Masonry's abilities to teach virtue and the overall character of the fraternity. Even Masonic apologists like Harris could not deny the existence of "base and unworthy" members. But they could use the attacks as a means of encouraging brothers toward proper conduct. Acknowledging criticism, first, provided an occasion for encouraging virtue. As Hector Orr warned brethren in 1798, Masonic values would be celebrated in vain if "our lives give the lie to our pretensions." William Bentley similarly recognized that not all brothers had reached the stage of "True Masons" who were "the most enlightened, and the most Benevolent of men"; he warned listeners in 1797 of the necessity of "becoming what ye ought to be": brothers needed to "deserve" this "character" they claimed. The possibility of immoral members also spurred exhortations to uphold high admission standards. Walter Colter considered the matter so important that he suggested, "It were better for us to reject three who *are* worthy of admission, than admit one who is *not*." Even Salem Town, who expected the universal spread of the fraternity during the millennium, warned brothers that at present admitting the right men was "vitally" important.[61] Claims that Masons accepted only those of high virtue fitted uneasily with arguments for Masonry's ability to teach it, but the results of both assertions were the same: a vindication of the fraternity's honor and a bid for its members to be recognized as the men of virtue and talent who were the natural aristoi of the new Republic.

A second argument about the fraternity's membership was more difficult to answer. As early as 1796, Joseph Dunham identified the question, "Why are not ladies initiated into these Mysteries?" as one "which has excited the curiosity and wonder, not only of *that* sex, but of the world at large." Benjamin Gleason noted the same issue in 1805 as "a capital Quere, at the present day." [62] Despite the prevalence of this question, Masons never agreed, as they had on the question of unworthy members, on a single line of response. Brothers variously suggested that women could not attend secret meetings without scandal, that women would cause jealousy within the brotherhood, and that Freemasonry was designed to soften men, providing moral improvement that women did not require. More commonly, brothers pointed to the exclusion of women from colleges and governments, noting that no one questioned that practice. "It would be as great a burlesque upon female delicacy," Charles Train argued in 1812, "to be raised to the sublime degree of Master Mason, as to be honoured with a commission in the American army, or with the degree of L.L.D." [63]

The heart of what Train called "the most plausible, and weighty objection" to the fraternity, however, did not lie primarily in actual membership policy. As Train and others pointed out, nearly all organized social life remained segregated by sex, even on the village level. Benjamin Whitman, a southeast Massachusetts lodge master, did not even know of women who showed any "anxiety to be admitted to the knowledge of [Masonic] secrets." Still, the issue needed to be cleared up, particularly because the question seems to have been raised most often in New England villages, where Masonry was still relatively new around the turn of the century. A popular belief that Masonry might accept women into their nighttime meetings behind closed doors would arouse widespread criticism. "Were women to be admitted to our Lodges," the Reverend brother Ezra Ripley of Concord, Massachusetts, pointed out in 1802, "though they should be pure, as angels are, they could not avoid infamous charges from the envious and uncharitable world abroad." [64] He probably did not need to suggest to his brothers that they themselves would also face similar attack.

Ultimately, however, the issue of women's involvement was one of ideology rather than sociology, a challenge to perceived incongruities in Masonic arguments rather than any strong insistence on women's participation. Female and male reformers in the 1790s launched a broad challenge to traditional gender roles, calling for increased women's education, greater equality within marriage, and new recognition for women's important role in child rearing. Such attacks on received ideas troubled many Americans, including brother Samuel Sumner Wilde. Though he carefully stated that he did not believe "that the pursuits of science are unsuitable to the female mind," he also warned strongly against erasing the boundaries between women's and men's "character and pursuits." An "inattention to this necessary distinction," he argued, would do more than anything else "to encrease the present disorders in the world, and to make confusion worse confounded." In the face of such reactions, post-Revolutionary Americans could not allow women to enter political life, but they could invest women's private roles with larger significance. Women's attitudes and activities increasingly seemed to epitomize morality, religion, and refinement, new roles that seemed congruent with key parts of the values brothers now claimed were peculiarly Masonic. As Whitman noted, the question of women's exclusion from the fraternity arose because brothers argued that "Masonry has such charms . . . the *institution* is bottomed upon such noble and Godlike principles, and has the happiness of mankind for its consummate object," all areas in which women seemed to have a particularly important role.[65]

The comments of an anonymous Worcester, Massachusetts, woman who published *Observations on Free Masonry* in 1798 suggests the ways that Masonic language could be used both to celebrate virtues that were now placed within women's sphere and to emphasize its new importance. While professing admiration for Masonry's exclusion of women, she also claimed to have been "initiated . . . at my birth" because "*Faith, Hope* and *Charity* presided." As she grew, "my three godmothers, ere the dawn of reason expanded my ideas, laid the foundation of a masonic structure, Benevolence and Philanthropy, in my breast." Women could not become Masons, she argued, partly because the fraternity "was ordained . . . to *level* the masculine character of the other sex with the feminine softness of ours," suggesting that men needed external institutions to teach key values that women inherently possessed. She expected better treatment in heaven's "Universal Lodge," however, where "all distinctions are annihilated," not just between different classes and nations but between sexes. There, "the widow's son [the murdered grand master Hiram Abiff] rank[s] no higher than her daughters, provided the latter are clothed in their necessary *Jewels,* Innocence and Virtue."[66]

The new views of Masonry and women thus forced brothers to share the same symbolic space—a joint tenancy that at times forced brothers to reconfigure their praise in order to distinguish the fraternity beyond the values of love and virtue increasingly represented by women. They approached the issue of exclusion gingerly, generally in a separate section on apologetics and with extensive compliments to "the most fair, and most excellent part of creation." Especially during a period when they were meeting the challenge of alleged association with the subversive Illuminati, Masons clearly wanted the exclusion of women to be taken for granted. Their new arguments, however, moved too close to disputed gender boundaries for the issue to be safely ignored. The attempt to defend Masonry's gender lines required brothers to make arguments less congenial to their preferred rhetorical strategies. Rather than praising Masonry's refining and spiritualizing influence, orators sometimes found themselves exalting the fraternity's connection with the manual labor of operative masons and with wartime "fields of blood." Ultimately, however, questions about women's exclusion also acknowledged the force of brothers' arguments. Critics now viewed Masonry, not as a tavern club engaged in dissipated revels or a badge of elite social standing, but as a charitable and moral institution comparable to the key institution where both men and women were free and accepted, the church.[67]

Questions about the fraternity persisted. All Masons, let alone all Americans, could not fully agree that their fraternity was, as one orator claimed in

1797, "designed in Providence . . . to revive the glories of the golden age, and to assist the maturing reason of men to liberate them from the labyrinth of ignorance, superstition and prejudice." But even objections to the fraternity paid tribute to the power of its new explanations.[68]

Charles Willson Peale had a different sort of complaint about the fraternity, one that sums up post-Revolutionary Masonry's symbolic role—and suggests another issue that requires examination. In 1802, Peale moved into Philadelphia's State House, the site of the signing of the Declaration of Independence and the writing of the federal Constitution. Peale, however, was not the only tenant. The legislature had earlier given permission to the city's Masons to hold meetings in the hall. Peale found the brothers bad neighbors. "He complains," noted deputy grand master James Milnor, "that the sittings of the lodges are continued at so late an hour as to occasion him great inconvenience." The difficulties that followed, ending in the fraternity's departure, were on many levels ironic, for the brotherhood and Peale's Philadelphia Museum professed the same enlightened desires.[69]

The Masons and the museum both sought to inculcate learning and morality. Just as the fraternity carefully planned its lodge halls and its rituals to teach moral and intellectual truths, so Peale arranged his portrait gallery of exemplary heroes to inspire morality and his natural history collections to illustrate the categories of enlightened knowledge. Peale even considered naming his museum the "Temple of Wisdom," but decided against it because of the title's religious connections. Masonry had no such scruples. It openly identified itself with the acknowledged sources of the sacred, even identifying its halls as temples and its brothers as priests.[70]

If the comparison between Masonry and the museum suggests the power and scope of the fraternity's new rhetoric—its link to the values expressed in both Independence Hall and the new United States Capitol—their cohabitation also suggests both that they operated in the physical world and that their high-minded ideals were not entirely divorced from self-interested motives. For Peale, the museum provided his primary source of income; yearly receipts in this period averaged about forty-seven hundred dollars. As the busy and increasingly wealthy museum keeper complained, Masons also were more than symbolic priests and teachers. The fraternity's activities affected other parts of life—particularly the economic and political spheres that post-Revolutionary Americans believed peculiarly the domain of men. As Peale's museum did for its keeper, the fraternity provided practical benefits for its brothers—something that Hiram Hopkins realized one day while watching a Masonic ceremony in upstate New York.[71]

CHAPTER SEVEN

Preference in Many Particulars

Charity and Commerce, 1790–1826

Hiram Hopkins was not a Mason when he attended the capstone laying of the Erie Canal's ten combined locks in Lockport, New York, on June 24, 1825, but what he saw and heard there excited him. The procession of nearly three hundred brothers caught his eye first. "I saw among the brotherhood, distinguished by their aprons and sashes," he recalled later, "several of my youthful associates, and others of my acquaintances, among whom were the Elders and many of the members of our Presbyterian Church." At the lock, Hopkins watched as the brothers poured the ceremonial corn, oil, and wine upon the capstone and listened to an oration. According to Hopkins's later account, the speaker "portrayed, in lively colors, the benefits of the institution—that it was the handmaid of Religion and that on the existence of this order depended much of our scientific knowledge—that it had been upheld and supported by all the wisest and best of men in every age, from the building of Solomon's Temple to the present time, including among its distinguished followers and patrons, the Apostles, and immediate disciples of our blessed Saviour." Hopkins was deeply moved. "My feelings," he remembered, were "excited to a high degree by all these things." [1]

More than powerful ideas and public honor, however, intrigued Hopkins. He also knew "that masons had preference in many particulars." Hopkins's first thoughts of joining the fraternity had arisen earlier when his cousin Eli Bruce suggested that Hopkins run for town constable. The flattered would-be candidate, however, discovered that Bruce, the county sheriff, had to consider whether his duty lay in supporting his expected opponent, a Masonic brother. The ceremony at the locks reawakened Hopkins's interest. He "petitioned immediately" to the local lodge. [2]

As Hopkins realized, post-Revolutionary Masonry involved more than high-minded symbols. Fraternal membership also provided practical advantages. Through its rapidly expanding network of lodges, Masonry offered brothers charity, economic aid, and even political advantage. Post-Revolutionary Masons increasingly emphasized their obligation to support their brothers, not only providing for them and their families in times of distress but also giving them preferential treatment in commerce, employment, and voting. Members even had an obligation, Seth May reminded brothers shortly after Hopkins's experience at the locks, to risk their "lives in the service of a[n endangered] brother." In such a situation, he insisted, they should "not hesitate a moment."[3]

Fraternal concern held particular importance for the men who flocked into Masonic lodges after the Revolution. The growth of commerce and geographical mobility created particular difficulties for the merchants, artisans, and professionals who continued to make up the bulk of the fraternity. For these men, the "union, friendship, brotherly love, and mutual sympathy" forged by Masonry provided ties that proved useful in a wide range of economic activities.[4] In each of these contexts, brothers discovered advantages that both eased their characteristic difficulties and (less successfully) balanced particular interests and public advantages. Needy strangers caught up in the mobility and uncertainty of post-Revolutionary society found Masonry's charitable activities a means of supplementing or even replacing the frayed bonds of family and neighborhood. In the more tightly knit localities, the fraternity helped newcomers enter social and economic networks, encouraging the communal cooperation that fostered individual success as well. Finally, Masonry facilitated long-distance trade, offering an ideal of broader familial concern that helped create and maintain ties with men beyond the locality.

These uses, Masons believed, involved more than establishing selfish advantage. Building fraternity in a world increasingly made up of strangers, their order encouraged the concern and watchfulness that made society more than a collection of unconnected and amoral individuals. "Reciprocal benefits," an orator told Portland, Maine, brothers in 1799, "are necessary to the end of our creation." As a result, "a community is happy or miserable in proportion to the prevalence or neglect of this principle" of mutual involvement.[5] Masonry, brothers argued, helped build this happiness and, just as important, expanded it to meet the needs of a changing society where stable local bonds could no longer be taken for granted.

Masonry's new practical significance, however, could be interpreted differently. The benefits provided by the fraternity might actually undermine rather than advance the public good. Masonic charity increasingly went solely to brothers, and fraternal ties could be used to build close ties in business dealings, in both cases slighting the often-superior claims of nonmembers. Ironically, the success of the brotherhood in building a network of fraternal concern and compassion raised the anxieties of outsiders excluded from these benefits. By the 1820s, these tensions no longer seemed resolvable, and many Americans turned against the fraternity.[6]

Such a view of the fraternity, as (in the words of these later opponents) "allied to the selfish desires of the human heart," misunderstood the conflicting desires and uses that the fraternity attempted to satisfy. Rather than fostering a unique selfishness, Masonry actually expressed post-Revolutionary Americans' tangled ambivalences about their changing society and economy. Americans did not generally rush headlong into a world of disconnected individuals and unregulated economic interactions. The history of Masonry suggests that even Americans' most commercially minded individuals attempted to preserve the close ties and personal concern of smaller communities even as they also pursued the opportunities offered by wider commerce. Understanding this complex interweaving of individual benefits and social improvement —and the reasons why Antimasons would later reject the entire enterprise as hopelessly corrupt—requires examination of both the practice and ideas of Masonry's charity, economic aid, and political benefits.[7]

1. The Most Charitable and Benevolent of the Human Race

When Anne Royall arrived in New York City in February 1825, she had, she recalled later, "not one cent upon earth." She had assembled her fare by begging in the streets of Philadelphia, arriving in New York "a total stranger, in the pelting storm." Royall had only one asset, her late husband's Masonic membership. Turning to the fraternity, she received more than just immediate relief. The brothers also sponsored a benefit performance at a member's theater that featured, besides two plays, a "Masonic Monologue" and a "Grand Masonic Transparency." Three hundred Masons and others attended the evening. Royall received $180 for her trip to New England.[8]

As the response of the New York brethren suggests, charity seemed one of the most significant purposes of post-Revolutionary Freemasonry. The lodge's charity funds, the revived American Union Lodge argued in 1810, were "the grand object of the institution." "Relief" now joined "Brotherly Love" and "Truth" in summations of key Masonic principles.[9] As the promoter of Royall's benefit suggested in a newspaper advertisement, Masonry

> knows its office, each endearing tie
> of soft-eyed genuine Philanthropy.[10]

Royall's discussion of her trip and her experiences, first described in a book published through the intervention of a brother, provides insight into the growing prominence attached to philanthropy within Masonry and its larger context. In her dependence upon the fraternity, Royall took advantage of its extraordinary post-Revolutionary expansion, a growth that made Masonry nearly ubiquitous in small towns as well as larger seaboard cities. This expanded fraternity, Royall often suggested in her later writings, helped create a fictive family that eased some of the dangers of being a total stranger. Royall's experiences also make clear the limitations of post-Revolutionary charitable institutions. As she knew, no other organization reached so far or served so many needs as the brotherhood. Brothers were, she concluded in her description of the New York benefit, "the most charitable and benevolent of the human race." [11]

Royall's trip from Alabama in 1823 to New England in 1825 depended heavily upon her exploitation of Masonic ties. Although she exaggerated in claiming that she "applied to none but Masons," members often provided crucial aid. In Virginia, brother Thomas Ritchie, editor of the Richmond *Enquirer,* intervened after a local innkeeper refused to take in the nearly penniless woman. In Baltimore, Royall arranged an interview with the marquis de Lafayette, the Revolutionary hero who was just beginning his triumphal tour of communities—and Masonic lodges—in every state in the Union. Brother Lafayette's letter opened further Masonic doors, including presumably those in New York City.[12]

Royall's reception in that city, like her entire journey, exploited Masonry's amazing post-Revolutionary growth. Brothers had long boasted of the fraternity's universality; after the Revolution it became omnipresent as well. Lodges met in each of the larger cities she visited as well as in the smaller towns like Portland, Maine; Carlisle, Pennsylvania; Wheeling, Virginia; and Savannah, Georgia, in all of which she met brothers during later journeys. As the grand master of Pennsylvania suggested in 1810, the boundaries of the fraternity were already "co-extensive with our territorial limits." "It has grown with the nation's growth and strengthened with her strength." [13]

This expansion partly reflected a population that more than tripled in the forty years after 1790. But Masonry grew even more rapidly. According to the grand master of New York in 1860, his state's population had tripled in the first quarter of the century; lodge membership grew fourfold. By the time Royall arrived in New York in 1825, fully forty-four lodges met in that city, twice as many as in 1812. Even in the earlier year, Masonic meetings were not difficult to find. According to a Masonic guidebook, a dedicated (and energetic) brother in September 1812 could have attended a city lodge nearly every weeknight of the month—and most of those nights had a choice of lodges. Four met on September 1 alone.[14]

By 1825, however, New York City was no longer the center of the state's Masonry. If the fraternity grew within the city, it virtually exploded outside it. "We are lost in admiration at [Masonry's] extraordinary progress," marveled grand master De Witt Clinton in 1806: "Every day produces new applications for lodges, and every place witnesses them." At the end of the Revolution, he pointed out, the state had only about ten lodges. Now there were nearly one hundred. These new lodges met primarily outside the city; by 1825, ninetenths of the state's lodges were located there. As Clinton noted, "Masonry has erected her temples, as well in the most remote frontier settlements, as in the most populous villages and cities." The growth that amazed Clinton continued and even accelerated after 1806. Over the next four years, the grand lodge chartered more than seventy new lodges; and by 1825, nearly five hundred lodges met in New York State, so many that its city and country lodges had divided three years before, largely over the proper means to oversee the exploding number of lodges.[15]

New York provided the most fertile soil for post-Revolutionary Masonry, but other areas also experienced rapid growth. In 1812 alone, Philadelphia lodges initiated nearly three hundred new brothers. The thousand Masons that attended the rededication of the grand lodge hall eight years later formed only a small fraction of the members of the state's nearly 100 lodges. Similar growth occurred elsewhere. Virginia in 1820 sponsored 114 lodges; Kentucky, where organized Masonry began only after the Revolution, 45. A national meeting two years later estimated—probably conservatively—that American Masons numbered about eighty thousand. As the leader of the Pennsylvania fraternity had noted a dozen years before, the order had expanded "beyond our most sanguine expectations."[16]

"Wherever a Mason may sojourn . . . whether in prosperity, or adversity," Salem Town boasted in the 1810s, "the same interchange of feelings and brotherly affections . . . exists in every country and every nation." As Town implied, post-Revolutionary Masonry was not simply larger; it was also more useful, helping to form a community of concern that both supplemented and reached beyond older ties. Royall's experience suggests that such close fraternal ties were particularly significant in a society where people and goods moved more rapidly and over longer distances than ever before. Only Masonry, brothers claimed, could create ties that survived these rapid changes. "No human tie," argued Royall in her description of her New York experiences, "is so strong or so much to be relied upon as that between Masons."[17]

Royall's other ties had clearly proved unreliable. Family and neighborhood provided little comfort. Her husband, the wealthy western Virginian planter and brother William Royall, had died in 1812, and his estate remained in litigation for the next eight years. Although finally given a widow's dower in 1819, the debts built up through years of legal expenses left Royall nearly penniless. Her neighborhood provided little comfort. Local residents had long resented her advancement from daughter of William Royall's housekeeper to Royall's wife, particularly because the two had admittedly "cohabited without marriage." Remaining in the area also made prosecution by creditors more likely. The new territory of Alabama offered a fresh start but further weakened her connections with older acquaintances.[18]

If Royall's neighborhood ties proved distinctly unhelpful, family bonds were similarly weak. Continual movement had loosened kin networks. Royall had been born in Maryland, but her parents moved to western Pennsylvania when she was three. Ten years later, her mother, having outlived two husbands, moved to western Virginia, where, after several stays of varying lengths, she became William Royall's housekeeper. By the time Anne Royall lost her bid to retain the estate in 1819, her mother had lived in at least three different places in two different states. Anne's niece helped her after William Royall's death, but a quarrel over money between Anne and her niece's new husband completed her isolation.

Royall's abrasive personality exacerbated her difficulties. Her assertiveness and flair for self-promotion allowed her to write more than a dozen books and, after 1830, edit and publish a Washington newspaper—where according to legend she secured an interview with John Quincy Adams by commandeering his clothes while he swam naked in the Potomac. But her independence had a price. Her tart tongue and lack of conventional feminine deference alienated many and cost her much goodwill as well as a broken leg from an angry Vermont shopkeeper who threw her out onto the icy street.

Despite these peculiarities, New York brothers believed that Royall's situation exemplified the difficulties Masonry counteracted with its comprehensive concern. As Seth May noted in another context that same year, fraternal aid needed to go beyond supplying food and shelter for the neediest. "The duties . . . we have religiously avowed to perform," he argued, even included a willingness to provide education for poor children of Masons. Individually and collectively, members sought to provide for the well-being of brothers and their families in a variety of ways. New York City lodges had already supported fifty children in the city's Free Schools from 1808 to 1818, providing clothing as well when needed. Later, Independent Royal Arch Lodge, a participant in the Free School program, also agreed to sponsor a child in Ceylon under the care of a missionary brother, requesting that he be called "Hiram Abiff." Such lodge activities were supplemented by grand lodge charity—the New York State body spent more than twenty-one hundred dollars in 1813, or more than 80 percent of that year's total expenditures—and by the individual giving upon which Royall relied.[19]

Although growing in range and amount, brothers' charity failed to keep pace with demand. Post-Revolutionary lodges increasingly limited their aid to brothers and their dependents. Colonial Masons had similarly given aid primarily to other Masons, but their emphasis on universal love and community leadership also encouraged them to emphasize their concern for all. Post-Revolutionary brothers found taking care of their own members difficult enough. When American Union Lodge re-formed in Marietta, Ohio, in 1790, its first bylaws noted that its "charity ought not to be circumscribed to narrow bounds," but provide explicitly for the relief of "others, not of the Fraternity." Thirty years later, the group aimed its sights less grandly. Its 1819 revised bylaws left out the section on outsiders and spoke only of the need for the standing charity committee to examine "the situation of distressed Brethren." So heavy did calls upon the Canton, Ohio, lodge become that it was forced in 1825 to limit aid to "travelling masons in indigent circumstances," without an explicit lodge vote, to two dollars.[20]

Despite this action, fraternal charity remained ad hoc and discretionary, varying widely by place and year. Attempts to institutionalize charity usually failed. The Free School program established in New York City lapsed after less than a decade. South Carolina's and Massachusetts's Masonic orphanages, like Ohio's project of a manual labor school, never got beyond the planning stages. Aid to individuals also varied greatly. Although a single Philadelphia lodge in 1800 gave away the substantial sum of one thousand dollars, all the other city lodges combined failed to distribute that much.[21]

This lack of system created strengths as well as weaknesses—particularly because it allowed brothers to adapt to individual circumstances and (sometimes) to provide exceptional aid. Salem Town considered one case so extraordinary that he included it in a short memoir written later in life. Traveling down to Georgia to head a school in the 1820s, Town became acquainted with a New York blacksmith making the same trip, a Freemason whom Town recalled as a man who "had little or no means before hand, but [who] was very industrious." Soon after their arrival, the blacksmith died, leaving his wife and two children "destitute among strangers." Noting the situation, the local lodge paid for the family's return "to their friends at the north." Town accompanied them, handing over the hundred dollars that remained when they were back among their family. "It was," Town recalled, "a moment in my life not easily forgotten." "If left in Georgia in her circumstances, and unbefriended," he believed, the widow would "have remained, in all probability, a child of sorrow and suffering all her life." The sick and penniless Anne Royall received a similarly generous reception upon arriving in Alexandria near the beginning of her trip. Not only did the local lodge master provide her with room and board, but he assigned one of his servants to aid her recovery, a level of concern, she wrote, that "exceeds the most extravagant romance."[22]

Although such extravagance was undoubtedly rare, these incidents made a deep impression on post-Revolutionary Americans like Town and Royall. Both lived in a world where they were sometimes total strangers, where people moved more often and over longer distances. Large cities in particular included, Royall noted later, "vast numbers of strangers," leading the editors of both the Philadelphia and the Charleston city directories to call their volumes a "strangers' guide." The weakening of family and neighborhood ties went beyond urban centers. Charles G. Finney's uncle believed that the young man who had already left his upstate New York home to attend secondary school in relatively rural Litchfield, Connecticut, would also be "much among strangers."[23]

If the experience of being a stranger became increasingly common, it did not immediately become any less troubling. Outsiders were still much more likely to be executed for crimes than longtime community residents. Even upstanding strangers lacked the interdependencies and ties of obligation (what Masons sometimes called the "mutual exchange of good offices") that softened life's unpredictability. The successful Albany, New York, printer (and sometime Masonic brother) Solomon Southwick recalled in 1821 that he was "cast upon the world in early life, with no compass to guide, no friendly hand to direct my way." Significantly, the oration at the canal locks, which so impressed Hiram Hopkins, spent nearly as much time celebrating the canal's ability to link separated families as praising Masonry. "The young couple," the speaker suggested, could now leave "the family homestead" without "their aged parents . . . conjur[ing] them not to leave them now that they stand as it were, tottering on the brink of the grave." "That tender connection among men" which existed previously, noted brother De Witt Clinton in 1793 (years before he championed the canal), has been "reduced to nothing" by "the infinite diversities of family, tribe, and nation."[24]

Masonry actively attempted to recreate this connection. Finney's uncle, worried about his nephew's move from home, recommended Masonry for just that reason. "It would be of service to me," the future evangelist recalled his uncle saying, "because if a Freemason I should find friends everywhere." Benjamin Gleason noted in 1798 that Masons lose "the name of *Stranger,*" the term of address often used for outsiders. Masonic charity and friendship, however, ultimately went even further. Rather than just neighbors, Masons were brothers, part of the same family and thus united by even closer bonds. Membership, Gleason suggested, provided "the *peculiar privilege*" of being called by "the endearing and honorable appellation of BROTHER."[25]

The new emphasis on the practical uses of familial relations extended the older metaphor of fraternity. More than an expression of common humanity, despite divisions, Masonic brotherhood now included close, even emotionally charged, bonds of obligations. As Royall noted, Masonic fraternity created "claims of a sacred nature." Such claims, Clinton explained, formed ties of "artificial consanguinity" that operated "with as much force and effect, as the natural relationship of blood." "I could not have been gladder to see them," Royall wrote of a reunion with two Maryland Masons, "had they been brothers, as in fact they were."[26]

In a 1797 address that reveals a final aspect of Masonic charity, the Reverend brother Thaddeus Mason Harris conventionally suggested that people possess "companionable propensities and affectionate dispositions" that make social interaction necessary for human existence. But, he went on to say in a more original observation, determining the proper limits of friendship caused problems. Clearly, no one could be friends with everyone. Yet the other extreme of exclusive individual friendship also created difficulties. Intimacy often proved misplaced, wasted on "worthless men" or those of "mean and interested views." Even more solid friendships sometimes were unable to meet the stress of adversity. "Some *medium*" was required, Harris suggested, "where our affections may be exercised without being partial and without being indiscriminate."[27]

Not surprisingly, Harris believed that Masonry resolved this difficulty, providing a "desirable mean between the diffusedness of general regard and the contractedness of individual attachment." On one hand, the fraternity was "founded on a liberal and extensive plan," extending its benevolence "to every individual of the human race." Yet Masonry also created "a community of interests." Fraternal ties "realized that *constancy* of affection which friendship boastingly promises, but frequently fails to retain; and that *tender sympathy* which fraternal love ought ever to express."[28]

Despite Harris's confidence, however, Masonry could not fully resolve the tension between general regard and individual attachment. The ideological demands of universal love coexisted uneasily with the expanding practical needs of a brotherhood that increasingly included men without the relative financial security of the colonial elite. As Harris also suggested, this difficulty was not solely Masonic. Contemporary benevolent associations proved even less able to juggle these conflicting demands. Unlike Masonry, these societies almost universally limited themselves either to mutual aid for a select group of friends or to broader charity for others. For post-Revolutionary brothers, the power of Masonry lay in its ability to hold together these distinct and often contradictory cultural demands. As Harris argued, the fraternity offered "the affectionate embrace of large philanthropy."[29]

For post-Revolutionary brothers, philanthropy first required universal concern. "I need not remind you," the Reverend brother Daniel Poor wrote to a Massachusetts lodge from his mission in Ceylon, "that our institution is founded upon those broad principles of benevolence and morality which the Governor of the Universe revealed to men." Such values, he warned, "absolutely forbid us to regard a part of the human family, however numerous, as the whole."[30] Brotherhood needed to extend beyond the fraternity. As a song written for a Newburyport, Massachusetts, celebration noted:

> Nor, to Craftsmen alone
> Is our sympathy shown—
> The world are our brothers—their weal is our own.[31]

Lodge actions as well as individual benevolence reinforced this ideal. Although aid primarily went to brothers, Masonic giving could reach beyond the fraternity. Poor's celebration of Masonic universality came in response to a lodge's aid to a Ceylonese child. Lodges also contributed to public libraries, schools, churches, and relief of imprisoned debtors. Pennsylvania brothers donated some three thousand dollars to ease the suffering caused by the 1793 yellow fever epidemic. Troy, New York, Masons subsidized the purchase of firewood for the poor during the hard winter of 1828.[32]

In seeking to uphold the broader dimensions of charity, brothers responded to increasingly insistent ideological demands. Universal love, a key part of colonial Masonry's enlightened discourse, gained new importance after the Revolution. A wide variety of religious positions emphasized God's love as well as (or even in place of) his wrath and the centrality of benevolent activities in religious duties. At the same time, political theory stressed the importance of virtuous concern for others as a primary bond holding together a republican society free from coercive structures of authority.[33] Finally, according to enlightened social theory, unselfish concern for the poor and helpless represented the man of sentiment's reaction to the sight of suffering. According to a song written by a Newburyport woman, Masons epitomized this sympathetic ability to respond imaginatively to the feelings of others:

> There's a chord in the heart of each Mason, that bleeds
> And trembles with pain, at the wounds of another.

Another poem similarly claimed:

> Our hearts, no vile distinctions know,
> But vibrate strong to ev'ry chord of woe.[34]

The importance attached to this universal sympathy increasingly forced brothers to justify their growing attention to their own members. As Edmund Richmond noted in 1801, people sometimes questioned whether the fraternity's "private affections" were compatible with "general benevolence." Brothers first responded that particular loyalty only increased universal benevolence. Furthermore, brothers suggested, Masonry's charge to "prefer a brother to a friend" did not require vile distinctions, a claim they reinforced with a biblical passage Harris incorporated into a charge he wrote to close a lodge meeting. "Every human being," it argued, "has a claim upon your kind offices." Therefore, "we enjoin it upon you 'to do good unto *all*,' while we recommend it more 'especially to the household of the *faithful*.'"[35]

Masonry's attempt to balance these two sides reveals its peculiar cultural and social position. As the heir to the prestige and enlightened vision of the colonial elite, Masonry sought to perpetuate its reputation for public leadership and guardianship. But the fraternity's Revolutionary transformation allowed the admission of brothers without the wealth and relative security of earlier Masons, expanding the demands upon the fraternity. Other charitable organizations felt these conflicting demands. But, unlike Masonry, they could concentrate their attention on one side or the other.

Organized benevolence expanded dramatically in post-Revolutionary

America. Royall's 1820s travel account noted more than forty charity groups in New York City and more than thirty in Philadelphia. Yet she substantially underestimated benevolent activity. Philadelphia city directories for the time Royall visited reveal nearly two hundred charitable organizations, with purposes ranging from mutual aid to orphanages to missions. This growth was not limited to urban areas. Even outside Boston, Massachusetts residents organized nearly three hundred benevolent societies in the 1820s and 1830s alone.[36]

"Friendly societies" for mutual aid formed the most popular of these groups. Nearly one hundred friendly associations met in Philadelphia during the mid-1820s, so many that their creators found it difficult even to choose a distinctive name. City residents could join the Penn Beneficial Society, the Pennsylvania Beneficial Society, the Pennsylvania Benefit Society, the Pennsylvania Benevolent Society, the Pennsylvania Union Benevolent Society, the Union Society of Philadelphia, and the Union Beneficial Society. The Washington Beneficial Society (not to be confused with the Wayne, Warren, Whitefield, and Wesleyan Beneficial Societies) claimed to be "the largest and most respectable Beneficial Society in the United States," with a vice-president, an electing committee, and a school committee in each of the city's wards. Occupational groups also practiced mutual aid. Philadelphia's Musical Fund Society sought not only "to advance the art" but "to relieve distressed professors of music." Like London's ubiquitous box societies, these groups brought together people, usually all men, who paid into a central treasury while healthy in order to receive support for themselves when sick or injured and aid to their families after their death. Members, after an initiation fee, typically paid in about thirty-seven cents each month and could expect three to four dollars during each week of sickness, money for burial expenses, and aid for the widows and orphans.[37]

According to the Philadelphia handbook used by Royall in compiling her travel account, these friendly societies "were originally established to prevent the degrading reflections arising from the circumstance of being relieved, while sick, by public or private charity: the members [of mutual aid associations] may demand their relief as a *right*." In distinguishing such institutions from other charities, the handbook did not mean to deny the benevolent purposes of mutual aid. A member of Philadelphia's Provident Society proudly noted in 1810 that his group stood "second to none in works of benevolence." But charity could also imply subordination and dependence, a link reinforced by post-Revolutionary changes in charitable activities. Particularly in cities, elites increasingly created groups that sought to aid others rather than themselves. While clearly benevolent in intent, however, such organizations also recalled the aristocratic paternalism rejected by republican ideology.[38]

Beneficial societies distinguished themselves from such personal dependence by encouraging fraternal involvement as well as financial aid. Rather than the merely monetary relationship of health or life insurance (enterprises whose beginnings can partly be traced to these associations) or the narrow focus of charitable hospitals, orphanages, or schools, friendly societies provided a broad range of services. The rituals and conviviality of their meetings drew participants closer together. Society-appointed physicians provided medical care. Sick members also received regular calls from a visiting committee. The Provident Society orator even argued that the group aided its members "more by the many personal services which we can and do render, than by the small sums we give." [39]

This involvement, however, was possible only because mutual aid societies limited their concern. Access to money and friendship came with a daunting range of conditions. Typically, groups accepted only healthy men aged twenty-one to forty-one, precisely the ages when sickness and death were least likely. Residence seems not to have been a specific requirement for membership in many societies, but regulations typically required attendance at the annual meeting or payment of a fine. Even sick members received aid from most societies only if they had been members for more than a year. As a toast to "our sister Societies" proposed by the Provident Society noted, the "honey" of friendship needed to be "well secured from the drones." [40]

Mutual aid societies were often restrictive in yet another way. Many were organized around the smaller loyalties of the early-nineteenth-century city, easing the difficulties of creating mutuality but also reinforcing accepted lines of division by uniting neighborhoods, occupations, opinions. Even the names of the Northern Liberty Benevolent Society, the Christian Benevolent Society, and the Wesleyan Beneficial Society proclaimed particular loyalties. Ethnic groups also formed organizations restricted to their particular heritage. In the mid-1820s, Philadelphia residents of French, German, Irish, and African descent all sponsored their own mutual aid associations. Other ethnic organizations helped new immigrants. The American Friendly Institution admitted only "native[-born] Americans" to their friendship.

Despite these limitations, contemporaries almost universally celebrated charitable associations as exemplars of the benevolence that held society together. Boston Baptist minister Samuel Stillman proclaimed these organizations "undoubted evidence of the improved state of society, and a delightful exemplification of the benevolent affections, which the ever blessed God hath implanted in our nature for very important purposes." New York Masonic brother John Vanderbilt was even more enthusiastic. The more than forty "benevolent combinations" working in "the immense, unbounded field of charity" created "a glorious cause for exaltation." [41]

Masons seemed fellow laborers in the cause. Brother James Carter believed the fraternity rested "upon the broad base of universal philanthropy" that impelled other benevolent associations. "At this time . . . when Bible, Missionary, Peace, and other societies designed to ameliorate the condition of the human race are rapidly multiplying," wrote the Danvers, Massachusetts, lodge, "surely we as members of the most ancient and most extensive of them all, should be highly inexcusable were we to stand idle spectators of that glorious work which Freemasonry was especially designed and peculiarly calculated to perform."[42]

Outsiders also recognized this kinship. The Reverend Thomas Gray included the fraternity in his 1805 discussion of Boston's charities, as had another non-Mason, the Reverend Samuel Stillman, four years before. The prominent place of brothers in benevolent activities reinforced this standing. Harris and C. P. Sumner (Charles Sumner's father), both Masons, wrote songs for the Female Asylum meeting at which Stillman spoke. Brother Israel Israel played a major role in relieving sufferers in the 1793 Philadelphia yellow fever epidemic. As one of the earliest and the most successful charitable associations, the fraternity also inspired other groups, both directly, as in the case of Gloucester's 1780s Masonic Fire Society (or, presumably, Philadelphia's later Hiram Beneficial Society), and indirectly, as in that same city's Provident Society's almost Masonic claim that "benevolence, friendship and sociability" formed the "tripod of our society."[43]

But brothers also claimed that their fraternity transcended the limitations of similar groups. Masonry, James Carter argued, "differs from other benevolent associations less in the object it has in view," helping individuals and improving society, "than in the means of obtaining it." The fraternity, he noted, "most happily combines the leading objects of all benevolent associations." Through this combination, Masonry avoided both the narrow self-regard of mutual aid societies that offered friendship only to members, and the remoteness of charitable associations that paternalistically helped outsiders and often required donations rather than personal involvement from its members. Masonic fraternity instead attempted to create mutuality with both local brothers and the world. "The *true Mason*," Harris explained, "looks as much to the welfare of his colleague as to his own." The Reverend William Bentley went even further: "Our friendship is not begun in disinterested love," he argued provocatively. "We have an interest in each other." Such comprehensive friendship attracted the projectors of a new Reading, Massachusetts, lodge in the 1790s. They hoped to incorporate the town's Mechanic Society in their broader organization.[44]

Two further elements also distinguished Masonry. First, the fraternity extended beyond the locality. Rather than the "straightened and contracted" close friendship of most societies, Masonry was universal, extending even beyond the broadest benevolent societies, which, except for a handful of religious organizations, limited themselves only to a single locality. Masonic universality involved a willingness to ignore what Harris called the "petty distinctions and partial considerations, irrational prejudices and contracted sentiments" that destroyed "the friendly intercourse of mankind." "Masonry," he proclaimed, "breaks down these formidable barriers."[45]

Besides this immense vision of the fraternity as what another orator called "one grand inclosure, aiming to embrace the whole family of man," Masonry was distinctive because it taught morality. Other organizations, based more on financial contribution than on fraternal concern, lacked the ability or the inclination for such discipline, a consideration that ultimately convinced Salem minister and brother William Bentley to abandon his notion of uniting his local lodge with the town's Marine Society. "Masonry has an object beyond the Marine Society," he decided, "a design to urge the social passions." The fraternity, brothers argued, even trained members to practice philanthropy outside the lodge itself. "Works of Charity are the *least appropriate* and the *least useful* Scope of our Order," John Ernst argued in 1801. Not that these were insignificant, but the "formation of man . . . is of far more importance," leading to even greater results. Through "the Exercises of brotherly love," Masonry makes "the severest Duties of universal Philanthropy . . . more habitual and easy to him."[46]

Ultimately, Masonry's true parallel among benevolent organizations was the church. Both groups preached a mutual concern that began with, but was not to be limited to, their members. At the same time, they also provided moral training. But churches were not generally well organized for charity and, despite the rise of denominational organizations, still tended to be local or regional rather than national or international. Masons sometimes argued that the church's lack of success in spreading sympathy made their order necessary. "Were . . . the unanimity, love, equality, generosity, and disinterestedness" that characterized the early church and modern Freemasonry true among "professing Christians *now*," Harris argued, "Free Masonry would be less necessary among them."[47]

Not surprisingly, religious metaphors for the fraternity came easily to brothers and their supporters. Harris's comments about the church came after a comparison of Masonry with "the state of the primitive Christians." Just as these early Christians "had all things common," so too the brotherhood formed "a community of interests" that "makes the prosperity of each individual the object of the whole, [and] the prosperity of the whole the object of the each individual." "Thousands and thousands" of brothers "have one heart, one hand—the heart of benevolence, the hand of charity." Royall praised Masonic brothers in similarly sacred terms: "Like fire on the altar, charity and benevolence . . . that sacred spark which came down from heaven, has been preserved by masons."[48]

For Royall such benevolence could be found only in the brotherhood. She could not turn to family or community, ties worn thin by continual movement and change. Unfortunately, this same rootlessness also made other benevolent groups similarly inadequate. Royall could not (or perhaps simply would not) remain long enough in a locality to join a so-called friendly society, nor would she submit to the dependence required for other sorts of aid. In her friend-less state, Masonry alone transcended both particular bonds and geographical boundaries.

Though it provided aid for a fragmented and mobile society, the frater-nity did not celebrate this state of affairs. Indeed, Masons explicitly resisted this fragmentation. Unlike specialized charitable institutions that expected individuals to pick and choose among them, the fraternity proposed a uni-versal organization that united the world as fictive kin with common inter-ests. Masonry sought to create an enlightened family, rejecting the coercion, hierarchy, and exclusion of strangers that held other groups together but pro-moting the same close and affectionate loyalties. Providing not just the ne-cessities of existence but the love and concern of a family, Masons, Royall concluded, were "the most benevolent class on earth."[49]

II. Bound to Regard You as a Mason

The cure for political dissension, the Reverend brother Mason Locke Weems advised the New Jersey Legislature in December 1801, lay in following the ad-vice of "that great Masonic Saint" who counseled, "Love one another." "Yes best of patriots[,] let us as little children *love one another*," Parson Weems ex-horted, "and there shall be no more schism in the national body." The effect of his address, Weems wrote to his employer, Mathew Carey, was electric. "The Gov'r press'd my fist," he recalled, "thank'd me for my performance— insisted I sh'd print it." So impressed was the governor that he began a sub-scription for the pamphlet without first consulting Weems. The Council alone requested fifty copies. The resulting piece gave Masonry a prominent place. Weems included his lodge affiliation on the title page and dedicated it to the governor as his "Affectionate Countryman and Masonic brother."[50]

As these details suggest, Weems used Masonry as more than grist for the considerable rhetorical talents that led to the legendary cherry tree incident in his *Life of Washington*. The fraternity also provided aid in his other great passion, selling books. Masonic activities allowed him to beard potential cus-tomers. "Hope to vend some to-morrow at the Masonic Meeting 16 Miles from this," he wrote in the month of his address to the legislature. Two months later, he noted, "Tomorrow I set off for Newtown to be ready to utter the Masonic Oration—God grant I may sell some Bibles etc. etc." The identifi-cation of himself as a Masonic brother on his publications similarly served commercial purposes, underlining his moral authority and encouraging frater-nal patronage. Nearly all Weems's early works cited his affiliation on the title pages. His first production was dedicated to George Washington and signed, "On the square of Justice, and on the Scale of Love, I remain, Most Honored General, Your very sincere friend, And Masonic Brother. . . ." After Wash-ington's death, Weems further capitalized on the great man's fame by writing the extremely popular *Life of Washington*. By the time the cherry tree incident appeared in a later version of the book, the author identified himself (with at best considerable exaggeration) as the "Former Rector of Mt. Vernon Parish." Nearly all the early editions, however, noted instead Weems's fraternal standing.[51]

Weems was an extraordinarily inventive salesman and writer, but his employment of fraternal ties for the benefit of himself as well as his society was not unusual. Like Weems, American brothers discovered new economic uses for their fraternity in the years after the Revolution. This application of the fraternity to the problem of making a living was not the result of a clearly thought-out, coherent program. Unlike the Masonic doctrines of love that Weems taught, the fraternity's economic functions had few long-standing traditions. Instead, like Weems's entire bookselling career, Masonry's practical uses were improvised in response to new economic circumstances.

For Weems, as for other post-Revolutionary brothers, Masonry's newfound ability to provide personal economic advantage also seemed a means of healing the growing division between private advantage and the public good. Within the smaller-scale economic networks that encompassed a large proportion of most people's activities, fraternal values and activities reinforced the ideals of mutual concern and friendship even as they helped establish and reinforce individual economic standing. This dual role seemed particularly appealing to newcomers and young men attempting to establish their place in the world as well as, more generally, to occupational groups like merchants, professionals, and artisans who needed to attract clients and to build trustworthy credit relationships.[52]

Encouraging synergy between public and private benefits, however, proved more problematic than expected, particularly in long-distance commercial relationships. The ideas of mutuality and friendship helped ease the difficulties of this broader trade, but Masonic ties also increased brothers' ability to pursue selfish actions. The post-Revolutionary fraternity encouraged economic involvement among brothers even at the expense of worthy outsiders, creating in practice the very exclusivity that its teachings rejected in theory. Later opponents of the fraternity considered this situation a paradigm of all fraternal activity, a ruthless desire for self-seeking advancement cloaked in public pronouncements of morality and universal concern. But this was clearly not the brothers' original intention. The inconsistencies within Masonry's economic meanings were part of a larger series of ambivalences with which Americans faced the post-Revolutionary transformation of economic life. Just as important, they were much less apparent within the local networks like the one that the young Henry Clay entered in 1797.[53]

Henry Clay painted a dramatic picture of his arrival in Lexington, Kentucky: "I went as an orphan, who had not yet attained the age of majority," he told the United States Senate in an 1842 farewell oration, "poor, penniless, with-

out the favor of the great." In stressing his credentials as a self-made man—
a term he might have coined—Clay conveniently ignored the presence of his
mother and stepfather just outside Lexington and his two brothers already
living in the town. He also slighted his Masonic ties. Introduced into the fraternity by his legal mentor in Richmond, Virginia, Clay joined the Lexington
lodge soon after his arrival. The brothers there played an important role in his
success. Brother James Brown, Kentucky's first secretary of state, sent Clay
cases and helped him learn the intricacies of local law. Clay soon became
Brown's brother-in-law as well, marrying, like Brown, into the wealthy and
influential Hart family. Clay had undoubtedly already met his future wife's
brother at lodge meetings. Although he did not mention the fraternity in his
1842 recital of his early years, Clay's account, perhaps not surprisingly, used
a familial metaphor to describe his welcome. "Scarce had I set my foot upon
[Kentucky's] generous soil," he noted, "when I was seized and embraced with
parental fondness . . . and patronized with liberal and unbounded munifi-
cence." [54]

Clay's contrast between his arrival and his reception involved more than an
oratorical flourish. As "the deep sensibility and difficult utterance" that (according to the Senate recorder) marked the delivery of this passage suggests,
the description dramatically represented a fundamental issue, a key tension
within post-Revolutionary economic relations. [55] Clay's images of the solitary
self-made men and the friendly community rhetorically separated the complex connections between individual and communal advantage. By introducing newcomers into the community as well as reinforcing the ideal of loving
mutual exchange, the fraternity helped balance the sometimes conflicting desires for individual economic success and a harmonious society.

Both the circumstances of post-Revolutionary society and the fraternity's
particular social configuration heightened the importance of easing this natural tension between individual and social interests. Although mutual aid provided a basis for survival, the growth of mobility and commerce made these
obligations seem less compatible with advancement. Other voluntary associations and institutions helped resolve some of this conflict, but Masonry's
ideals and structures made it particularly useful. The connection can be seen
in a case considered by the Danville, Virginia, lodge in 1823.

When K——, a lodge member, required a cosigner for a personal note of
indebtedness, he turned to a Masonic brother. C—— barely knew K——, but
his fraternal relationship led him to agree. When payment was demanded,
however, K—— refused to honor the note, forcing C—— to pay the substantial sum of sixty-five dollars. K——'s Danville, Virginia, lodge considered the
matter in 1823 and acted decisively. "Their neglect to deal with Brother K. at
an earlier date," the brothers confessed, "left the impression to be made on
the mind of a comparative stranger that he, Brother K., was worthy of the
trust and confidence of the community." They repaid C—— the entire sum. [56]

The case suggests the complexity of Masonry's attempt to encourage both individual and communal benefits. Fraternal practices and teaching first reinforced brothers' reputation and facilitated their economic activities. These benefits were particularly significant for newcomers, providing screening and moral training that reassured potential trading partners and provided a means of resolving disputes. As a member of the Virginia grand lodge noted in 1798, lodges sought "to guard the conduct of their members both in society and private life." The Danville lodge made the same point, arguing that Masonic membership provided a recognized measure of moral respectability. Fulfilling the same function, a Cincinnati, Ohio, lodge rejected petitioners in 1807 for "want of character" and "want of moral character." Through its rituals, fellowship, and ideals of mutual concern, the lodge brought together men in a setting that encouraged friendship and interaction.[57]

As the Danville lodge realized, C——'s willingness to help his brother K—— grew at least partly out of fraternal loyalties. In an analogous situation in Pennsylvania, William Nelson similarly cosigned a brother's note from "motives purely Masonic." Early Lexington Lodge members Basil Duke and Frederick Ridgely created a partnership for importing drugs and medicine, as did their brothers and fellow physicians Benjamin Dudley and James Fishback. When Clay, soon to be speaker of the Kentucky House, left town for several months in early 1807, he left his cases to Jesse Bledsoe, William T. Barry, and James January, all fellow lodge members.[58]

Such connections made Masonic membership particularly useful for mobile men like C——, still a "relative stranger" in Danville. Joining a lodge often served as an early step in settling into a new location. Lexington's Jesse Bledsoe followed his close friend Clay's example of joining a lodge while establishing a legal practice. Salem, Massachusetts, minister William Bentley similarly decided that the British surgeon "Mr. Haynes" planned to "establish himself in this part of the country" when he met "with the Brethren this evening." For these new brothers, membership in the fraternity provided some of the advantages offered by letters of recommendation, helping reassure brothers and outsiders alike that a member possessed moral character and trustworthiness. Even for "uncivilized and wandering" Masons in Asia and Africa, Clark Brown told Vermont brothers in 1808, "the avenues of favor and protection always lie open."[59]

For John Clay, Henry's brother by blood and membership, these advantages seemed particularly clear. Forced to leave Lexington in 1804 because of economic difficulties, John wrote to Henry regarding a certificate attesting to his Masonic standing before arriving at his destination in New Orleans. The document would help reassure people who were otherwise unlikely to trust an outsider with a record of business failure. "I beg leave again to impress it upon you," he later wrote anxiously to Henry when the certificate failed to arrive promptly, "that you would attend to that business early as possible."[60]

Aiding the prospects of individual brothers, however, formed only part of Masonry's tasks. By spreading friendship and mutual interaction, members believed that the fraternity also laid the foundations of a harmonious and civilized society. "Without discharging the demands of mutual dependence," brother Amos Stoddard argued typically in 1797, "mankind would live like brutes, and be the perpetual enemies of each other." Weems's address to the New Jersey Legislature four years later used the same image, suggesting that "man without society" was only "a miserable Ourang Outang, who lives in-finite degrees below that state of dignity and happiness for which he was cre-ated." Masons believed their order encouraged that higher state. Since mutual involvement formed the foundation of community happiness, Stoddard sug-gested, teaching and exemplifying this morality formed "the great duty of masons."[61]

The Masonic ideal of loving mutuality extended to business relationships as well. Brother Clark Brown warned New Hampshire brothers that "the advan-tage taken of necessity and ignorance in commercial intercourse" was merely another example of the "guile, injustice and cruelty" that resulted from ignor-ing the sympathy taught by "the moral and benevolent design of Christianity and Free-masonry." In contrast, members pledged in the Master Mason's de-gree ceremony not to "wrong . . . a brother . . . to the value of one cent." South Carolina grand master William Loughton Smith termed "*A scrupulous adherence to our engagements . . .* a high masonick virtue." On the other hand, "There is no being more despicible than a tricky character, one who is always on the watch to overreach his neighbor and take advantage of his credulity and indulgences." "A strict observance of good faith between man and man," Smith concluded, "enlivens the toilsome path of business."[62]

In reinforcing this good faith, brothers sought to maintain the cooperation and mutual involvement required by local economies. To survive and pros-per, community members needed to share or exchange labor, tools, goods, and favors. This interdependence created complex webs of obligations that extended beyond business. Within this world, flexible adaptation to personal circumstances (largely what Smith meant by "indulgences") became an essen-tial economic virtue, reinforcing continuing relationships and cushioning the difficulties of economic uncertainty. These networks of obligation did not foreclose economic success; in theory and often in practice, they helped nur-ture it.[63] A New York brother later argued that the earliest merchants of Troy, New York, succeeded, not because of their competitive zeal, but because "they supported each others' credit" and "readily united in measures calculated to promote the interest of the village." "By . . . general co-operation," grand mas-ter Smith told South Carolina brothers, "nations prosper, while individuals promote their own and each other's welfare." Yet too much attention to self-interest led to difficulty. "The great difficulty" facing Masonry and society in general, Stoddard believed, "is to make [people] sensible of [their] dependence and of their interest to obey its dictates." "Our passions of sympathy and revenge"—concern for others and a desire to enjoy and profit from their failures—"often meet in collision—they constantly war in our breasts."[64]

Stoddard's martial metaphor expressed the peculiar tensions of post-Revolutionary economic life. If conflict between personal and communal advantage had always been inherent in the American economy, social and economic changes intensified this battle. The expansion of individual movement disrupted the carefully balanced obligations of community networks while the spread of trade and production for the market brought people into greater contact with and dependence upon outsiders, relative strangers whose own economic survival did not necessarily depend upon mutual concern. All this would be expressed and justified by an ideology that glorified independence. But these changes did not render Masonry's ideals of mutuality and personal morality obsolete. Indeed, the problems of a system in which growing commercial impersonality coexisted with continued personal obligations made Masonry's teachings of friendship, trust, and reputation even more relevant. Henry Clay's involvement with the Baltimore merchant (and seemingly non-Mason) William Taylor suggests the difficulties created by post-Revolutionary economic changes—and the significance of Masonic practices and ideals.

Clay's work for Taylor primarily involved collecting unpaid bills from Taylor's extensive Kentucky activities, money that, according to Taylor's instructions, was then to be sent to Baltimore by means of banknotes. This type of paper possessed great disadvantages. Banknotes could easily be irretrievably lost in transit, could be acquired only at a premium, and were often scarce. After extensive searching Clay informed Taylor in 1802 that "this Country is almost exhausted of all the light money." But banknotes had one major advantage. They represented a corporate obligation that bypassed the uncertainties of individuals. As Taylor warned Clay, "I have but slender relyance on The punctuality of people in The Country."[65]

Clay's activities suggest that Taylor's fears were well-founded. As debtors often realized only too well, legal action was slow and often inefficient. One mercantile house, Clay warned Taylor, demanded further depositions merely as a means of "procrastination." Another of Taylor's debts was settled only when Clay offered to postpone payment for the amount of time court proceedings would last. But legal recourse was not always possible. Joseph Kelly, who owed Taylor more than one thousand dollars, simply moved away. His debt was ten years old by the time Taylor discovered his whereabouts. Despite Clay's subsequent efforts, part of the money remained outstanding five years later.[66]

In such a setting, where even a well-heeled merchant employing a talented and influential attorney experienced insuperable problems, careful assessments of circumstances and character became essential. Wealth alone did not suffice, as Clay emphasized in cautioning Taylor against a potential business partner. "The character which I have received of Sheppard," he wrote, "is that he has the means, tho' not generally the disposition, to pay his debts with ease." Alternatively, confidence in a person's character could overcome other doubts. Despite Taylor's demands for banknotes, Clay accepted two personal notes in 1803, explaining that one was from "an intimate acquaintance" and the other involved "men of wealth and respectability."[67]

Personal obligation posed problems within localities as well. Even local trade created chains of debt that extended far beyond the neighborhood. Tennessee merchant John Overton was nearly bankrupted when his business partner (and Masonic brother) Andrew Jackson accepted the notes of a Philadelphia acquaintance only to find, after Jackson passed them on to to another firm, that he continued to be responsible for their repayment. Such a situation, where intervening and secondary actors often assumed the risks of another, became the subject of an almost apocalyptic warning in the 1837 *Autobiography* of Philadelphia publisher Mathew Carey, Weems's sometime employer and perhaps his Masonic brother. Although a bank board member, Carey still had to find personal securities for his bank loans. In turn, he provided the same assistance to others, a practice that led him to lose about thirty thousand dollars. "Let me then urge on the reader, who is not already sunk in this devouring vortex—would to Heaven, I could say it in a voice of thunder, shun, as you would shun temporal perdition, the rocks and quicksands of endorsation." But even Carey had to admit that his actions involved a moral obligation. "I was obliged to apply to my friends for endorsements," he explained, "and had, of necessity, to reciprocate this dangerous kindness."[68]

In such a situation, Masonry had clear economic relevance. Although his Masonic membership is not clear, Mathew Carey cited the fraternity's sacred obligation when caught in a tight spot with a debtor. He was forced, he told Joseph Clarke in 1794, to be "more troublesome and more importunate with you than my inclination would otherwise prompt me to be" because of the enormous financial demands upon him. "I assure you by the oath of a freemason," he continued, "that my payments in the month of January are 7000 dollars and . . . I shall find it hardly possible to raise that sum."[69] "Had I not belonged to the same Fraternity and been bound to regard you as a Mason," Ohio merchant John McCorkle wrote to Indiana's John Tipton after the latter lost his temper in a dispute over credit, "I should have treated your threatenings with their merited contempt."[70]

Another incident involving Tipton makes clearer the Masonic meaning of these interactions. In the middle of an 1819 letter to Tipton, Jonathan Woodbury of Hardensburgh, Indiana, began again, this time with the salutation "Dear Brother." Having started the letter with the more impersonal "Dear Sir," Woodbury's nod to their common affiliation betrayed uneasiness at having to inform Tipton that he had passed along a counterfeit banknote. Tipton had the obligation, moral if not necessarily legal, to make good the money, but Woodbury clearly realized the difficulties of compelling payment from ninety miles away. His anxiety proved unfounded. Tipton quickly sent a new note, inspiring Woodbury to write a extended celebration of the Masonic virtues exhibited by Tipton's "punctual attentions to remiting to me the money withou[t] an equivocation, from the rules of rectitude and justice." "Whilest we walk by the plumb and act on the square of justice," Woodbury wrote, "it augments the love of man, to man." "In fact, there is no other way ever yet found out, that will render mankind happy here, and I presume it will Secure happiness hereafter." "I am," he ended the letter, "Dear Brother, Yours Sincerely. . . ."[71]

As Woodbury suggested, Masonry's economic ethic discouraged what brother Hezekiah Niles called "the mere calculating spirit of trade, and sole attention to dollars and cents." Rather than encouraging brothers to succeed in an amoral world of self-seeking, Masonry strove to embed economic activities in a larger vision of personal responsibility and mutuality. This attempt to advance members' economic interests within the context of a larger social vision can be seen as well in Masonic discipline, an activity that also had clear implications for both economic benefit and communal ideals.[72]

Had Tipton not accepted his duty, McCorkle or Woodbury could have taken his complaint to the brotherhood. The Lynchburg, Virginia, lodge considered an analogous situation in 1796, when Samuel Scott wrote to his Masonic brother James Mozeley in "abusive Language" about a promised "Parcell of corn." The lodge determined the agreement between the two to be ambiguous and set a new date for delivery. As a Virginia brother suggested two years later, lodges sought to "admonish . . . the vicious" and, if unsuccessful, "finally, to suspend or expel from the benefits of masonry all incorrigible transgressors." Some state bodies, as had Virginia the year before, extended the lodge's oversight to brothers unaffiliated with any local lodge.[73] The disciplines of brotherhood, many members believed, included forswearing legal action against all but the most recalcitrant brothers. "Masons," Clark Brown suggested, "ought . . . to settle all disputes and grievances among themselves." Even when a lodge could not resolve a case, Brown argued, the parties should not go to civil courts, but appeal to the grand lodge, the "Supreme Court of masonic judicature." So important did this principle seem that Pennsylvania in 1820 seriously considered making Brown's metaphor an actuality by establishing its own courts "for the adjustment of differences and of disputed accounts between Masons."[74]

More than the difficulties of implementation caused brothers to abandon the plan. Formal courts would have undermined an additional goal of Masonic discipline. Just as much as justice and fraternal harmony, lodges also sought to rehabilitate offenders, aiming, Tipton wrote about another case, "to correct his follies, improve his knowledge and make him more usefull to society." Significantly, the Danville lodge gave K—— only a warning about the incident with C——, before expelling him after another offense two years later. As the long interval suggests, lodge discipline sought changes of heart. When Otis Robbins made reparation for his thefts as collector of taxes and regained "the confidence and good opinion of his brethren and the Community," the Massachusetts grand lodge voted to "receive" the expelled member back "with kindness."[75]

Such Masonic discipline formed part of a larger post-Revolutionary reaction against legalism. Following the biblical ideal that also inspired Masonic practices, religious groups like Methodists and Presbyterians discouraged legal actions among their members. The 1790s movement for legal reform, centered in the Democratic-Republican party, drew upon these attitudes and a more general anger against lawyers to demand a court system that would be more responsive to local standards and individual situations. Brother Felix Grundy of Kentucky spearheaded this campaign's greatest success.[76]

More commercially oriented men such as Henry Clay (Grundy's lodge brother) almost universally opposed these attempts. Many promoted instead an alternative vision of legal requirements that judged contracts solely by their written terms rather than their fairness or mutuality, a position that, among other advantages, allowed creditors greater legal protection. But this new legalism represented more a desire for ultimate recourse than a model for commercial relations. The growing popularity of Masonry among lawyers and men engaged in extensive commerce suggests that they too feared a system dominated by self-seeking, impersonal competition and held in check only by legalities interpreted by outsiders. Instead, Masonry offered a vision of a society bound by ties of morality and friendship, what Weems called "the square of Justice, and . . . the Scale of Love."[77]

In promoting this society, Masonry once again shared important functions with other voluntary associations. Henry Clay's membership in Lexington's debating society and in the Jeffersonian Republican party, like his Masonic ties, boosted his legal business and helped form alliances that could be used for economic advantage. Others joined churches that offered fraternal ties and practical aid. As in its charity, however, Masonry attempted to be more comprehensive than any of these other groups. It combined moral culture and close friendship with a broader inclusiveness that made room for newcomers and outsiders. As a look at the social characteristics of lodges suggests, these increasingly separated goals seemed particularly significant in the years after the Revolution not only because they responded to larger social and economic changes but because they fitted the experiences and desires of a particular range of ages, occupations, and aspirations.[78]

For Henry Clay, Lexington Lodge provided more than a means of gaining the trust and confidence of his new neighbors. Through his membership and

Table 10. Occupations in Lexington, Kentucky, Directory, 1806, and of Lodge Members, 1794–1810

Occupation	Lexington Directory[a]	Lexington Lodge[b]
Merchant	28 (11.3%)	35 (30.4%)
Professional	22 (8.9%)	34 (29.6%)
Government official	5 (2.0%)	6 (5.2%)
Luxury goods artisan	11 (4.5%)	6 (5.2%)
Mercantile-related artisan	4 (1.6%)	1 (.9%)
Building crafts artisan	38 (15.4%)	7 (6.1%)
Other artisanal	109 (44.1%)	11 (9.6%)
Retailer	27 (10.9%)	7 (6.1%)
Agriculturalist		8 (7.0%)
Other	3 (1.2%)	

[a] 247 of 247 listed.   [b] 115 of 167 identified.

Sources: J. Winston Coleman, Jr., *Masonry in the Bluegrass; Being an Authentic Account of Masonry in Lexington and Fayette County, Kentucky, 1788-1933* (Lexington, Ky., 1934); William M. Stuart, "Masonry North and South: Two Remarkable Lodge Records," *Am. Lodge Res. Trans.*, II (1936-1938), 449-460; *Kentucky Gazette (and General Advertiser)* (Lexington), 1790-1817; *Charless' Kentucky, Tennessee, and Ohio Almanack for the Year 1807* . . . (Lexington, Ky., 1806), rpt. in J. Winston Coleman, Jr., *Lexington's First City Directory . . . 1806* (Lexington, Ky., 1953); Hopkins, ed., *Papers of Clay*, I.

(by 1802 if not earlier) leadership in the local brotherhood, he established fraternal ties with some of the most influential men in his profession. Nearly one-quarter of Lexington Lodge members during the period of Clay's fullest participation belonged to the legal community, including most of the city's leading lawyers, men like James Brown (his early benefactor) and Felix Grundy (his later rival).[79] Just as important, the lodge also brought together court officers and judges who could ease Clay's path through a new legal system. The state attorney general, the county sheriff, the county clerk of Jessamine County, the clerk of the circuit court, and the United States district judge all belonged to the lodge (Table 10).

The legal profession's continued importance in Masonic lodges illuminates the social limits of Masonry's Revolutionary transformation. Although it grew beyond the colonial elite, the fraternity did not become simply a cross-section of the larger population. Specific ages, occupations, and aspirations all

Table 11. Age at Membership of Jordan Lodge Members, Danvers, Massachusetts, 1808–1827

Age at Joining	Proportion of Membership	Age at Joining	Proportion of Membership
1–19	.7%	32–33	5.9%
20–21	3.7	34–35	2.9
22–23	19.1	36–37	3.7
24–25	23.5	38–39	1.5
26–27	14.7	40–44	8.8
28–29	11.8	45–49	2.2
30–31	2.2	60–69	.7

Note: Of 144 members, 136 were identified. Members who were affiliated, that is, who received degrees elsewhere, are excluded.

shaped the post-Revolutionary fraternity. Young men establishing an independent economic identity, professionals, merchants, and artisans who needed support and connections, and ambitious men all entered the fraternity in large numbers partly because it spoke directly to central economic issues in their lives. Although, as someone who later became a grand master and a national political figure, Clay can hardly be considered typical, the young lawyer who entered Lexington Lodge at the end of the eighteenth century fitted a pattern established by numerous post-Revolutionary brothers.

According to strict Masonic standards, Clay should not even have been a Mason when he arrived in Lexington. He had been made a brother in Richmond, Virginia, when he was only twenty, one year shy of the minimum age accepted by all official bodies. The willingness to breach the rule, not uncommon in the period, suggests the popular acceptance of Masonic initiation as a part of a particular phase of life. New members often were in the ill-defined segment of the male life cycle in which a young man (generally in his late teens to his late twenties) left his parents' household, established an occupation, and got married.[80] More than one-half the members of the Danvers, Massachusetts, lodge joined by age twenty-five; more than three-quarters entered the lodge before they were thirty. Only 1 of the more than 130 identifiable members joined after the age of fifty (Table 11). Even outsiders recognized this relative youth. A Maine orator complained that some people believed the fraternity "a mere matter of amusement to young men."[81]

Economic needs as much as amusement helped attract these men. Membership eased the difficult transition to independent economic existence outside the parental household. Like newcomers, young men often needed to establish a commercial reputation and networks of business and credit. Masonry was particularly helpful in laying these foundations because, unlike many other organizations for the young, the fraternity also included older men. Although Clay joined a Lexington debating society about the same time he entered the town's lodge, his interest waned after only a few years. He continued within the lodge until 1824, however, more than a quarter of a century.[82]

Specific occupational groups as well as particular ages also distinguished Masonry. Lawyers and other professionals formed a central element within Lexington Lodge and the national fraternity. Merchants, shopkeepers, and artisans made up the bulk of the rest. Lodges in both village and urban settings illustrate the contours of this membership and the conditions that shaped it.

Lexington had, as Clay noted later, "a bar uncommonly distinguished by eminent members," but even the hordes of lawyers attracted by the uncertainties of Kentucky land titles did not form a majority of the lodge membership.[83] Of the some three-quarters of the members that worked outside the legal profession, men engaged in trade made up the largest group. Nearly one-third of the whole (30.4 percent) were merchants. Government officials (5.2 percent), artisans, shopkeepers, and innkeepers (27.9 percent), and other professionals (7.0 percent) from Lexington and elsewhere made up the bulk of the rest. Their concentration within the lodge can be seen by comparing Masonry's regional membership with the village's occupational structure. Although professionals, merchants, and government officials made up almost two-thirds of the lodge, they numbered, according to the 1807 town directory, fewer than one-quarter of the village residents (Table 10).

Both Ark Lodge in Geneva, New York, and Jordan Lodge in Danvers, Massachusetts, show a similar range (Table 12).[84] These northern lodges attracted a smaller proportion of professionals, about 15 percent in each, perhaps because, unlike Lexington, neither was a county seat or major court center. More than one-quarter of Ark brothers (27.5 percent) engaged in trade, a group similar in size to Lexington Lodge, but only one-twentieth of the Jordan members (5.0 percent) were merchants, not surprising for a small town outside the major commercial center of Salem. Instead, artisans and shopkeepers made up the bulk of the Danvers brothers (47.2 percent) as well as a number labeled manufacturers (7.5 percent) by a later local historian. Even in the midst of a heavily agricultural area of upstate New York, men who primarily farmed made up only about one-tenth of the Geneva lodge (11.8 percent). Among the Lexington brothers, such agricultural employments characterized a small, barely noticeable element.[85]

This variation in particular proportions can also be seen in urban lodges. City bodies tended to draw men slightly lower on the social scale than the eminent lawyers that filled Lexington's lodge hall. Boston and Philadelphia's earliest Ancient groups continued to attract high proportions of artisans and

Table 12. Occupations of Members of Ark Lodge, Geneva, New York, and Jordan Lodge, Danvers, Massachusetts, 1807–1827

Occupation	Ark Lodge, 1807–1819[a]	Jordan Lodge, 1808–1827[b]
Merchant	14 (27.5%)	8 (5.0%)
Professional	10 (19.6%)	22 (13.8%)
Government official	2 (3.9%)	
Manufacturer		12 (7.5%)
Luxury goods artisan	4 (7.8%)	
Building crafts artisan	2 (3.9%)	9 (5.7%)
Other artisanal	12 (23.5%)	56 (35.2%)
Retail	1 (2.0%)	10 (6.3%)
Agricultural	6 (11.8%)	20 (12.6%)
Seagoing		21 (13.2%)
Other		1 (.6%)

[a] 51 of 96 identified.   [b] 159 of 172 identified.

Sources: Stelter, *History of Ark Lodge No. 33;* Thompson, ed., *Index to the Newspapers Published in Geneva;* Massey, *History of Freemasonry in Danvers, Massachusetts.*

shopkeepers (Table 13). More than two-thirds of Philadelphia's Lodge No. 2 belonged to these groups in both 1792–1795 and 1820. The post-Revolutionary membership of St. Andrew's Lodge in Boston (1790–1820) actually included proportionately more artisans than before the war. Although such mechanics had made up about one-quarter of the earlier lodge, they now accounted for nearly two-thirds (63.5 percent). The memoir of a leading member noted many "North End Mechanics." [86]

Urban lodges, however, included more than artisans. Both groups attracted a number of merchants, nearly one-tenth of each lodge. Indeed, two of the period's wealthiest traders, Philadelphia's Stephen Girard and New York City's John Jacob Astor, also belonged to lodges in their respective cities. Astor's Holland Lodge attracted a substantial number of that city's leaders in the 1790s. Headed for years by De Witt Clinton, this lodge consisted primarily of merchants (47.6 percent) and professionals (18.8 percent). Only about one-fifth of the lodge (19.6 percent) were smaller-scale artisans and retailers (Table 14). [87]

Although a variety of economic and cultural factors drew particular men into the fraternity, the nearly universal predominance of professionals, mer-

Table 13. Occupations of Members of St. Andrew's Lodge, Boston, and Lodge No. 2, Philadelphia, 1790–1820

Occupation	St. Andrew's 1790–1820[a]	Lodge No. 2 1792–1795[b]	Lodge No. 2 1820[c]
Merchant	5 (9.6%)	4 (8.7%)	2 (7.4%)
Professional	2 (3.8%)	4 (8.7%)	5 (18.5%)
Luxury goods artisan	3 (5.8%)		2 (7.4%)
Mercantile-related artisan	13 (25.0%)		
Building crafts artisan	8 (15.4%)	7 (15.2%)	3 (11.1%)
Other artisanal	9 (17.3%)	16 (34.8%)	9 (33.3%)
Retail	8 (15.4%)	8 (17.4%)	3 (11.1%)
Seagoing	2 (3.8%)	4 (8.7%)	1 (3.7%)
Other	2 (3.8%)	3 (6.5%)	2 (7.4%)

[a] 52 of 61 identified. [b] 46 of 91 identified. [c] 27 of 33 identified.

Sources: The Lodge of St. Andrew, and the Massachusetts Grand Lodge . . . 5756–5769; Barratt and Sachse, *Freemasonry in Pennsylvania,* II, 3, 64, 67, 69, 212–213; Philadelphia directories.

chants, and artisans highlights common economic issues that made Masonry attractive. First, for all but the best-connected, these occupations tended to be difficult to enter. Securing clients without the ties and reputation built through family and neighborhood was difficult. As a non-Mason wrote to Clay in 1804 about a silversmith moving to Lexington, "I need not suggest much to your extended and discriminateing mind the utility and importance of having influential friends in the commencement of business among strangers." His concerns were entirely understandable, for the new silversmith would have vied for business with two Masonic brothers who had been in Lexington for years, including Edward West, crafter of the first county seal. Men in these fields also depended upon credit for their livelihood, placing a further strain upon the resources required to establish a trade or profession. "'Tis not reasonable further indulgence should be given," Lexington merchant brother John Jordan lectured his customers in September 1802; but he was forced to ask for payment again the following year. More than one-third of the men in the Geneva Lodge sample experienced some form of debt difficulty, a list of troubles that ranges from bringing suit to recover money to seeking exemption from imprisonment for their own debts.[88]

The primary occupations represented in the lodge were also relatively rare.

Table 14. Occupations of Members of Holland Lodge No. 8, New York City, 1787–1800

Merchants (99): 47.6%
   91 merchants, agent for British packets, auctioneer, broker, commission merchant, counting house, fur trader, vendue master, wine merchant

Professionals (39): 18.8%
   23 attorneys, 11 physicians, 2 counselors-at-law, druggist and apothecary, physician and surgeon, schoolmaster

Government officials (5): 2.4%
   Chief clerk in Department of War, clerk in Treasury, clerk in Department of War, notary public, president of the United States (George Washington)

Foreign dignitaries (5): 2.4%
   3 foreign aristocrats, secretary of the ministry of the United Netherlands, Swedish consul

Banking and financial (6): 2.9%
   3 bank tellers, banker and businessman, clerk in bank, insurance broker

Artistic (4): 1.9%
   2 organists, printer/publisher of directory/Shakespeare gallery, portrait painter

Luxury goods artisans (3): 1.4%
   Bookseller, engraver, hairdresser

Mercantile-related artisans (3): 1.4%
   2 ship chandlers, ship carpenter

Building crafts (7): 3.4%
   4 painters and glaziers, 2 upholsterers, painter

Other artisans (9): 4.3%
   2 tailors, baker, butcher, distillery, furrier, shoemaker, tanner and currier, wheelwright

Retailers (19): 9.1%
   7 grocers, 7 shopkeepers, 2 taverners, hardware store, tavern and boardinghouse, coffeehouse

Seagoing (8): 3.8%
   5 shipmasters, 2 mariners, captain of the cutter

Other (1): .5%

Note: 208 of 315 identified.
Source: *Sesquicentennial Commemorative Volume of Holland Lodge No. 8 of the Ancient and Honorable Fraternity of Free and Accepted Masons* (New York, 1938), 148–162; New York directories.

Although only three lawyers belonged to the Danvers lodge, these brothers probably still made up a substantial portion of the town's bar. In villages like Danvers or Lexington, Masonry brought together men who shared the cosmopolitan attitudes and broader learning that often characterized merchants and professionals. In urban areas that could offer more specialized social and occupational organizations, the fraternity failed to attract these men in such large numbers.

Besides specific ages and occupations, the fraternity also attracted men with broader economic horizons. The professional, mercantile, and artisanal groups that swelled membership rolls tended to be at the forefront of post-Revolutionary economic change. Clay later told neighbors that he had expected only modest success when he arrived in Lexington. Whether or not this was so—he had, after all, studied with the attorney general and former governor of Virginia—he expanded his horizons quickly. His clients soon included not only Tennessee brother Andrew Jackson but merchants from Chillicothe, Richmond, Pittsburgh, and Philadelphia. Clay's wealth grew with his practice, eventually including thousands of acres of land as well as investments in salt, hemp, hotels, and the Kentucky Insurance Company. His defense as a young state legislator of that corporation's move into banking helped establish a political career that steadfastly promoted active government aid to the economy.[89]

As an example of and a spokesman for broader economic development, Clay provided a pattern for many other Masonic brothers whose occupations and cosmopolitan outlook led them to seek advantage beyond local trading networks. Both Andrew Jackson and his vice-president and Masonic brother Richard Mentor Johnson (who studied with Lexington brother James Brown) became so involved in stores and land speculation that their legal practice became only a minor part of their activities. Not surprisingly, a number of leading national spokesmen for economic development belonged to the fraternity, including Clay himself, Hezekiah Niles, and Mathew Carey. On a more local level, more than one-eighth of all Ark Lodge members appear in the town's newspaper supporting calls for roads, canals, and other internal improvements.[90]

Masonry thus attracted the very men most likely to experience the tensions Clay dramatized in his farewell speech, the feeling of entering new territories without trustworthy guides (literally as well as figuratively) and the desire for a friendly community. Masonry spoke to both sides of this difficulty. It provided economic benefits for ambitious young men engaged in commercial, professional, and artisanal occupations even as it reinforced the mutual involvement that encouraged both economic gain and social harmony. The broader horizons of these men also encouraged involvement in political action and concern for the community. Ironically, however, these same men were also expanding their economic activities in ways that increased the tension between individuals and their society, an irony suggested by an incident involving John Tipton.

In April 1829, James F. D. Lanier, a Madison, Indiana, lawyer, wrote to Tipton, now the federal Indian agent at Fort Wayne, about the possibility of doing business. "Whilst we were together at the grand lodge last winter," the Madison lawyer reminded Tipton, "you gave me assurances of getting a contract for the supply of some goods to the Indians." Tipton's action, Lanier suggested, would fulfill the ideals of brotherly charity, helping not only to pay his deceased father's debts (which he felt to be "an *honorary* obligation," if not a legal one) but also to support "an aged mother[, a] wife[,] and four little children." "Your compliance will confer an obligation to be remembered and repaid," Lanier further promised, signing the letter, "Yours fraternally." Tipton responded in a brotherly manner. While Lanier asked for only a one-thousand-dollar contract, Tipton provided a three-thousand-dollar one.[91]

The exchange between Lanier and Tipton reveals the powerful benefits available through Masonic ties. Living more than one hundred miles apart, Tipton clearly lacked personal knowledge of Lanier's circumstances. But Lanier could appeal to their common fraternity in a letter that also portrayed the proposed contract as a charitable act and a means to gain future benefits. Indeed, Tipton seems to have accepted Lanier's suggestion that the transaction created a debt that went beyond the exchange of money and goods. Lanier later supported Tipton's senatorial aspirations in his region and served as legal mentor to one of Tipton's sons.[92]

As Lanier's successful attempt at persuasion suggests, Masonic ties could be useful in long-distance trading relationships as a means of gaining advantage over competitors who lacked such a fraternal bond. Masonry brought Tipton and Lanier together, even though they lived many miles from each other, not only because of their contact in meetings but because of a new Masonic doctrine that encouraged brothers to enter into such relationships by recommending preference to Masons over outsiders. This ideal helped brothers negotiate the often confusing post-Revolutionary economy, providing Tipton with one means of differentiating between ambitious and willing contractors. But these new uses of Masonry also created a deeper tension between the fraternity's claim to promote the public good and its use for individual profit. In practice, brothers such as Lanier could use Masonry to create a particular identity very much like the sects, parties, and nationalities that the fraternity claimed to supersede. Rather than simply establishing universal brotherhood and social unity, fraternal ties also created exclusive ties that brothers could exploit for their own advantage.

The fraternity first provided increased personal contacts. While Weems visited Masonic meetings to sell books, Lanier advanced his commercial interests by meeting with brothers from different parts of the state in the grand lodge. Glover Perrin, an upstate New York innkeeper, found an even more creative means of using his membership. He placed Masonic emblems on his tavern sign, he told a visiting De Witt Clinton in 1810, "to prevent his debtors from seizing the house." Fraternal advantages could extend beyond individual transactions. Tipton and Clay both asked Masonic brothers to provide letters of introduction. Appealing to a more anonymous audience, Weems noted his membership on his title pages just as other brothers identified themselves in advertisements. Robert Brookhouse, a Salem, Massachusetts, goldsmith and jeweler, placed Masonic symbols on his trade card. Besides noting his "extensive assortment of Ready-made Clothing," J. T. Jacobs and Company also included a large Masonic emblem in its 1824 advertisement in the New York city directory, explicitly addressing readers already looking for help in the area.[93]

The "Southern and Western Merchants" that Jacobs hoped to entice into his store would be drawn not just by an increased likelihood of personal consideration but by a Masonic ideal that explicitly promoted business activities between brothers. In the years after the Revolution, brothers established a new doctrine of "preference," a requirement that brothers "prefer" each other in business "before any other person in the same circumstances." "Around this altar," the master reminded the brothers in a charge often given at the closing of a lodge, "you have solemnly and repeatedly promised to befriend and relieve, with unhesitating cordiality . . . every brother who shall need your assistance." This aid, members were instructed, went beyond charitable relief. "Strangers and foreigners" who were Masons were also "to be recommended for employment if an opportunity offers." "Masons in every situation of life," suggested an enthusiastic brother's proposal for a Masonic directory of occupations, "must be inclined, in unison with the principles of that brotherly love, on which . . . the order is founded, to give a preference to brethren who want employment, or who have articles for disposal of which they stand in need." [94]

Masonic ties did more than promote broad moral standards; they actually guided the paths of trade. Such direction was particularly useful in the post-Revolutionary economic order. As the desire for a Masonic directory suggested, choosing among a multitude of possible employers, suppliers, and potential customers was a complex task in an economy of small firms. Even the period's largest businesses continued to be overwhelmingly personal. Despite his extensive practice, Henry Clay never took on a partner. Even banks were run by (and to a large extent for) a small group. Inevitably, such a system made relationships beyond the locality difficult. The obligations and mutual concern that characterized community interactions tended to diminish over distance. "When I left Kentucky," former Kentucky secretary of state James Brown wrote to his lodge brother Henry Clay after moving to New Orleans, "I counted on being somewhat cheated in my old accounts—Settle it as well as you can and I shall be content." Brown's attempt to preserve good relations

Figure 15. Tavern Sign. Trapshire, New Hampshire, circa 1819. *Courtesy of Scottish Rite Museum of Our National Heritage, 91.008.4. Photography by David Bohl*

J. T. JACOBS & CO.

MERCHANT TAILORS,

Corner of Maiden-Lane and Nassau Street,

Respectfully inform their friends and the public that they have now on hand an extensive assortment of

READY-MADE CLOTHING,

consisting of Frock Coats, Dress Coats, Coatees, Pantaloons and Vests, assorted sizes of the latest fashions, and a superior style of workmanship. Summer Coatees, Round Jackets and Pantaloons of Canton Camblets, Bombazines, Bombazetts, Circassians, Sinchew, Pongees, striped Denmark Satin, Drillings plain and striped, Florentines, &c. &c. Children's Dresses and Youths' Clothing constantly on on hand.

J. T JACOBS & Co. assure their friends and the public, that their present assortment comprises as fresh and as great a variety as can be found in the city. All of which they will sell at reduced prices.

Southern and Western Merchants are respectfully invited to call and examine their Stock of Clothing, which will be sold on the lowest possible terms, by the case or package, for cash or approved endorsed paper.

Figure 16. Advertisement, J. T. Jacobs and Co., Merchant Tailors. *From Thomas Longworth,* Longworth's American Almanac, New-York Register, and City Directory *(New York, 1824). Courtesy American Antiquarian Society*

by refusing to press his contractual rights perhaps reflected earlier experience. After Brown sued the Virginian Elisha Hall "to compel the payment of a small sum," Hall prepared a pamphlet so slanderous that Brown felt compelled to publish a sixty-page rejoinder rebutting the charges.[95]

In a society where long-distance relationships threatened such dangerous consequences, Masonry provided valuable aid in choosing (on moral and practical levels) between the scores of Lexington lawyers or New York clothing shops. But this use of Masonry also helped subvert the fraternity's larger ideals. In this context, brotherly ties operated much like the older, more particular loyalties of family, sect, nationality, and neighborhood. Particularly in the less well marked commercial paths of the colonial period, these ties of obligation had played an important role in facilitating economic life and encouraging distant partners to look beyond narrow self-interest. But Masonry opposed the parochialism of these identifications. It recommended instead a voluntary society open to all men based on merit rather than particular ties. Ironically, Masonic brotherhood, when applied to post-Revolutionary business, could become another example of the primitive corporate solidarity created by these older distinctions. "As by a kind of magic spell," claimed one orator, "the language of the craft, at all times and in all places, can call into action the sympathetic and benevolent affections."[96]

Weems's desire both to promote virtue and to sell books through Masonry thus turned out to be more ambiguous than he or other Masons realized. Beyond the locality, the fraternity entered the more contested frontiers of economic change, a world where the balance between social and individual good seemed less certain. Masonry's expanded post-Revolutionary reach allowed brothers opportunities for creating and maintaining economic relationships that, in their scramble for survival and success, they could hardly afford to ignore. Exploiting the various meanings of Masonic ties, however, created a disjunction between the brothers' search for personal advantage and their professed concern for the common good. While public explanations of the fraternity emphasized its attempt to restrain selfish actions, its everyday workings provided increased opportunities for them, allowing Lanier to gain government business at the expense of other willing (and perhaps as needy) merchants. Members "bound to regard [brothers] as a Mason" challenged the parochial communities of family, neighborhood, and sect but ironically also created a new kind of exclusivity that undermined the fraternity's emphasis on moral and intellectual merit. Ignoring or dismissing countervailing Masonic tendencies, later opponents of the fraternity would see this difficulty more clearly—and less charitably.

In 1792, Salem minister William Bentley copied into his diary a prayer that presaged the larger issues raised by post-Revolutionary Masonry's growing practical importance. The text described the fraternity as "a Temple to th[e] praise" of the "universal Creator." "It is formed," it stated, "of those rich materials with which heaven is built and . . . it is of the same proportions upon which thy world was fashioned." The temple's pillars rested on both a base of "pure Self Love" and a base of "Social Happiness."[97]

As Bentley realized, Masonry held such a significant place in post-Revolutionary America because it seemed to exemplify the highest standards of both heaven and earth. The order's expansion, then just beginning, took it into nearly every part of the nation and extended its reach among the nation's political, commercial, and cosmopolitan leaders. Except for a few nagging questions and a small band of vocal sectarians, Americans largely acquiesced in the brothers' extraordinary claims about their order. Pennsylvanians rejected by a local lodge even took to petitioning the grand lodge to obtain admission.[98]

This standing, Bentley's prayer pointed out, depended greatly upon the fraternity's ability to get the proportions right. Masonry convinced many of its role as "the handmaid of Christianity," but the temple could hardly claim to be more significant than the church itself. Even more dangerously, the fraternity's balance of pure self-love and social happiness could easily degenerate into selfishness. Masonry's practical uses fitted brothers' economic needs too well not to be used sometimes to gain economic advantages at the expense of others.

The bases of Masonry's temple thus stood in tension. As the prayer suggested, the fraternity's cultural and practical uses—its links to the widely shared ideals of virtue, education, and religion, its charitable activities, and its ability to facilitate local and long-distance commerce—helped to hold together society, to unite what expansion and change threatened to tear asunder. But Masonry's ability to identify itself with the early national order by encompassing its tensions also created problems. Colonial Masonry had made a place for itself by playing a secondary part in a larger social and cultural setting. The post-Revolutionary fraternity placed itself at the center of society. This attempt to embody, to incarnate, the foundations of its world would exalt Masonry—and create the contradictions that would later nearly destroy it. The fraternity's great expansion (in ideological and practical importance as well as size) produced insupportable tensions that would be ruthlessly exposed when the early national order began to crumble in the 1820s. One of the key focuses of this attack lay in the political advantages that Hiram Hopkins and others realized were part of the fraternity's benefits.

CHAPTER EIGHT

In Almost Every Place
Where Power Is of Importance

Politics, 1790–1826

Although relatively unknown, Daniel Tompkins was a serious candidate for New York State governor, a more established state politician assured a worried Solomon Southwick in 1807. Southwick, an Albany newspaper editor and political insider as well as a disillusioned Mason, believed the thirty-three-year-old Tompkins was too closely linked to New York City to win election to the state's highest office. The politician attempted to set Southwick's mind at ease by citing Tompkins's Masonic connections. As a former official of the fraternity, the candidate had visited a number of upstate lodges, and, the politician predicted, "they will turn out to support him." [1]

Tompkins won the election, eventually going on to become vice-president of the United States and, at the same time, grand master of New York. Thinking back years later as a bitter opponent of Masonry, Southwick believed he had found the key to Tompkins's success: "I now seriously believe," he wrote in 1827, "that he made his debut on the political stage, through their influence." [2]

The truth of the matter was somewhat more ambiguous. Southwick was almost certainly wrong about the particulars of the case. Tompkins's chief rival, Morgan Lewis, was himself a brother—and a later New York grand master. Furthermore, as Masons repeatedly argued, the fraternity brought together a wide range of political beliefs and loyalties—and explicitly prohibited discussing them within the lodge.

If Southwick's specific suspicions were misplaced, however, his broader concern about the fraternity's influence pointed to something important, the close ties between Masonry and post-Revolutionary political life. Reflecting the fraternity's occupational composition, cosmopolitan ideals, and high social standing as much as its political uses, lodges included substantial numbers of politically active and aware men. The results of this involvement were more intricate, and more revealing, than either Southwick or his Masonic brothers claimed. While Masonry failed to sustain an important partisan role, it offered an important means by which Americans adapted older styles of politics to the new situations created by the Revolution.[3]

Within the narrower realm of partisan activities (the success or failure of particular candidates, policies, or parties), Masonry had only intermittent and inconsistent impact. Although party spirit and conflicting political loyalties sometimes overwhelmed admonitions to harmonious brotherhood and fraternal neutrality, Masonry generally discouraged overt partisanship, thereby helping delay the development of full-scale political parties until the 1820s and 1830s. The range of different positions and affiliations within the fraternity as well as the longtime Masonic prohibition on direct political involvement within the lodge hindered any sustained attempts to use the fraternity to serve a particular group or party.[4]

If Masonry had only minor impact on partisan politics, it clearly played a role in more fundamental political questions about the ordering of power and authority. The fraternity did not, despite Southwick's charge, anoint individual candidates. As an organization of national reach and high social standing, however, Masonry formed part of the post-Revolutionary infrastructure of power and authority, helping to constrain, channel, and facilitate political activities. Within this broader realm, Masonry helped both to open up and to restrict participation. The broadened social composition of the lodge as well as its ideology of fraternity and equality offered growing numbers of men both high social standing and fraternal connections with powerful men. At the same time, however, exclusive brotherhood also helped consolidate a privileged group. The fraternity offered relatively well-to-do men with cosmopolitan learning greater opportunities to communicate and cooperate with each other while proclaiming commitment to the public will and the general welfare.

This ambiguity fitted well into the period's political developments. The Revolution and its attendant social changes challenged the colonies' elite-dominated system of personal connections between prosperous men linked by family, neighborhood, and patronage. Yet greater popular participation within new political structures did not immediately destroy older forms. Nationally organized mass political parties run by professional operatives and emphasizing democracy and public opinion would not develop for a generation. Despite periods of intense partisan divisions in the intervening years, political organization and activity continued to be directed by a political leadership that, while it was wider and more inclusive, still tended to be made up of men who were relatively more wealthy and cosmopolitan.[5]

As Antimasons like Southwick recognized (sometimes only dimly), post-Revolutionary Masonry's ability to expand the circles of politically active men and to increase their power made the fraternity a pillar of early national political culture. Tompkins's election might not have been directed by the fraternity, but his membership was not completely irrelevant to his standing either.

Every New York governor but one from Tompkins's predecessor in 1804 to the late 1820s would also be a brother. The complex role of Masonry in both partisan politics and the more fundamental work of organizing power began with the high concentration of political leaders within the fraternity. Once again, the case of Henry Clay is instructive.[6]

1. The Most Influential and Respectable Men

Although Clay eventually outshone all other Kentucky politicians, in his early years he was merely a promising junior member of the lodge, following a path blazed by his lodge brothers through the Kentucky House and the United States Congress. Lawyer Edmund Bullock had already headed the Kentucky Assembly before Clay began his legal training. Captain John Fowler started his ten-year stint in Congress about the time Henry Clay arrived in Lexington. Brother Buckner Thruston became a United States senator the year before Clay partly because Clay shifted votes to defeat the candidate supported by Felix Grundy, himself a Lexington Lodge member and a former congressman. Even Clay's 1811 election to the speakership of the United States House of Representatives, the high point of his nascent career, had already been foreshadowed by a lodge brother's brief term earlier that same year as president pro tem of the Senate. More than one-fifth of all Lexington Lodge members during the years before Clay's national prominence served in the Kentucky or United States legislature. Lexington brothers' political involvement extended beyond the peaks of state and national politics. Locally, nearly one of eight held the post of town trustee. A substantial number also held appointive posts on the bench or in the bureaucracy. Altogether, almost half of the Lexington members held some public office.[7]

Clay's membership in Lexington Lodge thus brought him more than contact with professional colleagues and potential clients; he also could claim fraternity with some of the most powerful men in the town and state. Although Lexington brothers were particularly prominent, their extensive political involvement was not accidental or fortuitous. A high proportion of American brothers sought and held political office. This extensive participation partly grew out of the fraternity's popularity among occupations that tended to encourage political interest and involvement. At the same time, the fraternity's expanded yet still exclusive social range allowed it to become a center for aspiring and established leaders that could provide the connections and status necessary for attaining public office.

These characteristics allowed Masonry to fit into the broader patterns of political activity. In the years after the Revolution, republican ideals and the expansion of elective offices helped open up political involvement beyond the narrow circles of gentry and urban elites that had dominated colonial politics. Opportunities for aspiring leaders multiplied. Yet these changes,

Table 15. Public Offices Held by Ark Lodge Members, Geneva, New York, 1807–1819

National
  1 congressman (2 others decline nomination to run)

State
  7 assemblymen (3 others candidates), 1 state senator

County
  12 justices of the peace

Village
  12 assessors, 10 trustees, 8 constables, 6 collectors, 3 inspectors of common schools, 2 commissioners of highways, 2 fire wardens, 2 presidents, 2 treasurers, coroner, overseer of the poor, sheriff, surveyor, town clerk

---

Note: 44 of 96 identified.
Source: John H. Stelter, *History of Ark Lodge No. 33, F. and A.M.: 1807–1957* (Geneva, N.Y., [1957]); Gary B. Thompson, ed., *Index to the Newspapers Published in Geneva, New York* (Geneva, N.Y., 1981–).

like Masonry's own Revolutionary transformation, did not open up political power to all. The increased opportunities for men of lesser social standing represented more an expanded definition of elite status than a completely open system. Through its continued prestige and its increased identification with fundamental values, the fraternity reinforced these political changes. Masonry, as a voluntary institution that fulfilled a broad range of uses and enrolled only a fraction of the population, could never completely dominate officeholding, but its peculiar characteristics attracted many local, state, and national leaders.[8]

When Henry Clay finally reached the heights of national politics as speaker of the House in 1811, he had beside him a number of Masonic brothers. Four of the eight-member congressional delegation from his state, including both senators, belonged to the fraternity. The disproportionate political influence of Masons extended beyond Kentucky. President James Madison's cabinet included an even greater Masonic representation. Of the thirteen men who served during the War of 1812, at least seven were brothers. The Geneva, New York, lodge shows a similar concentration on the local level. Just as in Lexington, nearly half the Geneva members held some political office. More than a tenth served as state or national legislators (Table 15).[9]

Both direct and indirect factors help explain this involvement. To a certain extent, the brothers' extensive political involvement must have been self-perpetuating. The presence of successful politicians within lodges attracted other leaders—and men who sought to emulate them. But other characteris-

tics deepened Masonry's attraction. The occupations that dominated the fraternity (lawyers, merchants, and prosperous artisans) tended to be the same
groups most heavily involved with politics and policy issues. Masonry's cosmopolitan values and connections further attracted men whose economic and
intellectual activities oriented them beyond the locality, just the sort of men
likely to be aware of and active in larger political issues. The high standing of
the fraternity within the community allowed ambitious men to identify themselves with widely shared public values and to participate in prestigious public rituals. Finally, Masonic membership, unlike some other badges of elite
status, provided connections that reached beyond the locality.

The post-Revolutionary fraternity's social range gave it further political
relevance. By expanding downward and outward during its Revolutionary
transformation, the order adapted to the new political and social geography
of early national America, as brother Daniel Delavan realized unhappily in
1798. "Good god[,] has the Masonick Instatution come to this?" the later
Westchester County sheriff wrote to Masonic brother Pierre Van Cortlandt,
the president of New York's first constitutional convention, upon learning that
Radical Republican and brother Samuel Young hoped to head a new lodge.
"Unless that there is a Check Post to the Progress of Such fellows," Delavan
vowed, "I as to my Self will be a Shamed to own my Self a mason."[10]

Masonry, however, was hardly as open as Delavan feared. The fraternity
never became merely a replica of the entire society. Like Young, a longtime
member of the state legislature, brothers often continued to possess above-
average wealth and learning. The fraternity's relatively high cultural tone—
Clay's lodge brother John Rowan fought a duel with a non-Mason after
arguing over who was the better classical scholar—and the unanimous vote
required for initiation placed limits on the fraternity's democratization. High
fees created an even more conspicuous barrier. An 1820 committee of the
grand lodge of New York reported that charges for the first three degrees
ranged from thirteen dollars in Connecticut to twenty-nine dollars in South
Carolina. New York, like Ohio, required twenty dollars at a time when even
skilled workers generally made less than two dollars a day. Furthermore, initiation fees made up only part of a continuing financial commitment that also
included outlays for refreshments and dues.[11]

As a result, the post-Revolutionary fraternity, despite its widened social
range, remained a center for social and political leaders even into the 1820s.
"Some of the principal citizens of Batavia were connected with it," remembered Samuel Greene of New York, one of Masonry's most active opponents
after 1826. When he was initiated into the fraternity in the mid-1820s, his
sponsor was the county surrogate, the state probate officer in the region. In the
"thickly settled portions of the state," Pennsylvania's grand lecturer similarly
reported in 1829, "the lodges generally are composed of the most influential
and respectable men in the respective neighborhoods."[12] "What is Masonry
now?" William Brainard asked in 1825. "It is powerful," he answered indis-

creetly but accurately. Although it drew upon a wide social range, it included "men of rank, wealth, office and talent . . . in almost every place where power is of importance." [13]

Post-Revolutionary Masonry's combination of relative social inclusiveness and exclusive honor allowed it to fit the new contours of post-Revolutionary political involvement, to adapt to the growing range of men seeking office. The domination of the colonial fraternity by the principal people matched their political and social power. With its Revolutionary transformation, the early national order could meet the needs of a political nation that had itself grown beyond its earlier bounds. Yet this broader political elite, like the fraternity itself, remained exclusive. Relatively well-to-do men with wider cultural horizons still tended to hold the more prominent offices and to take the initiative in organizing politics.

Like its colonial predecessor, post-Revolutionary Masonry continued to bring together a wide range of politically influential men. But the fraternity's size and scope also gave it growing importance within a similarly expanding political arena. Ironically, however, Masonry's high concentration of leaders made some forms of political activity more difficult.

11. We Have Nothing to Do with Politics

"Brethren," noted an 1824 newspaper's plea "To the Masonic Fraternity," "Your former grand master, and Senior Grand Warden are now candidates for the support of the 'free and accepted' electors of New-York." Both De Witt Clinton and Cadwallader D. Colden, candidates for governor and state Senate, were brothers, and their campaign newspaper sought the votes of "the 'free and accepted' electors" on that basis: "If there be any virtue in the cardinal principles of our faith," the piece urged, "[they] will receive your undivided suffrage." [14]

Clinton and Colden won the election. But, as in the case of Tompkins's first gubernatorial term, the influence of Masonry is unclear. The newspaper editor conveniently failed to mention that the candidate for lieutenant governor on the same ticket was not a brother and, even more tellingly, that Clinton's opponent was himself a Mason. Clinton himself consistently rejected such political uses of the fraternity. The ideals of Masonry, he had argued thirty years before, "spurn the contracted views of faction." "Masonry has her politics," he suggested, "but not the politics of a day, a party," or even "a country." [15]

The 1824 appeal, however, reveals some of the key elements of the ambiguous relationship between Masonry and partisan politics. As the newspaper article suggests (if indeed the author was a brother), the heat of political battle might overwhelm Masonic scruples. But countervailing forces kept this intermittent fever in check, making Masonry only an inconsistent tool for party politics. The fraternity's long-standing opposition to political activity and discussion, reinforcing the larger culture's opposition to parties and political divisions, created a strong barrier to Masonic partisanship. In any case, the fraternity simply could not have worked well as a party instrument, being paradoxically both too large and too small to be entirely useful, uniting a membership that was both diverse and a minority within the larger community. As Clinton suggested, Masonry had its politics, but it was seldom the partisan warfare of which Antimasons suspected the fraternity.

The partisan weaknesses of Masonry, however, did not stop some politicians from seeking such advantage, especially during a period when partisan fires often burned brightly. In 1799, a disgruntled Mason complained that a group of Connecticut brothers had sent a list of approved candidates for the state's upper house "to most of the lodges in this state" five years previously, asking the recipient to present it to his lodge "in such a manner as to give it success." The obligation of the Royal Arch degree (one of a series of additional rituals added after the Revolution) required members, according to some versions of the pledge, to seek other Royal Arch Masons' "political preferment in preference to another of equal qualifications." Although this clause seems not to have been included everywhere, it formed part of the folk wisdom accepted by Hiram Hopkins's circle in Lockport, New York. His friends advised the new Mason to receive the degree in order to neutralize the advantage of Hopkins's presumed Royal Arch opponent.[16]

Such attempts to turn Masonic brotherhood to political advantage faced important cultural obstacles. Hopkins's cousin (and patron) declared that he would support the yet uninitiated Hopkins in an earlier election despite the membership of Hopkins's rival. In what might have been another popular gloss on Masonic beliefs, Hopkins's cousin reasoned that his Masonic obligations did not require him "to go against my interests." Even more important than such informal rules of thumb, official prohibitions of Masonic involvement in politics blocked explicit participation. Opposition to discussion of party issues remained part of what brothers had begun to call the "landmarks" of the order. The Connecticut attempt to mobilize brothers in favor of a single slate, according to the author, "no where met with a very cordial reception"; he himself "communicated" his copy "to the *flames,* instead of the *lodge.*"[17]

The fraternity's decisive response to instances when party affairs influenced official actions further reveals the strength of this prohibition. At a time when political competition seemed more the result of opponents' moral depravity than an honest difference of opinion (the New York newspaper characterized Clinton's opponents as "a knot of foul conspirators reeking from the swamps of corruption"), Masonic groups could not entirely avoid partisanship. The Maryland grand lodge, at the height of the 1790s war fever against France, sent an address to President John Adams that virtually called for war. Even then the brothers also noted, "It is a maxim of the Masonic Fraternity, and which is most religiously adhered to, never to interfere in Political subjects." Although undoubtedly seen by the authors as part of the tradition of loyal addresses proclaiming support for the government, a majority of grand lodge members believed the action violated fundamental Masonic doctrine. They repudiated the address and censured the grand master who had instigated it.[18]

A similar situation occurred in the ironically titled lodge of Amity during 1811. In that year, the Zanesville, Ohio, lodge brothers rejected two members of the local Tammany Society, a controversial Radical Republican group. "Some brethren," wrote the state's grand master rebuking the action, "have determined to prevent the admission of . . . applicants . . . in consequence of their being members of the Tammany Society," but "we, my Brethren, have nothing to do with politics." He urged them, "Apply the compass to restrain your prejudices and the square to test your actions."[19]

Masonry's composition as well as its official and unofficial teachings restrained the partisan uses later opponents claimed to discern within Masonry. First, the fraternity could not encompass all the politically active men of an area, let alone the entire electorate. Although strategically placed, membership seldom reached much more than 10 percent of the adult white male population, leaving many people outside its ties. The New York City newspaper editor might have viewed his Masonic appeal as comparable to the article following his addressed to "the Sons of Erin," another interest group that might be expected to look favorably on Clinton.[20]

If the fraternity was too small to assure success even in the best of circumstances, it was also, paradoxically, too large. Masons "have ever been, and are now, found attached to different political parties," noted an upstate New York newspaper in 1828, pointing out that both Henry Clay and Andrew Jackson belonged to the fraternity. Like those two rivals, Masons often found themselves on different political sides. Clay belonged to the same lodge as his earliest legislative antagonist, Felix Grundy. A closer examination of the figures involved in the Zanesville, Ohio, Tammany case reveals further complexities. Dr. John Ham, one of the rejected men, was an important Tammany leader, but so too was his father-in-law, Dr. Isaac Van Horne, at the time not only a member of the Zanesville lodge but its second officer. The mastermind of the entire Tammany scheme, Radical Republican Thomas Worthington, belonged to another lodge, as did his chief rival, the moderate Republican governor Return Jonathan Meigs, Jr.[21]

The fraternity's opposition to partisan wrangling also played another significant role, reinforcing the general belief that political divisions were illegitimate expressions of personal ambition and moral failure. As a poem "On Parties" published by Lexington brother John Bradford in 1796 noted:

> Both make the public good their plea,
> The end of all their wishes;
> With half an eye a man may see,
> Both want the loaves and fishes.[22]

Masonic doctrines of noninvolvement and neutrality helped encourage this antiparty sentiment. Bringing together men of different parties in a setting that stressed unity, the fraternity helped blunt the partisan divisions that threatened to divide society into warring factions.[23]

Masonry's attempt to remove itself from such disputes, however, ironically made the fraternity more politically significant. By hindering the development of political parties, the antiparty sentiments that Masonry reinforced placed even greater demands on informal politics, the personal cooperation between leaders that the fraternity helped encourage.

III. Men of All Parts of the Union Mingling Together

On April 14, 1798, the grand lodge of North Carolina laid the cornerstone of the Main Building, the central building of the nation's first state university. The procession to the site included the governor, his Council, and the judges of the state's highest court, all, the grand lodge noted, "under the direction and superintendence of the Most Worshipful William R. Davie, grand master." A former member of the Federal Constitutional Convention and a major general in the state militia, Davie had spearheaded the creation of the new school, a role that led contemporaries to call him the school's "founder" and "father." His central place in the ceremony would be confirmed the next year when the state legislature elected him governor.[24]

This connection between the post and Masonry was not unusual. Although the governor in 1798 did not belong to the fraternity, he was exceptional. Only seven other non-Masons served in the office under the state's Revolutionary constitution. During the years between 1776 and 1836, the eighteen brothers that served as governors held office, on average, more than twice as long as their non-Masonic counterparts. In all, Masons served a total of forty-eight of the sixty-one years.[25]

The links between Masonry and North Carolina politics were close. The fraternity might have played only a minor role in partisan activities, but it reinforced post-Revolutionary political structures in fundamental ways. The fraternity first created networks that encouraged communication and cooperation between politically active men. Just as important, Masonry helped constitute an elite that could plausibly claim to be enlightened and republican—and could address the sometimes contradictory cultural and practical demands placed upon them.

These roles were particularly important because they responded to crucial problems created by post-Revolutionary political culture. In the years after Independence, Americans attempted to purify and open up older forms of politics. But they did not thereby immediately accept either the democratic structures or the political partisanship that would develop in the 1820s and 1830s. North Carolina's constitution adopted in 1776 illustrates this development.

The governor was elected every year, reducing the dangers of accumulated power and allowing replacement when a leader strayed from the popular will. But the constitution also placed the election in the hands of the legislature, not the people. Masonry helped facilitate this adaptation of the small-scale politics of elite connections to Revolutionary ideology and the new structures created in North Carolina and elsewhere, creating channels of communication and cooperation that eased the difficulties of organizing politics on a new scale in a political culture where challenges to elites provided a central theme. The significance of the fraternity during this intermediate stage between the aristocratic politics of the colonial period and the democratic forms of the Jacksonian era can be seen first in another case involving Masonic public officials.[26]

John Eaton had barely settled into his new post as secretary of War after President Andrew Jackson's 1829 inauguration, when Washington residents began to spread rumors about him and his new wife. According to gossip, the secretary had committed adultery with the new Mrs. Eaton even before her previous husband had died. Jackson was outraged at the charge. Eaton was not only a longtime supporter and friend but also a Masonic brother, a circumstance that made the charge even more unbelievable. Jackson dispatched another Mason, Congressman Richard Mentor Johnson, to persuade cabinet members to receive the Eatons socially, an act of loyalty that later helped Johnson gain the vice-presidency.

Jackson gave his assessment to the Reverend Ezra Stiles Ely of Philadelphia. "The high standing of Mr. Eaton as a man of moral worth and a Mason gives the lie direct in my estimation to such a charge [of adultery], and ought to do it, unless the facts of his alleged guilt shall be clearly and unequivocally established." That Mrs. Eaton's father and first husband were themselves Masons further undermined the credibility of the charges. "Every person who is acquainted with the obligations of masons must know that Mr. Eaton, as a mason, could not have criminal intercourse with another mason's wife, without being one of the most abandoned of men." As Jackson's next letter to Ely noted, such an action would have "burst the bonds of masonry."[27]

The Masonic ties that bound Jackson to Eaton reinforced a brother's position in less extreme circumstances as well. Through the connections built in local lodges and in capital cities, Masons created networks of trust, friendship, and communication that facilitated political activity. These ties were not always strong enough to overcome personal and factional rivalry (brothers in Jackson's cabinet participated in the ritual shunning of Mrs. Eaton), let alone the sometimes deep chasms between different parties and their leaders. Fraternal ties opened connections and pathways of communication; they did not determine the messages or the results. Still, the fraternity had particular relevance within the expanded arenas created by post-Revolutionary political structures. For leaders and aspiring politicians eager to gain a hearing within their locality and beyond, Masonic ties could help overcome the obstacles created by more particular loyalties and the lack of continuing personal inter-action.

Even individual Masonic groups often reached beyond the locality. Non-urban lodges seldom drew entirely upon a single village. Only about half of the members of the Ark Lodge of Geneva, New York, came from Geneva itself. One-third traveled from surrounding towns. One in seven lived even further away. Lexington Lodge shows a similar pattern. Some two-fifths of the members lived beyond the village, with most of these men traveling from a different county. The higher-degree bodies that developed after the Revolution usually encompassed an even broader range of residences. About two-thirds of all Geneva's higher-degree brothers lived outside that town. For politically active men, this wide-ranging membership provided ample opportunity for build-ing connections with other political leaders. In Lexington Lodge, Henry Clay met with speakers of the Kentucky House like Louisville's Robert Breckin-ridge and Bourbon County's Green Clay, a veteran of more than two decades in the Virginia and Kentucky legislatures (Table 16).[28]

Masonic ties could also unite men at the centers of government as well. As late as 1838, even after years of active agitation against the fraternity, former Indiana grand master and senator John Tipton noted "men of all parts of the Union mingling together as brethren of the masonic family" at a Wash-ington, D.C., celebration. The North Carolina grand lodge similarly brought together political leaders from a variety of localities. Besides a midyear meet-ing in Halifax, the state body also assembled in Raleigh during the yearly legislative session, an event that drew the state's leading politicians. The grand lodge meeting held in November and December 1797, the last before the Uni-versity of North Carolina cornerstone laying the following spring, elected to its highest offices North Carolina's secretary of state and solicitor general, the clerk of the governor's Council, a former congressman, and three of the four commanding officers of the state militia. Among the fifty-some other partici-pants at the meeting were nineteen members of the sitting legislature (more than one-third of all the brothers present), the federal attorney general of the district, a former speaker of the North Carolina House who was already the namesake of a county, and a judge of the Supreme Court of Law and Equity. The last also served as the state treasurer. In all, some 70 percent of the atten-dees held or had held high state office. Another 10 percent would gain such office in the next decade.[29]

These Masonic connections facilitated communication and cooperation be-yond the locality. In a state where the legislature met for only a single month each year, North Carolina's fraternity helped regulate the election of the gov-ernor in a way that addressed the various claims of individuals and regions. In all, North Carolina's eighteen Masonic governors came from fourteen dif-

Table 16. Residential Distribution of Masons, 1794–1827

Residence	No.	%
Lexington, Ky., Freemasons, 1794–1810[a]		
Lexington	83	61.5
Fayette County	12	8.9
Outside Fayette County	40	30.0
Ark Lodge, Geneva, N.Y., 1807–1819[b]		
Geneva	41	50.6
Surrounding towns	27	33.3
Other Seneca or Ontario County	12	14.8
Other	1	1.2
Royal Arch Chapter, Geneva, N.Y., 1809–1822[c]		
Geneva	36	36.7
Surrounding towns	27	27.6
Other Seneca or Ontario County	30	30.6
Other	5	5.1
Jordan Lodge, Danvers, Mass., 1808–1827[d]		
Danvers	51	64.6
Contiguous towns	14	17.7
Next layer of towns	1	1.3
Surrounding counties	12	15.2
Other	1	1.3

[a] 135 of 167 identified.   [b] 81 of 96 identified.   [c] 98 of 137 identified.   [d] 79 of 172 identified.

Sources: J. Winston Coleman, Jr., *Masonry in the Bluegrass; Being an Authentic Account of Masonry in Lexington and Fayette County, Kentucky, 1788-1933* (Lexington, Ky., 1934); *Kentucky Gazette (and General Advertiser)* (Lexington), 1790-1817; *Charless' Kentucky, Tennessee, and Ohio Almanack for the Year 1807 . . .* (Lexington, Ky., 1806), rpt. in J. Winston Coleman, Jr., *Lexington's First City Directory . . . 1806* (Lexington, Ky., 1953); James F. Hopkins, ed., *The Papers of Henry Clay*, I, *The Rising Statesman, 1797-1814* (Lexington, Ky., 1959); John H. Stelter, *History of Ark Lodge No. 33*, and *History Royal Arch Masonry, Geneva, New York, 1809-1964* (Geneva, N.Y., 1964); Thompson, ed., *Index to the Newspapers Published in Geneva*; Dudley A. Massey, *History of Freemasonry in Danvers, Massachusetts from September, 1778, to July, 1896 . . .* (Peabody, Mass., 1896).

ferent counties. At least thirteen had previously held grand lodge office. The problem of identifying trustworthy men from a range of localities might also have encouraged Masonry's significance on the national level. More than half of all Andrew Jackson's cabinet members were brothers, coming from a wide range of states, including Michigan, New Jersey, North Carolina, and Louisiana.[30]

Masonic ties could also be used by aspiring individuals seeking favor and advancement. John Tipton's connection with James F. D. Lanier, formed in Indiana grand lodge meetings, involved not only business transactions but Lanier's political support for Tipton. Michigan brother Colonel John Anderson drew upon his Masonic ties in 1818 to expedite his claims in Congress. Anderson had already got two bills passed before the five hundred dollars he offered to North Carolina brother Lewis Williams "as part pay, for [the] extra trouble I give you" became public knowledge. Speaker Henry Clay, another brother, brought Anderson to the House for a public rebuke.[31]

As the Anderson case suggests, fraternal loyalties often had to be subordinated to other duties and considerations—including the moral values also preached by the order. Grand master Davie, during his term as governor, similarly encouraged the successful prosecution of his deputy grand master, Secretary of State James Glasgow. Glasgow's land frauds had become public through incriminating material presented by another brother, Andrew Jackson.[32] Just as important, Masonry's very exclusivity, the quality that made its ties useful, also limited its effectiveness. Despite the high concentration of important political leaders who belonged to the fraternity in North Carolina and Lexington, Kentucky—greater perhaps than in most other areas—not all leaders belonged to the fraternity. Personal appeals to Masonic fraternity, not always effective even among brothers, carried little weight with nonmembers.

Masonry's political significance, however, did not depend entirely upon the ability of brothers to get special favors. Its ability to structure connections and friendship across local lines gave it particular importance within a post-Revolutionary political system that inconsistently demanded both partisan organization and nonpartisan rhetoric.[33]

Besides making more offices elective, the state and federal governments established during the Revolutionary period also created larger districts. Contests that had previously been limited largely to single localities now spread over counties and even entire states. In this new system, local elites had to attract the votes of relative strangers and challenge their counterparts in other towns, a situation that virtually required broader political organization extending beyond personal bonds. New York's governors had to win statewide elections, a requirement that reinforced both Southwick's concerns about Tompkins's city background and the advantages of his Masonic connections. In large districts, where leading men often did not know each other, common membership in a fraternity provided a valuable tie.

Such connections also aided recruitment for other positions. Government appointments often depended upon recommendations by an influential leader who might be approached through Masonic ties. President and brother George Washington regularly sought advice from Revolutionary war officers like his Maryland Masonic brother Otho Holland Williams. Similarly, Washington later approached North Carolina grand master Davie for suggestions about staffing the army being created for the expected war with France in the late 1790s, suggesting that "Officers of *celebrity* in the Revolutionary Army" deserved precedence. For the many men who lacked such a background, Masonic membership might gain Davie's attention—and reinforce claim to inclusion in the next category Washington suggested, "gentlemen of Character, [and] liberal education."[34]

The expanded scale of operations created by the Revolution, requiring candidates to reach outside their localities and leaders to seek out appointees they barely knew, paradoxically encouraged both partisan activities and nonpartisan values. Forced to operate in larger districts and polities, political leaders needed to mobilize potential voters and gain the support of influential leaders beyond the range of personal connection. They were also forced to compete with notables from other locations. At the same time, the expanded range of people and interests involved in politics also inspired policy differences (and the distinctive visions of the public good that became intertwined with them). But the post-Revolutionary proliferation of interest and constituencies that encouraged partisanship also helped sustain antipartisan values. By appealing to higher goals that transcended divisions (at least rhetorically), leaders gained the moral authority necessary to speak to a broader audience—thus reinforcing the significance of the language of the common good at a time when bitter divisions and often ferocious political infighting might have threatened to make it merely an outmoded political language.[35] Masonry would not, perhaps could not, become a key factor in determining these political conflicts—indeed, it deliberately set itself outside them. But the fraternity, a universal organization built (like the Republic itself) upon voluntary connections rather than false hierarchies helped leaders lay claim to the continuing ideal of nonpartisan attachment to the public good.

The resulting disjunction between structural needs and ideological demands in post-Revolutionary politics increased the importance of other kinds of connections. The party organizations developed by the Federalists and the Jeffersonian Republicans depended heavily upon informal ties built around patronage, family, neighborhood, religion, and ethnicity.[36] Freemasonry played a similar role, helping leaders to make contacts and to encourage cooperation. The fraternity's peculiar features, furthermore, made it particularly useful for this purpose. Unlike ties based on blood or residence, Masonry encompassed large numbers of diverse men and could be expanded even further.

As a result, brothers could use the fraternity in politics much as they did in their economic activities, as a means of both advancing their own self-interest and asserting their desire for social harmony and progress. This tension between public and private advantages would be reinforced by a final ambiguity within the fraternity's political role. While Masonry in some ways seemed to open up leadership, it also helped reinforce the advantages of the elite, a dual purpose that can be seen in an incident that took place in Lexington, Kentucky, the year before Henry Clay's arrival.

In 1796, the town's trustees (a majority of whom were Masons) explained to the public the need for both further public improvements and the increased revenues to pay for them. Even if the prevailing taxes for the next five years could be entirely dedicated to the purpose, they warned, the money would "be insufficient to build stone bridges, to make sewers for carrying off the water, to sink wells and erect pumps . . . and to make such other repairs, as are necessary for the health, safety, and convenience of their fellow-citizens." Something further needed to be done. The trustees turned to Lexington Lodge, which had already received state authorization for a lottery. With the cooperation of the brotherhood, the trustees created another lottery based upon the lodges, circumventing a legislature dominated by agrarian suspicions of town spending. The resulting "Chances of Insurance on the Lottery Authorised by Law" used rules taken almost directly from the brother's model. Although a group of trustees, all of them Masons, guaranteed the town's interest, the new local lottery would have the same number of tickets, the same prizes, and the same winning numbers as the fraternity's.[37]

The close cooperation between lodge and town seen in the Lexington lottery suggests some of the ways that Masonry helped to redefine American political leadership in the years after the Revolution. For brothers as well as many outsiders, Masonry represented a republican adaptation of the eighteenth-century ideal of enlightened men working together to advance the common good. The expanded fraternity, open to all men of merit and virtue, helped identify a leadership group that could meet the new cultural and practical demands placed upon them by the Revolution and its legacy. At the same time, however, Masonry also helped these elites consolidate their power, impeding more complete democratization.

By both opening up politics and limiting participation to a select group, Masonry mediated one of the central tensions of post-Revolutionary political culture. Americans continued to hold to the ideal of public-spirited cooperation among its leaders. Yet they also rejected the close ties of family and economic interest that had previously made such collaboration possible. By encouraging bonds seemingly based upon disinterested friendship and limiting brotherhood to the worthy, Masonry helped meet some of these conflicting demands.

Masonry's first role, broadening the boundaries of political leadership, can be seen as part of its support of enlightened values. Like the Revolutionaries, Masonry claimed to reject the older means of organizing society, the paternalism of patronage ties as well as the narrow loyalties of family, neighborhood, and nation. The fraternity instead, members argued, brought together all worthy men, bridging the divisions created by particular loyalties. Because of this openness and broad reach, Masonry could reject the particular interests of a small group in favor of the good of the whole. As the North Carolina grand lodge argued the year of the university cornerstone ceremony, Masonry created a "chain of union between the charitable and benevolent of all countries and nations."[38]

The broadened social range of the post-Revolutionary fraternity gave new significance to these older claims. Rather than being a public expression of a narrow elite, early national Masonry opened its honor to lesser men like Clay or Jackson who were attempting to rise without the traditional prerequisites of wealth, family, or influential connections. Masonry instead sought, as George M. Bibb told Lexington Lodge in 1804, to "unite all men in one grand lodge."[39]

Masonry's attempt to democratize the prerogatives of the colonial elite fitted well into the ideological demands of the Revolution. Well-to-do men could no longer claim leadership simply because of their social position. Annual elections like those for the Kentucky House or for the entire North Carolina government forced continual recourse to the people through elections that, argued the Democratic Society of Kentucky (a group whose leadership was dominated by Lexington brothers), should be "free from party or religious prejudices, and unaffected by [candidates'] occupation, fortune, or connections." Instead of these irrelevant qualifications, voters should reward, in terms used by grand master Davie to praise donors to the state university, "liberal, disinterested and patriotic exertions for the happiness and welfare of the state." Lexington Lodge brother Green Clay similarly summed up this tradition while announcing his candidacy for governor in 1808: "My own happiness, and that of my family, [is] inseparably blended with the welfare of the state."[40]

By challenging older definitions of status, however, Masonry also helped create and reinforce new ones. Even in their public statements, brothers claimed that Masonry united the virtuous and talented, defending their exclusiveness on grounds that only worthy men could learn Masonry's lessons of morality and friendship. Just as important, however, Masonic membership in actuality was not determined solely by the virtue and talents it cited as membership criteria. Wealth, cosmopolitan learning, social standing, and political power all tended to be overrepresented in lodges. Masonry brought together these relatively privileged men, reinforcing their earlier advantages by encouraging them to watch out for each other's interest and providing them with increased opportunities for cooperating. Lexington's town lottery would not have been possible without such close ties.[41]

In helping to establish a republican aristocracy, Masonry can be seen as an heir to the colonial ideal of gentility. The great changes of the late eighteenth century, seen in the rise of Ancient Masonry, blurred the boundaries of gentlemanly status and fragmented the supposed unity of political, cultural, and social standing. The rise of relatively cosmopolitan artisans and lesser merchants within the cities and provincial elites outside meant that learning could no longer be considered an exclusive badge of elite status. At the same time, Revolutionary ideals of republicanism called into question attempts to link social and economic power with political position.

As a key symbol of these Revolutionary values, Freemasonry helped transcend this growing fragmentation, joining the politically active with men of cosmopolitan economic and cultural interests. The fraternity, of course, could not restore the dominance of colonial gentlemen. American society was becoming too large and complex, too divided by political and geographic lines, for any small group (or any one vision of the public good) to control society. But Masonry could bring together substantial numbers of men with plausible claims to social and political authority—and reinforce their standing.

This ambiguous post-Revolutionary position was not so much at odds with republican ideals as it was a part of its ideological tensions. Many Americans feared the power of what the Lexington Democratic Society called "*undue, aristocratical influence,*" but they also believed that this corruption could be combated only by electing leaders who, because of their character, would rise above it. Only informal cooperation among those whom Lexington gubernatorial hopeful Green Clay called "the best men" could avoid the "spirit of dissention" criticized by the Democratic Society.[42]

The synergy of Masonry and post-Revolutionary political culture in promoting men praised by both Thomas Jefferson and John Adams as the "natural aristoi" can be seen in one of the oldest brothers in Andrew Jackson's cabinet, Louisiana's Edward Livingston. A member of one of New York's most prominent colonial families, Livingston had served as deputy grand master of that state about the time the still relatively unknown Daniel Tompkins had visited upstate lodges on his rise to the governorship. Livingston's brother (through Masonry as well as blood) held even higher offices and played a larger role in establishing the post-Revolutionary political system. Longtime New York grand master and state chancellor Robert R. Livingston, besides serving on the committee that drafted the Declaration of Independence, had been a leading figure in writing New York's Revolutionary constitution, whose restrictions on popular control allowed him and his followers to maintain their political standing well into the next century—and continued the opportunities for the informal politics that Masonry increasingly facilitated.

The similarity of this republican leadership to its colonial predecessors provided one of the foundations of the movement against Freemasonry of the 1820s and 1830s. Not coincidentally, this opposition developed during a period of ferment that transformed early national political culture as well. Both the New York and the North Carolina constitutions, which had propelled so many brothers into their highest offices, would be replaced. The new North Carolina constitution adopted in 1836 directed that the governor be elected in a statewide contest by a broadened electorate, a change that encouraged greater public participation and virtually required even broader political organization. Both these results made Masonry less central to the state's politics. As in New York (which had changed its constitution more than a decade before), North Carolina brothers continued to be elected to the state's highest office, but they no longer dominated the position. Fraternal ties held less significance in a political culture that deeply distrusted the nonpartisan stance taken by Masonry and its attempted balance between inclusiveness and exclusivity.[43]

The link between Masonry and the University of North Carolina went beyond the central role of brothers in its creation, the fraternity's laying of the cornerstones of its first two buildings, or even the temporary lodge that initiated a number of professors after the 1798 ceremony. On a larger level, the fraternity and the school played similar roles in post-Revolutionary society. The university (just as much as the fraternity) brought together politically aspiring men from a variety of localities, states, and regions. Furthermore, the university and the fraternity, with their broad geographical reach and diverse memberships, could not be used easily or consistently for explicit partisan purposes. Finally, they both claimed to serve the public good. According to Governor Alexander Martin, a Mason, the college would be created, not for the benefit of a few, but "for the cause of humanity."[44]

Just as important, the two institutions helped define the post-Revolutionary social order in the same way. Like Masonry, the university also sought to open up leadership and status to a broader range of men. Learning and merit provided the primary criteria for admission. Yet the school, again like the fraternity, also helped to define an elite group. According to a mid-nineteenth-century historian, some earlier North Carolinians recognized this connection, arguing that the proposed school formed "one step towards a permanent aristocracy." By bringing young men together with their peers from influential families as well as providing social experiences that eased them into high social and political circles, the university helped create a republican aristocracy based on knowledge and virtue as well as family or fortune.[45]

The college, of course, made greater demands on its members. Besides drawing almost exclusively from a narrow range of ages and requiring residence in the same locality, it imposed financial burdens that went far beyond

Masonry's fees. "It is not in the power of more than one person in a hundred to avail himself of the institution," complained a contemporary. Such limits on participation allowed universities to form networks of informal politics even into the twentieth century. Ironically, Masonry's greater availability, its ability to meet republican calls for openness, made it an easier mark for democratic attacks. By opening up higher status and broader connections to more people than did colleges, the fraternity became a more potent symbol of republican ideals and a more pervasive means of helping build political stability in a time of confusion and conflicting demands. Masonry's greater ability to meet these challenges, however, would also make it a clearer target for attempts to change politics when the post-Revolutionary system began to come unglued. These tensions would be heightened even further because activities and attitudes within the lodges were also changing dramatically during the years when many Americans were overwhelmed by the high claims as well as the great advantages of the ancient and honorable society.[46]

CHAPTER NINE

Into the Secret Place

Organization and Sacrilization, 1790–1826

Although Hiram Hopkins decided to take further degrees primarily for political gain, this objective faded as he advanced. His expected opponent, a higher-degree Mason, failed to enter the race for town collector, and Hopkins won easily, but the new Lockport, New York, official continued his Masonic career. He became first a Mark Mason, then a Past Master, a Most Excellent Master, and, finally, in August 1826, a Royal Arch Mason. The last promised a great deal. According to Thomas Smith Webb's influential handbook of Masonry, the Royal Arch ceremony was "indescribably more august, sublime, and important than all which precede it." It was "the summit and perfection of Ancient Masonry." In a long ceremony that Hopkins recalled as "two or three hours of hard labour," he "learned . . . to raise the living arch by 3 times 3, that night in Open Chapter." The Arch represented the Masons' word lost during the building of Solomon's Temple with the murder of Hiram Abiff. More than a means of identifying craftsmen, the word was revealed to be nothing less than the secret name of God. Even before this extraordinary revelation, Hopkins was convinced of Masonry's significance. By the time he finished the Most Excellent Master ceremony, he had come to believe the rituals of almost incomparable worth. "I thought," he recalled, "that nothing excelled the masonic degrees, except the Christian religion, and thought they were but little surpassed even by that."[1]

Hopkins's excitement marked the success of a generation of attempts to remodel the order, to make its internal life conform to the high expectations created by the fraternity's growing public prestige. The world within Masonry created by these enthusiastic brothers added another layer to the post-Revolutionary fraternity's increasing complexities. Earlier brothers had described Masonry as a badge—a public symbol—of high social status and a means of creating universal love. After the fraternity's Revolutionary transformation, brothers began to argue that it also exemplified the highest values of religion and the Republic. At the same time, Masonry began to provide a powerful means of meeting the physical and psychological needs of an increasingly confusing world. Hopkins had been enticed into the fraternity because of these public expectations and beliefs. Inside the lodge rooms, he discovered yet another attraction. The fraternity, brothers now argued, was not simply an exemplification of universal processes but a sanctified institution whose values and experiences transcended the ordinary world. As "I approach this degree," confessed a renegade Mason revealing the secrets of the Royal Arch ritual in 1827, "I feel myself more than ever as standing upon 'holy ground.' " [2]

The higher degrees provided the locus of this change. Spreading first through the new Ancient lodges during the Revolutionary period and undergoing extensive adaptation in America, these degrees grew rapidly after 1800. New York alone had 125 Royal Arch chapters by 1827, more than the number of lodges in the entire country fifty years before. Tennessee possessed 19 chapters, 1 for every two lodges. These bodies were only one part of a bewildering variety of new degrees and organizations emerging after the Revolution. The supreme council of Charleston in 1802 claimed to preside over thirty-three distinct steps. Furthermore, they suggested, its members possessed an additional nineteen degrees that could also be given. Although De Witt Clinton had no direct connection with this group, he ultimately served not only as New York's grand master but as the founding head of the national General Grand Royal Arch chapter, the sovereign grand commander of the Sovereign Grand Consistory, the thrice illustrious grand master of the Grand Encampment of New York, and the grand master of the General Grand Encampment of the United States. [3]

Such formidable titles masked organizational weakness. Over time, two rival systems would emerge in America, the York Rite and the Scottish Rite. Hopkins's degrees belonged to what later became the York, or American, Rite, a series of degrees extending beyond the Royal Arch into the Knights Templars and Knights of Malta. These British degrees spread into America through Ancient groups like the Fredericksburg, Virginia, lodge (the site of the first recorded Royal Arch ceremony on the American continent in 1753) and Boston's St. Andrew's Lodge (the founder of the first American Royal Arch chapter in 1769). They became pervasive, however, only after Thomas Smith Webb regularized and spread them from New York and New England around the turn of the century. Another series of degrees grew out of the Charleston supreme council. Later called the Scottish Rite because of Continental belief in the importance of the Scots in Masonry, this primarily French degree system was known at the time as the Council, Sublime, or Ineffable degrees. Even this seemingly fundamental split, however, emerged fully only in the mid-nineteenth century. The post-Revolutionary situation was much more confusing. Despite their attempt to bring, as their motto suggested, "order out of chaos," the Charleston supreme council quickly faced a rival body in New York. Webb's series of York Rite degrees became more popular than both. Yet even his system could not be fixed permanently. Another Mason succeeded in introducing an additional set of "Cryptic Degrees" into the York Rite in the 1810s.[4]

The popularity of the higher degrees, however, rested, not on organizations, but on their ability to speak to issues of great importance to post-Revolutionary Americans. In these rituals, Masons explored new ways of thinking about themselves and their world far removed from the neoclassical Enlightenment portrayed in other parts of Masonry. The new degrees first revalued private life, giving it a new significance as a retreat from and a preparation for public activity. Within this private sphere, furthermore, strong emotions spoke directly to a person's identity, now defined as an inner self. These new beliefs made Masonry a pioneer in new cultural territories, helping post-Revolutionary Americans redefine the enlightened gentility of the eighteenth century—and begin to create the Romantic sentimentalism of the nineteenth. For many Americans, post-Revolutionary Masonry, celebrating medieval knights and glorifying the lodge as a sanctuary, provided the earliest and most powerful expressions of these immense cultural developments.[5]

These changes did not remain segregated in the new, higher degrees. They spread into other parts of Masonry as well, increasing the importance of the fraternity's internal activities. For many enthusiastic brothers, Masonry was no longer primarily a public symbol or a means of promoting the universal ideals of benevolence. Now the fraternity itself became sacred. As a result, members began to pay increasing attention to the order's inner workings. Many brothers became obsessed with the standardization and memorization of rituals, a matter that had been of little moment to colonial brothers. Carefully organized and regulated Masonic structures now seemed essential to fulfilling the fraternity's sacred mission.

This new focus on internal matters helped change Masonry from a relatively ad hoc association to a complex institution whose values and experiences differentiated it from the rest of society. Of course, this withdrawal affected only parts of the fraternity. Masonry continued to serve as a symbol of public values and to provide valuable practical benefits. But the new emotionalism and organization spreading outward from the higher degrees gave Masonry a solidity that attracted the fervent allegiance of men such as Hiram Hopkins. The fraternity's diverse ideas and purposes heightened this attraction. By uniting public, disinterested leadership and private interests, public roles and private retreat, Masonry brought together values that seemed increasingly distinct. Opponents would later argue that such attempts at unification formed a clear and present danger to both religion and the Republic. But this conclusion seemed very far from the minds (and the hearts) of brothers like Hiram Hopkins who experienced the new inner life of the lodge and found it more compelling than even their highest expectations.

1. The Lodge of Instruction

When Royal Arch Mason the Reverend William Bentley attended the installation of Henry Fowle as the first master of Boston's Mount Lebanon Lodge in 1801, he found its hall "superbly decorated." Fowle "sat in an arch upon columns decorated, and in the keystone an eye motto, He seeth in secret." The minister discovered similar elegance when his own Essex Lodge moved to new quarters six years later. "Handsomely decorated," the new hall had "the officers enthroned and . . . supplied with badges and the Apartment with furniture far above the Antient style." [6]

Earlier Masons had paid little attention to these matters. Before 1800, Bentley's lodge "sat at a board covered with a cloath and supported by legs." [7] The changes noted by Bentley reveal post-Revolutionary Masonry's new atmosphere, a literal and metaphorical remodeling of the fraternity's practices and attitudes that expressed the new sanctity portrayed in the higher degrees and the increasingly high place Masonry played in the new Republic. Rituals and organizations that had previously seemed merely the means of establishing the order now became ends in themselves. At the same time, brothers also created a web of institutions and structures that made Masonic organization as distinct from its predecessors as its new internal splendor differed from its older informality.

These changes gave post-Revolutionary Masonry a new aura of permanence. Despite their guarded doors, colonial lodges had not been clearly distinguished from the outside world. Indeed, many slipped easily in and out of existence. The huge early national investment in teaching and organization made later Masonic bodies seem increasingly distinct, built upon rules and patterns that applied only to the fraternity. Of course, these developments were not entirely unparalleled. Other organizations similarly developed new bureaucracies and rules to cope with their expanding size and aspirations. Masonry, however, differed in its attempt to distinguish itself so clearly from the outside world. The public was not welcome, except on rare occasions, in the new lodge rooms, nor was it to know anything about the rituals that so many brothers memorized so intently. Just as much as the higher degrees, with their extraordinary divergence from earlier ideas and patterns, Masonry's reorganization made it distinctive, differentiating it from its surroundings at the same time that other aspects of Masonry claimed that the fraternity exemplified and led society.

In 1818, Mount Lebanon master Henry Fowle complained of "Gothic barbarity" within Masonry. The occasion for his complaint lay, not in the complexities of the higher degrees, but in the lack of those qualities in the lower. Local lodges needed to perform their rituals—what came to be called the "work"—in ways befitting Masonry's importance. "Ignorance and Inconsistencies . . . abound" in the lower degrees, he suggested to Thomas Smith Webb, "for want of a uniform and rational system of work and labor."[8]

Fowle's complaint was more ritual lament than new insight. For some twenty years, he and Webb had been seeking to remake Masonic ceremonies. Without accurate and pure ceremonies, reformers believed, true Masonry could hardly be said to exist. To implement this dramatically different view of the fraternity at a time when it was expanding far beyond its older bounds, brothers labored to create new structures and practices that distinguished Masonry from the outside world.

In the decades after 1790, other Masons came to the same conclusions as Fowle. The 1807 Pennsylvania grand master termed the lack of "correctness and skill" in ritual "a radical evil." "A correct and uniform mode of working and lecturing," the Connecticut grand lodge declared in 1818, "is of vital importance to the interests of Masonry." The alarm expressed at these variations marked a radical shift in attitudes. Previous Masons had given little attention to the matter. "Our mode of working is sufficiently uniform to answer every valuable purpose," resolved the Connecticut state body complacently in 1807, only eleven years before its alarming discovery of diversity. Indeed, before this post-Revolutionary outburst of anxiety, the fraternity possessed no institutional means of transmitting or supervising ritual practices. Brothers learned the ceremonies informally, following local or individual practice. In the District of Columbia (where these older practices persisted), the grand master in 1818 discovered in visits that hardly any two of his lodges worked alike.[9]

Post-Revolutionary reformers, however, began to see ritual differently, viewing it not simply as a means of entry into an honorable company but as a sacred body of knowledge whose very wording was of utmost importance. According to a resolution passed by the Pennsylvania grand lodge in 1820, "Every deviation from the established mode of working is highly improper, and cannot be justified or countenanced."[10] The founders of speculative Masonry had believed the ritual the fragmentary and imperfect remains of an ancient rite. Entranced by these claims, later-eighteenth-century English and American brothers had sought to renew this connection, but, unlike the earlier brothers, they refused to believe the original details irrecoverable. William Preston, the key figure in this movement in England, found that his search for proper ritual practice in the 1760s was "rather discouraged" by its "rude and imperfect state," "the variety of modes established in our meetings, and the difficulties which I encountered in my researches." In attempting this restoration, Preston and his American successors fixed rituals that had never been fully regularized before, adapting them to new expectations. By 1772, Preston had polished and systematized older practices into a coherent whole whose nonsecret portions were published as *Illustrations of Masonry,* a work that went through twelve English editions in the next forty years.[11]

This new English interest affected the American fraternity only in the 1790s. For most the version of Preston they received came through the adaptations of Thomas Smith Webb, whose 1797 *Freemason's Monitor* (as its subtitle *Illustrations of Masonry* suggests) drew heavily upon Preston's work. Webb's further reorganization and adaptation of Preston's lectures became the foundation of ritual practice in nearly all the United States. Selling more than sixteen thousand copies in ten years, the *Monitor* went through eight editions in Webb's lifetime. In turn, it became a model and a source for numerous American imitators, including Jeremy L. Cross's widely diffused *Masonic Chart*. By 1826, the Webb and Preston volumes formed such a part of Masonic consciousness that William Morgan entitled his unauthorized exposé of the new rituals *Illustrations of Masonry*.[12]

Establishing a coherent and consistent ritual formed only the first step in the campaign for uniformity. The revised work still had to be spread to individual lodges and Masons. Post-Revolutionary Masons used a variety of means to encourage, as the Reverend George Richards stated in 1806, "every member of this ancient and honorable fraternity, to obtain a complete knowledge of the PRESTONIAN lectures." Informal tutoring became widespread. Charles G. Finney, an instructor before he became a celebrated evangelist, recalled that he "paid the strictest attention to what [brothers] called their lectures and teachings," becoming "what they call a 'bright Mason'; that is . . . I committed to memory their oral teachings," and taught them to brothers. Fowle traveled to all the New England states as well as New York teaching the lectures more formally to interested lodges.[13]

Webb similarly acted as a bright Mason, but he also realized that further measures were needed to reach the goal of a consistent ritual. He strongly encouraged the original and widest-spread means of this instruction, lectures by the lodge master or his appointee during lodge meetings. In Providence, Rhode Island, Webb also added a weekly gathering devoted solely to teaching the ritual.[14] His song extolling "the Mason's glory" celebrated the active brother

> Whose prying mind doth burn,
> Unto complete perfection,
> Our mysteries to learn;
> Not those who visit lodges
> To eat and drink their fill
>
> . . . .
>
> But only those whose pleasure,
> At every lodge, can be,
> T'improve themselves by lectures,
> In glorious Masonry.[15]

Of course, not all Masons burned for the careful memorization of lengthy rituals. *Jachin and Boaz*, an unauthorized English exposé of the first three degrees that was often reprinted in America, sometimes provided a crib for brothers seeking a shortcut. Grand lodges also appointed official traveling lecturers to spread the new versions of the ceremonies. Benjamin Gleason became the first American grand lecturer in 1805, accepting a new Massachusetts position after it was declined by Fowle. More than three-quarters of the nation's other pre-1830 grand lodges created a similar office. Indeed, the role became so common that one Vermont lodge collected money for a sick brother, John Barney, so that he could travel to Boston to learn the Webb ritual from its source and then be able to support himself.[16]

Grand lecturers, either paid by the state body or approved to contract individually with lodges, formed only part of a wide range of official programs. Kentucky brothers tried for years to find an effective (and inexpensive) means of instruction. Their grand lodge appointed committees to inspect lodge rituals in 1800 and 1804, chose a grand lecturer in 1807, created district inspectors in 1814, and the following year, still unsatisfied, instructed the grand master to teach the subordinate lodge representatives at grand lodge meetings.[17]

The sometimes obsessive interest in ritual purity suggests the growing distinction enthusiastic brothers attempted to draw between Masonry and the outside world. At a time when many Americans vigorously attacked religious formalism, Masonry developed a set of rituals that required exacting performance from even its newest members. This development might not have been entirely without parallel. The spread of formal schooling to broader numbers of Americans at a time when recitation still formed a primary means of instruction might have acclimated the predominantly young men who joined the fraternity to the new Masonic forms. Furthermore, skilled artisans, who had experienced the discipline of entering the mystery of a craft, and lawyers, whose profession required strict attention to words, might have seen the demands of ritual purity as similar to their own disciplines. Still, the function of fraternal teaching lay, not in linking Masonry to other experiences, but in separating it from them. Ritual purity required that the fraternity become a distinctive body with its own rules and logic, a development encouraged as well by the growing attention given the fraternity's organization.[18]

The new complexity and solidity of Masonic structures can be seen in Henry Fowle's superbly decorated Mount Lebanon Lodge and the organizations that grew up around it during the years after its 1801 creation. Lodges themselves seemed more permanent. Brothers willing to pay a stated sum could be declared "life members." Such a status ensured a perpetual claim upon Masonic charity, another fraternal activity that was becoming increasingly regularized. The Massachusetts grand lodge created a separate Lodge Charity Fund in 1811. Eight years later, Mount Lebanon and other city lodges formed the Boston Masonic Board of Relief. Boston lodges also organized the Masonic

Board of Directors, a committee that appointed a secretary, a superintendent, and (for several years) a general agent to manage Boston's Masonic Hall.[19] The institutions surrounding Mount Lebanon did not stop with the city. After 1802, the lodge formed a part of a Masonic district headed by a district deputy grand master who visited each lodge once a year to oversee the payment of dues, the reporting of membership matters, and the accuracy of the ritual.[20] The activities of these new officers as well as the appointment of grand lecturers could be followed by the brethren in the annual proceedings published by the grand lodge.

This web of structures represented a vast change from the earlier fraternity. The Massachusetts provincial grand lodge had consisted of a few officers meeting with the representatives from a handful of lodges. Most local groups seem to have ignored these meetings and would have had trouble even learning about its decisions. Unlike later state groups that published their proceedings as often as twice a year, the Massachusetts provincial grand lodge printed only one official pamphlet in its almost sixty years of existence. The post-Revolutionary development of organization in large part responded to the fraternity's extraordinary growth. But post-Revolutionary brothers went beyond merely attempting to perpetuate older patterns. They created new structures that paralleled the post-Revolutionary attempt of churches, charities, and other groups to expand and regularize their activities. In so doing, however, these groups established an institutional culture that separated them from local societies and customs. As a secret society and the largest voluntary association in America, Masonry extended this trend even further.

Although urban lodges like Mount Lebanon often required a complexity of organization unnecessary in villages or rural areas, nearly all state bodies expanded their activities. "The system of Deputy District Grand Masters," Mississippi's grand master recalled in 1852, "was once general in the United States." By 1830 more than two-thirds of all the state grand lodges instituted such a system of districts, headed by what were sometimes also called grand inspectors or grand visitors. The Pennsylvania state body even created district grand chaplains.[21]

The higher degrees added further Masonic strata. The supreme council recommended two separate levels of local bodies for the Sublime degrees. Webb's more popular degrees prescribed Mark lodges, Royal Arch chapters, and Knights Templars commanderies.[22] Of course, few villages could support the full range of degrees. Lockport, New York, resident and Royal Arch companion Hiram Hopkins had to travel to Rochester when he sought to become a Knight Templar. But after the turn of the century increasing numbers of brothers were, like Hopkins, within reach of a variety of Masonic organizations. Boston's Henry Fowle served as an officer in eight different bodies, holding some twenty different positions ranging from junior warden of St. Andrew's Lodge to deputy grand high priest of the state Grand Royal Arch chapter and deputy general grand master of the General Grand Encampment of the United States.[23]

The expansion of fraternal organizations allowed Masonry to provide employment for some. State officers often received payment for their duties. Philadelphia lodges hired a full-time tyler (or doorkeeper) who lived in the Masonic Hall and stood guard at meetings. Grand lodge secretaries commonly were compensated for increasingly complex and onerous duties that included keeping not only the minutes but the membership rolls of a rapidly expanding institution. After 1800 the Virginia grand lodge paid its secretary two hundred dollars per year. The larger New York State body offered six hundred dollars. Traveling lecturers had little choice but to live off their Masonic work. In Massachusetts, Benjamin Gleason, the first American grand lecturer, contracted to receive a minimum of one thousand dollars for the year. Besides teaching the Webb work in many different parts of the country, Jeremy L. Cross also supported himself by not only selling regalia and ritual equipment but providing charters for his new Cryptic degree system. Opportunities even developed beyond the organization itself. Several editors launched Masonic magazines. St. Andrew's Lodge and chapter member Charles W. Moore established a weekly Masonic newspaper in 1824.[24]

As the examples of Cross and Moore suggest, the higher degrees encouraged the emergence of a cadre of strongly committed brothers. Not only the intense rituals but the organizations themselves encouraged increased identification with Masonry. Membership itself demanded substantial investment. Although Webb's first Knights Templars body, formed in Providence in 1802, required possession of the first three degrees as well as the next four Royal Arch degrees, it still charged initiates twenty-five dollars. Three years later, the new grand body formed over Rhode Island and Massachusetts raised the fees to a minimum of thirty dollars, more than half a month's wages for a skilled laborer, thereby creating a strong barrier against the merely curious. The new bodies also required increased participation in their organizations and rituals, areas that overlapped, since officers usually played a designated part in the degree ceremonies. Besides the high priest that presided over the Royal Arch chapter, companions chose a king, a scribe, a Royal Arch captain, a captain of the host, a principal sojourner (to lead the initiates through the degree), and grand masters of the First, Second, and Third Veil. New York's Morton Commandery of Knights Templars required sixteen officers.[25] The state and national bodies that supervised these local groups created even more opportunities for brothers.

As a result, higher-degree membership tended to be defined largely by Masonic interest rather than occupational or cultural standing. Steep fees and expenses surely kept many poorer brothers from the higher-degree bodies, but their occupational composition suggests no major differences between higher-degree and lodge-degree bodies. In Boston, professionals seem to have been

Figure 17. The Master's Carpet. An attempt to standardize Masonic symbols. *Engraving by Amos Doolittle, from Jeremy Cross,* The True Masonic Chart *(New Haven, Conn., 1819). Courtesy of Scottish Rite Museum of Our National Heritage, Library, 14.1, C951, 1820a. Photography: John Miller Documents*

Table 17. Occupations of Members of St. Andrew's Royal Arch Chapter, Boston, 1769–1823

Occupation	1769–1800[a]	1817–1823[b]
Merchant	16 (15.5%)	6 (8.6%)
Professional	11 (10.7%)	12 (17.1%)
Government official	2 (1.9%)	2 (2.9%)
Banking and financial		2 (2.9%)
Artistic	1 (1.0%)	
Military	4 (3.9%)	
Luxury goods artisan	8 (7.8%)	3 (4.3%)
Mercantile-related artisan	8 (7.8%)	8 (11.4%)
Building crafts artisan	5 (4.9%)	7 (10.0%)
Other artisanal	19 (18.4%)	12 (17.1%)
Retail	16 (15.5%)	13 (18.6%)
Seagoing	11 (10.7%)	1 (1.4%)
Other	2 (1.9%)	4 (5.7%)

[a] 103 of 196 identified.   [b] 70 of 133 identified.

Sources: Chapman, *St. Andrew's Royal Arch Chapter,* 124–128, 138–162; Boston directories, 1789, 1796, 1798, 1800, 1803, 1805, 1813, 1816, 1818, 1821–1823, 1825, 1826; *By-laws of St. Andrew's Royal Arch Chapter, Boston* (Boston, 1866); Henry J. Parker, "The Masonic Register of Boston Masons, 1733–1800," MS, Massachusetts Grand Lodge Library, Boston.

drawn more and artisans drawn less to St. Andrew's Royal Arch chapter than to its associated lodge (Table 17), but Philadelphia shows little consistent difference in these categories (Table 18). Geneva's Masonic bodies, where the comparison can be made more directly, also exhibit a profile similar to Philadelphia's except in the higher proportions of professionals in the Mark Lodge and Royal Arch chapter (Table 19).

The primary occupational distinction lay in the proportionately greater involvement of ministers in higher-degree bodies. Although no ministers joined St. Andrew's Lodge in Boston between 1790 and 1820, five joined its Royal Arch chapter between 1817 and 1823 alone. More than one-quarter of all the new 1820–1828 members of the Providence, Rhode Island, Knights Templars body set up by Webb were clergymen. Drawing upon biblical themes and ideas, the Webb bodies in particular helped cement the growing rapprochement between the fraternity and religion.[26]

Table 18. Occupations of Philadelphia Masons, Harmony Chapter No. 52, and Knights Templars, Union Chapters Nos. 1 and 2, and St. John's Commandery No. 4, 1794–1831

Occupation	Harmony 1808[a]	Union 1794–1814[b]	St. John's 1819–1831[c]
Merchant	5 (11.6%)		4 (7.0%)
Professional	2 (4.7%)	2 (5.1%)	13 (22.8%)
Government official	2 (4.7%)	2 (5.1%)	3 (5.3%)
Banking and financial	3 (7.0%)	2 (5.1%)	
Artistic	2 (4.7%)		
Luxury goods artisan	6 (14.0%)	3 (7.7%)	7 (12.3%)
Mercantile-related artisan	3 (7.0%)	1 (2.6%)	1 (1.8%)
Building crafts artisan	1 (2.3%)	5 (12.8%)	2 (3.5%)
Other artisanal	15 (34.9%)	15 (38.5%)	19 (33.3%)
Retail	1 (2.3%)	8 (20.5%)	7 (12.3%)
Seagoing	3 (7.0%)		
Other		1 (2.6%)	1 (1.8%)

[a] 43 of 61 identified.   [b] 39 of 52 identified.   [c] 57 of 77 identified.

Sources: John Curtis, *Centennial Celebration and History of Harmony Chapter, No. 52, Royal Arch Masons from . . . 1794 to . . . 1894* (Philadelphia, 1894), 17–18, 99–101; Philadelphia Directories, 1802, 1806–1811, 1813, 1814, 1828–1833; Julius F. Sachse, *The History of the Masonic Knights Templars in Pennsylvania, 1797–1919* (Philadelphia, 1919), 64–67, 77–79; George W. Kreamer, *St. John's Commandery* (Philadelphia, 1901), 293–295.

Besides this extensive clerical interest, the most telling characteristic of higher-degree brothers was their Masonic activity. Twenty-six of the twenty-eight Geneva Lodge officers elected in this period joined higher-degree bodies, making up nearly one-fifth (19 percent) of their total membership.[27] Of the fourteen founders of the Richmond Royal Arch Chapter No. 3 in 1792, nine held grand lodge office in the next three years. The Rochester Templar body formed in 1826 included not only the orator who so impressed Hiram Hopkins the previous year but also the junior warden, treasurer, and master of the city's lodge. The last served as the head of the Royal Arch chapter as well. Not surprisingly, Hiram Hopkins also had been a lodge officer before taking further degrees.[28]

Table 19. Occupations in Geneva, New York, Higher-Degree Bodies, 1812–1819

Occupation	
Merchant	13 (22.8%)
Professional	17 (29.8%)
Government official	1 (1.8%)
Luxury goods artisan	2 (3.5%)
Building crafts	1 (1.8%)
Other artisanal	13 (22.8%)
Retailer	1 (1.8%)
Agriculture	9 (15.8%)

Note: 57 of 137 identified.
Sources: John H. Stelter, *History Royal Arch Masonry Geneva, New York, 1809–1964* (Geneva, N,Y., 1964), 18; Gary B. Thompson, ed., *Index to the Newspapers Published in Geneva, New York.* (Geneva, N.Y., 1981–).

This committed membership helped speed Masonry's transformation. Former Mason David Bernard noted in 1829 that only "a very small proportion of Masons, comparatively speaking, ever advance any further than the third degree."[29] This fraction probably ranged somewhere between one-quarter (the proportion of Royal Arch chapters to lodges in mid-1820s New York) to one-half (the proportion of Geneva, New York, lodge members who went beyond the original degrees). Despite their relatively small numbers, however, higher-degree members held disproportionate power. Their membership in groups built around ritual, their official positions in these additional bodies, and their lower-degree leadership all encouraged the development of Masonry from its earlier institutional informality.

Although expressed in Masonic language, the fraternity's growing emphasis on rules and structures paralleled developments in other groups. Post-Revolutionary voluntary associations expanded even more rapidly than Masonry itself. New England alone contained some fifteen hundred charitable societies by 1820. Although many of these groups remained purely local, a number attempted to expand and to reduce their dependence on the vagaries of local interest and patronage. Charitable associations sometimes hired paid secretaries, agents, and social workers. Political parties developed more slowly, but the tasks of organizing and spreading information increasingly became a full-time occupation. Churches created extensive new organizational infrastructures.[30] Even among the officially localistic Baptists, growth spurred the development of formal church associations that printed their minutes. The Presbyterian Church similarly began publishing the proceedings of their General Assembly in 1789, a clear indication of the growing importance assigned to centrally defined rules known to all. Methodist structure set out deliberately to insulate the institution from local custom and control. Besides having full-time bishops at its head, its circuit riders and its rotation of even residential ministers helped encourage ministerial loyalty to the organization rather than to a specific locality.[31]

Just as in Masonry, the expansion of these organizations helped create identities that spanned localities, allowing associations to move beyond parochial local customs and struggles. The fraternity, however, differed from other associations in crucial ways. Charities, parties, and (to a lesser extent) churches all sought publicity and growing membership as their central goal. The impetus behind the growth of Masonic institutions, however, lay primarily in strengthening the boundaries that differentiated the fraternity from the world. Fraternal leaders believed Masonry sacred in the fullest sense, not just connected to divine tasks and aims but also separated from common things. Consequently, Masonic organizations were not simply pragmatic means to an end. According to brothers like Webb and Fowle, they literally housed the secret name of God.

Such attitudes help explain the angry responses to the Maine grand lodge's 1824 decision to accept a "solemn affirmation" rather than an oath in its initiation rites. According to their reasoning, precise wording was less important than preserving meaning, especially when adaptation would allow more scrupulous Christians to join the fraternity. The grand lodges of Pennsylvania, Delaware, Tennessee, Missouri, and Illinois, however, saw things differently. Ritual changes now seemed a dangerous challenge to Masonic fundamentals. The Illinois body concluded that even this single innovation invalidated the entire process. They resolved that they would "not recognize as a Freemason, a person initiated in the manner proposed by the Grand Lodge of Maine."[32]

II. The Rugged Road

At first glance, brother Thomas Smith Webb's career typifies the nineteenth-century self-made man. Born the sixth child of a marginal Boston mechanic in 1771, Webb apprenticed as a bookbinder after receiving a public school education. Having served his time, he moved to Keene, New Hampshire, at the age of nineteen. He failed to find sufficient work there and returned to Boston. Soon afterward, Webb moved to Hartford, Connecticut, for a yearlong stay that began his upward climb. Becoming a wallpaper manufacturer, he moved to Albany, New York, to establish his new trade. His successful ventures there, which also included a bookselling partnership, eventually won him the first vice-presidency of the Albany Mechanics Society. Seeking even greater opportunities, he moved to Providence, Rhode Island, where he also manu-factured cotton and sold fire insurance. By the time he returned to Boston about 1814, Webb was a colonel in the militia, a member of the school com-mittee, and the grand master of Rhode Island. Boston's Handel and Haydn Society, a group he helped found, chose him as its first conductor. Webb now proclaimed himself a "gentleman," joined an Episcopalian church, and wrote songs about "fair beauty" and the "power of truth." His eulogist singled out Webb's "urbanity of manners" for particular notice.[33]

Another side of Webb's activities, however, fits less easily into the story of a rising gentleman. As perhaps the most influential Mason in post-Revolu-tionary America, Webb regularized and organized not only the original three degree rituals but a series of higher degrees that portrayed a world seemingly far removed from his urbane manners and his taste for Handel and Haydn. The Royal Arch ritual he revised, experienced later by Hiram Hopkins, in-volved members' clanging pots and pans as well as pushing and shoving initi-ates. His Knights Templars degree began in a room painted completely black and ended with the candidate drinking wine from a human skull.

The bizarre world Webb and his associates created within these degrees, seemingly so distant from respectable public life, actually spoke powerfully to their experiences and perceptions. If cornerstone ceremonies represented the public side of the fraternity's ideas, the higher degrees expressed the anxieties and inner conflicts created by the attempt to live up to these expectations in a rapidly changing society. Webb's new degree rituals provided stories that helped brothers comprehend their experiences. Instead of the polished self-presentation of gentlemen sure of their standing, the higher-degree rituals portrayed a cold world where success came only by struggle, an experience made bearable only by the honor won by activity and the refreshment offered by warm private spaces.

These new categories formed a part of the larger reshaping of the Enlighten-ment. Within the ceremonies created or revised in the 1790s and early 1800s, Masons thought through and experienced ways of envisioning an opposi-tion that would become central to much nineteenth-century thinking—the cold public world of struggle and competition versus the affective private sphere. Challenging the genteel vision of the previous century, which had seen only the public as honorable, the new rituals better fitted the experiences of brothers like Webb who lived far from the social and cultural settings imag-ined by eighteenth-century gentlemen. This remapping can be seen clearly in the Knights Templars degree, the highest rank in Webb's system and one upon which he had particular influence.

The culmination of Webb's Templar ceremony occurred in the Knights Tem-plars' meeting hall, where twelve lighted candles arranged in a triangle represented Jesus' disciples. The candidate extinguished one to symbolize Judas's betrayal, then was led about as a "pilgrim penitent" carrying a human skull to view scenes of Jesus' death and Resurrection. Finally, the candidate knelt while the extinguished candle was relit to symbolize his new membership, allowing him not only to become a knight but to fill the place "made vacant by the death of Judas Iscariot."[34]

The extraordinary conflation of Masonry, knighthood, and membership among Jesus' disciples formed only one version of a theme of honor and advancement that occurred again and again in the higher degrees. "The rites and mysteries developed in this degree," the high priest told initiates during the Royal Arch ceremony, "have been handed down through a chosen few." In the previous degree (the Most Excellent Master), only "those, who had proved themselves to be complete masters of their profession, were admitted" to the capstone laying of Solomon's Temple. According to Webb's description, they fully deserved this honor: "None but the meritorious and praiseworthy, none but those who through diligence and industry have advanced far towards perfection . . . can be admitted to this degree of masonry." The first three degrees "entered," "passed," and "raised" brothers; the Royal Arch ceremony "exalted" them.[35]

The image of the "chosen few," so important to Webb's degree system, became virtually an obsession in the less explicitly Christian Supreme Council degrees. Most of their thirty additional degrees portrayed increasing levels of honor among the temple workmen. In the Sublime Knights Elected, the fifteen knights selected in the previous tenth degree joined a new order "to make room for raising other worthy brethren." To a select twelve of this "grand chapter of illustrious knights," Solomon then "gave . . . command over the twelve tribes." Further degrees dubbed the initiates "Prince of Jerusalem," "Grand Pontiff," "grand master of all Symbolic Lodges," and "Prince of Masons."[36]

According to both sets of degrees, becoming a Prince, a Pontiff, or a Most Excellent Master involved more than simply a recognition of previous standing. The rituals instead emphasized that only vigorous activity made exaltation possible. The Knights Templars candidate vowed at the beginning of the degree to use his sword "in defense of the Christian Religion," protection the ritual later expanded to "innocent maidens, destitute widows," and "helpless orphans." In the Council system, the Elected Knights gained their position by tracking down and executing one of Hiram Abiff's murderers. Many of the same knights received an even higher order in the following ceremony "as a reward for the[ir] zeal and integrity." Even degrees unrelated to knighthood reflected this new emphasis. The color red, particularly associated with the Royal Arch degree, symbolized, according to Webb and others, fervency and zeal.[37]

This zeal was necessary because standing could no longer be taken for granted. According to the degree ceremonies, society was fluid and uncertain. The new Knight Templar took his place among the twelve disciples only after a lengthy period as a pilgrim, someone outside normal social ties. Before depicting a pilgrim penitent within the asylum, the candidate had already passed through two other periods as a pilgrim. At the ceremony's beginning, the initiate was dressed in humble clothing and forced to beg for food and water at various locations in the meeting room for "seven years." The candidate next became a pilgrim warrior for another term. Only then could he reach Jerusalem. These probationary periods, according to the explanation given later, represented "the great pilgrimage of life through which we are all passing." Pilgrim status, furthermore, involved more than a brief period of humility before honor. Even after they gained their new position as a knight and an apostle, the ritual warned, initiates could still expect only "a rough habit, coarse diet, and severe duty."[38]

The image of an uncertain world appears again and again in Webb's work. His 1813 grand master's address to Rhode Island lodges spoke of the "cold damps of a selfish world." In his Royal Arch ritual, the climax of the first set of Masonic degrees, the candidates travel from Babylon to Jerusalem along the "rugged road," an area of the hall littered with debris, bricks, and stones. "We are," the Knights Templars initiate was told, "all weary pilgrims."[39]

As Webb suggested, this rugged road involved more than entering a new Masonic position; it expressed the liminality, the in-betweenness, of life itself, a subtle yet important shift away from key elements within the ideals of enlightened gentility. Colonial gentlemen had seen honor as a badge of status, a recognition of social position and the attributes peculiar to that station. The degree rituals rejected this identification. Honor, they argued instead, was open to all who possessed the proper ability and zeal. Such a belief also suggested crucial differences in the means of achieving status. According to the canons of gentility, good breeding and proper character made even difficult actions look easy and natural. The higher degrees repudiated this ethic of effortlessness, exalting instead the vigorous activity necessary for success in a disorderly and confusing world. For weary pilgrims on a rugged road, a machinelike universe with a foreordained hierarchy of status held neither explanation nor comfort.[40]

The celebration of vigorous activity within an uncertain world expressed the experiences of men forced to struggle for a place in society. Webb's rise took him to four states before he could return to his native city as a "gentleman." Even then his position was insecure. Within four years he moved to Ohio to recoup his uncertain fortunes. The experiences of the more settled Henry Fowle, a close associate of Webb and the leader of Boston's first Knights Templars organization, further suggests the brothers' own rugged road. The son of a Medford tailor who became a block-and-tacklemaker, Fowle found himself teetering on the edge of bankruptcy shortly after opening a shop in Boston. Only an unexpected order on the day before he had booked passage to New York prevented him from leaving. Fowle eventually prospered to the point where he could buy the Reverend Samuel Mather's Mansion House. But even then difficulties arose. The Embargo and subsequent events, he recalled, again "reduced me almost to beggary." Upon reaching retirement age, he sold his revived business to his son, whose failure to follow the agreed terms left Fowle in penurious retirement.[41]

The experience of the cold world represented in the higher degrees extended beyond a few Boston leaders. The social changes that lay behind Masonry's new practical significance, geographical mobility, spreading market, fragmentation of the colonial gentry, and rising political partisanship all created risks and anxieties as great as the opportunities they presented for middling men such as Fowle and Webb.[42] The higher degrees represented as well the opening wedge of what would become a widespread cultural response. The Revolutionary generation attempted to break the link between social standing and political position, arguing that leadership and honor should not be determined by wealth or other extrinsic measures. Nineteenth-century Americans expanded this idea into an "individualism" that rejected the power of social categories to determine behavior and belief. Fittingly, the term entered the language only in the 1820s, the decade before Alexis de Tocqueville noted the tendency of "each citizen to isolate himself from the mass of his fellows and withdraw into the circle of family and friends," into a "little society formed to his taste."[43]

Tocqueville's belief that the American "gladly leaves the greater society to take care of itself," however, misread the situation. Rather than withdrawing from the public sphere, Americans were actually entering it in increasing numbers. What had changed was the felt power of the social order as a determinant of position. Warning against submission to "badges and names," Ralph Waldo Emerson argued that social relationships and social standing did not (or at least should not) determine identity in any way: "Society everywhere is in conspiracy against the manhood of every one of its members." Masonry's connection with Emerson's message of self-reliance was complex. Clearly the new, higher degrees, in themselves and in their rituals, created badges of status identifying and proclaiming position and identity. But, like Emerson, the higher degrees also rejected the idea that society fixed an individual's standing. The new rituals argued that men established their own position through struggle against a hostile society. Even the new Templars, ranked among the twelve disciples of Jesus himself, could expect only "constant warfare with the lying vanities and deceits of the world."[44]

When brother George Washington died in late 1799, the Reverend Thaddeus Mason Harris, a Royal Arch Mason of Charlestown, Massachusetts, delivered a "Fraternal Tribute" that reveals another part of the Masonic remapping of the world. According to brother Harris, the lodge provided a haven for Washington. At its meetings, Washington "found *relief* from his cares, or *strength* to rise above them." "When harassed by the fatigues of war or the concerns of public life," Washington "was fond of seeking the *refreshment* and enjoying the *serenity* always to be found within the peaceful walls of the Lodge."[45]

The new vision expressed in post-Revolutionary Masonry did not deny opportunities for comfort and stability, anymore than it foreclosed honor and station. Masons instead imagined new spheres, what Tocqueville called "little societies," that could be counterpoised to the increasingly problematic public. Brothers identified the lodge as one of these private spheres. This shift in Masonic rhetoric, taking place alongside rather than replacing the lodge's public purposes, made the fraternity a pioneer in another central nineteenth century metaphor, the idea of a private world distinguished by love and cooperation. By redefining Washington, Harris helped to revalue previously unimportant experiences, providing them with a significance they had lacked for actual colonial gentlemen like Washington.

During the years after Harris's 1800 address, the description of Masonry as a private space became increasingly common. With the opening of the lodge, Harris wrote in 1801, "the busy world is shut out and with it, all its perplexities, and cares, and sorrows." South Carolina brothers by 1807 similarly referred to their meetings as a "sacred retreat." The Universalist minister Hosea Ballou used the same image in an 1808 Vermont address, noting that brothers left "the bustle of a noisy world" to enter "that celestial retreat, beneath the sacred bowers of innocence, where . . . the sons of science repose in safety." Not surprisingly, this idea formed a part of higher-degree rituals as well. The Knights Templars ceremony concluded within their hall, significantly called the "asylum," their place of refuge. A prayer in the Royal Arch ritual elaborated further: "We thank thee that amidst the pains and calamities of our present state, so many means of refreshment and satisfaction are reserved to us, while travelling the *rugged path* of life."[46]

This new sense of Masonry as "separated . . . from common society" did not involve a repudiation of other roles. The image of retreat instead formed another layer of fraternal rhetoric, joining rather than displacing the more public images of honor and moral leadership. Indeed, brothers argued that the two parts of Masonry were intimately linked. Masons retreated because they needed to prepare for their other duties. "We leave the world behind," argued the Reverend William Bentley in 1797, "not to hate it, but to assemble all [God's] blessings into our bosoms, and to go abroad to scatter them."[47]

Brothers also left the world behind, Bentley might have said, to explore a new realm that would become increasingly important in the following decades. The significance of this new cultural construction can be seen by looking at how it modified colonial gentility and how this adaptation in turn would be taken up and reshaped. Harris's 1800 picture of Washington provides a point of comparison for each.

Harris's descriptions clearly misread the centrality of public honor in the lives of Washington and other colonial gentlemen. Washington attended Masonic functions almost exclusively upon public occasions. Indeed, after his earliest visits to the lodge in the 1750s, he perhaps never again witnessed degree ceremonies. Washington's Masonic career, like his life as a whole, fitted the older assessment of public life as the only source of honor. In this civic vision, retreat from the public world meant denying humankind's fundamental sociability, a negative image symbolized by the hermit's Hobbesian selfishness. Eighteenth-century genteel ideals had widened but not destroyed this space by redrawing the public sphere to include social interaction as well as political service. At the same time, politeness also widened the gap between these public and private areas by defining a wide range of activities as unacceptable. Although private life was not necessarily insignificant, it could never be honorable.[48]

Harris's picture of Washington made poor history, but it helped create a powerful myth. In the years after the Revolution, Americans revalued the private. The result was the creation of a series of private—or perhaps more accurately semipublic—spheres that, like the family and education, received increased attention and honor. As with the lodge, these semipublic activities often were defined partly as places of preparation for moral activity. The central ideals of this shift, and their connection with Masonic ideas, can be seen in both Weems's biography of Washington and the new valuation of women and the family.[49]

Brother Mason Locke Weems's revisions of his immensely popular Washington biography vividly suggest this development. First published in 1800, the book's early versions presented Washington as the exemplary public gentleman. While the title page of one edition promised "much light on the *private* as well as *public* life and character," the work still began by calling Washington "this truly great man" and moved into his military career by the end of the first page. Even the short account of Washington's schooling emphasized his judicious leadership. Among his schoolmates, Weems claimed, "a reference to him was the usual mode of deciding all differences." More tellingly, only these early editions mention his Masonic membership.[50]

Later versions of the book dramatically shifted this emphasis away from public deeds. By 1806, Weems suggested that *"private life"* was of greater significance, since it provided the "foundation of all human excellence." These neglected areas of Washington's life, Weems complained, had been consigned to "the *back rooms,*" like "old *aunts* and *grandmothers.*" Instead of continuing the practice followed by European "grandees" (and Weems's earlier versions), the author argued that he would not be taken in by the "ensigns of character," the symbols of social standing. "A public character," he warned, "is often an artificial one." Instead, he would present Washington as "what he really was" by exhibiting his *"private virtues."*[51]

These revisions suggest the leveling tendencies of this new division of life. By representing the private Washington, Weems hoped to make the great man more accessible. Scenes of "the Demigod" in "elegant orations," he argued, only distanced Washington: "Who among us can hope that his son shall ever be called, like Washington, to direct the storm of war, or to ravish the ears of deeply listening Senates?" Children could understand little of such "high character." It was "like setting pictures of the Mammoth before the *mice.*" Indeed, common private life brought out greatness more fully. Anyone, Weems argued, could "act greatly" when he was "the *burning focus* of unnumbered eyes." Harris's 1800 "fraternal tribute" similarly suggested that imagining Washington as a brother made him "less majestic but more engaging." The great man would not, he assured his listeners, "disdain the humble honors we pay."[52]

The most dramatic and far-reaching results of the reshaping of private life, however, lay, not in reshaping Washington's image, but in the new importance given to women and the family. The household, the realm of women, received little attention in the genteel vision of the colonial period. In Weems's metaphors, the family belonged "behind the curtain," "below the clouds," in "the *back rooms*" rather than in the public parlor of genteel manners and civic power. The Revolution and its attendant social changes changed this valuation, arguing that motherhood fulfilled public purposes. By training children in self-denying virtue, mothers played a key role in upholding a Republic without traditional governmental restraints. By the 1830s, this ideal had become linked to another image, that of the household as not only the proper place for women but also a place where their values influenced others. This ideology of domesticity portrayed the home (as the household now came to be called) as a separate sphere where feminine influence created a peaceful retreat from the competitive, amoral masculine world.[53] By linking to the public world what had formerly seemed private, these new ideals gave new standing to the family and women's roles. A number of mid-nineteenth-century women even took advantage of this connection to enter the public sphere, agitating for temperance, humanitarian endeavors, or even women's rights by claiming that their particular responsibility for morality made such actions necessary.[54]

The vision of Masonry seen in Harris's Washington and elsewhere reveals some of the complexities of these changes. According to Harris, the lodge fulfilled functions that would be ascribed almost exclusively to the home half a century later. The terms Harris underlined in the passage, *"refreshment," "serenity," "relief,"* and *"strength,"* all played central roles in an ideology of domesticity that also promised refuge from what he called "fatigues" and "concerns." The correspondence between the home and the lodge suggests a larger reorganization of public and private spheres, a development that included but went beyond the family. Indeed, the decisive gendering of the private as female seems to have occurred only after it became defined as a retreat from and a preparation for the public world. Perhaps not coincidentally, Weems's biography of Washington, despite its glorification of the private, portrays Washington's father, not his mother, as the family's central figure.[55] The image of the lodge as a retreat also formed part of a post-Revolutionary reshaping of male gender roles. Masonic rhetoric portraying the lodge as a separate sphere of refreshment helped create a fundamental model of masculinity in which men, rather than being strictly community members, private beings, or, alternatively, citizens, participated by turns in both a peaceful private sphere and an uncertain, troublesome public world.[56]

For both the lodge and home, these new definitions gained power by using religious metaphors. Just as women and children became angels and the home a place of worship, so the Masonic meeting came to be a temple and an asylum, a sanctuary where the world could not penetrate. Lodges, which before had been "installed," now were "consecrated," set apart from common things. Not surprisingly, even Washington became part of this new image. "As punctually as he attended public worship in the church," claimed the popular Masonic orator the Reverend George Richards, "would he attend private worship in the lodge." [57]

III. The Thick Veil

According to De Witt Clinton, the higher degrees that so entranced Hiram Hopkins posed a real danger. At times, he warned in 1793, "the genuine degrees of Freemasonry have been considered as initiative steps into more elevated orders, and more sublime mysteries" invented "with a view of gain or of gratifying that taste for frivolous parade which is the natural companion of frivolous minds." Thirty-two years later, he complained to the New York grand lodge of "frivolous pageantry and fantastic mummery, equally revolting to good taste and genuine Masonry." "To the magnificent temple of the Corinthian order," he lamented, "there have been added Gothic erections, which disfigure its beauty and derange its symmetry." [58]

Although Clinton did not reject all higher degrees (he went on to become the national leader of a number of Webb bodies), his criticisms are significant, for they underline the extent to which the new rituals departed from the standards of eighteenth-century Masonry and the genteel, enlightened culture in which it grew. The higher degrees as a whole expressed an aesthetic, a theory of education, and a vision of the self that challenged the canons of public decorum followed by Washington and Webb. Clinton's critique referred first to artistic issues. Rather than following the standards of decorum prescribed by neoclassical aesthetics, he complained, higher-degree rituals engaged in frivolity, emotional excitement for its own sake. The issue of taste, however, involved more than narrowly artistic standards. The new, higher-degree aesthetics encouraged a taste for Romantic art, but they also expressed and helped create new ways of thinking about education and even identity itself. Rather than attempting to polish external self-presentation, as gentility recommended, the higher degrees sought, through emotional assault, to reach an interior self that could be changed only by breaking down outward defenses. The rituals, despite Clinton's protestations about frivolity and fantasy, actually had a serious purpose. Like the neoclassical models that Clinton followed, the seemingly frivolous higher degrees sought to teach morality. They did so, however, in a way that prefigured a new view of human psychology.[59]

Thomas Thompson, the grand master of New Hampshire, considered the higher degrees even more worrisome. They were "new, fanciful, and mock degrees," he told the grand lodge in 1808, "made up of pomp, pageantry, and show with loftily high sounding titles of kings; high priests, princes, scribes . . . all unmasonic and imposing." But the Knights Templars degree seemed the most dangerous. It was "a compound of enthusiasm and folly." "Of all the Masonic titles there is none so truly ridiculous in America as that of the Knights Templars."[60]

A skull formed the primary prop for the end of the ritual adapted and standardized by Thomas Smith Webb. After the candidate returned from a depiction of Jesus' passion and resurrection, the grand commander took the skull carried by the initiate and poured wine into it. This "fifth libation," the commander explained, was "emblematical of the bitter cup of death, of which we must all, sooner or later, taste." Drinking from it himself to show the seriousness of the request, he then passed the skull to the candidate for the final obligation. Giving "testimony of my belief of the mortality of the body and the immortality of the soul," the candidate vowed, "As the sins of the whole world were laid upon the head of our Savior, so may the sins of the person whose scull this once was, be heaped upon my head, in addition to my own; and may they appear in judgment against me, both here and hereafter, should I violate or transgress any obligation in Masonry." He then drank.[61]

The scene aroused strong reactions. A Rhode Island Baptist minister recalled that the experience "shocked me at the time more than I can express." According to Avery Allyn, later a strong opponent of the order, his initial refusal to take the libation and "the *profane* oath" caused the knights to surround him with drawn swords. Even such a committed Mason as Henry Fowle responded with trepidation. Although head of St. Andrew's Royal Arch chapter and a later founder of the national Templar organization, he hesitated for some time before organizing an encampment of knights in Boston because, he recalled, of "a conscientious scruple whether we should be able to live up to the moral and religious obligations they impose."[62]

Figure 18. The Fifth Libation. Antimasonic representation of Knights Templars
ceremony. *From Avery Allyn, A Ritual of Freemasonry (Philadelphia, 1831).*
Courtesy American Antiquarian Society

The Templar ritual represented the most awe-inspiring and overwhelming
of the higher degree ceremonies, but it represented an extension of elements
common to all. As Clinton and Thompson suggested, the ceremonies con-
travened the basic premises of neoclassical aesthetics, their emphasis on simplicity, rationalism, and reserve. The "beautiful Simplicity" celebrated by the
Spectator formed a key element in these genteel standards. "I shall not," De
Witt Clinton conventionally declared in 1823, "step aside to embellish or to
dazzle; to cull a flower or to collect a gem": "Truth, like beauty, needs not
the aid of ornament." Complexity seemed dangerous because it disrupted
the calm necessary for rational thought. Clinton complained in 1825 of the
"fanciful speculations of visionary men" about Masonic history, typically recommending an attempt "to sober down our minds to well-established facts."
"Enthusiastic friends of our Institution have done it much injury." According
to the neoclassical theories he still followed, gentility demanded a certain distance and reserve.[63]

The higher degrees, on the other hand, deliberately set out to "dazzle." In
elaborate rituals—lasting sometimes for hours—brothers employed decora-
tions, costumes, and props that in the end made their halls resemble a theater
more than a conventional club room. Officers played the principal characters
in the narratives that made up the bulk of the ceremonies. The high priest,
king, prelate, and captain of the host all represented historical personages in
the Royal Arch ritual taken by Hopkins. They were costumed accordingly.

The presiding high priest wore a multicolored robe with a mitre and breast-plate; the king (the second officer), a scarlet robe and a crown.[64] The initiate who played the central figure in this participatory theater passed by, and sometimes over and through, elaborate stage sets. The Royal Arch ceremony required a burning bush, two trapdoors, three veils colored blue, scarlet, and purple, respectively, and a pile of brickbats, stones, and rubble. The Select Master's degree in the Cryptic Rite prescribed nine different veils. These props sometimes created highly theatrical effects. In the Royal Arch ritual, an unseen companion speaks from the burning bush, and in the Most Excellent Master degree a fire rises without being set.

Rejecting the neoclassical ideal of simplicity, the higher degrees also worked under a different set of suppositions in their treatment of morality. The road to virtue, they argued implicitly, lay, not in sobering down, but in stirring up emotions. The Knights Templars ritual began with the initiate left blindfolded in the "Chamber of Reflection," a room often painted black and lit with a single candle. The candidate then removed his blindfold to discover himself sitting at a table bearing the skull and crossbones. In this unnerving setting, the candidate promised in writing to defend the Christian religion and obey the rules of the order. Similar uses of excited emotions occur in other degrees. The initiate in the Past Master's degrees was placed into the master's chair as presiding officer, only to find his attempts to establish order met by boisterous opposition. Finally, forced to resign in frustration, the candidate received a lecture on the necessity of preparation for any office.

The importance of emotional extravagance and enthusiasm in the higher degrees did not imply a complete rejection of the genteel standards upheld by Clinton and Thompson. The continued importance of such values can be seen clearly in the life of the self-proclaimed "gentleman" Thomas Smith Webb, the most important American adapter and proponent of the Templar degree. Under Webb's baton, the Handel and Haydn Society started its career by using a book whose material, the title page boasted, was "Chiefly Selected or Adapted from Modern European Publications." Webb's own songs suggested a genteel message similar to the enlightened neoclassical music celebrated in the group's title and in its original music. Using high poetic diction, his works celebrated the "pow'r and majesty" of "fair Truth." One even invoked Apollo, asking that "discord be set at defiance."[65]

Post-Revolutionary Masons referred to the complexity and excitement of these degrees as well as Masonry in general, not as discordant or enthusiastic, but as "sublime." Fowle called the Templar degrees "those Sublime Orders," and the Council degrees were commonly known as the "sublime degrees." Masonry as a whole became "the sublime science." Baltimore's Elijah Stansbury even called it the "sublimest institution ever devised by man."[66]

The use of the term, a central concept in the rethinking of neoclassicism, suggests that the higher degrees were not merely the result of fanciful minds.

Figure 19. The Chamber of Reflection. Where the Knights Templars initiate promised
to keep the rules of the order. *From Avery Allyn*, A Ritual of Freemasonry
(Philadelphia, 1831). Courtesy American Antiquarian Society

Instead, they formed part of a larger shift in transatlantic aesthetics in the century after Addison and Steele attacked "Goths in Poetry" who used "the extravagances of an irregular Fancy" to hide their inability to achieve "the beautiful Simplicity of the Greeks and Romans"—and early speculative brothers
scorned the Middle Ages as a decline from the glorious Augustan era. These
changes were extraordinarily complex, but they can partly be seen as the result of growing tension between two themes that helped shape early Masonry,
rational order and sympathetic emotions.[67]

Both these ideals played central roles in the English elite's late-seventeenth-
century attempt to restore their political and religious authority. Rationalism
attacked the uncontrolled enthusiasm of the sectaries. Sympathetic feelings
about others' distress refuted the mechanistic selfishness that Hobbes cited as
a justification for tyrannical power. Yet the emotional responses that seemed
to prove society natural also could be used to challenge the rational calm of
neoclassical decorum. By the middle of the eighteenth century, the new genre
of the novel increasingly celebrated sentiment as a revelation of individual
moral purity. At the same time, theoretical concern about the undeniable
artistic power of seeming disorder encouraged an increasing interest in the ir-

regular (sometimes called the picturesque) and the overwhelming (sometimes called the sublime). These new tendencies laid the foundation of Romantic aesthetics. Strong feelings rather than reason now seemed the source of the deepest insights. Orderly and sober expressions appeared too prosaic, too stultifying, to comprehend the imagination's response to life's diversity and complexity.[68]

America participated in these developments slightly later. Most prominent and cosmopolitan critics and artists continued to adhere to neoclassical standards through the early decades of the nineteenth century. Romanticism emerged full-blown in America only in the 1830s.[69] Yet this late acceptance among the literati does not, as the higher degrees reveal, constitute the entire history of American aesthetics. Like the rise of American novel reading (also suspected as dangerous by neoclassical thinkers), the popularity of the higher degrees reveals shifting tastes within less exalted ranks. Webb himself can be linked to these literary changes. The bookstore and lending library in Albany that he owned in the mid-1790s (about the time he began revising the higher degrees) included, besides important enlightened works, the new and influential gothic novels of Ann Radcliffe.[70] Webb's higher Masonic degrees, including the gothic journeys of the Templars, allowed Americans to experience, even literally to embody, cultural currents that came to dominate much of the nineteenth century.

Ultimately, however, both proponents and critics of the new rituals believed more was at stake than definitions of art. Clinton and Thompson based their critiques not just on the "taste for frivolous parade," or bad art, but on "enthusiasm and folly"—dangerous moral principles. The rituals' innovative aesthetics, their anticlassical complexity, and their heightened emotionalism and sublimity sought to do more than provide an interesting experience. Just as much as neoclassical literature, they attempted to provide training in virtue. An understanding of this goal requires going beyond aesthetic ideas to broader questions about the nature of the universe, education, and the self.

"You have hitherto only seen the thick veil that covers the S.S. [Sanctum Sanctorum] of God's temple," King Solomon told the seven "Secret Masters" in that Sublime degree. "Your fidelity, zeal and constancy have gained you this favour I now grant you, of shewing you our treasure, and introducing you into the secret place." Along with the idea of public honor, the image of secret wisdom open to only a select few formed the heart of the sublime degrees. The Cerneau supreme council (a New York body related to these sublime rituals) labeled members of the first three degrees respectively as "neophite," "adept," and "wise man." Its more powerful rival, the Charleston supreme council, would not even concede that wisdom could be achieved by the third degree. Only "a man of science"—a Mason of the higher degrees—could preside over a lodge, argued the "Grand Inspector Generals." These early degrees were "merely symbols of the superior or sublime degrees" and had originated only "as a test of the character and capacity of the initiated, before they should be admitted to the knowledge of the most important mysteries."[71]

In the years after the Revolution, the idea of hidden wisdom expressed within these Sublime degrees grew increasingly popular in Masonry as a whole. The vision of secret knowledge can partly be traced to Masonry's pre-Enlightenment heritage, but its deeper meanings pointed toward ideas of education and the self that would become dominant in the nineteenth century. Like Masonic wisdom, this new set of ideals suggested, the foundations of identity lay in a secret place, within the heart, that could be addressed only through strong impressions and expressed fully only through overflowing emotions. Although set in biblical or medieval times, the post-Revolutionary higher degree rituals actually formed part of a larger transformation of enlightened gentility that created the Victorian world of sentimentalism and the interior self.

The Webb higher-degree rituals created a similar aura of mystery and secret knowledge. The Royal Arch degree dramatized this vision most fully. There the deepest knowledge of all, the "ineffable name of God" revealed to Moses at the burning bush, lay literally buried beneath the ruins of the temple. Taking the part of workmen rebuilding the temple after the Babylonian captivity, the initiates in the degree accidentally discovered the ark of the covenant in an underground vault where Solomon, King Hiram, and Hiram Abiff had hidden it during the building of the temple. The overseers then opened the ark to find the book of the law and a *"key"* to the ark's symbols. The *"three mysterious words"* there, the lost Mason's word now called "the *grand omnific* royal arch word," turned out to be the name (and thus the key to the identity) of the deity, a secret title that could be spoken only in groups of three forming triangles with their arms and feet. Even in the position that Hopkins called the "Living Arch, by 3 times 3," the word was not repeated whole. Instead, each participant pronounced a syllable in turn, giving, according to the ritual, "the name of Deity in three languages—Jah-bul-lun, Je-ho-vah, G-o-d." At the climax of the discovery in the ceremony, the companions did not even say it aloud. They merely raised the living arch.

Numbers as well as words held deep significance in the higher degrees. The Royal Arch ritual invested the number seven (the degree was the seventh in the sequence) as well as three and nine (the Trinity and its square) with mystical meaning. Only three initiates could be exalted at once, each beginning with a rope tied around his body seven times. They finally passed through three veils to face the three overseers of the work. In the previous Webb ritual, the initiate wore a rope wrapped six times, entered the hall after six knocks, was led around the lodge six times, and kissed the Bible six times.

The new importance of mystery in post-Revolutionary Masonry marked

Figure 20. *The Masonick Minstrel*. By David Vinton, frontispiece (Dedham, Mass., 1816). *Courtesy American Antiquarian Society*

a recovery of an underutilized but central Masonic element. From the beginning, British Masons connected their fraternity with the ancients' mystical wisdom. Although they took advantage of the fraternity's mysterious
reputation, colonial American brothers virtually ignored this link. Post-
Revolutionary Masons recovered this resource. Although the degrees ultimately played an important part in establishing new ways of thinking, the
mysteries of the higher degree rituals in many ways formed part of a cultural
tradition that had largely been driven out of learned culture in the generations
after Newton.[72]

This esoteric tradition, like the Masonic higher degrees, gave great importance to mysteries and numbers. In the treasure seeking that became increasingly common in post-Revolutionary America, guides with deep spiritual knowledge sought to retrieve treasure buried in the earth. The treasure
seeker and Mormon prophet Joseph Smith even claimed, like the Royal Arch
ritual, to have found God's word buried underneath the earth. Thomas Smith
Webb's Albany bookstore helped publish a work purporting to provide "a revealed knowledge of the Prophecies and the Times" in 1796—just about the
time Webb began to concentrate on the higher-degree rituals. The volume's
author, the English seer Richard Brothers, interpreted London's loud thunder
in 1791 as portending the city's imminent destruction. Only his pleading with
the deity turned away the impending "fire from heaven" and a "large river . . .
coloured with human blood." Brothers also claimed that God instructed him
"to write the Chronology of the world," a fascination with "prophetic numbers" that Webb's partner had attempted to satisfy the previous year with a
book, *The Signs of the Times,* predicting the Second Coming in 1864.[73]

The similarities between Masonry and such activities underline how extensively the higher degrees repudiated important elements of the Enlightenment. Hoarding knowledge seemed dangerous, even superstitious, to enlightened thinkers whose central project required the spread of information. Even
though Clinton suggested that the preservation of secret wisdom was one
of early Masonry's central functions, significantly, he believed such activities necessary only before the invention of the printing press. Then, like good
enlightened gentlemen, the brothers happily shared their accumulated knowledge. For Clinton, as for other enlightened thinkers, the spread of knowledge
to all naturally led to ethical improvement, what Clinton called "the sunshine
of" not only "mental" but "moral illumination."[74]

The new degrees were not entirely part of the older esoteric tradition
either. With other key elements in Masonry celebrating more openness, post-
Revolutionary brothers generally did not seek a return to the secretive world
of magi and adepts where, as a history of Freemasonry published in the 1820s
by a member of a Boston Royal Arch chapter explained of Egypt, "knowledge
. . . was carefully concealed from the vulgar."[75] Just as important, the ceremonies actually went far beyond the esoteric tradition to pioneer new models

Figure 21. The Living Arch by Three times Three. The triangles in which Royal Arch Masons pronounced or portrayed the secret name of God. *From Avery Allyn*, A Ritual of Freemasonry *(Philadelphia, 1831). Courtesy American Antiquarian Society*

of human psychology. This shift can be seen in two elements that played important roles in the higher degrees, their physicality and their strong emotions.

Hiram Hopkins's description of his Royal Arch initiation as "two or three hours *hard labour*" might have been merely a reference to the symbolic work of rebuilding the temple, but other elements of the ritual suggest that he might have been speaking less metaphorically, for the process of exaltation must have been exhausting. The ceremony began with members' tying up the initiates with ropes. After being loosed, the men had to crawl over a large pile of debris. They also passed three times under another "living arch," one with fewer mystical and more physical meanings. For this part of the ceremony, two rows of companions formed a line, each linking hands with those on the opposite side. The initiates then crawled between the rows as knuckles, knees, and feet poked, prodded, and crushed them.

Such a gauntlet had no parallel in earlier degrees—or in the ideals of gentility. Even the compass placed against the bare skin in the Entered Apprentice's degree involved no direct physical contact. When touching occurred in the raising of the initiate playing Hiram, it was carefully ritualized as "the five points of fellowship." The strenuous exertions of the Royal Arch degree would have seemed ungenteel to enlightened gentlemen. George Washington's face on the day he left the presidency, John Adams recorded, "was as serene and unclouded as the day," though nearly everyone else was teary-eyed. The controlled Washington recorded in his diary that it was "much such a day as yesterday in all respects." For gentlemen such as Washington, politeness required careful restraint of outward expressions.[76] In the higher degrees, breaching this decorum was precisely the point. Physical contact and pain broke down the surface of calm and stability that had been the goal of genteel education. The rituals sought to penetrate directly to a person's moral center, now defined, not as outward self-presentation, but as inner character. The exhaustion, the physical pummeling, and the terror experienced in the degrees all sought to encourage the emotional responses necessary to change deeply ingrained habits and tendencies.

These changes went deeper than simply moving the center of educational attention. They also helped create a new way of thinking about the foundation of human identity, about the self. Locke and the Enlightenment discredited the centuries-old model of human psychology as a collection of disparate feelings, attitudes, and desires struggling for dominance. In place of these warring faculties, the Enlightenment posited a more unified mechanical consciousness. Post-Revolutionary thinkers kept this sense of relative consistency, but pushed the center inward. Instead of a seething mass of conflicting tendencies or a machine driven by sense experience, this new model suggested, humans had an internal core of identity that could be educated and relied upon for guidance.[77]

These changes can be seen in many different areas. Late-eighteenth-century novels, like much contemporary political thinking, centered on fears of hypocrisy. The novel of seduction, the most popular genre, portrayed a trusting young woman being taken in, for a time at least, by a deceitful man who hid his true nature. Two other important works (both published in 1798), the *Memoirs of the Notorious Stephen Burroughs of New Hampshire* and Charles Brockden Brown's *Wieland*, similarly turned around the manipulation of appearances. Stephen Burroughs impersonates a minister and then becomes a

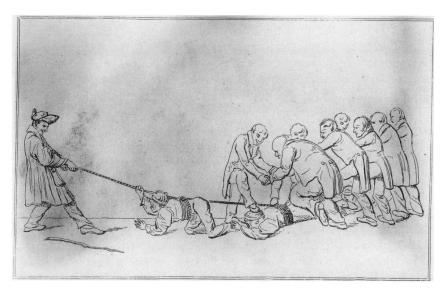

Figure 22. The Living Arch. Representing the trials of life and the attempt to break down the defenses resisting moral education. *From Avery Allyn,* A Ritual of Freemasonry *(Philadelphia, 1831). Courtesy American Antiquarian Society*

counterfeiter. In *Wieland,* a ventriloquist connected with the Illuminati (two very different modes of concealing reality) disrupts a genteel family circle. As an anonymous reviewer in 1819 noted of Brown: "He loves . . . to impress you with the self-dependence of characters, plotting, loving, suspecting evil, devising good, in perfect secrecy. Sometimes, when he would exhibit strength of mind and purposes to most advantage, he takes away all external succour."[78] A more clearly enunciated expression of the new vision of the self can be seen among a group that often condemned early novels, evangelical Christians. They too envisioned an inner identity. This "spiritual heart," Charles G. Finney argued, "lies [in] back of all [the mind's] other voluntary affections and emotions" and gives them "their character." Like Masonic education, evangelical preaching by Finney and others involved breaking through outward defenses in order to speak directly to the true inward self.[79]

Besides the presumed power of the impressions made by such intense lessons, the significance of emotions as evidence of inner states can be seen clearly in one of Webb's higher degrees. A section in the Most Excellent Master's lecture tells of an excited workman at the dedication of Solomon's Temple who found the event so deeply moving that, filled with "reverential awe," he ascended directly to heaven.[80]

As the event suggests, emotions within higher-degree rituals (as in novels and evangelical conversions) became increasingly important morally as well as aesthetically. Excited feelings provided not only a means of reaching the true self but of revealing it more directly than sober rationality. In Weems's attempt to make the impassive Washington an image of this new economy of self, the great man's expressive face revealed his virtue. Even in church, he suggested, neighborhood women "would sometimes wander from the cold reading-preacher, to catch a livelier devotion from [Washington's] *mind-illumined face*." Such beliefs would lead to the weepy sentimentalism so popular in the nineteenth century that portrayed emotional expression (particularly as expressed in tears) as pure expressions of a true inward self. The 1819 effusions of a Pennsylvania Mason about another eighteenth-century classical hero, the Massachusetts Ancient grand master Joseph Warren, suggest the increasing removal of genteel restraint upon emotions. "Oh brave, generous and noble Warren!" exclaimed Lewis Deffebach to a man who once wore an Augustan toga for a public oration. "Would that the spot that contains thy relics were here, freely would I fall prostrate by its side; kneel upon it, and with the tears of genuine affection and gratitude, bedew the sacred mound!" [81]

The shifting views of aesthetics, psychology, and the self explored in the post-Revolutionary higher degrees finally reached Clinton. Although not entirely unaffected by these changes, Clinton modeled himself primarily on the ideals of eighteenth-century gentility and Enlightenment. His lifelong interest in nature grew out of an attempt to understand and to categorize the visible world, not to learn its transcendent lessons of morality and to be overwhelmed by its sublimity. The flowers of fancy that became so important to later Americans seemed to Clinton only to disrupt sober reason. Indeed, he believed the idea of hidden depths and strong emotions more characteristic of superstition than of true morality.

But even the man whom his opponents dubbed the "Magnus Apollo" could not halt these immense cultural changes. The New York Knights Templars eulogist of Clinton felt obliged to portray him as a man whose inner feelings gushed in deep revelation of his inner purity. The 1828 funeral oration characterized Clinton as a man "enraptured with the principles of the institution." Rather than the spokesman of simplicity and sobriety, the eulogist considered Clinton, in a metaphor significantly drawn from medieval Catholicism, "an ardent votary at our shrine." [82]

In 1801, Henry Fowle learned of a renegade Mason giving the Royal Arch and Knights Templars degrees under the cover of the charter and jewels of a subordinate lodge. He determined to "immediately arrest them" by sending brother Benjamin Russell, a fellow member of St. Andrew's Royal Arch chapter and the grand marshal of the grand lodge. Russell hastened to the meeting room, pushing in the half-opened door with such force that he threw the tyler across the room. Clapping his hand on the leader's shoulder, he proclaimed (in Fowle's account), "I arrest you, Sir, in the name of the Grand Lodge of Massachusetts." The astonished man quickly regrouped, pointing out that they were giving the Royal Arch, not a lower degree, and thus, according to Masonic jurisprudence, Russell's authority did not extend to the meeting. Russell, noting that he was also grand king of the grand chapter, proceeded to seize them again in the name of that body.[83]

The language of legality came naturally to active brothers who saw themselves protecting sacred rites. Both the increasingly solid structures they were building and the higher degrees that formed a distinct private world helped promote a sense that defending Masonic rules and rituals fulfilled the requirement of the Knights Templars oath to wield their sword for the "Christian religion." Even the offending Boston brother seems to have accepted this ideal. He defended himself, not by questioning Russell's right to invade the room, but by citing Masonic legalities.

Ultimately, however, the sense of empowerment provided by the sacrilization of Masonry proved a double-edged sword. The fraternity's separation from public attitudes and standards as well as its growing institutional infrastructure provided brothers with a loving community that compensated for the confusion of the outside world. But the sectarian side of Masonry, with its emphasis on emotionally charged loyalty and distinction, created tension with the fraternity's public portrayal of itself as disinterested leader and practical helper. The fraternity's romantic, secret world fitted uneasily into the classical columns of its exterior.

In the generation after the Revolution, Masonry's ability to embody the period's diverse cultural demands gave it enormous power. The continued elaboration of these elements, however, also prepared the way for Masonry's ultimate fall. In 1826, upstate New York brothers spirited away a Mason who presumed to break his sacred oaths and publish the fraternity's secrets. Like Fowle and Russell earlier, these brothers believed Masonry so significant that its rules transcended the Republic's. The resulting uproar revealed the complex layers of the post-Revolutionary fraternity—and the internal contradictions it had created. From the perspective of the attempt to purify and reshape American society in the 1820s, Masonry's tensions seemed, not a creative attempt to deal with the cross purposes of its culture, but an attempt to deceive the public: another example of the hypocritical visible front hiding true inward identity. The fraternity's post-Revolutionary success, its ability to encompass disparate and even conflicting demands, thus prepared the way for its eventual failure.

In 1818, the Pennsylvania grand lodge reported that the furnishings of its new hall were being destroyed by "the almost total Exclusion of a fresh supply of Air" during lodge meetings. This suffocation can be seen as a symbolic problem as well. By separating its internal activities from the outside world, post-Revolutionary Masonry created a heady new atmosphere. As a newly exalted Hiram Hopkins would soon learn, however, it could be dangerous— and, with the right spark, highly inflammable.[84]

PART FOUR

Masonry and Democracy

CHAPTER TEN

The Lion and the Crows

Antimasonry, 1826–1840

After the August 1826 ceremony in which Hiram Hopkins received the Royal Arch degree, his guide drew him aside to warn him that a stonemason in nearby Batavia, New York, was publishing a book revealing Masonry's secrets. According to the guide, the treacherous brother, William Morgan, would even disclose the Grand Omnific Royal Arch Word, the secret name of God that Hopkins had learned that evening. Hopkins was appalled. "If Morgan was guilty of such an outrage upon the laws of Masonry," he later remembered thinking, "it was just for him even to lose his life." Hopkins and other Masons often discussed Morgan's threat to "publish Masonry" in the weeks to come. Many brothers wanted to send Morgan out of the country by force. Hopkins would have gone even further. "I thought," he recalled, "he deserved to die." [1]

These discussions placed Hopkins near the center of an event that would transform American Masonry. The attempts of Hopkins's brothers to deal with Morgan set off a firestorm of criticism that virtually destroyed the order's standing in American society. Over the next decade and a half, Masonry lost more than half of its members and virtually ceased creating new lodges. Just as important, the impact and implications of this Antimasonic movement went beyond the fraternity. Antimasonry's new organizational models and belief in the significance of public opinion and the conscience provided experience and examples that American organizers and reformers would draw upon for the next generation and beyond.

These changes, however, would not have been possible had not angered upstate brothers like Hiram Hopkins determined to prevent William Morgan's disclosures. As the book drew closer toward publication, Masons increased pressure upon the ex-brother and his business partner, Batavia printer David C. Miller. Miller and his friends successfully thwarted an attempt to burn down his printing office on September 10. The following day, brothers had Morgan arrested on a trumped-up charge and taken to Canandaigua. After the original charges against him proved groundless, he was imprisoned under a hastily devised indictment for a two-dollar debt. The next day, a menacing group of strangers, some carrying clubs, seized Miller on a similarly manufactured charge, even holding him for a time in a nearby town's lodge room. A magistrate released Miller later that day. Morgan suffered a worse fate. That evening, a stranger paid Morgan's bail and then helped force him into a carriage while Morgan cried, "Murder! Murder!"[2]

Hopkins played a small role in the abduction, helping his cousin, Niagara County sheriff Eli Bruce, prepare a cell for the expected prisoner. But the kidnappers bypassed the jail, and Hopkins grew increasingly anxious. "It would be best to bring him back," he advised brothers more closely involved in Morgan's kidnapping over the next few months, until one finally told him privately it was already too late—Morgan had been killed. Although the precise fate of the abducted author remains uncertain even today (Morgan was never seen again, dead or alive), both Hopkins and the final state prosecutor to examine the case shared the common Antimasonic conviction that Morgan was murdered. The conspirators had probably originally attempted to take Morgan to Canada and perhaps on to Europe only to have their plans break down at the last minute. After holding Morgan for about a week at Fort Niagara, the increasingly harried brothers might have decided that destroying the evidence of their misdeeds was the least unpalatable option.[3]

Lacking conclusive evidence of murder, prosecutors could press only lesser misdemeanor charges of conspiracy and kidnapping. Even then, success remained elusive, in large part because Masons used their position and influence to impede legal action. Hopkins, acting upon Bruce's instructions, packed Niagara County juries with brothers. Other Masons fled before they were forced to testify. Less friendly outsiders were sometimes pressured to withhold cooperation. Despite some twenty trials and three successive special prosecutors appointed by the state, only a handful of convictions resulted, all followed by minor jail terms. Bruce, a central conspirator, received the longest sentence, thirty months.[4]

The brotherhood largely escaped punishment. And it prevented the publication of all but the first three degree rituals, which appeared as *Illustrations of Masonry* a month after the abduction. But it lost the larger battle in the court of public opinion. Its high-handed actions catalyzed a dramatic revaluation of post-Revolutionary Masonry. Over the next ten years, the resulting outcry crippled the fraternity in the South and nearly destroyed it in the North. Thousands of brothers left the fraternity. Vocal ex-Masons joined with similarly aroused outsiders to create an active opposition to the fraternity, a shift spurred by Hiram Hopkins's testimony against his former patron and brother, Eli Bruce, in court—and against his fraternity in print. Although Hopkins had once judged Masonry nearly equivalent to Christianity, he now believed almost precisely the opposite. He had been "trained," he decided, in the "school" of Satan.[5]

Ultimately, however, the Morgan incident was only the spark that set off these changes. Other circumstances provided the fuel and fanned the flames. Antimasons organized their protest on a new scale, using a wide range of activities and publications to shape public opinion. Faced with an active opposition concentrating on a single purpose, the more comprehensive, and thus more diffuse, fraternity could not withstand the pressure. Whether formally or informally, most American brothers ended their affiliation. The success of this Antimasonic agitation rested on more than effective organization. The new opposition expressed a growing disenchantment not just with Masonry but with the entire social and cultural order it embodied. The fraternity's doctrine of preference, its higher degrees, and its attempt to link itself with Christianity, Antimasons argued, all pointed to a conspiracy to undermine true religion and republican values. In making this argument, Masonry's opponents drew upon, and in turn helped advance, a nascent attack upon the larger post-Revolutionary social order. The Antimasonic critique explored and popularized the powerful ideals of conscience, public opinion, and purified religion that reinforced the growing cultural dominance of democracy and evangelicalism.

Unable to reply convincingly, members either joined the opposition, halted their lodge activities, or attempted to preserve Masonry in secret. These few remaining brothers presided over the fraternity's revival in the 1840s, a resurgence that eventually allowed Masonry to recover its previous size. The fraternity, however, would never regain its post-Revolutionary role as a central emblem of religion and the Republic.

1. The Concentration of Great Numbers on a Single Point

This transformation had been entirely unexpected. Less than two weeks before Morgan disappeared, Batavia, New York, brother Henry Brown printed a letter in a newspaper asking why "some of the masons . . . took alarm" at Morgan's "intention to publish the secrets of masonry." Not only was such concern "indiscreet," he argued; it was "unnecessary." Morgan could not harm the fraternity, any more than "a handful of mud" thrown at the sun would "arrest its course, or extinguish its beams." "The lion might as well have been alarmed because an army of kites or crows, had threatened to invade his proud domains."[6]

Of course, Brown would be proved wrong. The handful of mud would dim the sun; the flock of birds, dethrone the king of beasts. But the revolution occurred only because the insurgents recognized the fraternity's power. Like Brown, Antimasons knew that Masonry could not be defeated by a direct assault upon older structures. Within the locality, strategically placed brothers often wielded traditional means of influence, employing economic pressure, oral attacks, and official power to quell sporadic opposition and doubts. Antimasonry, however, built pressure on a different level, addressing a larger public opinion rather than local communities or a narrow range of elites. Antimasonic newspapers, public meetings, and even lobbying campaigns bypassed the power of such local notables, thus encouraging local changes through translocal means. In these activities, Antimasons pioneered the methods of modern pressure groups and single-issue organizations, including creating the first third-party in American history.

Masonry's size and comprehensiveness, the foundation of its earlier strength, now hindered a strong public defense. Its supporters and purposes were too various to mobilize effectively. Less than three years after the Morgan incident, Brown felt compelled to justify the complacency of his earlier letter by explaining that "the above article, it will be recollected, was written at a time when the masonick in[s]titution stood higher, perhaps, than at any former period." [7] Within a few years, Masons would lose the battle for public support and often find themselves having to choose between commitments that had once seemed inextricably linked, their local standing and their Masonic membership. Before examining the organizational efforts that created this extraordinary reversal of fortune, a brief outline of the Antimasonic movement and its results may be useful.

Antimasonry did not begin as a revolutionary attempt to dethrone the fraternity—or to challenge the larger social order. It originally sought merely to discover Morgan's fate and perhaps secure his return. Concerted action began two weeks after Morgan's disappearance when a group of concerned Batavians met to discuss the case. Similar assemblies were soon convened along the route traveled by the abductors, with each appointing a "Morgan committee" to investigate the crime. As this task proceeded, it became clear that strategically placed Masons and their sympathizers were covering up the truth and hindering punishment of kidnappers who were themselves brothers. For many committeemen and area residents, this fraternal intransigence shifted the focus of concern. By the beginning of 1827, the nearly universal desire for justice became a more divisive attack on Masonry itself. The various "Morgan committees" (or at least those members who had turned against the fraternity) convened more than a hundred meetings in nearly every town in western New York. Rather than simply seeking further information and punishment for the guilty, these assemblies began to attack Masonry itself, even recommending local candidates who could be trusted to support the Morgan investigations. The attack on the fraternity expanded over the following year. A major meeting of former Masons in Le Roy on July 4, 1828, issued a "Declaration of Independence from the Masonic Institution." The following month a statewide Antimasonic convention met in Utica. [8]

The transformation of reaction to a small-town crime into an assault upon a worldwide fraternity took less than two years. Over the next five years, this new opposition to Masonry spread throughout virtually the entire northern United States. Newspapers played a key role in spreading this message. Solomon Southwick pledged his Albany newspaper, the *National Observer,* to the cause before the middle of 1827. The *North Star,* of Danville, Vermont, began its long-running attack on Masonry the same year.[9] Since most established newspapers shunned the movement as too divisive, Antimasonic activists soon made creating new papers a priority. New York leaders in late 1828 sponsored a new organ in Hartford, Connecticut. By then, newspapers supporting the cause had already begun appearing in Ohio's Western Reserve and Lancaster County, Pennsylvania. Within two years, more than a hundred Antimasonic papers appeared through the North. Public meetings and conventions also spread the opposition to the fraternity. Massachusetts, Connecticut, Michigan, and Vermont all held their first statewide assemblies in 1829. Indiana Antimasons met early the following year, in preparation for the movement's first national convention that fall. Volunteer local and state committees helped organize these assemblies and provide the central direction of the movement. These groups also sponsored publications and traveling speakers.[10]

Although this organization never extended into the South (only scattered meetings opposed the fraternity there), by the early 1830s the Antimasonic movement had virtually saturated the rest of the country. Even then the two primary themes first enunciated in upstate New York formed the heart of the message. Antimasons first argued that Masonry's secrecy, exclusivity, and power all made it incompatible with a republican society based on equal rights and popular sovereignty. Just as important, the fraternity opposed Christianity itself, particularly through its bloody initiation oaths. America could be saved only by driving Masons out of church and office—and eventually destroying the lodges themselves. The attempt to defeat such a powerful group created intense conflict—with angry words and mob action on both sides. A prominent Boston brother later recalled the period as a time of "unmitigated violence and virulence."[11]

The powerful opposition to the fraternity soon expanded into the political arena. Not surprisingly, western New York led the way, choosing an Antimasonic ticket in 1827 that elected nearly one-eighth of the state Assembly. Although substantial numbers of Antimasons resisted politicizing opposition to the fraternity, leaders in other northern states soon followed New York's lead. Pennsylvanians first proposed an Antimasonic ticket in 1828; Vermonters made the move the following year. In the following decade, both states elected an Antimasonic governor: Pennsylvania, acting in cooperation with the Whig party, in 1835, and Vermont for four straight years, from 1831 to 1834. Other Antimasonic parties, particularly in New England and areas settled by New Englanders, achieved lesser successes. In yet other states, including Illinois, Missouri, and the entire South, Antimasons failed to organize politically at all. Generally, the party proved most effective where a single party possessed overwhelming strength, allowing the Antis (as they were often called) to become the democratic and egalitarian voice of opposition to Andrew Jackson. In 1831, however, the new party seemed so promising that New York leaders engineered a run for the presidency. In the first national nomination convention in American history (held in fall of that year), they selected as their candidate the former United States attorney general William Wirt, despite his lukewarm support for Antimasonry. Wirt eventually gained about 8 percent of the national vote, attracting a plurality in Vermont that won his only electoral votes. Perhaps energized by this respectable showing in 1832, the party reached its high point the following year. Vermont's Antimasonic governor, William A. Palmer, attracted a majority of the state's voters for the first and only time while Massachusetts candidate John Quincy Adams also gained the party's largest totals. By 1834, however, signs of decline appeared almost everywhere as the Democrats and the new Whig party stepped up their organizing. Within two years, Antimasonic parties in nearly all states had virtually ceased their independent existence, usually entering, either formally or informally, the emerging Whig coalition.[12]

This place in the new party formed perhaps the greatest legacy of Antimasonic politics. Successful Antimasonic candidates (again like the former United States senator Palmer and the former president Adams) usually were prominent politicians who had already staked out positions similar to other anti-Jackson groups. The particularly Antimasonic elements of the party program encountered stiff resistance. Although legislatures in a number of states investigated the fraternity, Antimasons failed to institute registration of lodges and members, to restrict their oaths, and to prevent the appointment of brothers to office.[13]

Political Antimasonry ultimately failed; the movement itself largely succeeded. It never reached its ultimate goal of destroying the fraternity, but it destroyed the foundations of public acceptance and high status that supported Masonry. Defections from the fraternity increased dramatically in the late 1820s. Many lodges simply stopped meeting. By the middle of the 1830s, northern Freemasonry virtually ceased to exist. Whereas nearly five hundred lodges had met in the mid-1820s in New York, only twenty-six still had enough energy to send a representative to the grand lodge meeting in 1837. Almost two-thirds of all Indiana lodges had been closed by same year. Illinois, Michigan, and Vermont no longer even held annual grand lodge meetings. New members proved even harder to come by. The entire Connecticut fraternity initiated only twelve men in 1836. Providence, Rhode Island, brothers admitted no one at all during the entire decade. Even the southern fraternity, where there was no Antimasonic party and virtually no Antimasonic organization, would be seriously damaged by the new attitudes about Masonry.[14]

The decline of the American fraternity, ironically, also helped weaken its opponents as well, making organizing and political activity seem less press-

ing. By the end of the 1830s, Antimasonic activity, if not Antimasonic sentiment, was clearly waning, an opening that allowed the few brothers who had
resisted the Antimasonic assault to renew more public Masonic activities. In
1839, New York created its first new lodge since 1828. By 1843, the Indiana
grand master believed that "the cloud" of Antimasonic feeling "is fast dis-
appearing." The Vermont grand lodge re-formed three years later. But this
revival would be slow and incomplete. The Rhode Island grand lodge did not
charter a new lodge from 1825 to 1856. There as elsewhere, the fraternity regained its previous membership only after the mid-1850s. Despite dramatic
increases in their states' population, both the New York and Massachusetts
grand lodges still presided over fewer lodges in 1860 than in 1825.[15]

Hiram Hopkins first attacked the fraternity openly around the end of 1828,
when he appeared as a witness against Eli Bruce, but he did not (in his phrase)
"come out in the public prints" until the following spring. In September 1829,
he wrote a letter to a cousin in Vermont that was printed in the state's leading
Antimasonic newspaper. The following year, it appeared as a Boston pamphlet.[16]

The spread of Hopkins's testimony through "the public prints" reveals the
new dimensions of Antimasonic organization. Rather than seeking merely to
reach local leaders, opponents of Masonry sought to change the accepted
values of the entire community, what was coming to be called public opinion. Through a variety of methods, Antimasons mobilized local pressure even
over the objections of local leaders, creating what contemporaries called an
"agitation." Harsh words, riots, and the ballot box aroused public opinion to
eject prominent brothers from leadership of both government and the church.
Through this agitation, Antimasons helped shift the character of the American
public sphere, the arena in which people attempted to debate and to decide
questions about public policy and attitudes. This transformed public sphere,
swelled in succeeding years by mass political parties, abolitionism, and temperance, included many more people than ever before—and more organizations attempting to sway them.[17]

The original Morgan committees established in upstate New York around
the end of 1827 had been made up of what one contemporary labeled "highly
respected citizens." But the rise of opposition to Masonry soon shifted the
movement's social meanings. Rather than expressing community opinion
through the filter of local notables, this new agitation challenged the influence
of those leaders. To win support for their radical program, Antimasons over
the next few years mounted an extraordinary educational campaign to transform public opinion. Even a strong critic of the agitation was forced to admit
that "there never was a party more active, more resolute, or more persever-
ing."[18]

Public meetings provided the first means of building support. The many assemblies and conventions that met in the years after 1826 sought to do more than express public concern and discuss strategy. Leaders also used the gatherings to spread information. Preparation of statements for the published proceedings formed a central (sometimes the central) activity of these meetings. After the June 1832 New York State convention, committee members ordered the distribution of fifteen thousand pamphlets and broadsides containing its resolutions and addresses. Zealous Antimasons also gave local lectures that often reenacted Masonic rituals as well as rehearsed arguments against the fraternity. Avery Allyn, one of the most active of these lecturers, spoke to audiences in Pennsylvania, New York, Connecticut, Rhode Island, and Massachusetts. An upstate New York opponent even painted a picture of Morgan's imprisonment and exhibited it, an unhappy brother noted, before "the admiring eyes of thousands." [19]

Even more than public meetings, print formed the heart of the Antimasonic movement. Lecturers could be harassed or denied meeting places, and meetings ignored outside their immediate neighborhoods; but, once in print, books, handbills, and pamphlets could not be easily silenced. Since most existing newspapers refused to consider the issue, Antimasons formed their own newspapers throughout the Northeast. By 1830 Pennsylvania alone supported 53. The national convention that year counted 124 "founded exclusively on the principle of opposition to Freemasonry," an astonishing one-eighth of the nation's newspapers. [20] And these formed only part of the printed offensive against Masonry. An Antimasonic book helped stir Hopkins to make his public renunciation. In turn, Hopkins's piece became one of the numerous pamphlets devoted to the cause, some of which were distributed by the Boston Young Men's Antimasonic Tract Society. When a St. Andrew's brother died within the Masonic Hall in 1827, activists posted quickly prepared placards around both Boston and New York City alleging foul play. [21]

Besides publications and meetings, Antimasons also aroused public attention through political action, moving further than previous reform organizations had thought possible or acceptable. From the movement's beginnings, Antimasons realized the need for sympathetic public officials. Within a year after Morgan's disappearance in New York and within four years in the rest of the Northeast, Antimasons organized their own political party, the first third-party in American history. The new Antimasonic party sought to ban Masons from appointive public office, to register Masonic members and organizations, and to prohibit Masonry's extrajudicial oaths. Party leaders also pioneered the legislative public hearing as a means of investigation and publicity. Rhode Island (1831), Massachusetts (1834), and Pennsylvania (1835) all created legislative committees to consider the fraternity's dangers. Although such occasions seldom brought the political gains Antimasonic leaders anticipated, their testimony and findings provided ammunition for further agitation. [22]

In moving into the electoral realm, Antimasons challenged older expectations about the political process. Established political culture (if not established practice) rejected special-interest politics, attempts to enact particular pieces of legislation rather than to seek the good of the whole. But Antimasons infuriated by Masonic cover-up of the Morgan affair came to believe that they needed at least to keep brothers out of sensitive office. To do this, they argued, they were "driven by *necessity* to the Ballot Box." From there, only a short step led to a more organized party. Although many Antimasons still resisted the move, the political vanguard employed the increasingly powerful idea of public opinion. Older beliefs had suggested that campaigns to change people's attitudes should generally remain out of the political arena. But the new idea that public policy merely followed public opinion allowed Antimasons to organize politically. As John Quincy Adams, the movement's best-known political leader, reasoned in 1833, "It is . . . the duty of pure and disinterested Antimasonry to operate, as well as it can, upon public opinion; and one of the most effective modes of thus operating is the ballot box." Indeed, voting formed "perhaps, the mildest of all possible forms of operating upon public opinion—by public opinion itself."[23] Adams recognized that culture and political life were inextricably bound together, that each influenced the other—a position that rejected both the older notion that the elite established society's direction and the newer myth that the voice of people naturally repeated the voice of God. Unfortunately, the fraternity that became the target for this assault would be unable to take advantage of this new insight.

Both during and after the storms of Antimasonry, brothers often adopted a persona of injured innocence. Through the "sweeping denunciations . . . so prodigally lavished against" Masons, a group of Monroe County, New York, Masons complained in 1829, Antimasons destroyed "the peace and harmony of neighborhoods and of society." Admittedly, characterizations such as Pennsylvania Antimason Thaddeus Stevens's attack on "the principles and company of Neroes and Calligulas" were extreme even in a period of rhetorical harshness. But brothers were not always as innocent as they claimed. Many fought back with as much venom as their opponents. Fear of Masonic anger delayed Hiram Hopkins's break with the fraternity. According to his account, "My pride has caused much suffering in my mind." "I foresaw, in vivid colours, my destiny by Freemasonry, should I renounce the institution." Brothers, he knew from experience, "would endeavor by all their art to '*derange my business* and *destroy my character.*'" Although in the end Hopkins's public stand did not cost him as much as he feared—"Their efforts . . . have in a good degree proved unvailing"—still the expectation of private ruin and public humiliation proved a strong check to action. "The idea of continually being branded with the epithets of '*traitor, purjured villian*' and the like, would have caused me rather to lose my *right hand* than to come out against my *once* friends."[24]

The brothers' response to the torrent of Antimasonic agitation reveals the limits of fraternal power. Brothers possessed powerful local leverage: they could deploy official authority, economic clout, and local gossip to obstruct opponents. Yet the same circumstances that allowed the Masonic counterattack some local success ultimately hindered an organized and persuasive campaign. Like the other structures of power that came under attack in the Jacksonian era, the fraternity could not withstand the new methods of organization.

Brothers resisted Antimasonry, first, by use of their official authority. During the Morgan incident and its aftermath, well-placed Masons often took advantage of their positions to foil attacks. Niagara County sheriff Eli Bruce instructed his cousin and deputy, Hiram Hopkins, to select a grand jury for a key Morgan investigation that would be at least three-quarters Masonic—enough to ensure a sympathetic response but not enough, Bruce thought, to "arouse suspicion." Brothers also used official power directly against Antimasonic agitation itself. Avon, New York, magistrates arrested Thomas Hamilton, an early Antimasonic lecturer, twice within four days in November 1827, the second time presumably because they expected a more sympathetic justice. Avery Allyn, a more prominent lecturer who (like Hamilton) reenacted Masonic rituals, was taken into custody fifteen times. Yet attempts at silencing such men were ultimately unsuccessful. Because addresses on, and even demonstrations of, Masonry broke no law, neither Hamilton nor Allyn was ever convicted.[25]

Economic pressure provided another weapon. As editor of Albany's *National Observer,* one of the first newspapers to espouse Antimasonry, ex-Mason Solomon Southwick experienced what Hopkins later feared, Masonic attempts to *"derange my business."* According to Southwick's July 1827 complaint, "The OBSERVER has been proscribed in every direction by masonic zealots." Subscriptions were canceled; advertisements, removed. Other parts of Southwick's business also felt the strain. "By direct or indirect management," he noted, incidental "job-work, to no small amount" had been "diverted." "In short," Southwick charged, "every artifice, worthy of a dark, corrupt and rotten cause, has been resorted to for the purpose of destroying every source of its prosperity." A witness in the case against Eli Bruce successfully persuaded the grand jury to excuse him because, he argued, testifying would lead to his economic ruin. A would-be editor in Philadelphia similarly suggested in 1829 that "fear of incurring masonic displeasure, and perhaps vengeance," explained the lack of an Antimasonic outlet in that city. Four years later in Worcester, Massachusetts, probate judges sympathetic to the fraternity prevented notaries from placing their notices in Antimasonic papers.[26]

Attacks on opponents' character also could be used to repress criticism. According to an Antimasonic agitator at the Massachusetts convention held at the end of 1829, "Masons were in the uniform habit of stigmatizing seceders as 'perjured villains,' 'drunkards,' and as destitute of moral honesty." These attacks "were circulated throughout the land; everybody heard them." After an Antimasonic address in Belchertown, Massachusetts, Baptist minister David Pease received a letter from one of the town's leading Masons warning that "the curses of God and man are upon you." Because Pease was "a blasphemer . . . thou art, never to be forgiven." "Hell is your portion," the letter concluded, "and that, and ten times worse, you *deserve*." Such strong words, literally condemning Pease to a fate worse than death, became so common that Antimasons believed "floods of Masonic calumny" part of a concerted plan of countermeasures.[27]

These counterattacks sometimes culminated in mob action. The Antimasonic lecturer Avery Allyn found that "often the windows and doors" of the places where he spoke "were broken and battered with stones and other missiles." Sometimes the entire house was "torn down." The 1831 Massachusetts Antimasonic convention complained angrily about extensive attempts "to disturb public meetings by *noise and riots,* or to attack them by Masonic mobs." "Masonic riots, noise, mobs, and confusion," it charged, "are the orders of Freemasonry."[28]

Although they could cause local havoc, however, Masons could not easily emulate their adversaries' organized agitation. Brothers sometimes attempted to use publicity to strengthen their position. Nearly all the Masonic bodies in New York and surrounding areas published resolutions disavowing involvement in the case, expressing regret about Morgan's disappearance, and asserting that Masonic principles would not allow such "gross violations." In New England alone, John Quincy Adams noted, these protests were "numerous." More than sixteen hundred Massachusetts brothers signed a "Declaration" written by a St. Andrew's brother in 1831. But protestations of virtue could easily be overdone. The author of the Massachusetts declaration advised Connecticut brothers against releasing their statement separately in each town. "Only the *united* weight and respectability of the names," he argued, could "produce conviction on the public mind."[29]

More sustained rebuttal proved difficult. Unlike their opponents, brothers established only a handful of papers to support their cause. Even the most successful, Charles W. Moore's *Boston Masonic Mirror,* decided in June 1832 to include more material of "general interest." The term "Masonic" remained in the title but was printed in much smaller letters. The paucity of Masonic newspapers created a decided disadvantage. Few newspapers not founded for the purpose supported Antimasonry, but nearly as few actively defended the fraternity. Indeed, Masonry's structure itself impeded organized action. Although reforming brothers had worked for a generation to strengthen supervisory organizations, local bodies (and the rituals only they could perform) remained the center of the fraternity. State organizations and their national counterparts in the higher degrees used most of their limited income for bookkeeping and charity, so support for a newspaper or extensive controversial publications was virtually impossible. Even on the local level, many brothers maintained only a limited connection with the fraternity's organizations. Even the enthusiastic Mason Salem Town remained unaffiliated with a lodge for much of his life. "If [Antimasons] do succeed," wrote Moore, "their success must, in great measure, be attributed to the inertness—the lukewarmness of those who are the most interested and who should be the most active, of their opponents." [30]

As much as its structure, Masonry's dual commitment to exclusiveness and secrecy forestalled effective defense. A majority of American adult men had no ties to the fraternity. To them, as to all women, brothers could no more than affirm Masonry's honor and good intentions, the very qualities the Morgan incident had called into question. An active opposition to Antimasonry, furthermore, might have simply seemed to fulfill its charges about the fraternity's power—and about the ways that Masonic funds, supposedly dedicated to charity, were used for less noble purposes. In the end, ironically, Masonry could not fight back effectively because of the same factors that previously made it popular. A more inclusive order might have muffled broader questioning. A smaller fraternity made up entirely of strongly committed members might have organized a powerful defense. Yet either of these options would have required a very different fraternity, one that had lost its extraordinarily fruitful tension between inclusiveness and exclusivity—and one that would never have attracted strong opposition in the first place.

The combination of strong, yet limited, Masonic reaction and continuing Antimasonic agitation created intense local battles that eventually shifted public attitudes about the fraternity, an often contentious process visible in the church in Belchertown, Massachusetts (namesake of the Masonic colonial governor and boyhood home of Salem Town). The town's Congregational minister, the former Yale tutor the Reverend Lyman Coleman, had been extremely successful since his arrival in 1825, revitalizing the Sunday school and fostering widespread revival. Yet despite his obvious religious gifts, zealous Antimasons found Coleman too indifferent to the fraternity's dangers. Although he did not belong to the fraternity, he failed to denounce Masonry fully. Within a year after the height of the revival, Antimasons made things so difficult for him that he requested a dismissal. Weary brothers and their remaining supporters fled the church as well. [31]

If broader agitation provided Antimasonry's driving force, local responses made it successful. As in Belchertown, Antimasons seldom succeeded in erasing all loyalty to Freemasonry. But they did something just as significant. Their angry and often intemperate attempts to drive brothers (and their sympathizers) from public office, the church, and the lodge eroded older presumptions in Masonry's favor. Eventually the burden of proof shifted onto the fraternity, forcing many brothers to choose between membership and public approval.

Like other reformers over the next decade, Antimasons believed their issue an apocalyptic battle between good and evil that admitted of no compromises. As a delegate to the 1829 Massachusetts convention noted in biblical language, Antimasons were not fighting "against anything of flesh and blood but . . . against principalities and powers." Purity could be recovered only through the complete expulsion of what one opponent called "*Anti-Christ*." Masonry's former sanctity increased fears of this corrupting influence. "Freemasonry once appeared to us beautiful, like whited sepulchre," a New York woman noted, but "like it we find it is full of dead men's bones and an uncleanliness." The recent revelations about the fraternity exposed it as "a demon, and offspring of him who reigns in the bottomless pit." "O forsake free masonry for Christ," pleaded a Baptist minister. "Come out of Babylon." [32]

Even the destruction of American Masonry would not end the threat. As a committee of the 1831 Massachusetts state convention cautioned, other nations would still be plagued by the fraternity, and unsuspecting later generations might allow it to creep back in. A Belchertown lecturer warned Antimasons that their opponent might take on another name "for the purpose of deception, until it could recover what has been lost." Such attitudes probably lay behind the refusal of the town's Antimasons to accept the proposals by local Masons in 1832 for "peace and reconciliation." Although brothers pledged not to attend or even communicate with lodges, the town's Antimasons rejected this surrender. Only complete renunciation and repentance could preserve society—and save their souls. Outsiders who refused to condemn Masonry also became the object of Antimasonic scorn. "Respectable" people "are stigmatized in ridiculous slang, by the wretched nicknames of 'Jacks' and 'Bats,' and other similarly indecent and indecorous appellations," complained a Masonic newspaper in 1829, "for no other reason than that they choose to hold themselves aloof from the present excitement." [33]

Such polarizing demands for unconditional surrender created intense local turmoil. Even fifty years later, a leading New York abolitionist judged that "no subject, except that of slavery, has ever produced intenser excitement in this country than broke out" over the fraternity. At Batavia, two or three thousand Antimasons showed up on the June St. John's Day in 1827 to protest a Masonic celebration that attracted only two hundred brothers. The hotter-headed members of the crowd threw stones and drove a wagon back and forth through the procession. A Phelps, New York, mob broke into the lodge room and burned the charter in the street. In Hornellsville, New York, children played with the Royal Arch chapter's jewels after opponents scattered the contents of the chapter room. "None but those who have witnessed it," recalled a New York Masonic leader, "can justly appreciate the condition of things at that time, and to what extent feeling was carried." [34]

Beyond the streets, the battle raged most strongly over two key institutions, government and the church. Even Antimasons who feared a single-issue political party usually supported what their opponents called "proscription," the removal of brothers from government and the judicial system. Belcher-town Antimasons engineered a vote to remove adhering Masons from the jury list. As the build-up to the expulsion of that town's minister suggests, the church formed an even more divisive battleground. A Belchertown dea-con who retained his Masonic membership became the first focus of anger. Some opponents of the fraternity forsook their customary pew on Sacrament Sunday to avoid receiving communion from a Mason. Soon the more scrupu-lous opponents of Masonry completely refused to attend the ceremony or even prayer meetings for fear brothers might be there. Ministers, whether because they were brothers or because they simply (as in Belchertown) refused to con-demn Masonry fully, also became a target. Such attempts to drive Masons and their sympathizers from churches often failed. Some individual congregations and Baptist associations (a number of which had already opposed the frater-nity before 1826) officially proscribed Masons. But most denominations re-mained divided on the issue and took no official stand. Even the New England Methodist Conference, which eventually banned its ministers from Masonic membership, also counseled congregations to accept ministers who had been Masons even if they still refused to condemn the fraternity completely.[35]

Although the more extreme definitions of Antimasonic purity never gained universal support, they helped change public opinion. In the years from 1826 to the mid-1830s, the burden of proof shifted dramatically. Masons, previ-ously presumed innocent, now faced a skeptical public. By the early 1830s, public opinion had moved so decisively that some proposals for reconcilia-tion by brothers and "jacks" suggested terms that seemed less compromise than capitulation. A number of 1831 National Republican conventions in Ver-mont recommended such a strange bargain. To patch up the divisions created by Antimasonic politics, which they condemned as "hallucination and blind eagerness," the convention requested that Masons seeking to end Antimasonic proscription renounce their membership. William Leete Stone, a moderate New York City newspaper editor and brother, had originally been a strong Masonic defender. Even in 1832, he argued that the fraternity taught "moral virtues and duties, and . . . religious truths" and that its lodge meetings ex-hibited the most "grave, orderly, and decorous conduct" he had seen in any "societies of men." Yet Stone still recommended "a voluntary, simultaneous, and universal abandonment of speculative Freemasonry in the United States." "There is no use in contending, at this late hour, that the principles on which it was built, are moral, benevolent, and virtuous," he argued, for "public opin-ion is against it."[36]

Not only had larger public sentiment turned against the fraternity, but many brothers who remained unconvinced by Antimasonic arguments recog-nized the dangers of opposing the attack. Hopkins had earlier feared that a public stand against the fraternity would ruin his local standing. Increasingly, continued membership threatened the same outcome. Not surprisingly, most brothers sought to preserve their reputation. Even in 1828, an upstate New York lodge complained about the difficulties of attracting members to meetings. Many Masons, the more zealous member noted, "neglected (as they say) to attend." Others did not want to give "offense to their brethren of the churches to which they belonged." Some stayed away "to preserve peace in their domestick circles." Still others feared "rendering themselves unpopular." Less than a year later, a convention that included representatives from the same brothers' lodge declared that they were "unwilling to submit tamely to the sweeping denunciations which have been so prodigally lavished against them." But such a clear expression of the people's will could not be resisted.[37] They voted to surrender their charters.

"Every thing is done now by societies," remarked William Ellery Channing, the spiritual leader of American Unitarianism, in a perceptive 1829 discussion of the larger implications of the rising tide of Jacksonian agitations. "One of the most remarkable circumstances or features of our age is the energy with which the principle of combination . . . is manifesting itself. . . . Would men spread one set of opinions or crush another? They make a society." Such organization was made possible "by modern improvements . . . especially . . . the press." "So various and rapid are the means of communication," he suggested, "that . . . an impulse may be given in a month to the whole country . . . and a voice like that of many waters be called forth from immense and widely separated multitudes.[38]

Channing's comments perceptively noted the shift in power created by the new attempt to direct opinion. In the midst of these agitations, the older expectations that elites should control politics and public life, under assault for a generation, simply crumbled. Not surprisingly, the inordinate influence of the powerful became a central theme of reform and political rhetoric, including, of course, the Antimasonic attack on the Ancient and Honorable society. As a leader in a church closely associated with such social elites, the Unitarian Channing felt strongly the dangers of larger organizations that challenged loyalties created by family, neighborhood, and patronage. Although agitation increased involvement in public affairs, Channing pointed out, organizers also sought to mediate and limit opinion—thus channeling it to their own purposes. Such groups, Channing complained, tended to "menace . . . individuality of character." In large part, the minister might simply have been complaining of the declining ability of individual elites to control decision making, what he celebrated as "that delicate kindnesses, which once flowed from the more prosperous to the less prosperous members of a large family, and which bound society together." But Channing also recognized a larger paradox in the democratizing public sphere of the late 1820s and 1830s. Even as humble people gained more say in public affairs, new institutions also shaped and limited this expression to fit their own agendas. Reform organizations and political parties did not seek merely to reflect attitudes. They sought to change and use them for their own advantage. In Channing's resonant metaphor, the new agitations allowed "public opinion" to be "shackled."[39]

Antimasonry played a key role in this shift. The movement was at the forefront of a shift in American reform from earlier religious causes that generally recommended relatively uncontroversial measures such as religious education, missionary activity, and Bible distribution. The new reformers agitated for divisive measures like ending drinking or slavery, purposes that required changing public opinion rather than simply providing better means for expressing it. Like the earlier Antimasons, these groups quickly learned the limitations of local activity. By the time William Lloyd Garrison (a delegate to the 1832 Massachusetts Antimasonic convention) founded the first national journal of immediate abolitionism in 1831, more than one of every ten newspapers in the country were already devoted to a reform, the extermination of Masonry. Antimasons also prepared the even more troubled way to political action, providing explanation and example for later temperance and abolitionist reformers. Perhaps not coincidentally, Myron Holley, an active Antimason who termed remaining fears of political involvement "a degrading slavery," would be a key figure in the creation of the first abolitionist party.[40]

Just as immediate abolitionists in many ways followed the trail blazed by Antimasonry, northern opponents of abolition used the same weapons of local authority as the earlier brothers. Established men in the mid-1830s again used rioting, official action, and harsh words to beat back challenges to their local standing. Despite the immediate success of many of these actions, antiabolitionist activities, like the assault on Antimasonry, ultimately proved ineffective against new types of agitation. Publications, public meetings, and informal networks allowed abolitionists to press their attacks despite local disfavor. Indeed, canny reformers often turned attacks on themselves against the perpetrators by publicizing them.[41]

In the end, Masonry's defeat can be seen as prefiguring the fate of other institutions and practices challenged by reformers, a parallel seen in the case of the total-abstinence phase of the temperance movement. Alcohol, like Masonry, had been an accepted and even esteemed part of everyday experience, providing a ritual of sociability even at funerals and clerical ordinations. Yet these beverages lacked strongly committed participants that could organize an effective defense. Brewers, distillers, and liquor sellers, the groups with the greatest stake in the practice, were too diffused and localized to defend their activities over the long term. Furthermore, drinkers (again like Masonic brothers) were forced to admit the existence of abuses. As with other older practices—even the more cosmopolitan fraternity—drinking served too many diverse purposes and embodied too many compromises to be defended easily. Like Antimasons, temperance advocates mobilized a broad coalition around one purpose and eventually succeeded, if not in destroying its enemy, at least in dramatically weakening it. Channing called this "the grand Manoeuvre to which Napoleon owed his victories . . . the concentration of great numbers on a single point."[42] Through its assault, Masonry's opposition defeated an immense and seemingly invincible foe at the height of its powers. Although a brother at the beginning of the troubles had predicted it could not be done, the crows had defeated a lion.

11. A Stupendous Mirror

For Hopkins, publicly turning against the fraternity required an agonizing re-appraisal that took more than two and a half years after Morgan's abduction. Not just fear of Masonic retaliation kept Hopkins silent. Despite his "disgust and perfect abhorrence of the masonic institution," he still believed himself bound by his degree obligations, oaths that called for his mutilation and death should he betray the order's secrets. Breaking those promises would mean "committing the most awful perjury, morally, that men could commit." As a result, Hopkins "mourned in secret places during nearly two years." Finally, amid fears that he would remain upon this "*bed* of sin" for the rest of his life, his reading in the Bible and Antimasonic literature convinced him: "My ma-sonic obligations were not binding upon *me,* nor any mason." The sin "con-sisted in *taking* these abominable oaths," not in breaking them.[43]

Although many of the movement's critics considered Antimasonry simply "deluded and infatuated men . . . blindly and zealously persecuting their innocent and worthy neighbors," heated rhetoric and sensational appeals to prejudice alone could not persuade scrupulous men such as Hopkins to reject the fraternity. They needed strong, compelling arguments. Just as brothers had shaped explanations of their order to post-Revolutionary values and con-cerns, Antimasons drew upon and helped advance a developing critique of earlier ideas about what it meant to be, in Hopkins's phrase, "patriots and Christians." Antimasonry became part of a massive attempt to purify and re-vitalize American society—a vast, disparate movement that included attacks on the "corrupt bargain," the Second Bank of the United States, drinking, and slavery. By emphasizing conscience, public opinion, and evangelical Chris-tianity, Antimasonry helped lay the foundation for a redefined social and cultural order. At least one Mason glimpsed this role as early as 1829. Anti-masonry, he complained, "has placed the *publick mind of the country in what may be justly termed the incipient stage of a revolution.*"[44]

Brother Henry Brown, who had warned against Masonic overreaction to Morgan's publishing plans, found the subsequent opposition to the fraternity even more troubling. Wondering in 1829 whether his account of the events would be comprehensible to "strangers living remote from the scene," he interrupted his narrative of reactions to Morgan's disappearance to confess that "the effect of all this . . . cannot be well described." Only "the aid of history," he suggested, would allow outsiders to "credit" his account. The Morgan affair needed to be seen as part of a long train of "popular excitements" that had killed Socrates and Jesus and led to the "delusion" of the Popish Plot and the "frenzy" of the Salem witchcraft cases. Under slightly different circumstances, Brown concluded, Antimasonic anger would undoubtedly "have terminated in the massacre of all masons in the vicinity."[45]

The theme of "excitement" that Brown and others made the cornerstone of their attack on Antimasonry could not be answered directly. After all, Antimasons could not deny that they were stirring up one of the most extensive agitations yet seen in America and using, as a moderate opponent of the fraternity admitted, "every term of vituperation supplied by a language that is sufficiently copious in epithets." But Antimasonry was not simply a frenzy; nor was it, as its detractors (and some later scholars) charged, primarily an attempt to reassert older ways in the face of change. Although such concerns clearly played some role, Antimasonry also helped to articulate and establish a new set of ideas that shaped the rest of the nineteenth century.[46]

Antimasonic responses to the charge of excitement reveal the movement's novelty. Instead of denying the term itself, opponents of Masonry instead challenged its foundations, the underlying models of society and psychology that made "excitement" a term of abuse. Instead of believing the populace easily deluded and prone to irrationality, Antimasons argued that public opinion was ultimately reliable. Even common people, they suggested, could be trusted to decide public affairs—as long as they were not hindered by aristocracies that subverted public wisdom. This faith in democracy ultimately rested on confidence in individual judgment.

Antimasonry had not originally advanced such a comprehensive critique. Even critics of the movement admitted that its original impetus lay in a laudable desire for justice in the Morgan affair. But the abduction and subsequent Masonic intransigence led many people to reconsider the fraternity's broader implications, furnishing what an early Antimasonic convention called "a bloody text which afforded matter for fearful comment." In pondering this "new complexion," concerned citizens became convinced that they had discovered a larger danger, a fraternal conspiracy seeking, the 1831 Massachusetts convention noted, "to corrupt, and, ultimately, to undermine and destroy all our civil and religious institutions." Myron Holley's address for the 1830 national Antimasonic convention suggests the larger menace Antimasons saw in the fraternity. "Revealed freemasonry is a stupendous mirror, which reflects, in all their horrors, the exact features of that vast spirit of crime, with which this nation is now wrestling, for all that makes life desirable."[47]

Seeing Masonry as a microcosm of society's worst elements, Antimasons challenged not just the fraternity but the larger post-Revolutionary order it had come to represent. In placing public opinion and conscience at the center of their thinking, the opponents of Freemasonry were not inventing new ideas, but they were giving them new meanings that directly addressed the tensions and contradictions of the post-Revolutionary order—thus helping to clear the stage for the democratic and evangelical ideology of liberty and self-control that would in various forms dominate the nineteenth century. "The time of reformation and moral revolution," Reuben Sanborn argued in 1828, "has dawned upon the land of pure republicanism, and genuine Christianity."[48]

To Antimasons, one of Masonry's most pressing dangers lay in its affront to what the 1830 national convention judged "the only just government of human origin, that of public opinion." "To this government," it argued, "freemasonry is wholly opposed." The order's secrecy allowed brothers to hide their actions from the public eye and to defy the public will; it established an aristocracy that supported "the exclusive privilege of individuals with the prerogative of power." Against this "rank and fashion . . . power and wealth," Antimasons argued, they had only one advantage, the very public opinion that Masons sought to destroy.[49]

The early weakness of Antimasonry made its adherents fully aware of their reliance on prevailing sentiment. Lacking a foothold in political parties and originating in the newly settled and less influential areas of New York (even a supporter felt compelled to explain to the state legislature that "the people at the west were not exactly crazy"), Antimasonry faced a herculean task. Masonic power, New York State Senator John Crary complained in 1828, was "gigantic." As the fraternity "has spread itself through this Union," warned an upstate New York convention the same year, "it has insinuated and connected itself with almost every interest, either of a private or public nature." To defeat a group that claimed it could not be destroyed even by government, Antimasons had only the people's will. "You ask what is to be done with all the power, the wealth, the talents, and the influence of the fraternity," Frederick Whittlesey told the New York state convention of 1828. "There is one engine, and one only, which can be successfully arrayed against it," he answered, "and that is *public opinion*. Public opinion is the law of this land."[50]

In contrast to their own "open appeal to PUBLIC OPINION," the fraternity's opponents argued that Masonry's secrecy and oaths allowed it to circumvent the people's will and gain "undue advantage over the common citizen." According to alarmed Pennsylvania legislators in 1836, their own governor had given offices to men who had applied explicitly as brother Masons and even pardoned criminals upon petition of their lodge. Members furthermore swore to keep each other's secrets, allowing criminals to plot with impunity and forcing good men to learn and be silent about these sordid deeds. Finally, the characterization of Masonry as an aristocracy was reinforced by the titles brothers claimed for themselves. "Have they a longing for the faded liveries of the rotten Aristocracies of Europe?" asked a renouncing Mason. "Or, is it to prepare us for slavery, that they have introduced the lordly names of 'MOST WORSHIPFUL,' of 'KNIGHTS,' of 'KINGS' and 'HIGH PRIESTS'?" As Thaddeus Stevens's 1834 resolution in the Pennsylvania legislature averred, Masonry formed "a regularly organized kingdom within the limits of this republic."[51]

The fraternity's huge size and power caused particular alarm. Opponents recognized how quickly American Masonry had grown after the Revolution. "A cool observer cannot but look back with astonishment" at this development, an upstate New York convention noted in 1828. Such unprecedented growth could reflect only selfish and dangerous ends. "For what purpose have *two thousand lodges* been organized in these United States?" T. F. Talbot ominously asked the 1828 New York State convention. "Why are six hundred thousand men united together by mysterious ties, the nature of which are studiously concealed from their countrymen?"[52]

In making these arguments, Antimasons formed the vanguard of a larger reshaping of ideas about government. In the years after the rise of Antimasonry, attacks on aristocracies in the name of public opinion became central to the language of opposition, reform, and change. Of course, public opinion in one sense had been at the heart of the Revolution. But for the Revolutionary generation popular sovereignty had generally been ultimate more than immediate. Long-standing political theory, as far back as ancient Greece, suggested that too much influence by the people, the democracy, led to anarchy and chaos. Popular feelings needed to be led and, if necessary, ignored for the sake of the public good. James Madison's 1791 discussion of "public opinion" admitted it to be "the real sovereign" that "must be obeyed by the government"—but only, he cautioned, in some "cases." In others, "it may be influenced by the government." The belief that leaders should stand between often-mistaken public desires and public-spirited decisions continued to be popular through the 1820s. As the new president John Quincy Adams told members of Congress in 1825, they should not be "palsied by the will of our constituents."[53]

Like Madison and Adams before them, critics of Antimasonry argued that rational leaders needed to resist the will of erring common people. New York State legislators often followed this line of argument in discussions of the Morgan case. Considering the call for a state investigation in 1828, the speaker of the House "alluded to various instances in the history of England, to show the effect of popular excitement and the injurious effect flowing from it." Another member similarly warned the House of the need "to free themselves from the contagion of this excitement—boldly to stem the current of popular feeling." Acting governor Enos Throop, a leader in the rising Democratic party that loudly proclaimed the power of the people's will, would praise legislators in 1830 for resisting popular calls for quick action. The feelings of excitement, he noted happily, "give evidence of speedily subsiding into their natural and healthful channel."[54]

Antimasons, like other insurgents of the period, angrily challenged attempts to limit public opinion. They realized that calls like a New York State official's for "Calm inquiry . . . deliberate decision . . . and . . . impartial, unbiased judgment" by "independent" men usually left powerful institutions like Masonry undisturbed. Presuming to dictate measures in defiance of the express will of the people, warned an Antimasonic state senator, was "treating the people like children that do not know what is good for themselves." Excitement was a sign of freedom, Antimasons argued, an affirmation that individuals would resist oppression. In what became a common term for the entire movement, Judge Enos Throop (although later a strong critic of Antimasonry) had earlier called the desire for justice in the Morgan affair "a blessed spirit." The "strong feeling of virtuous indignation" aroused by the crime, he suggested in 1827, reinforced "the spirit which brought us into existence as a nation, and a pledge that our rights and liberties are destined to endure." [55]

Antimasonic championing of public opinion helped legitimize it as the authoritative expression of the public good. Radical members of the Democratic party even argued that the people's will determined ultimate standards of value. Democratic historian and party leader George Bancroft believed "the common judgment in taste, politics, and religion is the highest authority on earth and the nearest possible approach to an infallible decision." [56] Other shades of the political spectrum might have added more qualifications, but all except the most conservative stressed the significance of the people's voice. As an aspiring Whig legislator in 1836, Abraham Lincoln promised, if elected by the county's voters, "I shall be governed by their will." [57]

Groups of people that attempted to resist this will rather than be governed by it came to be called "aristocracies," another older term that gained new significance in the Jacksonian era. Antimasonry helped renew and refocus the older attack on such privileged men who sought their own good rather than the public's. Rather than a group of individuals, however, Antimasons attacked an institution. Their concept of the fraternity as a "hydra-headed monster" (to quote Hiram Hopkins's cousin, Safford Hopkins) helped formulate a critique that would later be turned against other organizations. Both the Jacksonian Democrats' assault on the "monster" Bank of the United States (the defining moment in the rise of the party) and the immediate abolitionist attack on the South as the "slave power" (the period's most radical movement for reform), appropriated terms pioneered by Antimasons. Each painted its enemy as an entrenched institution that possessed undue power and demanded special treatment.

In assailing a group that had embodied the central social tensions of the post-Revolutionary period, Antimasonry acted as a precursor of later nineteenth-century changes. Like Jefferson, the fraternity had attempted to repudiate a formal and closed aristocracy without denying the need for leaders of republican virtue and talents. For Antimasons and others who sought a society where all possessed an equal say in public affairs, such a compromise now seemed, not the Revolution's embodiment, but its opposite. Masonry, one of its earliest opponents argued, perpetuated "the aristocratical principles of Europe" in defiance of the principle of "equal rights and privileges." By contrast, as Safford Hopkins suggested, Antimasonry asserted "the cause of the people, *versus* Masonry." [58]

Behind Antimasonic faith in the people lay another central idea, the power of conscience that Hiram Hopkins emphasized in describing his struggles to renounce Masonry. Even when he attempted to justify his actions and to remain in the fraternity, he wrote: "I *felt* its evil influence. I felt it was *opposed to a good conscience*." He "attempted to smother conviction" because he knew that Masons persecuted opponents, particularly former members who *"had left it for conscience sake."* In the end, he turned against the fraternity: "Had I no conscience, I should probably have said nothing." [59]

Hopkins's repeated insistence on the role of conscience reveals another layer in Antimasonry's attacks. Just as the concept of public opinion established new ways of thinking about republican institutions, so the idea of conscience pointed to a reshaping of ideas about humanity's moral nature. The belief in a trustworthy internal compass first shaped reformers' methods. Since this moral faculty always pointed directly to the truth, the spread of what Antimasons called "information" would naturally lead people to oppose the fraternity. The idea of conscience could also be turned against the fraternity itself. Because its oaths bound people to follow Masonry rather than their conscience, opponents argued, the fraternity posed a serious roadblock to morality. Only Masonry's destruction could remove the external restraints that kept people like Hopkins enslaved.

The power of conscience also provided a response to critics who derided Antimasonry as an excitement. Rather than holding that rational powers would be usurped by emotion, agitators argued that truth often prevailed because of it. "Excitement is not fanaticism," a loss of moral judgment, T. F. Talbot claimed at the first New York State Antimasonic convention in August 1828. "What great moral benefit, let me ask, was ever conferred upon mankind which was not produced by *excitement*? How was the Christian religion itself propagated but by *excitement*?" Myron Holley asserted that strong emotions actually encouraged higher moral values. "Whence originate the purest virtues, and the most exalted achievements, of created intelligences but from powerful excitements?" [60]

Believing that people were naturally drawn to the truth by a conscience that irresistibly recognized true morality, Antimasons argued that strong feelings, although often helpful, were not always necessary. The simple truth about Masonry's dangers, if presented plainly, would lead people to proper conclusions. "The great end to be accomplished is the diffusion of INFORMATION," noted a speaker at the 1830 Massachusetts Antimasonic convention. "If that be thoroughly done, we hold that the event is sure." Of course, doubters might remain. A New York State orator in 1828 warned against expecting aid from "the timid, the selfish, or the willfully ignorant." Still, another Antimason argued, the movement would be successful because it provided facts "sufficient to convince every candid, honest, and intelligent mind." "The general diffusion of correct information," concluded the 1831 Massachusetts convention, was "all that appears necessary to insure a complete triumph of the cause." [61]

If "the best feelings of our nature," as Holley argued, call people "to be antimasons," Masonry attacked the true principles of morality. The most insistent Antimasonic complaint centered on the fraternity's effect on religion. According to opponents, Masonry adopted the pose of piety while actually undermining true faith. This attack on Masonry as "anti-Christian" seems to have emerged only after opponents realized its political dangers. "The public mind is already somewhat awake to its dangerous tendency upon our civil liberties," suggested Jedediah Hotchkin in 1828, "but in attempting to expose its gross impiety, I am well aware that I am touching another and more delicate chord, which may vibrate in tones of opposition that have never yet been awakened." "I consider," he declared, "masonry as warring against religion." [62]

This new note in the chorus of opposition soon swelled dramatically. Criticizing Masonry's religious results soon became as widespread as discussions of its political tendencies. The fraternity had falsely "worn the mantle of religion," even seeking to convince people that it could "bring men to heaven." Masonry's public claims to religious efficacy seemed dangerously at odds with the fraternity's irreligious secret practices. Just "as the Babylonians carried away the furniture of the house of God to deck their own," wrote a New York woman, "so did Masons borrow ornaments from religion, to decorate an institution that was red with the blood of murdered innocence." Masonry's crime lay, not in the vague religiousness that some before and after complained of, but in its attempt to present itself as fully and uniquely Christian. According to Hotchkin, the fraternity provided "much that is calculated to excite the abhorrence of all who have a holy jealousy for the sanctity of the institutions of the Christian religion." [63]

The religiously charged atmosphere of the higher degrees seemed particularly troublesome. The Royal Arch ritual (led by a "High Priest") required a brother to speak the fundamental Old Testament revelation of God at the burning bush, using God's sacred name, "the most solemn appellation by which the Supreme Being is known," to give the ceremony "a zest." Although such rituals seemed to convey holiness, they still allowed non-Christians to participate, debasing the sacred and falsely promising salvation through Masonry rather than God and the church. As a result, Masonry's "gross impiety" was "wresting from very many of the fellow creatures their inheritance to . . . [heaven's] incorruptible joys." [64]

Masonry seemed to subvert religion and morality in this life as well as the

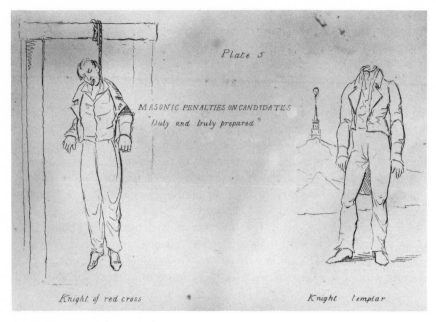

Figure 23. Masonic Penalties. *From Avery Allyn,* A Ritual of Freemasonry
(Boston, 1831). Courtesy American Antiquarian Society

next. The obligations undertaken in each degree ritual forced brothers to obey
Masonic rules rather than their conscience, the only faculty that could rescue
them from the fraternity's degradation. Through such means, even an "honest man" could be "drawn into a snare, and chained by an oath to iniquity
all his days." Myron Holley considered Masonic oaths that required public
silence in the face of a guilty brother's confessions, or even the misdeed itself,
a "crime." Because "a moral agent" thereby "voluntarily forgoes the use of his
understanding," taking the oaths was "worse than self-murder." These same
restraints on conscience led another pioneering Antimason to judge the fraternity not just "blasphemous, murderous, anti-republican, and anti-Christian"
but literally "demoralizing." [65]

Through this indictment, Antimasonry helped clarify and popularize new
ways of thinking about moral duties that would soon become widely accepted, most notably among evangelical Christians. Charles G. Finney, a
former Mason and a key figure in the emerging evangelical world, used terms
that followed Antimasonic rhetoric to describe his role as an evangelist. Like
the earlier movement, Finney in the mid-1830s recommended appealing to
the power of conscience through truth and excitements. Although in an ideal
world, he conceded, emotionalism would not be necessary, in the present
situation "to expect to promote religion without excitements is unphilosophi-

cal and absurd." "There must be," he argued, "excitement sufficient to . . . roll back the tide of degradation and sin." But these feelings could be useful only if they affected the inner moral sense. "The only way to secure *sound* conversions is to deal faithfully with the conscience," Finney advised ministers. "If attention flags . . . appeal to the feelings . . . but do your *work* with conscience." Through the direct appeal of the truth, "the Spirit of God urges the truth home upon [the listener] with such tremendous power as to induce him to turn." The power of truth broke "the chain that binds" the sinner.[66]

Antimasonic ideas also intersected with another primary part of the emerging evangelical program, the desire to change society. Like Antimasons, evangelicals attacked both attempts to provide religious sanction for nonreligious purposes and the promiscuous mixing of the converted and the unconverted. The two groups also attempted to mobilize a purified religious opinion in order to reform society. The idea of a trustworthy inner guide provided Antimasons and evangelicals the psychological reinforcement that could even allow them to resist the other source of Jacksonian-era authority, public opinion. "Let every one settle it as a principle," exhorted immediate abolitionist and Antimason William Lloyd Garrison, "that his conscience, and not his lay or spiritual leaders, must be his commander. It matters not whether we are with the multitude or the minority. . . . What is the tongue of reproach, compared to the sting of guilt?"[67]

The idea of a virtually infallible inner guide extended beyond evangelical circles. Conscience stood at the center of the new moral philosophy that emerged in American colleges during the 1830s. In the period's most successful text, *The Elements of Moral Science,* Francis Wayland placed "the supremacy of conscience" at the heart of his discussion, calling it "the most authoritative impulse, of which we find ourselves susceptible." Other reformers similarly stressed the significance of what Wayland called "the constant monitory power of conscience." The Universalist minister Adin Ballou created the utopian community of Hopedale to show that social order could depend upon "man's being and doing right from the law of God written on his heart, without the aid of external bonds and restraints." "It is every man's privilege," he argued, "by the grace of God, to attain to such a state." Noting that "conscience, like reason and judgment, is universal," George Bancroft used the idea to justify his faith in the public's judgment. "In questions of practical duty conscience is God's umpire, whose light illumines every heart."[68]

Such ideas repudiated the intellectual framework of post-Revolutionary Masonry's ritual training. As the world came to seem more confusing, brothers had intensified their rituals to nurture the morality that undergirded the larger society. Particularly through the higher degrees recommended in Webb's *Freemason's Monitor,* Masons attempted to inculcate virtue through a vigorous assault upon initiates' psychological defenses. Their ordeals, the grand lodge of Maine suggested in 1824, sought "to bind the conscience to the cause of virtue," providing strict training and guidance necessary to control the inner self. Significantly, Freemasons referred to their guidebook, not their conscience, as their monitor.[69]

Although the power of conscience seemed to make Masonry's strenuous rituals dangerous, in other ways the new ideas represented simply an extension of the fraternity's teachings. The antebellum idea of conscience built directly upon the older theories of the moral sense and natural benevolence that had been identified with Masonry from its beginnings. And the new defense of excitement represented an expansion of the fraternity's use and defense of strong feelings in its rituals. But perhaps this common lineage merely magnified Masonry's dangers. Even though it attempted to spread moral discipline, the fraternity still seemed threatening to its opponents because it was another large institution exercising external coercion. Only the conscience, Antimasons argued, provided a safe ground for morality in a world where, as the higher degrees had also suggested, institutions were untrustworthy or tyrannical and individuals needed to be self-reliant. Perhaps contrasting this independence with what he considered Masonry's moral suicide, Myron Holley argued in 1830, "Freedom, in every beneficial sense, is the soul of antimasonry."[70]

III. These Desperate Fanatics

Only a few months before the first national Antimasonic convention in 1830, New York's outgoing grand master hailed the election of Morgan Lewis as grand master of the state's brothers. "Freemasonry can now enroll on her list of patrons another soldier of the Revolution," rejoiced Elisha King. With "the most important offices . . . filled by men enjoying the affections and confidence of an intelligent community, we may reasonably hope that the apprehension and prejudices which have been recently excited . . . will, ere long, be dissipated." In turn, Lewis magnanimously suggested that most of the fraternity's opponents should not be treated too harshly. They were "to be contemplated more in pity than in anger." Their leaders, however, deserved less consideration. They "certainly had the power . . . rather to stifle than to fan the embers of discord, until they had blown them into a flame of persecution." Noting the movement's connections "with political party views," Lewis argued that "the conclusion is irresistible that they have been actuated by sinister and selfish, not by virtuous and laudable motives." The excitement encouraged by Antimasonic leaders was "better adapted to the darkness of the middle ages than to the enlightened period of the present day."[71]

Masonry's response to its opponents failed as decisively in its arguments as in its organization. Just as the structures that helped the fraternity grow during the post-Revolutionary period proved a liability by 1830, so too ideas that had previously been compelling lost their power. Labeling their opponents as deluded or demagogic had been successful for brothers before, but now these arguments failed to counter their opponents' democratic and evangelical arguments.

That Masonry remained trapped in older explanations should not seem surprising. Its celebration of enlightened leaders enjoying the confidence of the community and using their power in the name of virtue, learning, and religion had helped bring the order to the pinnacle of its popularity. Although these themes continued to be seductive, they proved ineffective against challenges in the name of the people and their internal convictions, arguments that pointed directly at the old order's most vulnerable elements. Masons presented a convincing case only when they criticized Antimasonry in the name of individual liberty. Even this argument did little to defend the fraternity itself. Brothers might condemn the excesses of the new order, but, like the entire Masonic counterattack, their arguments did little to prevent the passing of the old.

As Lewis suggested, Masonic interpretation of the Antimasonic movement began at the same point as the Antimasons themselves, with the anger generated by the abduction of Morgan. But the two groups disagreed about the nature of the transformation that followed. While Antimasons suggested they had revealed the fraternity's true nature, Masons argued that evil men had attempted to use popular feeling for their own ends, deluding the people into a superstitious persecution. Confronting this excitement required a twofold strategy: exposing the true nature of these dangerous leaders and broadcasting the evil tendencies of their ideas. Only such intervention could reverse the success of what a Masonic editor judged "moral depravity . . . permitted to stalk abroad at noon-day."[72]

Restoring society's proper balance first required unmasking Antimasonic leaders. As Lewis suggested, Masonic rebuttal usually implied that these men had the power and duty to direct popular feeling into correct channels, yet they had instead encouraged and even strengthened its worst tendencies— literally misled the public. Only immoral demagogues who rejected rational argument and the public good would so play upon unhealthy popular feelings. According to one of Antimasonry's angriest opponents, "In cases of extreme agitation, it often, alas, too often, becomes indispensable that the names of individuals should be brought before the publick, and their characters delineated . . . with such force, that the people may no longer be hood-winked by their deceptions, or misled by their hollow-hearted professions."[73]

Masons proposed various reasons for these deceptions. Some New Yorkers argued that Antimasons were merely Federalists. E. B. Grandin, a Wayne, New York, newspaper editor, perceived "the old 'cloven foot' of *Federalism*" in the movement. "It is now," he argued, "ANTI-MASONIC FEDERALISM." "But a new name for the true old fashioned federal principles of other time," judged another. Defenders of Masonry more commonly portrayed opponents as lesser men seeking advancement. "Nothing short of the facilities [Antimasonry] afforded to broken down demagogues, would have induced [Myron Holley] again to attempt to rise," complained a New York brother. "But after all, who are they?" asked a Boston editor about the 1831 petitioners against the state's grand lodge. "Where are the merchants?—where the lawyers?—where the physicians?—where the clergymen?—where the respectability of the community?"[74] Both lines of attack identified a lust for wealth and power as the ultimate motive of Antimasonic leaders. The new grand master Morgan Lewis found this conclusion "irresistible," carrying the overwhelming power of truth. "These desperate fanatics [would] drench this land of freedom with the blood of its sons!" warned a less moderate writer. "And for what? Office, office!" Even protestations of sincerity could not be credited. Clearly, wrote another brother, "the men who manage the Anti-masonick excitement do not desire the destruction of Masonry—nay, they would do all in their power to sustain it. . . . By opposing the institution and vilifying its members they obtain their bread."[75]

In portraying leaders as designing manipulators, Masonry's defenders cast the people as dupes. "The weak-minded and the ignorant . . . the prejudiced and depraved" provided the foundation for Antimasonic power. Brothers admitted that "honest and respectable citizens" had also been "induced to join in the accursed crusade." Both groups, however, were "deluded" or "infatuated," literally made foolish under the influence of what an Indiana Democratic congressman called "those who rouse the rable to do harm." "Good men," noted the *Craftsman* of Rochester, New York, have always feared "designing men" who play on "publick feeling." "Therefore, it has been their object to secure by wholesome bonds, and good institutions, the peace of society, and the preservation of order." But "when these chords are unloosened," society's "bonds . . . are burst from their fastening" by "popular ferment." Then "all the dread evils of an unorganized society . . . are suffered to have their sway." "The natural result of the operation of such a party as Anti-Masonry," the article concluded apocalyptically, "is revolution, civil war, and bloodshed."[76]

Only one argument was persuasive in the larger arena. Neither calls for elites to exert greater authority nor accusations of popular stupidity and irrationality proved successful against democratic insurgents. Only Masons' attempts to identify their plight with attacks on liberty were compelling. Antimasonic attempts to persecute and proscribe Masons could lead to "indiscriminate intolerance and proscription" against all sorts of groups, a Pennsylvania paper argued. "Honest difference[s] of opinion" should be "tolerated" and "firmly protected," protested another critic of Antimasonry. Indeed, "civil liberty" depended upon keeping these distinctions outside politics and public policy.[77] Antimasonry, particularly in its political manifestations, found itself forced to answer what an 1833 Vermont Antimasonic convention

Figure 24. Antimasonic Apron. *By W. Cammeyer, Jr., Albany, New York, 1831. Prints and Photographs Division, Library of Congress, LC-USZ62-92279*

called "the cry of proscriptions that have so often been urged against the principles of Antimasonry," explaining again and again that not voting for a Mason hardly abridged a candidate's rights. Clearly, the charge of proscription struck a deeper chord, resonating with the growing rejection of government interference as an attack on liberty, a theme that would be as powerful as Antimasonry's ideas in shaping nineteenth-century American thinking. Even people who rejected Masonry itself could find the argument persuasive. Although Mosely Kendall believed Masonry "a compound of folly and wickedness," he turned against Antimasonry as well in 1830: it had "usurped the rights of conscience and freedom."[78]

The attack on Antimasonry as intolerant and prone to persecution helped stem its political tide, shutting the new party out of majority status in all but a single state. The argument also helped prevent a renewed attack when Masonry revived in the 1840s. But Kendall's argument also points up the ultimate weakness of the critique, its irrelevance to the larger question of the fraternity's survival. Complaints of persecution might hinder organized Antimasonry, but they did little to save Masonry itself. Defending the order was more difficult than attacking its opponents. The glorifications of Masonry that had flourished in the post-Revolutionary period almost universally disappeared after 1826, particularly because Antimasons sought out indiscreet claims that could be turned against the brothers.[79] Defenses of the fraternity generally stuck to specifics, omitting references to Masonry's exalted position or God's special care. Timid Geneva, New York, brothers defended Masonry as *"simply a widely extended charitable institution."* Even one of the most assertive voices within the fraternity, the editor of the *Craftsman,* argued that the newspaper was never "intended to defend . . . the Masonick institution, and to prove that its existence is necessary." Rather, its "chief design . . . is to oppose a faction, who have taken it upon themselves to misdirect the honest feelings of the community, and . . . rise to power on the ruin of better men." Upon such evil men, "all reason and argument would be lost." [80] The ultimate result of such tactics was not surprising. Seeing themselves as an island of enlightenment in a sea of darkness, brothers who attempted to stand against Antimasonry could complain of the excesses of the new order but do little to preserve the fraternity that increasingly came to symbolize the old.

In choosing the seventy-five-year-old Morgan Lewis as their grand master, the New York grand lodge provided an unwitting emblem of the brotherhood's failure to comprehend the new world portended by Antimasonry. Electing a wealthy notable who had been a staff officer in the Revolution, a state governor twenty-three years before, and a powerful Hudson River landlord through his marriage into the great Livingston family, the brothers hoped to link themselves to key symbols of the post-Revolutionary Republic. But accumulating patrons to deflect criticism missed the point, for the issue of patrons — prominent men claiming special status and influence — lay at the heart of the attack. Masons continued to exhort the prominent to exercise power against an unstable people even after Antimasonry proved the appeal of democratic values. The residual power of these older ways of thinking sustained a small band of brothers that kept the fraternity from complete destruction, but could hardly hold back the larger triumph of the new ideas about religion and the Republic embodied in Antimasonry.

In the mid-1840s, Frederick Whittlesey, a member of one of the first Morgan committees and the main speaker at the 1828 New York state convention, paused in his history of the now-defunct Antimasonic party to refute allegations that it had been merely the creation of a few ambitious men. "It was emphatically a spontaneous movement of the people themselves," he insisted. Indeed, they had created it "not only in the absence of, but in defiance of the counsels of political leaders." The new party was originally formed without the patronage of experienced men, and it was "based upon principles before unknown in the political history of the state." [81]

Whittlesey's argument caught the revolutionary character of Antimasonry, its extraordinary challenge to an established order. But his comments failed to distinguish between Antimasonry's two crucial innovations. Opponents of Masonry first pioneered new means of agitation, printing, meeting, and politicking to change public opinion on a single issue. At the same time, and just as important, Antimasons also explored and popularized new ways of thinking that opposed widely accepted beliefs. By elevating conscience and public opinion as the test of religion and republicanism, Masonry's opponents helped lay the foundation for the cultural dominance of democracy and evangelicalism. Brothers fought back, but their inability to break free from older means of organization and argument virtually doomed their cause.

Antimasonry's pioneering role can be seen in the subsequent development of its ideas. Over the following decade, Democrats called most loudly for the supremacy of public opinion; reformers emphasized the power of conscience. Besides suggesting the way that Antimasonry preceded these later divisions, these debates also point to the ways that, by the 1830s, the older ideals that Antimasonry had attacked in Masonry no longer commanded authority. Arguments that the people lacked wisdom or needed leaders to guide them, even if still acceptable in some settings, virtually guaranteed larger unpopularity. The ideas clarified and popularized by the fraternity's opponents now dominated public discussions. What had been the hope of a speaker at the 1828 New York state convention had actually come to pass. Playing upon both the western New York origins of Antimasonry and the fraternity's idea of illumination from the East, he suggested, "We trust *light* has arisen in the west, which will soon spread its rays over our whole country." [82]

Losing the Right to Reverence

Masonry's Decline and Revival

In March 1829, a convention of Monroe County, New York, brothers decided to surrender the charters of the county's Masonic bodies. Masonry had not condoned the abduction of Morgan, they protested, nor was the fraternity "in any wise dangerous to either civil or religious liberty, or opposed to the Christian religion." Nonetheless, too many people had turned against the order for it to continue. "Unprincipled men" had perverted "virtuous indignation" about the Morgan affair to create "a monstrous infatuation." The time had come to admit that "all the absurd imputations and extraordinary charges which have been so industriously arrayed against the Fraternity" had swayed "publick opinion." They warned brothers: "A reckless opposition to the confirmed publick sentiment cannot be defended. . . . You are hotly pursued by the evil genius of a rapacious prejudice, which nothing can propitiate short of your unconditional submission."[1]

Living just east of Batavia, where the excitement began, Monroe County brothers were among the first to face the broader consequences of Antimasonic agitation and argument that nearly all American brothers would confront over the next decade. Unable to defend the fraternity convincingly, most Masons eventually gave up their fraternal activities. Some, like Hiram Hopkins, renounced Masonry publicly. Others, like the Monroe County brothers, officially surrendered their charters. Most, however, simply severed their connection silently, refusing to attend meetings or to pay dues. Even in areas without an organized political party or agitation, the attack undermined Masonry's prestige and appeal. The northern fraternity was especially hard-hit. But southern groups also experienced serious decline in numbers and enthusiasm. Ten years after the Monroe County meeting, substantial segments of American Masonry had virtually ceased organizational existence.

If the Monroe County brothers were right that public sentiment would turn fully against them, they were less perceptive in their belief that Americans as a whole demanded unconditional submission. Even zealous Antimasons targeted Masonry's post-Revolutionary adaptations more than its earlier incarnations. In the 1840s, American Masonry, shorn of these later elements, began to revive; thirty years later, it had recovered its membership losses. The new order, however, still bore the impress of the sweeping denunciations of those earlier years. It would never again recover the exalted position that had once seemed Masonry's just due.

Nearly three years after the Monroe County meeting, some sixteen hundred Massachusetts brothers signed another declaration, one with a very different purpose. The Boston brothers insisted that they "*can neither renounce nor abandon*" their affiliation, adding their "fervent declaration and hope" that, even if Americans "deprive Freemasons of their civil rights[,] . . . a vast majority of the Fraternity will still remain firm." The signers included nearly all the remaining members of St. Andrew's Lodge, the pioneering Ancient lodge that had been headed by Paul Revere and now included on its rolls Charles W. Moore, the editor of the *Boston Masonic Mirror* and the author of the declaration. The determination of Moore and his lodge brothers, however, could not reverse the fraternity's decline. While St. Andrew's had enrolled twenty-five new members in the five years up to 1827, it admitted only seven in the following seventeen (Table 20).[2]

If the noise of charge and countercharge, renunciation of membership and declaration of loyalty, played the largest role in altering public opinion, the fraternity's more quiet inability to attract new members and keep the old affected the order just as deeply. Ultimately, Antimasonry succeeded not so much because it induced men such as Hopkins to renounce the fraternity publicly as because it destroyed American faith in Masonry. This loss of legitimacy dried up interest in the North, where public anger burned brightly, and in the South, where the agitation hardly penetrated. Even lodges that persevered often did little else, surviving mostly because of older leaders whose opinion of Masonry had been fixed in the more successful days that Charles Moore and his Boston declaration sought to recall.

"The agitation which convulses the North did not pass the Potomac," noted brother and Supreme Court chief justice John Marshall in a perceptive 1833 analysis of southern Masonry. "The case of Morgan . . . produced no other excitement in this part of the United States, than is created by crimes of uncommon atrocity." The effect of Antimasonry on the fraternity "was silent, rather arresting its progress and directing attention from the society, than inducing any open, direct attack on it." As Marshall pointed out, the lack of a "Mason excitement" in the South did not mean that the fraternity remained unaffected.[3] Although agitation never became more than sporadic and failed to inspire political organization, still the South felt deeply the impact of Antimasonry. The slow starvation seen in St. Andrew's Lodge helps explain the quieter difficulties of the southern fraternity better than the monstrous infatuation visible to the upstate New York brothers.

Table 20. New Members, St. Andrew's Lodge, Boston, 1822–1843

Year	Members Admitted	Year	Members Admitted
1822	10	1827	1
1823	5	1831	1
1824	3	1836	3
1825	4	1837	1
1826	3	1843	1

Source: Lodge of St. Andrew, Massachusetts Grand Lodge, 5756–5769, 229, 240.

Nearly everywhere else in the lower South, the effects of Antimasonry threatened a slow death for the fraternity. The 1836 Alabama grand lodge judged "the spirit of Masonry" there "to be languishing." Lacking a quorum, the state body had been unable even to open the previous year. Alabama's Grand Royal Arch chapter experienced even more serious difficulties; it met only once during the entire decade. The grand master of neighboring Georgia noted hopefully to an 1831 meeting of his grand lodge that "the demoniac spirit of anti-Masonry" had "not yet entered our lodges," but his audience already sensed the danger. Facing declining attendance, the delegates proposed that a quorum be constituted by only five, rather than ten, lodges. The proposition failed because the necessary two-thirds of the state's forty-two lodges did not respond. After failing to meet at all for two years, the attendees at an 1835 grand lodge meeting simply declared the requisite number present and revoked the charters of all but sixteen lodges.[4]

"The gloom and disarray of Anti-Masonic rule" complained of by a Georgia brother also affected the upper South. South Carolina's grand lodge could not find a clergyman to serve as grand chaplain from 1827 to 1840. By 1829, only one-third of the state's lodges had reported to the grand lodge in the previous three years. At the group's December meeting, a speaker suggested that Masonry had served its purposes and should now disband. In Lodge No. 10 of Richmond, Virginia, one of the city's most prestigious lodges, the remaining members received only one request for initiation between February 1830 and December 1838 (and rejected it). Farther west, Kentucky Freemasonry also declined. Rob Morris estimated that the number of brothers in the state fell by one-half during the 1830s. Representation in grand lodge meetings dropped even more precipitously. Although fifty lodges had sent representatives in 1826, a decade later only eleven did so. Morris's assessment of Kentucky Masonry in 1859 summarized the situation of the entire southern fraternity: "There was no antimasonic Conventions, no public secessions, nor scandalous scenes," he wrote, "yet the general neglect of Masonry in Kentucky, and its failure for many years to effect any of [its] higher purposes . . . prove clearly enough that, had not the torrent of antimasonic opposition expended itself in a brief ten years, the Order in Kentucky . . . would have died out from sheer neglect."[5]

While this torrent substantially weakened Masonry in areas without strong Antimasonic organization, Antimasonry proved more successful where it was concentrated. Beleaguered northern brothers found metaphors of natural disasters like Morris's flood the most effective way to explain the movement's effects. According to an 1829 Vermont convention, "it burst upon us like the sudden explosion of a volcano, spreading the seeds of discord in families, in churches and in societies." An Ohio grand officer called the movement a "tornado." Whether seen in geological, biological, or meteorological terms, however, Antimasonry virtually destroyed northern Masonry. Two grand lodges shut down; the Michigan state body simply folded; Vermont Masonry survived only in the most technical sense. For ten years after 1836, three Vermont grand lodge officers met every two years to open and then promptly close the state body. Indiana officers appointed a committee in 1834 to "enquire into the expediency of this Grand Lodge *surrendering its Charter*," a process that might have failed only because they never possessed one to give up.[6]

The situation in New York, the center of post-Revolutionary growth and enthusiasm as well as the Morgan excitement, suggests the dimensions of Masonic decline. The June 1827 grand lodge meeting attracted representatives from 228 lodges; ten years later, only 45 appeared, fewer than had sometimes been warranted in a single year before. Losses occurred in all parts of the state. Near the western center of the Morgan affair, only 2 lodges survived. Even in New York City, almost three-quarters of the lodges folded (Table 21).[7] Surviving lodges often maintained only a tenuous existence, remaining open because a few resolute members were willing to defy public scorn. Most of the dozen remaining members of New York City's Clinton Lodge in the mid-1830s had served previously as lodge master. The seven members who kept alive Geneva's Ark Lodge, dubbed by later Masons the "immortal seven," met only under conditions of utmost secrecy, avoiding main roads in traveling to the meetings and entering one by one through a back door.[8]

Facing such dogged commitment, Antimasonry could not achieve complete success without unpopular legal measures. Even as the shifting climate of opinion dried up the source of new members and drove out older brothers through personal doubts or simple fear of disapproval, a handful of committed brethren kept their faith in Masonry. They provided the foundation for a new age of Masonic popularity that rose from the ashes of Antimasonic persecution.

The openings that made this return possible can be glimpsed in the "Report on the Effect of Freemasonry on the Christian Religion" approved by the 1830

Table 21. Lodges Represented at New York Grand Lodge Annual
Communications, 1827–1840

Year	No. of Lodges	Year	No. of Lodges
1827	228*a*	1834	53
1828	130*b*	1835	49
1829	87	1836	—
1830	77	1837	26
1831	71	1838	46
1832	52	1839	43
1833	56	1840	46

a 14 new warrants.   *b* 2 new warrants.

Source: Jesse B. Anthony, *Review of the Grand Lodge Transactions of the State of New York, 1781–1852* (Troy, N.Y., 1869), 68, 77, 78.

national Antimasonic convention. The statement followed many of the main trails being blazed by the movement. Convention members termed Masonic ceremonies "odious" because they blended "the holiest ceremonies of religion with the most revolting of human follies." They also attacked Masonic oaths for creating "a mental slavery." But, surprisingly, the report also attempted to exempt perhaps the majority of Masons from its harshest criticisms. Speaking of the recent influx of clergymen and Christian believers into the lodges, the report noted that "many of them are masons of only three degrees." They were thus, before the revelations of Morgan and others, "as ignorant of the unrevealed iniquity of the institution . . . as those who never passed the threshold of a lodge." [9]

The report clearly sought more to attract wavering brothers to Antimasonry than to persuade Masonry's opponents to accept the original three degrees: Antimasons wanted to destroy all Masonry. Still, certain aspects attracted particular anger. As the 1830 address suggested, the higher degrees epitomized Masonry's dangers: the growth in the fraternity's size and reputation, the special advantages enjoyed by brothers, and the claimed connection between Masonry and Christianity. The Antimasonic emphasis on the higher degrees suggests that its quarrel was ultimately, not with the fraternity in the abstract, but the particular shape Masonry had taken after the Revolution. The critique helps explain the future path of the fraternity. When Masonry began to revive after 1840, it shed many of the elements that had made it so troubling, elements that had been nurtured in the higher degrees.

Even the abduction itself might have been related directly to the higher de-

Figure 25. Master Mason's Certificate. The permanence of Masonry.
By Robert Macoy, 1854. Courtesy American Antiquarian Society

grees. The novelty of Morgan's enterprise lay in its threat to reveal the newer
York Rite rituals. Lower-degree ceremonies had long been publicly available
in America. At least eighteen editions of *Jachin and Boaz*, the popular 1762 English exposé of the first three degrees, appeared in America from 1790 to 1826.
By the 1810s, even the son of Massachusetts grand master Isaiah Thomas sold
copies in his Boston bookstore.[10] But Morgan proposed something different:
to disclose Masonry's mysteries all the way to the Royal Arch's secret name

of God. Outraged upstate New York brothers frustrated this part of his intention. Their attempts to hinder publication, which even included attempting to snatch the manuscripts from Morgan's wife after they abducted her husband, prevented the resulting book from going beyond the first three degrees.[11]

The higher-degree rituals (which others revealed in succeeding years) fueled the growing movement against the fraternity. Morgan's abduction seemed prefigured in the Royal Arch degree oath, which, whether it specifically included or excluded murder and treason (the evidence was unclear), certainly bound initiates to help brothers and keep their secrets in all other cases. Masonry's religious evils seemed epitomized by the degree's burning bush episode, where an unseen companion spoke the words of God to Moses—thus, horrified Antimasons noted, sacrilegiously "personating the deity." Even the titles of the Royal Arch chapter's two primary officers, high priest and king, confirmed Masonry's interlocking religious and political dangers. So strong was the Antimasonic concentration on these higher degrees that a Massachusetts activist praised John Quincy Adams's extended condemnation of the first degree as a necessary corrective. "It has been supposed," he wrote sarcastically, "that men must have taken at least *seven* such oaths, before they were really undeserving public confidence." [12]

The 1830 convention's partial absolution of lower-degree Masons thus pointed to central elements of the Antimasonic indictment. The attack expressed discontent primarily over the dramatic changes in the fraternity during the years following the Revolution. Even leaving aside the difficulties of organizing a comparable agitation without the widespread communication and transportation networks of the 1820s and 1830s, the Antimasonic movement would have been virtually unthinkable in the previous century. The colonial fraternity had been too small in size and aspiration to arouse such concentrated anxiety. Just as important, earlier Masonry lacked the post-Revolutionary order's ideological weight, its claims to encompass the important qualities of science, virtue, and religion—and it lacked the higher degrees that intensified brothers' commitment. Linked to the broader transformations of the 1820s and 1830s, such pretensions (what one convention called the fraternity's "flaunting banners") fueled an extraordinary explosion.[13]

Ironically, however, Antimasonry's success also paved the way for the fraternity's return, since it clipped the very authority—the ability of Masonry's banners to flaunt rather than just wave—that had energized the movement. A few remaining brothers, generally cautious about drawing attention to themselves, could not provide the plausible demon that opponents required. By the late 1830s, Antimasonry had spent its energy. The slow and relatively private nature of the fraternity's return over the next decade or so further soothed fears.[14]

But Antimasonry's success cannot be measured simply by the number of brothers who left or who returned. The movement's victory lay, rather, in its humbling of Masonic pretensions. Antimasons decisively demystified the order, making its secrets available for a few cents in a bookstore or a tavern and allowing people to voice a distaste that would have been unbecoming when Masonry seemed a central emblem of religion or the Republic. The destruction of brothers' openly expressed dreams of splendor and grandeur and the end of American society's willingness to credit post-Revolutionary Masonry's high claims allowed the fraternity to return — but only in another incarnation. Just as the post-Revolutionary swelling of Masonry's numbers and pretensions shaped and energized Antimasonry, so the fires of opposition molded a new fraternity.[15]

Nearly sixty years after the abduction of William Morgan, Albert Pike, the key figure in the mid-nineteenth-century revival of the Scottish Rite, wrote bleakly to its Southern Supreme Council. American Masonry, he warned, "in vain appeals to its antiquity and former prestige to protect it from irreverence." Besides a renewed Roman Catholic opposition to Masonry, he noted, other fraternal groups "jostle it in the struggle for precedence." Legitimate Masonry "has . . . gained popularity while losing its right to reverence."[16]

By 1884, Masonry had experienced extraordinary growth. Its membership rolls far exceeded their pre-1826 peak. But brothers had accommodated their order to a lesser place in society. As Pike pointed out, Victorian America no longer accorded Masonry its older role as the cornerstone of the Republic. While the fraternity's aid and sociability continued to meet important needs, other groups entered the social space that Masonry had previously occupied virtually alone. Brothers moderated their claims to a special relationship with Christianity, emphasizing instead a vague ethical symbolism. This new emphasis diffused older tensions, but the resulting decline in assertions that Masonry embodied God's special providence also made the fraternity less compelling. As Pike observed, Masonry had regained an important place in society, but it could no longer claim to be its symbolic center.

Although it began in the 1840s, the growth that Pike noted accelerated strongly in the 1850s and 1860s. In 1855, four thousand brothers marched in the procession dedicating Philadelphia's new hall, quadrupling the turnout at the earlier 1820 event. The occasion marked only the beginning of the state's fraternal revival. Over the next 20 years, more men joined the fraternity there than in the previous 125. Presiding over the aftermath of a war in which military lodges introduced a new generation of young men into the fraternity, President Andrew Johnson himself laid the cornerstone of the new Massachusetts Masonic temple in 1867. The higher degrees experienced similarly explosive popularity. The Knights Templars' military theme encouraged thousands to join a group that periodically sponsored literal encampments on the edges of cities and towns. Under the direction of Albert Pike, the sublime degrees blossomed into a genuinely popular Scottish Rite. Johnson received the entire range of the new ceremonies in the White House.[17]

But this revival, as Pike also pointed out, was selective. A bewildering variety of new groups now claimed a share of Masonry's former status as a symbol of fraternity and cosmopolitanism. New state and national institutions organized Americans in the space between their localities and their larger governments, making Masonry's national and international reach seem less threatening—but also less necessary. Ironically, the prodigies of organization achieved by Antimasons might also have made the fraternity's size less terrifying. Even Masonry's unique status as a male fraternity bound together by love and secret rituals began to be challenged. Other orders now provided charitable aid for mobile Americans, spread ideals of brotherhood, and initiated members into a closely knit fraternity. Odd Fellowship had been only a minor order before Antimasonry and had been caught in the crossfire, but it grew quickly in the 1840s as Masonry only slowly regained public confidence. The increased availability of Masonic ritual (made possible not only by the expanding midcentury membership but, ironically, by Antimasonic exposés) allowed other groups to borrow extensively from the older fraternity. By the 1860s, fraternal orders bound together by rituals had become virtually the standard means of forming a larger social organization. In 1866 alone, Americans borrowed Masonic forms to build organizations for farmers in the Grange, for Southern recalcitrants in the Ku Klux Klan, and for the Union soldiers who fought them in the Grand Army of the Republic.[18]

At the same time that a transformed institutional landscape denied Masonry a central place in the American imagination, the loosening of the fraternity's tight embrace of Christianity also calmed religious anxieties. Brothers no longer regularly presided at the dedications of church buildings, and their earlier claims of special providence moderated into a general religiousness. These diffuse religious ideas once again placed the fraternity among the many institutions that sought to spread morality. Whereas the post-Revolutionary higher degrees had promised direct contact with historical and sacred truth, the new Masonic culture, partly expressed in rituals transformed once again during the 1840s and 1850s, emphasized the fraternity's symbolic aspects. "In fact," noted a leading ritualist in a discussion of the Royal Arch degree, "the name of God must be taken, in Freemasonry, as the symbol of TRUTH, and then the search for it will be nothing but the search after truth, which is the true end and aim of the masonic science of symbolism."[19]

As Pike perceptively noted, post-1830s Masonry regained its membership at the expense of the qualities that allowed the earlier fraternity to command widespread awe. The taming of this power can perhaps best be seen in the lack of interest in reviving the attack on the resurgent order. Some Antimasonic veterans continued to be concerned. The evangelist Charles G. Finney bewailed Masonry's reappearance in an 1859 book, and Thaddeus Stevens investigated the mystical ties between congressional brothers and his archenemy Andrew Johnson during the impeachment drive, but only a few sectarian Christians attempted a larger public campaign. This waning of Antimasonic resolve underlines the earlier movement's success in destroying the powerful hold of Masonry on the public imagination during its first hundred years in America.

The Jacksonian-era assault on Masonry domesticated it—pushing it further into private life and taming its power as a very public symbol of the Republic and its values. Ironically, this humbling resulted from changes that Masonry had helped create. During the century after 1730, the fraternity played a key role in helping Americans remake their social order, shaping and symbolizing the transition from the aristocratic hierarchy of the eighteenth century to the democratic individualism of the nineteenth. Masonry's development reveals this process as a two-stage revolution in which the major changes of the late eighteenth century would be extended a generation later in the 1820s and 1830s, upsetting a careful republican equilibrium symbolized most fully by the fraternity.

In large part, these changes centered on three major configurations of Masonry's key themes of liberty (the boundaries between public and private that determine participation and freedom from control) and equality (the balance between social inclusiveness and exclusion). The fraternity's enlightened foundations, based on an instinctive and natural sociability and organized around polished self-presentation in the public world, proved attractive to colonial elites, but these values became even more significant when lesser men took up the fraternity in the midst of a widespread attempt to transform the social order. Viewed from a later perspective, however, these Revolutionary changes seem incomplete. Americans attempted to expand liberty from communal oversight and to redefine government as a sort of separate sphere insulated from economic, factional, and familial interests; but few wished to give up completely the moral order and personal concern that regulated authority and provided relief for people facing increasing mobility and commercialism. In the same way, post-Revolutionary Americans rejected aristocratic domination, but few sought to jettison completely the ideal of a leadership group distinguished by particular qualities. Masonry helped people to think through and experience these redefinitions—making them seem natural without denying the ambivalence people felt about them.

The ambiguities that proved so fruitful in the generation after the Revolution, however, became a liability when Jacksonian-era Americans pushed the changes of the Revolution even further. Masonry could not easily adapt to a public world where individuals claimed full participation on the basis of complete equality and to private spheres that were severed from public life. The massive assault on the fraternity that began in 1826 sought to destroy an institution whose exclusiveness and attempt to straddle public and private experiences seemed to threaten the new definitions of society. In the end, however, Antimasonry actually ended up reshaping the fraternity to fit this new social order, categorizing it as one of a series of private spheres in which individuals organized themselves rather than as a divinely inspired institution uniquely connected to enlightenment, religion, and the Republic. By midcentury, the revived, domesticated fraternity could command respect— but seldom reverence.[20]

One Sunday soon before his death in 1871, the aged and senile Father Edward Taylor sat quietly by the window in full Knights Templars regalia. A Methodist minister who influenced both Emerson's prose style and Melville's portrait of Father Mapple, Taylor had been an active brother in the 1820s, during the height of American Masonry's power and prestige. So central did the order seem to Taylor that he accepted membership in the Odd Fellows only after reserving his first allegiance to the earlier fraternity. During the height of Antimasonry, he had defied the Methodist hierarchy's ban on membership. Now only his uniform spoke of the days when he and so many others had seen the Ancient and Honorable Society as the embodiment of their highest values (and, for many, their deepest longings). But the silent Father Taylor might have been pondering what brother Albert Pike noted a few years later: "The Freemasonry of the United States is not what it was in the days of the Fathers."[21]

Rather unexpectedly, the study of Masonry poses a problem not so much of finding materials as of making sense of them. Eighteenth- and nineteenth-century Masons left few vivid narratives or confessions, and the remaining primary sources at first glance seem unrewarding. Official records of local lodges and their supervisory bodies confine themselves almost entirely to notations of attendance and degrees given. Masonic sermons and orations number in the hundreds but are often formulaic and unrevealing. Exposés of degree rituals describe practices that often appear merely bizarre. Only juxtaposing these different materials and placing them in their broader historical context reveals their larger importance. This study attempts to interpret these primary sources and the rich results of more than two centuries of research by Masonic antiquarians in the light of our knowledge of the American past. More recent works by historians on the fraternity and related topics (such as the valuable works of Margaret C. Jacob, David Stevenson, Dorothy A. Lipson, and Kathleen S. Kutolowski) can be traced in the Notes. The primary sources and antiquarian studies of Masonry are less accessible—and less familiar to historians. This note attempts to provide a guide for the scholar attempting to unravel some of their complexities.

Three major types of these sources constitute the foundation of my study. The numerous sermons and addresses given to the fraternity during this period (usually by Masons themselves) often provide the most accessible means of understanding Masonic self-perceptions. I have identified more than four hundred of these addresses published in America from 1750 to 1830. The earliest oration I discovered (from 1734) is printed for the first, and probably only, time as "The First Masonic Discourse Delivered in America," *Freemasons' Monthly Magazine,* VIII (August 1849), 289-293. As a basic list of its successors, I used the card catalog of the American Antiquarian Society (now available online), a firm foundation that can be supplemented with Richardson Wright, "The American Masonic Sermon," and "Bibliography of Printed Masonic Sermons," *American Lodge of Research Transactions,* III (1939-1940), 209-242, with additions in IV (1944-1945), 343. Other Masonic bibliographic aids are Josiah H. Drummond, *Masonic Historical and Bibliographical Memoranda,* 2d ed. (Brooksville, Ky., 1882), helpful on grand lodge proceedings; J. Hugo Tatsch, "American Masonic Journalism, 1811-1840," *American Lodge of Research Transactions,* III (1938-1939), 48-71; and Rob Morris, *The History of Freemasonry in Kentucky, in Its Relations to the Symbolic Degrees . . .* (Louisville, Ky., 1959). The proceedings of the different grand lodges (discussed below), particularly those of Pennsylvania and Maryland, sometimes contain addresses.

These orations and sermons generally provide a less technical understanding of Masonry than the second group of sources, lodge and grand lodge records. Local lodge histories based primarily upon minutes abound. Julius F. Sachse, *Old Masonic Lodges of Pennsylvania: "Moderns" and "Ancients," 1730-1800 . . .* , 2 vols. (Philadelphia, 1912), provides a wide sampling of these. Norris S. Barratt and Julius F. Sachse, *Freemasonry in Pennsylvania, 1727-1907, as Shown by the Records of Lodge No. 2, F. and A.M. of Philadelphia, from the Year A.L. 5757, A.D. 1757,* 3 vols. (Philadelphia, 1908-1910), provides a full record of the earliest Philadelphia Ancient lodge. Boston's St. Andrew's Lodge minutes are available on microfilm at the Grand Lodge of Massachusetts Library, Boston. Grand lodge records are usually more accessible and more valuable. After the Revolution, they were often published annually; these can be followed by looking under "Freemasons" in the two series of *American Bibliography,* by Charles Evans, and by Ralph A. Shaw and Richard Shoemaker. The collected proceedings published later by nearly every grand lodge are usually less comprehensive than those printed at the time, but their lack in depth is more than made up for by their ease of use and their coverage of an unbroken series of years. In my work, I have used most heavily those of Virginia (ed. John Dove), Pennsylvania, New York, Ohio, and Massachusetts. The last has published the only two sets of colonial grand lodge minutes that survive (as *Proceedings in Masonry: St. John's Grand Lodge, 1733-1792; Massachusetts Grand Lodge, 1769-1792 . . .* (Boston, 1895)). Charles Thompson McClenachan, *History of the Most Ancient and Honorable Fraternity of Free and Accepted Masons in New York . . . ,* 4 vols. (New York, 1888-1894), and Edward T. Schultz, *History of Freemasonry in Maryland . . . ,* 3 vols. (Baltimore, 1884-1887), are compilations that include much grand lodge material as well as local histories and some discussion. Albert Gallatin Mackey, *The History of Freemasonry in South Carolina, from Its Origin in the Year 1736 to the Present Time . . .* (1861; Columbia, S.C., 1936), one of the classic works of Masonic antiquarianism, is similar but includes more historical research.

The final set of sources for the history of Masonry is the largest. Masons have been studying their fraternity since at least James Anderson's history of the grand lodge in his 1738 *Constitutions* (a facsimile is published in G. W. Speth, ed., *Quatuor Coronatorum Antigrapha: Masonic Reprints of the Lodge Quatuor Coronati, No. 2076, London,* VII [Margate, 1890], a series with a number of other valuable reprints). The 1723 *Constitutions* was reprinted in Pennsylvania by Benjamin Franklin in 1738 and is available in facsimile in Pennsylvania Grand Lodge, *Proceedings of the Right Worshipful Grand Lodge of . . . Pennsylvania. . . Bi-centenary of the Birth of . . . Benjamin Franklin . . .* (Philadelphia, 1906), 225-318. But the first great landmark of modern Masonic history—excepting Mackey's volume—is Robert Freke Gould, *The His-*

tory of Freemasonry: Its Antiquities, Symbols, Constitutions, Customs . . . , 4 vols. (London, 1885). Gould, heavily influenced by the emerging scientific ideal of history, collected a substantial number of relevant sources into his four volumes, although his writing is often so dense as to be unreadable. A number of editions revised by others have appeared. I have used most often the version edited by Dudley Wright, *Gould's History of Freemasonry throughout the World,* 6 vols. (New York, 1936), a revision that dramatically increases the readability of the work and includes much new research. The only other general history I have found helpful is Henry Wilson Coil, *Freemasonry through Six Centuries,* 2 vols. (Richmond, Va., 1967, 1968). Albert Gallatin Mackey, *The History of Freemasonry: Its Legends and Traditions, Its Chronological History, with an Addenda by William James Hughan,* 7 vols. (New York, 1905–1906), and Henry Leonard Stillson and William James Hughan, *History of the Ancient and Honorable Fraternity of Free and Accepted Masons and Concordant Orders* (Boston, 1910) provide some different material but are generally less helpful than Gould and Coil. *Ars Quatuor Coronati* contains many useful articles on the early years of Freemasonry; their reprints provide some valuable original sources. Douglas Knoop et al., eds., *The Early Masonic Catechisms* (Manchester, 1943), also reprints many of the pamphlets and exposés of the 1720s and 1730s, including the most important of all, Samuel Pritchard, *Masonry Dissected* (London, 1730). Knoop and G. P. Jones also wrote the best histories of the early years of speculative Masonry: *A Short History of Freemasonry to 1730* (Manchester, 1940); and *The Genesis of Freemasonry: An Account of the Rise and Development of Freemasonry in Its Operative, Accepted, and Early Speculative Phases* (Manchester, 1947). The grand lodge's own set of essays on different chronological periods, English Grand Lodge, *Grand Lodge, 1717-1967* (Oxford, 1967), has some valuable material on the early years and is also good on post-1730s Masonry, an area on which Gould has little of analytical interest to say. Another helpful source is Henry Carr, ed., *The Collected "Prestonian" Lectures, 1925-1960* (London, 1967).

The 1936 Wright revision of Gould contains essays on all the American grand lodges, but they tend to be unsystematic. Coil is more helpful, but the best general Masonic study of the early American fraternity is Jacob Hugo Tatsch, *Freemasonry in the Thirteen Colonies* (New York, 1933). Melvin Maynard Johnson, *Freemasonry in America Prior to 1750* (Cambridge, Mass., 1917) and its expanded version, *The Beginnings of Freemasonry in America . . .* (New York, 1924) are exceptionally full collections of sources that can be supplemented with David MacGregor, "Items Relating to Freemasons and Freemasonry Taken from New York Newspapers up to 1740," *American Lodge of Research Transactions,* II (1936–1938), 406–437. On Pennsylvania, there is a great deal of relevant material in Sachse, *Old Masonic Lodges of Pennsylvania,* Barratt and Sachse, *Freemasonry in Pennsylvania,* and in Pennsylvania Grand Lodge, *Franklin Bi-centenary.* Thomas C. Parramore, *Launching the Craft: The*

First Half-Century of Freemasonry in North Carolina (Raleigh, N.C., 1975), and Gerald D. Foss, *Three Centuries of Freemasonry in New Hampshire . . .* , ed. Enzo Serafini (Concord, N.H., 1972), are more recent general state studies. Wayne A. Huss, *The Master Builders: A History of the Grand Lodge of Free and Accepted Masons of Pennsylvania,* 3 vols. (Philadelphia, 1986–1989), is a particularly valuable work by a historian. The key source for Masonic affiliations during the Revolutionary period is Ronald E. Heaton, *Masonic Membership of the Founding Fathers* (Washington, D.C., 1965).

After the Revolution, American Masonic historiography becomes much more diffuse and unanalytical. *The American Lodge of Research Transactions* often contains valuable articles, especially on New York, the base of the journal. Local lodge histories, the seemingly inevitable product of almost every lodge that lasted more than a century, vary in quality but, with the grand lodge proceedings, provide the most valuable sources on this period of growth and institutionalization. Thomas Smith Webb, *The Freemason's Monitor: or, Illustrations of Freemasonry* (originally published Albany, N.Y., 1797; a "new and improved edition," Salem, Mass., 1821, is the version I used most often), is very useful on matters of organization and ritual. Webb, of course, does not include the secret sections of the latter, material that can be followed in David Bernard, *Light on Masonry: A Collection of All the Most Important Documents on the Subject of Speculative Free Masonry . . .* (Utica, N.Y., 1829); and Avery Allyn, *A Ritual of Freemasonry . . .* (Boston 1831). John W. Carter, *The World's Wonder; or, Freemasonry Unmasked . . .* (Madisonville, Tenn., 1835), is a derivative of Allyn (itself taken at least partly from Bernard). William Morgan, *Illustrations of Masonry . . .* (1st ed., Batavia, N.Y, 1826, with many later reprints) is also useful on the first three degrees.

Three basic sources provide an introduction to the higher degrees, a subject almost incomprehensible to the scholar approaching the subject for the first time. For the York or American Rite, Herbert T. Leyland's full biography, *Thomas Smith Webb: Freemason, Musician, Entrepreneur* (Dayton, Ohio, [1965]), provides a very helpful introduction as well as throwing light on a number of related matters. The Scottish Rite has two valuable official histories, which treat some of the key issues in detail: Ray Baker Harris, *History of the Supreme Council (33°) Mother Council of the World, Ancient and Accepted Scottish Rite . . . Southern Jurisdiction, U.S.A., 1801–1861* (Washington, D.C., 1964); and Samuel Harison Baynard, Jr., *History of the Supreme Council, (33°) Ancient Accepted Scottish Rite of Freemasonry, Northern . . . Jurisdiction . . . ,* 2 vols. (Boston, 1938).

Introduction

1. Temple R. Hollcroft, "Salem Town: Partial Autobiography and Masonic Biography," *American Lodge of Research Transactions,* V (1949–1951), 240–266.

2. Salem Town, *A System of Speculative Masonry . . .* (Salem, N.Y., 1818) (quotation at 55).

3. See, for example, Richard Hofstadter, *The Paranoid Style in American Politics and Other Essays* (New York, 1965); and David Brion Davis, "Some Themes of Counter-Subversion: An Analysis of Anti-Masonic, Anti-Catholic, and Anti-Mormon Literature," *Mississippi Valley Historical Review,* XLVII (1960–1961), 205–224.

4. Robert Darnton, *The Great Cat Massacre and Other Episodes in French Cultural History* (New York, 1984), 5.

5. See Clifford Geertz, "Ritual and Social Change: A Javanese Example" (1959), in Geertz, *The Interpretation of Cultures: Selected Essays* (New York, 1973), 142–169. My use of the term "social order" argues that, in real life, theory and practice each have two primary tendencies. First, they are intimately intertwined. Each attempts to influence the other and to bring the other into harmony with it. But both theory and practice also aim for internal coherence, making sense within themselves. Habits and customs shape people's life, often despite the complaints of moralistic critics, and people often act pragmatically rather than according to grand theory. But cultural life is often no more coherent. Intellectuals point out inconsistencies in theories, attempting either to rethink these incongruities or to challenge the theories themselves. This study is about the complex ways in which these two axes intersect and change each other.

6. Henry D. Thoreau, "Resistance to Civil Government" (1849), in Thoreau, *Reform Papers,* ed. Wendell Glick (Princeton, N.J., 1973), 70–71.

Chapter One

1. Michael Spurr, "William Stukeley: Antiquarian and Freemason," *Ars Quotuor Coronatorum,* C (1987), 113–130; *Dictionary of National Biography,* s.v. "Stukeley, William"; Stuart Piggott, *William Stukeley: An Eighteenth-Century Antiquary,* rev. ed. (New York, 1985), esp. 77.

2. Scholarly work on British Freemasonry generally emphasizes either the enlightened or the mysterious side of the fraternity to the virtual exclusion of the other. David Stevenson, *The Origins of Freemasonry: Scotland's Century, 1590–1710* (Cambridge, 1988), sees links to the hermetic tradition as primary. Margaret C. Jacob, *Living the Enlightenment: Freemasonry and Politics in Eighteenth-Century Europe* (New York, 1991), and Jacob, *The Radical Enlightenment: Pantheists, Freemasons, and Republicans* (London, 1981), stress the enlightened side. Norman Hampson's review of Jacob, *Living the Enlightenment* (*Times Literary Supplement,* June 12, 1992, 9), also makes this point.

3. Samuel Pritchard, *Masonry Dissected* (London, 1730), in Douglas Knoop et al., eds., *The Early Masonic Catechisms* (Manchester, 1943), 109.

4. Ibid., 117–120, gives the earliest information on this degree. The connection between the exclamation and the Master's Word, given by Pritchard as "Machbenah," is unclear.

5. These early references to Masonry are included in nearly all histories of Masonry. For convenient compilations, see Henry Carr, "A Collection of References to the Mason Word," *AQC*, LXXXV (1972), 217–241; and Stevenson, *Origins of Freemasonry*, 125–135, 217–230.

6. Robert Plot, *Natural History of Stafford-shire* (1686), quoted in Stevenson, *Origins of Freemasonry*, 223–224; *Tatler*, no. 166, May 2, 1710, in Donald F. Bond, ed., *The Tatler* (Oxford, 1987), II, 419–420; see also no. 26, June 9, 1709 (I, 200). Stevenson, attempting to downplay nearly all 17th-century English references to nonoperative Masonry, discounts Plot's account even while admitting that "there is a ring of truth about these details." Stevenson's view of Plot as overly credulous is common (see also *DNB*, s.v. "Plot, Robert"), but Stuart Piggott, the leading scholar of contemporary antiquarians, calls his volume "sensible and often percipient" (*William Stukeley*, 22).

7. These quotations are from the copy of the "Old Charges" that Masonic historians refer to as the Buchanan Manuscript from the later 17th century. It is reprinted in Robert Freke Gould, *Gould's History of Freemasonry throughout the World*, ed. Dudley Wright, 6 vols. (New York, 1936), I, 55–60. These documents are discussed in all histories of early Masonry. For a modern summary, see Stevenson, *Origins of Freemasonry*, 18–23.

8. For examples of the London Masons Guild's attempt to restrict nonmembers from working in their trade, see Robert Freke Gould, *The History of Freemasonry: Its Antiquities, Symbols, Constitutions, Customs . . . ,* 4 vols. (London, 1906), II, 271–273. The fullest discussion of ritual manuscripts is in Henry Carr, "An Examination of the Early Masonic Catechisms," *AQC*, LXXXIII (1970), 337–357, LXXXIV (1971), 293–307, LXXXV (1972), 331–348. See also Knoop et al., eds., *Early Masonic Catechisms*.

9. Gould, *Gould's History of Freemasonry*, ed. Wright, I, 253–258, discusses the derivation of the term, as does Stevenson, *Origins of Freemasonry*, 11. Although noting the use of the term "free stone" to refer to easily carvable stone that thus required a skilled worker, both suggest that freemanship represented the primary meaning of the term.

10. Stevenson, *Origins of Freemasonry*, 15–17 (on earlier practices), and 25–76, 190–216 (on Scottish lodges). Stevenson (216–226) suggests that English lodges were only temporary meetings called for the initiation of fellows. Henry Carr, "The Transition from Operative to Speculative Masonry," in Carr, ed., *The Collected "Prestonian" Lectures, 1925–1960* (London, 1967), 421–438, suggests a more regular movement of nonoperatives into groups outside the company structure. The apparent preexisting definition of the four lodges at the 1717 creation of the grand lodge and their claims for precedence soon after seem to suggest a more formal sort of organization than Stevenson suggests, although not perhaps the developmental clarity implied in any simplified schema. The Scottish experience is carefully studied in Stevenson, *Origins of Freemasonry*, and *The First Freemasons: Scotland's Early Lodges and Their Members* (Aberdeen, 1988). Stevenson's evidence, however, suggests that Scottish lodges were still ultimately formal trade (if not political) organizations in ways that English lodges were not. See E. Conder, Jr., "The Masons Company of the City of London, and the Lodge of Accepted Masons Connected with It," *AQC*, IX (1896), 128–150.

11. Joseph M. Levine, *The Battle of the Books: History and Literature in the Augustan Age* (Ithaca, N.Y., 1991). For examples of the power of this belief, see J. G. A. Pocock, *The Ancient Constitution and the Feudal Law: A Study of English Historical Thought in*

the Seventeenth Century (Cambridge, 1957); Theodore Dwight Bozeman, *To Live Ancient Lives: The Primitivist Dimension in Puritanism* (Chapel Hill, N.C., 1988). For a broader discussion of American primitivism, see Richard T. Hughes and C. Leonard Allen, *Illusions of Innocence: Protestant Primitivism in America, 1630–1875* (Chicago, 1988).

12. Pico Rattansi, "Newton and the Wisdom of the Ancients," in John Fauvel et al., eds., *Let Newton Be!* (Oxford, 1988), 185–202. Frank E. Manuel, *Isaac Newton: Historian* (Cambridge, Mass., 1963), describes Newton's extensive work on ancient chronology.

On Newton's alchemy, the fullest studies are by Betty Jo Teeter Dobbs: *The Foundations of Newton's Alchemy: or, "The Hunting of the Greene Lyon"* (Cambridge, 1975), and *The Janus Faces of Genius: The Role of Alchemy in Newton's Thought* (Cambridge, 1991). For other work on Newton, see the contributions by Penelope Gouk, John Henry, and Jan Golinski, in Fauvel et al., eds., *Let Newton Be!* 101–168. My downplaying of magic above rests on arguments that, while recognizing the importance of alchemy and ancient wisdom for Newton, suggest a distinction between him and earlier magi. The work of Brian Vickers is particularly helpful: "Introduction," in Vickers, ed., *Occult and Scientific Mentalities in the Renaissance* (Cambridge, 1984), 1–56, and "Analogy versus Identity: The Rejection of Occult Symbolism, 1580–1680," 95–164. Dobbs, *Janus Faces of Genius*, attempts to show how Newton's alchemical beliefs were integrated into his other thinking, an argument that, while it shows the importance of occult ideas, also makes it more difficult to describe his alchemy as an alternative tradition opposed in major ways to other intellectual discourses. All this work, however, also makes it clear that late-17th- and early-18th-century British intellectuals, epitomized by Newton, believed that new forms of knowledge and inquiry could be combined with the recovery of ancient wisdom (sometimes through nonrational means), a dynamic tension between what came to be called science and what came to be called superstition that would be lost in subsequent years. The relationship of this debate to early speculative Freemasonry is discussed later.

13. Conder, "The Masons Company of the City of London," *AQC*, IX (1896), 128–150. See also the earlier discussion of lodges and the sources noted there.

14. *The Constitutions of the Free-Masons: Containing the History, Charges, Regulations, etc. of That Most Ancient and Right Worshipful Fraternity* (Philadelphia, 1734; rpt. of London, 1723), 59 (hereafter cited as *Constitutions* [1723]); John Hamill, *The Craft: A History of English Freemasonry* (London, 1986), 64.

15. *Constitutions* (1723), 80; Alex Horne, *The York Legend in the Old Charges* (London, 1988). See note 10 above for discussions of the nature of English lodges.

16. On these developments, see especially Knoop, *Early Masonic Catechisms;* and Carr, "Examination of Early Masonic Catechisms," *AQC*, LXXXIII (1970), 337–357, LXXXIV (1971), 293–307, LXXXV (1972), 331–348.

17. Pritchard, *Masonry Dissected*, in Knoop et al., eds., *Early Masonic Catechisms*, 111.

18. The song is from *Constitutions* (1723), 91. The blindfold used in later years is not mentioned in Pritchard, *Masonry Dissected*, in Knoop et al., eds., *Early Masonic Catechisms*, but might have been either unmentioned or a part of the practices in some lodges. For the later Master's degree, see *Jachin and Boaz: An Authentic Key to the Door of Freemasonry* (London, 1762). For the classic exposition of initiation rites, see the work of Victor W. Turner: for example, *The Ritual Process: Structure and Anti-Structure* (Chicago, 1969); "Passages, Margins, and Poverty: Religious Symbols of

Communitas," in Turner, *Dramas, Fields, and Metaphors: Symbolic Action in Human Society* (Ithaca, N.Y., 1974), 231–271; "Are There Universals of Performance in Myth, Ritual, and Drama?" in Richard Schechner and Willa Appel, eds., *By Means of Performance: Intercultural Studies of Theatre and Ritual* (Cambridge, 1990), 8–18. For application to later Masonic rituals, see Mark C. Carnes, *Secret Ritual and Manhood in Victorian America* (New Haven, Conn., 1989), esp. 32–33.

19. Pritchard, *Masonry Dissected*, in Knoop et al., eds., *Early Masonic Catechisms*, 110.

20. Carr, "An Examination of the Early Masonic Catechisms," *AQC*, LXXXIII (1970), 335; Douglas Knoop and G. P. Jones, *A Short History of Freemasonry to 1730* (Manchester, 1940), 96; Pritchard, *Masonry Dissected,* in Knoop et al., eds., *Early Masonic Catechisms*, 114. Informal explanations of symbols are hinted at in Carr, "An Examination of the Early Masonic Catechisms," *AQC*, LXXXIII (1970), 348. "Brother Euclid's Letter to the Author against Unjust Cavils," in James Anderson, *The New Book of Constitutions of the Antient and Honourable Fraternity of Free and Accepted Masons* (London, 1738), 226–228, seems to suggest something similar in arguing that the many exposés of the 1720s were inadequate; "All of 'em put together don't discover the profound and sublime Things of *old Masonry*" (226). Using symbolism that was universal among later Masons, the author, writing in 1738, describes brothers of lower social status being respectful to their betters "tho' on the *Level*, yet always within *Compass,* and according to the *Square* and *Plumb*" (228).

21. Carr, "Collection of References to the Mason Word," *AQC*, LXXXV (1972), 217–241.

22. [Martin Clare], "A Defence of Masonry, Occasion'd by a Pamphlet Call'd Masonry Dissected," in W. Smith, *The Free Masons's Pocket Companion,* 2d ed. (London, 1738), 105–111, 116–119; *Constitutions* (1723), 92; Pigott, *William Stukeley,* 71. The author of "A Defence" is identified as Martin Clare by William James Hughan in Albert Gallatin Mackey, *The History of Freemasonry: Its Legends and Traditions, Its Chronological History, with an Addenda by William James Hughan,* 7 vols. (N.Y., 1905–1906), VII, 2005. Hughan suggests that the piece was originally published separately in 1730 and then as part of *Constitutions* (1738).

23. *Constitutions* (1723), 35; "Brother Euclid's Letter," in *Constitutions* (1738) 227. The fullest study of popular magic is Keith Thomas, *Religion and the Decline of Magic* (New York, 1971). For the continued appeal of this tradition in America, see also Jon Butler, *Awash in a Sea of Faith: Christianizing the American People* (Cambridge, Mass., 1989).

24. On hermeticism, see, especially, Yates, *Giordano Bruno and the Hermetic Tradition;* and John L. Brooke, *The Refiner's Fire: The Making of Mormon Cosmology, 1644–1844* (New York, 1994), 9–29.

25. Manuel, *Isaac Newton: Historian,* 149.

26. Ibid., 93, 97 (quoting Newton; for Stukeley's and others' reaction, see 107); James E. Force, *William Whiston: Honest Newtonian* (Cambridge, 1985), 24; John Bunyan, *Solomon's Temple Spiritualiz'd; or, Gospel-Light Fetcht out of the Temple at Jerusalem . . .* (London, 1688); Force, *William Whiston,* 21; Stukeley, *Memoirs of Newton,* 18. Thomas Godwyn, *Moses and Aaron: Civil and Ecclesiastical Rites, Used by the Ancient Hebrews . . . ,* 2d ed. (London, 1626), went through 12 editions in the century; Knoop and Jones, *Short History,* 41–42. Hamill, *The Craft,* 108, cites a midcentury manuscript ritual drawn largely from Bunyan's book.

27. *Constitutions* (1723), 18, 23n.

28. Richard H. Popkin, "The Deist Challenge," in Ole Peter Grell et al., eds., *From*

Persecution to Toleration: The Glorious Revolution and Religion in England (Oxford, 1991), 195–215; see also Frank E. Manuel, *The Eighteenth Century Confronts the Gods* (Cambridge, Mass., 1959).

29. *DNB*, s.v. "Stukeley, William"; Manuel, *Isaac Newton: Historian*, 89–102, 122–138.

30. Manuel, *Isaac Newton: Historian*, 161–163 (294 n. 68, suggesting that Newton later changed his views); Manuel, *The Religion of Isaac Newton* (Oxford, 1974), 92.

31. Piggott, *William Stukeley*, 98. See also William Stukeley, *Stonehenge, a Temple Restor'd to the British Druids* (1740; New York, 1984), 2–4.

32. *Constitutions* (1738), 143; Popkin, "Deist Challenge," in Grell et al., eds., *From Persecution to Toleration*, 202 n. 41; *Constitutions* (1723), 18, 25–26.

33. See Manuel, *The Eighteenth Century Confronts the Gods*.

34. Robert P. Kraynak, *History and Modernity in the Thought of Thomas Hobbes* (Ithaca, N.Y., 1990), makes a similar argument about Hobbes's view of the inadequacy of history.

35. Piggott, *William Stukeley*, esp. 145, 156. See also Stuart Piggott, *The Druids* (London, 1968), 152–174. For a similar reaction to Whiston's millennial theories in 1750, see Force, *William Whiston*, 24.

36. Pritchard, *Masonry Dissected*, in Knoop et al., eds., *Early Masonic Catechisms*, 119.

37. Spurr, "William Stukeley," *AQC*, C (1987), 126, 127; see the 1723/4 Engraved List of lodges London, in *AQC*, XXIX (1916); *Constitutions* (1723), 83–87, 88–90; Piggott, *William Stukeley*, 70. Stukeley was chosen master at the 1721 creation of the lodge, but was not listed in that position in the 1723 *Constitutions* (81–82).

38. On the Kit-Cat, see *DNB*, s.v. "Cat, Christopher"; Peter Smithers, *The Life of Joseph Addison*, 2d ed. (Oxford, 1968), 92–93, 243–244, 422.

39. *Constitutions* (1723), 48.

40. Hogarth was a grand steward in 1735 (Gould, *Gould's History of Freemasonry*, ed. Wright, I, 360). *Constitutions* (1723), 54, explicitly warned brothers against "all excess."

41. Piggott, *William Stukeley*, 15, 53–55, 113–114, 124, 118–119; *DNB*, s.v. "Stukeley, William."

42. *Oxford English Dictionary*, s.v. "Club" (see also the *Spectator*'s common use of the term "knot" in connection with club in Donald F. Bond, ed., *The Spectator*, 5 vols. [Oxford, 1965], I, 289 [no. 68, May 18, 1711], 309 [no. 72, May 23, 1711]); Peter Earle, *The Making of the English Middle Class: Business, Society, and Family Life in London, 1660–1730* (Berkeley, Calif., 1989), 241–242. On clubs, see Robert J. Allen, *The Clubs of Augustan London* (Cambridge, Mass., 1933); M. D. George, *London Life in The Eighteenth Century* (London, 1925), 266–268; David Allen, "Political Clubs in Restoration London," *Historical Journal*, XIX (1976), 561–580; John Brewer, "Commercialization and Politics," in Neil McKendrick, John Brewer, and J. H. Plumb, *The Birth of a Consumer Society: The Commercialization of Eighteenth-Century England* (Bloomington, Ind., 1982), 217–230.

43. Bond, ed., *The Spectator*, I, 39–43 (no. 9, Mar. 10, 1711); Allen, *The Clubs of Augustan London*, 178–179.

44. Bond, ed., *The Spectator*, III, 506 (no. 403, June 12, 1712); Roy Porter, *English Society in the Eighteenth Century* (London, 1982), 60–61; E. A. Wrigley, "A Simple Model of London's Importance in Changing English Society and Economy, 1650–1750," *Past and Present*, no. 37 (June 1967), 44–70.

45. Bond, ed., *The Spectator*, I, 293, 294 (no. 69, May 19, 1711) (on the Exchange,

see I, 293 nn. 1, 3); Isaac Kramnick, *Bolingbroke and His Circle: The Politics of Nostalgia in the Age of Walpole* (Cambridge, Mass., 1968), 47; *British Mercury*, Aug. 2, 1712, quoted in Michael Harris, *London Newspapers in the Age of Walpole: A Study of the Origins of the Modern English Press* (Rutherford, N.J., 1987), 155. See also G. A. Cranfield, *The Development of the Provincial Newspaper, 1700-1760* (Oxford, 1962).

46. Daniel Defoe, *A Tour through the Whole Island of Great Britain*, 2 vols. (1724-1727; London, 1962), I, 12; Peter Borsay, *The English Urban Renaissance: Culture and Society in the Provincial Town, 1660-1770* (Oxford, 1989). See also Ian K. Steele, *The English Atlantic, 1675 to 1740: An Exploration of Communication and Community* (New York, 1986), 114-117, 138-140.

47. *Constitutions* (1723), 48, 83. See also Bond, ed., *The Spectator*, I, 45 (no. 10, Mar. 12, 1711), where Addison writes of "My good Brothers and Allies, . . . the Fraternity of Spectators who live in the World without having any thing to do in it."

48. Bond, ed., *The Spectator*, I, 42 (no. 9, Mar. 10, 1711), 512 (no. 125, July 24, 1711). On the Brothers Club, see Kramnick, *Bolingbroke and His Circle*, 11; see also Irvin Ehrenpreis, *Swift: The Man, His Works, and the Age*, II (Cambridge, Mass., 1967), 502-504. Swift extended the group's kinship metaphor beyond the members to their relations, allowing him to refer to his members' wives as his sisters. Jonathan Swift, *Journal to Stella*, ed. Harold Williams, 2 vols. (Oxford, 1948), I, 293-294.

49. *Constitutions* (1723), 48, 54, 93.

50. Bond, ed., *The Spectator*, I, 510 (no. 125, July 24, 1711); *Constitutions* (1723), 48.

51. Bond, ed., *The Spectator*, I, 423-424 (no. 101, June 26, 1711); Geoffrey Holmes, *British Politics in the Age of Anne* (London, 1968); Gary Stuart De Krey, *A Fractured Society: The Politics of London in the First Age of Party, 1688-1715* (Oxford, 1985). J. H. Plumb, *The Growth of Political Stability in England: 1675-1725* (London, 1967), suggests a growing stability under the ministry of Robert Walpole. Other works emphasize the continuing importance of divisions. See Linda Colley, *In Defiance of Oligarchy: The Tory Party, 1714-1760* (Cambridge, 1982); E. P. Thompson, *Customs in Common* (New York, 1991); Paul Kléber Monod, *Jacobitism and the English People, 1688-1788* (Cambridge, 1989); and Nicholas Rogers, *Whigs and Cities: Popular Politics in the Age of Walpole and Pitt* (Oxford, 1989).

52. See Gordon Rupp, *Religion in England, 1688-1791* (Oxford, 1986); Geoffrey Holmes, *The Trial of Doctor Sacheverell* (London, 1973); Holmes and W. A. Speck, *The Divided Society: Parties and Politics in England, 1694-1716* (New York, 1968), 49-57. Hoadley gave his controversial sermon in the period between the preliminary planning and the actual formation of the grand lodge.

53. N. Barker Cryer, "The De-Christianizing of the Craft," *AQC*, XCVII (1984), 34-46, discusses Christian elements within early Masonry.

54. *Constitutions* (1723), 48.

55. Ibid., 48-49. On Arbuthnot, see George A. Aitken, *The Life and Works of John Arbuthnot, M.D., Fellow of the Royal College of Physicians* (1892; New York, 1968). For the more bizarre Jacobitism (and personal life) of the duke of Wharton, see the *DNB*, s.v. "Wharton, Philip, Duke of." According to the 1738 *Book of Constitutions* (114), the election of the duke as grand master in 1722 was opposed by many of "the better sort" within the fraternity, a statement that remains obscure despite much speculation. Jacob, *Radical Enlightenment*, 130-132, makes a good deal of Masonry's connection with Whigs.

56. *Constitutions* (1723), 55.

57. Swift, *Journal to Stella*, ed. Williams, II, 505-506; Bond, ed., *The Spectator*, I, 487 (no. 119, July 17, 1711); Borsay, *Urban Renaissance*, 275.

58. *The English Theophrastus; or, The Manners of the Age* (London, 1702), quoted in *OED*, s.v. "Politeness"; Chesterfield quoted in Porter, *English Society in the Eighteenth Century,* 320. "What is opposite to the eternal Rules of Reason and good Sense," Steele argued in the *Spectator,* "must be excluded from any Place in the Carriage of a Well-bred Man" (Bond, ed., *The Spectator,* I, 323 [no. 75, May 26, 1711]). See also Lawrence E. Klein, *Shaftesbury and the Culture of Politeness: Moral Discourse and Cultural Politics in Early Eighteenth-Century England* (Cambridge, 1994); Klein, "Liberty, Manners, and Politeness in Early Eighteenth-Century England," *Hist. Jour.,* XXXII (1989), 583–605; Robert W. Malcolmson, *Popular Recreations in English Society, 1700–1850* (Cambridge, 1973).

59. *Constitutions* (1723), 37, 55, 93.

60. Ibid., 25–28, 37, 41. Howard D. Weinbrot, *Augustus Caesar in "Augustan" England: The Decline of a Classical Norm* (Princeton, N.J., 1978), suggests that, unlike Masonic practice, contemporaries commonly portrayed the emperor as an emblem of despotism.

61. See Margaret C. Jacob, *The Cultural Meaning of the Scientific Revolution* (Philadelphia, 1988), 143–144, 186, 189; John Stokes, "Inaugural Addresss: Life of John Theophilus Desaguliers," *AQC,* XXXVIII (1925), 285–308; Calhoun Winton, *Sir Richard Steele, M.P.: The Later Career* (Baltimore, 1970), 152, 203, 246–247; Rae Blanchard, "Was Sir Richard Steele a Freemason?" Modern Language Association of America, *Publications,* LXIII (1948), 903–917; *Pennsylvania Gazette* (Philadelphia), Aug. 13, 1730; R. William Weisberger, "Benjamin Franklin: A Masonic Enlightener in Paris," *Pennsylvania History,* LIII (1986), 165–180.

62. Bond, ed., *The Spectator,* I, 268 (no. 62, May 11, 1711), and see also III, 5 (no. 409, June 19, 1712); and Anthony Ashley Cooper, third earl of Shaftesbury, *Characteristics of Men, Manners, Opinions, Times,* ed. John M. Robertson, 2 vols. in 1 (1711; Indianapolis, Ind., 1964), I, 221–222, II, 11.

63. Piggott, *William Stukeley,* 38, 55, 56; for the Roman Knights, see 55, and for the similar comments of yet another knight, 24.

64. [John Arbuthnot], *An Essay on the Usefulness of Mathematical Learning, in a Letter from a Gentleman in the City to His Friend in Oxford* (Oxford, 1701), in Aitken, *The Life and Works of John Arbuthnot,* 409–435 (quotations at 412, 414); J. T. Desaguliers, *The Newtonian System of the World, the Best Model of Government: An Allegorical Poem* (London, 1728).

65. *Constitutions* (1723), 37, 93.

66. James Hoopes, *Consciousness in New England: From Puritanism and Ideas to Psychoanalysis and Semiotic* (Baltimore, 1989), 1–64; J. G. A. Pocock, "The Significance of 1688: Some Reflections on Whig History," in Robert Beddard, ed., *The Revolutions of 1688: The Andrew Browning Lectures, 1988* (Oxford, 1991), 271–292, esp. 285–292. Pocock also argues that enlightened ideas sought to reinforce state power, but see later for an argument that the Enlightenment sought to exclude the possibility of absolutism.

67. For attempts to bring together the immense literature on these changes, see Keith Wrightson, *English Society, 1580–1680* (London, 1982); C. G. A. Clay, *Economic Expansion and Social Change: England, 1500–1700,* 2 vols. (Cambridge, 1984).

68. Thomas Hobbes, *Leviathan,* ed. A. D. Lindsay (London, 1914), 64, 66; E. M. W. Tillyard, *The Elizabethan World Picture* (New York, 1944), is the classic exposition of the older view of society. For a discussion of its fate that (perversely, I would suggest) ends with Hobbes, see Stephen L. Collins, *From Divine Cosmos to Sovereign State: An Intellectual History of Consciousness and the Idea of Order in Renaissance England* (New York, 1989). On the strains of the late-Elizabethan and early Stuart period, see David

Underdown, *Revel, Riot, and Rebellion: Popular Politics and Culture in England, 1603–1660* (Oxford, 1985), especially chap. 2; Lawrence Stone, "Social Mobility in England, 1500–1700," *Past and Present,* no. 33 (April 1966), 16–55; and Christopher Hill, *The World Turned Upside Down* (London, 1977).

69. Shaftesbury, *Characteristics,* ed. Robertson, I, 262n; Hoopes, *Consciousness in New England,* 1–64. For discussions of Shaftesbury, see Klein, *Shaftesbury and the Culture of Politeness,* and, "Liberty, Manners, and Politeness," *Hist. Jour.,* XXXII (1989), 583–605; and Stanley Grean, *Shaftesbury's Philosophy of Religion and Ethics: A Study in Enthusiasm* (Athens, Ohio, 1967).

70. Shaftesbury, *Characteristics,* ed. Robertson, I, 74; see also D. D. Raphael, ed., *British Moralists, 1650–1800,* 2 vols. (Oxford, 1969), I, 175–176. On the 18th-century significance of Shaftesbury, see Klein, "Liberty, Manners, and Politeness," *Hist. Jour.,* XXXII (1989), 583–605; Basil Willey, *The English Moralists* (London, 1964), 220–221; John Mullan, *Sentiment and Sociability: The Language of Feeling in the Eighteenth Century* (Oxford, 1988); John K. Sheriff, *The Good-Natured Man: The Evolution of a Moral Ideal, 1660–1800* (University, Ala., 1982). See, for a later example of ideas, Adam Smith, *The Theory of Moral Sentiments,* ed. D. D. Raphael and A. L. Macfie (Oxford, 1976).

71. Randolph Trumbach, *The Rise of the Egalitarian Family: Aristocratic Kinship and Domestic Relations in Eighteenth-Century England* (New York, 1978). For a description of inheritance practices in Britain and America, see Toby L. Ditz, *Property and Kinship: Inheritance in Early Connecticut, 1750–1820* (Princeton, N.J., 1986), esp. 24–37.

72. *Constitutions* (1723), 50, 51, 55, 56; Douglas Knoop and G. P. Jones, *The Genesis of Freemasonry: An Account of the Rise and Development of Freemasonry in Its Operative, Accepted, and Early Speculative Phases* (Manchester, 1947), 303.

73. Knoop and Jones, *Genesis of Freemasonry,* 303.

74. Shaftesbury, *Characteristics,* ed. Robertson, I, 84–86; see I, 273, for a discussion of "good breeding." Chesterfield quoted in Willey, *The English Moralists,* 275.

75. Stone, "Social Mobility in England, 1500–1700," *Past and Present,* no. 33 (April 1966), 16–55.

76. Pritchard, *Masonry Dissected,* in Knoop et al., eds., *Early Masonic Catechisms,* 110.

77. *Constitutions* (1723), 92.

78. *Constitutions* (1738), 111, 115, 142.

79. T. M. Carter, "Provincial Warrants," part 1, *AQC,* XLI (1929), 43–121, provides a full treatment of the growth of lodges.

80. *Constitutions* (1723), 90.

81. Knoop and Jones, *Short History,* 129; Spurr, "William Stukeley," *AQC,* C (1987), 126.

82. Duncan Campbell Lee, *Desaguliers of No. 4 and His Services to Freemasonry* (London, 1932), esp. 15.

83. See Earle, *The Making of the English Middle Class,* chap. 1, "The Middle Station," for a helpful definition of the middle class. It should be emphasized that this group was not the broad group it later became; Earle estimates that only a bit more than 5% of the population in 1700 belonged to it. See also Geoffrey Holmes, *Augustan England: Professions, State, and Society, 1680–1730* (London, 1982).

84. *Constitutions* (1723), 81–82; *Constitutions* (1738), 110; Arthur L. R. Heiron, *Ancient Freemasonry and the Old Dundee Lodge, No. 18,* 2d ed. (London, 1921) (see 22 for the midcentury list). Douglas Knoop et al., eds., *Early Masonic Pamphlets* (Manchester, 1945), 3, mentions the concentration of high-ranking men in certain lodges. Little work

has been done on English Masonry's social composition. For hints as to the social standing of Masonry in the 1760s, see also T. W. Hanson, *The Lodge of Probity No. 61, 1738-1938* (Halifax, Yorks., 1939); and John Brewer, "Commercialization and Politics," in Brewer, Plumb, and McKendrick, *The Birth of a Consumer Society,* 217-224.

85. Knoop and Jones, *Genesis of Freemasonry,* 302-303; English Grand Lodge, *Grand Lodge, 1717-1967* (Oxford, 1967), 75; *Constitutions* (1723), 316.

86. See Knoop, *Early Masonic Pamphlets;* Henry Sadler, *Masonic Facts and Fictions, Comprising a New Theory of the Origins of the "Ancient" Grand Lodge . . .* (London, 1887), 39.

87. *An Ode to the Grand Khaibar* (London, 1726), 2, 3, 4; Ronald Paulson, ed., *Hogarth's Graphic Works: First Complete Edition,* 2 vols. (New Haven, Conn., 1965), I, 108.

88. Gould, *History of Freemasonry,* III, 129-130, cites these articles. See also Paulson, ed., *Hogarth's Graphic Works,* I, 107-108, II, plate 46. On popular anti-Catholicism in this period, see Linda Colley, *Britons: Forging the Nation, 1707-1837* (New Haven, Conn., 1992), 11-54.

89. Gould, *History of Freemasonry,* III, 332. Jacobs, *Living the Enlightenment,* discusses European Masonry. See James Knowlson, *Universal Language Schemes in England and France, 1600-1800* (Toronto, 1975), 140-141, on French as a cosmopolitan language in this period.

90. On communication (and miscommunication), see Steele, *The English Atlantic.*

91. Jacob Hugo Tatsch, *Freemasonry in the Thirteen Colonies* (New York, 1933), 28; Pennsylvania Grand Lodge, *Proceedings of the Right Worshipful Grand Lodge of . . . Pennsylvania . . . Bi-centenary of the Birth of . . . Benjamin Franklin . . .* (Philadelphia, 1906), 87-90, 133-134; Melvin Maynard Johnson, *Freemasonry in America Prior to 1750 . . .* (Cambridge, Mass., 1917), 62-67. The extension of authority Franklin mentions is not noted in either the records of the Massachusetts or the London grand bodies; both, however, are incomplete. In a summary of previous grand lodge actions written around 1738 or 1739, the Massachusetts secretary noted a deputation appointing Franklin the first grand master, "which was the beginning of Masonry there." See Massachusetts Grand Lodge, *Proceedings in Masonry: St. John's Grand Lodge, 1733-1792; Massachusetts Grand Lodge, 1769-1792 . . .* (Boston, 1895), 4. See, on these actions and the resulting claims for priority, Henry Wilson Coil, *Freemasonry through Six Centuries,* 2 vols. (Richmond, Va., 1967-1968), I, 261-275.

92. William Bordley Clarke, *Early and Historic Freemasonry of Georgia, 1733/4-1800* (Savannah, Ga., 1924); Tatsch, *Freemasonry in the Thirteen Colonies,* 73-77. The evidence for Oglethorpe's involvement is circumstantial. For the controversy over the date of the Norfolk lodge's founding, see Tatsch, *Freemasonry in the Thirteen Colonies,* 114-129; the other Virginia Lodges were located in Botetourt County and Williamsburg (134).

93. Massachusetts Grand Lodge, *Proceedings in Masonry,* 482-483. Besides this grand lodge notation, there is no other evidence of the Charleston lodge.

94. Ibid., 402-403.

95. Mackey, *The History of Freemasonry,* 433-451. This document was endlessly reprinted in America through the 19th century. I have used the text found in William Smith, *Ahiman Rezon Abridged and Digested . . .* (Philadelphia, 1783), 1-11.

Chapter Two

1. For the incident discussed here and in subsequent paragraphs, see Pennsylvania Grand Lodge, *Proceedings of the Right Worshipful Grand Lodge of . . . Pennsylvania . . . Bi-centenary of the Birth of . . . Benjamin Franklin . . .* (Philadelphia, 1906), 97–104 (hereafter cited as *Franklin Bi-centenary*); Leonard W. Labaree et al., eds., *The Papers of Benjamin Franklin* (New Haven, Conn., 1959–), II, 187, 198–204; *Pennsylvania Gazette* (Philadelphia), Feb. 14, 1737/8; *Minutes of the Provincial Council of Pennsylvania, from the Organization to the Termination of the Proprietary Government,* 16 vols. (Harrisburg, Pa., 1838–1860), IV, 276–277.

2. The term "anglicization" was popularized by John M. Murrin, "Anglicizing an American Colony: The Transformation of Provincial Massachusetts" (Ph.D. diss., Yale University, 1966), to describe 18th-century institutional change. Since then, the concept has come to mean primarily the imitation of English social, cultural, and material life. T. H. Breen, "Creative Adaptations: Peoples and Cultures," in Jack P. Greene and J. R. Pole, eds., *Colonial British America: Essays in the New History of the Early Modern Era* (Baltimore, 1984), 221–223, summarizes many of these recent discussions. In more recent essays, he argues that British goods were the key to this anglicization. See Breen, "An Empire of Goods: The Anglicization of Colonial America, 1690–1776," *Journal of British Studies,* XXV (1986), 467–499; " 'Baubles of Britain': The American and Consumer Revolutions of the Eighteenth Century," *Past and Present,* no. 119 (May 1988), 73–104. See also Jack P. Greene, "Search for Identity: An Interpretation of the Meaning of Selected Patterns of Social Response in Eighteenth-Century America," *Journal of Social History,* III (1969–1970), 205–211. Both Greene and Breen seem to see the process primarily as one of attempted replication of another culture; Greene refers to "empty cultural borrowing" (211). See also Greene, *Pursuits of Happiness: The Social Development of Early Modern British Colonies and the Formation of American Culture* (Chapel Hill, N.C., 1988), 175. Richard L. Bushman, "American High-Style and Vernacular Cultures," in Greene and Pole, eds., *Colonial British America,* 352, suggests that the process went beyond imitation, involving striving for "an ideal" with "power of its own apart from the repetition of English behavior." In *The Refinement of America: Persons, Houses, Cities* (New York, 1992), 30–60, Bushman stresses European origins more strongly. I would suggest that the power of this ideal also developed from the particular circumstances of American elites within America (most notably the need to establish still-insecure authority in the midst of continued factionalism discussed in this chapter), a formulation suggested by Bernard Bailyn's classic discussion of political ideology in *The Origins of American Politics* (New York, 1968).

3. *Boston Gazette,* July 2, 1739, article reprinted in *Virginia Gazette* (Williamsburg), Aug. 10, 1739. Boston's First Lodge and its Modern grand lodge are often referred to by Masonic historians and antiquarians as St. John's Lodge—it took that name officially in the 1780s upon merging with the remaining Boston Modern lodges—and the St. John's grand lodge. Both sets of terms were in use in the 18th century. See Massachusetts Grand Lodge, *The Constitutions of the Ancient and Honorable Fraternity of Free and Accepted Masons . . .* (Worcester, Mass., 1792), 114, 134; the Ancient grand lodge (discussed in Chapter 3) was also known as the Massachusetts grand lodge.

4. David MacGregor, "Items Relating to Freemasons and Freemasonry Taken from New York Newspapers up to 1740," *American Lodge of Research Transactions,* II (1936–1938), 421. The first known American newspaper reference to Masonry is *Weekly News-Letter* (Boston), May 25, 1727. MacGregor's article supplements the careful

compilation of early sources (up to 1750) in Melvin Maynard Johnson, *The Beginnings of Freemasonry in America . . .* (New York, 1924).

5. *Virginia Gazette*, Dec. 2, 1737, Aug. 26, 1739; Carl Bridenbaugh, ed., *Gentleman's Progress: The Itinerarium of Dr. Alexander Hamilton, 1744* (Pittsburgh, 1992), xix, 19; *Franklin Bi-centenary*, 59-60.

6. Mrs. Conway Robinson Howard, ed., "Extracts from the Diary of Daniel Fisher, 1755," *Pennsylvania Magazine of History and Biography*, XVII (1893), 273; *Pennsylvania Gazette* (Philadelphia), June 20, 26, 1755; *Franklin Bi-centenary*, 141-148; William Smith, *A Sermon Preached in Christ-Church, Philadelphia . . . the 24th of June, 1755 . . .* (Philadelphia, [1755]). The London grand lodge did not have its own building until 1776; see John Hamill, *The Craft: A History of English Freemasonry* (London, 1986), 47-48. Hamill also discusses English processions (83-84).

7. R. Alonzo Brock, ed., "Journal of William Black," *PMHB*, II (1878), 43-44, describes a 1744 Philadelphia procession of the provincial government with many of the same elements as the later Masonic procession; for a complete description of another Modern public ceremony, see the 1768 installation of John Rowe as provincial grand master in Massachusetts Grand Lodge, *Proceedings in Masonry: St. John's Grand Lodge, 1733-1792; Massachusetts Grand Lodge, 1769-1792 . . .* (Boston, 1895), 148-161 (hereafter cited as Massachusetts Grand Lodge, *Proceedings in Masonry*).

8. On the developments of processions, see Peter Clark and Paul Slack, *English Towns in Transition, 1500-1700* (London, 1976), 131. On their significance to the 18th century, see E. P. Thompson, "Patrician Society, Plebeian Culture," *Jour. Soc. Hist.*, VII (1973-1974), 382-405. See also Sean Wilentz, ed., *Rites of Power: Symbolism, Ritual, and Politics since the Middle Ages* (Philadelphia, 1985); and, on later American rituals, David Waldstreicher, "Rites of Rebellion, Rites of Assent: Celebrations, Print Culture, and the Origins of American Nationalism," *Journal of American History*, LXXXII (1995-1996), 37-61; Albrecht Koschnik, "Political Conflict and Public Contest: Rituals of National Celebration in Philadelphia, 1788-1815," *PMHB*, CXVIII (1995), 209-248; and Len Travers, "Hurrah for the Fourth: Patriotism, Politics, and Independence Day in Federalist Boston, 1783-1818," Essex Institute, *Historical Collections*, CXXV (1989), 129-161. Rather surprisingly, colonial ceremonies outside the Virginia tidewater have been little studied. For Virginia, see Rhys Isaac, *The Transformation of Virginia, 1740-1790* (Chapel Hill, N.C., 1982); and A. G. Roeber, "Authority, Law, and Custom: The Rituals of Court Day in Tidewater Virginia, 1720-1750," *William and Mary Quarterly*, 3d Ser., XXXVII (1980), 29-52. Historians who have shown some attention to colonial public rituals include Carl Bridenbaugh, *Cities in the Wilderness: The First Century of Urban Life in America, 1625-1742* (New York, 1938); Bridenbaugh, *Cities in Revolt: Urban Life in America, 1743-1776* (New York, 1955); and Richard L. Bushman, *King and People in Provincial Massachusetts* (Chapel Hill, N.C., 1985).

9. For a summary of the widening gap, see the articles by Gloria L. Main, Lois Green Carr, and Lorena S. Walsh in "Toward a History of the Standard of Living in British North America: Forum," *WMQ*, 3d Ser., XLV (1988), 116-170; and Breen, "Empire of Goods," *Jour. Brit. Stud.*, XXV (1986), 467-499. Jack P. Greene has written extensively on the coalescence of elites. See, for example, *Pursuits of Happiness*, esp. 69-71, 92-99, 127-130, 147-149. For a fuller explication of this development, see Greene, "The Growth of Political Stability: An Interpretation of Political Development in the Anglo-American Colonies, 1660-1760," in John Parker and Carol Urness, eds. *The American Revolution: A Heritage of Change* (Minneapolis, Minn., 1975), 26-52. See also Bruce C. Daniels, ed., *Power and Status: Officeholding in Colonial America* (Middletown, Conn.,

1986); Thomas L. Purvis, *Proprietors, Patronage, and Paper Money: Legislative Politics in New Jersey, 1703-1776* (New Brunswick, N.J., 1986), 68, 95-96; David W. Jordan, "Political Stability and the Emergence of a Native Elite in Maryland," in Thad W. Tate and David L. Ammerman, eds., *The Chesapeake in the Seventeenth Century: Essays on Anglo-American Society* (Chapel Hill, N.C., 1979), 243-273, and Carole Shammas, "English-Born and Creole Elites in Turn-of-the-Century Virginia," 274-296. John M. Murrin suggests an American "growth of oligarchy," in "Political Development," in Greene and Pole, eds., *Colonial British America*, 442-445.

10. Albert Gallatin Mackey, *The History of Freemasonry in South Carolina, from Its Origin in the Year 1736 to the Present Time* ... (1861; Columbia, S.C., 1936), 15-16, 18-22; *Boston Gazette*, July 2, 1739.

11. Richardson Wright, "Masonic Contacts with the Early American Theater," *Am. Lodge Res. Trans.*, II (1936), 161-187. The first recorded musical concert in America was held in 1731 at the inn of Peter Pelham, later the master of a Boston lodge (O. G. Sonneck, *Early Concert-Life in America (1731-1800)* [Leipzig, 1907], 251). The Pennsylvania Masonic Hall dedicated in 1755 was used by the Dancing Assembly and later for a course on natural and experimental philosophy. The popular English performance, the *Lecture on Heads,* was performed in 1766 at the hall as well. Carl Bridenbaugh and Jessica Bridenbaugh, *Rebels and Gentlemen: Philadelphia in the Age of Franklin* (1942; London, 1962), 355; Kurt L. Garrett, "Palliative for Players: The Lecture on Heads," *PMHB*, CIII (1979), 168-169.

12. Richardson Wright, "Masonic Wares," *Am. Lodge Res. Trans.*, II (1934-1938), 544-545; Mackey, *History of Freemasonry in South Carolina*, 25; see also *South Carolina Gazette* (Charleston), Dec. 8, 1759, Jan. 7, 1764 (hereafter cited as *SCG*); Hunter Dickinson Farish, ed., *Journal and Letters of Philip Vickers Fithian, 1773-1774: A Plantation Tutor of the Old Dominion* (Williamsburg, Va., 1943), 93.

13. Smith, *Sermon Preached in Christ-Church* (1755), 9; Perez Morton, *An Oration; Delivered at the King's-Chapel in Boston, April 8, 1776, on the Re-Interment . . . of . . . Grand-Master Joseph Warren* ... (Boston, 1776), 8; Michael Smith, *A Sermon Preached in Christ-Church* ... (Newbern, N.C., 1756), 11.

14. William Brogden, *Freedom and Love: A Sermon . . . in the City of Annapolis . . . the 27th of December, 1749* (Annapolis, Md., 1750), 10, 12.

15. Samuel Clarke, *A Discourse concerning the Unchangeable Obligations of Natural Religion* ... (1706), in D. D. Raphael, ed., *British Moralists, 1650-1800,* 2 vols. (Oxford, 1969), I, 209-210. On Clarke's significance in America, see Norman Fiering, *Jonathan Edwards's Moral Thought and Its British Context* (Chapel Hill, N.C., 1981), 22-23, 91-92 n. 96, 377.

16. Fiering, *Jonathan Edwards's Moral Thought*, 126, argues that "in interpreting Edwards's thought one must always begin with his concept of love"; see 7-93, 283, 301-305, for discussions of Clarke's influence on Edwards. Charles Brockwell, *Brotherly Love Recommended* ... (Boston, 1750); Gilbert Tennent, *Brotherly Love Recommended* ... (Philadelphia, 1748), 3; Samuel Dunbar, *Brotherly Love, the Duty and Mark of Christians* ... (Boston, 1749); Joseph Morgan, *Love to Our Neighbors Recommended* ... (New London, Conn., 1727; 2d ed., Boston, 1749; 3d ed., Boston, 1749).

17. Thomas Pollen, *Universal Love: A Sermon Preached in Trinity-Church, at Newport, in Rhode-Island . . . on the 24th Day of June, 1757* (Boston, 1758), 13.

18. Smith, *Sermon Preached in Christ-Church* (1755), 12; Arthur Browne, *Universal Love Recommended . . . Boston . . . the 1st of October, 1755* (Boston, 1755), 8; Pollen, *Universal Love,* 13; Sydney V. James, *Colonial Rhode Island: A History* (New York,

1975), 186-228, 294-313, discusses religion and politics in 18th-century Rhode Island. Hermann Wellenreuther, "The Quest for Harmony in a Turbulent World: The Principle of 'Love and Unity' in Colonial Pennsylvania Politics," *PMHB*, CVII (1983), 537-576, suggests that "love and unity" were key values in 18th-century Pennsylvania politics, although he associates the ideals specifically with Quakers. Diversity in politics, religion, and national origins is a key theme in modern historiography. For a sampling, see Gary B. Nash, *The Urban Crucible: Social Change, Political Consciousness, and the Origins of the American Revolution* (Cambridge, Mass., 1979); Bernard Bailyn, *The Peopling of British North America: An Introduction* (New York, 1986); Sally Schwartz, *"A Mixed Multitude": The Struggle for Toleration in Colonial Pennsylvania* (New York, 1987). South Carolina was an exception to this general fragmentation, for reasons discussed in Robert M. Weir, " 'The Harmony We Were Famous For': An Interpretation of Pre-Revolutionary South Carolina Politics," *WMQ*, 3d Ser., XXVI (1969), 473-501.

19. Browne, *Universal Love Recommended* (1755), 11, 20.

20. Benjamin Franklin, *Benjamin Franklin's Autobiography,* ed. J. A. Leo Lemay and P. M. Zall (New York, 1986), 77-78.

21. On political divisions and the continued friendship of Franklin and Morris, see ibid., 129-130. Bernard Kusinitz, "Masonry and the Colonial Jews of Newport," *Rhode Island Jewish Historical Notes*, IX (November 1984), 180-185; Harvey Newton Shepard, *History of Saint John's Lodge of Boston . . .* (Boston, 1917), 47-48.

22. Browne, *Universal Love Recommended* (1755), 20. The samples of 138 Boston and 55 Philadelphia Modern Masons were compared with similar samples of Ancient Masons and with roughly contemporaneous tax lists (see Chapter 3). The list of Philadelphia Modern Masons in Wayne A. Huss, *The Master Builders: A History of the Grand Lodge of Free and Accepted Masons of Pennsylvania,* 3 vols. (Philadelphia, 1986-1989), I, 287-89, compiled independently, seriously underestimates the number of merchants in St. John's Lodge.

23. The other Masonic lodges in Philadelphia probably contained more men of lower social status (Huss, *Master Builders,* I, 30). The Boston sample contains members from all of the local lodges.

24. Bridenbaugh and Bridenbaugh, *Rebels and Gentlemen,* 200-202, discusses Smith.

25. J. T. D., "Notice of Ezekiel Price, Esquire, Member of the Historical Society," Massachusetts Historical Society, *Collections,* VIII (Boston, 1802), 85. As Thomas M. Doerflinger points out in *A Vigorous Spirit of Enterprise: Merchants and Economic Development in Revolutionary Philadelphia* (Chapel Hill, N.C., 1986), 11-58, merchants were a diverse group. For evidence that the Moderns were usually at the higher occupational levels, see the discussion of the Ancient lodges in Chapter 3.

26. Stephen Botein, "The Legal Profession in Colonial North America," in Wilfrid Prest, ed., *Lawyers in Early Modern Europe and America* (New York, 1981), 129-146, discusses the growing importance of lawyers. On Gridley's power, see John Adams, "Diary," *The Works of John Adams,* ed. Charles Francis Adams (Boston, 1850-1856), I, 54, II, 146.

27. This category is the most diverse of the four and the one that least reflects 18th-century usage. I have categorized these men in this way because my reading suggests a roughly equal social standing for most members of this group.

28. Huss, *Master Builders,* I, 30; Shepard, *History of Saint John's Lodge,* 15-16.

29. "The First Masonic Discourse Delivered in America," *Freemasons' Monthly*

Magazine, VIII (August 1849), 289–293 (quotations from 290–292) (hereafter cited as "First Masonic Discourse").

30. Ibid., 291; Shepard, *History of St. John's Lodge,* 47, transcribes the entries regarding Pelham's initiation.

31. For information on Charles's father, Peter Pelham, the shopkeeper, engraver, painter, and sometime innkeeper who later married John Singleton Copley's mother and served as master of Boston's Third Lodge, see *Dictionary of American Biography,* s.v. "Pelham, Peter"; Shepard, *History of St. John's Lodge,* 59.

32. Labaree et al., eds., *Papers of Franklin,* I, 232.

33. Massachusetts Grand Lodge, *Proceedings in Masonry,* 62.

34. Melvin Maynard Johnson, "Freemasonry in Massachusetts," in Robert Freke Gould, *Gould's History of Freemasonry throughout the World . . . ,* ed. Dudley Wright, 6 vols. (New York, 1936), V, 319, and Frederic E. Manson, "Freemasonry in Pennsylvania," VI, 155–156; "The Grammatical Construction of the Ritual," *Freemasons' Monthly Magazine,* XXV (1866), 100. Johnson, *Beginnings of Freemasonry in America,* 375–376, exaggerates only slightly in arguing "the actual ritual of the early days in America is an unfathomable mystery."

35. For these later changes, see Chapter 9.

36. Julius F. Sachse, *Old Masonic Lodges of Pennsylvania: "Moderns" and "Ancients," 1730–1800 . . . ,* 2 vols. (Philadelphia, 1912), I, 96 (see also 97); for practices in Philadelphia's Third Lodge that differed from early Boston practices, see Sachse, *OLMPa,* I, 1, 89; Melvin Maynard Johnson, *Freemasonry in America Prior to 1750 . . .* (Cambridge, Mass., 1917), 52–54; "First Masonic Discourse," 290.

37. Brogden, *Freedom and Love* (1750), 12; Letter from Boston First Lodge to Grand Master of English Grand Lodge, June 24, 1737, in Johnson, *Beginnings of Freemasonry in America,* 156–158.

38. On changes in the boundaries between public and private, see Chapter 9. The centrality of public activities and appearances in pre-19th-century society can be glimpsed in Richard Sennett, *The Fall of Public Man* (New York, 1977), 47–122.

39. America's growing trade and communication with England is traced imaginatively in Ian K. Steele, *The English Atlantic, 1675 to 1740: An Exploration of Communication and Community* (New York, 1986); see also Breen, "Empire of Goods," *Jour. Brit. Stud.,* XXV (1986), 467–499. The significance of English officials is suggested in John Clive and Bernard Bailyn, "England's Cultural Provinces: Scotland and America," *WMQ,* 3d Ser., XI (1954), 200–213. On buildings, see the perceptive comments of Bushman, "American High-Style and Vernacular Cultures," in Greene and Pole, eds., *Colonial British America,* 349–352, and *Refinement of America,* 130–180. On similar developments in the architecture of England's provincial towns, see Peter Borsay, *The English Urban Renaissance: Culture and Society in the Provincial Town, 1660–1770* (Oxford, 1989), 41–59, 101–113.

40. "First Masonic Discourse," 292–293; [William Smith], *Some Thoughts on Education* (New York, 1752), 12, 11. The fullest account of these larger changes is Bushman, "American High-Style and Vernacular Cultures," in Greene and Pole, eds., *Colonial British America,* and *Refinement of America,* 3–203. Isaac, *Transformation of Virginia,* provides a rich anthropological reading of genteel practices, although he neglects the significance of both sympathy and condescension, an issue highlighted by Stow Persons, *The Decline of American Gentility* (New York, 1973), 29–36, esp. 35–36. John F. Kasson, *Rudeness and Civility: Manners in Nineteenth-Century Urban America* (New York, 1990), 1–33, suggests, unlike the argument here, that 18th-century manners and society became less differentiated by class.

41. *Franklin Bi-centenary*, 106–110.

42. Ibid., 110–114; also reprinted in Labaree, *Papers of Franklin*, II, 198–202.

43. Franklin, *Autobiography*, ed. Lemay and Zall, 44–45.

44. Ibid., 51.

45. [Smith], *Some Thoughts on Education* (1752), 6, 11–12, 13, 14.

46. *SCG*, Dec. 27, 1738. On clubs, see Bridenbaugh, *Cities in the Wilderness*, 275, 436–437, 440–441; Daniel R. Gilbert, "Patterns of Organization and Membership in Colonial Philadelphia Club Life, 1725–1785" (Ph.D. diss., University of Pennsylvania, 1952). See also Bushman, "American High-Style and Vernacular Cultures," in Greene and Pole, eds., *Colonial British America*, 352, 358, on the importance of the "select company" in genteel practices; in *Refinement of America*, he gives almost no attention to clubs. Important discussions of clubs in later periods are Richard D. Brown, "The Emergence of Urban Society in Rural Massachusetts, 1760–1820," *JAH*, LXI (1974–1975), 29–51; Don H. Doyle, "The Social Functions of Voluntary Associations in a Nineteenth-Century American Town," *Social Science History*, I (1977), 333–356; and Doyle, *The Social Order of a Frontier Community: Jacksonville, Illinois, 1825–1870* (Urbana, Ill., 1978), 178–193. On Charleston social life, see Hennig Cohen, *The South Carolina Gazette, 1732–1775* (Columbia, S.C., 1953); Frederick P. Bowes, *The Culture of Early Charleston* (Chapel Hill, N.C., 1942).

47. *SCG*, Dec. 9 1732; James H. Easterby, *History of the St. Andrew's Society of Charleston, South Carolina, 1729–1929* (Charleston, S.C., 1929).

48. The German society continued the decreasing particularism visible in the St. Andrew's and South Carolina Societies; originally limited only to those of German parents and language, it soon became open to others. George J. Gongaware, comp., *The History of the German Friendly Society of Charleston, South Carolina, 1766–1916* (Richmond, Va., 1935); *SCG*, Dec. 17, 1735; *Rules of the Fellowship Society . . . 1762* (Charleston, S.C., 1774).

49. *SCG*, Mar. 4, 1732, Apr. 14, 1733, Aug. 14, 1749, Jan. 8, 1750; Mark A. De Wolfe Howe, ed., "Journal of Josiah Quincy, Jr., 1773," Massachusetts Historical Society, *Proceedings*, XLIX (1915–1916), 424–481.

50. *SCG*, Mar. 17, 1757. See *Rules of the St. Coecilia Society* (Charleston, S.C., 1774); Howe, "Journal of Josiah Quincy," MHS, *Proceedings*, XLIX (1915–1916), 442.

51. *SCG*, Oct. 15, 22, 1753, Mar. 14, 1754.

52. The only references to the group, beyond a stray reference in a letter, are newspaper announcements of their festivals. See Eliza Lucas to Miss Bartlett (ca. March 1742), in Elise Pinckney, ed., *The Letterbook of Eliza Lucas Pinckney, 1739–1762* (Chapel Hill, N.C., 1972), 32; *SCG*, Mar. 26, Sept. 5, 19, 1741, Apr. 3, 1742, Mar. 14, 1743, Mar. 3, 1744; *Boston Weekly News-Letter*, Aug. 2, 1744, reprints a London piece about the Scald Miserable Masons, a mock Masonic group, that also cites the Ubiquarians.

53. Bridenbaugh, *Cities in Revolt*, 163, cites a Boston "Society of Callicoes"—they did "no business at all"—who held a charter from London.

54. John Gordon, *Brotherly Love Explain'd and Enforc'd* (Annapolis, Md., 1750), 12.

55. Allen D. Candler, comp., *The Colonial Records of the State of Georgia* (Atlanta, 1904–1916), V, 179, XX, 141.

56. Massachusetts Grand Lodge, *Proceedings in Masonry*, 44, 160–161 (the 134 Freemasons present collected £28 1s. 4d.); Manson, "Freemasonry in Pennsylvania," in Gould, *Gould's History of Freemasonry*, ed. Wright, VI, 159.

57. Mackey, *History of Freemasonry in South Carolina*, 17; Ossian Lang, "Freemasonry in New York," in Gould, *Gould's History of Freemasonry*, ed. Wright, VI, 42.

58. Shepard, *History of Saint John's Lodge*, 40; Sachse, *OMLPa*, I, 83, 84, 85–86, 97.

59. *Franklin Bi-centenary,* 69n; Shepard, *History of Saint John's Lodge,* 12–13. Philadelphia's Third Lodge had a similar rule about spending (Sachse, *OMLPa,* I, 91). Hamill, *The Craft,* 80, suggests that pre-1816 English lodges made no distinction between meeting and convivial time.

60. Massachusetts Grand Lodge, *Proceedings in Masonry,* 2, 160. The Reverend John Wesley, although not known to be a Mason, attended a Masonic dinner in Savannah in 1737. He had previously preached a sermon to the brothers. Harold E. Davis, *The Fledgling Province: Social and Cultural Life in Colonial Georgia, 1733–1776* (Chapel Hill, N.C., 1976), 172.

61. *Franklin Bi-centenary,* 145; Mackey, *History of Freemasonry in South Carolina,* 35, 42 (see also 16).

62. "First Masonic Discourse," 292.

63. On the role of kinship ties in commerce, see Bernard Bailyn, *The New England Merchants in the Seventeenth Century* (1955; New York, 1964), 79–80, 87–91; and W. T. Baxter, *The House of Hancock: Business in Boston, 1724–1775* (New York, 1965), 197–202. For an attempt to assess actual brotherly relations, see Daniel Blake Smith, *Inside the Great House: Planter Family Life in Eighteenth-Century Chesapeake Society* (Ithaca, N.Y., 1980), 178–189. For other influential studies of 18th-century family life, see Jay Fliegelman, *Prodigals and Pilgrims: The American Revolution against Patriarchal Authority, 1750–1800* (Cambridge, 1982); and Lawrence Stone, *The Family, Sex, and Marriage in England, 1500–1800* (New York, 1977), esp. 221–269. Rather surprisingly, Fliegelman's discussion of the attack on patriarchal power does not consider the idea of brotherhood. Wilson Carey McWilliams, *The Idea of Fraternity in America* (Berkeley, Calif., 1973), considers social science and political theory rather than 18th-century practice and meanings.

64. The classic study of the importance of patronage in the 18th-century world is Lewis Namier, *The Structure of Politics at the Accession of George III,* 2d ed. (London, 1957). For discussions of patronage in early American politics, see Bernard Bailyn, *The Origins of American Politics* (New York, 1968); Robert Zemsky, *Merchants, Farmers, and River Gods: An Essay on Eighteenth-Century American Politics* (Boston, 1971), 52–62; and Stanley Nider Katz, *Newcastle's New York: Anglo-American Politics, 1732–1753* (Cambridge, Mass., 1968). For details of Allen's career, see Norman Sonny Cohen, "William Allen: Chief Justice of Pennsylvania, 1704–1780" (Ph.D. diss., University of California, Berkeley, 1966); *DAB,* s.v. "Allen, William"; and Bridenbaugh and Bridenbaugh, *Rebels and Gentlemen,* 184–191.

65. Franklin to Smith, May 3, 1753, in Labaree et al., eds., *Papers of Franklin,* IV, 475.

66. [William Smith], *An Answer to Mr. Franklin's Remarks, on a Late Protest* (Philadelphia, 1764), 15; Benjamin Franklin, *The Autobiography of Benjamin Franklin: A Genetic Text,* ed. J. A. Leo Lemay and P. M. Zall (Knoxville, Tenn., 1981), 1. Lemay and Zall follow this change through the intervening French translations (lvi). On Allen's later patronage of Benjamin West, in conjunction with James Hamilton, see E. P. Richardson, "West's Voyage to Italy, 1760, and William Allen," *PMHB,* CII (1978), 3–26.

67. Franklin, *Autobiography,* ed. Lemay and Zall, 51, 84.

68. Ibid., 100; Benjamin Franklin to Peter Collinson, May 21, 1751, in Labaree et al., ed., *Papers of Franklin,* IV, 134. On Franklin's subsequent use of post office patronage to aid his family and friends, see Gordon S. Wood, *The Radicalism of the American Revolution* (New York, 1992), 77.

69. Smith, *Sermon Preached in Christ-Church* (1755), 10.

70. *Franklin Bi-centenary,* 125–128; Sachse, *OMLPa,* I, 52–53.

71. Labaree et al., eds., *Papers of Franklin*, II, 202–204. An earlier draft is printed on 202–203n. Presumably Franklin's parents learned of the incident from articles in Boston papers; see II, 204 n.7.

72. Ibid., II, 204.

73. Mackey, *History of Freemasonry in South Carolina*, 21–25. Mackey suggests this hiatus might only have been the result of a 1741 regulation by the grand lodge of England that forbade publication of lodge proceedings or names of attendees, but no evidence has survived about any Masonic activity at all in Charleston during this period. On rival Masonic groups in the years just before the Revolution, see Chapter 3.

74. Although he belonged to a different Masonic faction (see Chapter 3), George Washington shows a similar attitude. Outside of official statements and replies to Masonic invitations, Washington seems to have mentioned the fraternity in personal correspondence only once. Another letter, Daniel Campbell to George Washington, June 28, 1754, also suggests that Washington referred to the lodge in a previous, undiscovered letter. W. W. Abbot et al., eds., *The Papers of George Washington*, Colonial Series, I, *1748–August 1755* (Charlottesville, Va., 1983), 151–152.

75. Anne Rowe Cunningham, ed., *Letters and Diary of John Rowe, Boston Merchant, 1759–1762, 1764–1779* (Boston, 1903), 14, 16, 34–37, 133, 148, 174, 176–177, 275 (hereafter cited as Rowe, *Diary*).

76. Ibid., 133–136.

77. James Thomas Flexner, *George Washington: The Forge of Experience (1732–1775)* (Boston, 1965), 251.

78. Bonfires were lit and houses illuminated for the occasion in Charleston (*SCG*, Nov. 16, 1753). In Savannah, the court, two of whose three members were Masons, marched from the Assembly Room with the court officers to hear a discourse on law and justice. *Georgia Gazette* (Savannah), July 8, 1767.

79. Rowe, *Diary*, 141–142 (Gridley), 231 (Inman), 287 (Box). Gridley's pallbearers included the lieutenant governor and James Otis; the coffin was followed by the family; the "Coaches, Chariots, and Chaises" of the marchers finished the procession. Public display at funerals was not new; see M. Halsey Thomas, ed., *The Diary of Samuel Sewall, 1674–1729*, 2 vols. (New York, 1973), where such events are a regular activity. On genteel drinking practices, see Peter Thompson, " 'The Friendly Glass': Drink and Gentility in Colonial Philadelphia," *PMHB*, CXIII (1989), 549–573.

80. Flexner, *Washington*, 268; Rowe, *Diary*, 244. As Chapter 3 notes, Revere was also a Mason, but a member of a less socially prominent faction.

81. Rowe, *Diary*, 116, 169; Directors of the Library Company to John Penn, Aug. 8, 1738, in Labaree et al., eds., *Papers of Franklin*, II, 207. Mackey, *History of Freemasonry in South Carolina*, 4–16, includes all the known participants in Charleston Masonry during the 1730s.

82. "First Masonic Discourse," 293; *Boston Evening-Post*, Jan. 7, 1750/1; Massachusetts Grand Lodge, *Proceedings in Masonry*, 14, 15; [Joseph Green], *The Grand Arcanum Detected* . . . (Boston, 1755); Smith, *Sermon Preached in Christ-Church* (1755), 15. On Green's Masonic satires, see David S. Shields, "Clio Mocks the Masons: Joseph Green's Anti-Masonic Satire," in J. A. Leo Lemay, ed., *Deism, Masonry, and the Enlightenment: Essays Honoring Alfred Owen Aldridge* (Newark, Del., 1987), 109–126. For further discussion of Green, see Shields, *Oracles of Empire: Poetry, Politics, and Commerce in British America, 1690–1750* (Chicago, 1990), 131–136, 188–191.

83. Joseph Green, *Entertainment for a Winter's Evening* . . . (Boston, 1750). A second edition appeared the same year, and the piece was reprinted again in 1795.

84. Ibid., 8–9, 11.

85. Ibid., 14.
86. Ibid., 15.
87. Ibid., 12, 15.

Chapter Three

1. For Franklin's funeral and the fraternity, see Pennsylvania Grand Lodge, *Proceedings of the Right Worshipful Grand Lodge of . . . Pennsylvania . . . Bi-centenary of the Birth of . . . Benjamin Franklin . . .* (Philadelphia, 1906), 167-169; and *Pennsylvania Gazette* (Philadelphia), Apr. 21, 1790. The grand lodge's failure to remark Franklin's death contrasts markedly with its extensive commemoration of George Washington — an Ancient Mason — 10 years later. Norris S. Barratt and Julius F. Sachse, *Freemasonry in Pennsylvania, 1727-1907, as Shown by the Records of Lodge No. 2, F. and A.M. of Philadelphia from the Year A.L. 5757, A.D. 1757*, 3 vols. (Philadelphia, 1908-1910), II, 167, 252-256, 258-270.

2. Neither historians of Boston nor historians of the fraternity itself note the significance of these changes. See Esther Forbes, *Paul Revere and the World He Lived In* (Boston, 1942), 59; Alfred F. Young, "George Robert Twelves Hewes (1742-1840): A Boston Shoemaker and the Memory of the American Revolution," *William and Mary Quarterly*, 3d Ser., XXXVIII (1981), 584; Young, "English Plebeian Culture and Eighteenth-Century American Radicalism," in Margaret Jacob and James Jacob, eds., *The Origins of Anglo-American Radicalism* (London, 1984), 203; Dorothy Ann Lipson, *Freemasonry in Federalist Connecticut* (Princeton, N.J., 1977), 49-50 (suggesting some social distinctions); Wayne Huss, *The Master Builders: A History of the Grand Lodge of Free and Accepted Masons of Pennsylvania*, 3 vols. (Philadelphia, 1986-1989), I, 27-28, 32-35. Huss's dissertation, "Pennsylvania Freemasonry: An Intellectual and Social Analysis, 1727-1826" (Ph.D. diss., Temple University, 1984), argues that Pennsylvania Freemasonry was made up of "men from all occupations, all social classes, all wealth levels and all nationalities" (9-10). His analysis, however, does not include the pre-Revolutionary Ancient lodges, and his subsequent history of the grand lodge, while continuing to suggest the fraternity's wide social range, narrows this broad claim (*Master Builders*, I, 30, 53).

3. On artisans in the Revolutionary era, see Gary B. Nash, "Artisans and Politics in Eighteenth-Century Philadelphia," in Jacob and Jacob, eds., *Origins of Anglo-American Radicalism*, 162-182; Charles S. Olton, *Artisans for Independence: Philadelphia Mechanics and the American Revolution* (Syracuse, N.Y., 1975), 33-34; and Eric Foner, *Tom Paine and Revolutionary America* (New York, 1976). On the rise of areas outside the principal seaports, see Gregory H. Nobles, "Breaking into the Backcountry: New Approaches to the Early American Frontier, 1750-1800," *WMQ*, 3d Ser., XLVI (1989), 641-670; D. W. Meinig, *The Shaping of America: A Geographical Perspective on Five Hundred Years of History*, I, *Atlantic America, 1492-1800* (New Haven, Conn., 1986), 288-295; and Lois Kimball Mathews, *The Expansion of New England: The Spread of New England Settlement and Institutions to the Mississippi River, 1620-1865* (Boston, 1909), 108-170. On the South, see, especially, Carville Earle and Ronald Hoffman, "Staple Crops and Urban Development in the Eighteenth-Century South," *Perspectives in American History*, X (1976), 7-78.

4. Barratt and Sachse, *Freemasonry in Pennsylvania*, I, 20.

5. Ibid.

6. Robert Freke Gould, *The History of Freemasonry: Its Antiquities, Symbols, Constitutions, Customs . . .* , 4 vols. (London, 1906), III, 208 (hereafter cited as Gould, *History of Freemasonry* [1906]). See also J. R. Clarke, "The Formation," part 2, "1751 to 1813," in English Grand Lodge, *Grand Lodge, 1717-1967* (Oxford, 1967), 92-105; T. O. Haunch, "The Formation," part 1, "1717 to 1751," 77-78, discusses the 1739 ritual. Some Masonic historians now deny these changes were ever made, suggesting that the English and Irish grand lodges might have diverged in organizing their third-degree ceremonies. See Colin Dyer, *William Preston and His Work* (Shepperton, Middlesex, 1987), 39-41. Henry Wilson Coil, *Freemasonry through Six Centuries,* 2 vols. (Richmond, Va., 1967-1968), II, 17-18, summarizes the major ritual and organizational differences between the Ancients and Moderns.

7. Clarke, "The Formation," part 2, "1751 to 1813," in *Grand Lodge, 1717-1967,* 85-89. For statistics, see T. M. Carter, "Provincial Warrants," part 1, *Ars Quotuor Coronatorum,* XLI (1929), 106. Grand masters in the 1740s attempted to halt the development of new lodges while older ones were languishing, perhaps slowing the spread of Masonry by preventing circles of acquaintances from forming their own lodges.

8. Gould, *History of Freemasonry* (1906), III, 186; Coil, *Freemasonry through Six Centuries,* II, 10.

9. Coil, *Freemasonry through Six Centuries,* II, 6; John Hamill, *The Craft: A History of English Freemasonry* (London, 1986), 50.

10. Gould, *History of Freemasonry* (1906), III, 188, 191-192. Clarke, "The Formation," part 2, "1751 to 1813," in *Grand Lodge, 1717-1967,* 92-93, discusses the social standing of the English Ancients. The social history of English Freemasonry in general awaits a serious study.

11. Clarke, "The Formation," part 2, "1751 to 1813," in *Grand Lodge, 1717-1967,* 93.

12. Gould, *History of Freemasonry* (1906), III, 190. The history of British Masonry during the next half-century is virtually uncharted territory. The main outlines of growth can be traced in Carter, "Provincial Warrants," part 1, *AQC,* XLI (1929), 43-121. By 1813, the Ancient grand lodge had become so influential that it was able to merge with the Moderns (always the larger body) on terms of equality. The Ancients, after a slow period between 1765 and 1785, expanded quickly afterwards, setting the stage for the union. The Moderns similarly recovered from the downturn of the 1740s, growing most notably in the provinces after 1760. On English Freemasonry, see also John Money, "The Masonic Moment: or, Ritual, Replica, and Credit: John Wilkes, the Macaroni Parson, and the Making of the Middle-Class Mind," *Journal of British Studies,* XXXII (1993), 358-395; Money, "Freemasonry and the Fabric of Loyalism in Hanoverian England," in Eckhart Helmuth, ed., *The Transformation of Political Culture: England and Germany in the Late Eighteenth Century* (London, 1990), 235-271; Money, *Experience and Identity: Birmingham and the West Midlands, 1760-1800* (Montreal, 1977), 136-140; Margaret C. Jacob, *Living the Enlightenment: Freemasonry and Politics in Eighteenth-Century Europe* (New York, 1991), 52-72; and John Brewer, "Commercialization and Politics," in Neil McKendrick, John Brewer, and J. H. Plumb, *The Birth of a Consumer Society: The Commercialization of Eighteenth-Century England* (Bloomington, Ind., 1982), 217-224.

13. Charles Burnes of Otway's Regiment was a member of No. 2 (Barratt and Sachse, *Freemasonry in Pennsylvania,* I, 26). On Blackwood: ibid., 30. The minutes never refer to Blackwood by rank, but the later partial erasure of the passage may also suggest a military connection.

14. Massachusetts Grand Lodge, *Proceedings in Masonry: St. John's Grand Lodge,*

1733-1792; Massachusetts Grand Lodge, 1769-1792 . . . (Boston, 1895), esp. 54–55, 104–106. *The Lodge of St. Andrew, and the Massachusetts Grand Lodge* . . . *5756-5769* (Boston, 1870), contains a great deal of scattered information on the new Boston group.

15. For the later history of the Boston Moderns, see Harvey Newton Shepard, *History of Saint John's Lodge of Boston* . . . (Boston, 1917); and Melvin M. Johnson, "St. John's Grand Lodge, 1775-1787," in Massachusetts Grand Lodge, *Proceedings of the Most Worshipful Grand Lodge* . . . *of Massachusetts for the Year 1931* (Boston, 1932), 189–201. A close reading of the documents printed by Johnson suggests that he considerably exaggerates the organizational health of the Moderns during this period. On loyalism, see Chapter 4.

16. George Brooks, the Philadelphia Ancient master, is identified in the 1756 Philadelphia valuation (Hannah Benner Roach, "Taxables in the City of Philadelphia, 1756," *Pennsylvania Genealogical Magazine,* XXII [1961], 9–41) and in Barratt and Sachse, *Freemasonry in Pennsylvania,* I, 11 n. 3. Gary B. Nash, *The Urban Crucible: Social Change, Political Consciousness, and the Origins of the American Revolution* (Cambridge, Mass., 1979), 400, gives probate data for Philadelphia that suggest a similar ranking for Brooks's estate at his death. Robert Francis Seybolt, *The Town Officials of Colonial Boston, 1634-1775* (Cambridge, Mass., 1939), provides information on public officeholding in that city.

17. John Hancock first attended the lodge Sept. 9, 1762, and last appears in the minutes Feb. 8, 1764; see the manuscript minutes of the lodge on microfilm at the Grand Lodge of Massachusetts library in Boston; Hancock never signed any of the various constitutions of the lodge scattered through the minutes, a formal requirement of membership (although one that was often ignored). This neglect perhaps explains his absence from the lodge's later membership roster. For information on Warren, see John Cary, *Joseph Warren: Physician, Politician, Patriot* (Urbana, Ill., 1961), 56–57, and the lodge minutes.

18. The Massachusetts valuations are indexed in Bettye Hobbs Pruitt, ed., *Massachusetts Tax Valuation List of 1771* (Boston, 1978). The number of merchants in Table 2 perhaps overstates their importance in occupational composition of St. Andrew's. Of the 32, at least 2 lived in the West Indies. Three more are identified by John W. Tyler, *Smugglers and Patriots: Boston Merchants and the Advent of the American Revolution* (Boston, 1986), as merchants, but listed themselves in 1762 as artisans (see *The Lodge of St. Andrew,* 241-242). Their stated occupations were japaner and painter, stationer and bookbinder, and ropemaker.

19. On mechanics, see also Carl Bridenbaugh, *The Colonial Craftsman* (Chicago, 1961). Edith J. Steblecki, *Paul Revere and Freemasonry* ([Boston], 1985), is a good study of Revere's relationship to the fraternity and is especially valuable on the relationship between his business and his Masonic membership.

20. Only about 37% (23 of 65) of the Philadelphia Ancients could be found on the 1756 list, in itself an indication of the lower status of the group.

21. David P. McKay and Richard Crawford, *William Billings of Boston: Eighteenth-Century Composer* (Princeton, N.J., 1975), 124-131.

22. Franklin used the term "the middling sort" in "Plain Truth" (1747), in Leonard W. Labaree et al., eds., *The Papers of Benjamin Franklin* (New Haven, Conn., 1959–), III, 199, 201. Alexander Graydon, *Memoirs of His Own Time: With Reminiscences of the Men and Events of the Revolution,* ed. John Stockton Littell (1811; Philadelphia, 1846), 40 (see also 80); McKay and Crawford, *William Billings,* 128. P. J. Corfield, "Class by Name and Number in Eighteenth-Century Britain," *History,* LXXII (1987),

38–61, suggests that 18th-century British writing—particularly after midcentury— shows a growing confusion about the terminology of social divisions. Although Corfield finds a wide variety of usage, she argues that a two-part model of society was losing ground, particularly after midcentury, to a three-part model. This formulation seems a better description of American practices than the common view that colonial Americans nearly always divided their society into three. See Jackson Turner Main, *The Social Structure of Revolutionary America* (Princeton, N.J., 1965), 221–239; and compare Carl Bridenbaugh, *Cities in Revolt: Urban Life in America, 1743–1776* (New York, 1955), 136, 146, with 283, 284.

23. McKay and Crawford, *Billings,* 33; Forbes, *Paul Revere and the World He Lived In,* 27–29; Annie Russell Marble, *From 'Prentice to Patron: The Life Story of Isaiah Thomas* (New York, 1935), 8–17, 235; Isaiah Thomas, *Three Autobiographical Fragments* (Worcester, Mass., 1962), 19–20. A further indication of the different level of cosmopolitan experience can be seen in the Ancients' attempts to get charters from Britain. The Boston Ancients applied to the Scottish grand lodge in 1754 and received their charter six years later after a bizarre series of errors that included the near seizure of a box containing payment—the Bostonians lacked a Scottish connection to draw money upon—and the Scottish attempt to send the document to "Boston, Virginia" (Massachusetts Grand Lodge, *Proceedings in Masonry,* 438–439). In Philadelphia, a ship's captain belonging to a Modern lodge refused to carry the draft when he discovered its purpose; it took six months before the brothers could find someone else to take it to England.

24. McKay and Crawford, *William Billings,* 47, 53, 127; Hans Nathan, *William Billings: Data and Documents* (Detroit, Mich., 1976), 17, where Billings, in his first appearance in print, contrasts singing with instrumental music, "which would serve those whose Leisure and Purse can afford the Expence of procuring them."

25. Nathan, *Billings: Data and Documents,* 21; McKay and Crawford, *William Billings,* 44–45; Kenneth Silverman, *A Cultural History of the American Revolution: Painting, Music, Literature, and the Theatre* . . . (New York, 1976), 44–45.

26. Forbes, *Paul Revere and the World He Lived In,* 109, 214; Marble, *From 'Prentice to Patron,* 65–66, 72; William Coolidge Lane, "The Printer of the Harvard Theses of 1771," Colonial Society of Massachusetts, *Publications,* XXVI, *Transactions, 1924–1926* (Boston, 1927), 1–15; Isaiah Thomas, *The History of Printing in America,* ed. Marcus A. McCorison (New York, 1970), 265.

27. Rhys Isaac, "Evangelical Revolt: The Nature of the Baptists' Challenge to the Traditional Order in Virginia, 1765 to 1775," *WMQ,* 3d Ser., XXXI (1974), 345–368; Massachusetts Grand Lodge, *Proceedings in Masonry,* 449.

28. *Lodge of St. Andrew,* 196–197; Massachusetts Grand Lodge, *Proceedings in Masonry,* 239–242, 454; Barratt and Sachse, *Freemasonry in Pennsylvania,* I, 134–135; William Smith, *A Sermon Preached in Christ-Church, Philadelphia . . . December 28, 1778* (Philadelphia, 1779), 36. Smith switched allegiance to the Ancient grand lodge after the Modern's decline.

29. Julius F. Sachse, *Old Masonic Lodges of Pennsylvania: "Moderns" and "Ancients," 1730–1800* . . . , 2 vols. (Philadelphia, 1912), I, 250 (hereafter cited as Sachse, *OMLPa*).

30. "Inland" or "interior" elites, the term I use for these brothers in villages or cities outside the earlier principal ports, is clearly not an ideal term. Many of the new Ancient lodges, especially after the Revolution, were away from the seaboard. But such pre-Revolutionary Ancient lodges as Port Royal and Fredericksburg, Virginia, or Gloucester, Massachusetts, were closely tied to the Atlantic. Nor could these loca-

tions be called part of the backcountry or the frontier. The area around Port Royal and Fredericksburg had been settled since the early 18th century. A better term might be "provincial" elites, since these groups were clearly secondary leadership groups compared to the urban principal people. But "provincial" is confusing, since the term can be used for all parts of the colonies as well as for leaders on the provincial or colony-wide level. In this sense, these secondary towns were the provinces of the provinces.

31. R. Walter Coakley, "The Two James Hunters of Fredericksburg: Patriots among the Virginia Scotch Merchants," *Virginia Magazine of History and Biography*, LVI (1948), 3–21, tracing a significant local firm; Oscar H. Darter, *Colonial Fredericksburg and Neighborhood in Perspective* (New York, 1957), esp. 62. See also John W. Reps, *Tidewater Towns: City Planning in Colonial Virginia and Maryland* (Williamsburg, Va., 1972), 198–202, 213. "Port Royal," recalled the Reverend Jonathan Boucher, who lived there in the 1750s, "was inhabited by factors from Scotland and their dependents" (Marshall Wingfield, *A History of Caroline County, Virginia from Its Formation in 1727 to 1924* [Richmond, Va., 1924], 17).

32. Gordon S. Wood, *The Radicalism of the American Revolution* (New York, 1992), 124–145, dramatizes some of the social meanings of this expansion. Joseph A. Ernst and H. Roy Merrens, " 'Camden's Turrets Pierce the Skies!': The Urban Process in the Southern Colonies during the Eighteenth Century," *WMQ*, 3d Ser., XXX (1973), 568–571, discuss Virginia's urban places.

33. Ronald E. Heaton and James R. Case, *The Lodge at Fredericksburgh: A Digest of the Early Records* (Silver Spring, Md., 1981).

34. Ibid., 84.

35. This group, founded in 1766, met near Valley Forge (Sachse, *OMLPa*, I, 211–212).

36. The list included 62 people; it "reads like 'who is who' in Caroline for the decade 1752–62," states T. E. Campbell, *Colonial Caroline: A History of Caroline County, Virginia* (Richmond, Va., 1954), 145, 365. On Gloucester: Massachusetts Grand Lodge, *Proceedings in Masonry*, 228; Pruitt, *Massachusetts Tax Valuation List of 1771*. On the Sargent family and its relationship to Boston, see Christine Leigh Heyrman, *Commerce and Culture: The Maritime Communities of Colonial Massachusetts, 1690–1750* (New York, 1984), 163–166.

37. Sachse, *OMLPa*, I, 126–130. Lodges chartered by Massachusetts grand lodges before the merger are listed in Massachusetts Grand Lodge, *Proceedings in Masonry*, 482–486.

38. Peter Oliver, *Peter Oliver's Origin and Progress of the American Rebellion: A Tory View* (1781), ed. Douglass Adair and John A. Schutz (San Marino, Calif., 1961), 27; Carl Bridenbaugh, ed., *Gentleman's Progress: The Itinerarium of Dr. Alexander Hamilton, 1744* (Pittsburgh, 1992), 31.

39. Oliver, *Peter Oliver's Origin and Progress,* ed. Adair and Schutz, 128; entry for Oct. 24, 1758, in L. H. Butterfield et al., eds., *Diary and Autobiography of John Adams* (Cambridge, Mass., 1961), I, 54.

40. On Smith: Sachse, *OMLPa*, I, 200–202. Neither Jones nor Remington appears afterward in the *Pennsylvania Gazette* in any clear reference to Philadelphia. Jones had advertised and called in debts in the newspaper a number of times before. For earlier references, see *Pennsylvania Gazette*, Feb. 25, 1729, Feb. 3, 1730, Feb. 6, 1732, Feb. 13, 1734, May 19, 1737 (the last advertises "speedy relief" from "the Venereal Disease"). Jones served as the steward for the 1729 feast of the Ancient Bretons (Mar. 4, 1729). An Evan Jones was elected a Philadelphia County assessor for a number of

years (Oct. 7, 1742, Oct. 6, 1743, Oct. 4, 1744, Oct. 3, 1745), and an Evan Jones was later a Bucks County coroner and innkeeper (Oct. 3, 1751, Nov. 10, 1757, July 29, 1762; see also George W. Neible, comp., "Account of Servants Bound and Assigned before James Hamilton, Mayor of Philadelphia," *Pennsylvania Magazine of History and Biography,* XXXII [1908], 243). Remington does not appear in the *Pennsylvania Gazette* at all, but see "Extracts from Minutes of Proceedings of New Jersey Courts," *PMHB,* XXXVII (1913), 361-368, where a John Remington is noted in Cumberland County, New Jersey. The experience of Edward Shippen III suggests a similar use of the country as an escape. When his new bride's previous husband appeared—he had been previously thought dead—the couple moved to Lancaster rather than face the scandal in Philadelphia. Randolph Shipley Klein, *Portrait of an Early American Family: The Shippens of Pennsylvania across Five Generations* (Philadelphia, 1975), 70-72.

41. Darter, *Colonial Fredericksburg,* 99-100, 113; Nash, *Urban Crucible,* 409-411; Klein, *Portrait of an Early American Family,* 72. See also Allan Kulikoff, *Tobacco and Slaves: The Development of Southern Cultures in the Chesapeake, 1680-1800* (Chapel Hill, N.C., 1986), maps 6, 7 (pp. 126, 127).

42. Campbell, *Colonial Caroline,* 206, 227; Douglas Southall Freeman, *George Washington: A Biography,* I, *Young Washington* (New York, 1948), 234 (266-268 incorrectly dates Washington's initiation); Heaton and Case, *Lodge at Fredericksburgh,* 91.

43. Sachse, *OMLPa,* I, 211-212; Heaton and Case, *Lodge at Fredericksburgh,* 3.

44. Carl Bridenbaugh, *Myths and Realities: Societies of the Colonial South* (1952; New York, 1971), 146; Lorenzo Sabine, *Biographical Sketches of Loyalists of the American Revolution . . . ,* 2 vols. (1864; Port Washington, N.Y., 1966), I, 508.

45. Wingfield, *History of Caroline County,* 103; Coakley, "The Two James Hunters of Fredericksburg," *VMHB,* LVI (1948), 3-21.

46. On Scottish commerce in the Chesapeake, see J. H. Soltow, "Scottish Traders in Virginia, 1750-1775," *Economic History Review,* 2d Ser., XII (1959), 83-98; Jacob M. Price, "The Rise of Glasgow in the Chesapeake Tobacco Trade, 1707-1775," *WMQ,* 3d Ser., XI (1954), 179-199.

47. William Moseley Brown, *Freemasonry in Virginia (1733-1936)* (Richmond, Va., 1936), photograph facing 80; George Weedon to James Hunter, Sept. 9, 1783, University of Virginia MSS, Alderman Library, University of Virginia, Charlottesville; Wingfield, *History of Caroline County,* 103. Alexandria Lodge also assisted in the ceremony (F. L. Brockett, *The Lodge of Washington: A History of the Alexandria Washington Lodge, No. 22 . . . 1783-1876* [Alexandria, Va., 1876], 44).

48. William Moseley Brown, *Freemasonry in Winchester, Virginia, 1768-1948* (Staunton, Va., 1947), 27-28, 44; Sachse, *OMLPa,* I, 283-284.

49. Forbes, *Paul Revere and the World He Lived In,* 398-399; Massachusetts Grand Lodge, *Proceedings of the Most Worshipful Grand Lodge . . . of Massachusetts . . . 1792-1815* (Boston, 1905), 75; *Constitutions of the Ancient and Honorable Fraternity of Free and Accepted Masons,* 2d ed. (Worcester, Mass., 1798), 223, 224-226. On Adams and music, see McKay and Crawford, *William Billings,* 66-67.

50. *Massachusetts Spy* (Boston), Jan. 16, 1772.

51. Gordon S. Wood, *The Creation of the American Republic, 1776-1787* (Chapel Hill, N.C., 1969), 170-172; Rosemarie Zagarri, "Representation and the Removal of State Capitals, 1776-1812," *Journal of American History,* LXXIV (1987-1988), 1239-1256. For a sensitive study of the South Carolina shift, see Jerome J. Nadelhaft, *The Disorders of War: The Revolution in South Carolina* (Orono, Maine, 1981), 136-138, 211.

52. Isaiah Thomas, *An Oration: Delivered in . . . Lancaster . . . Massachusetts, on . . .*

the Twenty-fourth of June, 1779 . . . (Worcester, Mass., 1781), 6, 7–8. On the appeal of these republican ideas to later artisans, see the works discussed in Daniel T. Rodgers, "Republicanism: the Career of a Concept," *JAH*, LXXIX (1991–1992), 24–31.

Chapter Four

1. The grand lodge unanimously approved the letter; see Pennsylvania Grand Lodge, *Reprint of the Minutes of the Grand Lodge of Free and Accepted Masons of Pennsylvania,* 12 vols. (Philadelphia 1895–1907), I, 32–35.

2. Ibid.

3. Norris S. Barratt and Julius F. Sachse, *Freemasonry in Pennsylvania, 1727-1907, as Shown by the Records of Lodge No. 2, F. and A.M. of Philadelphia from the Year A.L. 5757, A.D. 1757,* 3 vols. (Philadelphia, 1908–1910), I, 399.

4. Perez Morton, *An Oration; Delivered at the King's-Chapel in Boston, April 8, 1776, on the Re-Interment . . . of . . . Grand-Master Joseph Warren . . .* (Boston, 1776), 7; Esther Forbes, *Paul Revere and the World He Lived In* (Boston, 1942), 303.

5. On the recovery of Warren's body, see Forbes, *Paul Revere and the World He Lived In,* 301–302.

6. Julius F. Sachse, *Old Masonic Lodges of Pennsylvania: "Moderns" and "Ancients," 1730-1800 . . . ,* 2 vols. (Philadelphia, 1912), I, 281 (hereafter cited as Sachse, *OMLPa*); Barratt and Sachse, *Freemasonry in Pennsylvania,* I, 291–294; Ossian Lang, *History of Freemasonry in the State of New York* (New York, 1922), 57.

7. E. G. Storer, comp., *Records of Freemasonry in the State of Connecticut, with Brief Accounts of Its Origins in New England and Proceedings of the Grand Lodge,* 2 vols. (New Haven, Conn., 1859–1861), I, 86–87; Nathaniel Wheadon, "St. Patrick's Lodge No. 4," *American Lodge of Research Transactions,* II (1934–1935), 107–111; Sachse, *OMLPa,* I, 281.

8. The first Ancient lodges in Charleston, formed during the war, may also be related to the disorder of the Moderns there.

9. Thomas Sherrard Roy, *Stalwart Builders: A History of The Grand Lodge of Masons in Massachusetts, 1733-1978,* 2d ed. (Boston, 1980), 53–62; Harvey Newton Shepard, *History of Saint John's Lodge of Boston . . .* (Boston, 1917), 69; Massachusetts Grand Lodge, *Proceedings in Masonry: St. John's Grand Lodge, 1733-1792; Massachusetts Grand Lodge, 1769-1792 . . .* (Boston, 1895), 217–221, 222. On Massachusetts Moderns in this period, see Melvin Maynard Johnson, "St. John's Grand Lodge, 1775–1787," in Massachusetts Grand Lodge, *Proceedings of the Most Worshipful Grand Lodge of . . . Massachusetts for the Year 1931* (Boston, 1932), 189–208. Johnson argues that the Modern grand lodge continued to operate regularly during the war, but examination of his careful compilation suggests otherwise.

10. Anne Rowe Cunningham, ed., *Letters and Diary of John Rowe, Boston Merchant, 1759-1762, 1764-1779* (Boston, 1903), 307 (Apr. 8, 1776) (hereafter cited as Rowe, *Diary*).

11. Ibid., 292 (Apr. 19, 1775), 297 (Jan. 12, 1776), 301–302 (Mar. 11, 1776) (for looting by the army), 305 (Mar. 26, 1776).

12. Ibid., 245 (May 27, 1773), recording the incident with Hallowell; Shepard, *History of Saint John's Lodge,* 57; Massachusetts Grand Lodge, *Proceedings in Masonry,* 220.

13. *The Lodge of St. Andrew, and the Massachusetts Grand Lodge . . . 5756-5769* (Boston, 1870), 113, 167–168.

14. Massachusetts Grand Lodge, *Proceedings in Masonry*, 299. *Lodge of St. Andrew*, 234-236, says these petitions were for membership, but this would be extremely unlikely.

15. Massachusetts Grand Lodge, *Proceedings in Masonry*, 457-458; Howard P. Nash, "William Walter, First Grand Master of Masons in New York," *Am. Lodge Res. Trans.*, II (1934-1935), 59-87. Nash, "Origins of the Grand Lodge of New York," *Am. Lodge Res. Trans.*, III (1939-1942), 278-402, 518-625, provides an exhaustive examination of the matter that attempts to identify every member of the lodges involved.

16. Lang, *Freemasonry in New York*, 57. A remnant of St. John's Lodge, No. 3, which had removed its charter and its meetings out of the city, continued to meet and finally received a charter from the Ancient grand lodge.

17. Barratt and Sachse, *Freemasonry in Pennsylvania*, I, xiii, 291-294; Lodge No. 2 did not meet from July 21, 1777 to Nov. 6, 1778 (I, 290).

18. *St. George's Lodge in the Revolution: Read before the Lodge . . . September, 1914 by Its Secretary* (Schenectady, N.Y., 1917). On this lodge, see also *Sesquicentennial History: St. George's Lodge* (Schenectady, N.Y., 1924). On Arnold, see Lang, *Freemasonry in New York*, 58.

19. F. L. Brockett, *The Lodge of Washington: A History of the Alexandria Washington Lodge, No. 22 . . . 1783-1876* (Alexandria, Va., 1876), 20.

20. Charles S. Plumb, *The History of American Union Lodge No. 1, Free and Accepted Masons of Ohio, 1776 to 1933* (Marietta, Ohio, 1934), 61-68; Barratt and Sachse, *Freemasonry in Pennsylvania*, I, 399-401.

21. Barratt and Sachse, *Freemasonry in Pennsylvania*, I, 403.

22. Ibid., 403-404; Pennsylvania Grand Lodge, *Reprint of the Minutes*, I, 32-35; *Lodge of St. Andrew*, 276.

23. See Barratt and Sachse, *Freemasonry in Pennsylvania*, I, 406-408, for the Pennsylvanians' rambling discussion about implementing their proposal.

24. Nash, "Origins of the Grand Lodge of New York," *Am. Lodge Res. Trans.*, III, 291-293.

25. *Lodge of St. Andrew*, 245.

26. Pennsylvania Grand Lodge, *Proceedings of the Right Worshipful Grand Lodge of . . . Pennsylvania . . . Bi-centenary of the Birth of . . . Benjamin Franklin . . .* (Philadelphia, 1906), 87-90.

27. Massachusetts Grand Lodge, *Proceedings in Masonry*, 301-303; and see St. Andrew's to the Grand Lodge of Massachusetts, Dec. 21, 1782, 548-549. The statement about Scotland was recalled by a past master of the lodge in the 1880s (*Lodge of St. Andrew*, 105-106). Paul Revere's new lodge, Rising States Lodge, sued to gain possession of St. Andrew's property; an arbitrator divided it.

28. Sachse, *OMLPa*, I, 122-125; Pennsylvania Grand Lodge, *Reprint of the Minutes*, I, 97-98. The case of Virginia's independent grand lodge, formed in 1778, is traced in John Dove, ed., *Proceedings of the M. W. Grand Lodge of Ancient York Masons of the State of Virginia, from Its Organization, in 1778, to 1822 . . .* (Richmond, Va., 1874), 1-9.

29. Plumb, *American Union Lodge*, 45-47.

30. Sidney Hayden, *Washington and His Masonic Compeers*, 6th ed. (New York, 1867), 375-384; Henry J. Parker, *Army Lodges during the Revolution* [Boston, 1884], 12. On Paterson, see Thomas Egleston, *The Life of John Paterson, Major-General in the Revolutionary Army* (New York, 1894). Putnam was initiated July 26 shortly after being made commander of a regiment of light infantry. Plumb (*American Union Lodge*, 53) gives the date as July 26 while James R. Case ("Nominal Roll of Those on Record

in the Minutes of American Union Lodge, 1776-1783," *Am. Lodge Res. Trans.*, VI [1956], 356-401), without noting the disagreement, records June 26. See Rowena Buell, comp., *The Memoirs of Rufus Putnam and Certain Official Papers and Correspondence* (Boston, 1903), 85. The June ceremonies included not just Putnam's commander in chief but also fellow colonels of his brigade; see John M. Merriam, "The Military Record of Brigadier General John Nixon of Massachusetts," American Antiquarian Society, *Proceedings*, N.S., XXXVI (1926), 61; James C. Odiorne, *Opinions on Speculative Masonry, relative to Its Origins, Nature, and Tendency* (Boston, 1830), 259.

31. Ronald E. Heaton and James R. Case, *The Lodge at Fredericksburgh: A Digest of the Early Records* (Silver Spring, Md., 1981), 41, suggests that 33 of the 74 who were "commissioned as general officers of the Continental army" were or became Masons (it is difficult to tell in many cases when an officer first became a Mason). I presume that they mean those were commissioned with the rank of general, since all field officers after the first year of the war were appointed ultimately by Congress. I have used the number 78 instead of 74 as the base for the computation, following Jonathan Gregory Rossie, *The Politics of Command in the American Revolution* (Syracuse, N.Y., 1975), 219-221.

32. Charles Royster, *A Revolutionary People at War: The Continental Army and American Character, 1775-1783* (Chapel Hill, N.C., 1979), is the most sophisticated study of the Continental army and its officer corps, but does not discuss Freemasonry. Sidney Kaplan, "Veteran Officers and Politics in Massachusetts, 1783-1787," *William and Mary Quarterly*, 3d Ser., IX (1952), 29-57, is one of the few scholarly works to mention Masonry among the Revolutionary officers (31-32). Yet while the article briefly discusses the order as one of the elements in creating "group solidarity" among Massachusetts officers after the Revolution, it does not look at how Masonry met the needs of these soldiers during the war.

33. Buell, comp., *Memoirs of Rufus Putnam*, 131-134; Charles S. Hall, *The Life and Letters of General Samuel Holden Parsons, Major General in the Continental Army . . . 1737-1789* (Binghamton, N.Y., 1905), 82, 109, and letter dated May 22, 1779 (241-242); Rossie, *Politics of Command*, 220. Parsons's eventual advancement to major general came after his complaints about the promotion of William Smallwood, who had become a brigadier general about five weeks after Parsons's supposed rival. Richard H. Kohn, "American Generals of the Revolution: Subordination and Restraint," in Don Higginbotham, ed., *Reconsiderations on the Revolutionary War: Selected Essays* (Westport, Conn., 1978), 118.

34. See Royster, *Revolutionary People at War*, esp. 88-96, 207-210; Don Higginbotham, "Military Leadership in the American Revolution," in *Leadership in the American Revolution* (Washington, D.C., 1974), 91-111; Gerhard Kollman, "Reflections on the Army of the American Revolution," in Erich Angermann et al., eds., *New Wine in Old Skins: A Comparative View of Socio-Political Structures and Values Affecting the American Revolution* (Stuttgart, 1976), 153-176; and Robert Middlekauff, "Why Men Fought in the American Revolution," *Huntington Library Quarterly*, XLIII (1980), 144-145.

35. David Ramsay, *The History of the Revolution of South-Carolina, from a British Province to an Independent State*, 2 vols. (Trenton, N.J., 1785), II, 143-144, and his similar complaint about American officers in *The History of the American Revolution*, 2 vols. (Philadelphia, 1789), I, 331-332; John Adams to Nathanael Greene, Aug. 4, 1776, in Robert J. Taylor et al., eds., *Papers of John Adams* (Cambridge, Mass., 1977-), IV, 435. On 18th-century theory of military rank, see Victor Daniel Brooks, "American

Officer Development in the Massachusetts Campaign, 1775-1776," *Historical Journal of Massachusetts,* XII (1984), 8-18. See also Gordon S. Wood, *The Radicalism of the American Revolution* (New York, 1992), 84-87.

36. Higginbotham, "Military Leadership," in *Leadership in the American Revolution,* 96, 99-100. For a different argument that fails to take into account the large differences of wealth and status among American elites, see Kohn, "American Generals," in Higginbotham, ed., *Reconsiderations on the Revolutionary War,* 119; and James Kirby Martin and Mark Edward Lender, *A Respectable Army: The Military Origins of the Republic, 1763-1789* (Arlington Heights, Ill., 1982), 107. For a contemporary view that also highlights the importance of men below the highest levels, see Alexander Graydon, *Memoirs of His Own Time: With Reminiscences of the Men and Events of the Revolution,* ed. John Stockton Littell (1811; Philadelphia, 1846), 285. Note also the case of the artisan Paul Revere, who became a colonel wearing a sword and powdered hair during the Revolution (Forbes, *Paul Revere and the World He Lived In,* 331-332).

37. Tupper was promoted to brigadier general at the end of the war. See Samuel P. Hildreth, *Biographical and Historical Memoirs of the Early Pioneer Settlers of Ohio . . .* (Cincinnati, Ohio, 1852), 217-219; see also *Dictionary of American Biography,* s.v. "Tupper, Benjamin." On Putnam: Buell, comp., *Memoirs of Rufus Putnam,* 9-10.

38. Taylor et al., eds., *Papers of John Adams,* IV, 435; Buell, comp., *Memoirs of Rufus Putnam,* 54.

39. Plumb, *American Union Lodge,* 16-17; Sachse, *OMLPa,* II, 129.

40. Hall, *Life and Letters of Parsons,* 103, 161; Sachse, *OMLPa,* II, 76.

41. Quotation from William Smith, *A Sermon Preached in Christ-Church, Philadelphia . . . December 28, 1778* (Philadelphia, 1779), 13; Sachse, *OMLPa,* II, 3-14. John Baer Stoudt, "Song from an Orderly Book," *Am. Lodge Res. Trans.,* III (1938-1939), 166-167; Benjamin M. Nead, "A Sketch of General Thomas Procter . . . ," *Pennsylvania Magazine of History and Biography,* IV (1880), 468-469.

42. Plumb, *American Union Lodge,* 40. Washington Lodge, formed by Paterson and Greaton after the 1779 celebration, initiated more than 100 men in less than a year. Massachusetts Grand Lodge, *Proceedings in Masonry,* 284.

43. Plumb, *American Union Lodge,* 8; residences and ranks identified in Henry P. Johnston, *The Record of Connecticut Men, in the Military, and Naval Service, during the War of the Revolution, 1775-1783* (Hartford, Conn., 1889); *Massachusetts Soldiers and Sailors of the Revolutionary War,* 17 vols. (Boston, 1896-1908), I, 541; Ronald E. Heaton, *Masonic Membership of the Founding Fathers* (Washington, D.C., 1965). Kaplan, "Veteran Officers and Politics in Massachusetts," *WMQ,* 3d Ser., IX (1952), 31, wrongly suggests that American Union "at first admitted New Englanders alone."

44. George Washington to John Hancock, Sept. 21, 1775, in W. W. Abbot et al., eds., *The Papers of George Washington,* Revolutionary War Series (Charlottesville, Va., 1985-), II, 26; the petition requesting higher pay that Washington supported is printed, II, 32-33. Sidney Kaplan, "Rank and Status among Massachusetts Continental Officers," *American Historical Review,* LVI (1950-1951), 318-326.

45. General Orders, Cambridge, July 4, 1775, in Abbot et al., eds., *Papers of George Washington,* Revolutionary, I, 54, George Washington to John Hancock, Sept. 21, 1775, II, 26.

46. James Kirby Martin, "A 'Most Undisciplined, Profligate Crew': Protest and Defiance in the Continental Ranks, 1776-1783," in Ronald Hoffman and Peter J. Albert, eds., *Arms and Independence: The Military Character of the American Revolution* (Charlottesville, Va., 1984), 119-140. On the Seven Years' War, see Fred Anderson, *A People's*

Army: Massachusetts Soldiers and Society in the Seven Years' War (Chapel Hill, N.C., 1984).

47. Royster, *Revolutionary People at War*, 233.

48. Parker, *Army Lodges*, 10-12.

49. While a chaplain with a New Jersey militia unit, Philip Vickers Fithian lodged in the community; see Robert Greenhalgh Albion and Leonidas Dodson, ed., *Philip Vickers Fithian: Journal, 1775-1776* (Princeton, N.J., 1934), 203. On the Albany fraternity: William Stuart, "Daniel Shays, Rebel," *Am. Lodge Res. Trans.*, III (1938-1939), 185-187; Heaton, *Masonic Membership*, s.v. "Greaton, John"; Odiorne, *Opinions on Speculative Masonry*, 259. Colonel Benjamin Tupper also was initiated in a local lodge. See Case, "Nominal Roll of American Union Lodge," *Am. Lodge Res. Trans.*, VI (1956), 394; this article (356-401) provides a good deal of information on lodge brothers.

50. Barratt and Sachse, *Freemasonry in Pennsylvania*, I, 319-321. There were also nonmilitary men in almost all these categories.

51. Jacob Hugo Tatsch, *Freemasonry in the Thirteen Colonies* (New York, 1933), 202-227, lists all Revolutionary military lodges. On Otho Holland Williams's Pennsylvania lodge, see Sachse, *OMLPa*, II, 53-55. The Massachusetts Moderns had created an earlier lodge in 1756 under Richard Gridley often known as the Crown Point Lodge (Massachusetts Grand Lodge, *Proceedings in Masonry*, 59-60, 109). During the British occupation of the city, the Ancient grand lodge of Pennsylvania (then dominated by Tories) granted a warrant to a Scottish lodge in the British army that had lost its warrant, the document later returned by Parsons (see later, and Sachse, *OMLPa*, I 361-368).

52. Camp religion has received little attention from historians. For the outlines of the system of Continental chaplains, see Charles H. Metzger, "Chaplains in the American Revolution," *Catholic Historical Review*, XXXI (1945), 31-79. See also Jon Butler, *Awash in a Sea of Faith: Christianizing the American People* (Cambridge, Mass., 1990), 209-212; Howard Lewis Applegate, "Organization and Development of the American Chaplaincy during the Revolutionary War," *Picket Post*, LXVIII (1960), 19-21, 37-41; Applegate, "Duties and Activities of Chaplains," *Picket Post*, LXI (1958), 10-15, 39-41. On the importance of religion in the New England troops of the Seven Years' War, see Anderson, *A People's Army*, 155-157, 210-218.

53. Charles Thompson McClenachan, *History of the Most Ancient and Honorable Fraternity of Free and Accepted Masons in New York . . .*, 4 vols. (New York, 1888-1894), I, 333-334; Tatsch, *Freemasonry in the Thirteen Colonies*, 213.

54. General William Thompson, for example, became a Mason in Philadelphia's Lodge No. 3 by dispensation because, according to lodge records, he was "under the necessity (being Prisoner on Parole) of going speedily to New York." Heaton, *Masonic Membership*, s.v. "Thompson, William."

55. Odiorne, *Opinions on Speculative Masonry*, 259; Massachusetts Grand Lodge, *Proceedings in Masonry*, 275; Pennsylvania Grand Lodge, *Reprint of the Minutes*, I, 353; Plumb, *American Union Lodge*, 153-154; Sachse, *OMLPa*, II, 3 (see also the French print of Indian loyalist and Freemason Joseph Brant facing p. 4). John N. Hubbard, *Sketches of Border Adventures, in the Life and Times of Major Moses Van Campen, a Surviving Soldier of the Revolution* (Bath, N.Y., 1842), 165-170, notes a similar instance of brother Joseph Brant pledging to save the life of a brother. For the case of Captain John M'Kinstry, also saved from death at the hands of loyalist Indians, see "Col. John M'Kinstry," *American Masonic Register*, II (December 1822), 154, and the letter from C. H., II (February 1823), 190-191. C. H., who knew M'Kinstry and Brant later in their

lives, is identified as Charles Holt in Luther Pratt, *A Defence of Freemasonry, in a Series of Letters Addressed to Solomon Southwick, Esq., and Others, in Which the True Principles of the Order Are Given, and Many Late Misrepresentations Corrected* (Troy, N.Y., 1828), 104. For instances of Masonic kindness to prisoners and the shipwrecked, see *American Masonic Register,* II (February 1823), 191-192; and Pratt, *Defence of Freemasonry,* 110-120, a passage that reprints this periodical piece and notes more examples.

56. Sidney Kaplan, "Pay, Pension, and Power: Economic Grievances of the Massachusetts Officer of the Revolution," *Boston Public Library Quarterly,* III (1951), 15-34, 127-142. Charles Royster's brilliant depiction of the Continental soldiers (*A Revolutionary People at War*) argues that officers' hardships and their growing realization of the weakness of civilian support encouraged officers to identify more fully with the ideal of disinterested republican virtue. For the enlisted men's mutinies and the Newburgh "conspiracy," see Martin and Lender, *A Respectable Army,* 161-165, 186-194; Carl Van Doren, *Mutiny in January: The Story of a Crisis in the Continental Army* . . . (New York, 1943); and Martin, "A 'Most Undisciplined, Profligate Crew,'" in Hoffman and Albert, eds., *Arms and Independence,* 119-14.

57. On alternative military cultures, see Anderson, *A People's Army.* See also Middlekauff, "Why Men Fought in the American Revolution," *Huntington Library Quarterly,* XLIII (1980), 135-148, esp. 144. Margaret C. Jacob makes a similar argument that Masonry provided a concrete demonstration of enlightened principles in *Living the Enlightenment: Freemasonry and Politics in Eighteenth-Century Europe* (New York, 1991).

58. Mercy [Otis] Warren, *History of the Rise, Progress, and Termination of the American Revolution,* 3 vols. (Boston, 1805), III, 290. Knox's proposal for the Cincinnati quoted in Minor Myers, Jr., *Liberty without Anarchy: A History of the Society of the Cincinnati* (Charlottesville, Va., 1983), 15. Washington used the same phrase in *A Circular Letter, Addressed to the State Societies of the Cincinnati, by the General Meeting, Convened at Philadelphia, May 3, 1784, Together with the Institution, as Altered and Amended* (Philadelphia, 1784), 3. For a Masonic use of the phrase, see William Smith, *A Sermon Preached in Christ-Church, Philadelphia . . . the 24th of June, 1755* . . . (Philadelphia, [1755]), 9.

59. *The Institution of the Society of the Cincinnati* . . . (New York, 1784), 9; Myers, *Liberty without Anarchy,* 32-34, 53; Heaton, *Masonic Membership,* s.v. "Steuben, Friedrich"; New York Society of the Cincinnati, *Extract of the Proceedings . . . on the Fourth of July, 1786* . . . (New York, 1786), 3-10. The importance of this badge in the thinking of the society's founders may help explain their controversial rule limiting future membership to eldest sons. Since the order could be awarded only to officers and served as a unique emblem of Revolutionary virtue, only a single member of each generation could be invested with it.

60. Myers, *Liberty without Anarchy,* 31, 136. A similar proportion (36%) of original Pennsylvania Cincinnati members were Freemasons (136).

61. On the connections between fears of the military and the Cincinnati, see, for example, Richard H. Kohn, *Eagle and Sword: The Beginnings of the Military Establishment in America* (New York, 1975), 13. Myers, *Liberty without Anarchy,* is the fullest account of the group. See also Edgar Erskine Hume, "Early Opposition to the Cincinnati," *Americana,* XXX (1936), 597-638; Wallace E. Davies, "The Society of the Cincinnati in New England, 1783-1800," *WMQ,* 3d Ser., V (1948), 3-25; Kaplan, "Veteran Officers and Politics in Massachusetts," *WMQ,* 3d Ser., IX (1952), 29-57; John E. Van Domelen, "Hugh Henry Brackenridge and the Order of the Cincinnati," *Western Pennsylvania Historical Magazine,* XLVII (1964), 47-53.

62. Warren, *History,* III, 278, 280, 286, and discussing the order in III, 279–293. On Warren's larger agenda, see Lester A. Cohen, "Explaining the Revolution: Ideology and Ethics in Mercy Otis Warren's Historical Theory," *WMQ,* 3d Ser., XXXVII (1980), 200–218.

63. The aristocratic Philip Schuyler, for example, complained of the election of George Clinton as the New York governor during the war, since "Clinton's family and connections do not entitle him to so distinguished a preeminence." Yet, he continued, Clinton "is virtuous and loves his country, he has ability and is brave," and thus deserved support. Philip Schuyler to John Jay, July 3, 1777, quoted in Alvin Kass, *Politics in New York State, 1800–1830* (Syracuse, N.Y., 1965), 140.

64. Plumb, *American Union Lodge,* 92–98. Rufus Putnam chaired the first meeting at Marietta in 1790.

65. Sachse, *OMLPa,* II, 27. Don Higginbotham suggests that militia rank brought greater political advantage than involvement in the Continental army: "The American Militia: A Traditional Institution with Revolutionary Responsibilities," in Higginbotham, ed., *Reconsiderations on the Revolutionary War,* 89–90. See also the thwarted attempt to use Continental army officers in the postwar Virginia militia: Harrison M. Ethridge, "Governor Patrick Henry and the Reorganization of the Virginia Militia, 1784–1786," *Virginia Magazine of History and Biography,* LXXXV (1977), 427–439.

66. Odiorne, *Opinions on Speculative Masonry,* 260. For Sewall's Antimasonic involvement, see his diary in Charles Elventon Nash, *The History of Augusta: First Settlements and Early Days as a Town* . . . (Augusta, Maine, 1904), 480, 488, 489, 493. The Pennsylvania quotation is from Sachse, *OMLPa,* II, 76.

Chapter Five

1. William S. Baker, "Washington after the Revolution, 1784–1799," *Pennsylvania Magazine of History and Biography,* XX (1896), 363–364; Glenn Brown, *History of the United States Capitol,* I, *The Old Capitol, 1792–1850* (Washington, D.C., 1900), 14–16; Wilhelmus Bogart Bryan, *A History of the National Capitol* . . . , I, *1790–1874* (New York, 1914), 213; On the Masonic aspects of the ceremony, see William L. Cummings, "Ceremonial of Cornerstone Laying," *American Lodge of Research Transactions,* I (1930–1933), 153–154; Len Travers, " 'In the Greatest Solemn Dignity': The Capitol Cornerstone and Ceremony in the Early Republic," in Donald Kennon and Barbara Wolanin, eds., *A Republic for the Ages* (forthcoming).

2. Thomas Jefferson to Benjamin Latrobe, July 12, 1812, in Andrew A. Lipscomb and Albert Ellery Bergh, eds., *The Writings of Thomas Jefferson,* 20 vols. (Washington, D.C., 1903), XIII, 179.

3. *Directory and Stranger's Guide, for the City of Charleston . . . 1825* . . . (Charleston, S.C., 1824), 12–18, 20–22, 126–130.

4. Salem Town, *A System of Speculative Masonry* . . . (Salem, N.Y., 1818), 63.

5. De Witt Clinton, *An Address Delivered before Holland Lodge, December 24, 1793* (New York, 1794), 4.

6. Benjamin Gleason, *An Oration, Pronounced at Montreal, (Lower Canada,)* . . . *June 24, A.L. 5812,* 2d ed. (Boston, 1812), 6.

7. Pennsylvania Grand Lodge, *Reprint of the Minutes of the Grand Lodge of Free and Accepted Masons of Pennsylvania,* 12 vols. (Philadelphia, 1895–1907), I, 267.

8. John A. Clark, *An Address Delivered to the Masonic Fraternity, of Ark Lodge, Geneva . . . June 25, A.L. 5827* (Geneva, N.Y., 1827), 3–4, 7, 8.

9. Ibid., 11-12; F. L. Brockett, *The Lodge of Washington: A History of the Alexandria Washington Lodge, No. 22 . . . 1783-1876* (Alexandria, Va., 1876), 74.

10. Clark, *Address, Delivered to the Masonic Fraternity, of Ark Lodge, Geneva* (1827), 8-9; Clinton, *Address Delivered before Holland Lodge, 1793,* 3; Thaddeus Mason Harris, *Masonic Emblems Explained . . .* (Boston, 1796), 19 ("Erroneous Principles in Education," *Universal Asylum, and Columbian Magazine,* II [August 1791], 101, similarly notes that "sensible objects strike the most forcibly on the imagination"). On the broader implications of enlightened theories of knowledge and education, see Walter Jackson Bate, *From Classic to Romantic: Premises of Taste in Eighteenth-Century England* (1945; New York, 1961); Ernest Lee Tuveson, *The Imagination as a Means of Grace: Locke and the Aesthetics of Romanticism* (Berkeley, Calif., 1960), 33-40; and Jay Fliegelman, *Prodigals and Pilgrims: The American Revolution against Patriarchal Authority, 1750-1800* (Cambridge, 1982).

11. Chapter 9 discusses this new attention to ritual and preparation more fully. The song, written by Thomas Smith Webb, is ubiquitous in Masonic works after the turn of the century. See James Moore and Cary L. Clarke, *Masonic Constitutions; or, Illustrations of Masonry; Compiled by the Direction of the Grand Lodge of Kentucky . . .* (Lexington, Ky., 1808), 182-183.

12. Timothy Swan to B. Pierce, [after July 6, 1803], Timothy Swan Papers, 1783-1844, box 11, folder 2, American Antiquarian Society, Worcester, Mass.; Thomas Smith Webb, *The Freemason's Monitor; or, Illustrations of Masonry* (Albany, N.Y., 1797), 51-52; Webb, *The Freemason's Monitor; or, Illustrations of Masonry . . . ,* new ed. (Salem, Mass., 1821), 33 (hereafter cited as Webb, *Freemason's Monitor* [1821]); Dagobert D. Runes, ed., *The Selected Writings of Benjamin Rush* (New York, 1947), 119; Clark, *Address Delivered to the Masonic Fraternity, of Ark Lodge, Geneva* (1827), 9.

13. Clarence Cook, ed., *A Girl's Life Eighty Years Ago: Selections from the Letters of Eliza Southgate Bowne* (New York, 1887), 109-110; "On the Supposed Superiority of the Masculine Understanding," *Universal Asylum, and Columbian Magazine,* II (July 1791), 9; Benjamin Rush, "Of the Mode of Education Proper in a Republic" (1798), in Runes, ed., *Selected Writings of Benjamin Rush,* 92 (see also 95-96). See also Simeon Doggett, "A Discourse on Education . . ." (1797), in Frederick Rudolph, ed., *Essays on Education in the Early Republic* (Cambridge, Mass., 1965), 158-159. Discussions of changing women's roles can be found in Jan Lewis, "The Republican Wife: Virtue and Seduction in the Early Republic," *William and Mary Quarterly,* 3d Ser., XLIV (1987), 689-721; Mary Beth Norton, *Liberty's Daughters: The Revolutionary Experience of American Women, 1750-1800* (Boston, 1980); and Linda K. Kerber, *Women of the Republic: Intellect and Ideology in Revolutionary America* (Chapel Hill, N.C., 1980).

14. In highlighting this shift in the role of virtue, I do not wish to deny that intermediate thinkers had helped shift the discussion, perhaps even before the Revolution. See Gordon S. Wood, *The Radicalism of the American Revolution* (New York, 1992), 95-225.

15. Samuel Harrison Smith, "Remarks on Education: Illustrating the Close Connection between Virtue and Wisdom . . ." (1798), in Rudolph, ed., *Essays on Education in the Early Republic,* 170, 183. See John B. Radner, "The Art of Sympathy in Eighteenth-Century British Moral Thought," in Roseann Runte, ed., *Studies in Eighteenth-Century Culture,* IX (Madison, Wis., 1979), 189-210; Fliegelman, *Prodigals and Pilgrims,* 230-235. For a discussion of the need for education in a republic, see Melvin Yazawa, "Creating a Republican Citizenry," in Jack P. Greene, ed., *The American Revolution: Its Character and Limits* (New York, 1987), 282-309.

16. Clinton, *Address Delivered before Holland Lodge, 1793,* 4-5. On Clinton, see

Steven E. Siry, *De Witt Clinton and the American Political Economy: Sectionalism, Politics, and Republican Ideology, 1787-1828* (New York, 1990), 255-280, esp. 260-261.

17. See William Symmes, *An Oration, Delivered in the Meeting House of the First Parish in Portland, June 24th, 5796* . . . (Portland, Maine, 1796), 7; Samuel S. Wilde, *An Oration, Delivered at Pownalborough . . . June 24th, 5799* . . . (Wiscasset, Maine, 1799), 8-9.

18. De Witt Clinton, "Address before the Free School Society in the City of New York" (1809), in William W. Campbell, *The Life and Writings of DeWitt Clinton* (New York, 1849), 310; Noah Webster, "On the Education of Youth in America" (1790), in Rudolph, ed., *Essays on Education in the Early Republic,* 57, 65-66.

19. Brockett, *The Lodge of Washington,* 74; David Everett, *An Oration, in Vindication of Free Masonry . . . at Washington, N.H . . . September 28, A.L. 5803* . . . (Amherst, N.H., 1804), 3.

20. Gleason, *An Oration, Pronounced at Montreal* (1812), 6; Wilkes Allen, *The Duties of Freemasonry Illustrated and Enforced . . . at Chelmsford, (Massachusetts) . . . October 12, A.D. 1809* . . . (Boston, 1809), 17.

21. Clinton, *Address Delivered before Holland Lodge, 1793,* 4.

22. Ibid.

23. Past grand master Josiah Bartlett, address at installation of new grand master of Massachusetts, Dec. 27, 1810, in Massachusetts Grand Lodge, *Proceedings of the Most Worshipful Grand Lodge . . . of Massachusetts . . . 1792-1815* (Cambridge, Mass., 1905), 476.

24. James D. Hopkins, *An Oration, Pronounced before the Portland Lodge . . . 24th June, A.L. 5801* . . . (Portland, Maine, 1801), 12; John Cleland, "On the Real Secret of the Freemasons," in Cleland, *The Way to Things by Words, and to Words by Things . . .* (London, 1766; rpt. Menston, England, 1968), 108-123; Thomas Paine, "Origin of Freemasonry" (1805; first published 1810), in Philip S. Foner, ed., *The Complete Writings of Thomas Paine . . . ,* 2 vols. (New York, 1945), II, 830-841. The Maine grand lodge instituted inquiries in the 1820s to discover "whether any vestiges of ancient Masonry can be discovered in Palestine, and the countries adjoining." *Proceedings of the Grand Lodge . . . of the State of Maine, I, 1820-1847* (Portland, Maine, 1872), 80, 137, 163, 176.

25. Henry Mellen, *Sketches of Masonic History in an Oration Delivered July 25th A.L. 5798 . . . Portsmouth, before the Grand Lodge of New-Hampshire . . .* (Portsmouth, N.H., 1798), 11.

26. Clinton, *An Address Delivered before Holland Lodge, 1793,* 3; *The Echo; or, Columbian Songster . . . ,* 2d ed. (Brookfield, Mass., [1800]), 198 (song 28).

27. Charles S. Plumb, *The History of American Union Lodge No. 1, Free and Accepted Masons of Ohio, 1776 to 1933* (Marietta, Ohio, 1934), 208; Nelson Gillespie, *Centennial History of Apollo Lodge, No. 13, . . . Troy, New York . . .* (Troy, N.Y., 1898), 41-42; Brockett, *The Lodge of Washington,* 85-86; Alexandria-Washington Lodge, "Circular: Dear Sir, The Members of Alexandria Washington Lodge . . . ," broadside (Alexandria[?], 1812).

28. Nathaniel Very, *Nathaniel Very's Renunciation of Freemasonry* (Worcester, Mass., 1830), esp. 5, 13.

29. Ibid., 7, 13.

30. *Proceedings of the Grand Lodge . . . of the State of Maine,* I, 25-26; Thomas C. O'Donnell, "The Beginnings of Masonry in the Schoharie Valley," *Am. Lodge Res. Trans.,* II (1936), 204; Preserved Smith, *A Masonick Discourse, Delivered at Greenfield, Massachusetts . . . June, 26th, A.L. 5798* (Greenfield, Mass., 1798), 11.

31. De Witt Clinton, "The Address of De Witt Clinton" to the Grand Lodge of New

York, Sept. 29, 1825, in Charles Thompson McClenachan, *History of the Most Ancient and Honorable Fraternity of Free and Accepted Masons in New York,* 4 vols. (New York, 1888-1894), II, 433, 435, 436; "Address to the New York Free Academy" (1809), in Campbell, *Life and Writings of Clinton,* 311; Clinton to William D. Foot, Dec. 4, 1823, in James Renwick, *Life of Dewitt Clinton* (New York, 1840), 327.

32. Clinton, "Address before the Free School Society" (1809), in Campbell, *Life and Writings of Clinton,* 312, and "Address before the Phi Beta Kappa Society of Union College" (1823), 331; Washington to Alexander Hamilton, Sept. 1, 1796, in John C. Fitzpatrick, ed., *The Writings of George Washington,* XXXV (Washington, 1940), 199, and "Farewell Address," Sept. 19, 1796, XXXV, 230. On ignorance, knowledge, and government, see Melvin Yazawa, *From Colonies to Commonwealth: Familial Ideology and the Beginnings of the American Republic* (Baltimore, 1985) 167-194; Yazawa, "Creating a Republican Citizenry," in Greene, ed., *The American Revolution,* 282-302; and Jean V. Matthews, *Toward a New Society: American Thought and Culture, 1800-1830* (Boston, 1991), 18-19.

33. De Witt Clinton, "Final Address to the State Legislature" (1828), in Campbell, *Life and Writings of Clinton,* 309-310; Jefferson to John Adams, Oct. 28, 1813, in Lester J. Cappon, ed., *The Adams-Jefferson Letters: The Complete Correspondence between Thomas Jefferson and Abigail and John Adams,* 2 vols. (Chapel Hill, N.C., 1959), II, 390.

34. Hector Orr, *A History of Free Masonry . . . Bridgewater . . . June 30th, A.L. 5797* (Boston, 1798), 7; Webb, *Freemason's Monitor* (1821), 214; Frederick Dalcho, comp., *An Ahiman Rezon, for the Use of the Grand Lodge of South-Carolina, Ancient York-masons . . .* (Charleston, S.C., 1807), 136; Clinton, *Address before Holland Lodge, 1793,* 8.

35. Caleb Cushing, *An Address Delivered at Lynn . . . June 24, A.L. 5826* (Newburyport, Mass., 1826), 25.

36. Smith, *Masonick Discourse, Delivered at Greenfield, Massachusetts* (1798), 8; Anne Royall, *The Black Book; or, A Continuation of Travels, in the United States,* 3 vols. (Washington, D.C., 1828-1829), II, 12.

37. Cummings, "Ceremonial of Cornerstone Laying," *Am. Lodge Res. Trans.,* I (1930-1933), 153-156. *Report of the President, Vice Presidents . . . of the Bunker Hill Monument Association . . .* (Boston 1832), 14; and Massachusetts Grand Lodge, *Proceedings of the Most Worshipful Grand Lodge . . . of Massachusetts . . . 1815-1825* (Cambridge, Mass. 1905), 541-552, note some Massachusetts ceremonies. Further examples are cited in Thomas L. Parramore, *Launching the Craft: The First Half-Century of Freemasonry in North Carolina* (Raleigh, N.C., 1975), 127-131; William Mosley Brown, *Freemasonry in Virginia (1733-1936)* (Richmond, Va., 1936), 100 n. 9, 128; *Proceedings of the Grand Annual Communication of the Grand Lodge of Virginia . . . 1817* (Richmond, Va., 1818), 5, 18-19. On a 1791 District of Columbia ceremony, see *Proceedings of the Right Worshipful Grand Lodge . . . of Pennsylvania . . . at Its Celebration of the Sesquicentennial Anniversary of the Initiation of Brother George Washington into the Fraternity of Freemasons . . . A.D. 1902-A.L. 5902* (Philadelphia, 1902), 157.

38. T. O. Haunch, "The Constitution and Consecration of Lodges under the Grand Lodges of England," *Ars Quotuor Coronatorum,* LXXXIII (1970), 1-62, discusses British evidence.

39. Clark, *Address, Delivered to the Masonic Fraternity, of Ark Lodge, Geneva* (1827), 7; Smith, *Masonick Discourse, Delivered at Greenfield, Massachusetts* (1798), 9; Thaddeus Mason Harris, *Discourses, Delivered on Public Occasions, Illustrating the Principles . . . of Free Masonry . . .* (Charlestown, Mass., 1801), 184.

40. Edward T. Schultz, *History of Freemasonry in Maryland . . . ,* 3 vols. (Baltimore,

1884–1887), II, 200; William Bentley, *A Discourse, Delivered at Amherst, August 10, 1797 . . . at the Installation of the Benevolent Lodge . . .* (Amherst, N.H., 1797), 19; Clark Brown, *The Utility of Moral and Religious Societies, and of the Masonick in Particular . . . Putney, Vt. . . . June 24th, 1814 . . .* (Keene, N.H., 1814), 14.

41. Elbridge Henry Goss, *The Life of Colonel Paul Revere,* 2 vols. (Boston, 1891), II, 483–484, 485.

42. Ibid., II, 479; Thomas Jefferson, "A Bill for the More General Diffusion of Knowledge," in Julian P. Boyd et al., eds., *The Papers of Thomas Jefferson* (Princeton, N.J., 1950–), II, 527; Thaddeus Mason Harris, *A Charge, Delivered before the Officers and Members of the Grand Lodge of . . . Massachusetts . . . June 24th, A.L. 5795.* (Worcester, Mass., 1795), 9.

43. For the membership of Holland Lodge to 1800, see Chapter 6. Thomas Bender, *New York Intellect: A History of Intellectual Life in New York City, from 1750 to the Beginnings of Our Own Time* (New York, 1987), 46–88, discusses post-Revolutionary intellectual life in that city, giving particular attention to Clinton, Pintard, and Holland Lodge (57–60).

44. Susanne K. Sherman, "Thomas Wade West, Theatrical Impressario, 1790–1799," *WMQ,* 3d Ser., IX (1952), 10–28; Wayne A. Huss, *The Master Builders: A History of the Grand Lodge of Free and Accepted Masons of Pennsylvania,* 3 vols. (Philadelphia, 1986–1989), I, 70; Pennsylvania Grand Lodge, *Reprint of the Minutes,* I, 408–409. For Latrobe's membership, see Charles P. Rady, *History of Richmond Randolph Lodge, No. 19 . . .* (Richmond, Va., 1888), 16; Talbot Hamlin, *Benjamin Henry Latrobe* (New York, 1955), 196.

45. Huss, *Master Builders,* I, 73–74, 93. Hamilin, *Benjamin Henry Latrobe,* 196, notes that Latrobe, Strickland's teacher, also prepared a design for the Philadelphia hall. Strickland joined the fraternity on or soon after his 21st birthday. For more on the hall and its architect's membership, see Agnes Addison Gilchrist, *William Strickland: Architect and Engineer, 1788–1854* (Philadelphia, 1950), 2, 21, 34, 45–46, 59. John Money, *Experience and Identity: Birmingham and the West Midlands, 1760–1800* (Montreal, 1977), 136–140, notes a similar Masonic interest in music, drama, and books in late-18th-century provincial England. On Rowson, see Charles C. Perkins and John S. Dwight, *History of the Handel and Haydn Society, of Boston, Massachusetts,* 2 vols. (Boston, 1883–1893), II, 33, 42, 44, 51. For a Masonic poem by Rowson, see Harvey Newton Shepard, *History of Saint John's Lodge of Boston* (Boston, 1917), 81–82.

46. David Longworth, *Longworth's American Almanac, New York Register, and City Directory* (New York, 1816), 11. For materials decorated with Masonic symbols, see Scottish Rite Masonic Museum of Our National Heritage, *Masonic Symbols in American Decorative Arts* (Lexington, Mass., 1976); John D. Hamilton, *Material Culture of the American Freemasons* (Hanover, N.H., 1994).

47. Robert W. Reid, "Some Early Masonic Engravers in America," *Am. Lodge Res. Trans.,* III (1938–1942), 97–125; Barbara Franco, "Masonic Imagery," in James F. O'Gorman, ed., *Aspects of American Printmaking, 1800–1950* (Syracuse, N.Y., 1988), 10, 21–24. Paul Revere was also active in this new Masonic market; see Edith J. Steblecki, *Paul Revere and Freemasonry* ([Boston], 1985), 70–75, 108–113.

48. Smith, *Masonick Discourse, Delivered at Greenfield, Massachusetts* (1798), 9.

49. Cushing, *An Address Delivered at Lynn* (1826), 27; Claude M. Fuess, *The Life of Caleb Cushing,* 2 vols. (New York, 1923), I, 63, 44.

50. William Bentley, *The Diary of William Bentley, D.D., Pastor of the East Church, Salem, Massachusetts,* 4 vols. (Salem, Mass., 1905–1914), II, 329 (Jan. 10, 1800); Bent-

ley, *Discourse, Delivered at Amherst* (1797), 10; Greville Bathe and Dorothy Bathe, *Jacob Perkins: His Inventions, His Times, and His Contemporaries* (Philadelphia, 1943); *Dictionary of American Biography,* s.v. "Perkins, Jacob."

51. Henry A. Pochman, *German Culture in America, 1600-1900: Philosophical and Literary Influences* (Madison, Wis., 1957), 53-54. On Bentley, see Richard D. Brown, *Knowledge Is Power: The Diffusion of Information in Early America, 1700-1865* (New York, 1989), 197-217; and Louise Chipley, "William Bentley, Journalist of the Early Republic," Essex Institute, *Historical Collections,* CXXIII (1987), 331-347.

52. Henry McRaven, *Nashville: "Athens of the South"* (Chapel Hill, N.C., 1949), 64; Wilkins Tannehill, *Sketches of the History of Literature, from the Earliest Period to the Revival of Letters in the Fifteenth Century* (Nashville, Tenn., 1829), esp. iii. On Tannehill's early career, see Sam B. Smith et al., eds., *The Papers of Andrew Jackson* (Knoxville, Tenn., 1980-), II, 261 n. 3.

53. James Gilreath, "American Book Distribution," American Antiquarian Society, *Proceedings,* XCV (1985-1986), 540. Brown, *Knowledge Is Power,* discusses what he calls "the Communications Revolution" and its effects on individual lives. William J. Gilmore, *Reading Becomes a Necessity of Life: Material and Cultural Life in Rural New England, 1780-1835* (Knoxville, Tenn., 1989), studies its effect on a community. See also David Jaffee, "The Village Enlightenment in New England, 1760-1820," *WMQ,* 3d Ser., XLVII (1990), 327-346; Cathy N. Davidson, *Revolution and the Word: The Rise of the Novel in America* (New York, 1986), 15-97.

54. Bentley, *Diary,* II, 329 (Jan. 10, 1800). See Chapter 7 for a discussion of the Lexington, Kentucky, lodge.

55. Franklin Bowditch Dexter, *Biographical Sketches of the Graduates of Yale College . . . ,* 6 vols. and suppl. (New York, 1885-1913), IV, 623-625; [John Woodworth?], *The Spunkiad; or, Heroism Improved* (Newburgh, N.Y., 1798); Very, *Renunciation of Freemasonry,* 13. On Gorton, see John Woodworth, *Reminiscences of Troy from Its Settlement in 1790 to 1807 . . . ,* 2d ed. (Albany, N.Y., 1860), 68-70; and A. J. Weise, *History of the City of Troy . . . to . . . 1876* (Troy, N.Y., 1876), 112.

56. Cushing, *An Address Delivered at Lynn* (1826), 25.

57. [Hannah Mather Crocker], *A Series of Letters on Free Masonry* (Boston, 1815), 7. The date of this incident is not provided by Crocker's account, but it must have been before early 1798.

58. Bentley, *Diary,* II, 379 (July 11, 1801), III, 321 (Sept. 20, 1807). On Hall, see Charles H. Wesley, *Prince Hall: Life and Legacy* (Washington, D.C., 1977), esp. 217-219; and Henry Wilson Coil et al., eds., *A Documentary Account of Prince Hall and Other Black Fraternal Orders* ([St. Louis, Mo.], 1982), esp. 38-41. As Coil points out, W. H. Grimshaw, *Official History of Freemasonry among the Colored People in North America* (New York, 1903), often cited as a key source, is extremely unreliable. William D. Piersen, *Black Yankees: The Development of an Afro-American Subculture in Eighteenth-Century New England* (Amherst, Mass., 1988), 59, is similarly inaccurate. Schultz, *History of Freemasonry in Maryland,* II, 409, notes a rejected 1822 petition by a group of African-Americans to the grand lodge of Maryland.

59. Jeremy Belknap to Ebenezer Hazard, Mar. 2, 1788, Belknap Papers, Massachusetts Historical Society, Boston; Coil et al., eds., *Documentary Account,* 121. Hall's death notice in the *Boston Gazette,* Dec. 7, 1807, and *Independent Chronicle* (Boston), Dec. 7, 1807, refers to him simply as "Master of African Lodge."

The African Lodge publications are Prince Hall, *A Charge Delivered to the Brethren of the African Lodge on the 25th of June, 1792 . . .* (Boston, 1792) (reprinted in Dorothy

Porter, ed., *Early Negro Writing, 1760–1837* [Boston, 1971], 63–69, hereafter cited as Hall, *Charge* [1792]); Hall, *A Charge Delivered to the African Lodge, June 24, 1797* . . . (Boston, 1797) (also in Porter, *Early Negro Writing,* 70–78, hereafter cited as Hall, *Charge* [1797]); John Marrant, *A Sermon Preached on the 24th Day of June 1789* . . . (Boston, 1789). A earlier draft of this last is in Prince Hall, "Letters and Sermons, 1787–1802," MS book held by the Prince Hall Grand Lodge, Boston. I have used the microfilm copy at the Grand Lodge of Massachusetts, Boston. The nearly illegible heading suggests that Prince Hall had a hand in preparing the piece for press; the published version is quite different from the manuscript. As master of the lodge, Hall also presented a loyal address to the governor during Shays's Rebellion.

60. Harry E. Davis, "Documents Relating to Negro Masonry in America," *Journal of Negro History,* XXI (1936), 413; Hall, *Charge* (1792), 64. The first "duty of a Mason," Hall told the brothers in 1792, is belief in God, his unity, his creation of all things, and his governance of "all things here below by his almighty power" (Hall, *Charge* [1792], 64).

61. Hall, *Charge* (1792), 66–67; Marrant, Draft Address, in Hall, "Letters and Sermons" (unpaginated); Marrant, *Sermon,* 20. The presence of these lives in the lodge minutes suggests that they were read at lodge meetings.

The persecution of the early church also was of great significance for Hall. Although he made no explicit connection between these years and his own situation of "the daily insults . . . in the streets of Boston" and the "bulwark of envy, pride, scorn and contempt, which is so visible to be seen in some and felt," the parallels seem clear (Hall, *Charge* [1797], 70, 72). "The [weak]," he wrote of the early church, "Prevailed against the strong and Mighty[. F]or what were the Apostles and followers of Christ but poor week contemptible persons[?] . . . And who were the Enemies to Christ and his Followers? They were men of the Greatest Note, persons of Repute and Honour: they were Rich [?] and Wealthy [?] great and Mighty. But . . . the son of man with his [?] poor despised Apostles prevailed against those who . . . [? were?] of the Greatest" ("Remarks," in Hall, "Letters and Sermons").

62. See *Charge* (1792), 65, 68.

63. Basic biographical data on Crocker can be found in *DAB,* s.v. "Crocker, Hannah Mather," and *Notable American Women,* s.v. "Crocker, Hannah Mather." The illiteracy of many members of African Lodge is noted in Hall, *Charge* (1797), 77.

64. [Crocker], *Series of Letters,* 8, 9.

65. Ibid. On Samuel Mather (Harvard College, 1723), see Clifford K. Shipton, *Biographical Sketches of Those Who Attended Harvard College* . . . , Sibley's Harvard Graduates, VII (Boston, 1945), 216–238, esp. 226. The Queen of Sheba is referred to in "A Short Address, From the Mistress of St. Ann's Lodge," *Columbian Centinel* (Boston), Feb. 24, 1798; also in [Crocker], *Series of Letters,* 20–21. Three years after publishing her discussion of Masonry in 1815, Crocker went on to produce a 100-page pamphlet on "the real rights of women," stressing that God "has endowed the female mind with equal powers and faculties, and given them the same right of judging and acting for themselves, as he gave to the male sex" (H. Mather Crocker, *Observations on the Real Rights of Women, with Their Appropriate Duties, Agreeable to Scripture, Reason, and Ccommon Ssense* [Boston, 1818], 5).

66. [Crocker], *Series of Letters,* 7.

67. "A Short Address, from the Mistress of St. Ann's Lodge," *Columbian Centinel,* Feb. 24, 1798; this poem was later reprinted in [Crocker], *Series of Letters,* 20–21, where the date is wrongly given as 1778. *Notable American Women,* s.v. "Crocker, Hannah Mather," repeats this error.

68. [Crocker], *Series of Letters,* 8; Norton, *Liberty's Daughters,* and Kerber, *Women of the Republic,* attribute these changes to the Revolution.

69. Hall, *Charge* (1797), 73.

Chapter Six

1. Salem Town, *A System of Speculative Masonry . . .* (Salem, N.Y., 1818), 13, 22, 37, 67. For Town's account of his experience, see Temple R. Hollcroft, "Salem Town: Partial Autobiography and Masonic Biography," *American Lodge of Research Transactions,* V (1949–1951), 240–266.

2. This transformation has been virtually unnoticed by historians—or at least not taken seriously. The historiography of Masonry and post-Revolutionary religion shows a wide disagreement about the relationship of the two, with historians taking almost every position except Salem Town's. This chapter argues that Town's close identification of Masonry with Christianity (if not his belief that they were ultimately the same) was the widest-spread view of the fraternity in these years. Jon Butler, *Awash in a Sea of Faith: Christianizing the American People* (Cambridge, Mass., 1990), 235–236, links Masonry to the occult world of folk magic. Dorothy Ann Lipson and Kathleen Smith Kutolowski see Masonry as more related to rational religion. Lipson contends that Masons and clergy saw the fraternity as a protest against Connecticut orthodoxy. "The similarity between deism and Freemasonry," she argues, "is so pervasive that it is difficult to distinguish them" (*Freemasonry in Federalist Connecticut* [Princeton, N.J., 1977], 123–124). Somewhat less sweepingly, Kutolowski labels the fraternity "secular and universalist . . . threatening religious canons" ("Freemasonry and Community in the Early Republic: The Case for Antimasonic Anxieties," *American Quarterly,* XXXIV [1982], 559). David M. Ludlum, *Social Ferment in Vermont, 1791–1850* (1939; rpt. New York, 1966), 86–133, similarly sees a strong undercurrent of religious antagonism. Paul Goodman's work on Antimasonry suggests less antagonism, judging pre-1826 Masonry "vaguely Christian" and contending that post-Revolutionary churches viewed the fraternity with "tolerance or indifference" (*Towards a Christian Republic: Antimasonry and the Great Transition in New England, 1826–1836* [New York, 1988], 11, 57).

3. *Masonic Mirror: and Mechanic's Intelligencer* (Boston), II (Apr. 15, 1826), 121.

4. Hector Orr, *An Oration, Delivered November 3d, A.L. 5797, by Request of Fellowship Lodge, in Bridgewater . . .* (Boston, 1797), 4

5. Henry Crocker, *History of the Baptists in Vermont* (Bellows Falls, Vt., 1913), 288.

6. De Witt Clinton, "Address before the American Bible Society" (1823), in William W. Campbell, *The Life and Writings of DeWitt Clinton* (New York, 1849), 308.

7. This typology of sectarian and nonsectarian attitudes draws upon a long tradition in religious studies that goes back at least to Ernst Troeltsch, *The Social Teaching of the Christian Churches,* trans. Olive Wyon (New York, 1931). See also Sidney E. Mead's work on denominationalism, especially *The Lively Experiment: The Shaping of Christianity in America* (New York, 1963). Curtis D. Johnson, *Islands of Holiness: Rural Religion in Upstate New York, 1790–1860* (Ithaca, N.Y., 1989), uses a similar scheme, referring to a sectarian "island mentality" (see 22–30, 89–93, 145–158). Although Johnson provides a sometimes sensitive account of these positions, I see much more development over time toward nonsectarian attitudes.

8. David Benedict, *A General History of the Baptist Denomination in America . . . ,* 2 vols. (Boston, 1813), I, 340. Stephen Wright, *History of the Shaftsbury Baptist Asso-*

ciation, from 1781 to 1853 (Troy, N.Y., 1853), 57, 92–93; William G. McLoughlin, *New England Dissent, 1630–1833: The Baptists and the Separation of Church and State,* 2 vols. (paginated continuously) (Cambridge, Mass., 1971), II, 759–760, for discussion of New England Baptist action.

9. North Carolina Grand Royal Arch Council Transcriptions, June 24, 1825, folder 17, J. Ray Shute Papers, Southern Historical Collection, University of North Carolina, Chapel Hill. *A History of Spartanburg County . . . ,* American Guide Series ([Spartanburg, S.C.], 1940), 82–83, notes a Baptist church council in northern South Carolina that expelled a Masonic minister. A Quaker disciplinary action against a Mason in southern Virginia is mentioned in W. Asbury Christian, *Lynchburg and Its People* (Lynchburg, Va., 1900), 13, although it is unclear whether the issue was Masonic membership or the ritual use of a sword.

10. J. R. Shute, "An Interesting Church Decision," *Nocalore,* V (1935), 127–128.

11. Wallace Selden Boardman, *Historical Sketch of the Baptist Church in Addison, Vermont, 1797: 1919* (n.p., 1919), 5; "A New Inquisition," *American Masonic Register, and Ladies' and Gentlemen's Magazine,* I (March 1821), 241–249; *Proceedings of the Centennial Celebration of the Presbyterian Church, of Greensburg, Penn'a., . . . 1888 . . .* (Greensburg, Pa., 1888), 50–52.

12. Shute, "An Interesting Church Decision," *Nocalore,* V (1935), 127–128; Wright, *History of the Shaftsbury Baptist Association,* 57; Benedict, *A General History of the Baptist Denomination,* I, 340–342; McLoughlin, *New England Dissent,* II, 760.

13. Benedict, *A General History of the Baptist Denomination,* I, 340–342.

14. "'New Inquisition' Defeated," *American Masonic Register,* I (July 1821), 438–439. This article includes a piece from an unidentified source.

15. De Witt Clinton, *An Address Delivered before Holland Lodge, December 24, 1793* (New York, 1794), 7; *Proceedings of the Grand Lodge of North Carolina and Tennessee, from A.L. 5804, A.D. 1804 to A.L. 5840, A.D. 1840,* 1816 (n.p., n.d.) 13. Clinton played a major role in New York's 1806 removal of civil disabilities for Roman Catholics (*Dictionary of American Biography,* s.v. "Clinton, DeWitt"). The idea that Masonry transcended sectarian differences might have been a part of an incident reported by George Washington Dame, *Historical Sketch of Roman Eagle Lodge No. 122 . . . 1820–1895* (Danville, Va., 1939), 11; having trouble reviving a lodge in Prince Edward County in 1839, Dane was told by an older Mason that the last master of the local lodge, a physician, "held and taught that Freemasonry was an older and better religion than the Church." He even had a dying patient join the lodge "as the surest plan of salvation."

16. *Extracts from the Minutes of the General Assembly, of the Presbyterian Church, in the United States of America, A.D. 1817* (Philadelphia, 1817), 15. Sidney E. Mead's works provide the fullest account of this growing denominationalism. See, for example, Mead, *The Lively Experiment,* esp. 103–133, and *The Nation with the Soul of a Church* (New York, 1975). Nathan O. Hatch, *The Democratization of American Christianity* (New Haven, Conn., 1989), and "The Christian Movement and the Demand for a Theology of the People," *Journal of American History,* LXVII (1980–1981), 545–567, shows how these themes affected even ardent evangelicals.

17. *Extracts from the Minutes of the General Assembly, of the Presbyterian Church,* 1817, 13–14.

18. Harvey Newton Shepard, *History of Saint John's Lodge of Boston* (Boston, 1917), 81–82. Rowson's husband, William, performed the song.

19. Samuel Stillman, *A Discourse Delivered before the Members of the Boston Female Asylum, Friday, Sept. 25, 1801* (Boston, 1801), 3, 5. Three of the songs listed as sung

at this meeting (pp. 16-18), the only ones with authors listed, were written by Freemasons, the Reverend Thaddeus Mason Harris and C. P. Sumner (the father of Charles Sumner).

20. "New Inquisition," *American Masonic Register,* I (March 1821), 241-249; *Proceedings of the Centennial Celebration of the Presbyterian Church of Greensburg, Penn'a.,* 50-52; *Extracts from the Minutes of the General Assembly, of the Presbyterian Church, 1817,* 13-14; *Extracts from the Minutes of the General Assembly, of the Presbyterian Church, in the United States of America, A.D. 1820* (Philadelphia, 1820), 176, 178, 185.

21. Albert Gallatin Mackey, *The History of Freemasonry in South Carolina, from Its Origin in the Year 1736 to the Present Time . . .* (1861; Columbia, S.C., 1936), 186.

22. Francis Barclay, *A Sermon, Delivered at Easton . . . 24th of June, 1806 . . .* (Easton, Pa., 1806), 3. See also Pennsylvania Grand Lodge, *Reprint of the Minutes of the Grand Lodge of Free and Accepted Masons of Pennsylvania,* 12 vols. (Philadelphia, 1895-1907), II, 279.

23. Quoted in Charles Thompson McClenachan, *History of the Most Ancient and Honorable Fraternity of Free and Accepted Masons in New York,* 4 vols. (New York, 1888-1894), II, 181. Although this prayer can be traced back to the Irish grand lodge in 1730, it seems not to have been used in America until after the Revolution. N. Barker Cryer, "The De-Christianizing of the Craft," *Ars Quotuor Coronatorum,* XCVII (1984), 39.

24. See Avery Allyn, *A Ritual of Freemasonry . . .* (Boston, 1831) for the rituals of these degrees. Chapter 9 provides a fuller discussion.

25. See, for example, the "Rule for the Guidance of Christian Freemasons," in the most popular handbook of the period: Thomas Smith Webb, *The Freemason's Monitor; or, Illustrations of Masonry . . . ,* new ed. (Salem, Mass., 1821), 322-324.

26. Daniel Burhans, *A Sermon, Delivered at Lanesborough . . . June 24, A.L. 5807 . . .* (Pittsfield, Mass., [1807]), 19n; Edward T. Schultz, *History of Freemasonry in Maryland,* 3 vols. (Baltimore, 1884-1887), II, 481; Ezra Ripley, *A Masonic Sermon, Preached at Greenfield, Massachusetts, on 24th June, A.D. 1802 . . .* (Greenfield, Mass., 1802), 4.

27. Samuel Andrew Peters, *"Vox Clamatus in Deserto" . . .* (New York, 1807), 11; Schultz, *History of Freemasonry in Maryland,* II, 204.

28. For examples, see Mackey, *History of Freemasonry in South Carolina,* 198-199; and Joseph H. Hough, comp., *Origins of Masonry in the State of New Jersey, and the Entire Proceedings of the Grand Lodge, from Its First Organization, A.L. 5786* (Trenton, N.J., 1870), 238.

29. Pennsylvania Grand Lodge, *Reprint of the Minutes,* III, 377, 388, 422, 537-538; Schultz, *History of Freemasonry in Maryland,* II, 585; Christian, *Lynchburg and Its People,* 29, 63, 72, 88-89, 105.

30. Charles Albert Snodgrass, *The History of Freemasonry in Tennessee, 1789-1943 . . .* (Nashville, Tenn., 1944), 75; for the Maryland debate, see Maryland Grand Lodge, *Extract of Proceedings . . . 14th of May, A.D. 1804* (Baltimore, 1804), 2; *Extract of Proceedings . . . 12th . . . of November A.D. 1804* (Baltimore, 1804), 3; *Extract of Proceedings . . . Tenth Day of November A.D. 1806* (Baltimore, 1806), 3.

31. Henry F. May, *The Enlightenment in America* (New York, 1976), 252-277; and Butler, *Awash in a Sea of Faith,* 218-220, discuss some elements of this change. May suggests that post-1800 Congregational and Presbyterian clergy believed "they were fighting a two-front war. Certainly concerned to extirpate infidelity, they were equally hostile to ignorant enthusiasm, and believed deeply that learning must go hand in hand with piety" (321). Mark A. Noll, *Princeton and the Republic, 1768-1822 . . .* (Prince-

ton, N.J., 1989), traces the attempt to foreclose the more religiously corrosive elements of rationalism by reasserting Christian specifics at Princeton in the years after 1800. For explicitly Christian elements in earlier British Masonry, see Cryer, "The De-Christianizing of the Craft," *AQC*, XCVII (1984), 34–74.

32. Town, *System of Speculative Masonry*, 175–176; I have found no other evidence of belief in this millennium in my reading, although Town is cited in Gustavus F. Davis, *Free-masonry an Honourable Institution: An Address, Delivered in Haverhill, Mass. . . . June 25, A.L. 5827* (Boston, 1827), 8.

33. The committee declared that "this satisfactorily accounts for the unexampled spread of Masonry through our country of late years." *An Abstract of the Proceedings of the Antimasonic State Convention of Massachusetts, Held in Faneuil Hall, Boston, May 19 and 20, 1831* (Boston, 1831), 24–25. See also Goodman, *Towards a Christian Republic*, 19.

34. Increase N. Tarbox, ed., *Diary of Thomas Robbins, D.D., 1796–1854*, 2 vols. (Boston, 1886–1887), I, 87, 76, 63.

35. For the fullest account of this incident, see Vernon Stauffer, *New England and the Bavarian Illuminati* (New York, 1918). More recent discussions include Joseph W. Phillips, *Jedidiah Morse and New England Congregationalism* (New Brunswick, N.J., 1983), 73–101; Lipson, *Freemasonry in Federalist Connecticut*, 99–104; Stephen E. Berk, *Calvinism versus Democracy: Timothy Dwight and the Origins of American Evangelical Orthodoxy* (Hamden, Conn., 1974), 125–132.

36. Morgan's prayer in Josiah Bartlett, *An Address: Delivered at . . . Charlestown, Massachusetts . . . February 22, 1797 . . .* (Charlestown, Mass., 1797), 12–16; Jedidiah Morse, *A Sermon Delivered before the Grand Lodge . . . of Massachusetts . . . at Concord . . . June 25th, 1798* (Leominster, Mass., 1798). Neither the fullest study of the controversy nor the latest biography of Morse notes his earlier prayer. See Stauffer, *New England and the Bavarian Illuminati;* and Phillips, *Jedidiah Morse.*

Illuminati Sermon: Jedidiah Morse, *A Sermon, Delivered at the New North Church in Boston, on May 9th, 1798 . . .* (Boston, 1798), 22n. On Masonry—which is not mentioned in the text—see 21n–22n, 25n. Morse notes that "at the head of which [the fraternity] stands the immortal Washington," probably a reference to the common misconception that Washington was general grand master (22n). The same unwillingness to offend the American fraternity can be seen in two of the earliest and most important attacks after Morse. See David Tappan, *A Discourse Delivered in the Chapel of Harvard College, June 19, 1798 . . .* (Boston, 1798), 14–16n; Timothy Dwight, *The Duty of Americans, at the Present Crisis . . . Fourth of July, 1798* (New Haven, Conn., 1798), 32. Although claiming that Masonry had become corrupted even before the Illuminati and a conspiracy led by Voltaire (10–12), Dwight argues that uncorrupted Masons should not be upset by Robison's argument. "On my mind no impression, disadvantageous to the ancient Free Masonry, was made by reading the book." He notes that Robison himself was one of these uncorrupted Masons (32).

37. Jedidiah Morse, *A Sermon, Exhibiting the Present Danger . . .* (Charlestown, Mass., 1799), 46; see also 33.

38. See, for example, Benjamin Whitman, *An Oration, Delivered at Taunton, (Massachusetts) before King David's Lodge . . . September 13th, 5798 . . .* (New Bedford, Mass., 1798); Clark Brown, *Christian Charity, the Perfection of Every Moral System . . . June 24, 1799 . . .* (Greenfield, Mass., 1799); Caleb Prentiss, *A Sermon Delivered before Mount Moriah Lodge: At Reading . . . June 24 . . . 1799 . . .* (Leominster, Mass., 1799); Seth Payson, *A Sermon, at the Consecration of the Social Lodge in Ashby . . . June, A.D.*

1799 . . . (Amherst, N.H., 1800). For a rare mention of the issue in a Masonic address outside New England, see Seth Paine, *An Eulogy, on General George Washington, Pronounced in the Friendship Lodge . . . 22d of February, 1800* (Charleston, S.C., 1800), 18–19. The difficulties caused by the extreme Federalism and war fever of some leading Baltimore Masons in 1798 partly involved their response to charges of opposition to government. Maryland grand master Belton was censured by the grand lodge for calling for a military unit of Masons, allowing a military lodge on his own authority, and sponsoring a public address to the president that virtually justified the expected war. See Schultz, *History of Freemasonry in Maryland,* I, 257–274, 407–408.

39. [Roger] Viets, *A Sermon, Preached before the . . . Masons, at Granby, in Connecticut . . . on the 9th July 1800* (Hartford, Conn., 1800), 4; McLoughlin, *New England Dissent,* II, 760.

40. Frederick W. Hotchkiss, *A Sermon, Delivered at the Installation of Pythagoras Lodge . . . Lyme, Connecticut, October 7th, 1800* (New London, Conn., 1800), 5–6; Viets, *A Sermon, Preached before the . . . Masons, at Granby,* 8.

41. Tarbox, ed., *Diary of Thomas Robbins,* I, 171, 198, 326, 327.

42. James Johnson, *A Sermon Preached at the Anniversary Meeting . . . at St. Albans, Vermont . . . June 24, 1826* (1826), quoted in Ludlum, *Social Ferment in Vermont,* 94.

43. This categorization of rationalist, orthodox, and evangelical follows Hatch, *Democratization of American Christianity,* esp. 35.

44. Tarbox ed., *Diary of Thomas Robbins,* I, 76, on Strong's Masonic membership; Dudley A. Massey, *History of Freemasonry in Danvers, Massachusetts from September, 1778, to July, 1896 . . .* (Peabody, Mass., 1896), 147–161. For Robbins's relationship with Strong, see *Diary,* and the letter from Robbins in William B. Sprague, *Annals of the American Pulpit; or, Commemorative Notices of Distinguished American Clergymen of Various Denominations . . . ,* 9 vols. (New York, 1859–1869), II, 37–38; see 34–41, for Strong's career and reputation. Lipson, *Freemasonry in Federalist Connecticut,* 176–177, tries to suggest Masonic hostility to missionary activities, referring to "antimission Masons" (179), even though she discusses the two ABCFM missionaries (178).

45. Taylor: Richard A. Harrison, *Princetonians, 1769–1775: A Biographical Dictionary* (Princeton, N.J., 1980), 111–115; McWhorter: James McLachlan, *Princetonians, 1748–1768: A Biographical Dictionary* (Princeton, N.J., 1976), 194–199. Taylor served as acting president again in 1799 before Jonathan Edwards, Jr., began his term. Harrison, *Princetonians, 1769–1775,* 370–375, gives information on John Noble Cumming, local lodge founder and a trustee in MacWhorter's Newark, New Jersey, church. Another prominent Presbyterian, the Reverend James Muir of Alexandria, preached at the local memorial service for Washington as well as assisting at the graveside ceremony during the funeral. Washington's clergyman, Episcopalian Thomas Davis, was also a brother and performed the Episcopal services at the tomb (*The Lodge of Washington and His Masonic Neighbors* [Alexandria, Va., 1928], 30–31, 40). On Muir's career, see Sprague, *Annals of the American Pulpit,* III, 516–521. For another southern Presbyterian brother, see Cumming's College of New Jersey classmate, Thomas Harris McCaule, who was grand chaplain of Georgia upon his death. (Harrison, *Princetonians, 1769–1775,* 407–409).

46. On Wesley, see Harold E. Davis, *The Fledgling Province: Social and Cultural Life in Colonial Georgia, 1733–1776* (Chapel Hill, N.C., 1976), 172. On Wainwright, see Sprague, *Annals of the American Pulpit,* V, 610–617. His appointment is noted in *Masonic Mirror: and Mechanic's Intelligencer,* II (July 8, 1826), 218. The Lutheran Frederick Schaeffer, soon to be a Columbia professor, is noted by a contemporary as "one

of the most prominent ministers of his denomination" (Sprague, *Annals of the American Pulpit,* IX, 145).

On Griswold, see Sprague, *Annals of the American Pulpit,* V, 415–425. His membership is noted in *History of St. Johns Commandery Number One . . . Knights Templars . . . from 1802–1902* (Providence, R.I., 1902), 245.

Three Episcopal clergymen: On Henry William Ducachet of New York City, see William J. Duncan, *History of Independent Royal Arch Lodge, No. 2 . . . of the State of New York* (New York, 1904), 93. On Frederick Dalcho of Charleston, a key figure in the early history of the Scottish Rite in America, see Sprague, *Annals of the American Pulpit,* V, 560–562. On Milnor: Pennsylvania Grand Lodge, *Reprint of the Minutes,* III, 64; Sprague, *Annals of the American Pulpit,* V, 562–571; and John S. Stone, *A Memoir of the Life of James Milnor, D.D., Late Rector of St. George's Church, New York* (New York, 1848), a volume published by the American Tract Society.

47. Although Hatch (*Democratization of American Christianity,* 35) places Universalists in his populist category (roughly the evangelicals of this discussion) because of their style, their theological stance perhaps places them in the rationalist group for this purpose. For the affiliation of Massachusetts ministers, see the membership file in the Grand Secretary's Office, grand lodge of Masons in Massachusetts, Boston. The Reverend Abner Kneeland, later convicted of blasphemy in a celebrated Boston court case, acted as a grand chaplain of the Pennsylvania grand lodge, following the example of another important Universalist, the Reverend George Richards. On Kneeland, see Pennsylvania grand lodge, *Reprint of the Minutes,* V, 5, 33, 46, 75, 270, 283. Except in the notation at V, 126 (probably a mistake), Kneeland acted only as grand chaplain, pro tem. Richards is noted in Norris S. Barratt and Julius F. Sachse, *Freemasonry in Pennsylvania, 1727–1907, as Shown by the Records of Lodge No. 2, F. and A.M. of Philadelphia from the Year A.L. 5757, A.D. 1757,* 3 vols. (Philadelphia, 1908–1910), I, 298n. Richardson Wright, "George Richards: Preacher, Teacher, and Masonic Editor," *Am. Lodge Res. Trans.,* IV (1944–1945), 346–351.

48. Tarbox ed., *Diary of Thomas Robbins,* I, 90. Robbins was referring to the attempt of the British government to control seditious societies in the midst of the French Wars. Actually, the Masons were specifically exempted from some of the law's more onerous requirements.

49. Sprague, *Annals of the American Pulpit,* VI, 145–148, 229–235; *History of St. Johns Commandery, Number One, Knights Templars,* 245.

50. Sprague, *Annals of the American Pulpit,* VI, 400–407. Bradley later published *Some of the Beauties of Free-masonry; Being Extracts from Publications . . . with Introductory Remarks, Designed to Remove the Various Objections Made against the Order . . .* (Rutland, Vt., 1816). The Mormon leader Brigham Young owned a copy (D. Michael Quinn, *Early Mormonism and the Magic World View* [Salt Lake City, Utah, 1987], 240).

51. "Methodism and Freemasonry," *Masonic Mirror: and Mechanic's Intelligencer,* II (May 6, 1826), 150. Aaron Lummus's introduction to "An Address, Delivered at Ashburnham, A.L. 5825 . . . ," *Masonic Mirror: and Mechanic's Intelligencer,* II (Mar. 18, 1826), 89, suggests that he had visited Masonic groups in Massachusetts, Rhode Island, and New Hampshire while preaching in 138 different towns. This sermon continues in II (Mar. 25, 1826), 97, II (Apr. 1, 1826), 105–106. Aaron Lummus was the assistant secretary of the conference and, from 1829 to 1831, an editor of a Methodist newspaper. James Mudge, *History of the New England Conference of the Methodist Episcopal Church, 1796–1910* (Boston, 1910), 168, 362–363.

52. On Mudge, see *History of St. Johns Commandery, Number One, Knights Templars,*

244; Sprague, *Annals of the American Pulpit*, VII, 230–235; and Mudge, *History of the New England Conference*, esp. 46. On Taylor, see Membership File, Grand Secretary's Office, Grand Lodge of Masons in Massachusetts, Boston; and James Mudge, *History of the New England Conference*, 91–92. On Sias, see *History of St. Johns Commandery, Number One, Knights Templars*, 243; Mudge, *History of the New England Conference*, esp. 78–79. Ludlum, *Social Ferment in Vermont*, 106, notes that Sias commanded the Knights Templars in Boston during the 1825 reception of Lafayette.

53. Schultz, *History of Freemasonry in Maryland*, II, 238. On Dow, see Hatch, *Democratization of American Christianity*, esp. 36–40.

54. *Masonic Mirror: Science, Literature, and Miscellany*, N.S., I (Apr. 24, 1830), 337–338.

55. Massachusetts Grand Lodge, *Proceedings of the Most Worshipful Grand Lodge . . . of Massachusetts . . . 1815–1825* (Cambridge, Mass. 1905), 541–552. For the 1829 ceremony at a Sandy Bay, Massachusetts, Universalist Church, see *Masonic Mirror: Science, Literature, and Miscellany*, N.S., I (July 25, 1829), 26, which also cites a piece from an Albany, New York, paper noting that "the corner stones of several edifices, dedicated to divine purposes, were laid."

56. *Masonic Mirror: and Mechanic's Intelligencer*, II (Sept. 23, 1826), 311; "The Church of All Denominations," *American Masonic Register*, I (July 1821), 414; *Extract from the Proceedings of the Most Ancient Fraternity of Free and Accepted Masons of the State of Louisiana, Held in the City of New-Orleans* (New Orleans, La., 1828), 9–14. The Mississippi grand lodge in 1826 laid the cornerstone of a Methodist Episcopal Church in Port Gibson (*Proceedings of the Grand Lodge of Mississippi . . . from Its Organization July 27th, 5818 . . . [to] 5852* [Jackson, Miss., 1882], 54–57).

57. *Masonic Mirror: Science, Literature, and Miscellany*, N.S., I (Apr. 24, 1830), 337–338.

58. Ibid., 337.

59. John P. Payson, *Masonic Oration Delivered before . . . Columbian Lodge, Convened at Deerfield, New-Hampshire, December 27th, A.L. 5799* (Portsmouth, N.H., 1800), 18; Richard Rosewell Eliot, *A Discourse, Delivered at Athol, at the Consecration of Harris Lodge, October 13, 1803–A.L. 5803 . . .* (Greenfield, Mass., 1804), 19–20.

60. Thaddeus Mason Harris, *Discourses, Delivered on Public Occasions, Illustrating the Principles . . . of Free Masonry . . .* (Charlestown, Mass., 1801), 176.

61. Harris, *Discourses, Delivered on Public Occasions*, 177; Hector Orr, *A History of Free Masonry . . . Bridgewater . . . June 30th, A.L. 5797* (Boston, 1798), 23, 24; William Bentley, *A Discourse, Delivered at Amherst, August 10, 1797 . . . at the Installation of the Benevolent Lodge . . .* (Amherst, N.H., 1797), 27, 16; Walter Colton, *Masonic Obligations; An Address, Delivered before Washington Chapter, No. 6 and St. John's Lodge, No. 2, Middletown, June 24th, A.L. 5826* (Middletown, Conn., 1826), 12–13; Town, *System of Speculative Masonry*, 200.

62. Joseph Dunham, *An Oration, Delivered at Hanover, before the Franklin Lodge* (Hanover, N.H., 1797), 18; Benjamin Gleason, *A Masonic Address, etc. Pronounced before the Brethren of Mount Moriah Lodge, at Reading . . . June 24th, A.L. 5805 . . .* (Boston, 1805), 9. This question of excluding women had been considered originally in England; see George Smith, *The Use and Abuse of Freemasonry* (London, 1783), 349–366, where a similar range of reasons is given; and Brother C——, "A Charge Delivered in the *Union lodge*, at *Exeter*, in *Devon*, . . . A.L. 5770," in *The Free-Mason's Pocket Companion* (New London, Conn., 1794), 10–11. For a discussion of women's exclusion in a later period, see Mark C. Carnes, *Secret Ritual and Manhood in Victo-*

rian America (New Haven, Conn., 1989), 81–89. Carnes argues more generally that gender was an issue because men were attempting to separate themselves from feminine worlds. I argue that it was problematic earlier primarily because both women and Masonic brothers were occupying the same cultural ground.

63. Charles Train, *A Masonic Oration, Pronounced at Framingham, June 24, A. L. 5812* (Boston, 1812), 15.

64. Ibid., 15; Whitman, *Oration, Delivered at Taunton* (1798), 12; Ripley, *Masonic Sermon, Preached at Greenfield, Massachusetts* (1802), 16.

65. Samuel S. Wilde, *An Oration, Delivered in Pownalborough . . . June 24th, 5799* (Wiscasset, Maine, 1799), 17n; Whitman, *An Oration, Delivered at Taunton* (1798), 18. Caleb Cushing later married Wilde's daughter. Important discussions of the reshaping of gender roles include Jan Lewis, "The Republican Wife: Virtue and Seduction in the Early Republic," *William and Mary Quarterly,* 3d Ser., XLIV (1987), 689–721; Mary Beth Norton, *Liberty's Daughters: The Revolutionary Experience of American Women, 1750–1800* (Boston, 1980); and Linda K. Kerber, *Women of the Republic: Intellect and Ideology in Revolutionary America* (Chapel Hill, N.C., 1980).

66. [Abigail (Blodget) Stickney Lyon], *Observations on Free Masonry; with a Masonic Vision, Addressed, by a Lady in Worcester, to Her Female Friend* (Worcester, Mass., 1798), 4, 5, 8. See also the case of Hannah Mather Crocker discussed in Chapter 5. The willingness of these women to identify themselves with Masonic values perhaps suggests that the intense anxiety about gender roles expressed by Wilde was less common within the fraternity than the desire to recommend further female education and to grant women's activities greater equality with men's. Benjamin Gleason, still serving as the grand lecturer of the Massachusetts grand lodge in 1806, suggested to Bristol County, Massachusetts, brothers that "the improvements and refinements of some succeeding age . . . may add the last polishes and finishing to the picture" (of Masonry and perhaps of society in general) and allow women to become "in all our conventions, a *sister* and a *companion* with her *brother* man." Benjamin Gleason, *An Oration, Pronounced before the "Bristol Lodge," in Norton, and in the Presence of the Associated Celebrating Lodges of Bristol County, on St. John's Anniversary, June 24th, A.L. 5806* (Boston, 1806), 18.

67. James Mann, *An Oration, Addressed to the Fraternity of Free Masons, in the Presence of a Large Concourse of People, on the Tenth of October, in Wrentham . . .* (Wrentham, Mass., 1798), 28; Amos Stoddard, *A Masonic Address, Delivered before. . . . Kennebeck Lodge . . . Hallowell, Massachusetts; June 24th, . . . 5797* (Hallowell, Mass., 1797), 20.

68. David Leonard, *An Oration, Pronounced at Nantucket, December 27, 1796 . . .* (New Bedford, Mass., 1797), 8.

69. Barratt and Sachse, *Freemasonry in Pennsylvania,* I, 294–296.

70. Sidney Hart and David C. Ward, "The Waning of an Enlightenment Ideal: Charles Willson Peale's Philadelphia Museum, 1790–1820," *Journal of the Early Republic,* VIII (1988), 396. On Peale's museum, see also David R. Brigham, *Public Culture in the Early Republic: Peale's Museum and Its Audience* (Washington, D.C., 1995), esp. 35–50; Charles Coleman Sellers, *Mr. Peale's Museum: Charles Willson Peale and the First Popular Museum of Natural Science and Art* (New York, 1980).

71. Hart and Ward, "The Waning of an Enlightenment Ideal," *Jour. Early Republic,* VIII (1988), 401; Sellers, *Mr. Peale's Museum,* 195. Before its final sale to P. T. Barnum around 1849, Peale's museum had been on exhibit at Philadelphia's Masonic Hall. Barnum had already exhibited there as well (Sellers, *Mr. Peale's Museum,* 306,

308–310). On the museum's finances, see also Brigham, *Public Culture in the Early Republic*, 83–106.

Chapter Seven

1. Hiram B. Hopkins, *Renunciation of Free Masonry* (Boston, 1830), 5. On the ceremony, see also *Albany Argus* (New York), July 8, 1825. For another brother drawn to the fraternity by a Masonic public appearance—in this case a Masonic funeral—see David Pease, *The Good Man in Bad Company; or, Speculative Freemasonry a Wicked and Dangerous Combination* . . . (Brookfield, Mass., 1831), 19.

2. Hopkins, *Renunciation of Free Masonry*, 5.

3. Seth May, "Address, Delivered at the Installation of the Officers of Temple Lodge, Nov. 19, A.L. 5825," *Masonic Mirror: and Mechanics' Intelligencer* (Boston), II (May 6, 1826), 145. Avery Allyn, *A Ritual of Freemasonry* . . . (Boston, 1831), 71, suggests that this willingness formed part of the Master Mason's obligation.

4. Clark Brown, *The Utility of Moral and Religious Societies, and of the Masonick in Particular . . . Putney, Vt. . . . June 24th, 1814* . . . (Keene, N.H., 1814), 21–22.

5. Amos Stoddard, *An Oration, Delivered in the Meeting House of the First Parish in Portland . . . June 24th, 5799* . . . (Portland, Maine, 1799), 11.

6. Recent discussions of Masonry tend to follow the broad outlines of this earlier debate. Historians generally suggest that Masonry affected society primarily through its aid to individuals. Paul Goodman and Charles Sellers stress the fraternity's benefits to mobile men, in Goodman, *Towards a Christian Republic: Antimasonry and the Great Transition in New England, 1826–1836* (New York, 1988), esp. 12, 14, 41; and in Sellers, *The Market Revolution: Jacksonian America, 1815–1846* (New York, 1991), 281–282. Conrad Edick Wright sees Masonry simply as another example of a "mutual" charity, although, like other fraternal groups, "the most removed from their own communities" (*The Transformation of Charity in Postrevolutionary New England* [Boston, 1992], 105). Dorothy Ann Lipson provides the fullest discussion of these issues, covering discipline, charity, and aid to mobile individuals. Like Randolph A. Roth, she does not take very seriously Masonic claims to seek the public good rather than particular interests of the members; see Lipson, *Freemasonry in Federalist Connecticut* (Princeton N.J., 1977), 200–227, 244–248; Roth, *The Democratic Dilemma: Religion, Reform, and the Social Order in the Connecticut River Valley of Vermont, 1791–1850* (Cambridge, 1987), 98–101. By contrast, Kathleen Smith Kutolowski and Don Harrison Doyle consider not just these personal benefits but the ways that Masonry (and, for Doyle, other voluntary groups) helped to knit society together. In particular, Doyle notes the significance of Masonry's moral training, a topic virtually ignored by other historians. But he (as does Kutolowski) tends to ignore the conflict between the individual and society that others see as inherent in the situation. See Kutolowski, "Freemasonry and Community in the Early Republic: The Case for Antimasonic Anxieties," *American Quarterly*, XXXIV (1982), 545–548; Doyle, *The Social Order of a Frontier Community: Jacksonville, Illinois, 1825–1870* (Urbana, Ill., 1978), 156–193. This chapter attempts to combine these approaches, examining Masonic claims to seek both individual advantage and public benefits—while attempting to explain how later opponents of the fraternity could see these same desires as utterly incompatible.

7. *An Abstract of the Proceedings of the Antimasonic State Convention of Massachusetts, Held in Faneuil Hall, Boston, May 19 and 20, 1831* (Boston, 1831), 62. Historians

have increasingly located the growth of a competitive, individualistic society during the years after the Revolution. See, especially, Joyce Appleby, *Liberalism and Republicanism in the Historical Imagination* (Cambridge, Mass., 1992); and Gordon S. Wood, *The Radicalism of the American Revolution* (New York, 1992). Paul Goodman's study of Antimasonry sees the fraternity as a symbol of this capitalist transformation (*Towards a Christian Republic*). This study suggests more internal conflict within commercially minded individuals. Steven Watts similarly views the period from the Revolution to the War of 1812 as marked by "half-conscious motives, unintended consequences, [and] frequent self-deception" in this rise of self-seeking individualism. But Masonry reveals neither the almost pathological dysfunction nor the clear-cut resolution during the War of 1812 suggested by Watts (*The Republic Reborn: War and the Making of Liberal America, 1790–1820* [Baltimore, 1987], quotation at xviii). Donald B. Cole, *The Presidency of Andrew Jackson* (Lawrence, Kans., 1993), argues that Jackson, like his followers, showed "ambivalence toward . . . the new economy" (x). The fullest discussions of the ways mutualism and competition could coexist appear in studies of economic practice. See Christopher Clark, *The Roots of Rural Capitalism: Western Massachusetts, 1780–1860* (Ithaca, N.Y., 1990), 21–117; Daniel Vickers, "Competency and Competition: Economic Culture in Early America," *William and Mary Quarterly*, 3d Ser., XLVII (1990), 3–29.

8. Anne Royall, *The Black Book; or, A Continuation of Travels in the United States*, 3 vols. (Washington, D.C., 1828–1829), II, 11, discusses her earlier experiences in New York, providing the personal details missing in her *Sketches of History, Life, and Manners in the United States* (New Haven, Conn., 1826). See also Bessie Rowland James, *Anne Royall's U.S.A.* (New Brunswick, N.J., 1972), 136–137; Richardson Wright, "Anne Royall, Masonic Protagonist," *American Lodge of Research Transactions*, I (1930–1933), 177–193, discusses Royall, paying particular attention to her discussions of Masonry.

9. Charles S. Plumb, *The History of the American Union Lodge No. 1, Free and Accepted Masons of Ohio, 1776 to 1933* (Marietta, Ohio, 1934), 143–144; Thomas Smith Webb, *The Freemason's Monitor: or, Illustrations of Masonry . . .*, new ed. (Salem, Mass., 1821), 27 (hereafter cited as Webb, *Freemason's Monitor* [1821]). See also Thaddeus Mason Harris, *Discourses, Delivered on Public Occasions, Illustrating the Principles . . . of Free Masonry . . .* (Charlestown, Mass., 1801), 71.

10. James, *Royall's U.S.A.*, 135.

11. Royall, *Black Book*, II, 11. Wright, *Transformation of Charity*, provides the fullest account of the development of charity in the years after the Revolution and discusses much of the literature on charity (199–206).

12. Royall, *Black Book*, II, 117; James, *Royall's U.S.A.*, 99–101, 114–117.

13. Grand master James Milnor's Circular Address to the Philadelphia Lodges, in Pennsylvania Grand Lodge, *Reprint of the Minutes of the Grand Lodge of Free and Accepted Masons of Pennsylvania*, 12 vols. (Philadelphia, 1895–1907), II, 489.

14. William J. Duncan, *History of Independent Royal Arch Lodge, No. 2 . . . of the State of New York . . .* (New York, 1904), 106; *Hardcastle's Annual Masonic Register, for the Year of Masonry, 5812* (New York, 1811), 4–8; Charles Thompson McClenachan, *History of the Most Ancient and Honorable Fraternity of Free and Accepted Masons in New York . . .*, 4 vols. (New York, 1888–1894), II, 232 (hereafter cited as McClenachan, *New York*).

15. De Witt Clinton, *An Address Delivered by the Most Worshipful the Honorable DeWitt Clinton, Esq. to the Grand Lodge, of the State of New-York, at His Installation into the Office of Grand Master, on the 19th of June, 1806* (New York, 1806), 13;

McClenachan, *New York,* II, 351–377, 445–454; Ossian Lang, *History of Freemasonry in the State of New York* (New York, [1922]), 96–107.

16. *Grand Lodge of the Most Ancient and Honorable Fraternity of Free and Accepted Masons of Pennsylvania . . . 6th December . . . 1819* [Philadelphia, 1819], 5–11; John Dove, ed., *Proceedings of the M. W. Grand Lodge of Ancient York Masons of the State of Virginia, from Its Organization, in 1778, to 1822 . . .* (Richmond, Va., 1874), 584–586; grand master James Milnor's Circular Address to the Philadelphia Lodges, Pennsylvania Grand Lodge, *Reprint of the Minutes,* II, 489. Rob Morris, *The History of Freemasonry in Kentucky, in Its Relations to the Symbolic Degrees* (Louisville, Ky., 1859), 294–295, counts 1,451 brothers in that state that same year. The figure of 80,000 United States Masons in 1822 (McClenachan, *New York,* II, 342) equals about 4.85% of the eligible adult white male population of about 1,650,000 noted in the 1820 census (calculated by dividing the white male population for the ages 14–25 in half to approximate the population in that category at least 21 years of age and thus eligible for Masonic membership, then adding this number to the higher-age categories). *The Statistical History of the United States from Colonial Times to the Present* (Stamford, Conn., 1965), 10 (Series A 70–85).

17. Salem Town, *A System of Speculative Masonry . . .* (Salem, N.Y., 1818), 161–162; Royall, *Black Book,* II, 183.

18. James, *Royall's U.S.A.,* 69. James is the best biography of Royall. I draw upon it extensively for the discussion in the following paragraphs.

19. May, "Address, Delivered at the Installation of the Officers of Temple Lodge, Nov. 19, A.L. 5825," *Masonic Mirror: and Mechanics' Intelligencer,* II (May 6, 1826), 145; McClenachan, *New York,* II, 230–238. Duncan, *History of Independent Royal Arch Lodge, No. 2,* 85–86. The New York grand lodge spent $2,141.50 on charity in 1813 (McClenachan, *New York,* II, 245–246). The Boston Board of Masonic Relief, made up of the city's lodges, spent $667.11 in 1822 (Massachusetts Grand Lodge, *Proceedings of the Most Worshipful Grand Lodge . . . of Massachusetts . . . 1792–1815* [(Cambridge, Mass., 1905]), 419–420).

20. Plumb, *American Union Lodge,* 118, 216; Herbert T. O. Blue, *The History of Canton Lodge No. 60 . . . of Ohio, 1821 to 1946* (Canton, Ohio, 1946), 20. The Massachusetts Ancient grand lodge distributed "the remains" of their June 1791 feast to the jail. Massachusetts Grand Lodge, *Proceedings in Masonry: St. John's Grand Lodge, 1733–1792; Massachusetts Grand Lodge, 1769–1792 . . .* (Boston, 1895), 379.

21. McClenachan, *New York,* II, 230–238; Albert Gallatin Mackey, *The History of Freemasonry in South Carolina, from Its Origin in the Year 1736 to the Present Time . . .* (1861; Columbia, S.C., 1936), 209–210 (1825); Massachusetts Grand Lodge, *Proceedings of the Most Worshipful Grand Lodge . . . of Massachusetts . . . 1815–1825* (Cambridge, Mass., 1905), 485–495 (1824); Ohio Grand Lodge, *Proceedings of the Grand Lodge . . . of Ohio . . . from 1808 to 1853 Inclusive,* 2 vols. (Columbus, Ohio, 1857–1858), I, 252, 270, 279–280 (1834); Pennsylvania Grand Lodge, *Reprint of the Minutes,* I, 455–456.

22. Temple R. Hollcroft, "Salem Town: Partial Autobiography and Masonic Biography," *Am. Lodge Res. Trans.,* V (1949–1951), 246–247; Royall, *Black Book,* I, 140.

23. Royall, *Sketches of History, Life, and Manners,* 259; Thomas Wilson, *The Philadelphia Directory and Stranger's Guide, for 1825* (Philadelphia, 1825); *Directory and Stranger's Guide, for the City of Charleston . . . 1825 . . .* (Charleston, S.C., 1824); Charles G. Finney, *The Character, Claims, and Practical Workings of Freemasonry* (Cincinnati, Ohio, 1869), v–vii.

24. Solomon Southwick, *An Address, Delivered by Appointment, in the Episcopal*

Church, at the Opening of the Apprentices' Library, in the City of Albany, January 1, 1821 (Albany, N.Y., 1821), iv; Francis Higgins Cuming, *An Address Delivered at the Laying of the Cap-Stone . . . June 24th, 1825 . . .* (Lockport, N.Y., 1825), 11; De Witt Clinton, *An Address Delivered before Holland Lodge, December 24, 1793* (New York, 1794), 10.

25. Finney, *Character, Claims, and Practical Workings of Freemasonry,* v-vii; James J. Tyler, *The Last Crusade of Rev. Charles G. Finney* (rpt. from Grand Lodge of Ohio Proceedings [1950]), 3-4; Benjamin Gleason, *A Masonic Address, etc. Pronounced before the Brethren of Mount Moriah Lodge, at Reading . . . June 24th, A.L. 5805 . . .* (Boston, 1805), 5. See, for example of *"Stranger,"* Morris Birkbeck, *Notes on a Journey in America,* 3d ed. (1818; rpt. New York, 1966), 81.

26. Royall, *Sketches of History, Life, and Manners,* 199; Clinton, *Address Delivered before Holland Lodge, 1793,* 10; Royall, *Black Book,* I, 313.

27. Thaddeus Mason Harris, *A Discourse, Delivered at Bridgewater, November 3, 1797, at the Request of the Members of Fellowship Lodge . . .* (Boston, 1797), 12-13.

28. Harris, *Discourse, Delivered at Bridgewater* (1797), 13, 14.

29. Thaddeus Mason Harris, *A Masonick Eulogy, Pronounced at Worcester, Massachusetts, Twentyfourth of June, A.L. 5794 . . . before . . . Morning Star Lodge . . .* (Worcester, Mass., 1794), 11.

30. Dudley A. Massey, *History of Freemasonry in Danvers, Massachusetts from September, 1778, to July, 1896 . . .* (Peabody, Mass., 1896), 156.

31. *Masonic Mirror: and Mechanics' Intelligencer,* II (May 13, 1826), 153.

32. For debtor's aid, see Raymond A. Mohl, *Poverty in New York, 1783-1825* (New York, 1971), 125; Wayne A. Huss, *The Master Builders: A History of the Grand Lodge of Free and Accepted Masons of Pennsylvania,* 3 vols. (Philadelphia, 1986-1989), I, 62 (yellow fever); Nelson Gillespie, *Centennial History of Apollo Lodge, No. 13 . . . Troy, New York . . .* (Troy, N.Y., 1898), 69-70. For other examples of Masonic charity, see Chapters 5 and 6.

33. See, for example, Joseph Haroutunian, *Piety versus Moralism: The Passing of the New England Theology* (New York, 1932). A broader view is sketched by Thomas L. Haskell, in Thomas Bender, ed., *The Antislavery Debate: Capitalism and Abolitionism as a Problem in Historical Interpretation* (Berkeley, Calif., 1992), 107-160.

34. *Masonic Mirror: and Mechanics' Intelligencer,* II (May 13, 1826), 153; Donald Fraser, *An Interesting Companion for a Leisure Hour . . .* (New York, 1814), 121.

35. Edward Richmond, *A Sermon, Preached October 21st, 1801, at the Consecration of the Rising Star Lodge, in Stoughton . . .* (Boston, 1801), 16; Harris, *Discourses, Delivered upon Public Occasions,* 279. An argument similar to Harris's is made in Thomas Gray, *The Value of Life and Charitable Institutions: A Discourse Delivered before the Humane Society . . . June 11th, 1805* (Boston, 1805), 10-11.

36. Royall, *Sketches of History, Life, and Manners,* 209. On Philadelphia: Robert Desilver, *The Philadelphia Directory for 1824 . . .* (Philadelphia, 1824), esp. xxxix-lxxv; Wilson, *Philadelphia Directory for 1825,* esp. xxxvii-xxxix. On the earlier growth of such associations in Philadelphia, see John K. Alexander, *Render Them Submissive: Responses to Poverty in Philadelphia, 1760-1800* (Amherst, Mass., 1980), 122-141. On Massachusetts: Richard D. Brown, "The Emergence of Urban Society in Rural Massachusetts, 1760-1820," *Journal of American History,* LXI (1974-1975), 40-41; see also Wright, *Transformation of Charity.*

37. Desilver, *Philadelphia Directory for 1824,* 1; Wilson, *Philadelphia Directory for 1825,* xiv. For an example of costs and benefits, see the rules of the American Friendly Institution in Desilver, *Philadelphia Directory for 1824,* xxxix. On English friendly soci-

eties, see M. Dorothy George, *London Life in the Eighteenth Century* (1925; New York, 1965), 301-303, 398 nn. 89-90, 403 n. 139, n. 141; John Langton and R. J. Morris, ed., *Atlas of Industrializing Britain, 1780-1914* (London, 1986), 194-195. On the New England experience, see Wright, *Transformation of Charity*, 30-31, 65-67.

38. Thomas Wilson, *Picture of Philadelphia, for 1824* . . . (Philadelphia, 1823), 278; John Vallance, *An Oration, Delivered before the Provident Society, of Philadelphia, April 3d, 1810* . . . (Philadelphia, [1810]), 9-10. Wright, *Transformation of Charity*, 65-82, 147-157, makes this distinction between "mutual" and "fiduciary" charity. Even the Philadelphia Dispensary, one of the city's largest private organizations, required that a needy sick person receive the recommendation of a subscriber before receiving aid.

39. Vallance, *Oration, Delivered before the Provident Society* (1810), 10. James Mease, *Picture of Philadelphia* . . . (Philadelphia, 1811), 276-277, gives information on the Provident Society's aid. From April 1795 to April 1811 it provided $992 to 52 sick members and $2,251 to widows. Priscilla Ferguson Clement, *Welfare and the Poor in the Nineteenth-Century City: Philadelphia, 1800-1854* (Rutherford, N.J., 1985), 208 n. 24, suggests that, while private organizations probably provided aid to more people than public welfare in this period, still the private aid was "typically, extremely small." This conforms to Wayne A. Huss's figures on the Pennsylvania Grand Lodge's charity fund, which suggests that the average disbursement from 1792 to 1809 was about $12. Huss, *Master Builders*, I, 62-63.

40. Vallance, *Oration, Delivered before the Provident Society* (1810), 15-16.

41. Wright, *Transformation of Charity*, 115-133; Samuel Stillman, *A Discourse, Delivered before the Members of the Boston Female Asylum, Friday, Sept. 25, 1801* . . . (Boston, 1801), 3; John Vanderbilt, Jr., *An Address, Delivered in the New-York Free School, on the 27th Day of December, 1809* . . . *on the Introduction of Fifty Orphan and Helpless Children Belonging to the Masonic Fraternity* . . . (New York, 1810), 15. On the expansion of institutions in New England, see Wright, *Transformation of Charity*, 51-111.

42. James Carter, *Oration, Delivered at Groton* . . . *June 24, A.L. 5821* . . . (Worcester, Mass., 1821), 17; Massey, *History of Freemasonry in Danvers, Massachusetts*, 148.

43. Stillman, *Discourse Delivered before the Members of the Boston Female Asylum* (1801), 5, 16-18 (songs); Gray, *The Value of Life and Charitable Institutions* (1805), 14; J. H. Powell, *Bring Out Your Dead: The Great Plague of Yellow Fever in Philadelphia in 1793* (Philadelphia, 1949), esp. 177-179 (on Israel); William Bentley, *The Diary of William Bentley, D.D., Pastor of the East Church, Salem, Massachusetts*, 4 vols. (Salem, Mass., 1905-1914), II, 246; Vallance, *Oration, Delivered before the Provident Society* (1810), 15-16, 2. The Provident Society's emblem was a hive of bees, a symbol commonly used by Masons. *Rules and Orders, Agreed to Be Observed by a Masonick Fire Society, Instituted at Glocester, August 18th, Anno Domini, MDCCLXXXIX* (Boston, 1789).

44. Carter, *Oration* (1821), 1; William Bentley, *A Discourse, Delivered in Roxbury, October 12, 5796; before the Grand Lodge of* . . . *Massachusetts* . . . (Boston, 1797), 16; Bentley, *Diary*, II, 246.

45. Harris, *Masonick Eulogy, Pronounced at Worcester* (1794), 8.

46. Henry Channing, *A Discourse Delivered in New-London, at the Request of Union Lodge* . . . *June 30, 1796* (New London, Conn., 1796), 5; Bentley, *Diary*, I, 270 (July 2, 1791); John Frederick Ernst, *Oration with a Suitable Prayer, Delivered before the Grand Royal Arch Chapter for* . . . *New-York* . . . *Third Day of February, A.L. 5801* (Albany, N.Y., [1801]), 11.

47. Harris, *Discourse, Delivered at Bridgewater* (1797), 14. Charity within churches (rather than within religious benevolent associations) has been given surprisingly little attention. See M. J. Heale, "Patterns of Benevolence: Charity and Morality in Rural and Urban New York, 1783-1830," *Societas—A Review of Social History,* III (1973), 337-359; and Clement, *Welfare and the Poor in the Nineteenth-Century City,* 142-143.

48. Harris, *Discourse, Delivered at Bridgewater* (1797), 13, 14; Royall, *Black Book,* II, 12.

49. Wright, "Royall," *Am. Lodge Res. Trans.,* I (1930-1933), 182.

50. M. L. Weems, *The True Patriot* (Philadelphia, 1802), 5. For Weems's own description of the event, see Weems to Carey, Dec. 3, 1801, in Paul Leicester Ford, ed., *Mason Locke Weems: His Works and Ways,* 3 vols. (New York, 1929), II, 208-210.

51. Weems to Carey, Dec. 25, 1801, Feb. 19, 1802, in Ford, ed., *Mason Locke Weems,* II, 216, 229. Weems, *The Philanthropist; or, A Good Twelve Cents Worth of Political Love Powder* (n.p., [1799]), 3. On the *Life of Washington* and Weems's other works, see Ford, ed., *Mason Locke Weems,* esp. I, 1-29. Watts, *The Republic Reborn,* 141-151, portrays Weems similarly as someone who united "money and morality." The best study of Weems's bookselling is James Gilreath, "Mason Weems, Mathew Carey, and the Southern Booktrade, 1794-1810," *Publishing History,* X (1981), 27-49. For a brief biography, see Lewis Leary, *The Book-Peddling Parson: An Account of the Life and Works of Mason Locke Weems . . .* (Chapel Hill, N.C., 1984). See Chapter 9 for a cultural analysis of *The Life of Washington.*

52. Doyle, *Social Order of a Frontier Community,* 157, similarly writes of "the paradoxical needs of the voluntary community for individual opportunity and social discipline," although his work, concerned primarily with a later period, does not single out Masonry.

53. The distinction between local exchange and long-distance trade is made by Clark, *Roots of Rural Capitalism,* esp. 28-38, 69-71. Local economic ties are vividly portrayed in John Mack Faragher, *Sugar Creek: Life on the Illinois Prairie* (New Haven, Conn., 1986), 121-170, esp. 133-136. Vickers, "Competency and Competition," *WMQ,* 3d Ser., XLVII (1990), 3-29, similarly notes the coexistence of the two forms. The social meanings of economic change in this period are the subject of a large literature. Allan Kulikoff, "The Transition to Capitalism in Rural America," *WMQ,* 3d Ser., XLVI (1989), 120-144, provides a good introduction. See also James A. Henretta, *The Origins of American Capitalism: Collected Essays* (Boston, 1991); and, from a different perspective, Winifred Barr Rothenberg, *From Market-Places to a Market Economy: The Transformation of Rural Massachusetts, 1750-1850* (Chicago, 1992).

54. Calvin Colton, *The Life and Times of Henry Clay,* 2 vols. (New York, 1846), I, 36.

55. Colton, *Life and Times of Clay,* I, 35.

56. Only initials are used in George Washington Dame, *Historical Sketch of Roman Eagle Lodge No. 122 . . . 1820-1895* (Danville, Va., 1939), 22.

57. Dove, *Proceedings of the Grand Lodge of Virginia,* 186-187; Morris, *History of Freemasonry in Kentucky,* 121. For a local lodge's disciplinary activities, see William Mosley Brown, *Freemasonry in Staunton, Virginia . . .* (Staunton, Va., 1949), 30. Lodges did not always follow injunctions to watch carefully. Henry Clay's duels with Humphrey Marshall and later with his Masonic brother John Randolph of Virginia were ignored by his lodge and grand lodge. When the grand master of Kentucky, however, fought with a past master of the Lexington Lodge in 1818, the grand lodge suspended the two indefinitely. Charles Snow Guthrie, *Kentucky Freemasonry, 1788-1978: The Grand Lodge and the Men Who Made It* (n.p., 1981), 55-57.

58. Pennsylvania Grand Lodge, *Reprint of the Minutes,* I, 320, 345; James F. Hopkins, ed., *The Papers of Henry Clay,* I, *The Rising Statesman, 1797–1814* (Lexington, Ky., 1959), 261. Roth, *Democratic Dilemma,* 98–99, finds that Masons were more likely to form partnerships with each other than with nonmembers in Vermont's Connecticut Valley, although he suggests that churches provided an even more important means of creating partnerships. Paul E. Johnson, *A Shopkeeper's Millennium: Society and Revivals in Rochester, New York, 1815–1837* (New York, 1978), 29–30, gives Rochester examples.

59. Bentley, *Diary,* III, 26–27; Clark Brown, *The Moral and Benevolent Design of Christianity and Free-masonry, Discussed . . . June 24th, A.L. 5808 . . . Danville . . .* (Danville, Vt., 1808), 11–12.

60. Hopkins, ed., *Papers of Clay,* I, 140; 145 n. 3 discusses John Clay's move.

61. Amos Stoddard, *A Masonic Address, Delivered before . . . Kennebeck Lodge . . . Hallowell, Massachusetts: June 24th . . . 5797* (Hallowell, Mass., 1797), 3–4; Weems, *True Patriot,* 8.

62. Brown, *Moral and Benevolent Design of Christianity and Free-masonry,* 11; David Bernard, *Light on Masonry: A Collection of All the Most Important Documents on the Subject of Speculative Free Masonry . . .* (Utica, N.Y., 1829), 62; William Loughton Smith to the Grand Lodge, 1795, in Frederick Dalcho, *An Ahiman Rezon, for the Use of the Grand Lodge of South-Carolina, Ancient York-masons . . .* (Charleston, S.C., 1807), 153–155.

63. Clark, *Roots of Rural Capitalism,* 28–38, 69–71, and noting the economic benefits of this local system (71); Faragher, *Sugar Creek,* 121–170. See also Vickers, "Competency and Competition," *WMQ,* 3d Ser., XLVII (1990), 3–29.

64. David Buel, Jr., *Troy for Fifty Years: A Lecture . . . 21st December, 1840* (Troy, N.Y., 1841), 15–16; Dalcho, *Ahiman Rezon,* 153–155; Stoddard, *Masonic Address, Delivered before Kennebeck Lodge* (1797), 3–4.

65. Hopkins, ed., *Papers of Clay,* I, 70, 84.

66. Ibid., I, 40, 380–381, 779–780; Jonathan M. Chu, "Debt Litigation and Shays's Rebellion," in Robert A. Gross, ed., *In Debt to Shays: The Bicentennial of an Agrarian Rebellion* (Charlottesville, Va., 1993), 81–99, stresses the inefficiency of legal action as a means to recover debts.

67. Hopkins, ed., *Papers of Clay,* I, 39, 98.

68. Mathew Carey, *Autobiography* (1837; Brooklyn, N.Y., 1942), 42.

69. Mathew Carey to Joseph Clarke, Dec. 26, 1794, in Lea and Febiger Papers, Historical Society of Pennsylvania, Philadelphia, quoted in James N. Green, "From Printer to Publisher: Mathew Carey and the Origins of Nineteenth-Century Book Publishing," in Michael Hackenberg, ed., *Getting the Books Out: Papers of the Chicago Conference on the Book in Nineteenth-Century America* (Washington, D.C., 1987), 31. But see also a reference to a "Mr. M. Carey" (undoubtedly the same person) in the 1829 minutes of Pennsylvania Lodge No. 2, suggesting that Carey was not then recognized as a brother by the lodge. Norris S. Barratt and Julius F. Sachse, *Freemasonry in Pennsylvania, 1727–1907, as Shown by the Records of Lodge No. 2, F. and A.M. of Philadelphia from the Year A.L. 5757, A.D. 1757,* 3 vols. (Philadelphia, 1908–1910), III, 209.

70. John McCorkle to John Tipton, Apr. 26, 1826, in Glen A. Blackburn, comp., *The John Tipton Papers (Indiana Historical Collections,* XXIV–XXVI), 3 vols. (Indianapolis, Ind., 1942), I, 526–527.

71. Jonathan Woodbury to John Tipton, Apr. 11, June 13, 1819, ibid., I, 155–158.

72. *Weekly Register* (Baltimore), Aug. 1, 1812, quoted in Watts, *Republic Reborn,* 73.

On discipline, see Lipson, *Freemasonry in Federalist Connecticut,* 214–227. Lipson's useful discussion does not note the economic significance of Masonic discipline.

73. William Mosley Brown, *Marshall Lodge No. 39 . . . the Story of One of Virginia's Most Distinguished Lodges* (Staunton, Va., 1953), 117–118; Dove, *Proceedings of the Grand Lodge of Virginia,* 186–187, 210; see Pennsylvania Grand Lodge, *Reprint of the Minutes,* II, 57, for a similar rule extending oversight made by the Maryland grand lodge.

74. Brown, *Moral and Benevolent Design of Christianity and Free-masonry,* 22–23; Pennsylvania Grand Lodge, *Reprint of the Minutes,* IV, 280, 284.

75. Tipton to Henry Chase, Aug. 16, 1838, in Blackburn, *Tipton Papers,* III, 664; Massachusetts Grand Lodge, *Proceedings, 1815–1825,* 89–90; see also Ohio Grand Lodge, *Proceedings, 1808 to 1853,* 225–226.

76. See *Extracts from the Minutes of the General Assembly of the Presbyterian Church, of the United States of America, from A.D. 1789, to A.D. 1802 . . .* (Philadelphia, 1803), 5; *The Doctrine and Discipline of the Methodist Episcopal Church,* 19th ed. (New York, 1817), 46–48. Richard E. Ellis, *The Jeffersonian Crisis: Courts and Politics in the Young Republic* (New York, 1971), 111–129, discusses these movements. Kentucky established an arbitration law in 1795 that allowed for nonjudicial settlement of cases and, in 1801, created circuit courts presided over by a judge and two assistants. The assistants did not have to be trained in the law but did have to live in the county where the court was held. Pushed through by Felix Grundy, this system would not be changed until 1816 (123–156).

77. Lawrence M. Friedman, *A History of American Law* (New York, 1973), 232–238; Sellers, *Market Revolution,* 54; Weems, *The Philanthropist,* 3. On the importance of enforceability, see Clark, *Roots of Rural Capitalism,* 28–38; and Bruce H. Mann, *Neighbors and Strangers: Law and Community in Early Connecticut* (Chapel Hill, N.C., 1987), 34–46.

78. The implicit functions of voluntary associations have been extensively explored. For an excellent synthesis, see Doyle, *Social Order of a Frontier Community,* 156–193. On churches, see, as well, Donald G. Mathews, "The Second Great Awakening as an Organizing Process, 1780–1830: An Hypothesis," *Am. Quarterly,* XXI (1969), 23–43.

79. See Table 10 for sources. Since lodge records no longer exist, only scattered lists or references could be used, making it impossible to provide complete membership data or even to tell precisely when Clay entered the lodge or held office. The period 1794–1810 spans the period from beginning of the lodge to the start of Clay's national prominence. It also allows comparison with the 1807 directory of Lexington. *Charless' Kentucky, Tennessee, and Ohio Almanack for the Year 1807 . . .* (Lexington, Ky., 1806), reprinted in J. Winston Coleman, *Lexington's First City Directory . . . 1806* (Lexington, Ky., 1953).

80. The Kentucky grand lodge reaffirmed the minimum age of 21 in 1804, in *Proceedings of the Grand Lodge of Kentucky . . . Lexington . . . September . . . 1804* (Lexington, Ky., 1804), 7–8. Joseph Kett, *Rites of Passage: Adolescence in America, 1790 to Present* (New York, 1977), 11–107, is the fullest study of young men establishing themselves.

81. Samuel S. Wilde, *An Oration, Delivered at Pownalborough . . . June 24th, 5799* (Wiscasset, Maine, 1799), 19. Both Dorothy Ann Lipson and Paul Goodman report ranges similar to the range in Danvers in their studies of, respectively, a Connecticut and a Maine lodge. See Lipson, *Freemasonry in Federalist Connecticut,* 354 (appendix 4, table 8); Goodman, *Towards a Christian Republic,* 115–116. Wayne A. Huss, how-

ever, finds the mean age of men who became Masons in Pennsylvania in 1824 and 1825 was 29.7 years (*Master Builders,* I, 110).

82. Clay resigned from Lexington Lodge on Nov. 18, 1824. J. Winston Coleman, Jr., *Masonry in the Bluegrass; Being an Authentic Account of Masonry in Lexington and Fayette County, Kentucky, 1788–1933* (Lexington, Ky., 1934), 93.

83. Colton, *Life and Times of Clay,* I, 29.

84. Ark Lodge No. 160 of Geneva, New York (Ontario County) was chartered in September 1807. The 96 members who joined the lodge from that date to 1819 are identified in John H. Stelter, *History of Ark Lodge No. 33, F. and A.M.: 1807–1957* (Geneva, N.Y., [1957]). The closing date, 1819, was chosen to coincide with the first volume of Gary B. Thompson, ed., *Index to the Newspapers Published in Geneva, New York* (Geneva, 1981–). Identifications are based on Stelter or the information in Thompson.

Jordan Lodge of Danvers, Massachusetts, was chartered in December 1808; 172 men became members through January 1828, after which the lodge failed to meet until October 1845. Massey, *History of Freemasonry in Danvers, Massachusetts,* contains brief biographies of all identifiable members.

85. For other studies of Masonic membership outside larger cities, see Lipson, *Freemasonry in Federalist Connecticut,* 132–149, 351–355; Kutolowski, "Freemasonry and Community in the Early Republic" *Am. Quarterly,* XXXIV (1982), 543–561; Hal S. Barron, *Those Who Stayed Behind: Rural Society in Nineteenth-Century New England* (Cambridge, 1984), 25; Roth, *Democratic Dilemma,* 98–101. Huss, *Master Builders,* appendix G, tables 3 and 4 of vol. I (I, 297–299), is particularly useful because it is based on information provided by lodges for new initiates. Although classification by sector of the economy rather than by occupation makes precise comparison difficult (merchants and sailmakers, for example, appear in the same category), still the numbers suggest a profile similar to my own. Some of these studies, especially Lipson and Roth, find a higher proportion of farmers, but all find a greater proportion of non-agricultural occupations than in the population at large. These studies have led some historians (notably Lipson, Huss, and Kutolowski) to stress Masonry's openness to all men rather than just the wealthy. While this is true, the high proportion of well-to-do men even in their studies suggests that these scholars underestimate the fraternity's high standing in the community.

86. *A Memorial of the Half-Century Membership of R. W. Charles W. Moore in St. Andrew's Lodge* (Cambridge, Mass., 1873), 22, 25. The St. Andrew's brothers are from the list of members in *The Lodge of St. Andrew, and the Massachusetts Grand Lodge . . . 5756–5769* (Boston, 1870), 237–239. The Lodge No. 2 members are from contemporary lists of the entire membership at two points. Barratt and Sachse, *Freemasonry in Pennsylvania,* II, 212–213 and III, 64, 67, 69.

87. For another New York City lodge, see Duncan, *History of Independent Royal Arch Lodge, No. 2,* 64, 85–86, 91, which notes that the lodge was "composed largely of mariners" who often were recorded as transient members; some simply withdrew after their initiation (64). The few other studies of Masonic membership have generally concentrated on villages and towns. Huss, *Master Builders,* appendix G, table 4 of vol. I (I, 299) notes aggregates of 1824–1825 Philadelphia and non-Philadelphia initiates that suggest a similar distinction between urban and nonurban lodges. Paul Goodman's examination of Boston brothers who signed a declaration supporting Masonry in 1831 (*Towards a Christian Republic,* 156–157, 293 n. 25) reveals a similar profile. The sampled brothers in the tables were chosen to take advantage either of a full list of lodge members at a single point in time or of a corresponding city directory.

88. Hopkins, ed., *Papers of Clay*, I, 151; Coleman, *Masonry in the Bluegrass*, 39, 55; *Kentucky Gazette* (Lexington), Sept. 24, 1802, Dec. 27, 1803. A Baltimore Militia Toast to "The Mechanics of Baltimore" on the Fourth of July 1801 asked for "long bills" and "prompt pay." See also Charles G. Steffen, *The Mechanics of Baltimore: Workers and Politics in the Age of Revolution, 1763-1812* (Urbana, Ill., 1984), 237 (see also 192 for complaints about banks); Doyle, *Social Order of a Frontier Community*, 183-184. On lawyers, see Gerard W. Gawalt, *The Promise of Power: The Emergence of the Legal Profession in Massachusetts, 1760-1840* (Westport, Conn., 1979), 55-60, 109-115; and the vivid portrait of the young John Adams in Richard D. Brown, *Knowledge Is Power: The Diffusion of Information in Early America, 1700-1865* (New York, 1989), 93-96. On doctors, see Daniel H. Calhoun, *Professional Lives in America: Structure and Aspiration, 1750-1850* (Cambridge, Mass., 1965), 20-58. Of the 96 members of Ark Lodge (Geneva, New York) from 1807 to 1819, 34 (35.3%) appear in the newspaper as part of some debt-related problem. These include requests for payment of debt (14 members involved; 19 separate incidents), action to recover another's mortgage (11; 16 separate incidents), mortgage default (9), sheriff's sale of property (6), involvement in collecting others' debts (2), insolvency hearing (1), request for exemption from imprisonment for debt (1).

89. The fullest account of Clay's rise is in Bernard Mayo, *Henry Clay: Spokesman for the New West* (New York, 1927). See also Hopkins, ed., *Papers of Clay*, I.

90. Sam B. Smith et al., eds., *The Papers of Andrew Jackson* (Knoxville, Tenn., 1980-), esp. I, xxiv; Leland Winfield Meyer, *The Life and Times of Colonel Richard M. Johnson of Kentucky* (1931; New York, 1967), 290-342. On Niles, see Edward T. Schultz, *History of Freemasonry in Maryland . . .*, 3 vols. (Baltimore, 1884-1887), II, 714-717. On Geneva brothers, see Stelter, *History of Ark Lodge No. 33;* and Thompson, *Index to the Newspapers Published in Geneva.*

91. J. F. D. Lanier to John Tipton, Apr. 20, 1829, in Blackburn, comp., *John Tipton Papers*, II, 156-157; Tipton's compliance is noted in Tipton to Allen Hamilton et al., Oct. 27, 1829, II, 215. J. F. D. Lanier, *Sketch of the Life of J. F. D. Lanier* (New York, 1870), does not mention his Masonic ties.

92. Blackburn, comp., *Tipton Papers*, II, 821n, III, 603.

93. Clinton, "Private Canal Journal, 1810," in William W. Campbell, *The Life and Writings of DeWitt Clinton* (New York, 1849), 111; Thomas Longworth, *Longworth's American Almanac, New-York Register, and City Directory* (New York, 1824), 8. Brookhouse's card is reproduced as fig. 19 following p. 180, in Essex Institute, *Historical Collections*, CXIII (1977).

94. Webb, *Freemason's Monitor* (1821), 27; Dalcho, *Ahiman Rezon*, 37, 162; *Freemason's Magazine and General Miscellany*, II (January 1812), 265-266. The Pennsylvania grand lodge considered a similar scheme; see Pennsylvania Grand Lodge, *Reprint of the Minutes*, IV, 280-281.

95. Hopkins, ed., *Papers of Clay*, I, 221 (see also 207); James Brown, *An Address to the Public, Accompanied by Documents, Exposing the Misrepresentations, Calumnies, and Falsehoods, Contained in the Pamphlet of Elisha I. Hall, of Frederick County, Virginia* (Lexington, Ky., 1803), quotation from 5. Brown collected nearly 30 pages (the only known copy is damaged) of supporting letters, many from his Lexington Lodge brothers, to reinforce his case.

96. Brown, *Moral and Benevolent Design of Christianity and Free-masonry*, 11-12. On the importance of loyalties in trade, see, for example, Bernard Bailyn, *The New England Merchants in the Seventeenth Century* (1955; New York, 1964), 87-91; Fred-

erick B. Tolles, *Meeting House and Counting House: The Quaker Merchants of Colonial Philadelphia, 1682-1763* (Chapel Hill, N.C., 1948), 73-80 (see 51-80 for a description of Quaker life that strongly parallels post-Revolutionary Masonry).

97. Bentley, *Diary,* I, 379 (July 30, 1792).

98. See, for example, the two cases noted in Pennsylvania Grand Lodge, *Reprint of the Minutes,* IV, 142-143, 148-149, IV, 169, 177-178.

Chapter Eight

1. Solomon Southwick, *A Solemn Warning against Free-Masonry, Addressed to the Young Men of the United States* (Albany, N.Y., 1827), 135-136.

2. Ibid.

3. A number of scholars have noted the political activities of brothers: Kathleen Smith Kutolowski, "Freemasonry and Community in the Early Republic: The Case for Antimasonic Anxieties," *American Quarterly,* XXXIV (1982), 555-558; Dorothy Ann Lipson, *Freemasonry in Federalist Connecticut* (Princeton, N.J., 1977), 144-148; Ronald P. Formisano, *The Transformation of Political Culture: Massachusetts Parties, 1790s-1840s* (New York, 1983), 199. Paul Goodman, *Towards a Christian Republic: Antimasonry and the Great Transition in New England, 1826-1836* (New York, 1988), mentions this political involvement in Vermont (121). The broader implications of this activity have not received sustained attention.

4. Lipson, *Freemasonry in Federalist Connecticut,* argues that the fraternity in that state represented a form of dissent against Federalist hegemony. John L. Brooke, "Ancient Lodges and Self-Created Societies: Freemasonry and the Public Sphere in the Early Republic," in Ronald Hoffman and Peter J. Albert, eds., *The Beginnings of the "Extended Republic": The Federalist Era* (Charlottesville, Va., 1996), is the fullest attempt to argue that Masonry was a reflection of partisan loyalties. See also Brooke, *The Heart of the Commonwealth: Society and Political Culture in Worcester County, Massachusetts, 1713-1861* (New York, 1989), 242-251.

5. Ronald P. Formisano has been the leading figure in developing this view of the early Republic's politics. See *Transformation of Political Culture;* "Deferential-Participant Politics: The Early Republic's Political Culture, 1789-1840," *American Political Science Review,* LXVIII (1974), 473-487; "Boston, 1800-1840: From Deferential-Participant to Party Politics," in Formisano and Constance K. Burns, eds., *Boston, 1700-1980: The Evolution of Urban Politics* (Westport, Conn., 1984), 29-57; and *The Birth of Mass Political Parties: Michigan, 1827-1861* (Princeton, N.J., 1971). For a synthesis, see Joel H. Silbey, *The American Political Nation, 1838-1893* (Stanford, Calif., 1991), esp. 1-32. Harry L. Watson, although dissenting from Formisano and Silbey on some issues, also speaks of this period as "prepartisan," and refers to "informal" politics, in *Jacksonian Politics and Community Conflict: The Emergence of the Second Party System in Cumberland County North Carolina* (Baton Rogue, La., 1981), esp. 60-81. See also John Brooke's concept of "associational politics" (*Heart of the Commonwealth,* 243-247, 267-268). Gordon S. Wood, *The Radicalism of the American Revolution* (New York, 1992), 287-305, virtually ignores this transitional generation, moving almost directly from the 1790s to the 1820s in attempting to underline the impact of the American Revolution.

6. The only non-Mason to win election, 1804-1828, Governor Joseph C. Yates, held the office between 1822 and 1824 after soundly beating the disaffected Masonic

brother Solomon Southwick. For Southwick's own story of his earlier Masonic career, see Southwick, *Solemn Warning against Free-Masonry*, 70–80.

7. For sources, see Table 10. The multiple offices held by lodge members make a clear accounting difficult.

8. Jackson Turner Main, "Government by the People: The American Revolution and the Democratization of the State Legislatures," *William and Mary Quarterly*, 3d Ser., XXIII (1966), 391–407; Formisano, "Boston, 1800–1840," in Formisano and Burns, eds., *Boston, 1700–1980*, 35; Andrew R. L. Cayton and Peter S. Onuf, *The Midwest and the Nation: Rethinking the History of an American Region* (Bloomington, Ind., 1990), 65–83; Cayton, "Land, Power, and Reputation: The Cultural Dimension of Politics in the Ohio Country," *WMQ*, 3d Ser., XLVII (1990), 266–286. Daniel P. Jordan, *Political Leadership in Jefferson's Virginia* (Charlottesville, Va., 1983), sees little change during this period. For a fuller view, see Whitman H. Ridgway, *Community Leadership in Maryland, 1790–1840: A Comparative Analysis of Power in Society* (Chapel Hill, N.C., 1979). Ridgway, the fullest attempt to look at political leadership in this period, does not consider Masonry systematically.

9. *Biographical Directory of the United States Congress, 1789–1989*, Bicentennial Edition (Washington, D.C., 1989), 80, lists the Kentucky delegation to the Eleventh Congress. Of the four brothers, only Richard M. Johnson was not a Lexington Lodge member. For Johnson's membership, see *Proceedings of the Grand Lodge of Kentucky . . . Lexington, August, A.L. 5808–A.D. 1808* (Lexington, Ky., 1808), 15. On the cabinet, see William M. Stuart, "Masonry in the War of 1812," *American Lodge of Research Transactions*, I (1930–1933), 213–229. Kutolowski, "Freemasonry and Community in the Early Republic," *Am. Quarterly*, XXXIV (1982), 555–558; and Lipson, *Freemasonry in Federalist Connecticut*, 145–148, suggest a comparable level of political involvement for members in (respectively) Genesee County, New York, and around Pomfret, Connecticut.

10. Daniel Delavan to Pierre Van Cortlandt, Jan. 22, 1798, in Jacob Judd, ed., *Correspondence of the Van Cortlandt Family of Cortlandt Manor, 1815–1848*, vol. IV of *The Van Courtlandt Family Papers* (Tarrytown, N.Y., 1981), 415–416.

11. Charles Snow Guthrie, *Kentucky Freemasonry, 1788–1978: The Grand Lodge and the Men Who Made It* (n.p., 1981), 55; Charles Thompson McClenachan, *History of the Most Ancient and Honorable Fraternity of Free and Accepted Masons in New York*, 4 vols. (New York, 1888–1894), II, 331–332.

12. Samuel D. Greene, *The Broken Seal . . .* (Boston, 1870), 23–24; Pennsylvania Grand Lodge, *Reprint of the Minutes of the Grand Lodge of Free and Accepted Masons of Pennsylvania*, 12 vols. (Philadelphia, 1895–1907), VI, 51. Greene notes that other lodge members included his church's oldest deacon and a member of his church session. See also Hal S. Barron, *Those Who Stayed Behind: Rural Society in Nineteenth-Century New England* (Cambridge, 1984), 25. Other historians have been more anxious to stress the inclusiveness of the fraternity than its role as a center for men of high social standing. See Wayne Andrew Huss, "Pennsylvania Freemasonry: An Intellectual and Social Analysis, 1727–1826" (Ph.D. diss., Temple University, 1985); Kutolowski, "Freemasonry and Community in the Early Republic," *Am. Quarterly*, XXXIV (1982), 543–561; Lipson, *Freemasonry in Federalist Connecticut*; Randolph A. Roth, *The Democratic Dilemma: Religion, Reform, and the Social Order in the Connecticut River Valley of Vermont, 1791–1850* (Cambridge, 1987), 98–101. Besides seemingly suggesting that officeholding bore little relationship to social standing, these studies also discount the disproportionately high concentrations of well-to-do men in Masonry.

13. William Brainard, *A Masonic Lecture, Spoken before the Brethren of Union Lodge, New-London . . . January 24, A.L. 5825* (New London, Conn., 1825), 3; see also 16–17. Brainard's address was later reprinted by Antimasons as evidence of Masonry's dangerous political tendencies.

14. *National Union* (New York), Oct. 24, 1824. Most of this piece is quoted, somewhat inaccurately, in Norris S. Barratt and Julius F. Sachse, *Freemasonry in Pennsylvania, 1727–1907, as Shown by the Records of Lodge No. 2, F. and A.M. of Philadelphia, from the Year A.L. 5757, A.D. 1757 . . .* , 3 vols. (Philadelphia: 1908–1910), III, vii.

15. De Witt Clinton, *An Address Delivered before Holland Lodge, December 24, 1793* (New York, 1794), 7.

16. Avery Allyn, *A Ritual of Freemasonry* (Boston 1831), 128–130, for different versions of the oath; Hiram B. Hopkins, *Renunciation of Masonry* (Boston, 1830), 6–7. Rev. Nathan D. Whiting, of Ithaca, New York, testified in a 1832 legal deposition "that he has been *told, by Royal Arch Masons,* that the clause in the oath, relative to the *political preferment* by one Royal Arch Companion of another, originated in the Western part of the State of New York, and that the same was introduced into the oath by Mr. Cuos, who at that time held the office of Grand King of the Royal Arch Chapter of the State of New York, FOR POLITICAL PURPOSES." *Free-Masonry Unmasked: or, Minutes of the Trial of a Suit in the Court of Common Pleas of Adams County, Wherein Thaddeus Stevens, Esq. Was Plaintiff and Jacob Lefever, Defendant* (Gettysburg, Pa., 1835), 32.

17. Hopkins, *Renunciation of Masonry*, 4; *A Hint to Free-Masons* (Newfield, Conn., 1799), 7.

18. *National Union*, Oct. 24, 1824; Edward T. Schultz, *History of Freemasonry in Maryland . . .* , 3 vols. (Baltimore, 1884–1887), I, 256–275 (the address itself is on 257–258), 295–297, 408; *Proceedings of the Grand Lodge of Maryland, in the Committee of the Whole* (Baltimore, 1798). The censure was later reversed, although the grand lodge argued that their doing so reflected "no cause save Charity and Brotherly Love" (Schultz, *History of Freemasonry in Maryland,* I, 295). See also Lowell M. Limpus, "Grand Master Belton and the Jacobins," *Am. Lodge Res. Trans.,* VII (1959), 294–319.

19. Norris F. Schneider, *Lodge of Amity, No. 5 . . . Zanesville, Ohio, 1805–1955* (Zanesville, Ohio, 1955), 30–31. On the political controversy, see Andrew R. L. Cayton, *The Frontier Republic: Ideology and Politics in the Ohio Country, 1780–1825* (Kent, Ohio, 1986), 107–109.

20. Estimates include Kutolowski, "Freemasonry and Community in the Early Republic," *Am. Quarterly,* XXXIV (1982), 555 and n. 63; and Lipson, *Freemasonry in Federalist Connecticut,* 147. Thaddeus Stevens argued in an 1831 speech that brothers made up "but one-twentieth part of our voters" (*Free-Masonry Unmasked,* xi). For the 1822 estimate by a Masonic meeting of 80,000 brothers in the United States, approximately 5% of the adult white male population, see McClenachan, *History of Masons in New York,* II, 342. On Masonic appeal, see *National Union,* Oct. 24, 1824. On Clinton's standing among New York's Irish, see Dixon Ryan Fox, *The Decline of Aristocracy in the Politics of New York* (New York, 1919), 76–78, 233.

21. *Geneva Gazette and General Advertiser* (New York), Aug. 6, 1828. Many of Ohio's 1790s Federalist elite had also been brothers, including the first two judges of the Northwest Territory. On the Masonic involvement of these Ohio figures, see Schneider, *Lodge of Amity,* 29, 31; J. J. Tyler, *Chillicothe and the Beginnings of the Grand Lodge of Ohio . . .* (n.p., 1938), esp. 8–13.

22. *Kentucky Gazette* (Lexington), Oct. 15, 1796. Bradford's membership status is

unclear. He was certainly a Mason in 1824, but was not listed as a member of Lexington Lodge in 1802. Guthrie, *Kentucky Freemasonry,* 62, 40.

23. On opposition to parties, see, besides the works cited above on politics, Ronald P. Formisano, "Political Character, Antipartyism, and the Second Party System," *Am. Quarterly,* XXI (1969), 683–709. Don Harrison Doyle, *The Social Order of a Frontier Community: Jacksonville, Illinois, 1825–1870* (Urbana, Ill., 1978), 178–193, discusses the ways that voluntary societies blunted community divisions.

24. *An Abstract of the Proceedings of the Grand Lodge of North-Carolina, in the Year A.L. 5798, A.D. 1798* (Halifax, N.C., [1798]), 2–4. For the composition of the grand lodge that performed the ceremony, see *An Abstract from the Proceedings of the Grand Lodge of North-Carolina . . . Raleigh . . . 30th of November, A.L. 5797, A.D. 1797* (Halifax, N.C., 1798), 7. On Davie himself, see Blackwell P. Robinson, *William R. Davie* (Chapel Hill, N.C., 1957); R. D. W. Connor, comp., *A Documentary History of the University of North Carolina, 1776–1799,* 2 vols. (Chapel Hill, N.C., 1953), I, 504–509; see I, 236–240, for the October 1793 Masonic cornerstone laying of the new school's first building.

25. Earley Winfred Bridges, *The Masonic Governors of North Carolina* (Greensboro, N.C., 1937).

26. For the significance of governmental structures on political activity: Paul Goodman, "The First American Party System," in William Nisbet Chambers and Walter Dean Burnham, eds., *The American Party Systems: Stages of Development,* 2d ed. (New York, 1975), 56–89; Richard P. McCormick, *The Second American Party System: Party Formation in the Jacksonian Era* (Chapel Hill, N.C., 1966).

27. Andrew Jackson to Rev. Dr. Ezra Stiles Ely, Mar. 23, Apr. 10, 1829, in James Parton, *Life of Andrew Jackson,* 3 volumes (New York, 1860), III, 188–189, 193; Johnson's role in the affair is seen on 303–309. Ely may have been Jackson's Masonic brother; he was a grand chaplain of the Pennsylvania grand lodge in 1843 (Wayne A. Huss, *The Master Builders: A History of the Grand Lodge of Free and Accepted Masons of Pennsylvania,* 3 vols. [Philadelphia, 1986–1989], I, 157). Jackson's vehement reactions to the Eaton matter clearly reflected his touchiness about previous attacks on his late wife's virtue, but fraternal ties also helped reinforce his indignation. That same year, he again sided with a brother even against the claims of an aggrieved wife. Brother Sam Houston had suddenly resigned as governor of Tennessee to embark on a migration that would later lead to Texas, abandoning his new wife. Although the incident led to enormous public uproar, Jackson refused to condemn Houston. Houston's letter of gratitude revealed his perception of the incident as a sign of Masonic precepts. "You have acted," he wrote Jackson, "upon the great scale which prescribes benevolence and universal philanthropy" (Houston to Jackson, Sept. 19, 1829, quoted in Robert V. Remini, *Andrew Jackson and the Course of American Freedom, 1822–1832,* vol. II of Life [New York, 1981], 205). Remini does not note Houston's clear Masonic reference.

28. On Green Clay, see *Kentucky Gazette,* Mar. 1, 1808.

29. John Tipton, *Speech of the Hon. John Tipton, of the United S. Senate, M.E.H.P. Logan Chapter, Indiana, Delivered in the City of Alexandria, before the Grand Lodge and Royal Arch Chapter of the District of Columbia, June 25, 1838* (Washington, D.C., 1838), 5; *An Abstract from the Proceedings of the Grand Lodge of North-Carolina, 1797,* notes the brothers who attended the grand lodge meeting held in Raleigh from Nov. 30 to Dec. 5, 1797. Excluding the grand tyler (almost always more an employee than an officer) and the members of the grand lodge (p. 8) who are not specifically noted as attending in the minutes, I traced the remaining 52 men in John L. Cheney, Jr., ed., *North*

Carolina Government, 1585–1974: A Narrative and Statistical History (Raleigh, N.C., 1975); and William S. Powell, ed., *Dictionary of North Carolina Biography* (Chapel Hill, N.C., 1979–).

30. Bridges, *Masonic Governors of North Carolina;* William M. Stuart, "Andrew Jackson and Freemasonry," *Am. Lodge Res. Trans.,* I (1930–1933), 110–123.

31. Glen A. Blackburn, comp., *The John Tipton Papers (Indiana Historical Collections,* XXIV–XXVI), 3 vols. (Indianapolis, Ind., 1942), I, xv–xvi, III, 603; John A. Munroe, *Louis McLane: Federalist and Jacksonian* (New Brunswick, N.J., 1973), 74; James F. Hopkins, ed., *The Papers of Henry Clay,* II, *The Rising Statesman, 1815–1820* (Lexington, Ky., 1961), 424, 429–430.

32. Robinson, *William R. Davie,* 307–313. The Masonic affiliations of a number of the figures are noted in Thomas C. Parramore, *Launching the Craft: The First Half-Century of Freemasonry in North Carolina* (Raleigh, N.C., 1975), 165–169. The case involved land grants in Tennessee reserved for war veterans. The governor of Tennessee at the time, John Sevier, was also a Freemason.

33. Goodman, "The First American Party System," in Chambers and Burnham, eds., *American Party Systems,* 56–89; McCormick, *Second American Party System.* On the continuing opposition to political self-assertion, see Formisano, *Transformation of Political Culture,* 134–136.

34. On Williams, see Ridgway, *Community Leadership in Maryland,* 80–81. Ridgway does not note Williams's Masonic relationship to Washington (see Chapter 4). On Davie: Robinson, *William R. Davie,* 296–297.

35. Gordon S. Wood, "Interests and Disinterestedness in the Making of the Constitution," in Richard Beeman, Stephen Botein, and Edward C. Carter II, eds., *Beyond Confederation: Origins of the Constitution and American National Identity* (Chapel Hill, N.C., 1987), 60–109, argues that public acceptance of self-interest had begun replacing the rhetoric of the common good during the Confederation period, particularly among the Antifederalists.

36. See, for example, Cayton and Onuf, *The Midwest and the Nation,* 65–83; Formisano, *Transformation of Political Culture,* 149–168.

37. *Kentucky Gazette,* Jan. 2, Mar. 12, 1796.

38. North Carolina Grand Lodge, *Halifax, [N.C.], January 20 A.L. 5798 . . . The Most Worshipful . . .* (Halifax, N.C.[?], 1798).

39. *Kentucky Gazette,* Jan. 10, 1804.

40. Ibid., Aug. 31, 1793; *Kentucky Gazette and General Advertiser,* Mar. 1, 1808; Robinson, *William R. Davie,* 236.

41. For a parallel example of how informal groupings affected political life, see the discussion of boardinghouses in James Sterling Young, *The Washington Community, 1800–1828* (New York, 1966), 98–107, 110–142. Although later work has questioned Young's argument that these groups affected voting more than party, his study reveals a great deal about the type of informal politics that Masonry helped to support. Young does not consider the influence of fraternal affiliation.

42. *Kentucky Gazette,* Apr. 12, 1794; *Kentucky Gazette and General Advertiser,* Mar. 1, 1808. On the continued importance of elites in post-Revolutionary politics, see Formisano, *Transformation of Political Culture,* 128–148; and Robert H. Wiebe, *The Opening of American Society: From the Adoption of the Constitution to the Eve of Disunion* (New York, 1984). Wood, *The Radicalism of the American Revolution,* portrays the values of this enlightened aristocracy, but, like other historians, is too quick to suggest its downfall. The experience of Freemasonry suggests their later appeal. On the

continued importance of appeals to disinterestedness, see Pauline Maier, "The Transforming Impact of Independence, Reaffirmed: 1776 and the Definition of American Social Structure," in James A. Henretta et al., eds., *The Transformation of Early American History: Society, Authority, and Ideology* (New York, 1991), 194–217.

43. Stuart, "Andrew Jackson and Freemasonry," *Am. Lodge Res. Trans.*, I (1932–1933), 110–123. On political structures, see McCormick, *Second American Party System*, 104–119, 199–209; Charles Sellers, *The Market Revolution: Jacksonian America, 1815–1846* (New York, 1991), 112–113.

44. Governor Alexander Martin to the General Assembly, Nov. 2, 1790, in Connor, comp., *Documentary History of the University of North Carolina*, I, 79–80. The temporary lodge is discussed in Thomas Parramore, *Launching the Craft*, 159.

45. Fordyce Hubbard, *Life of William Richardson Davie, Governor of North Carolina* (1848), quoted in Robinson, *William R. Davie*, 228. See also Ronald Story, *The Forging of an Aristocracy: Harvard and the Boston Upper Class, 1800–1870* (Middletown, Conn., 1980), esp. 88–134.

46. "Ignoramus," *North-Carolina Journal* (Halifax), Feb. 6, 1793, in Connor, comp., *Documentary History of the University of North Carolina*, I, 209.

Chapter Nine

1. Hiram B. Hopkins, *Renunciation of Free Masonry* (Boston, 1830), 6–7; Thomas Smith Webb, *The Freemason's Monitor; or, Illustrations of Masonry . . .* , new ed. (Salem, Mass., 1821), 124 (hereafter cited as Webb, *Freemason's Monitor* [1821]).

2. *The Second Part; or, A Key to the Higher Degrees of Freemasonry . . . by a Member of the Craft* (Cincinnati, Ohio, 1827), in *Masonry Revealed and Illustrated by Eleven Seceding Members . . .* (Cincinnati, Ohio, 1850[?]), 111. The text of this pamphlet was often published (without attribution) in later editions of William Morgan, *Illustrations of Masonry . . .* (first published Batavia, N.Y., 1826). The rituals in this exposé differ significantly from the more carefully attested versions in Avery Allyn, *A Ritual of Freemasonry . . .* (Boston, 1831) and David Bernard, *Light on Masonry: A Collection of All the Most Important Documents on the Subject of Speculative Free Masonry* (Utica, N.Y., 1829).

3. *Circular throughout the Two Hemispheres . . . 4th Day of December, 1802* [Charleston, S.C., 1802], 3.
Despite the popularity of these degrees (and their significance for understanding Masonry), earlier historians have seldom paid much attention to them. For studies of Masonry that ignore the higher degrees, see Dorothy Ann Lipson, *Freemasonry in Federalist Connecticut* (Princeton, N.J., 1977); Paul Goodman, *Towards a Christian Republic: Antimasonry and the Great Transition in New England, 1826–1836* (New York, 1988); Kathleen Smith Kutolowski, "Freemasonry and Community in the Early Republic: The Case for Antimasonic Anxieties," *American Quarterly*, XXXIV (1982), 543–561. Mark C. Carnes, *Secret Ritual and Manhood in Victorian America* (New Haven, Conn., 1989), discusses higher-degree rituals in a later period.

4. The term "Ancient and Accepted Scottish Rite" was not used in America until the 1840s; see Ray Baker Harris, *History of the Supreme Council (33°) Mother Council of the World, Ancient and Accepted Scottish Rite . . . Southern Jurisdiction, U.S.A., 1801–1861* (Washington, D.C., 1964), 216. Harris provides the best introduction to the Scottish Rite; Herbert T. Leyland, *Thomas Smith Webb: Freemason, Musician, Entrepreneur* (Dayton, Ohio, 1965), the best start for the York Rite. Samuel Harrison Baynard, Jr.,

History of the Supreme Council, (33°) Ancient Accepted Scottish Rite of Freemasonry, Northern . . . Jurisdiction . . ., 2 vols. (Boston, 1938), considers the Scottish Rite in the North. Carnes, *Secret Ritual and Manhood*, esp. 133-139, discusses its later development. Eugene E. Hinman et al., *A History of the Cryptic Rite*, 2 vols. (paginated continuously) (Cedar Rapids, Iowa, 1931), is the fullest study of this series of degrees.

5. For an attempt at a synthesis, see Jean V. Matthews, *Toward a New Society: American Thought and Culture, 1800-1830* (Boston, 1991). See also Henry F. May, *The Enlightenment in America* (New York, 1976); Donald H. Meyer, *The Democratic Enlightenment* (New York, 1976). Neither May nor Meyer considers the larger cultural changes discussed in Jan Lewis, *The Pursuit of Happiness: Family and Values in Jefferson's Virginia* (New York, 1983). For an understanding of the ending point of this transformation, I have found helpful Daniel Walker Howe, *The Unitarian Conscience: Harvard Moral Philosophy, 1805-1861* (Cambridge, Mass., 1970); Karen Lystra, *Searching the Heart: Women, Men, and Romantic Love in Nineteenth-Century America* (New York, 1989); and Karen Halttunen, *Confidence Men and Painted Women: A Study of Middle-Class Culture in America, 1830-1870* (New Haven, Conn., 1982).

6. William Bentley, *The Diary of William Bentley, D.D., Pastor of the East Church, Salem, Massachusetts*, 4 vols. (Salem, Mass., 1905-1914), II, 403 (Nov. 23, 1801), III, 327 (Nov. 3, 1807); see also III, 301 (June 24, 1807). Fowle was Bentley's brother-in-law.

7. Ibid., II, 357 (Dec. 2, 1800); see also II, 11 (Mar. 20, 1793), for Bentley's 1793 description of another badly decorated lodge.

8. Leyland, *Webb*, 365-366.

9. Pennsylvania Grand Lodge, *Reprint of the Minutes of the Grand Lodge of Free and Accepted Masons of Pennsylvania*, 12 vols. (Philadelphia, 1895-1907), II, 280-281; E. G. Storer, comp., *The Records of Freemasonry in the State of Connecticut, with Brief Accounts of Its Origin in New England and Proceedings of the Grand Lodge*, 2 vols. (New Haven, Conn., 1859, 1861), I, 293, 195; Rob Morris, *The History of Freemasonry in Kentucky, in Its Relations to the Symbolic Degrees* (Louisville, Ky., 1859), 193. I have drawn examples from the early Republic in this paragraph, because colonial Masonic writers seldom even mention ritual matters. The Scottish Rite seems to have been an exception to this new concern. See Carnes, *Secret Ritual and Manhood*, 133-139, for a discussion of Albert Pike and his revision of its rituals in the 1850s.

10. Pennsylvania Grand Lodge, *Reprint of the Minutes*, IV, 243-244.

11. William Preston, *Illustrations of Masonry . . .*, 1st American, from 10th London, ed. (Alexandria, [D.C.], 1804), vii-viii; Colin Dyer, *William Preston and His Work* (Shepperton, Middlesex, Eng., 1987).

12. Thomas Smith Webb, *The Freemason's Monitor; or, Illustrations of Masonry* (Albany, N.Y., 1797), is the first edition. Sales figures for the work are from Leyland, *Webb*, 388; for imitators, see Samuel Cole, *The Freemason's Library and General Ahiman Rezon . . .*, 2d ed. (Baltimore, 1826 [1st ed. 1817]); Morris, *History of Freemasonry in Kentucky*, on the 1808 Kentucky Constitutions (111-115) and on Cross (224). Preston, *Illustrations of Masonry*, was also popular in America; according to Leyland, *Webb*, 74, it received its first American edition in 1796 (an edition not listed in Evans, *American Bibliography*) and two editions in 1804 (Shaw and Shoemaker, *American Bibliography*, 7115, 7116); see also the 1797 quotation of Preston in Enoch Huntington, *A Sermon, Preached at Middletown, June 28, 1797 . . .* (Middletown, Conn., 1797), 9. In 1804, the grand lodge of Kentucky subscribed for 20 copies (Morris, *History of Freemasonry in Kentucky*, 80).

13. George Richards, *Light against Light in Three Ranks! A Masonic Discourse . . .*

Gloucester, Massachusetts . . . June 24, 5806 . . . (Portsmouth, N.H., 1806), 28–29; Charles G. Finney, *The Character, Claims, and Practical Workings of Freemasonry* (Cincinnati, Ohio, 1869), v–vi; Henry Fowle, "Autobiography of the Late Brother Henry Fowle, Written in 1833," *Freemason's Monthly Magazine,* XXIV (1865), 364 (reprinted, with some adaptations and notes, as David H. Kilmer, ed., *The Autobiography of Henry Fowle of Boston [1766-1837]* [Bowie, Md., 1991] [quotation on 62–63]). See Hinman et al., *History of the Cryptic Rite,* 584–585, for an account by a student of Masonic rituals. According to the recollections of Samuel D. Greene, a leading Antimason, William Morgan served as a bright Mason before exposing the rituals in 1826 (*The Broken Seal . . .* [Boston, 1870], 33).

14. Leyland, *Webb,* 214. For examples of regular lecturing in lodges, see Edward Thomas Schultz, *The History of Concordia Lodge, No. 13 . . . from April 13, 1793, to March 18, 1881* (Baltimore, 1881), 35; and Julius F. Sachse, *Old Masonic Lodges of Pennsylvania: "Moderns" and "Ancients," 1730-1800 . . . ,* 2 vols. (Philadelphia, 1912), I, 275.

15. This song is ubiquitous in Masonic works after the turn of the century. I quote it here from James Moore and Cary L. Clarke, *Masonic Constitutions; or, Illustrations of Masonry; Compiled by the Direction of the Grand Lodge of Kentucky . . .* (Lexington, Ky., 1808), 182–183.

16. Solomon Southwick, *A Solemn Warning against Free-Masonry, Addressed to the Young Men of the United States* (Albany, N.Y., 1826), 75–76, claims that Thomas Smith Webb instructed him by using this volume. According to Southwick's account, the discovery of his copy by his wife and her mystification at its appeal helped encourage him to leave the fraternity. For John Barney, see Leyland, *Webb,* 349–350; Christie B. Crowell, "Freemasonry in Vermont," in Robert Freke Gould, *Gould's History of Freemasonry throughout the World . . . ,* ed. Dudley Wright, 6 vols. (New York, 1936), VI, 306.

Only 5 of the 26 (19.2%) grand lodges formed before 1830 failed to create some form of grand lecturer—Delaware, Louisiana, Maryland, Michigan, and Tennessee (but see Charles Albert Snodgrass, *The History of Freemasonry in Tennessee, 1789-1943 . . .* [Nashville, Tenn., 1944], 73). This trend continued after 1830. The Florida grand lodge, formed in 1830, established the position in its first year of operation (*Proceedings of the Grand Lodge of the Most Ancient and Honorable Fraternity of Free and Accepted Masons, of the State of Florida . . . from Its Organization, A.D. 1830, to 1859, Inclusive* [New York, 1859], 18). Mississippi chose a grand lecturer in 1833 (*Proceedings of the Grand Lodge of Mississippi . . . from Its Organization July 27th, 5818, to . . . 5852 . . .* [Jackson, Miss., 1882], 133, 135).

17. For Kentucky's various attempts at creating uniformity, see *Proceedings of the Grand Lodge of Kentucky, F. and A.M.: From October 1800 to November 1814,* I (rpt. Louisville, Ky., 1884), 8, 65, 95, 162, 328–329; *Proceedings of the Grand Lodge of Kentucky . . . August, A.L. 5815-A.D. 1815* (Lexington, Ky., 1815), 23–24; *Proceedings of the Grand Lodge of Kentucky . . . August, A.L. 5816-A.D. 1816* (Lexington, Ky., 1816), 21; *Proceedings of the Grand Lodge of Kentucky . . . August, A.L. 5817-A.D. 1817* (Lexington, Ky., 1817), 17–18, 29.

18. See W. J. Rorabaugh, *The Craft Apprentice: From Franklin to the Machine Age in America* (New York, 1986), on entrance into a craft; the post-Revolutionary printing of many of these secrets is discussed on 33–36. Such printed materials must have required the same precise study required in legal education. A vivid description of the rigors of this type of learning can be found in R. Kent Newmyer, *Supreme Court Justice Joseph Story: Statesman of the Old Republic* (Chapel Hill, N.C., 1985), 39–43.

19. Massachusetts Grand Lodge, *Proceedings of the Most Worshipful Grand Lodge . . .*

of Massachusetts . . . 1792-1815 (Cambridge, Mass., 1905), 465-468. Virginia created a fund similar to the Lodge Charity Fund in 1813; see John Dove, ed., *Proceedings of the M. W. Grand Lodge of Ancient York Masons of the State of Virginia, from Its Organization, in 1778, to 1822* . . . (Richmond, Va., 1874), 439-440, 455-456. On Board of Relief, see Massachusetts Grand Lodge, *Proceedings of the Most Worshipful Grand Lodge . . . of Massachusetts . . . 1815-1825* (Cambridge, Mass., 1905), 214; the grand lodge Committee of Charity helped organize this body. John T. Heard, *A Historical Account of Columbian Lodge . . . of Boston, Mass.* (Boston, 1856), 373, notes the Masonic Board of Directors of the Associated Societies of the town of Boston. St. Andrew's Lodge similarly formed "the Proprietors of the Green Dragon Tavern" to manage its hall; see *A Memorial of the Half-Century Membership of R. W. Charles W. Moore in St. Andrew's Lodge* (Cambridge, Mass., 1873), 25.

20. Massachusetts Grand Lodge, *Proceedings, 1792-1815*, 191-192; see also 340. Salem's Essex Lodge opposed the new officers as dangerous impositions on local lodge authority; see Bentley, *Diary*, II, 411-412 (Feb. 2, 1802); III, 6-7 (Feb. 1, 1802), 13 (Mar. 1, 1803), 16 (Mar. 14, 1803).

21. *Proceedings of the Grand Lodge of Mississippi 5818 to 5852*, 537; Pennsylvania Grand Lodge, *Annual Publication: Grand Lodge of the Most Ancient and Honourable Fraternity of Free and Accepted Masons of Pennsylvania* . . . (Philadelphia, 1828), 117. Of the 26 grand lodges formed before 1830, only South Carolina, Connecticut, Rhode Island, Tennessee, Missouri, Louisiana, and Michigan failed to create some form of inspectors (see the various grand lodge proceedings and histories). A proposal for a combination of grand visitors and grand lecturers came before the Tennessee grand lodge in 1822 but seems not to have been implemented (Snodgrass, *History of Freemasonry in Tennessee*, 73; see also 82 for a projected district system). On New York, see Arthur Alexis Bryant, "The District Deputy Grand Masters in New York State, 1855-1936, with Some Account of the Grand Visitors (1805-1849)," *American Lodge of Research Transactions*, II (1936-1938), 461-497.

22. The Webb bodies were the Royal Arch chapters and the Knights Templars commanderies. Mark lodges were sometimes created, although they were usually a first step to the organization of full chapters. The Supreme Council, in its 1802 manifesto, prescribed Sublime grand lodges (for degrees 4-14, sometimes known as Ineffable lodges or Lodges of Perfection), Councils of Princes of Jerusalem (15-16), and a Council of Grand Inspectors (17-32) (*Circular throughout the Two Hemispheres, 1802*, 3).

23. Alfred F. Chapman, *St. Andrew's Royal Arch Chapter, of Boston, Massachusetts* . . . (Boston, 1883), 26-27, summarizes Fowle's Masonic career. See also his "Autobiography," *Freemason's Monthly Magazine*, XXIV (1864), 205-, XXV (1865), 11-. Of course, ritual matters did not consume the time of all Masons. See St. Andrew's Lodge and chapter member Charles Moore's description of Joab Hunt, who "does not seem ever to have taken any active part in the working of its [St. Andrew's Lodge] Ritual, although he was always prompt and ready to serve on its charitable and other committees" (*Memorial of the Half-Century Membership of Charles Moore*, 22).

24. Massachusetts Grand Lodge, *Proceedings, 1792-1815*, 283-290; Hinman et al., *History of the Cryptic Rite*, contains a great deal of material on Cross, including his diary; for his peddling, see 188. On Moore, see *Memorial of the Half-Century Membership of Charles Moore*, 18. Publishers also aimed publications at Masons (or at curious outsiders). See, for example, John Lathrop, Jr., *The Gentleman's Pocket Register, and Free-Mason's Annual Anthology, for . . . 1813* (Boston, [1813]); Philo Astonomiae, *The Free-Mason Almanac, for the Year 1826* (Enfield, Mass., 1825).

25. *History of St. Johns Commandery, Number One . . . Knights Templars, Providence, Rhode Island . . . from 1802 to 1902* (Providence, R.I., 1902), 69; *Grand Commandery of Knights Templar, Massachusetts and Rhode Island, 1805–1905 . . .* (Central Falls, R.I., 1905), 114; William L. Gardner, *Historical Reminiscences of Morton Commandery, No. 4, Knights Templars . . . 1823, to . . . 1891* (New York, 1891), 12–13.

26. *History of St. Johns Commandery, Knights Templars, Number One*, 243–246.

27. In a further indication of Masonic involvement, 15 of the 19 Geneva brothers in the sample who formed a business partnership with another Mason belonged to a higher-degree body.

28. Floyd Wills Sydnor and William Shelton Gearheart, *A History of Richmond Royal Arch Chapter No. 3 . . . from Its Organization, March 12, 1792, to October 2, 1941 . . .* (Richmond, Va., 1942), 16–17; *Directory of the Village of Rochester* (Rochester, N.Y., 1827), 111; Hopkins, *Renunciation of Masonry*, 5.

29. Bernard, *Light on Masonry*, 77.

30. Conrad Edick Wright, *The Transformation of Charity in Postrevolutionary New England* (Boston, 1992); Carroll Smith Rosenberg, *Religion and the Rise of the American City: The New York City Mission Movement, 1812–1870* (Ithaca, N.Y., 1971); Richard D. Brown, "The Emergence of Urban Society in Rural Massachusetts, 1760–1820," *Journal of American History,* LXI (1974–1975), 29–51; Brown, "The Emergence of Voluntary Associations in Massachusetts, 1760–1830," *Journal of Voluntary Action Research,* II (1973), 64–73. On growing size of organizations, see the insightful discussion of the American Education Society in David F. Allmendinger, Jr., *Paupers and Scholars: The Transformation of Student Life in Nineteenth-Century New England* (New York, 1975), 54–63.

Partly as a reaction against narrow institutional histories, recent church historians seldom examine the growth of church organization after the Revolution. Jon Butler, *Awash in a Sea of Faith: Christianizing the American People* (Cambridge, Mass., 1990), 268–282, is an important exception. Hatch, *Democratization of American Christianity,* notes this building of organizations and strong leadership among the more popular denominations (see, for example, 9, 12, 56–58) but is clearly uncomfortable with a development that seems undemocratic. Russell E. Richey, *Early American Methodism* (Bloomington, Ind., 1991), similarly tries to redefine organization. Martin E. Marty, *Righteous Empire: The Protestant Experience in America* (New York, 1970), although considering what he calls "the invention of forms" (67–77) in this period discusses only local developments, reform societies, and charitable institutions. Donald M. Scott, *From Office to Profession: The New England Ministry, 1750–1850* (Philadelphia, 1978), illuminates the professionalization of the ministry.

31. While only 3 or 4 Baptist associations published their minutes before 1789, during the next three years some 21 different associations began the practice. These can be traced in Clifford K. Shipton and James E. Mooney, *National Index of American Imprints through 1800: The Short-Title Evans,* 2 vols. (Worcester, Mass., 1969), s.v. "Baptists." See also "Presbyterian Church in the U.S.A." The Protestant Episcopal Church began publication of its minutes in 1785. Walter B. Shurden, *Associationalism among Baptists in America: 1707–1814* (New York, 1980), esp. 51–58, notes (39) that twice as many Baptist associations were formed between 1780 and 1790 as in the entire colonial period. Hatch, *Democratization of American Christianity,* 81–93, discusses Methodism. See also Richey, *Early American Methodism,* 10, 19–20, 6–8. Universalists created their first national organization in 1790; see David Robinson, *The Unitarians and the Universalists,* Denominations in America, I (Westport, Conn., 1985), 58.

32. *Proceedings of the Grand Lodge . . . of the State of Maine,* I, *1820-1847* (Portland, Maine, 1872), 85, 95-97, 119, 134-137; Pennsylvania Grand Lodge, *Reprint of the Minutes,* IV, 409; John Corson Smith, *History of Freemasonry in Illinois, 1804-1829* (Chicago, 1903), 120-122.

33. Leyland, *Webb,* is an excellent biography. Further details of Webb's life can be found in Paul Dean, *An Eulogy, Delivered in Boylston Hall, Boston . . . on the Character of . . . Thomas Smith Webb . . .* (Boston, 1819) (quotation on 4); *Old Colony Collection of Anthems,* 2 vols. (Boston, 1818-1819), II, 159-161, prints "Fair Truth like Thine," with words by Webb.

34. Allyn, *Ritual of Freemasonry,* 252.

35. Morgan, *Illustrations of Masonry,* 116; Webb *Freemason's Monitor* (1821), 116, and see also 16, where Webb suggests that the degree "consists of a select few."

36. Webb, *Freemason's Monitor* (1821), 262-264, 268-270; *Circular throughout the Two Hemispheres, 1802,* 3, lists the degrees.

37. Allyn, *Ritual of Freemasonry,* 230-232, 237, 265-267; Webb, *Freemason's Monitor* (1821), 269. On the 10th degree, see Harris, *History of the Supreme Council, Southern,* 3; Webb, *Freemason's Monitor* (1821), 257-258.

38. Allyn, *Ritual of Freemasonry,* 249.

39. Leyland, *Webb,* 243; Allyn, *Ritual of Freemasonry,* 151, 247. The presence of Gothic novels such as Ann Radcliffe's *Mysteries of Udolpho* and *The Romance of the Forest* in the bookstore (see *Albany Register* [New York], May 27, 1796) and circulating library (Nov. 21, 1796) run by Webb and his Albany partners may provide a background for, and perhaps a specific influence on, Webb's views. Like his degrees, these books portray the values and practices of gentility being threatened by a hostile and confusing world.

40. On the genteel ethic of effortlessness, see Halttunen, *Confidence Men and Painted Women,* 93.

41. Fowle, "Autobiography," *Freemason's Monthly Magazine,* XXIV (1864), 205-, XXV (1865), 11-, and rpt. in Kilmer, ed., *Autobiography of Henry Fowle.* The backgrounds of the 10 members of the 1830 supreme council suggest a similar status as outsiders. Only 1 had been born in Charleston; 6 began life outside the United States. Nearly half, furthermore, were non-Protestants. Three of the council members were Roman Catholic; another was Jewish. Many of the early leaders in the council degrees were Jewish. Julius F. Sachse, comp., *Ancient Documents Relating to the A. and A. Scottish Rite in the Archives of the R.W. Grand Lodge . . . of Pennsylvania* (Philadelphia, 1915), 18-19.

42. Gordon S. Wood, *The Radicalism of the American Revolution* (New York, 1992), 124-369. Lewis, *Pursuit of Happiness* (New York, 1983), 40-105, connects this new sense of a confusing and dangerous world (especially as expressed in evangelical religion and changing images of death) with the declining power of the Virginia gentry.

43. On the history of the term "individualism," see Gillian Brown, *Domestic Individualism: Imagining Self in Nineteenth-Century America* (Berkeley, Calif., 1990), 203 n. 2. Alexis de Tocqueville, *Democracy in America* (1835-1840), ed. J. P. Mayer and Max Lerner, trans. George Lawrence (New York, 1966), 477. See also Richard O. Curry and Lawrence B. Goodheart, eds., *American Chameleon: Individualism in Trans-National Context* (Kent, Ohio, 1991).

44. Tocqueville, *Democracy in America,* 477; Ralph Waldo Emerson, "Self-Reliance," in *The Collected Works of Ralph Waldo Emerson,* II, *Essays: First Series* (Cambridge, Mass., 1979), 29, 30; Allyn, *Ritual of Freemasonry,* 247.

45. Thaddeus Mason Harris, *The Fraternal Tribute of Respect Paid to the Masonic Character of Washington, in the Union Lodge, in Dorchester, January 7th, A.L. 5800* (Charlestown, Mass., 1800), 9–10.

46. Thaddeus Mason Harris, *Discourses, Delivered on Public Occasions, Illustrating the Principles . . . of Free Masonry . . .* (Charlestown, Mass., 1801), 276; Frederick Dalcho, *An Ahiman Rezon, for the Use of the Grand Lodge of South-Carolina, Ancient York-masons . . .* (Charleston, S.C., 1807), 163 (also in Harris, *Discourses, Delivered on Public Occasions,* 278); Hosea Ballou, *An Oration, Pronounced at Windsor, before . . . Vermont Lodge, on the 27th December, A.L. 5808 . . .* (Windsor, Vt., 1809), 3–4; Allyn, *Ritual of Freemasonry,* 147.

47. Amos Maine Atwell, *An Address, Delivered before Mount-Vernon Lodge . . . February 22, 1800 . . .* (Providence, R.I., 1800), 8; William Bentley, *A Discourse, Delivered at Amherst, August 10, 1797 . . . at the Installation of the Benevolent Lodge . . .* (Amherst, N.H., 1797), 15.

48. J. G. A. Pocock, *The Machiavellian Moment: Florentine Political Thought and the Atlantic Republican Tradition* (Princeton, N.J., 1975), traces this civic tradition back to the Renaissance. The terms "public" and "private" as used here should not be viewed as sealed categories or as literal descriptions of actual practices, but as mental maps or templates for categorizing and understanding reality. This chapter, and the rest of the book, suggests that the terms illuminate important cultural divisions for the period before 1840. The terms "public" and "private" here and below involve more than Jürgen Habermas's concept of the "public sphere." I use "public" here to refer to groups and issues that possess more than individual and personal significance. See Jürgen Habermas, *The Structural Transformation of the Public Sphere: An Inquiry into a Category of Bourgeois Society,* trans. Thomas Burger with Frederick Lawrence (Cambridge, Mass., 1989). Karen V. Hansen, *A Very Social Time: Crafting Community in Antebellum New England* (Berkeley, Calif., 1994), proposes a third category of "the social" beyond the "public" and the "private." But Hansen defines the two older terms much too narrowly, seeing public as "the state and all state-related activities" and the private as "rooted in the activities of the household and nuclear family" (9; see also 1–28). For a discussion of the terms "public" and "private" that perhaps defines the public too broadly, see Mary P. Ryan, *Women in Public: Between Banners and Ballots, 1825–1880* (Baltimore, 1990). Ryan seems to suggest four different uses of "public": civic ceremonies, outdoor spaces, politics, and public discourse (esp. 16–17).

49. Karen Lystra argues that "this public-private division was a basic organizing principle of nineteenth-century middle-class culture" (*Searching the Heart,* 17). See also Louis P. Masur, *Rites of Execution: Capital Punishment and the Transformation of American Culture, 1776–1865* (New York, 1989), 102–109.

50. The quotations are from, respectively, Mason L. Weems, *A History of the Life and Death . . . of General George Washington . . .* (Georgetown, Va., 1800), title page, 5; Weems, *A History of the Life and Death of General George Washington,* 2d ed. (Philadelphia, 1800), 1. Washington's Masonic affiliation is noted in [Weems], *The Life and Memorable Actions of George Washington . . .* [Baltimore, 1800], 92–94; Weems, *A History of the Life and Death,* 1st ed., 60.

51. This material is first found in M. L. Weems, *The Life of Washington the Great . . . ,* 5th ed. (Augusta, Ga., 1806), and is quoted from Weems, *The Life of Washington,* ed. Marcus Cunliffe (Cambridge, Mass., 1962), 1–5. Cunliffe's version reprints the ninth edition, of 1809; later editions would remain the same (xix).

52. Weems, *Life of Washington,* ed. Cunliffe, 1, 2, 4, 8.

53. Ibid., 2, 3. For a rich discussion of the actual geography of later gentility, see

Halttunen, *Confidence Men and Painted Women,* 104-110. On the rise of what has come to be called "Republican Motherhood," see Linda K. Kerber, *Women of the Republic: Intellect and Ideology in Revolutionary America* (Chapel Hill, N.C., 1980); Mary Beth Norton, *Liberty's Daughters: The Revolutionary Experience of American Women, 1750-1800* (Boston, 1980); Ruth H. Bloch, "American Feminine Ideals in Transition: The Rise of the Moral Mother, 1785-1815," *Feminist Studies,* IV (1978), 100-126. On its roots in earlier ideas, see Rosemarie Zagarri, "Morals, Manners, and the Republican Mother," *Am. Quarterly,* XLIV (1992), 192-215.

On domesticity, see Nancy F. Cott, *The Bonds of Womanhood: 'Woman's Sphere' in New England, 1780-1835* (New Haven, Conn., 1977); Mary P. Ryan, *The Empire of the Mother: American Writing about Domesticity: 1830-1860* (New York, 1982); Mary Kelley, *Private Woman, Public Stage: Literary Domesticity in Nineteenth-Century America* (New York, 1984); Linda K. Kerber, "Separate Spheres, Female Worlds, Woman's Place: The Rhetoric of Women's History," *JAH,* LXXV (1988-1989), 9-39; Brown, *Domestic Individualism;* Lisa Norling, "'How Frought with Sorrow and Heartpangs': Mariners' Wives and the Ideology of Domesticity in New England, 1790-1880," *New England Quarterly,* LXV (1992), 422-446.

54. Mary P. Ryan, *Women in Public,* and "Gender and Public Access: Women's Politics in Nineteenth-Century America," in Calhoun, ed., *Habermas and the Public Sphere,* 259-288, provide a broader look at 19th-century women's relationship to the public. Kerber, "Separate Spheres, Female Worlds, Woman's Place," *JAH,* LXXV (1988-1989), 9-39, suggests convincingly that the idea of separate spheres cannot be seen as an objective description of reality, but her suggestion that it has outlived its usefulness seems to neglect its significance as a cultural construct that, I argue, went far beyond women's roles.

55. Harris, *Fraternal Tribute,* 9-10; Helena M. Wall, *Fierce Communion: Family and Community in Early America* (Cambridge, Mass., 1990), 147; Peter L. Berger, Brigitte Berger, and Hansfried Kellner, *The Homeless Mind: Modernization and Consciousness* (New York, 1973), 83-96; Garry Wills, *Cincinnatus: George Washington and the Enlightenment* (Garden City, N.Y., 1984), 35-53. Brown, *Domestic Individualism,* too closely identifies the values of the private sphere as domestic and thus feminine. John Tosh, "Domesticity and Manliness in the Victorian Middle Class: The Family of Edward White Benson," in Michael Roper and John Tosh, eds., *Manful Assertions: Masculinities in Britain since 1800* (London, 1991), 44-73, rightly warns against envisioning the domestic sphere as purely feminine. Donald Yacovone, "Abolitionists and the 'Language of Fraternal Love,'" in Mark C. Carnes and Clyde Griffen, eds., *Meanings for Manhood: Constructions of Masculinity in Victorian America* (Chicago, 1990), 85-95, shows that some antebellum men participated in a world of affection that parallels female friendships, but does not explore how these private spheres relate to the public world of assertion and competition.

56. Recent discussions of masculine identities include E. Anthony Rotundo, *American Manhood: Transformations in Masculinity from the Revolution to the Modern Era* (New York, 1993); Carnes and Griffen, eds., *Meanings for Manhood;* Roper and Tosh, eds., *Manful Assertions.* Carnes, *Secret Ritual and Manhood,* argues that mid-19th-century Masonic rituals expressed a desire to create a masculine identity. In connecting these ideas with the Revolutionary transformation of Masonry (see Chapters 3, 4, above) and the revision of rituals after the war, he misses, I would suggest, the transitional stage that helped create the image of the private sphere that only later became decisively gendered.

57. For an example of the term "consecration," see Bentley, *Diary,* III, 301 (June 24,

1807). Richards is quoted in *American Masonic Register,* I (September 1820), 8. On the use of religious language to discuss romantic love, see Lystra, *Searching the Heart,* 237–250.

58. De Witt Clinton, *An Address Delivered before Holland Lodge, December 24, 1793* . . . (New York, 1794), 15; Clinton, "The Address of De Witt Clinton" [to the Grand Lodge of New York, Sept. 29, 1825], in Charles Thompson McClenachan, *History of the Ancient and Honorable Fraternity of Free and Accepted Masons in New York* . . . , 4 vols. (New York, 1888–1894), II, 432–433.

59. Public criticism of the higher degrees was rare. For exceptions, see Thomas W. Thompson, *Valedictory of the Most Worshipful Thomas Thompson, Esq., Past Grand Master of Masons in and throughout . . . New Hampshire, at His Resignation . . . April 27, A.L. 5808* . . . (Portsmouth, N.H., 1808), 1–3.

60. Ibid., 1–3.

61. The Knights Templars ritual is printed in Allyn, *Ritual of Freemasonry,* 229–258; for confirmation from an earlier Masonic source, see the notation of the same Scripture passages in Webb, *Freemason's Monitor* (1821), 237–243.

62. *Rev. H. Tatem's Reply to the Summons of the R.I. Royal Arch Chapter,* 3d ed. (Warwick, R.I., 1832), 6; Allyn, *Ritual of Freemasonry,* 250n; Fowle, "Autobiography," *Freemason's Monthly Magazine,* XXIV (1864), 266–267 (Kilmer, ed., *Autobiography of Henry Fowle,* 35).

63. De Witt Clinton, "Address before the Phi Beta Kappa Society of Union College" (1823), in William W. Campbell, *The Life and Writings of DeWitt Clinton* (New York, 1849), 330; Clinton, "The Address of De Witt Clinton" [to the Grand Lodge of New York, Sept. 29, 1825], in McClenachan, *History of Masons in New York,* II, 431.

64. Webb, *Freemason's Monitor* (1821), 201–203.

65. Oliver Holden, *The Massachusetts Compiler* . . . (Boston, 1795); *Old Colony Collection of Anthems,* II, 159–161; Leyland, *Webb,* 352.

66. Fowle, "Autobiography," *Freemason's Monthly Magazine,* XXIV (1864), 267 (Kilmer, ed., *Autobiography of Henry Fowle,* 35); Schultz, *History of Concordia Lodge, No. 13,* 58. For the importance of the term to Harvard thinkers at about the same time, see Howe, *Unitarian Conscience,* 199–200.

67. My brief and necessarily schematic account is particularly influenced by Walter Jackson Bate, *From Classic to Romantic: Premises of Taste in Eighteenth-Century England* (1946; New York, 1961); and Lilian R. Furst, *Romanticism* (London, 1976), 15–38. For the idea of 18th-century thinking as "a self-transformation of its values and tastes," see James Engell, *The Creative Imagination: Enlightenment to Romanticism* (Cambridge, Mass., 1981) (quotation on ix).

68. For different aspects of sentiment, see G. J. Barker-Benfield, *The Culture of Sensibility: Sex and Society in Eighteenth-Century Britain* (Chicago, 1992); John Mullan, *Sentiment and Sociability: The Language of Feeling in the Eighteenth Century* (Oxford, 1988); Fred Kaplan, *Sacred Tears: Sentimentality in Victorian Literature* (Princeton, N.J., 1987); Jay Fliegelman, *Prodigals and Pilgrims: The American Revolution against Patriarchal Authority, 1750–1800* (Cambridge, 1982); John K. Sheriff, *The Good-Natured Man: The Evolution of a Moral Ideal, 1660–1800* (University, Alabama, 1982).

On the picturesque and the sublime, see Samuel H. Monk, *The Sublime: A Study of Critical Theories in Seventeenth-Century England* (1935; Ann Arbor, Mich., 1960); Ernst Cassirer, *The Philosophy of the Enlightenment,* trans. Fritz C. A. Koellm and James P. Pettegrove (Boston, 1951). On Romantic aesthetics, see David Perkins, "The

Construction of 'The Romantic Movement' as a Literary Classification," *Nineteenth-Century Literature,* XLV (1990), 129–143; Kaplan, *Sacred Tears;* Lilian R. Furst, *Romanticism in Perspective: A Comparative Study of Aspects of the Romantic Movements in England, France, and Germany* (London, 1969); René Wellek, "The Concept of Romanticism in Literary History," in Wellek, *Concepts of Criticism,* ed. Stephen G. Nichols, Jr. (New Haven, Conn., 1963), 128–198; Louis I. Bredvold, *The Natural History of Sensibility* (Detroit, Mich., 1962); M. H. Abrams, *The Mirror and the Lamp: Romantic Theory and the Critical Tradition* (London, 1953); Bate, *From Classic to Romantic.*

69. For a genealogy of Romanticism that relies on great minds, see Reginald Horsman, *Race and Manifest Destiny: The Origins of American Racial Anglo-Saxonism* (Cambridge, Mass., 1981), 160–164; Matthews, *Toward a New Society,* is slightly more cautious (see 74–76, 120–123). On criticism in the period, see William Charvat, *The Origins of American Critical Thought, 1810–1835* (New York, 1936); for the more popular side, see Cathy N. Davidson, *Revolution and the Word: The Rise of the Novel in America* (New York, 1986); Fliegelman, *Prodigals and Pilgrims.* Attempts to link these changes to social and political developments include William C. Dowling, *Poetry and Ideology in Revolutionary Connecticut* (Athens, Ga., 1990); Gordon Wood, introduction, in Wood, ed., *The Rising Glory of America, 1760–1820,* rev. ed. (Boston, 1990), 1–24; Michael T. Gilmore, *American Romanticism and the Marketplace* (Chicago, 1985); Linda K. Kerber, *Federalists in Dissent: Imagery and Ideology in Jeffersonian America* (Ithaca, N.Y., 1970). Ann Douglas, *The Feminization of American Culture* (New York, 1977), connects the rise of sentimentalism with a Victorian alliance between ministers and women. The prominence of clergymen in higher-degree Masonry suggests another path.

70. Radcliffe's *Mysteries of Udolpho* (1794) and *The Romance of the Forest* (1791) were available in both Webb's bookstore (see *Albany Register,* May 27, 1796) and circulating library (see Nov. 21, 1796).

71. Webb, *Freemason's Monitor* (1821), 258; Sachse, comp., *Ancient Documents Relating to the Scottish Rite,* 204; *Circular throughout the Two Hemispheres, 1802,* 2–3. Webb (*Freemason's Monitor* [1821], 69) showed a greater deference toward the original three degrees. He even suggested that the orders of knighthood culminating in the Knights Templars, while significant and related to the fraternity, were not, strictly speaking, "part of the system of freemasonry" (217). See also the responses to the *Circular throughout the Two Hemispheres, 1802,* the manifesto of the Charleston supreme council, whose attempt to subordinate the lower degrees aroused strong reaction: Ohio Grand Lodge, *Proceedings of the Grand Lodge . . . of Ohio . . . from 1808 to 1853 Inclusive,* 2 vols. (Columbus, Ohio, 1857–1858), I, 65; Bentley, *Diary,* III, 16 (Mar. 14, 1803); Pennsylvania Grand Lodge, *Reprint of the Minutes,* II, 97; Thomas Thompson to John Crawford, June 1803, in Edward T. Schultz, *History of Freemasonry in Maryland . . . ,* 3 vols. (Baltimore, 1884–1887), II, 55–58.

72. For the earlier tradition of ancient wisdom, see Chapters 1, 2.

73. Alan Taylor, "The Early Republic's Supernatural Economy: Treasure Seeking in the American Northeast, 1780–1830," *Am. Quarterly,* XXXVIII (1986), 6–34; Richard Brothers, *A Revealed Knowledge of the Prophecies and Times: Book the First* (Albany, N.Y., 1796), esp. iii, 48, 51 (the title page notes that the book was "also sold by Spencer and Webb"); J. Bicheno, *The Signs of the Times . . .* (Albany, N.Y., 1795). For the continued significance of this literature, see John L. Brooke, *The Refiner's Fire: The Making of Mormon Cosmology, 1644–1844* (New York, 1994), 3–58; D. Michael Quinn, *Early Mormonism and the Magic World View* (Salt Lake City, Utah, 1987).

74. Clinton, *Address Delivered before Holland Lodge, 1793*, 4. See Chapter 5 for further discussion of this argument.

75. Alex. Lawrie, "The History of Freemasonry," *Amaranth; or, Masonic Garland*, II (1829), 11.

76. John Adams to Abigail Adams, Mar. 5, 1797, in Charles Francis Adams, ed., *Letters of John Adams, Addressed to His Wife* (Boston, 1841), II, 244; entry for Mar. 4, 1797, in Donald Jackson and Dorothy Twohig, eds., *The Diaries of George Washington* (Charlottesville, Va., 1976–1979), VI, 236. The insecure Adams read Washington's expression as enjoying "a triumph over me." George Washington Parke Custis, the president's step-grandson, suggested later that Washington wept at the event. See Douglas Southall Freeman, *George Washington: A Biography*, 7 vols. (New York, 1948–1957), VII, 437 n. 202. See also the description of Benjamin Franklin in the 1770s in Michael Warner, *The Letters of the Republic: Publication and the Public Sphere in Eighteenth-Century America* (Cambridge, Mass., 1990), 94. For this ideal of restraint and its transformation in the post-Revolutionary period, see Lewis, *Pursuit of Happiness*.

77. James Hoopes, *Consciousness in New England: From Puritanism and Ideas to Psychoanalysis and Semiotic* (Baltimore, 1989); Perry Miller, *The New England Mind: The Seventeenth Century* (1939 Boston, 1961), 239–241; Howe, *Unitarian Conscience*, 41, 57; Louis P. Masur, " 'Age of the First Person Singular': The Vocabulary of the Self in New England, 1780–1850," *Journal of American Studies*, XXV (1991), 189–221. Lystra, *Searching the Heart*, esp. 28–55, summarizes this new cultural vision.

78. Larzer Ziff, *Writing in the New Nation: Prose, Print, and Politics in the Early United States* (New Haven, Conn., 1991), 54–82. Ziff connects this interest in false appearances with a growing belief that reality lies in outward representation: I would argue that it shows an increasing distrust in this belief. For later fears of hypocrisy, see Halttunen, *Confidence Men and Painted Women*, 33–55, 138–152. [E. T. Channing], review of William Dunlap, *The Life of Charles Brockden Brown . . .* (1815), *North American Review and Miscellaneous Journal*, IX (June 1819), 74.

79. Finney, "Sinners Bound to Change Their Own Hearts" (1836), in David Grimsted, ed., *Notions of the Americans, 1820–1860* (New York, 1970), 78. Evangelical Christianity has traditionally been viewed as the driving force behind the changes discussed in this section and, indeed, the entire chapter. See, for example, Lystra, *Searching the Heart*, 29–30; Lewis, *Pursuit of Happiness*, esp. 209–212. The history of Masonry suggests that other forces played important roles and that perhaps evangelicalism is a result as well as a cause of larger changes.

80. *The Second Part* (1827), in *Masonry Revealed and Illustrated* (Cincinnati, Ohio, 1850[?]), 109.

81. Weems, *Life of Washington*, ed. Cunliffe, 53; Lewis Deffebach, "Masonic Address . . . 24th of July Last, at Doylestown, Pennsylvania . . . ," *American Masonic Register*, I (December 1820), 131; and see the similar statement in John Lathrop, *An Address, Delivered before King Solomon's Lodge, Charlestown, on . . . June 24, A.L. 5811* (Boston, 1811), 9. On 19th-century weeping, see Kaplan, *Sacred Tears*.

82. *Proceedings of the Grand Encampment of Knights Templar of the State of New York, from Its Organization, 1814–1859* (New York, 1860), 65. For other Masonic commemorations of Clinton, see *Proceedings of the Grand Chapter Royal Arch Masons of the State of Tennessee: From Its Organization, I, 1826–56* (Nashville, Tenn., 1939), 16–17; and W. Samuel Rockwell, "Eulogy on Clinton, Pronounced at the Request of the Masonic Fraternity, in Milledgeville, Geo. 24th June, A.L. 5828," *Amaranth; or, Masonic Garland*, I (October 1828), 201–209.

83. Fowle, "Autobiography," *Freemason's Monthly Magazine,* XXIV (1864), 267–269 (Kilmer, ed., *Autobiography of Henry Fowle,* 36–38). On Russell, see Joseph T. Buckingham, *Specimens of Newspaper Literature, with Personal Memoirs, Anecdotes, and Reminiscences,* 2 vols. (Boston, 1852), II, 1–45.

84. Pennsylvania Grand Lodge, *Reprint of the Minutes,* IV, 90–91. The committee wrote of "no provision having been made for the Escape of the smoke and foul air, as well as dust from the stoves, etc."

Chapter Ten

1. Hiram B. Hopkins, *Renunciation of Free Masonry* (Boston, 1830), 7–8. For the rumor that Morgan would reveal the higher degrees up to the Royal Arch, see Samuel D. Greene, *The Broken Seal* (Boston, 1870), 42.

2. Besides Hopkins, *Renunciation of Free Masonry,* and Greene, *The Broken Seal,* other useful accounts of the Morgan incident by contemporaries include William L. Stone, *Letters on Masonry and Anti-Masonry, Addressed to the Hon. John Quincy Adams* (New York, 1832); Henry Brown, *A Narrative of the Anti-Masonick Excitement, in the Western Part of the State of New-York, during the Years 1826, '7, '8, and a Part of 1829* (Batavia, N.Y., 1829). Among later studies see, especially, William Preston Vaughn, *The Antimasonic Party in the United States, 1826–1843* (Lexington, Ky., 1983), 3–9; Ronald P. Formisano with Kathleen Smith Kutolowski, "Antimasonry and Masonry: The Genesis of Protest 1826–1827," *American Quarterly,* XXIX (1977), 139–165; A. P. Bentley, *History of the Abduction of William Morgan, and the Anti-Masonic Excitement of 1826–1830 . . .* (Mount Pleasant, Iowa, 1874).

3. Hopkins claimed that he learned of Morgan's whereabouts on Sept. 14, 1826, but only discovered that he had been murdered in January 1827 (Edward Giddins, *The Anti-Masonic Almanack, for the Year of Christian Era 1830* [Rochester, N.Y., 1829], unpag.). Formisano and Kutolowski, "Antimasonry and Masonry," *Am. Quarterly,* XXXIX (1977), 152–153, note the 1831 conclusion of Victor Birdseye that Morgan had been murdered, probably on September 19. This account agrees with the purported confession of Henry C. Valance, recorded in [Henry C. Valance], *Confession of the Murder of William Morgan, as Taken Down by Dr. John L. Emery, of Racine County, Wisconsin, in the Summer of 1848 . . .* (New York, 1849). Although timing is uncertain, this scenario is also backed up by the later account of J. T. Shedd (*A Brief Account,* 7–8), who lived near the scene of the crime and who claimed to have been told the story directly by one of the murderers.

4. Kidnapping became a felony in New York only in the wake of the Morgan episode (Formisano and Kutolowski, "Antimasonry and Masonry," *Am. Quarterly,* XXIX [1977], 156. This article provides the fullest and most carefully documented account to date of the trials. Hopkins's involvement in shaping juries is noted in Stone, *Letters on Masonry and Anti-Masonry,* 247. Bruce's own story appears in Rob Morris, *The Masonic Martyr: The Biography of Eli Bruce . . .* (Louisville, Ky., 1861).

5. Hopkins, *Renunciation of Masonry,* 5.

6. Brown, *Narrative of the Anti-Masonic Excitement,* 20, 23. Greene, *Broken Seal,* 38, records a similar Masonic comment about a mouse, "meaning the government of the people," and the Masonic lion.

7. Brown, *Narrative of the Anti-Masonic Excitement,* 23.

8. Stone, *Letters on Masonry and Anti-Masonry,* 167; Brown, *Narrative of the Anti-Masonick Excitement,* 63–64. Stone and Brown provide the best contemporary accounts of the beginnings of Antimasonry. David Bernard, *Light on Masonry: A Collec-*

tion of All the Most Important Documents on the Subject of Speculative Free Masonry . . . (Utica, N.Y., 1829), provides an essential compilation of early Antimasonic documents.

9. Solomon Southwick, *A Solemn Warning against Free-Masonry, Addressed to the Young Men of the United States* (Albany, N.Y., 1827), discusses Southwick's opposition to Masonry (see esp. 138–140). See also David M. Ludlum, *Social Ferment in Vermont, 1791–1850* (1939; rpt. New York, 1966), 115.

10. Dorothy Ann Lipson, *Freemasonry in Federalist Connecticut* (Princeton, N.J., 1977), 277; Vaughn, *Antimasonic Party*, 90, 153. Vaughn provides the fullest chronicling of the organizational details of both the Antimasonic movement and the party. For the extent of Antimasonic newspapers, see below.

11. *A Memorial of the Half-Century Membership of R. W. Charles W. Moore in St. Andrew's Lodge* (Cambridge, Mass., 1873), 27. The Antimasonic critique of the fraternity and American society is discussed below.

12. See Vaughn, *Antimasonic Party*. The most sophisticated studies of the party are Donald J. Ratcliffe, "Antimasonry and Partisanship in Greater New England," *Journal of the Early Republic,* XV (1995), 199–240; Paul Goodman, *Towards a Christian Republic: Antimasonry and the Great Transition in New England, 1826–1836* (New York, 1988), 105–245; and Ronald P. Formisano, *The Transformation of Political Culture: Massachusetts Parties, 1790s–1840s* (New York, 1983), 197–221. See also Kathleen Smith Kutolowski, "Antimasonry Reexamined: Social Bases of the Grass-Roots Party," *Journal of American History,* LXXI (1984–1985), 269–293; Robert O. Rupp, "Social Tension and Political Mobilization in Jacksonian Society: A Case Study of the Antimasonic Party in New York, Pennsylvania, and Vermont" (Ph.D. diss., Syracuse University, 1983); Michael F. Holt, "The Antimasonic and Know Nothing Parties," in Arthur M. Schlesinger, Jr., ed., *History of U.S. Political Parties,* 4 vols. (New York, 1973), I, 575–593. On Adams and the Antimasonic party, see Leonard L. Richards, *The Life and Times of Congressman John Quincy Adams* (New York, 1986), 43–54.

13. Ratcliff, "Antimasonry and Partisanship," *Journal of the Early Republic,* XV (1995), argues that Antimasonic politics primarily rallied forces already opposed to Andrew Jackson.

14. Dwight L. Smith, *Goodly Heritage: One Hundred Fifty Years of Craft Freemasonry in Indiana* (n.p., 1968), 79, 80; Vaughn, *Antimasonic Party,* 164, 169; John S. Gilkeson, Jr., *Middle-Class Providence* (Princeton, N.J., 1986), 152. For a fuller discussion of the decline of Masonry, see below, Epilogue.

15. Vaughn, *Antimasonic Party,* 53, 132; Smith, *Goodly Heritage,* 79–80; Henry W. Rugg, *History of Freemasonry in Rhode Island* (Providence, R.I., 1895), 111. See below, Epilogue, for a discussion of this Masonic revival.

16. Hopkins, *Renunciation of Masonry,* 1, 3, 11–12.

17. In this chapter, which is about how an issue gains public attention and comes to be controlled by public opinion, the term "public sphere" is used, as in Jürgen Habermas's influential formulation, to describe the space where issues of importance to the community are discussed. Discussions of the concept, however, seldom give due attention to the impact of institutions and organizations on this seemingly neutral sphere of discussions about public affairs. See Craig Calhoun, ed., *Habermas and the Public Sphere* (Cambridge, Mass., 1992).

18. *Boston Masonic Mirror,* Mar. 9, 1833, 2. The connection between Antimasonry and the Morgan affair is discussed perceptively in Ronald P. Formisano with Kathleen Smith Kutolowski, "Antimasonry and Masonry," *Am. Quarterly,* XXXIX (1977), 139–165.

19. *Evening Journal Extra: Anti-Masonic Republican State Convention* ([Utica, N.Y.,

1832]), 8; Avery Allyn, *A Ritual of Freemasonry* . . . (Philadelphia, 1831), xxiii; Brown, *Narrative of the Anti-Masonick Excitement,* 42. The painter, a former Mason, charged a 12½¢ entrance fee.

20. *An Abstract of the Proceedings of the Antimasonic State Convention of Massachusetts, Held in Faneuil Hall, Boston, May 19 and 20, 1831* (Boston, 1831), 34; William L. Cummings, *A Bibliography of Anti-Masonry,* 2d ed. (New York, 1963), 11–12. The convention committee counted 983 newspapers in the United States, with 124 explicitly identifying themselves as Antimasonic. A large number of these publications, 46, were located in Pennsylvania and New York. Daniel Hewett's enumeration of newspapers in 1828 suggested there were 681 newspapers then in operation; see C.S.B., "Daniel Hewett's List of Newspapers and Periodicals in the United States in 1828," American Antiquarian Society, *Proceedings,* N.S., XLIV (1934), 365–396. Wayne A. Huss, *The Master Builders: A History of the Grand Lodge of Free and Accepted Masons of Pennsylvania,* 3 vols. (Philadelphia, 1986–1989), I, 146, gives the location of that state's Antimasonic newspapers by county.

21. Hopkins, *Renunciation of Masonry,* 11, points to Bernard, *Light on Masonry,* as the catalyst for his open denunciation of Freemasonry. For tract society publications, see *Extract from the Proceedings of the First U. States Antimasonic Convention* . . . , Young Men's Anti-Masonic Association for the Diffusion of Truth, Publication no. 2 (Boston, 1833); John Quincy Adams, *Letters on the Entered Apprentice's Oath* (Boston, 1833); *Memorial of the Half-Century Membership of Charles Moore,* 22–23.

22. Goodman, *Towards a Christian Republic,* 8. Lipson, *Freemasonry in Federalist Connecticut,* 267–311, convincingly argues that the party was less important than the broader movement out of which it grew. For the use of a trial as a similar means of gathering information and gaining publicity, see *Free-Masonry Unmasked: or, Minutes of the Trial of a Suit in the Court of Common Pleas of Adams County, Wherein Thaddeus Stevens, Esq. Was Plaintiff and Jacob Lefever, Defendant* (Gettysburg, Pa., 1835). Norman B. Wilkinson, "Thaddeus Stevens: A Case of Libel," *Pennsylvania History,* XVIII (1951), 317–325, describes the court battle.

23. *Abstract of the Proceedings of the Antimasonic State Convention of Massachusetts, 1831,* 17; Adams, *Letters on the Entered Apprentice's Oath,* 23. The ideological significance of public opinion is discussed more directly below.

24. *Craftsman* (Rochester, N.Y.), I (Mar. 24, 1829), 49; *Free-Masonry Unmasked,* xiii; Hopkins, *Renunciation of Masonry,* 11.

25. Stone, *Letters on Masonry and Anti-Masonry,* 247; Brown, *Narrative of the Anti-Masonick Excitement,* 161–166; *Abstract of the Proceedings of the Antimasonic State Convention of Massachusetts, 1831,* 14 (see 41–47, for another example of an attempted legal prosecution).

26. Southwick, *Solemn Warning against Free-Masonry,* 138–140; Stone, *Letters on Masonry and Anti-Masonry,* 247; *Anti-Masonic Herald, and Lancaster Weekly Courier* (Lancaster, Pa.), June 5, 1829; *Antimasonic Republican Convention, of Massachusetts, Held at Boston, Sept. 11, 12, and 13, 1833* . . . (Boston, 1833), 10.

27. *A Brief Report of the Debates, in the Anti-Masonic Convention of the Commonwealth of Massachusetts, Held in Faneuil Hall, Boston, Dec. 30, 31, 1829, and Jan. 1, 1830* (Boston, 1830), 46; David Pease, *The Good Man in Bad Company; or, Speculative Freemasonry a Wicked and Dangerous Combination* . . . (Brookfield, Mass., 1831), 27. Pease identifies the author of this letter as a Mason "of no inconsiderable *magnitude* in B——" (p. 26).

28. Allyn, *Ritual of Freemasonry,* "Publisher's Preface," xxiii; *Abstract of the Proceedings of the Antimasonic State Convention of Massachusetts, 1831,* 15.

29. Brown, *Narrative of the Anti-Masonick Excitement*, 15, quoting the March 1827 statement of the Lyons Royal Arch Chapter; Adams, *Letters on the Entered Apprentice's Oath*, 17. The text of Charles Moore's "Declaration of the Freemasons of Boston and Vicinity" is reprinted in *The Lodge of St. Andrew, and the Massachusetts Grand Lodge . . . 5756–5769* (Boston, 1870), 247–249. Moore's advice: *Boston Masonic Mirror*, IV (June 30, 1832), 2. For the Connecticut and Rhode Island Declarations using Moore's text, see also *Boston Masonic Mirror*, IV (Mar. 2, 1833), 2; Rugg, *History of Freemasonry in Rhode Island*, 102–105.

30. Stone, *Letters on Masonry and Anti-Masonry*, 467, suggests that the *Craftsman*, a Masonic newspaper in Rochester, New York, "was established by masonic contributions, and patronised almost exclusively by them" (*Boston Masonic Mirror*, June 30, 1832, 2, Mar. 9, 1833, 2).

31. *The Nature and Fruits of Political Antimasonry, Practically Exhibited* (Northampton, Mass., 1835). On the church members and the split, see also Mark Doolittle, *Historical Sketch of the Congregational Church in Belchertown, Mass. . . . .* (Northampton, Mass., 1852). Doolittle was a Belchertown Mason during this period.

32. *A Letter Addressed by a Young Lady of Cazenovia, N.Y., to the Clergyman of the Church of Which She Is a Member* ([Cazenovia, N.Y., 1829]), 1, 2; Pease, *Good Man in Bad Company*, 18; *Brief Report, Anti-Masonic Convention, 1829, and 1830*, 14.

33. Pease, *Good Man in Bad Company*, 15; *The Nature and Fruits of Political Antimasonry*, 3–4; *Craftsman*, I (Mar. 31, 1829), 58. For another use of the term "Jack Mason," see *Boston Masonic Mirror*, N.S., III (Jan. 14, 1832), 225.

34. Elizur Wright, *Myron Holley; and What He Did for Liberty and True Religion* (Boston, 1882), 155; Brown, *Narrative of the Anti-Masonick Excitement*, 150–154; Jesse B. Anthony, *Review of the Grand Lodge Transactions of the State of New York, from the Years 1781 to 1852* (Troy, N.Y., 1869), 61; "Capitular Masonry in Steuben County, New York," *American Lodge of Research Transactions*, X (1967), 212. For other such incidents in New York, see Emmett Hawkins, "The Time of William Morgan," *Am. Lodge Res. Trans.*, XIV (1980), 41–53. And see Jesse B. Anthony, "The Morgan Excitement: An Exhaustive Account of That Historic Affair in the United States, Written from a Masonic Stand-point," in Henry Leonard Stillson and William James Hughan, eds., *History of the Ancient and Honorable Fraternity of Free and Accepted Masons, and Concordant Orders* (Boston, 1891), 529.

35. *The Nature and Fruits of Political Antimasonry*, 5; Goodman, *Towards a Christian Republic*, 63.

36. Rupp, "Social Tension and Political Mobilization," 238–239; Stone, *Letters on Masonry and Anti-Masonry*, 14, 20, 563, 564. Stone's public defense of Masonry is alluded to on 565. Stone and his work are discussed in Formisano and Kutolowski, "Antimasonry and Masonry," *Am. Quarterly*, XXIX (1977), 149–150. Perhaps a measure of the changed landscape after 1826 is the article's suggestion that scholars have "mistakenly" seen Stone's book as Antimasonic.

37. Herman A. Sarachan, *A History of Masonry in Monroe County: 1810–1970* (Rochester, N.Y., 1971), 29; *Craftsman*, I (Mar. 24, 1829), 49.

38. William E. Channing, "Remarks on Association," in *The Works of William E. Channing*, new ed. (Boston, 1875), 138–158 (quotations, 138–139).

39. Gordon S. Wood, *The Radicalism of the American Revolution* (New York, 1992), 271–305, fails to consider the crucial role of organization in undermining aristocracy. Channing, "Remarks on Associations," in *Works of William E. Channing*, 140, 147. 149.

40. For Garrison's attendance, see *Boston Masonic Mirror*, IV (Sept. 15, 1832), 2. See *The Address of the United States Anti-Masonic Convention Held in Philadelphia, Septem-*

ber 11, 1830 (Philadelphia, 1830), 19; and see also the biography of Holley by a leading abolitionist: Wright, *Myron Holley.*

41. Leonard L. Richards, *"Gentlemen of Property and Standing": Anti-Abolition Mobs in Jacksonian America* (New York, 1970).

42. Channing, "Remarks on Associations," in *Works of William E. Channing,* 139.

43. Hopkins, *Renunciation of Masonry,* 3, 4, 9, 10.

44. Mosely J. Kendall, "Renunciation of Antimasonry," June 21, 1830, *Boston Masonic Mirror,* N.S., II (July 3, 1830), 3; Hopkins, *Renunciation of Masonry,* 11; *Craftsman,* I (Feb. 24, 1829), 20.

45. Brown, *Narrative of the Anti-Masonick Excitement,* 119–149 (quotations from 119, 120, 138, 142, 149).

46. Stone, *Letters on Masonry and Anti-Masonry,* 229. Goodman, *Towards a Christian Republic,* portrays Antimasonry as an attempt to reject the larger social and cultural changes of the post-Revolutionary period. Lipson, *Freemasonry in Federalist Connecticut,* 267–311, similarly suggests that Antimasons attempted to keep "social morality" linked to its "orthodox, communitarian base." Daniel Walker Howe, *The Political Culture of the American Whigs* (Chicago, 1979), while convincingly attacking the older tradition of viewing Antimasonry as "paranoid," also suggests that the movement spoke "in the terminology of a vanished political culture" (55–56, 79). For this older assessment of Antimasonry as paranoid, see Richard Hofstadter, *The Paranoid Style in American Politics and Other Essays* (New York, 1965); and David Brion Davis, "Some Themes of Counter-Subversion: An Analysis of Anti-Masonic, Anti-Catholic, and Anti-Mormon Literature," *Mississippi Valley Historical Review,* XLVII (1960–1961), 205–224. For perceptive studies that recognize the importance of the idea of public opinion and democracy (if not conscience and religion) in Antimasonry, see Formisano, *Transformation of Political Culture,* 197–221; and Holt, "Antimasonic and Know Nothing Parties," in Schlesinger, ed., *History of U.S. Political Parties,* I, 575–593.

47. *Abstract of the Proceedings of the Antimasonic State Convention of Massachusetts, 1831,* 24; *Address of the United States Anti-Masonic Convention, 1830,* 11.

48. Reuben Sanborn, *Freemasonry, a Covenant with Death: A Discourse, Delivered at a Public Meeting in Hornby, Steuben County, June 3, 1828* (Bath, N.Y., 1828), 10.

49. "Speech of the Hon. John Crary, in the Senate of the State of N. York, March 25, 1828, On the Proposition of Appointing an Inquisitor in the Case of William Morgan," in Bernard, *Light on Masonry,* 450.

50. "Address to the People of the State of New York," Antimasonic Convention of the Twelve Western Counties of New York, Held at Le Roy, March 6th and 7th, 1828, in Bernard *Light on Masonry,* 422, 439; "Speech of the Hon. John Crary," 450; "Address to the Citizens of the State of New York" by the "Anti-Masonic State Convention, Proceedings of the Anti-Masonic N.Y. [*sic*] State Convention, Held at Utica, Aug. 4, 5, and 6, 1828," 487. See also the same point on public opinion made in "Address to the People of the State of New York [Le Roy, 1828]," 430.

51. *Abstract of the Proceedings of the Antimasonic State Convention of Massachusetts, 1831,* 17; "Oration of Herbert A. Read, Esq., Pronounced at Le Roy, July 4, 1828, to an Assembly of Nearly One Thousand Persons," in Bernard, *Light on Masonry,* 468; Alfred Creigh, *Masonry and Anti-Masonry: A History of Masonry, as It Has Existed in Pennsylvania since 1792* (Philadelphia, 1854), 108, 170; Nathaniel Very, *Nathaniel Very's Renunciation of Freemasonry* (Worcester, Mass., 1830), 15.

52. "Address to the People of the State of New York [Le Roy, 1828]," and "Speech of T. F. Talbot, Esq. in the Anti-Masonic New York State Convention, August 4, 5, and 6, 1828," in Bernard, *Light on Masonry,* 423, 493.

53. James Madison, "Public Opinion," for the *National Gazette*, Dec. 19, 1791, in William T. Hutchinson et al, eds., *The Papers of James Madison* (Chicago, Charlottesville, Va., 1962-), XIV, 170; John Quincy Adams, "First Annual Message," Dec. 6, 1825, in James D. Richardson, *A Compilation of the Messages and Papers of the Presidents, 1789-1897,* 10 vols. (Washington, D.C., 1900), II, 316. On public opinion, see also Benjamin Rush, "Thoughts on Common Sense," in Michael Meranze, ed., *Essays: Literary, Moral, and Philosophical* (Schenectady, N.Y., 1988), 146-150, for a similar discussion.

54. "Address to the People of the State of New York [Le Roy, 1828]," in Bernard, *Light on Masonry,* 438-439. Throop quoted in Frederick Whittlesey, "Political Anti-Masonry," chap. 38, of Jabez D. Hammond, *The History of Political Parties in the State of New-York,* 4th ed. (Buffalo, N.Y., 1850), II, 393.

55. Message of the Lieutenant Governor (Nathaniel Pitcher) to the Senate, Mar. 18, 1828, and "Speech of the Hon. John Crary," in Bernard, *Light on Masonry,* 432, 444; Whittlesey, "Political Anti-Masonry," in Hammond, *History of Political Parties in the State of New-York,* II, 376.

56. George Bancroft, "The Office of the People in Art, Government, and Religion: An Oration Delivered before the Adelphi Society of Williamstown College, in August, 1835," in Bancroft, *Literary and Historical Miscellanies* (New York, 1855), 410. John Ashworth, *"Agrarians" and "Aristocrats": Party Political Ideology in the United States, 1837-1846* (London, 1983), highlights the more extreme formulations presented by each political party but suggests that moderate Whigs adopted the ideals of democracy (148-150). As he notes, his examples of democratic Whigs are often drawn from former Antimasons (151-170). Howe, *Political Culture of the American Whigs,* also suggests respect for public opinion among Whigs and notes that the Republican party made it a key concern (236, 271-279, 301). John L. Brooke, *The Heart of the Commonwealth: Society and Political Culture in Worcester County, Massachusetts, 1713-1861* (New York, 1989), 327-328, points to a connection between Jacksonian arguments and Antimasonry, but suggests the link was created in eastern Massachusetts after 1830.

57. "To the Editor of the *Sangamo Journal,*" June 13, 1836, in Roy P. Basler, ed., *The Collected Works of Abraham Lincoln,* 11 vols. (New Brunswick, N.J., 1953-1990), I, 48. Lincoln noted in 1856, "Our government rests in public opinion" ("Speech at a Republican Banquet, Chicago, Illinois," Dec. 10, 1856, II, 385). Lincoln went on to identify " 'the equality of men' " as the center of "our political public opinion."

58. *An Address to All Honest Masons, in Eight Numbers,* in Bernard, *Light on Masonry,* 413 (these pieces were originally published in 1828 by the *Le Roy Gazette* [New York], 375); Hopkins, *Renunciation of Masonry,* 12.

59. Hopkins, *Renunciation of Masonry,* 3, 8, 9, 11.

60. Bernard, *Light on Masonry,* 497-498; "Address to the People of the State of New-York," in *Proceedings of a Convention of Delegates, from the Different Counties in the State of New-York, Opposed to Free-Masonry, Held at the Capitol in the City of Albany, on the 19th, 20th, and 21st Days of February, 1829* (Rochester, N.Y., 1829), 39. Holley's authorship is noted in Wright, *Myron Holley,* 168.

61. *Brief Report, Anti-Masonic Convention, 1830,* 34; "Speech of T. F. Talbot," in Bernard, *Light on Masonry,* 501; Hopkins, *Renunciation of Masonry,* 12; *Abstract of the Proceedings of the Antimasonic State Convention of Massachusetts, 1831,* 14.

62. *Address of the United States Anti-Masonic Convention, 1830,* 19; Jedidiah N. Hotchkin, *A Candid Appeal to Professors of Religion . . .* (New York, 1818 [1828]), 3-4.

63. *A Letter Addressed by a Young Lady of Cazenovia, N.Y.,* 2; Bernard, *Light on Masonry,* 62n; Hotchkin, *Candid Appeal,* 8. Goodman, *Towards a Christian Republic,*

80–102, pulls together some scattered references to women by Antimasons to suggest that they generally criticized the fraternity as hostile to women, but the issue of gender never became as significant in Antimasonic discourse as he suggests, partly because political action was so often the goal of their arguments. Indeed, Goodman cites nearly as many Masonic statements challenging Antimasonry on the grounds of its hostility to women.

64. Hotchkin, *Candid Appeal*, 3–14.

65. Vermont General Assembly Select Committee report, Nov. 8, 1832, in *Journal of the General Assembly of the State of Vermont, at Their Session Begun and Holden at Montpelier . . . on Thursday 13th October, A.D. 1832* (Danville, Vt., [1832]), 150; Wright, *Myron Holley*, 186; Bernard, *Light on Masonry*, x.

66. Charles Grandison Finney, *Lectures on Revivals of Religion*, ed. William G. McLoughlin (Cambridge, Mass., 1960), 11, 214, 196. On the power of truth, see also Sidney Earl Mead, *Nathaniel William Taylor, 1786–1858: A Connecticut Liberal* (Chicago, 1942), 35, 159–160.

67. *Liberator* (Boston), Jan. 26, 1833.

68. Francis Wayland, *The Elements of Moral Science* (New York, 1835), 30, 45. In an 1835 edition for secondary schools (*The Elements of Moral Science*, Abridged and Adapted to the use of Schools and Academies [Boston, 1835]), the chapter on the conscience is the second longest chapter in the work. On these issues and the period's moral philosophy, see D. H. Meyer, *The Instructed Conscience: The Shaping of the American National Ethic* (Philadelphia, 1972), esp. 9–14, 43–50.

Other reformers: Adin Ballou, *History of the Hopedale Community, from Its Inception to Its Virtual Submergence in the Hopedale Parish*, ed. William S. Heywood (Lowell, Mass., 1897), 17; Bancroft, "The Office of the People in Art, Government, and Religion," in Bancroft, *Literary and Historical Miscellanies*, 410. See Ronald G. Walters, *The Antislavery Appeal: American Abolitionism after 1830* (New York, 1978), 60–62, on conscience.

69. *Proceedings of the Grand Lodge . . . of the State of Maine*, I, *1820–1847* (Portland, Maine, 1872), 85, 95–97. See Chapter 9 for discussion of the changing psychology inherent in the higher degrees.

70. *Address of the United States Anti-Masonic Convention, 1830*, 20. Walters, *The Antislavery Appeal*, 60–62, seems to identify antebellum ideas of conscience too closely with the older idea of the moral sense.

71. Charles Thompson McClenachan, *History of the Most Ancient and Honorable Fraternity of Free and Accepted Masons in New York . . .* , 4 vols. (New York, 1888–1894), II, 607–609.

72. *Boston Masonic Mirror*, IV (June 30, 1832), 2.

73. *Craftsman*, I (Mar. 24, 1829), 51.

74. E. B. Grandin, "Renunciation of Anti-Masonry," *Craftsman*, I (Mar. 17, 1829), 43; "Correct Sentiment: Extract of a Letter from Cattaraugus County," *Craftsman*, I (Mar. 24, 1829), 51; "Myron Holley," *Craftsman*, II (Apr. 7, 1830), 59; *Boston Masonic Mirror*, N.S., II (Mar. 12, 1831), 294–295.

75. McClenachan, *History of Masons in New York*, II, 608; *Boston Masonic Mirror*, IV (Mar. 30, 1833), 1; *Craftsman*, I (June 16, 1829), 148. See also Brown, *Narrative of the Anti-Masonick Excitement*, 206.

76. *Craftsman*, I (Feb. 10, 1829), 4 (Feb. 24, 1829), 20; John Tipton to James B. Slaughter, Feb. 26, 1832, in Glen A. Blackburn, comp., *The John Tipton Papers (Indiana Historical Collections*, XXIV–XXVI), 3 vols. (Indianapolis, Ind., 1942), II, 534.

77. *Pennsylvania Argus* (Easton), reprinted in *Boston Masonic Mirror*, N.S., II (July

30, 1830), 38 (Aug. 7, 1830), 42. Ronald P. Formisano, *The Birth of Mass Political Parties: Michigan, 1827–1861* (Princeton, N.J., 1971), 60–67, discusses the strong strain of antiparty attitudes in Antimasonry. In the larger debate over Masonry, however, the strongest attacks on politicization and party discipline came from the Masons themselves. As argued above, political Antimasons had to persuade people to act politically.

78. "Address to the People of the State of Vermont," *Proceedings of the Anti-Masonic State Convention, Holden at Montpelier, Vt., June 26 and 27, 1833* (Montpelier, Vt., 1833), 30; *Boston Masonic Mirror*, N.S., II (July 3, 1830), 3. On the movement against government interference and toward negative liberty, see James A. Henretta, "The Slow Triumph of Liberal Individualism: Law and Politics in New York, 1780–1860," in Richard O. Curry and Lawrence B. Goodheart, eds., *American Chameleon: Individualism in Trans-National Context* (Kent, Ohio, 1991), 87–106; L. Ray Gunn, *The Decline of Authority: Public Economic Policy and Political Development in New York, 1800–1860* (Ithaca, N.Y., 1988); Robert H. Wiebe, *The Opening of American Society: From the Adoption of the Constitution to the Eve of Disunion* (New York, 1984), 241–251.

79. For example of such glorification, see the long excerpt from brother William Brainard's 1825 Connecticut oration: *A Masonic Lecture, Spoken before the Brethren of Union Lodge, New-London . . . January 24, A.L. 5825* (New London, Conn., 1825), in *Proceedings of a Convention of Delegates, Opposed to Free-Masonry, Held at Albany, 1829*, 11.

80. *Craftsman*, I (June 16, 1829), 147; (Mar. 3, 1829), 28.

81. Whittlesey, "Political Anti-Masonry," in Hammond, *History of Political Parties in the State of New-York*, II, 369–403 (quotations, 269, 378). Although Whittlesey was perhaps right that political leaders originally did not encourage Antimasonry, Kutolowski, "Antimasonry Reexamined," *JAH*, LXXI (1984–1985), 269–293, shows that established political leaders and their socioeconomic peers led the party later.

82. "Speech of T. F. Talbot," in Bernard, *Light on Masonry*, 491.

Epilogue

1. *Craftsman* (Rochester, N.Y.), I (Mar. 24, 1829), 49.

2. "The Declaration" is reprinted in *The Lodge of St. Andrew, and the Massachusetts Grand Lodge . . . 5756–5769* (Boston, 1870), 247–249. For the lodge's membership, see 239–240.

3. Joseph Ritner, *Vindication of General Washington from the Stigma of Adherence to Secret Societies* (Boston, 1841), 18. The effects of Antimasonry on the South have remained virtually unnoticed. Paul Goodman, *Towards a Christian Republic: Antimasonry and the Great Transition in New England, 1826–1836* (New York, 1988), 235, typically suggests that "Masonry flourished in the South." The lone exception is William Preston Vaughn, *The Antimasonic Party in the United States, 1826–1843* (Lexington, Ky., 1983), 170–171. "Masonic excitement" is used in Elijah Fletcher to Jesse Fletcher, Dec. 13, 1830, in Martha van Briesen, ed., *The Letters of Elijah Fletcher* (Charlottesville, Va., 1965), 119.

4. *Proceedings of the M.W. Grand Lodge of Ancient Free and Accepted Masons of the State of Alabama, from Its Organization in 1821, to 1839, Inclusive* (Montgomery, Ala., 1906), 396, 419 (see 433 for a more optimistic 1837 assessment); *Proceedings of the Grand Royal Arch Chapter of the State of Alabama, 1823–1852* (Montgomery, Ala., 1909), 171; William Henry Rosier and Fred Lamar Pearson, Jr., *The Grand Lodge of*

Georgia, Free and Accepted Masons, 1786–1980 (Macon, Ga., 1983), 44–70 (quotation at 62). An 1832 address to the Louisiana grand lodge spoke of "the brilliant state of Masonry" there; see *Extract from the Proceedings of the Grand Lodge of Free and Accepted Masons of the State of Louisiana . . .* (New Orleans, La., 1832), 4–5.

5. *Celebration of the One Hundredth Anniversary of the Grand Chapter of Royal Arch Masons of Georgia . . . April 12th, 1922* (n.p., 1922), 25; Albert Gallatin Mackey, *The History of Freemasonry in South Carolina, from Its Origin in the Year 1736 to the Present Time . . .* (1861; Columbia, S.C., 1936), 216–217, 241–242, 294–295; *History of Richmond Lodge No. 10 . . . 1780–1950* (Richmond, Va., 1952), 97–103; Rob Morris, *The History of Freemasonry in Kentucky, in Its Relations to the Symbolic Degrees* (Louisville, Ky., 1859), 34.

6. Vermont: *Craftsman*, I (Aug. 18, 1829), 219; *Early Records of the Grand Lodge of Free and Accepted Masons of the State of Vermont, from 1794 to 1846 Inclusive* (Burlington, Vt., 1879), 407–416 (at the end of 1845, the Vermont grand master petitioned the Massachusetts grand lodge to sanction their actions and allow them to resume their activities). Ohio: Ohio Grand Lodge, *Proceedings of the Grand Lodge . . . of Ohio . . . from 1808 to 1853 Inclusive*, 2 vols. (Columbus, Ohio, 1857–1858), I, 373. Michigan: *Transactions of the Grand Lodge of the Most Ancient and Honorable Fraternity of Free and Accepted Masons of the Territory of Michigan . . . June 24, A.D. 1826, A.L. 5826, and January 8, A.D. 1827, A.L. 5827* (Grand Rapids, Mich., 1883), 1–21 (the grand lodge, which first met in June 1826, had its last meeting on Aug. 8, 1827; it seems not to have met again until 1841). Indiana: Dwight L. Smith, *Goodly Heritage: One Hundred Fifty Years of Craft Freemasonry in Indiana* (n.p., 1968), 80, 81. Illinois: Vaughn, *Antimasonic Party*, 169.

For the effects of Antimasonry on other northern states, see Goodman, *Towards a Christian Republic*; and Vaughn, *Anti-Masonic Party*. The discussion of Pennsylvania in Wayne A. Huss, *The Master Builders: A History of the Grand Lodge of Free and Accepted Masons of Pennsylvania*, 3 vols. (Philadelphia, 1986–1989), I, 112–150, provides the best single study of Antimasonry's effects on the fraternity.

7. Charles Thompson McClenachan, *History of the Most Ancient and Honorable Fraternity of Free and Accepted Masons in New York*, 4 vols. (New York, 1888–1894), III, 11; *Proceedings of St. John's Lodge No. 1 . . . 1757–1932* [New York, 1932], 36; Vaughn, *Anti-Masonic Party*, 52. See also Jesse B. Anthony, "The Morgan Excitement: An Exhaustive Account of That Historic Affair in the United States, Written from a Masonic Stand-point," in Henry Leonard Stillson and William James Hughan, eds., *History of the Ancient and Honorable Fraternity of Free and Accepted Masons, and Concordant Orders* (Boston, 1891), 529–530.

8. *Proceedings of St. John's Lodge No. 1*, 37; Anthony, "The Morgan Excitement," in Stillson and Hughan, eds., *History of the Ancient and Honorable Fraternity*, 531.

9. "Report on the Effect of Freemasonry on the Christian Religion," in *Extract from the Proceedings of the First U. States Antimasonic Convention . . .*, Young Men's Anti-Masonic Association for the Diffusion of Truth, publication no. 2 (Boston, 1833), 83.

10. *American Bibliography*, s.v. "S., R., *Jachin and Boaz: An Authentic Key to the Door of Freemasonry*," lists five editions each in the 1790s and 1800s, six in the 1810s, and two (one in Spanish) from the 1820s. The largest number of these came from Boston (five) and New York City (four). Paul Dean, *Discourse, Delivered before Constellation Lodge* (Boston, 1829), 29, inaccurately claims it is "notorious to the world" that Morgan's book "is but a newly-vamped re-publication of an old English pamphlet." A more objective Masonic observer, William Leon Cummings, "Bibliography

of Anti-Masonry," *Nocalore*, IV (1934), 27, argues that Morgan "was fairly familiar with the active working of Lodges at that period." *Jachin and Boaz* appears in Isaiah Thomas, Jr., *Catalogue of Books for Sale ... August 1811* (Boston, 1811), 37. At 37½ ¢, Morgan's book cost less than one-third the price of Webb's *Monitor* ($1.25, p. 31) and one-sixth the price of the quarto edition of *Masonic Constitutions* ($2.50, p. 41, perhaps the Massachusetts version prepared by his father in the 1790s.). Solomon Southwick claimed in the 1820s that he bought *Jachin and Boaz* from Thomas Smith Webb's partner, possibly before Webb entered the business. Southwick, *A Solemn Warning against Free-Masonry, Addressed to the Young Men of the United States* (Albany, N.Y., 1827), 72.

11. William Morgan, *Illustrations of Masonry ...* (Batavia, N.Y., 1826), does not include material beyond the first three degrees. *The Second Part; or, A Key to the Higher Degrees of Freemasonry ... by a Member of the Craft* (Cincinnati, Ohio, 1827), presents a version of the later rituals that was sometimes included in editions of Morgan. It differs from the later, and more fully attested, account revealed by a Le Roy Convention of renouncing Masons in 1828 and published in David Bernard, *Light on Masonry: A Collection of All the Most Important Documents on the Subject of Speculative Free Masonry ...* (Utica, N.Y., 1829), and Avery Allyn, *A Ritual of Freemasonry ...* (Boston, 1831).

12. See the motion offered by Thaddeus Stevens in the Pennsylvania Legislature, Dec. 10, 1834, in Alfred Creigh, *Masonry and Anti-Masonry: A History of Masonry, as It Has Existed in Pennsylvania since 1792* (Philadelphia, 1854), 108. On Adams: John Quincy Adams, *Letters on the Entered Apprentice's Oath* (Boston, 1833), 4 — statement from the anonymous introduction.

13. "Address to the People of the State of New York," Antimasonic Convention of the Twelve Western Counties of New York, held at Le Roy, March 6th and 7th, 1828, in Bernard, *Light on Masonry,* 422.

14. The grand lodge of New York proved so opposed to public processions that a few enthusiastic brothers who marched in defiance of the body's vote were expelled. They formed their own St. John's grand lodge of the State of New York in 1857, a small body that lasted for 13 years. McClenachan, *History of Masons in New York*, III, 12–49.

15. The argument of Goodman, *Towards a Christian Republic,* that Antimasonry was a "long-run failure" (244) because Masonry later revived fails to take into account the larger impact of Antimasonry on the fraternity.

16. Albert Pike, "Allocution of the Grand Commander of the Supreme Council of the 33d Degree for the Southern Jurisdiction of the United States of America" (1884), reprinted in Alphonse Cerza, *Anti-Masonry: Light on the Past and Present Opponents of Freemasonry* (Fulton, Mo., 1962), 253–264.

17. On Pennsylvania ceremonies and growth, see Huss, *Master Builders*, I, 149–234. On the Scottish Rite and other higher degrees, see Mark C. Carnes, *Secret Ritual and Manhood in Victorian America* (New Haven, Conn., 1989), esp. 133–139. On Johnson, see William M. Stuart, "The Anti-Masonic Phase of Johnson's Impeachment," *Am. Lodge Res. Trans.*, II (1934–1938), 146–160.

18. Carnes, *Secret Ritual and Manhood,* esp. 6–9, notes these groups. Albert Pike also seems to have been a Klan leader (Stuart, "Anti-Masonic Phase of Johnson's Impeachment," *Am. Lodge Res. Trans.*, II [1934–1938], 152).

19. Albert G. Mackey, *The Book of the Chapter; or, Monitorial Instructions, in the Degrees of Mark, Past, and Most Excellent Master, and the Holy Royal Arch*, 4th ed. (New York, 1864 [1st ed., 1858]), 144–145. For a discussion of antebellum voluntary associations that stresses their common moral purpose, see Don Harrison Doyle, *The Social Order of a Frontier Community: Jacksonville, Illinois, 1825–1870* (Urbana, Ill.,

1978), 178–193. On changes within the fraternity after Antimasonry, see Huss, *Master Builders,* I, 163–165; and Carnes, *Secret Ritual and Manhood,* 25–30. Huss and Carnes provide the only scholarly examinations of this neglected period of Masonic history. For valuable discussions of late-19th-century Masonry, see Mary Ann Clawson, *Constructing Brotherhood: Class, Gender, and Fraternalism* (Princeton, N.J., 1989); Lynn Dumenil, *Freemasonry and American Culture, 1800–1930* (Princeton, N.J., 1984); William D. Moore, "The Masonic Lodge Room, 1870–1930: A Sacred Space of Masculine Spiritual Hierarchy," in Elizabeth Collins Cromley and Carter L. Hudgins, eds., *Gender, Class, and Shelter: Perspectives in Vernacular Architecture,* V (Knoxsville, Tenn., 1994), 26–39; and Moore, "Masonic Lodge Rooms and Their Furnishings, 1870–1930," *Heredom: The Transactions of the Scottish Rite Research Society,* II (1993), 99–136. John D. Hamilton, *Material Culture of the American Freemasons* (Lexington, Mass., 1994), esp. 95–102, 150–153, discusses and illustrates the material environment of Masonry beyond as well as during its first century in America.

20. Mackey, *History of Freemasonry in South Carolina,* 275.

21. Pike, "Allocution of the Grand Commander," in Cerza, *Anti-Masonry,* 255; Gilbert Haven and Thomas Russell, *Father Taylor, the Sailor Preacher* . . . (Boston, 1871), 311–312.